Yüan Thought

Neo-Confucian Studies
SPONSORED BY THE REGIONAL SEMINAR
IN NEO-CONFUCIAN STUDIES
COLUMBIA UNIVERSITY

Yüan Thought

Chinese Thought and Religion
Under the Mongols

Hok-lam Chan and
Wm. Theodore de Bary,
Editors

Columbia University Press
1982   NEW YORK

Library of Congress Cataloging in Publication Data
Main entry under title:

Yüan thought.

(Neo-Confucian studies)
Papers originally presented at a conference, Issaquah, Wash., Jan. 1978, sponsored by
the Committee on Studies of Chinese Civilization of the American Council of Learned
Societies.
Includes bibliographical references and
index.
Contents: Introduction / Wm. Theodore de
Bary—"Comprehensiveness" (t'ung) and
"change" (pien) in Ma Tuan-lin's historical
thought / Hok-lam Chan—Law, statecraft,
and the Spring and autumn annals in Yüan
political thought / John D. Langlois, Jr.—
[etc.]
1. Philosophy, Chinese—Congresses.
2. China—Religion—Congresses. I. Chan,
Hok-lam. II. De Bary, William Theodore,
1918–   . III. American Council of Learned
Societies. Committee on Studies of Chinese
Civilization. IV. Series.
B125.Y8   181'.11'09022   82-1259
ISBN 0-231-05324-X   AACR2

Columbia University Press
New York   Guildford, Surrey

Clothbound editions of Columbia University Press books
are Smyth-sewn and printed on permanent and durable
acid-free paper.

Neo-Confucian Studies

Preface

THIS SYMPOSIUM IS the outgrowth of a conference on Chinese thought under Mongol rule held at Issaquah, Washington, in January 1978 on the initiative of Professor Hok-lam Chan and with the sponsorship of the Committee on Studies of Chinese Civilization of the American Council of Learned Societies. The study of premodern Chinese thought has been the subject of a continuing series of conferences held under the auspices of the Subcommittee on Chinese Thought and Religion in recent years. These conferences have resulted in the publication of *Self and Society in Ming Thought* (1970), *The Unfolding of Neo-Confucianism* (1975), and *Principle and Practicality: Essays in Neo-Confucianism and Practical Learning* (1979). The present volume, by focusing on the Yüan period (1260–1368), an era of subjugation by the Mongols, represents a further stage in this continuing exploration of neglected aspects of Chinese thought and religion in the imperial era.

The papers presented here deal with areas of thought and religion that reaffirmed the classical heritage from the T'ang and Sung in response to alien rule, and provided the basis for further intellectual growth in the Ming and Ch'ing periods. They discuss the unique importance of this period for the testing of Chinese tradition when its survival was seriously threatened, as well as the continuing vitality and variety of Chinese thought in such difficult circumstances.

The conference organizer and participants wish to acknowledge the assistance of the Subcommittee on Chinese Thought and Religion of the American Council of Learned Societies for its support of conference expenses from funds of the Ford Foundation and the National Endowment for the Humanities. We are grateful to Professor Donald J. Munro, University of Michigan, for advice on the planning of the conference, to Professors Julia Ching of Toronto and Yan-shuan Lao of Ohio State for their contributions to the meeting itself, and to Professor James T. C. Liu of Princeton for his valued service as conference discussant. We would also like to thank Professor Judith Berling of Indiana University and Ms. Ruth Dunnell of Princeton for their indispensable service as conference rapporteurs, and also to Mr. Timothy Phelan of the University of Washington for help in typing the conference records as well as some of the papers for publication.

Explanatory Notes
and Abbreviations Used

THE STYLE OF this book in sinological matters follows that adopted in the earlier volumes on premodern Chinese thought published by Columbia University Press, but more specifically *Principle and Practicality: Essays in Neo-Confucianism and Practical Learning* (1979). Translation of Yüan official titles and terms is adapted from the established usage in Yüan historical studies, particularly that of *China Under Mongol Rule*, edited by John D. Langlois, Jr. (Princeton University Press, 1981), with certain alterations. The term *Kuo-tzu hsüeh* or *Kuo-tzu chien*, for instance, is rendered as "Imperial College" rather than "National University" to convey more precisely the original meaning.

The system of transcription of Mongol names follows that in A. Mostaert, *Dictionnaire ordos*, vol. 3, "Index des mots du mongol ancien" (Peking: Catholic University, 1944), and standardized by Professor Francis W. Cleaves in his articles in *Harvard Journal of Asiatic Studies*, with the following minor changes:

ǰ is replaced by j
č is replaced by ch
š is replaced by sh
ɣ is replaced by gh
q is replaced by kh

Thus the following common names are transformed as:

Činggis Qan   Chinggis Khan
Qubilai Qaɣan   Khubilai Khaghan

Abbreviations of Chinese titles and editions are identified at first appearance, except in the case of the following standard works:

PN   Po-na
SKCSCP   Ssu-k'u ch'üan-shu chen-pen
SPPY   Ssu-pu pei-yao

SPTK Ssu-pu ts'ung-k'an

SYHA *Sung-Yüan hsüeh-an,* compiled by Huang Tsung-hsi
     and amended by Ch'üan Tsu-wang

TSCC Ts'ung-shu chi-ch'eng

YS   *Yüan shih*

Contributors

JUDITH A. BERLING is Associate Professor of Religious Studies at Indiana University, Bloomington. She received her Ph.D. from Columbia and has taught at Stanford University. She is the author of *The Syncretic Religion of Lin Chao-en* (1980) and is currently working on the popularization of elite traditions and the interaction among religions in traditional China.

HOK-LAM CHAN is Professor of Chinese History at the University of Washington, Seattle, specializing in the later imperial dynasties. His recent publications include *Li Chih in Contemporary Chinese Historiography* (1980) and *Theories of Legitimacy in Imperial China* (1982). He is a principal contributor to the *Dictionary of Ming Biography* (1976), and is coeditor and contributor, with Igor de Rachewiltz, of *Yüan Personalities*, vol. 1, under preparation. He graduated from the University of Hong Kong and received his Ph.D. from Princeton University.

WING-TSIT CHAN is Professor of Chinese Philosophy and Culture Emeritus, Dartmouth College; Honorary Doctor of Humane Letters, Dartmouth College; Anna Gillespie Professor of Philosophy, Chatham College, and Adjunct Professor of Chinese Thought, Columbia University. He is also a member of Academia Sinica and president of the Society for Asian and Comparative Philosophy. Among his major works are *A Source Book in Chinese Philosophy* (1963), his translation, *Instruction for Practical Living and Other Neo-Confucian Writings by Wang Yang-ming* (1963), his translation of Chu Hsi's *Reflections on Things at Hand* (1967), and *Neo-Confucianism, etc.: Essays by Wing-tsit Chan* (1969).

JOHN W. DARDESS received his doctorate in Chinese from Columbia University in 1968 and is now Professor of History at the University of Kansas. He is the author of *Conquerors and Confucians: Aspects of Political Change in Late Yüan China* (1973) and several articles on Yüan and Ming history, and has completed a book manuscript on the founding of the Ming dynasty.

WM. THEODORE DE BARY is John Mitchell Mason Professor of the University at Columbia University, and author and editor of a number of books on Asian philosophy. He was Executive Vice-President for Academic Affairs and Provost at Columbia from 1971 to 1978. A former president of the Association for Asian Studies and a fellow of the American Academy of Arts and Sciences, he is also the editor and coauthor of *Self and Society in Ming Thought* (1970), *The Unfolding of Neo-Confucianism* (1975), and *Principle and Practicality: Essays in Neo-Confucianism and Practical Learning* (1979). His most recent work is *Neo-Confucian Orthodoxy and the Learning of the Mind-and-Heart* (1981).

HERBERT FRANKE is Professor Emeritus of Far Eastern Studies at the University of München, Germany, and President of the Bavarian Academy of Sciences. His field of special interest is the history of China under dynasties of conquest, and his publications include *Geld und Wirtschaft in China unter der Mongolenherrschaft* (1949), *Forschungsbericht Sinologie* (1953); with Wolfgang Bauer, *The Golden Casket* (1964), and with Rolf Trauzettel, *Das chinesische Kaiserreich* (1968). He is editor of *Sung Biographies* (1976), and coeditor and contributor of vol. 6 of the *Cambridge History of China: The Dynasties of Conquest* (forthcoming).

DAVID GEDALECIA is Associate Professor of History at the College of Wooster in Ohio. He received his M.A. and Ph.D. degrees from Harvard University in Chinese intellectual history and has published a biographical study of Wu Ch'eng and articles on Neo-Confucianism. He is currently pursuing his interests in Sung and Yüan thought.

JAN YÜN-HUA is Professor of Religious Studies at McMaster University, Hamilton, Canada. He was educated in China and India, receiving his Ph.D. from Viswa-Bharati University, Santiniketan. He has published widely on Sino-Indian religious relations, Chinese Buddhism, and Taoist thought, including a book, *A Chronicle of Buddhism in China* (1966), and numerous articles in professional journals. His current research interests are on the T'ang monk Tsung-mi and the Huang-Lao tradition of Taoism.

JOHN D. LANGLOIS, JR., is Associate Professor of History at Bowdoin College with an M.A. from Harvard University and a Ph.D. from Princeton University. He is the editor of *China under Mongol Rule* (1981), and the author of articles on the intellectual history of the Sung, Yüan, and early Ming periods. He is now working on a study of Ming legal history.

LIU TS'UN-YAN is Professor of Chinese at the Australian National University, Canberra, and has been a visiting professor at Columbia, Harvard, Hawaii, Malaya, Hong Kong, and Paris. With a Ph.D. and a D. Lit. from the University of London, he is also a Fellow of the Royal Asiatic Society and a Foundation Fellow of the Australian Academy of the Humanities. Among his many writings are *Buddhist and Taoist Influences in Chinese Novels* (1962); *Chinese Popular Fiction in Two London Libraries* (1967), and *Selected Papers from the Hall of Harmonious Wind* (1976).

TU WEI-MING is Professor of History at the University of California, Berkeley. He was educated at Tunghai University and Harvard University where he received his Ph.D. in 1968. His fields of interest include Confucianism, Chinese intellectual history, and religious philosophies of Asia. Among his publications are *Neo-Confucian Thought in Action* (1976), *Centrality and Commonality: An Essay on the Chung-yung* (1976), and *Humanity and Self-Cultivation: Essays in Confucian Thought* (1980). Currently he is working on Chu Hsi and Neo-Confucian humanism.

CHÜN-FANG YÜ is Associate Professor of Religion at Rutgers, the State University of New Jersey, specializing in the history of Chinese Buddhism since the Tang dynasty. She was trained at Tunghai University and Columbia University, where she received her Ph.D. Her publications include *The Renewal of Buddhism in China: Chu-hung and the Late Ming Synthesis* (1981), and several articles on Sung and Ming Buddhism. She is currently working on a study of Buddhism in Neo-Confucian China and a chapter on Ming Buddhism for the *Cambridge History of China*. vol. 8.

Contents

Wm. Theodore de Bary

Introduction

THE YÜAN or Mongol era in Chinese history is in many ways its least typical period. Never before had the country been so totally subdued by an alien conqueror far removed in his nomadic ways and tribal customs from the conventional picture of the stately Chinese dynasty. Shaken to its institutional foundations and exposed to foreign ideas and influences from the larger world which the Mongols had overrun, China somehow managed to survive all this intact. No earlier age, and perhaps no other civilization of comparable maturity and refinement, had undergone such violent displacement and yet emerged in such secure possession of itself.

In the domain of Chinese thought, as it might appear in hindsight, a similar outcome was predictable. The survival of Buddhism, for one thing, was not much in doubt, since many Mongols and much of the leadership already professed that faith. The Taoist religion too, in certain of its manifestations, appealed to the Mongol appetite for the magical and supernatural, and in others to the conqueror's interest in a teaching of acquiescence and passivity among his subjects. Confucianism, for its part, though early an object of contempt, probably invited no more animosity or repression than any other of the teachings tolerated or ignored in the far-flung Mongol empire. As conquerors with ambitions to universal rule, the Mongols shared at least this much with traditional Chinese dynasties: they easily assumed an air of lofty impartiality in the dispensing of favors or imposing of disabilities, intent on keeping the peace and avoiding sectarian conflict which might upset their control.

In these circumstances it would seem only a matter of time before Chinese tradition reasserted itself. If this is so, however, the nature of the outcome was still far from certain, and indeed what emerges as most significant about this extraordinary epoch in Chinese life is the striking adaptability of tradition to new circumstances, rather than simply its dogged persistence. The vastly superior numbers of the Chinese no doubt insured the massive survival of Chinese values and ethnic traits against all outside influences, yet the actual story of these times is most tellingly revealed in the opportunities which alien intrusion and improvisation provided for new ideas and institutions to get established. Of this the best example is the superseding of an earlier Confucian tradition by a new one, which fairly succeeded in coopting the conqueror himself. In this process Neo-Confucianism became for the first time a full-fledged state orthodoxy, an "orthodoxy" destined to affect the intellectual life and political culture not only of China but of all East Asia.

It would be misleading to cast the Mongols in the role of conscious innovators or bold planners of a new order in East Asia. Nevertheless their own ambitions drove them to take up new challenges and their essential pragmatism led them to accept new realities. On the one hand, within their vast empire they could promote the diffusion across Asia of new cultural elements such as Arab astronomy; on the other hand, given their overextended reach and the actual limits of their effective control, they allowed a large measure of autonomy in many areas, which left room for new cultural activities, including movements in popular literature, art, and religion, to spring forth from soil that had been well broken up by foreign disruptions.

Against this background it was not far-fetched for one knowledgeable non-Chinese observer, the late Yoshikawa Kōjirō[a] to suggest that the role of the Mongol ruler Khubilai Khaghan in thirteenth-century China compared to that of Tokugawa Ieyasu in early seventeenth-century Japan. Each of them, though no doubt conservative of his own interest in consolidating new-won power, proved adaptable with regard to means and ready to accept certain innovations, like Neo-Confucian education, which might serve that interest.[1]

In these circumstances even the most likely candidates for survival among Chinese institutions had to win out in the general competition with newer ways of doing things. Sometimes indeed it was the latter, or perhaps some hybrid, which won. The dyarchy which superimposed a Mongol pattern of military organization upon a native system of civil administration produced noteworthy adaptations in certain areas, as for instance in the new Mongol systems of provincial administration and military garrisons, which were to be perpetuated by the Ming and Manchu dynasties.[2] This fact has indeed attracted the attention of institutional historians, who are not unaware of Yüan contributions to the Chinese system, yet little study has been given to an even more significant product of Mongol-Chinese interaction, the new civil service examination sys-

tem which officially signaled the establishment of Neo-Confucian orthodoxy for ages to come. Perhaps just because this new system became such
a monumental fact of Chinese life in later centuries, it has come to be
taken for granted—another "inevitable" feature of the Chinese resurgence
under the Ming. And yet this view of it overlooks not only the change in
content of the examinations in the Yüan but also crucial adaptations in
form which were significantly affected by the Mongol-Chinese encounter, with its interplay between radically different cultural and social systems.

    In short, in the relatively open historical situation created by the
Mongol disturbance of Chinese institutions, it was possible for new elements to come to the fore and gain a place for themselves before things
closed in again under the Ming. In the early years of the conquest Chinese
culture lay exposed and, deprived of its usual dynastic connections and
supports, had to rely on its own inner resources. It cannot be supposed
that tradition simply held fast. Both what managed to endure from the
past and what sprang anew from the native soil—as for instance the remarkable flowering in the Yüan period of popular literature in the form
of drama, poetry and fiction—had to satisfy the needs or tastes of a larger,
more heterogeneous public, and had to seek out the common human
denominator in a multicultural society.

    Nevertheless the traditional order won a crucial first victory over the
newcomers when the Mongols were forced to recognize the need for
ruling agrarian China through the civil bureaucratic administration which
had been developed as part of the dynastic system. The initial acceptance
of this fact of life in China came with the Mongol Khan Ögödei's entrusting of the internal administration to the sinicized Khitan statesman
Yeh-lü Ch'u-ts'ai[b] (1189–1243), who proceeded to reconstitute a fiscal
administration of the familiar Chinese type.[3] Perhaps the second phase
could be seen as inaugurated in 1260 by the formal adoption of a new
Chinese-style reign name, signifying the resumption of Chinese dynastic
rule under the leadership of Khubilai. As the conclusive step in this development one may cite the institution of the new examination system
in 1313–1315 under Emperor Ayurbarwada (Jen-tsung[c], r. 1311–1320),
which confirmed the system of bureaucratic recruitment most characteristic of the great Chinese dynasties.

    If this sequence of developments in the Yüan seems to underscore
the continuing importance of the dynastic system, the first of the papers

in this volume reminds us that the strength of traditional institutions is
not to be judged from the tenure of dynastic regimes alone. Hok-lam
Chan's study presents for us the historical thought of Ma Tuan-lin[d] (1254–
1324/5), a survivor of the Southern Sung dynasty whose life and work
carried over into the Mongol period. Ma's scholarship was pursued largely
in isolation from the main political events of the time, and he can hardly
be reckoned as one of the influential thinkers of the Yüan period. Nevertheless his institutional history of China, completed in 1307, sums up
both the scholarly legacy of the Sung school and the lessons derived from
its critical study of Chinese history. In form and in substance it stands as
the culmination of China's social and cultural evolution up to that point.

Ma Tuan-lin exemplifies the type of broad learning and empirical
investigation which had become a hallmark of Neo-Confucian scholarship as advocated by the leader of that movement, Chu Hsi[e] (1130–
1200). He also offers a perspective on history which reflects the latter
philosopher's rather ambivalent view of the tension which exists between
ancient ideals and historical realities. Thus Ma presents a picture of the
model institutions of the ancient sage-kings as embodying the highest
standards against which to measure the strengths and weaknesses of the
historical dynasties. The latter, for him, fall far short of measuring up to
those ideals, and yet in contrast to many reformers of the Northern Sung
period who called for wholesale change and a "restoration of the ancient
order," Ma, like Chu Hsi, questions whether this can, or even should,
be attempted. Indeed, his doubts go beyond mere feasibility and extend
to the suitability of such reforms in the changed conditions of more recent times. What exists exists for some reason. History, and the consequences of the past, cannot simply be overruled. But what can reasonably
be done only becomes clear if one follows the long-term development of
institutions in the course of many dynasties, and observes the cumulative
effects of that process. Hence the need for general histories, comprehensive in time and extensive in their coverage of social and cultural institutions, to replace the standard histories of single dynasties. Only through
this kind of comprehensive investigation and "broad learning" can one
hope to arrive at a sound judgment as to what is in the long-range, general interest of mankind, rather than what serves simply the immediate
interests of a given dynasty.

Chief among the long-term trends seen by Ma is the steady centralization of power in the imperial dynastic system. This is regrettable but

only reflects the historical process by which the ancient system of public morality, stressing the common good, had yielded to a widespread preoccupation with personal gain and the pursuit of private interests, including the dynastic interest. If one could accomplish a moral reformation and the restoration of Confucian public morality, said Ma, it might be feasible to reestablish the ancient "feudal" pattern of government and do away with centralized despotism. Until such a moral transformation was accomplished, however, it would be unrealistic not to accept centralized bureaucratic administration as a fact of life, making such improvements or modifications in it as one could through constructive reformism. Better to improve the exercise of established power than dream of reversing history and returning to a primitive ideal.

In their own way Yüan rulers had to accept the same facts of history as Ma. They had to work through the same system rather than attempt to convert China to the Mongols' pastoral way of life. Nevertheless at the outset they were ill-adapted to the Chinese bureaucratic scene, and it took a major effort of Chinese scholar-statesmen to persuade the Mongols to accept the rule of law which was so much a part of the dynastic system. "Law" had more than one meaning for the Chinese. To some it represented "systems" characterized by rational procedures and regular routines. Under Khubilai an able corps of Chinese advisors devoted much of their time and many lengthy memorials to explaining the need for such a system of administrative law, which, to a considerable degree, Khubilai accepted.[4]

In the matter of legal codes, however, as John Langlois points out in his study, there was greater ambivalence on the part of both the Mongols and the Chinese. Khubilai set aside the preexisting Jurchen-Chin dynasty code, ostensibly as "too harsh." The meaning of this is unclear and a combination of reasons, both realistic and idealistic, may explain why Khubilai and his successors never got around to filling the legal void, with the result that the Yüan, alone among major dynasties, bore the stigma of being "law-less": of lacking a permanent code. Professor Langlois suggests that in an ethnically plural and multicultural society, a supposedly uniform code would have been strangely incongruous and inoperable. Moreover, as a conquest group in the numerical minority, the Mongols would find any legal limitation on the exercise of their own power a decided disadvantage. Chinese advocates of a legal code argued that the intent was to curb the abuses of subordinate officials. Thus they found themselves advocating, in effect, the centralization of authority which Ma Tuan-lin had deplored. Yet the Mongols as the principal power-holders could not fail to see that any legal restraint on the exercise of authority would fall most heavily on them.

For the Chinese' part, the need to accept these controlling power factors may have been seen, by the more Confucian-minded among them, as good reason to make virtue a necessity in the absence of law. Although scholars like Ma Tuan-lin had long since reconciled themselves to the need for law in the dynastic context, others with a more moralistic ap-proach to history and politics, according to Professor Langlois, saw the judgments rendered by Confucius in the *Spring and Autumn Annals* as a surer guide to the administration of justice than any law code. In this view the *Annals* illustrated the constant norms of justice, as applied by Confucians in given historical situations, with a sensitivity to human needs, a flexibility and finesse beyond anything that rigid adherence to a legal code could allow. From study of the *Annals*, then, the ruler and his surrogates could take Confucius as their model and approximate the jus-tice of the sage-king, administering personalized rule rather than the in-flexible and impersonal legal system inherited from the great dynasties. The ethical code of the Confucian gentleman was appealed to, then, as a higher law, more civilized than the legal codes of even benevolent despots.

How widespread this attitude was in the Yüan period remains a mat-ter of speculation. One may well doubt that it sufficed to explain the absence of a formal code in the Yüan or the feeling that such was dis-pensable. Yet a significant number of the Yüan scholar-officials holding this view of the *Annals* as a sure guide to justice were also identified with the Chu Hsi school, whose influence was spreading at this time. True, one need not have been a member of that school to hold such views; quite possibly, however, the moral enthusiasm generated by the new movement reinforced the idealism expressed in this interpretation of the *Spring and Autumn Annals*.

A rather different, though still Confucian, view of the essentials of rule and rulership is found in Professor Franke's study of Wang Yün[f] (1227–1304). As a member of the Hanlin Academy and court historian, Wang Yün bespoke a traditional Confucian statecraft largely unaffected by the new developments in Neo-Confucianism. He represented the po-litical culture surviving from the Chin dynasty, which had preceded the

Mongols in the occupation of North China and long been at odds with the Southern Sung. Wang personified the type of official whose bureaucratic credentials were attested by the old-style civil service examinations, putting primary emphasis on literary skills and bureaucratic know-how, rather than on ideological fitness. Theirs were the skills useful in the drafting of government documents and keeping of records. Scholars possessing them became solidly entrenched in the Hanlin Academy, which handled much of the government's paperwork. Though Wang Yün was not a major thinker, he possessed a scholarship and bureaucratic competence of no mean order, representing a style of Chinese learning which had flourished under foreign rule in the Tung-p'ing region of what is now Shantung province, with a high level of literary sophistication and political savoir faire. Where, however, the Sung school had deprecated the Han and T'ang dynasties as political models—an attitude seen also in the critique of dynastic codes—the political wisdom of this tradition drew heavily on the conventional lore associated with successful rulers of those great dynasties.

Wang Yün, from a Chinese family which got its political start under Jurchen rule, had had a long and distinguished career at court and in the provinces before he presented to the throne the two short guides to rulership which form the centerpiece of Professor Franke's study. In these works Wang distilled the essence of his accumulated learning and experience, presenting models of conduct and lessons of history for the edification of the ruler or heir apparent. For this he drew mainly on the classics and histories, but with special emphasis on the exemplary actions of the Han and T'ang monarchs.

Professor Franke underscores the very simple and practical nature of these lessons, their down-to-earth, nonmetaphysical character. Here, in effect, we have the hard core of the working Confucian tradition, absent the high-flown theories of the Sung philosophers. From this one can easily surmise that Wang pitched his message at the level of the common denominator between Chinese, Mongol, and Central Asian experience, not at the level of Chinese high culture. As texts thought worthy of translation into Mongol, they conveyed the essential message capable of penetrating the language barrier and breaking through cultural bounds.

Further significance is lent to this conclusion by comparison to earlier works in the same genre of imperial instruction. In form and in spirit Wang's writings come closest to the T'ang works, the *Examples of the*

Emperor (Ti fan)[g] attributed to T'ang T'ai-tsung[h] (r. 627–649), and *The Essence of Government in the Chen-kuan Era (Chen-kuan cheng-yao)),*[i] compiled by Wu Ching[j] (670–749) to record the essential spirit and substance of T'ai-tsung's rule. Wang's use of historical examples is also reminiscent of the work of Fan Tsu-yü[k] (1041–1098) in the Northern Sung and of Chen Te-hsiu[l] (1178–1235) at the end of the Southern Sung.[5] This latter resemblance, however, renders all the more strange and striking Wang's avoidance of any reference to these Sung models, or to the text of the *Great Learning*, which had become the main text for citation and discussion in the imperial instruction offered by members of the Ch'eng-Chu school. The most celebrated work of this type was Chen's *Extended Meaning of the Great Learning (Ta-hsüeh yen-i)*,[m] which had been presented to Khubilai before he formally ascended to power in China in 1260.[6] The *Extended Meaning* shared with Wang's work the honor of translation into Mongol—not just once, but several times. For Wang not to mention it, or the *Great Learning* itself, or Chu Hsi's views on the latter as the basic text for the ruler's self-cultivation, suggests that we have here a case of separate, if not competing, political traditions—the old line represented by Wang Yün and the Chin culture of the Tung-p'ing region, on one side, and on the other the Neo-Confucian movement which, just at this moment in history, was overtaking, though not fully displacing, the preexisting tradition. Elsewhere and on other occasions Wang Yün had paid tribute to Chu Hsi's outstanding contributions to the advancement of the Confucian Way. No doubt this reflected the rapid rise in prestige of Neo-Confucianism in his time. Nevertheless, Wang's own intellectual formation had been in the earlier culture, and his most authentic voice was not that of the Ch'eng-Chu school.

Since Neo-Confucianism is a form of Confucianism, and claims to preserve all that is essential in the latter, no clear line of demarcation can be drawn between them. At this juncture in Chinese history, however, and in Wang's rather unusual "typical case," we may see how things stood in the mind of an authentic Confucian, experienced in the ways of the Chinese political world, on the eve of Neo-Confucianism's penetration of the imperial citadel. Through his eyes, and through the writings of others like Ma Tuan-lin, we get a view of the most persistent realities of the Chinese dynastic tradition.

The Neo-Confucian's qualified acceptance of those same realities, but insistence also on a higher order of values which men might attain, is the subject of the next group of papers to be considered. Included among them are studies of four of the most influential Neo-Confucian teachers of the Yüan period, namely, Chao Fu,[n] Hsü Heng,[o] Liu Yin,[p] and Wu Ch'eng.[q] They represent the wave of the future, breaking over the rock of China's entrenched institutions and age-old problems, and then spreading beyond to other lands and people.

In the early decades of the thirteenth century Chu Hsi's teaching had become a vital force in the educational life of South China, but, given the hostility between the alien regimes in the North and the Southern Sung dynasty, communication was difficult and Chu Hsi had almost no following in north China. With the Mongol conquest of the South, however, and with China reunited, though under foreign rule, the relative isolation of the North ended. Meanwhile the high level of Confucian culture sustained under the Chin, and the familiarity with earlier philosophical developments of the Northern Sung, yielded a well-prepared and receptive audience for the new teaching. Wing-tsit Chan's study of "Chu Hsi and Yüan Neo-Confucianism" tells the dramatic story of how the highest expression of Sung culture, its "learning" or philosophy, survived the defeat of the dynasty itself and turned military subjection into cultural victory.

Professor Chan has already made impressive contributions to the study of the Chu Hsi school in the Southern Sung, Ming, and Ch'ing periods. Here, in tracing the transmission of the teaching through this stormy epoch, he identifies those characteristics of the movement which marked this initial phase in its growth, thus delineating the elements of continuity and discontinuity which are fused in the history of any great tradition. Against the background of earlier symposia which have highlighted different features of the movement, we may note the following significant observations by Professor Chan:

First is the predominance of the Chu Hsi school in the Yüan period and the failure of other Sung schools, notably that of Lu Hsiang-shan,[r] to perpetuate themselves. This dominance was largely achieved without the benefit of official endorsement or support, though the latter eventually confirmed Chu Hsi's teaching as the approved one. The reasons for this extraordinary survival power and inherent strength of the Chu Hsi school remain to be explained, but the fact itself is undoubted, given the evidence adduced by Professor Chan. Though Lu Hsiang-shan in the Sung, and Wang Yang-ming[s] in the Ming, are often referred to as leaders of the so-called "Lu-Wang[t] school," there was in fact no such school historically in the sense of a lineal succession or ongoing academy from the Sung into the Yüan and Ming.

Second, Chu Hsi's concept of the orthodox tradition (*tao-t'ung*)[u] was widely accepted by leading thinkers of the time, and helped give a sense of unity and common purpose to the members of the school.

Third, Chou Tun-i[v] and his concept of the Supreme Ultimate had importance for Yüan Neo-Confucians far beyond what was generally accorded to it in the later tradition.

Fourth, the *Elementary Learning* (*Hsiao-hsüeh*)[w] compiled under the direction of Chu Hsi was a major Neo-Confucian text along with Chu's version of the Four Books. By contrast, the *Reflections on Things at Hand* (*Chin-ssu lu*)[x] by Chu Hsi and Lü Tsu-ch'ien,[y] a basic anthology of the Ch'eng-Chu school much used in other periods, was little spoken of. This would seem to indicate that Yüan Neo-Confucians stressed basic ethical teachings, expressed in the simplest form and addressed to the layman as well as the scholar.

Fifth, a similar tendency may perhaps be seen in the relative weight given to the paired values of "abiding in reverence and the exhaustive investigation of principle (*chü-ching ch'iung-li*)."[z] Major Yüan thinkers showed a strong preference for the practice of reverence, and deemphasized the investigation of principle. Thus again the moral and religious aspect seems to have dominated over the intellectual and speculative. Not until the early Ming was an effort made to redress the balance.

In Professor Chan's study Hsü Heng (1209–1281) emerges as the leading intellectual figure of the age, an activist at court and the most influential teacher of the time, whose followers were to dominate the Yüan educational system. By contrast Wei-ming Tu has chosen as his subject a figure known primarily for his abstention from official service. This is Liu Yin (1249–1293), whose "eremitism" had earlier been cited by Frederick Mote as a form of subtle but unmistakable protest against Mongol rule. Hsü and Liu had long been cast as alternative models of Confucian commitment, since the story (almost certainly apocryphal but nonetheless celebrated) had been told of Liu's having chided Hsü for his readiness to serve the Mongols. Hsü replied that commitment to the Tao obliged one to respond to the call for public service in its behalf. Later, it is said, Liu gave as his reason for declining office that it was respect for the integrity of the Tao that obliged him to refrain from serving an unworthy regime.[7]

Professor Mote had already distinguished Liu Yin from the typical Taoist recluse, whose withdrawal from the public arena reflected a self-centered individualism and disassociation from politics, as well as from the typical Neo-Confucian loyalist, whose refusal to serve was grounded in a prior, and exclusive, loyalty to another dynasty. Instead of this, according to Mote, Liu's "eremetism" was a veiled protest by one whose political commitments were made clear in his polite refusal to be associated with a corrupt government.

Tu, by contrast, sees Liu's reluctance to serve, not primarily as a form of political protest but as fulfilling a commitment to a Neo-Confucian ideal of sagehood which went beyond politics. In this view Liu had been converted to Neo-Confucianism as an ethicoreligious calling which placed a supreme value on the achievement of individual integrity in conformity with the Way. Liu's decision not to serve in government was made on grounds that "were not exclusively political, for . . . the Confucian demand that a man serve society is primarily an ethicoreligious one. Moreover the basic Confucian commitment is to morality and culture rather than to any particular structure of power. . . ." Thus Liu was "impelled to choose morality and culture over politics by a profound sense of mission, and ultimate concern for personal purity and dignity as respect for the Confucian Tao."[8]

This deep sense of mission appears as a common characteristic of converts to Neo-Confucianism in the thirteenth century, about whom we have many accounts of a conversion-experience akin to being "born again."[9] In some sense, of course, they had been Confucian scholars all along, yet when Chu Hsi's works became available, it was for them much like a revelation or new testament. Until then the classics had been just so much antiquarian learning; now these texts came to have a much heightened significance and personal meaning in their lives. This was especially true of Chu's explication of the Four Books and his exposition of the *Elementary Learning* as a basic manual and guide to the moral life. Suddenly the light of reason shone over all things and the inspirational call to the personal achievement of sagehood had a catalytic and dynamizing effect on many individuals.

No less of a sense of mission than Liu Yin's was felt by the great southern scholar Wu Ch'eng (1249–1333), the central figure in David Gedalecia's paper. Gedalecia approaches his subject from a somewhat different angle, however. For him Wu's significance is less as someone who played a key role in Yüan developments than as a pivotal figure in the long-term development of Neo-Confucian ideas. In his own time, even though Wu had a reputation as perhaps the greatest classicist and philosopher of the day, he was not the subject of such great controversy as he became in the Ming period, when his role as an interpreter of orthodox Neo-Confucianism became a major issue.

This is not to say that Wu was uninvolved in the great issues of his time. He was in fact one of the most prominent of Neo-Confucians to express opposition to the resumption of the civil service examinations on the ground that they were too impersonal, mechanical, and competitive.[10] The learning they required was minimal and routinized, in contrast to the fullness of scholarship and virtue which had been associated with the Neo-Confucian sage as the model of self-cultivation and education. Wu stood as one of the last hold-outs against the new system, invoking the unchallengeable authority of Chu Hsi in behalf of his position. Thus the basic issue of principle over which he broke with the government was not one which put him into theoretical opposition to Chu Hsi, even though Chu was to become prominently identified with the new system through the use in the examinations of his versions of the Four Books.

The issue Gedalecia focuses on is the dual aim of "honoring the virtuous nature and maintaining constant inquiry and study" (*tsun te-hsing, tao wen-hsüeh*),[aa] a time-honored formulation of the balance to be maintained by Confucians between moral cultivation and scholarly inquiry. For Wu to be deeply concerned over maintaining this balance was not out of keeping with his position on the examination issue, since, in his view, the evil of the new system was precisely its neglect of moral cultivation and abandonment of the ideal of integrated learning. Nor was his stress on honoring the moral nature counter to the prevailing trend of thought in the Chu Hsi school. In Wing-tsit Chan's study of the Chu Hsi school in the Yüan it is his conclusion, too, that such an emphasis on the moral and religious aspect of self-cultivation had been a general tendency, with little said in the school about the "exhaustive investigation of principle."

It is true that the relative weight of moral and intellectual concerns had already been an issue in the encounter between Chu Hsi and Lu Hsiang-shan, as Wu Ch'eng himself pointed out. Thus the issue was certainly there for anyone who wished to stir up controversy over it. Chu Hsi himself, however, had belittled the difference between them and sought to avoid contention with Lu. The same may be said for a significant number of Chu's immediate followers, like Huang Kan[ab] (1152–1221), Wei Liao-weng[ac] (1178–1237) and Chen Te-hsiu.[11] They were inclined toward reconciliation, rather than partisan polemics. Indeed it may be said that Yüan thought in general inclined toward harmony and accommodation, so that in taking a generous view of Lu Hsiang-shan, Wu Ch'eng was quite in keeping with the spirit of the age and not, in most eyes, disqualified by this from being accepted as an authentic transmitter of the Ch'eng-Chu teaching.

As Professor Gedalecia reviews the growing controversy which later arose over Wu's orthodoxy, it becomes clear that the polarization of thought around the figures of Chu Hsi and Lu Hsiang-shan is more a product of the Ming than of the Sung and Yüan. Stresses then developed among divergent strains in the original teaching, as one tendency or another was pursued at the expense of the all-round balance Chu Hsi had sought to maintain among them—a balance which social and cultural change would in any case have rendered unstable. One benefit of this study, then, is that it helps us to see how we make problems for ourselves—how prone any age is to read its own problems into its past, and how not only our own conflicts but even the refinement of our methods of thought and analysis may easily contaminate the historical evidence we are dealing with.

In his study of "Confucianism, Local Reform, and Centralization in late Yüan China," John Dardess shifts the focus away from the leading thinkers and scholars of the age and directs it at the Confucian elite on the local level—in this case, activists who tried to put their principles to work in reform of the fiscal administration and military defense. Here Professor Dardess labels their reformist thought and activity as "Confucian" because the values invoked and the practices employed may be considered the stock in trade of the perennial tradition, rather than distinctive Neo-Confucian creations. The working ingredients in this historical situation are nonetheless a compound of old and new. Eastern Chekiang, the hotbed of reform, was also a seedbed of Neo-Confucian teaching. Shao-hsing,[ad] Yü-yao,[ae] Chin-hua,[af] etc., the cities and towns in which

activists started their Confucian reform programs, were also active centers
of Neo-Confucian thought and scholarship. The reformers themselves
drew inspiration from typical Neo-Confucian texts like the *Elementary
Learning,* and when they sought to improve local education they did so
by stressing the basic moral relations expounded in that text, and by
building halls for "Clarifying (or Manifesting) Moral Relations" (*Ming-
lun t'ang*)[ag] such as are found in Neo-Confucian academies throughout
East Asia. We have reason to believe then that their sense of mission and
their dedication to the cause of reform was not unconnected with the
renewed sense of commitment to the Way which Neo-Confucianism engendered in the Yüan statesmen who served Khubilai or even in the
philosophers and scholars who refused to serve the Mongol ruler. Indeed
the reformers themselves paid specific tribute to the Sung masters, as
much for their personal example as martyrs in the service of the Way, as
for their inspiring ideas.

Three things impress us as significant in this valiant, but in the end
unsuccessful, struggle for reform on the local level. First is the fact that
the reform leaders among the local elite were not limited to one ethnic
group, economic class or social function. There were significant numbers
of Mongols and Central Asians, along with Chinese, working together in
a common cause. Some had means, others had none. Some had official
status or civil service degrees, others lacked these. What brought them
together was their common education in Neo-Confucianism and their
shared sense of commitment to make the Way prevail in the world. This
moral activism and esprit de corps Dardess identifies as "Confucian
professionalism," using the latter term less in its modern connotation of
specialized function than in its original sense of a body of values which
one actively professes and works to uphold. From Dardess' evidence it is
clear that the spread of Neo-Confucian education in the Yüan era created
a distinct professional class, a moral and intellectual elite with a common
bond transcending race, social status or worldly means.

Second, struggling against corruption and maladministration in their
home regions, these grass-roots activists had a strong sense of the need to
mobilize support among the local populace and to achieve this by building a new spirit of moral and social solidarity among them. To this end
they tried to "restore" authentic Confucian rituals that celebrated the
common values of the community and structured human activities in
pursuit of shared goals. Much of this effort was based on classical models,

but the "neoclassical" inspiration for it came in significant measure from the Sung experience with reform and Chu Hsi's own sense, in an age characterized by corruption and incompetence at court, that educational, social, and economic reform must start at the local level.

Nevertheless, and this third point goes hand-in-hand with the second, according to Dardess reform on the local level required centralization of authority against divisive forces; it could not be completely self-contained but depended on a correlative effort by the central government. The problem of reform, to be manageable, had to be defined in terms of local needs and capabilities, yet autonomy on the regional level, if particularistic and self-serving, could intervene and come into conflict with any polity, local or national, grounded in an ethos of genuine commonalty (*kung*)[ah] and public service. Chu Hsi's whole educational approach, in his interpretation of the *Great Learning* as the key text and classical basis of public morality, was built on the idea of individual self-discipline in fulfillment of the highest good (which also served the common good) for man in society. Thus the ideology of reform was predicated on a universalistic ethic and a conception of the structured society as culminating in a true center, uniting power and justice.

Unfortunately for the noble men who sought to "rescue the times" in the mid-fourteenth century, the forces of fractious regionalism proved too strong, and the leadership of the Yüan court too weak, for the local reform to be sustained. It is Dardess' contention nonetheless that even this experience of frustrated reform served as a useful lesson for some of its leaders like Liu Chi[ai] (1311–1375) who, abandoning the Yüan as hopeless and unworthy, contributed their efforts to building the new Ming regime of Chu Yüan-chang.[aj]

The inclination to look to the center for direction has long been a fact of Chinese life, and this has been so irrespective of the differences among dynasties, conquerors, the type of governmental structure, and whether or not there was strong ideological guidance or dictation from above. Thus it is not surprising, when we turn to teachings or traditions other than Confucianism (which everyone assumes to be state-oriented or concerned with politics), that Professor Jan Yün-hua should consider the relations of Buddhism to the state, and the situation of Buddhists at the capital Ta-tu[ak] (modern Peking), to have prime significance for understanding the condition of even this relatively apolitical religion. One way or another, by favor or neglect, protection or persecution, the attitude of the ruling power was bound to have its effect on the organization of religion. Even in the studies of Professors Yü and Liu, though they deal with other topics, the omnipresence of the ruling power is evident.

Predisposed though the Mongols were from before the conquest to favor Buddhism, this gave no guarantee that Chinese Buddhists would have an easy time of it. In the early days of conquest military and political affairs preoccupied the new rulers, and patronage, when it came in more settled circumstances, tended to be dispensed with a view to maintaining peace and a balance among religious forces. Even influential Buddhist laymen at court, such as Yeh-lü Ch'u-ts'ai and Liu Ping-chung[al] (1216–1274), had to accept these ground rules and try to eschew partisanship. Under such conditions the Chinese Buddhist community in the capital region considered it an accomplishment, in the midst of the general devastation, that they could simply survive and transmit their teachings to the next generation. Hence in Professor Jan's judgment the most that Chinese Buddhists could aspire to was continuity, not creativity.

Still, these circumstances alone do not account for the lack of dynamism within the Buddhist community at this time. Under the surface veneer of religious toleration and ecumenical harmony, enough infighting was going on to stimulate the competitive drive of any movement. Among the Chinese and Tibetan Buddhists there was intense rivalry for the favor of the khans or the attention of the people. The various sects subordinated their differences only when faced by a common threat from encroachments of the Taoist clergy on their religious properties, or were challenged by spurious Taoist "scriptures" depicting Buddhism as a minor offshoot and deviation from Taoism. As of this time Chinese Buddhism was largely dominated by the Ch'an or Meditation sect, a movement which by its very nature lacked any principle of organization or cohesion. Its own "leaders," as Professor Yü's study of Chung-feng Ming-pen[am] (1263–1323) illustrates, felt a responsibility mainly for the transmission of the lamp of enlightenment from mind to mind, and very little for the functioning or administration of institutions, be they political, social, or even ecclesiastical. Thus, even within the Ch'an school the real question was whether or not a given transmission of teaching and practice could maintain itself.

In this respect Professor Jan points out the paradoxical situation of a teaching so noncommittal and so insistent on "wordless transmission" that it found itself on the verge of extinction unless something were done to record its essential teachings. Thus it had to be counted an achievement that the Ch'an schools succeeded at this time in putting into writing what had previously been left unsaid. As Professor Jan has it, when the Ch'an Master Ts'ung-lun[an] wrote that he tried to express in language the truth of the inexpressible, someone commented that "It is not that the Honorable Lun was so given to speech, but only that the Tao needed to be discussed. He therefore had no choice but to speak."[12]

There was another ironical moment in the history of Ch'an Buddhism when the Yüan regime decided that it was time to limit the number of tax- and draft-exempt monks by giving them examinations to determine their credentials as learned in Buddhist scripture. In a dramatic encounter with the Chancellor of State, the Ch'an master Hai-yün[ao] (1202–1257) averted this threat by disclaiming any competence in the reading of Buddhist scripture himself. Expressing incredulity that so eminent a monk could profess virtual illiteracy, the Chancellor asked "If you cannot read, how could you become a senior monk?" To which Hai-yün replied, shocking the court by his seeming temerity, "Is the honorable Great Official able to read [the scriptures]?"[13]

With his back against the wall, defending the essential faith, Hai-yün was willing to make an issue of whether or not genuine religious understanding could be put to a literacy test. Among his own coreligionists, however, he acknowledged the low estate to which the Buddhist clergy had fallen by their lack of study and discipline. This was indeed one of the reasons why he felt compelled to insure the continuity of instruction by compiling a record of the *koans* of the Ts'ao-tung[ap] school. Ch'an's radical denial of culture and insistence on the sole authority of the Ch'an master had to be abandoned if the authentic transmission itself could only be assured by cultural means. Ming-pen, too, felt this pressure when he conceded the practical need for the *hua-t'ou*,[aq] or *kung-an*[ar] (*kōan*), as a formula to put a stop to all conceptual formulations. He was as aware as Hai-yün of the deterioration of training and discipline, and the lack of true dedication among the monks. Hence the need for him to struggle with the problem of how one introduces some order and system into even a religion like Ch'an that forswears intellection and verbalization.

Leaders like Hai-yün and Ming-pen were successful enough in these efforts to insure at least the continuance of their own religious traditions, though in an uneasy, jostling coexistence with others. They knew well the tendency of the ruling power to bestow its ostentatious favors indiscriminately among the major faiths, and they accepted the polite conventions by which religions showed respect for one another as all members of the same spiritual family, each serving its respective function. Thus the studies of formal religion in this symposium are replete with instances of the silky syncretism which smoothed over the relations among religious groups in this time. Yet it was also typical of this Oriental "ecumenism" that in their seeming deference to one another each religion still managed to slip in a claim that it was somehow more equal than others or more lofty in its condescension.

A typical example is found in Yeh-lü Ch'u-ts'ai's formulation that "the Way of Confucius is for governing the world, the Way of Lao Tzu is for nourishing the nature, and the Way of Buddha is for cultivating the mind"—a view which he spoke of as "universally accepted in the past and present." When chided by his own Ch'an master for seeming to concede parity with Buddhism to Confucianism and Taoism, Yeh-lü disclosed a hidden reservation and an intentional ambiguity in this characterization. In his reading of it, Buddhism retained paramountcy through its control of the mind, while Confucianism, having to cede this crucial role to Buddhism, amounted in the end to no more than "the dregs of the Way."[14]

Given this attitude of outward deference and inward rejection of the three religions toward each other, little in the way of genuine interreligious dialogue actually took place. When, rarely, a serious debate was held, it was usually on the initiative of the ruler. Khubilai, on his part, was extraordinary for the eagerness with which he promoted open religious encounters at court and for the seriousness with which he appeared to follow the issues himself. In this role he seems to have prefigured the great Mogul Emperor Akbar (r. 1556–1605) in India, who held similar debates at court and took an active part in the religious encounters among Muslims, Hindus, and Christians. Indeed one may wonder if the rulers of these great conquest dynasties, presiding over such cultural diversity and yet endeavoring to construct some new polity in its midst, did not take a broader view and deeper interest in religion than was typical of either professional clergy or the more established dynasties.

With the plurality of cultures represented in the Mongol empire, with the presence in China of Muslims, Tibetan lamas, Nestorians, Roman Catholics, Jews and crypto-Manicheans, and with the extensive exchange among them on other levels of culture (especially material culture), it may seem striking that there was so little to show for the interaction in religion and philosophy. Striking, that is, if one can assume that a culturally open situation and tolerant rule are enough to foster philosophical or theological discussion. Yet one may well ask whether, in the given circumstances, it is on this level that one could expect to find evidence of cultural interchange, or whether it is under these conditions that significant religious or philosophical dialogue takes place. Up to this time the most fruitful discussions had been held, and the most impressive syntheses produced, in twelfth-century Sung China, though it was politically weak, militarily beleaguered, and culturally somewhat isolated. To judge from this a certain degree of cultural continuity and maturity, and an intense cultivation of intellectual and philosophical concerns, may rather be the precondition for erecting new and more complex structures of thought, even though it be at the cost of effectiveness in more practical matters.

In the Yüan conditions were perhaps too unsettled for this. With no established cultural direction, there was instead a groping for some consensus in values to serve as a common basis for action. And, it must be said, this was not to be found in the facile syncretisms then available. These were, in effect, agreements not to agree. Let everyone do his own thing: let the Confucians talk, let the Buddhists meditate, let the Taoists cultivate immortality. As Ming-pen, trying to sort things out, put it:

The Confucian Way is to govern the mind (chih-hsin)[as] and cultivate the mind (hsiu-hsin),[at] whereas the Buddhist Way is to brighten the mind (ming-hsin)[au] and awaken the mind (wu-hsin).[av] Governing and cultivation imply gradualness whereas brightening and awakening imply suddenness. The mind is, of course, the same. But the sudden approach is surely different from the gradual approach. This is because the worldly and the otherworldly are different. If our Buddha should decide to talk about the worldly Way, he would surely not forget to mention the theory of "rectifying the mind" and "making the will sincere." Suppose Confucius should decide to talk about the otherworldly Way, how can one be sure that he would not mention "emptiness of Mind" or "perfection of enlightenment"? When a person does not understand the great skill-in-means a sage employs in establishing his teaching, he will argue senselessly and merely add confusion.[15]

There can be no doubt that Ming-pen speaks for the Ch'an community when he refuses thus "to talk" or to "argue senselessly." Their "one great thing" was not to be done on the philosophical level, as the *hua-t'ou* pointedly asserted if it asserted anything. And under these circumstances, of course, there could be no significant dialogue, unless it be on Confucian—and now Neo-Confucian—terms. An indication of this is found in the further explanation which Yeh-lü Ch'u-ts'ai gave his master on the real meaning of his characterization of the Three Teachings. He quoted from the classic formulation in the *Great Learning:* "According to Tai's classic text one who wished to bring order to his state . . . would first rectify his mind. There has never been a case in which, one's mind being rectified, the state remained in disorder." From this Yeh-lu concluded that "the governing of the world is a byproduct of the controlling of the mind." [16] In his view, then, Buddhism, having claimed the mind as its special field of jurisdiction, automatically established its implicit authority over all else, and Confucianism's political function was likewise subject to this control.

Nor were the Neo-Confucians, for their part, unaware of these implications. Precisely for this reason they had disputed in the Sung whether the Buddhist mind was one which could be entrusted with such large responsibilities for the welfare of mankind. If Ming-pen could say, as Professor Yü reports, that the mind must be concentrated solely on the *hua-t'ou* of life-and-death, and should exclude all other concerns, the Neo-Confucians had to reject this as too self-centered an approach and too unpredictable a course on which to chart the way for human society. Hence they presented an alternative, a mind-and-heart of their own, more rational, moral, and socially concerned.

This had already been their problem in the twelfth century and if the dialogue now, such as we find it in Yeh-lü Ch'u-ts'ai and Ming-pen, is couched in the language of the *Great Learning,* this is because its linking of the "rectification of the mind-and-heart" with the concern for the "governance of men through self-discipline," as the Ch'eng brothers and Chu Hsi had so emphasized it, was already the focus of the dialogue in the Sung. [17]

To this dialogue, in fact, the great Ch'an master of the Sung, Ta-hui Tsung-kao[aw] (1089–1163) had himself contributed. Ta-hui, of course, had his own understanding of this "mind," but he acknowledged the centrality of the issue and of mind-rectification as the common ground among the Three Teachings. According to him, "The Dharmas of the sages of the Three Teachings—there isn't one that does not urge the good and forbid the bad, and rectify men's minds. If one's mind is not rectified, then one will be licentious and immoral, and profit will be one's only object. If one's mind is rectified, then one will be loyal and righteous and follow only principle. . . . You must know that in Confucian teaching, the first and most important thing is to rectify one's mind. When one's mind is rectified, then 'even in moments of haste and confusion' one does nothing that does not fit perfectly with this Tao."[18]

By the time of Ming-pen, a century and a half later, the leaders of the Neo-Confucian movement in the Yüan had made the doctrine of the *Great Learning*, as interpreted by Chu Hsi, the main focus of public discourse and the essence of the teaching which Hsü Heng and his disciples disseminated widely through the system of public instruction.[19] It is hardly surprising, then, that Buddhists who "decided to talk" about such matters, as Ming-pen puts it, would have recourse to the language of the *Great Learning* and the School of the Way. This had indeed become the consensus teaching, both in the schools and in the new system of civil service examinations. For Ming-pen this was not an article of faith or dogma but an option open to him, and one which, in the existing historical circumstances, it was natural for him to exercise in the way that he did. He spoke in the language of the Ch'eng-Chu school, tacitly recognizing Neo-Confucianism's increasing influence in the social and cultural arena. For in this arena it was giving new meaning and coherence to human life, encouraging men to believe in the possibility that some kind of rational and moral order could be brought out of the chaos around them.

What then about the other side of Ming-pen's equation: "should Confucius decide to talk about the otherworldly Way, how can one be sure that he would not mention 'emptiness of Mind' or 'perfection of enlightenment'?" Indeed one could not be sure. While Neo-Confucians resisted any tendency to "talk about an otherworldly Way," they certainly did discuss "enlightenment" and "emptiness of Mind." Instead of viewing it as another realm of "unworldly" truth, however, they saw it as a spiritual dimension of the human mind going beyond the purely rational and moral, which kept it open to new experience.[20] For them this realm of the spirit, as Chu Hsi affirmed it in his commentary on the *Great Learning*, offered the prospect of man's highest fulfillment by participation in the wondrous creative power of Heaven itself.[21] Chu recognized this human capability as something that could not be fixed, quantified, or wholly defined. Many of his followers in the Ch'eng-Chu school, too, including Huang Kan, Wei Liao-weng, Chen Te-hsiu, and Wu Ch'eng so understood it, and for this reason they were loathe in their own time to shut the door tight on either Lu Hsiang-shan or the Buddhists and Taoists.

This accounts, I believe, for the dominant spirit of reconciliation in the Ch'eng-Chu School and its Learning of the Heart-and-mind in the Yüan period. Later critics might tax them for being less than strictly orthodox, or more recently for being syncretists somewhat lacking in philosophical rigor, but one underestimates Chu Hsi, it seems to me, if one fails to appreciate his remarkable combination of toughness of mind, largeness of heart, and openness of spirit. It was these qualities in him which made him a worthy teacher for the Yüan, and in his followers too during this period, which rendered them something more than blind conformists repeating a dull routine. It is also these qualities of mind and spirit which contributed to a new phase in the growth of a rich and vital tradition, one that we, in this volume, have only begun to open up and explore.

NOTES

1. See Yoshikawa Kōjirō, "Shushigaku no hokuden zenshi"[ax] in *Uno Tetsujin sensei hakuju shukuga kinen Tōyōgaku ronsō* (Tokyo: Tōhō Gakkai, 1974), p. 1257.
2. See John D. Langlois, Jr., ed., *China Under Mongol Rule* (Princeton: Princeton University Press, 1981), Introduction, p. 12. For an account of the Yüan system of provincial administration and military garrisons, see Yang P'ei-kuei,[ay] *Yüan-tai ti-fang cheng-fu* (Taipei: Hao-han Publishers, 1975) and Ch'i-ch'ing Hsiao, *The Military Establishment of the Yüan Dynasty* (Cambridge, Mass: Harvard University Press, 1978), pt. 1. On the impact of these systems on the Ming and Ch'ing, see Charles O. Hucker, ed., *Chinese Government in Ming Times: Seven Studies* (New York: Columbia University Press, 1969), chaps. 1 and 2, and Robert H. G. Lee, *The Manchurian Frontier of Ch'ing Dynasty* (Cambridge, Mass: Harvard University Press, 1976), chap. 2.
3. See Igor de Rachewiltz, "Yeh-lü Ch'u-ts'ai (1189–1243): Buddhist Idealist and Confucian Statesman," in *Confucian Personalities*, ed. A. F. Wright and D. C. Twitchett (Stanford: Stanford University Press, 1962), pp. 189–216.
4. See Hok-lam Chan, "Liu Ping-chung (1216–74): A Buddhist-Taoist Statesman at the Court of Khubilai Khan," *T'oung Pao* (1967), 53(1–3):98–146.
5. See Wm. Theodore de Bary, *Neo-Confucian Orthodoxy and the Learning of the Mind-and-Heart* (New York: Columbia University Press, 1981), pp. 91–126. Hereafter cited as *Neo-Confucian Orthodoxy*.
6. *Ibid.* pp. 124–25.
7. See Frederick Mote "Confucian Eremitism in the Yüan Period" in A. Wright, ed., *The Confucian Persuasion* (Stanford: Stanford University Press, 1960), p. 218.
8. Tu Wei-ming, "Liu Yin's Confucian Eremitism," p. 264.
9. See W. T. de Bary, *Neo-Confucian Orthodoxy*, pp. 21–24.
10. *Ibid.*, pp. 59–60.
11. *Ibid.*, p. 150.
12. Jan Yün-hua, "Chinese Buddhism in Ta-tu," p. 397.
13. *Ibid.*, p. 388.
14. *Ibid.*, p. 384.
15. Chung-fang Yü, "Chung-feng Ming-pen and Chinese Buddhism in the Yüan," pp. 445–46.
16. Jan, "Chinese Buddhism in Ta-tu," p. 384.
17. See de Bary, *Neo-Confucian Orthodoxy*, pp. 31–34.
18. *Ta-hui P'u-chüeh ch'an-shih fa yü*[az] in *Taishō shinshū daizōkyō*, vol. 47, pp. 912c–13b. Cited by Miriam Levering in "Neo-Confucianism and Buddhism in the Sung as Movements within a Single *shih-tai-fu* Culture: Buddhist Interpretations of Confucian Discourse." Paper presented to the Columbia University Seminar on Neo-Confucianism, pp. 6–7.

19. See de Bary, *Neo-Confucian Orthodoxy*, pp. 44–45, 133, 141–43, 145–46.
20. See de Bary, *The Unfolding of Neo-Confucianism* (New York: Columbia University Press, 1975), pp. 164–88.
21. See de Bary, *Neo-Confucian Orthodoxy*, pp. 100–3, 145; *Principle and Practicality: Essays in Neo-Confucianism and Practical Learning* (New York: Columbia University Press, 1979), pp. 128–29.

GLOSSARY

a 吉川幸次郎

b 耶律楚材

c 仁宗

d 馬端臨

e 朱熹

f 王惲

g 帝範

h 唐太宗

i 貞觀政要

j 吳兢

k 范祖禹

l 眞德秀

m 大學衍義

n 趙復

o 許衡

p 劉因

q 吳澄

r 陸象山

s 王陽明

t 陸王

u 道統

v 周敦頤

w 小學

x 近思錄

y 呂祖謙

z 居敬窮理

aa 尊德性，道問學

ab 黃榦

ac 魏了翁

ad 紹興

ae 餘姚

af 金華

ag 明倫堂

ah 公

ai 劉基

aj 朱元璋

ak 大都

al 劉秉忠

am 中峰明本

an 從倫

ao 海雲

ap 曹洞

aq 話頭

ar 公案

as 治心

at 修心

au 明心

av 悟心

aw 大慧宗杲

ax 朱子学の北伝前史，宇野哲人先生白寿祝賀記念東洋学論叢

ay 楊培桂，元代地方政府

az 大慧普覺禪師法語，大正新修大藏經

Hok-lam Chan[a]

"Comprehensiveness" (*T'ung*) and "Change" (*Pien*) in Ma Tuan-lin's Historical Thought

INTRODUCTION

FOR ALMOST a century after China fell under the subjugation of the alien Mongols who founded the Yüan dynasty, Chinese civilization was put to a severe test of its viability and resilience. These nomadic conquerors, who came to rule China by force of arms, were alien to Chinese institutions and the Confucian value systems, and had to be persuaded of their worth before they allowed their continuance or reestablishment. To Chinese intellectuals living in this turbulent age, it was a time of serious crisis for their culture and more. In these dire circumstances, their urgent concern was to perpetuate their cultural heritage, convince the Mongol rulers of its value, and persuade them to extend patronage to it.[1] This intellectual response varied in modes and attitudes, and one of the significant efforts was the search for the meaning and lesson of the historical tradition for contemporary reference. Ma Tuan-lin[b] (1254–1324/5), author of the encyclopedic institutional history, *Wen-hsien t'ung-k'ao*[c] (Comprehensive Survey of Literary Remains), 348 *chüan*, is an outstanding example. He not only provided the most important documentation of the traditional heritage and institutions, but also expounded the classical concepts of "comprehensiveness" and "change" for understanding past ages. In this context he reflected upon the legacy of traditional institutions and value systems, their merits and faults. and sought to relate the historical experience to contemporary vicissitudes of alien domination.[2]

To understand Ma Tuan-lin's historical thought and his unique contributions, it is desirable, first of all, to place his *Comprehensive Survey* in the context of the historiographical development between the T'ang and Yüan dynasties. During these long centuries, Chinese historical writings, for generations dominated by the composition of the annal-biographical dynastic histories and chronological narratives under imperial auspices, made a significant breakthrough with the appearance of three comprehensive histories of the classical heritage and governmental institutions by private historians.[3] The first was the *T'ung-tien*[d] (Comprehensive Statutes) (801), 200 *chüan*, by Tu Yu[e] (735–812) of the T'ang; the second was the *T'ung-chih*[f] (Comprehensive Treatises) (1161), 200 *chüan*, by Cheng Ch'iao[g] (1104–1162) of the Southern Sung. These were continued and elaborated by Ma Tuan-lin's *Comprehensive Survey*. The importance of these three outstanding works, which collectively came to be known as *San T'ung*[h] ("three comprehensive compendia"), has long been acknowledged by traditional scholars as well as modern historians.[4] Not only did they provide an encyclopedic topical summation of the classical heritage and governmental institutions from legendary antiquity to the later imperial era that constituted a distinct genre in Chinese historiography, but they also revived and elaborated traditional views of the continuity and changes in history through a comprehensive investigation of the extant records.

There are several outstanding features in these three institutional encyclopedias that merit attention:

First, all three works undertook a comprehensive approach to the documenting and writing of history and aimed at presenting a broad survey of the imperial traditions and governmental institutions since the earliest times. They all used the word *t'ung*[i] in their title, alluding to "mastery of the subject" or "comprehensiveness," which, together with its related word *pien*,[j] meaning "change" or "transformation," expounded two seminal ideas in traditional Chinese historical thought and approaches to historical writing.[5] These ideas, emanating from ancient Chinese cosmogonical conceptions and the relationship between nature and man, were prominent in the *Book of Changes* and other Classics edited by Confucius for the preservation of the classical heritage and transmission of the teachings of the ancient sages. They were also echoed by the Taoist progenitors, Lao Tzu and Chuang Tzu, later Confucians such as Hsün Tzu, and the cosmologist Tsou Yen[k] (305–240 B.C.), although they differed in their philosophical discourses and in the interpretation of the historical process.[6] In various ways, they projected the view that it requires a command of the essentials of the history of all ages, and mastery of the keys to the changes in various stages before one can arrive at a proper understanding and judicious assessment of the lessons of human activities in the past.

It was Ssu-ma Ch'ien[l] (145–86? B.C.), author of the memorable *Shih chi*[m] (Records of the Historian), who applied these concepts to writing the first annal-biographical form of quasi-"universal" history of China from legendary antiquity down to his own time. His history contains not only the imperial annals, biographies, genealogical tables, but also, most important of all, monographs on institutions that seek to examine the continuity and changes in history. This ideal is most vividly elucidated in the concluding remarks of his autobiographical postface: "I wished to probe into all that concerns Heaven and Man, to master (*t'ung*) all the changes (*pien*) of the past and present, completing all as the work of a single tradition."[7] Ssu-ma Ch'ien's lofty principle, however, was abandoned by his successor Pan Ku[n] (A.D. 32–92) who, while continuing the annal-biographical tradition, chose a dynastic format for the composition of the *Han shu*[o] (History of the [Former] Han Dynasty), limiting the coverage to a single dynasty. Pan Ku's model was subsequently adopted by private and official historians for the composition of dynastic or standard histories, and Ssu-ma Ch'ien's ideal of a comprehensive, universal history fell into oblivion during the next several centuries.[8] It was revived in part by Liu Chih-chi[p] (661–721), author of the distinguished *Shih t'ung*[q] (Comprehensive Historiography), who produced a meticulous work of criticism of the craft of historical writing by drawing upon all the available compilations, and was finally enlivened by the authors of these three institutional encyclopedias although they also adopted a format that differed from the annal-biographical style of comprehensive, universal history.[9]

Secondly, all these three works were concerned with the documentation and investigation not of the rise and fall of rulers and dynasties, nor of the life and deeds of individuals of the past, but of the evolution of the imperial traditions and governmental institutions from their very beginning down to the time of composition. The sources encompass the imperial archives, government records, as well as canonical works, histories, official statutes, literary collections, and the comments and dis-

courses of scholar-officials of the past and present. They are classified
into various topics, and are either quoted at length to preserve the original documents and records, or are proportionately abridged as illustration
of observations or arguments on the subject in question. In many cases,
these authors freely introduced their own views and judgments to the
original documents and the opinions by the scholar-officials in order to
elucidate the written records and transmit their meaning to later generations. They reveal not only their methodology in these compilations but
also their perception of history in general and of the individual periods
in particular.

In all these works, moreover, the authors placed great emphasis on
the classification of source materials on the basis of the relative importance of the subject matter and the availability of the documents and
records. Tu Yu, who established the model for later compilations in his
Statutes, devised eight broad categories for his work: Food and Money,
Examinations and Official Promotions, Government Offices, Rites, Music, Army and Law, Prefectural System, and Border Defense.[10] These
were classified further into subsections under appropriate rubrics and all
the materials were arranged in a chronological order. Cheng Ch'iao, on
the other hand, divided his *Treatises* into two parts. The first part, called
Chi[r] (Annals) and *Chuan*[s] (Biographies), provides a comprehensive history from the earliest times down to the end of the Sui dynasty in the
annal-biographical style. The second part, called *Lüeh*[t] (Monographs),
contains twenty treatises on the Chinese cultural heritage and traditional
institutions. They include five novel categories such as family and clan,
philology, phonetics, capitals and flora, and insecta, and fifteen others
modelled on the *Statutes* that cover such topics as Classics, rites, music,
astronomy, arts, medicine, encyclopedias, and literature, in addition to
the principal governmental institutions.[11] Ma Tuan-lin, on the other
hand, though influenced by Cheng Ch'iao's innovations, went back to
the *Statutes* as the basic model and divided his *Survey* into twenty-four
sections dealing extensively with political, social, and economic institutions, and ignored many of the new classifications introduced in the
Treatises that are not directly related to political and institutional matters.

Finally, all the authors of these three institutional encyclopedias
shared a common view on the objectives of their work, and the purposes
which it would serve. This warrants historians' considering them together
in any appraisal of their worth. All three authors recognized the validity

of the Confucian views on history expounded, *inter alia*, in the *Shang shu*ᵘ (Book of Documents), the *Ch'un-ch'iu*ᵛ (Spring and Autumn Annals, 722–481 B.C.), and other classics, namely, that history should serve the purposes of moral didacticism, political persuasion, and conveying the lessons of the past to future generations. They did not, however, develop these concepts into a cosmological theory of historical causation, or an abstract moral-ethical philosophy of history, or propagate these views to lay down the grand principles governing the rise and fall of rulers and dynasties as did the Han scholars of the Five Agents school, or the metaphysical Neo-Confucian philosophers of the Sung dynasty. Instead, they sought to elucidate and perpetuate these Confucian concepts and views of history through a meticulous investigation into the organizations and functions of the traditional governmental institutions. They all wished that their work, by focusing on the concrete situations of institutional development and by delineating the nature of the changes, would enhance the understanding of practical statecraft and perpetuate the Confucian principles of government. These not only would serve, in the words of the late Étienne Balazs, as "guidance for bureaucratic practice" to contemporary rulers and public servants, but would also illuminate the ways of the ancient sage rulers for emulation by later rulers and scholar-officials to heed the mistakes of past dynasties.[12]

There are, of course, as shown later, noticeable differences among the three authors in the emphasis of their work. These reflect not only their scholastic temperament and their perceptions of history, but also the ideological predilections and intellectual trends of their time. Nevertheless, these varying emphases do not gainsay their homogeneity of outlook, and there are conspicuous traits of continuity in thought as well as in the methods of composition. Of these three institutional encyclopedias, Tu Yu's and Cheng Ch'iao's work have received considerable attention, but not much has been given to Ma Tuan-lin until recent decades, when mainland Chinese scholars have hailed him as a "progressive, scientific historian."[13]

The present essay is focused on Ma Tuan-lin's historical thought, in particular his concepts of "comprehensiveness" and "change" as keys to understanding history. It will show how his compendium surpassed its predecessors by broadening the scope of coverage, critically evaluating the written records, and formulating a judicious evolutionary view of history. This will serve to illustrate the continuous development and unique accomplishments of traditional historiography in the era of Mongol domination, and, more importantly, a salient dimension of the Chinese intellectual concern for the perpetuation of traditional institutions and Neo-Confucian values under alien conquest.

THE MAN AND HIS WORK

Ma Tuan-lin was descended from a scholar-official family in Lo-p'ing,[w] Jao-chou,[x] modern Kiangsi, but he left few primary sources for a reconstruction of his biography. It is quite extraordinary that, despite his later reputation, he is rarely mentioned in the writings of his contemporaries. There is no account of him in the *Sung shih*[y] (Sung History) nor the *Yüan shih*[z] (Yüan History), and only a sketch of his life in later sources such as the *Nan-Sung shu*[aa] (History of the Southern Sung) and the *Sung-Yüan hsüeh-an*[ab] (Philosophical Records of Sung and Yüan Confucians). The latter contain little information, as do the derivative biographies in the general histories of the Yüan period compiled by Ch'ing historians, including the *Hsin Yüan shih*[ac] (New Yüan History). Fortunately, his father Ma T'ing-luan[ad] (1222–1289) has a biography in the *Sung History*, and, together with the prefatory materials in the *Survey* and a few other references from the local gazetteers, we are able to present a fuller account of his life and career.[14]

Ma Tuan-lin's father, T'ing-luan, was a court official and scholar-historian of high repute under the later emperors of the Southern Sung. A *chin-shih* of 1247 in the reign of Li-tsung[ae] (r. 1225–1265), Ma T'ing-luan was appointed Instructor of a local school in Ch'ih-chou[af] (modern Anhwei) in 1253, and served as Supervisor of Archives in the Ministry of Finance and as Correcting Editor in the Imperial Library during the next three years. In 1256, however, he was cashiered on a trumped-up charge by the notorious Ting Ta-ch'üan[ag] (fl. 1263), then Assistant Executive of the Secretariat-Chancellery, for refusal to support his faction. Nevertheless, he earned respect for his integrity and uprightness, and was recalled, when Wu Ch'ien[ah] (1196–1262) became Right Grand Councilor in 1259, to be a Collating Editor of the Imperial Library and steadily advanced in rank. He was just appointed a Compiler in the Bureau of Military Affairs in 1260, then Chief Adviser to the Heir-apparent, and following that Vice-Director of Education, Auxiliary Academician of the Bureau of Hanlin Academicians, and, after serving concurrently as Compiler in the Institute of National History in 1263–1265, he was promoted to be an Executive of the Ministry of Rites.[15]

In 1265, upon the accession of Tu-tsung[ai] (r. 1265–1275), Ma became a veteran official and received appointment to a number of outstanding government positions. He served successively as Academician of the Tuan-ming Hall,[aj] Signatory Official of the Bureau of Military Affairs in charge of the compilation of military encyclopedias, and as Assistant Executive of the Secretariat-Chancellery. In 1269, he topped out his career as Right Grand Councilor and, concurrently, Commissioner of the Bureau of Military Affairs. In these new capacities, however, he came to clash with the notorious and powerful Chia Ssu-tao[ak] (1213–1275), the Senior Grand Councilor, and, to preserve his integrity and avoid possible disaster, he begged to retire in 1272, only to witness the fall of the dynasty to the Mongol invasion a few years later. It is said that in 1279, immediately after the conquest of Southern Sung, the Mongol emperor Khubilai Khaghan (r. 1260–1294) summoned T'ing-luan to court offering him an appointment, but he declined and remained in retirement until his death ten years later, at the age of 66.[16]

Ma T'ing-luan distinguished himself not only as an outspoken critic of the political factions and governmental maladministration, but also as an upright official historian noted for his impartial judgment and faithfulness to the craft of historiography. He had assumed charge, for several intervening years, of the archives in the Imperial Library and the Bureau of Military Affairs, and the compilation of veritable records and national histories in the Institute of National History. Therefore, he was able to gain access to the imperial archives and official documents, and accumulate a substantial collection of primary historical works which greatly facilitated his son's compilation of the institutional encyclopedia several decades later.

In addition to his official compilations, Ma T'ing-luan had written a general history in the chronological format called *Tu-shih hsün-p'ien*[al] (Review of History: Ten Days a Chapter) in 38 chapters, covering two thousand years from legendary antiquity down to the reign of Later Chou (951–960), and other miscellaneous works on the classics, philosophy, and literature. These works are all lost, but fragments of them have been retrieved from the Ming encyclopedia *Yung-lo ta-tien*[am] (The Great Works of Yung-lo) and were later printed in a collection called *Pi-wu Wan-fang chi*[an] (Literary Works of Pi-wu Wan-fang), 24 *chüan*, in *Yü-chang ts'ung-shu*[ao] (Collectanea from Yü-chang). It includes specimens of his memorials, essays, and poetry, as well as the surviving portions of the *Review of History*, 1 *chüan*, which provide some glimpses into his scholarship, his views on history, and the traces of his influence on his son's historical work.[17]

Ma Tuan-lin, *tzu* Kuei-yü,[ap] was born in 1254 when his father had already achieved some distinction in government, but we know little about his early years. It appears that he developed a penchant for scholarship, and a keen interest in historical writing under his father's tutelage. During his teen years, he pursued his study of the Neo-Confucian philosophy, particularly of Chu Hsi[aq] (1130–1200), under the instruction of Ts'ao Ching[ar] (1234–1315), a native of Hsiu-ning[as] (modern Anhwei), one of the leading disciples of the Chu Hsi school in the Southern Sung. In 1273, at the age of 19, Ma Tuan-lin topped the successful candidates in the prefectural examination at Jao-chou, and was subsequently appointed a *ch'eng-shih lang*,[at] a grade 8A Palace Gentleman at court by virtue of the *yin* (patronage) privilege. His career, however, was cut short three years later by the fall of the capital Lin-an[au] (present Hangchow) to the Mongol invasion, and he returned home to stay with his family until the end of the dynasty in 1279.[18]

Following the demise of the Sung, Ma did not seek an official appointment in the Mongol administration like some of his contemporaries. It is said that when the ex-Sung Grand Councilor Liu Meng-yen[av] (*chin-shih* of 1244), then serving as Minister of Personnel under Khubilai Khaghan, invited Tuan-lin to join the new government out of friendship with Ma T'ing-luan, he declined with the excuse of the advanced age of his father. Thereupon, at about the age of 30, he started work on his encyclopedia history of Chinese institutions.[19] In this undertaking, Ma Tuan-lin was motivated not only by his consuming interest in historiography, inspired by the distinguished T'ang and Sung historians, but also by a concern for the preservation of the records of the imperial heritage, particularly those of the Sung, under the rule of the Mongol conquerors. This was a task which nobly served the Confucian tradition, and at the same time provided an outlet for his talents after he had declined to serve in government. It was also a formidable task, but Ma Tuan-lin was greatly aided in the work of compilation by the rich collection of archival records and historical works available at his home, and, moreover, by the advice of his father who had put his experience and scholarship at his disposal.[20]

During the next twenty years, Ma spent his time almost exclusively on the composition of his institutional encyclopedia, hoping to fulfill his long cherished aspiration. It appears that, with the exception of brief service as Director of Studies (shan-chang)[aw] at a local school called Tz'u-hu Academy[ax] in Jao-chou shortly after his father's death in 1289, he held no other remunerative positions. There is little evidence of any association with other contemporary scholars, or any trace of their influence on his historical work. Finally in 1307, after two decades of work, Ma Tuan-lin completed his Comprehensive Survey of Literary Remains; he was then 53 years old, but had to wait another fifteen years before he saw his work in print.[21]

Ma Tuan-lin found an opportunity to publish his work when an emissary of Emperor Ayurbarwada (Jen-tsung,[ay] r. 1311–1320), the Taoist Wang Shou-yen,[az] arrived at his native place in January 1319 with the mission of searching out talented scholars for government service. Impressed by his work, Wang Shou-yen secured a copy of the Survey for presentation at court a few months later, and it received an enthusiastic response. Following this, Tuan-lin was given an appointment as Director of Studies of K'o-shan Academy[ba] in Ch'ü-chou,[bb] modern Chekiang, and an imperial order was issued to the authorities of Jao-chou for the publication of his work.[22] The manuscript was then transcribed, and in July 1322, three years later, Ma Tuan-lin was summoned to bring his own copy to the prefectural administration for collation and printing. The first official edition of the Survey was published in Jao-chou either at the end of this year or in the following year, when he was already 68 or 69 years old. Thereafter, he was given another appointment as instructor in a government school in T'ai-chou,[bc] Chekiang, but he asked for retirement three months later because of illness. It is reported that he died in the year following his retirement; this would place his death in 1324 or 1325, at the age of 70 or 71.[23]

Besides the Survey, Ma Tuan-lin is said to have left other collections of writings, including To-shih lu[bd] (Records on Miscellaneous Topics), 153 chüan; I-ken shou-mo[be] (Upholding the Roots of Righteousness), 3 chüan; and Ta-hsüeh chi-chuan[bf] (Collected Commentaries of the Great Learning), unclassified, and others. None of these works has survived, but they sufficiently attest to his versatile and prolific scholarship in the classics, philosophy, history, and literature.[24]

Essentially, the *Survey* follows the model of its two sister works both in its approach to history and in the organization and classification of source materials. Inasmuch as it also uses the word *t'ung* in the title, it purposes to be a comprehensive treatment of history and attempts to uncover all the traditional institutions since their inception in legendary antiquity. The title, *Wen-hsien t'ung-k'ao,* is derived from an often quoted saying of Confucius in the *Analects:*

I could describe the ceremonies of the Hsia[bg] dynasty, but Ch'i[bh] cannot sufficiently attest my words. I could describe the ceremonies of the Yin[bi] dynasty, but Sung cannot sufficiently attest my words. [They cannot do so] because of the insufficiency of their records (*wen*) and wise men (*hsien*).[25]

In Ma Tuan-lin's context, *wen* refers to the original documents, and *hsien,* related texts and opinions of the worthies. The latter part of the title, *t'ung-k'ao,* on the other hand, connotes "comprehensive survey" or "thorough examination," indicating that it attempts a continuous coverage and meticulous investigation of the source materials.[26]

In his "General Preface," Ma Tuan-lin lavishly extolled the comprehensive treatments of history by Confucius and Ssu-ma Ch'ien and the distinguished achievements of the T'ang and Sung historians. He praised Ssu-ma Ch'ien's *Records of the Historian* for tracing the causes of the rise and fall of rulers and dynasties, and for tracing the development of laws and institutions in an annal-biographical form of comprehensive, universal history. However, he heavily criticized Pan Ku's *History of the (Former) Han Dynasty* for confining the coverage to a single dynasty, and deplored this as a great disservice to a thorough and meaningful understanding of history. He also expressed admiration for Ssu-ma Kuang[bj] (1019–1086) and recognized the merit of his annalistic chronicle *Tzu-chih t'ung-chien*[bk] (*Comprehensive Mirror for Aid in Government*), but lamented that its format made it neglect the importance of institutional developments. He then stated the purpose of his own work:

It has always been my observation that periods of order or disorder, of the rise and fall of different dynasties, are not interrelated. The way the Chin came to power, for example, was not the same as the Han, while the fall of the Sui was quite different from that of the T'ang. Each period has its own history, and it is sufficient to relate events from the beginning to the end of the dynasty, without referring to the history of other dynasties or attempting to draw parapallels.

Laws and institutions, however, are actually interrelated. The Yin followed the rites of the Hsia, the Chou followed those of the Yin, and whoever follows the rites of Chou, though it be a hundred generations after, the way in which he takes from or adds to them may be known. This was the prediction already made by the Sage [i.e. Confucius]. Thus from the Ch'in and the Han down to the T'ang and the Sung, the regulations concerning rites, music, warfare, and punishments, the system for taxation and selection of officials, even the changes and elaborations in bureaucratic titles or the continuation and alterations in geography, although in the end not necessarily the same for all dynasties, did not suddenly spring into being at the beginning as something unique for each period. . . .

Therefore, as to the reasons or causes (ku) for the expansions and contractions [of institutions in each period], unless one makes a comprehensive and comparative study of them from beginning to end, it will certainly not be easy to discuss them. [The type of political history] that is not concerned with interrelated events has already been amply covered in Ssu-ma Kuang's book, but there is no work [that deals with institutions which] depend for their understanding upon historical continuity. Is it not fitting that scholars of our time should turn their full attention to this problem?[27]

Thereafter, Ma hailed Tu Yu's *Statutes* and acknowledged his indebtedness to it but also pointed out the pitfalls and weaknesses in its coverage of source materials, its classification of subject matter, and its observations and judgments. He then elaborated his method of composition and the meaning of the title of his work:

In ancient times, when Confucius spoke of the ceremonies of the Hsia and Yin dynasties, he greatly lamented the insufficient verification of the *wen* and *hsien* of those periods. The commentator explains: "What is *wen*? They are the written records. What is *hsien*? They are the opinions of the worthies." Now I was born a thousand and several hundreds of years later, and yet wish to deliberate on the events of a thousand and several hundreds of years before. Unless the truthful records in the historical narratives had been preserved, which made investigation possible, and the opinions of the past scholars were not too distant, which helped the discussion, even the sages would not make judgments without some basis.

I have often pondered that since I have inherited my father's profession and had a store of ancient chronicles in my home, not only have I [a rich collection of] books on the shelves but also [the benefit of] consultation with my father; thus I have sufficient access to both the written records (*wen*) and [the opinions of] the worthies (*hsien*). I have often worried that [if the records and information] were scattered and lost, I would have nothing to pass on to the wise men of later times. Thus I overcame my humble nature and shallow learning, jotted down occasional comments, widely searched for materials and classified them into various categories. . . . When I narrated past events, I based myself on the *Classics* and *History*, and consulted the *Comprehensive Essentials of Institutions (Hui-yao)*[bl] of all the dynasties as well as the biographies and works of the hundred schools. Whenever they were credible and verifiable, I followed them, but I would not record those that are strange and doubtful. These I call *wen*. When I commented on past events, I first consulted the memorials and discourses submitted by officials of that time, then the comments and deliberations made by recent scholars, as well as the random remarks of the noted worthies and the records of petty officials. If there was a single utterance or phrase that could rectify the errors of the established traditions and corroborate the authenticity of the historical narratives, I would select it and put it into the record. These are what I call *hsien*.

In the case of dubious remarks recorded in the historical works and the inconclusive deliberations reached by past scholars, I pondered and examined them, and when I came to a verdict, I put down my own views to be appended to these records. Therefore, I name my book *Comprehensive Survey of Literary Remains*, with 24 classifications in 348 *chüan*. . . .[28]

These remarks indicate that Ma Tuan-lin not only sought to propagate the traditions of the distinguished historians of the past, but also endeavored to improvise a distinctive framework to produce a more elaborate compendium of traditional governmental institutions. In this undertaking, he was evidently greatly indebted to Tu Yu and Cheng Ch'iao's work, since the *Statutes* provided the basic model for the compilation of institutional encyclopedias, whereas the *Treatises* further elaborated its format and expounded the concept of "comprehensiveness" as a guiding principle for developing a broad view of historical continuities.

In terms of coverage, the *Statutes* commences with the legendary Yellow Emperor and extends through the T'ien-pao[bm] reign (742–756) of the T'ang, with occasional references to the later eras down to Tu Yu's time in the commentaries. The *Treatises* also begins with the earliest times and concludes with the later T'ang, but the *Survey* broadens the scope of both the former works by tracing the development of governmental institutions to the reign of Ning-tsung[bn] (r. 1195–1225) of the Southern Sung. In organization, the *Statutes* is divided into eight categories dealing with economic, political, and military institutions, rites, music, and legal traditions, whereas the *Treatises* expands the divisions of the *Statutes* into twenty monographs or treatises with several novel innovations. Ma Tuan-lin, however, adopted some of the classifications of the *Treatises* and developed the basic categories of the *Statutes* into twenty-four sections in his own work.[29] They include: Land Taxes (7 *ch.*); Currency (2 *ch.*); Population (2 *ch.*); Services and Corvée (2 *ch.*); Customs and Tolls (6 *ch.*); Official Markets and Purchases (2 *ch.*); Local Tribute (1 *ch.*); National Expenditure (5 *ch.*); Examinations and Appointments (12 *ch.*); Schools (7 *ch.*); Government Offices (21 *ch.*); Imperial and Minor Sacrifices (23 *ch.*); Imperial Ancestral Temple (15 *ch.*); Court Rituals (22 *ch.*); Music (21 *ch.*); Army (13 *ch.*); Penal Law (12 *ch.*); Bibliography (76 *ch.*); Imperial Genealogy (10 *ch.*); Enfeoffment System (18 *ch.*); Astronomical Configurations (17 *ch.*); Prodigies of Nature (20 *ch.*); Geography (7 *ch.*); and Foreign Peoples (25 *ch*). These classifications thus embrace a broad spectrum of the Chinese traditional heritage and governmental institutions that far exceed the monographs or treatises in the dynastic histories as well as compendia compiled in the earlier periods.

As to the sources, the *Survey*, like its two predecessors, made full use of the original documents and published works on the classical heritage, ancient history, philosophy, and literature as well as political, social, and economic institutions, including the dissertations and judgments made by scholar-officials of the past and present in their respective works. The sources employed in the *Survey*, however, are much more extensive than either the *Statutes* or the *Treatises* because the work covers a longer time span and they are unique for the period from the late T'ang to the end of Sung since Ma Tuan-lin had inherited a rich collection of original documents and historical works from his father. These original sources were quoted either in full or were proportionately abridged under relevant sections and topics, and were discussed and analyzed by the author in numerous commentaries which abound with perspicacious views and carefully considered judgments.[30] In this sense, the *Survey* is not a mechanical compendium of written documents and historical works on the governmental institutions of the past dynasties. Rather, it is a monumental encyclopedia from a perceptive and erudite historian, who, being imbued with the lofty Confucian ideal, attempted to summarize and transmit the imperial heritage under different political vicissitudes wrought by the Mongol conquest of China. His work hence provides the basic sources not only for the composition of the later dynastic histories and compendia of governmental institutions, but also for the study and reappraisal of the totality of the Chinese historical heritage by scholars and historians of later periods.[31]

MA TUAN-LIN'S APPROACH TO HISTORY

In order to place Ma Tuan-lin's *Survey* in the proper historical perspective, it is imperative to probe into his approach to history, his views on the imperial heritage, and the methods which he employed in the composition of his institutional encyclopedia. First we must examine Ma's intellectual and scholarly background and delineate the ways in which he was indebted to past historians, particularly Tu Yu and Cheng Ch'iao, so as to provide a basis for an appreciation and evaluation of his achievements. It is quite clear, as already indicated, that Ma Tuan-lin was heavily influenced by his distinguished predecessors of the T'ang and Sung, but in compiling the *Survey*, he was able to set forth their ideas, make his own judgment of them, and put a distinctive stamp on his work.

In the first place, Ma Tuan-lin, along with Tu Yu and Cheng Ch'iao, like the earlier Chinese historians, all shared the Confucian perception of history and of the purposes of historical compilation. They believed their works, as institutional encyclopedias of the imperial heritage which purposed to document and illuminate the distinguished achievements of the past, would provide proper guidance on practical statecraft to contemporary rulers and bureaucrats, and would be used by later generations for reflection on the meaning of history and the lessons of the past.

Tu Yu, who lived in the later T'ang dynasty when classical Confucianism still predominated as the basic ideology of government and society, saw the mission of his *Statutes*, the first attempt to present a comprehensive documentation of governmental institutions since antiquity, as one of manifesting the kingly way and the principles of the ideal Confucian government. In order to illuminate and perpetuate the established way, the Tao, it is desirable for rulers to cultivate the people in accordance with the teachings of the ancient sages. This is feasible, however, only if the ruler can provide adequate food and subsistence for the people, since only then will people appreciate the rites and practice virtue. However, he also recognized the importance of establishing regular bureaucratic offices for administering and governing the people; this would in turn require a careful screening for qualified personnel. When all these prerequisites had been fulfilled, the ruler would then be able to use law to regulate the people, establish prefectures to accommodate them, and employ soldiers to defend the border regions against the intrusion of the nomadic peoples, so as to promote harmony and order, and achieve peace and prosperity. In this way, Tu Yu had taken a somewhat restricted approach to history in the composition of the *Statutes*, focusing primarily on those traditions and institutions that embodied the essentials of the Confucian vision of practical statecraft that could serve the ends of the

T'ang and later rulers, rather than attempt a grandiose compendium covering all the imperial heritage and governmental institutions.[32]

Cheng Ch'iao, on the other hand, while echoing Tu Yu's view on the objective of writing history and the relevance of the past to the present in his *Treatises*, laid out a more distinctive approach to historical composition. He placed great emphasis on the views of Confucius that in order to understand the past, one must first acquire a comprehensive purview of the records of all ages, in order to apprehend the genesis of all the happenings and grasp the keys to the changes in historical development. Harking back to Ssu-ma Ch'ien, who had so vividly exemplified the Confucian ideal of comprehensive history in his *Records of the Historian*, he lamented that later historians had limited themselves to single periods and dynasties, so that rulers and scholar-officials would fail to apprehend and master the causes of changes running through successive periods of history. Thus he labored through the historical records to identify the origins of the classical heritage, intellectual and cultural traditions, political, social, and economic institutions and organizations, and trace their evolution and changes in numerous meticulously documented classifications in his compendium. It was his hope that the *Treatises* would serve to overcome the parochial views of the contemporary Confucians and revive the lofty principle of comprehensively treated history, such that history would be made serviceable to rulers and scholar-officials and illuminate the ancient ideal of benevolent government and harmonious society.[33]

Ma Tuan-lin likewise reiterated the views and arguments of Tu Yu and Cheng Ch'iao in his *Survey* on the importance of understanding the past as a guide for action in the present and future. He cited the views of Hsün Tzu that the ways of the later rulers should approximate those of the later sage-kings, and that if one studies the ways of both the ancient and the later kings, he would have a clear perspective on the present and future. In his consuming interest in governmental affairs, however, Ma attached great importance to the study of institutions, laws, and statutes, more like Tu Yu than Cheng Ch'iao, since he argued that only when one had understood them would one be able to comprehend the essentials of the Confucian vision of good government and orderly society. He also followed Cheng Ch'iao in praising Ssu-ma Ch'ien's comprehensive treatment of history and criticizing Pan Ku for restricting the scope of his work to a single dynasty. This is because, he pointed out, while the political events of each period may not be related, all the institutional developments were interrelated. Therefore, he believed that only through a comprehensive investigation into the dominant governmental institutions since the earliest times could one grasp the imperial heritage, discern the lines of development, and understand the causes of all the changes to transmit the lessons of history to later generations.[34]

Secondly, Ma Tuan-lin, under the influence of Cheng Ch'iao, who had taken a skeptical attitude towards the doctrinal views of the classical heritage, also developed a more rational and pragmatic approach to the evaluation and interpretation of the historical records. This is seen in his reservations about the cyclical pulsations of the mystical cosmic powers in the Five Agents theory formulated by Tsou Yen as determinants of historical changes. It is also seen in his criticism of the arbitrary application of the Confucian principles of praise and blame attributed to the *Spring and Autumn Annals* for making judgments on the personalities and events of the past.

It was Liu Chih-chi, author of the distinguished *Comprehensive Historiography*, who set the tenor for criticism of both these traditions in historical writings in the heyday of the T'ang dynasty. He was highly critical of the mystical schemes of the Five Agents theory elaborated by the Han scholars, who saw in them the molding forces of history, and deplored the excessive recording of omenology in the historical annals as signs of good or bad government. In a skeptical spirit, he questioned whether these cosmological prodigies and natural oddities carried such moral messages, and preferred using human explanations, rather than invoking supernatural concepts, in accounting for the rise and fall of rulers and dynasties. Similarly, he cast doubt on the authenticity of the principles of praise and blame attributed to Confucius in the *Annals*, and contended that the latter were no more than contrived records of anicent history transmitted by the later Confucians. He objected, therefore, to the practice by official historians of invoking such arbitrary principles in the writing of dynastic history, because in his view, that betrayed the ideal of faithfulness and objectivity and perpetuated the distortion and prejudice in historiography.[35]

Tu Yu also appeared to have been influenced by these skeptical and rational attitudes towards the traditional historical writings since he did not include a section on the Five Agents in his *Statutes*, nor did he apply the principles of praise and blame in recounting historical events. It may be argued that these omissions do not sufficiently attest to his opposition to the mystical cosmic theory or to the principles of praise and blame attributed to the *Spring and Autumn Annals* since his work was primarily an encyclopedic compendium of governmental institutions. His relative silence on such important issues in the imperial heritage, however, at least shows his ambivalence in regard to these prevailing historiographical traditions. It is probable that Tu Yu, as a junior contemporary of Liu Chih-chi, was thoroughly influenced by his critical attitudes towards traditional historical writings and carried the new attitude into the composition of his own work, which itself significantly influenced later writers.[36]

It was Cheng Ch'iao who spelled out most concretely in the *Treatises* the rationale of his objection to these historiographical conventions. Cheng Ch'iao, who lived through the transition from the Northern to Southern Sung, was deeply exposed to the Neo-Confucian rational and metaphysical philosophies. He was more attracted, however, by the critical attitudes of the Sung scholars such as Ou-yang Hsiu[bo] (1007–1072) and Wang An-shih[bp] (1021–1086) towards the doctrinaire interpretation of the classical canons, and less so by the metaphysical speculation of philosophers such as Chou Tun-i[bq] (1017–1073) and Shao Yung[br] (1011–1077), who attempted to develop a cosmological or numerological theory for the interpretation of historical causation and human activities.[37] This attitude is clearly reflected in his approach to historical composition and interpretation. In his preface to the section on "Calamities and Auspicious Signs" (*tsai-hsiang*),[bs] he vigorously criticized two prevalent schools of thought in regard to a study of history that he considered as preposterous and misleading. The first, which he called "cheating people" (*ch'i jen chih hsüeh*),[bt] referred to the moralistic principles of the *Spring and Autumn Annals*; the other, dubbed as "cheating Heaven" (*ch'i t'ien chih hsüeh*),[bu] was directed against the mystical Five Agents theory. In both instances, he confronted the issues with bold skepticism and rational explanation that went beyond the preceding criticism of these established practices in traditional historical writing.[38]

In his criticism of the moralistic principles of the *Annals*, Cheng Ch'iao reiterated Liu Chih-chi's view that the work was only a documentary chronicle of ancient history, and though it recorded the good and bad deeds of the rulers and ministers, he did not believe that Confucius intended to transmit these records (as tradition would have it) to convey

implicit messages of a didactic or political sort. The belief that the principles of praise and blame were laid down by Confucius in the *Annals*,
he contended, was largely imputed by the authors of the three *Commentaries (chuan)*, the Tso, Kung-yang, and Ku-liang.[bv][39] It is preposterous
and misleading to insist, as did later historians, that Confucius edited the
Annals in such a way that each word carried the implication of praise
and blame. The assertion that there were such principles in the *Annals*,
he said, was tantamount to "cheating people" and should be challenged
and rebuked for the benefit of future generations. Furthermore, Cheng
Ch'iao boldly challenged the validity of the conventional criteria of moralistic judgment applied by official historians in their appraisal of historical personalities and political events. He objected to the practice of using
such epithets as *"k'ou"*[bw] (bandit), *"ch'ien"*[bx] (usurper), or *"i"*[by] (righteous) and *"ni"*[bz] (treacherous) for individual rulers or dynasties without
carefully weighing the historical evidence.[40] In his own eyes, the arbitrary application of these moralistic categories to historical writing, even
though they may have served to illuminate the virtuous and expose the
wicked, had inadvertently perpetuated distortion and prejudice at the expense of faithful recording and impartial historical judgment. These criticisms, however, should not be construed as Cheng Ch'iao's attempt to
cast away the principles of the *Spring and Autumn Annals*, or dissociate
himself from the basic values in this time-honored tradition. Rather, they
underlined his concern for rectifying the misrepresentation of canonical
authority.

Similarly, Cheng Ch'iao also repudiated the attempts of those official historians who invoked the mystical theory of the Five Agents school
as elaborated by Han historiographers when they attempted to relate cosmic
changes to political events and human affairs in the interpretation of
history. He was disdainful of the interdynastic linkage scheme laid out by
these earlier historians according to the successive domination of the five
cosmic powers, and he challenged the attribution of the rise and fall of
rulers and dynasties to these mystical forces. This was because, he argued, these five agents were only physical elements in the cosmic config-
uration, and there was no proof that they had any power over temporal
affairs, or that they were related to political changes, either in theory or
in practice. Though he recognized that there were natural calamities and
auspicious phenomena, he considered that they had little connection with
the rise and fall of rulers and dynasties, or with fortune and misfortune

in human affairs. The contention that these were interrelated, he said, was tantamount to "cheating Heaven," and were as absurd and misleading as the manipulation of praise and blame in judging personalities and events in the past. In his view, the rejection of this pseudohistorical, mechanistic theory of cosmic change would allow historians not only to give greater attention to human actions, but also to adopt a more flexible model for evaluating the past based on a thorough and objective investigation of the historical evidence.

In compiling his own work, Ma Tuan-lin was confronted by these same historiographical conventions, but like Cheng Ch'iao, he invoked no elaborate philosophy of history or alternative descriptive model. Instead, following in the steps of Cheng Ch'iao, he sought in a critical and rational spirit to clarify and modify these conventions within the existing historical framework. For instance, while he shared Cheng's skepticism on the validity of supernatural concepts for interpreting historical events, he took a somewhat more moderate attitude. In his "General Preface" to the Survey, he marshalled evidence from the Book of Documents through the History of the (Former) Han Dynasty on the manifestation of the cosmological prodigies and natural oddities, showing the contradictions in the correlations made between these occurrences and human activities.[41] While he did not contest the notion that cosmic forces gave rise to both natural calamities and auspicious phenomena, he challenged the logic of relating them to political affairs. As he pointed out, some of these occurrences had been interpreted as calamitous at one time, but auspicious at another time. That there was correlation between the two, he argued, was mainly asserted by the official historians for their own didactic and political purposes. Instead, he gave the definition "abnormal occurrences" (fan-ch'ang)[ca] to these extraordinary phenomena in the section on "Prodigies of Nature" (wu-i),[cb] and rather than fit them to some causal theory he simply admitted that there were inexplicable abnormalities in nature.[42] We should note, moreover, that Ma neither omitted the records on calamities and prodigies, nor the verdicts on human affairs and political events which earlier historians had arrived at in the context of the Five Agents theory. These should not be construed, whoever, as indicating any contradiction in Ma Tuan-lin's own view. It was his hope, as he clearly stated, that by preserving these pseudohistorical records, he could show later generations how fallacious it was to invoke and manipulate the Five Agents theory in the interpretation of historical events.

As to the principles of praise and blame attributed to the *Spring and Autumn Annals*, Ma Tuan-lin also raised doubts as to their applicability to historical events and personalities. In contrast to Cheng Ch'iao, who confronted the issue head-on, Ma approached the subject with a critical appraisal of the textual incongruities in the ancient chronicles. In the survey on "Bibliography" (*ching-chi*),[cc] he disputed the authenticity of the text of the *Annals* as transmitted by the Han scholars Liu Hsiang[cd] (77–6 B.C.) and his son Liu Hsin[ce] (d. A.D. 23), leaders of the Old Text School of Confucian classics, and challenged the historicity of their account of the meaning of the messages attributed to the ancient sages.[43] He pointed out, as the basis of his argument, that the *Annals* was reconstructed from the three *Commentaries*, by Tso, Kung-yang, and Ku-liang, each of whom transmitted the *Annals* independently with significant textual variations and even contradictions among themselves. These textual inconsistencies, he contended, suggest that either there were internal incongruities in these chronicles or they had been transmuted or distorted by later scholars, who deliberately interjected their own views and judgments in the name of the ancient sages in order to establish their own authority in the transmission of the classical canons.[44] In this way, Ma in fact challenged the contention that Confucius' editing of the ancient chronicles aimed at laying down principles of praise and blame, and implicitly censured the indiscriminate application of these criteria, attributed to the *Annals*, to other historical writings.

Thirdly, Ma Tuan-lin devoted great attention to the evolution of the political, social, and economic institutions since the earliest times in the tradition of his distinguished T'ang predecessor, Tu Yu. Following the *Statutes*, Ma divided his *Survey* into twenty-four sections with a more comprehensive and analytical survey of all the written records on governmental institutions extending from high antiquity down to the end of the Sung dynasty. The innovation which Ma Tuan-lin introduced to his compendium, however, did not alone lie in a more meticulous and systematic classification of the source materials, but in a more thorough and systematic evaluation of the historical evidence.

In brief, the *Survey* was superior to the *Statutes* in at least two major aspects. First, although Tu Yu placed "Food and Money" (*shih-hio*)[cf] in the leading categories of classifications of governmental institutions in his work, he assigned only 7 *ch.* to them. By contrast, he devoted 100 *ch.* to the "Rites" (*li*),[cg] drawing extensively from the *K'ai-yüan li*[ch] (Rites of the

K'ai-yüan Reign, A.D. 713–742), the principal collection of rites in his own time. This shows that Tu Yu was more interested in the functioning of rites in government over other political, social, and economic institutions. It also reflects the obsession of T'ang scholars with the omnipotence of the Confucian rites as the foundation of government.[45] Ma Tuan-lin, on the other hand, devoted only 60 *ch.* to "Rites" in his *Survey* although it covered a longer time span, whereas he assigned 27 *ch.* to "Food and Money" with a more judicious documentation and evaluation of the source materials, particularly for the period from the late T'ang down to the end of the Sung dynasty.

Second, Tu Yu saw the objective of his *Statutes* as providing guidance to rulers and scholar-officials so that they might ponder upon the past and select what was appropriate to be translated into practical administration. Thus he took laborious pains with the classification of the written records on institutions and documentation of the opinions expressed by scholar-officials of the past and present. He did not, however, attempt to discover the keys to the changes in institutions and practices, or address himself to the causes of these changes in a broad historical content.[46] Conversely, Ma Tuan-lin not only utilized the classifications of the *Statutes* to their full advantage, but also, more importantly, devoted great attention to the changes in institutions and reasons for these over several dynastic periods, with the hindsight of the political changes through the Sung, to the Mongol conquest of China. In this way, he was able to see beyond the horizons of his distinguished predecessors who were circumscribed by the ideological and political limitations of their own time.

Finally, Ma Tuan-lin was most distinctive for developing further the concepts of "comprehensiveness" and "change" in historical interpretation through a meticulous investigation into the records of traditional governmental institutions. In this respect, he was greatly indebted to Cheng Ch'iao, who had already set forth the view of universal history elaborated by Ssu-ma Ch'ien in the *Records of the Historian*. In his preface to the *Treatises*, Cheng Ch'iao introduced the term *hui-t'ung*,[ci] which literally means "meeting and linking," and hence "convergence and comprehensiveness," to expound his philosophy of history. He likened the principle of "meeting and linking," i.e., the continuous recording of human activities, to the many rivers flowing into the great sea. This principle he regarded as basic to all historical writing.[47]

In compiling the *Treatises*, Cheng Ch'iao saw its primary task as reviving the lofty aspiration of Ssu-ma Ch'ien in writing a universal history. The underlying principle of *hui-t'ung* or "meeting and linking," according to him, consists in the continuous recording of human activities, and the systematic classification of all the written records. We should note, however, that Cheng Ch'iao had taken a somewhat narrow definition of "comprehensiveness' in regard to historical compilation. For him the principle of *hui-t'ung* mainly referred to "classification" (*lei*),[cj] i.e., a systematic categorization of all available records in order to trace the sources of cultural and governmental institutions.[48] In his meticulous classification of historical records, the ancient classics were divided into 32 categories, the archaic writings into 6 categories, and the classical literature into 12 categories and 422 items.[49] His contention was that only by so doing could one discern the origin of all past developments. Indeed, no historian before Cheng Ch'iao had attempted such broad coverage of the classical heritage and devoted himself to such systematic evaluation of the historical records.

In general, Ma Tuan-lin agreed with Cheng Ch'iao's principle of comprehensiveness, and accepted the principle of *hui-t'ung* as the foundation of all historical writings. Nevertheless, he was dissatisfied, as were some of his contemporaries, with Cheng Ch'iao's narrow use of the concept. Therefore, while not rebuking Cheng Ch'iao for his notion of "classification," Ma expounded the concept of "*ku*"[ck] (reason or cause) to cast light on the nature of "change" in history. This concept was first spelled out when he enumerated the development of political, economic, and military institutions from the Ch'in and Han, down to the T'ang and Sung, showing how they evolved from one period to the next and were modified and expanded over time. He said, "as to the reasons or causes (*ku*) for the expansions and contractions (of institutions in each period), unless one makes a comprehensive and comparative study of them from beginning to end, it will certainly not be easy to discuss them."[50]

Ma Tuan-lin was interested in applying this critical approach to a thorough examination of the written records (*wen*) and the opinions of the worthies (*hsien*), in order to grasp meaningful problems, draw conclusions, and make judgments. In doing so, while propagating the idea of "comprehensiveness" in historical coverage, he postulated two distinct methods for evaluating past events. First, he sought to delineate the stages of development in history and clarify their significance by focusing on the evolution of dominant governmental institutions. Second, he attempted to uncover the reasons for historical changes by investigating the objective circumstances, without holding himself to doctrinaire and conventional interpretations. In this way, he hoped he could uncover the laws of change in the historical process.[51]

To illuminate the distinct stages of development in history, Ma Tuan-lin did not, as already noted, resort to any of the cosmological thories put forward by earlier philosophers. Instead, he identified the high points in the evolution of the principal governmental institutions through a periodization of Chinese history into two main stages, from legendary antiquity to the Ch'in, and from Ch'in-Han to the end of the Sung. He further subdivided the first phase into three periods based on the distinctive development and changes in the political and institutional spheres in ancient times. These periodizations are not too clearly established in regard to such categories as court rites, music, astronomical configurations, prodigies of nature and others, but they are apparent in the surveys on political, social, and economic institutions. Ma did not, however, devise a similar scheme of periodization for the later phase of ancient history after the feudal era, but singled out the distinctive stages of development in the principal governmental institutions from post-Ch'in to the end of Sung. His primary objectives were to identify the special characteristics in each period and find the keys to changes in the principal institutions and policies so as to develop an analytical interpretation of historical process.[52]

When speaking of the reasons for changes, Ma Tuan-lin often made such circumspect comments as "the things appropriate to the past and those appropriate to the present are different"; on other occasions, he explained "it could not have been avoided," or "it had to be like this."[53] In his "General Preface" when he examined the changes in the "Land Tax" (t'ien-fu)[cl] system from the reform of Shang Yang[cm] (d. 338 B.C.) of Ch'in to the innovation of Yang Yen[cn] (d. A.D. 781) in the T'ang, he concluded:

The system of taxing the landholdings of the people but putting no restriction upon the size of their holdings began with Shang Yang. The system of taxing people for the land they held, but taking no consideration of the number of adult or underage persons began with Yang Yen. Thus Shang Yang was responsible for abolishing the excellent well-field system of the Three Dynasties, and Yang Yen was responsible for the abandonment of the superior tsu, yung, and tiao[co] tax systems of the early T'ang. Scholars have spoken disdainfully of the changes made by these two men, but all later administrators have found it necessary to follow their methods. If they attempted to change back to the old ways [they found that], on the contrary, they only ended up in worse difficulty and confusion, and both the state and the people suffered. *This is because the things appropriate to the past and those appropriate to the present are different.*[54]

Similarly, when relating Yang Yen's two-tax *(liang-shui)*[cp] system, after quoting the opinion of the T'ang statesman Lu Chih[cq] (754–805) that the ancient sage rulers fixed the land tax on the basis of the capacity and productivity of the individual farmers, and not on a quota set up by the government to cover its estimated expenditure, he commented:

This is indeed a noteworthy opinion. However, it is in the nature of things that they are not uniform. Therefore, even though all men are human, they differ in talent and ability: some are ingenius and others mediocre. Though they all endeavor to make a living, they also vary in fortune: some are lucky and others not. There are those who through hard work and thrift accumulate a thousand cash, and the surplus of their ability could be extended to benefit others. There are also those who toil in the same routine and yet cannot save a bare sum and fall into debt for the rest of their lives. Even the sages could not regulate all men and make them equal. This is why the land tax was fixed on the basis of the landholdings, and measured against the income of the individual family to set up the quota of collection. Even though it is not the way to deal with things in better times, it was a plan to remedy troubled times. *It could not have been avoided, and should not be prejudged as wrong.*[55]

In another instance, commenting on the "hired labor" *(ku-i)*[cr] system of the T'ang and Sung in the survey on "Services and Corvée" *(chih-i)*,[cs] Ma made the following observation:

The reason the hired labor system had to be adopted was because, though one could not exempt those who had to perform such service from paying the levy, officials were put in charge of hiring the labor, so that their duties were different from those of the common people and much unnecessary expense could be spared. Even though the system could not have prevented the officials from engaging in corruption, yet the people, having paid the levy for hiring the labor, could be free from interference by the officials, and those who were greedy and wicked could not encroach upon the people. This kind of mutually-guarded relationship, though far from the ideal of the ancient times, still is the best way to remedy the chaos of the day, and *it had to be like this.*[56]

These comments indicate that Ma Tuan-lin had developed a consuming interest in finding the reasons for "change" in the historical process. Though he often placed great emphasis on the role of individuals in these changes, he did not ignore the objective circumstances that brought the changes about. It might seem that at times he took a some-what fatalistic view of the inevitability of certain historical changes, yet he supported this view with concrete documentary evidence.

MA TUAN-LIN'S VIEWS ON HISTORY

To enhance our understanding of Ma Tuan-lin's concepts of "compre-hensiveness" and "change," we may examine further his views on the stages of development in history and the reasons for the changes in the process. In his periodization schemes, Ma drew upon several key con-cepts in ancient Chinese thought to buttress his views on continuity and change. First, he invoked the notions of *kung*[ct] (public welfare or spirit of impartiality) and *ssu*[cu] (private interest or individual selfishness) as cri-teria for judging the subjective factors in history. Secondly, he adopted the terms *kuang*[cv] (brightness or heaven) and *yüeh*[cw] (darkness or earth), i.e., polar terms referring to the distinctive Chinese concept of cosmo-gony, as his criteria for judging the objective factors. These ideas emerge clearly in his "General Preface" as well as in his comments on the sepa-rate surveys dealing with key political, social, and economic institu-tions.[57]

In a nutshell, the antithetical concepts *kung* and *ssu* were central themes in ancient political thought, featured not only in the Confucian classics and the works of Mencius and Hsün Tzu, but also in the Taoist cannons and the treatises of the Legalist philosophers. These philosophers all agreed that the cultivation of a concern for the "public welfare" or a spirit of impartiality, and the suppression of "private interest" or individ-ual selfishness, were essential to a prosperous state and harmonious so-ciety. This means a sharing of profit by all, and the maintenance of impartial standards, in contrast to the pursuit of selfish gains or personal considerations. In the Confucian context, it meant the promotion of the principle of *i*[cx] (righteousness) rather than indulgence in *li*[cy] (selfish profit). The only differences among ancient thinkers lay in the means by which such goals were to be achieved. For instance, the Confucians emphasized moral cultivation, the Taoists, the elimination of human desires, and the Legalists, the use of authority, regulations, and punishments.[58] These ideas persisted into later times and were buttressed by the metaphysical interpretations of the Neo-Confucian philosophers since the Sung dynasty. They held that *kung* emanated from the "heavenly principles" (*t'ien-li*)[cz] and *ssu*, from "human desires" (*jen-yü*),[da] and that the cultivation of the former and elimination of the latter through self-cultivation are imperative to the promotion of the Tao and the realization of a moral-ethical, socio-political order. These ideas have been elucidated in various contexts by Neo-Confucian philosophers and statesmen such as the Ch'eng brothers, Ch'eng Hao[db] (1032–1085) and Ch'eng I[dc] (1033–1107), Chu Hsi in the Sung, Hsü Heng[dd] (1209–1281) during the early Yüan, and also the scholars and bureaucrats who attempted to introduce reform in local prefectures towards the end of the dynasty.[59] In articulating these concepts, Ma Tuan-lin adhered to conventional interpretations, but he did not resort to metaphysical speculations or moralistic judgments. Rather, he tried to invoke these time-honored values to develop his criteria for evaluating the subjective factors in specific political and institutional situations.

The terms *kuang* and *yüeh*, on the other hand, were loosely related notions in the ancient Chinese cosmogonic concepts pertaining to the genesis of all the myriad beings on earth since legendary antiquity. These Chinese philosophers believed that there was no separation between "brightness" and "darkness," or "heaven" and "earth" before "Creation," i.e., before the dawn of history. After "Creation," when history began, the two became separate and all myriad objects emerged along with the social and political organizations of the human race. These simple cosmogonic notions appeared not only in the Confucian classics but also in the Taoist and Legalist literature. They provided the basis for the development of more elaborate supernatural theories about the origin of the Chinese world order and its multifaceted civilization.[60] Ma Tuan-lin appears to have been the first historian to incorporate them into a scheme for the periodization of history. He devoted great attention to the period after the separation of *kuang* and *yüeh*, which gave rise to the differentiation between the management of heavenly affairs and that of human affairs, representing the polarity of religious and secular values in government. In his own view, this resulted in numerous cumulative changes in the political, social, and economic organizations of ancient societies, culminating eventually in the development of a unified bureaucratic empire.

First of all, Ma Tuan-lin focused on the evolution of the "Enfeoffment System" (*feng-chien*),[de] which he regarded as the dominant political institution and the key to an understanding of all spheres of human activity. In his "General Preface," he made no claim to special knowledge of the origin of the enfeoffment system, but pointed out that the number of feudal kingdoms had undergone remarkable contraction from Emperor Yü[df] down to the Chou kings, and there were numerous changes in the location of the fiefs as a result of migration and territorial expansion. This development, he said, was due to the fact that "all the ancient feudal lords, though they received fiefs from the Son of Heaven, won the trust of the people in their domain by practicing righteousness and cultivating them with virtue, so their people joyfully submitted to them." Therefore, their descendants inherited the land and ruled over it, and when they had to migrate to other places because of calamities and disasters, their people, out of loyalty to their rulers, went with them. Thus their settlements in time became capitals and cities. He then explained that this was because "in ancient times, the kings did not regard the country as their private property, nor did the lords treat their fiefs as their own; both the upper and lower ranks looked upon the land as the public property." The principal change, he averred, occurred when "Ch'in annexed the Six Kingdoms and introduced the 'prefectural system' (chün-hsien)[dg] over the empire, so that each foot of land and every single individual came to be regarded as the personal property of the ruler." This inaugurated a new era in the ruler-subject relationship.[61]

Ma then elaborated, in the preface to the survey on the enfeoffment system of state building, his notion of "public welfare" versus "private interest" in ancient society, and on the ascendancy of the latter as the main reason for the decline of this feudal institution. He said:

Both the enfeoffment and the prefectual systems were to divide the land in order to rule the people and we could not speak of the former [as the ruler's concern] for public welfare and the latter [as his concern] for private interest. However, only when [the ruler had] a heart of [i.e., concern for] the public welfare of the country could the enfeoffment system be made to work; otherwise, it would be better to have the prefectural system. If [the ruler did not have] a concern for the public welfare of the country, and yet tried to implement the enfeoffment system, it would become a source of disturbance. . . .

It began with Hsia that [the ruler regarded the country as the property] of one family. It began with Chou [that the ruler] enfeoffed the clan members of the same surname for the protection of the royal house. These two were all sages who made changes in institutions according to circumstances in order to provide regulations for the time, and we should not construe [their intention as] pursuit of private interest. However, if we compare them with Yao[dh] and Shun[di] of the earlier period, they were very narrow-minded. That is why the decline of the enfeoffment system began in the Hsia and culminated in the Chou. Hence, only one generation after Yü, when Ch'i[dj] had to wage a punitive campaign against Yu-hu shih,[dk] and another generation later, Chung-k'ang[dl] had to undertake chastisement against Hsi-ho.[dm] In such cases, the Son of Heaven had to wage war against the feudal lords, and the feudal lords refused to comply, even inter-fering with the campaigns of the Son of Heaven; these never happened before Yü's time, and they all began with Yu-hu. . . . Ever since that time, the Son of Heaven looked upon the heavenly seat as his private [property] and guarded it in perpetuity, and the feudal lords also looked upon their land and soldiers as their personal [property] and made use of them as they wished. If fortunately there were an enlightened and sagely king, he could persuade [the lords] with his virtue and control them with his might so that he could still make them submit. However, when [the kingdom] was in decline, even though people had not yet lost their heart, the feudal lords had already rebelled. As to the Chou kings who enacted the five-rank [investiture system] and established a succession of feudal fiefs, although they purposed to enfeoff all the close relatives and the virtuous worthies, the system could not in the end be extended to the Chi[dn] clan of a different surname. By the time of Kings Wen, Wu, Chao, and Mu,[do] when the fiefs were extended all over the country, the enfeoffment system became more elaborate and the regulations more complicated, and this indicates that people had become more narrow-minded. . . .[62]

Following this, Ma made the point that when the objective conditions changed, the system also had to be modified, so that the enfeoffment system inevitably gave way to the prefectural system in Ch'in times:

This is because, if the times were not the same as those of T'ang[dp] and Yü,[dq] and the kings themselves [not as virtuous as] Yao and Shun, it would be impos-sible to reestablish the enfeoffment system. But to say that since the prefectural system emanated from the [wicked] Ch'in, it must be replaced, is merely the opinion of [pedantic] scholars who do not apprehend the nature of the change. It is as if we placed ten thousand men in a community with store of merchandise and armed them with club and sword. If we want to insure that they would not seize the goods and thus try to restrain their behavior, we must have a ruler who possesses the integrity of Po I[dr] and I Yin,[ds] so that he could dispel or minimize their treacherous intentions. If we have no such person, it would be better to store away the club and sword, and strengthen the surveillance and control so that they would not act in a willful way. This is why in later times the hereditary enfeoffment system could not be reestablished, and why the prefectural system became such an excellent institution. Someone asked: "The fact that [the Great] Yü passed [his Hsia kingdom] to his son, and the Chou [kings] enfeoffed the clan members of the same surname, all were devices of the sages, and yet you delib-erately charge that they regarded the country as their own [private property] and consider them inferior to [the rulers] T'ang and Yü [i.e., Yao and Shun]. How is this?" I said: "It is because the world had long passed beyond that ancient stage. The sage could not turn against the times and could not use the ways of the ancients to rule the people, and we could not have understood the intention of the sages!"[63]

Next, Ma Tuan-lin dwelt on the evolution of governmental organizations and their respective functions as the basis of his criteria of periodization. In his comments in the survey on "Government Offices" (*chih-kuan*),[dt] he laid stress on the bifurcation of these offices into the management of heavenly affairs and human affairs, and the dominance of the latter as the most significant change in these institutions. He remarked:

As observed, all the government offices before the time of Emperor Yao of T'ang assumed the management of heavenly affairs, and those after the time of Yü and Hsia the management of human affairs. The laws and regulations of antiquity were simple and sparse, and we do not know the details. But we learn from the records of the classics and commentaries that since the time of Fu Hsi[du] down to Emperor Yao, most of the officials they appointed were given charge of the calendar and of explaining the seasons. This is because, in high antiquity, the methods for measuring time had not been established and since the way of heaven was vague and remote, only those who possessed sagely virtue would have the special knowledge. Therefore, positioning between heaven and earth, nourishing the myriad objects, regulating the four seasons and completing the work of the yearly cycle, these were the great deeds of the lord and his ministers. . . .

   After the four rulers [i.e., T'ai-hao,[dv] Yen Ti (Shen-nung),[dw] Shao-hao,[dx] Chuan-hsü[dy]], the successors all followed the precedents and filled such offices accordingly. By the time Shun became regent, even though he placed the "seven administrations of heavenly affairs" as the primal functions of government, yet he instituted the "nine offices" and made them responsible for human affairs without reference to heavenly affairs. This is because, having inherited the experience of the past sages, the methods of government were complete at the time of Yao, so that it would not be necessary to look for other worthies and wise men to take charge of these special duties. By the time of Chou the government system of the Three Dynasties had become more elaborate, but when we examine the appointment of officials made by King Ch'eng,[dz] among the "Three Dukes" (*san-kung*)[ea] and the "Three Elders" (*san-ku*),[eb] only two of their functions dealt with heavenly affairs, and those of the officials below the chief administrators were all concerned with human affairs, although the officials still bore the archaic titles. Moreover, [if we examine the responsibilities among the] so-called "Six Officers" (*liu-kuan*),[ec] the Heaven Officer was given charge of administration, the Earth Officer, education, the Spring Officer, rituals, the Summer Officer, Army, the Autumn Officer, punishment, and the Winter Officer, public works, without including the management of the affairs of heaven and earth and the four seasons. This is because by this time all the officers in charge of heavenly affairs had changed their roles and they occupied only an inferior rank in government.[64]

Finally, Ma Tuan-lin emphasized the changing character of the general population, and in particular the divergences in human talents due to changes in circumstances and occupations, as the yardstick for his periodization of ancient history. In his account of "Population" (*hu-k'ou*)[ed] in the "General Preface," he invoked his particular cosmogonical reference-point, the concept of the separation of *kuang* and *yüeh*, to show how the change of government functions from the management of heavenly affairs to the management of human affairs accounted for the radical transformation in political, social, and economic organizations. He said:

In ancient times, the population was sparse and all were men of talent and ability, whereas in later times population flourished but there were many mean and lazy people. They were all human beings. However, among the ancient people, when they were scholars (*shih*),[ee] they expounded the Tao and devoted themselves to studies; when they were farmers, they vigorously engaged themselves in agriculture, and when they became soldiers, they were adept at war and combat. Whatever their skills were called upon to accomplish, they performed well. Therefore, a state with one thousand *li* of territory and a community of ten thousand families all had adequate means to guard the kingdom in perpetuity and defend the castle for the people. When people were numerous, the kingdom became powerful, and when people were fewer, it became weaker. This is because in those times it was the people who helped found and maintain the kingdom. When the functions of *kuang* and *yüeh* [i.e., heavenly and earthly affairs] became separate, and social customs gradually diversified, people who were born at that time had fewer talents and less wisdom. Scholars were hamstrung by preoccupation with literary matters, and felt ashamed when offered armor and weapons, whereas the farmers contented themselves with ploughing and felt at a loss when questioned about literary matters. These later gave rise to the "nine schools" [of philosophers] and "hundred classes" of artisans, and even to the disciples of Buddhism and Lao Tzu. Thenceforth, people who depended for their livelihood on the land became more numerous every day, and though they thronged the streets and quarters, they were so weak physically that many of them could not fulfill their duties. That is why the number of the population could not be used to account for the strength or weakness of the state.[65]

These comments clearly set forth Ma Tuan-lin's criteria for dividing ancient history into three broad periods, i.e., (1) the period of legendary antiquity through T'ang and Yü (i.e., Yao and Shun); (2) the Three Dynasties of antiquity, i.e. Hsia, Shang, and Chou; and (3) the imperial period, commencing with the Ch'in unification of the Six Kingdoms. These periods were characterized, as previously noted, on the basis of a number of subjective as well as objective factors in historical development, and Ma tried to substantiate his argument with meticulous details drawn from the written records on the evolution of the principal governmental institutions. We may of course question the accuracy of these accounts, which is indeed challengeable in the light of modern scholarship, and yet, considering the knowledge about ancient history and the records available at Ma Tuan-lin's time, he used them with much critical acumen and objectivity. In addition, he left numerous judicious comments and perspicacious judgments on this long period of Chinese history that merit our attention and reflection.

First, Ma Tuan-lin placed great emphasis on the shift from the concern for "public welfare" to "private interest" as the basic subjective factor that both dictated the ruler-subject relationship and charted the direction of consequent changes in various spheres of human activities. In discussing the transition from the enfeoffment system to the prefectural system, he regarded the ages of T'ang and Yü as periods under which the rulers regarded the country as the public property of the people, whereas after the Hsia, they possessed it as the property of one family. Then, ever since the Ch'in unification, all the land under heaven had come to be considered the private property of the ruler. Ma did not, however, argue in favor of the archaic enfeoffment system over the subsequent prefectural system, as did some T'ang and Sung scholars, who regarded the former as exemplifying the ideal of decentralization whereas the latter reinforced the trend toward centralized imperial absolutism.[66] Instead, he placed great emphasis on the need for having rulers of high moral attainment who would make the feudal system work for the welfare of the people. He perceived that otherwise, it would be better to have a prefectural system because it provided a uniform standard of government. In these cases, Ma Tuan-lin did not, perhaps to the dismay of modern historians, tackle the basic social and economic issues, such as landownership, expansion of agriculture, or the rise in population, which appear to us today to have been more directly relevant to the change from one insitution to another.[67] Nevertheless, he made the important observation that "if the times were not the same as in the age of T'ang and Yü, and if the rulers were not [as virtuous as] Yao and Shun, it would not be possible to reestablish the enfeoffment system," and "the sage could not turn against the time and could not use the ways of the ancients to rule the people." This shows that, even though he did not spell out such conditions in terms of specific political and institutional development, he did emphasize the fact that when both the subjective and objective factors had given rise to these incremental changes, it would not be possible to restore the ideal norms of ancient society.

Secondly, Ma Tuan-lin invoked the concept of the separation of *kuang* and *yüeh*, which he had used as a yardstick for historical periodization, to illuminate the distinctive changes in class differentiation and power structure in ancient society. He believed that in the ancient era, when *kuang* and *yüeh*, i.e., the functions of service to heavenly and earthly affairs, or to religious versus secular matters, had not been well demarcated, the ruler was able to regulate and control the people by "practising righteousness and cultivating them with virtue." At that time the strength and weakness of the kingdom depended on the size of the population. However, after *kuang* and *yüeh* had become separate, i.e., when the political functions of the state had become diversified and the social organizations grew more complex, the ruler had to resort to power and surveillance to control the people, so that the size of the population alone did not constitute the strength or weakness of the feudal states. Thus the changing relationship between rulers and subjects reflected more than just erosion in the concern for *kung* (public welfare) versus *ssu* (private interest), which suggested moral degradation in the course of time, but also changes in the objective social and political circumstances. In a similar vein, Ma used the bifurcation of government offices and official prerogatives to illustrate the changes in the functions of the state, so as to strengthen his argument about the inevitable transformation of political and social organizations. This is clearly shown in his account of the evolution of the major government offices, from their earliest preoccupation with the management of heavenly affairs in the legendary era from Fu Hsi to Emperor Yao, to the subsequent concern with the management of human affairs since the Three Dynasties. In these cases, Ma did not elaborate the implications of the changes in reference to specific political and institutional development; nevertheless, he touched on an important issue in the historical process that buttressed his observation. This is the change from a simple political organization intended to promote the common good of man in the face of nature, to a complex organization designed by the ruler to regulate and control the people, putting his own personal interest over the benefit of the general population. This development, he contended, accounted for the new ruler-subject relationship after the Ch'in unification of the Chinese empire.

Finally, Ma tackled another important issue in his scheme of periodization that pertains to the changing nature of human behavior and social organizations. These changes were seen as a result of the divergence in human talents and abilities due to changes in life circumstances and occupations. In ancient times, he pointed out, because of the simple nature of society, wherein all men were required to undertake whatever was necessary to sustain life, there was no distinction between scholars, artisans, peasants, and soldiers. However, as mankind progressed and society developed, every individual was assigned a specific function according to his talent and ability, thus giving rise to class differentiations and specialized professions, and as a result, more complex human relationships. This trend of development, he contended, was inevitable because of the cumulative changes over periods of time, and though he cherished the Confucian harmonious relationship between the ruler and subjects, he did not advocate a return to the ancient ways of government since the objective circumstances that made these systems possible no longer existed. In this respect, Ma seemed to have exhibited a certain degree of fatalism, but he deeply believed that whatever the circumstances were, there was always room for human action to improve things. For this reason, he frequently alluded to the need for upholding the concern for public welfare over private interest under any and all political and institutional circumstances. This echoed the Neo-Confucian concern for moral cultivation by the ruler as well as his subjects, and by the scholar-officials in particular, since only with such a dedication to lofty principles would there be hope of a change toward the better. In this way, Ma Tuan-lin not only demonstrated a rational and objective approach to the interpretation of historical records, but also expounded an evolutionary view of history that accommodated the idealistic Neo-Confucian vision to the objectively observed cumulative changes in political and social institutions.

In like fashion, Ma extended his investigation into the later phases of history to expound his evolutionary view of political and institutional developments from the Ch'in and Han dynasties down to the end of the Sung. In reviewing this long period of history, he did not devise a clear-cut scheme of periodization, but focused attention on specific issues like the growth of centralized imperial authority, which had been a major concern of scholar-officials in the Sung dynasty.[68] In various places, he not only invoked abstract philosophical concepts as his basis for judgment, but also dwelt on the concrete historical situations in different periods.

Ma Tuan-lin again focused his inquiry on the evolution of the dominant political institution, the enfeoffment system, from the Ch'in to the Han period after the inauguration of the first bureaucratic empire. In his "General Preface," he delineated the changes in this institution that provided the inception of political centralization. He said:

Ever since the Ch'in annihilated the Six Kingdoms and placed the entire country under the prefectural system, every foot of land and every single person came to be regarded as the personal possession [of the ruler]. In the course of two generations, Liu [Pang]ᵉᶠ [d. 195 B.C.] Hsiang [Yü]ᵉᵍ [232–202 B.C.], and other bravos partitioned the empire and each ruled part of the territory as king. After Kao-tsuᵉʰ [Liu Pang, the Han founder, r. 202–195 B.C.] had eliminated Hsiang [Yü], he attacked and destroyed all the lords who either established themselves or were installed by Hsiang, and then divided the land to enfeoff [the princes of] Han, P'eng, Ying, Lu, Chang, Wu,ᵉⁱ and others. After that time, no one not a meritorious official of the Han could be made Prince. Several years later, however, there were altogether nine rebellions and all the feudal lords and princes not of the Liu surname were exterminated. Thereupon, [Kao-tsu] took away their land to make his sons, brothers, and relatives [princes of fiefs] such as Ching, Wu, Ch'i, Ch'u, Huai-nan,ᵉʲ and others. Thereafter, no one who did not have the surname of the Han house could become Prince. However, after a few generations, Chia Iᵉᵏ [201–169 B.C.], Ch'ao Ts'oᵉˡ [d. 154 B.C.], and others expressed great concern over the extraordinary power of the feudal lords. They felt that, as the close relatives were not given land and the distant ones could force the hands of the Son of Heaven, there would be worry for the preservation of the dynasty. Thereafter, [Emperor Ching,ᵉᵐ r. 157–141 B.C.] either divided up the states of the feudal lords] further, or reduced their land, and mobilized the six imperial armies to remove those strong enough to rebel, such as the [lords of the] Seven Kingdoms. . . . Thus, the further [the Han rulers] strengthened their surveillance and control, the more suspicious they became [towards their relatives and ministers]. . . . Ever since the reign of Emperor Ching and Emperor Wuᵉⁿ [r. 140–87 B.C.], [the Han rulers] forbade the feudal lords from administering the inhabitants [of their domain] and from appointing officials. In this way the feudal lords, though nominally rulers over their subjects, could only live on the stipend derived from the income of their fief, and could not exercise control over their land or soldiers.[69]

In these cases, Ma laid stress on the abolition of the enfeoffment system and the inauguration of the prefectural system as keys to the political and institutional changes in these periods. He made no explicit explanation of this development other than alluding to the changes in the power structure of government; instead, he emphasized the significance of the elimination of remnants of feudalism by the Han rulers. In his opinion, the abrogation of the privileges of the imperial princes and the strengthening of the surveillance system laid the groundwork of imperial absolutism.

Next, Ma Tuan-lin dealt with the development of the "Examinations and Appointments" (hsüan-chü)[eo] system after the Han period to substantiate his views on the rise of centralized imperial authority. In the same "General Preface," he commented:

Ever since the Han dynasties, all the Circuit Inspectors (tz'u-shih)[ep] and the local administrators were given the authority to appoint officials. Beginning with the Wei and Chin, [administrators from] the Chiu-p'in chung-cheng[eq] institution possessed a mandate to evaluate personnel [for official appointment]. They scrutinized [the candidates] on the basis of their reputation among the local community, and, having tested them in clerical positions, recommended them to the imperial court in order to promote the pure and the illustrious. Under this procedure, even though it was inferior to the ancient method of appointing officials on the basis of virtue and conduct, it was still possible to obtain people of talent and ability to serve in government. From the Sui onward, all the appointments of staff in the prefectures and subprefectures were made by officials in charge of the examination and selection of personnel, and all the literati began their official careers through the examination system. Ever since such officials were put in charge of the selection of government officials, the criteria for appointment came to rest on credentials, thus the junior clerks having custody of the dossiers acquired the power to make recommendations for promotion and demotion. Ever since the examination system was adopted for the selection of officials, the candidates were tested exclusively on their competence in literature. Thereafter, those who possessed such minimal skills were able to advance to a distinguished career. Ever since the literati began their careers on successful tests of their command of petty skills that concentrated on literature, while appointments were left to the deliberation of junior clerks in charge of the dossiers and recommendations were made exclusively on the basis of credentials, the ideal of selecting the virtuous and the capable was totally lost.[70]

Here Ma highlighted the significant changes in the official selection and promotion systems from the Han through the Sui dynasty. In this context, he stressed the shift in the power of appointment from the local administrators and gentry families to the bureaus in charge of personnel recruitment in the central government. These changes, he contended, not only enhanced the imperial authority, but also discarded the ancient ideal of selecting officials on the basis of their virtue and capabilities.

Furthermore, Ma Tuan-lin pointed out the changes which had taken place in the offices in charge of state administration in the central government to elaborate his views of the development of imperial absolutism. In his survey on "Government Offices," he made the following remarks:

As observed, although [rulers] after the Later Han established [the nominally highest offices of] the Three Dukes, the management of state affairs was [in fact] entrusted to the Chancellery and the Censorate, and the Master of Documents (*shang-shu*)[er] was the one actually responsible for the central administration. But at that time the Master of Documents only enjoyed a measure of access to the state administration, not yet having taken away all the authority of the Three Dukes. After the Wei and Chin, however, the Master of Documents became the real Chancellor, and the Three Dukes were relegated to become sinecures. How did this come to pass? It was because, under the Han, among the officials in charge of administration, both the Master of Documents and the Palace Writers (*chung-shu*)[es] were the personal servants of the Son of Heaven, and in later periods, all those treacherous ones who usurped the imperial authority also appointed their own staff to such offices. Nevertheless, the offices of these so-called Three Dukes had already been established in ancient times. Therefore, even on the transfer of the dynastic mandate, when imperial authority fell into private hands, the offices of the Three Dukes could not easily be ignored. For that reason, [rulers] deliberately appointed to these offices the elderly and sick who would not attend to their duties or those who would be reluctant to challenge the imperial prerogatives, [so that they could gain full control of power in their own hands].[71]

In these comments, Ma sought to illuminate the important changes in the power structure of government in these later dynasties as evidence of the acceleration of political centralization. The most distinctive features in this process, he pointed out, are that those officials who held high ranks need not have been those who possessed actual power, whereas those who gained such power need not have been those who held the rank of the Three Dukes. In his view, the fact that all these rulers, legitimate or otherwise, invested substantial authority in their personal staff rather than in high-ranking ministers was a significant departure from the ancient ideal of government and a principal means of enhancing the absolute power of the dynastic rulers.

In addition, Ma Tuan-lin paid special attention to the evolution of the dominant economic institutions and policies as illustrating the growth of centralized imperial authority since Ch'in and Han times. This is seen in his analyses and discussions of the development and changes in the

"Land Tax," "Customs and Tolls" (*cheng-ch'üeh*),[et] and "Official Markets and Purchases" (*shih-ti*)[eu] systems. In these cases, he did not, as mentioned earlier, address himself to such problems as land ownership and property rights that pertain to changes in the economic institutions and policies, but again based his argument on the statement that "before the Ch'in, the rulers regarded the country as the property of the people, whereas after that time, they looked upon the land as their personal property." Similarly, he seldom elaborated the reasons for these changes in specific institutional contexts, but instead stressed the significance of incremental changes over time, as, for instance, the unfeasibility of reestablishing the ancient enfeoffment and well-field systems. Often, he invoked the distinction between "public welfare" and "private interest" to buttress his argument that objective conditions had made inevitable the growth of imperial absolutism in the later dynasties. This is most vividly illustrated in the following comments in his "General Preface" dealing with the development of the "Customs and Tolls" and the "Official Markets and Purchases" systems since the Ch'in and Han:

There were two sources of state levies and tolls. The first was the [resources from] the mountains and rivers, such as salt, tea, and minerals. The second was the [resources from] the customs and markets such as liquor and commercial taxes. Those who were ashamed to speak of profit would say: "[They are collected] for the county magistrates for food, rent, clothing, and taxes; it is not the kingly way to compete with the common people for the profit of commerce and trade."

Those who were adept in discussing profit would say: "These treasures from the mountains and sea, heaven and earth, have been seized by strong and powerful people, and the aggregation of goods in the customs and markets has been controlled by the merchants and traders. If we seize them from the strong and powerful people, and from the merchants and traders, in order to defray the expenses of the state, we will not have to rely exclusively on the revenue and taxes of the people. This is the idea of revering the fundamental principle and discouraging the pursuit of mean occupations [i.e., emphasizing agriculture and deemphasizing commerce], and it should set the course for the state hereafter. Ever since this theory came to be accepted, later rulers who were bent on increasing the levies and tolls all used it as a pretext. When the levies had been exhausted, the government would seize the resources for their own profit, so that officials assumed control over boiling salt, brewing liquor, harvesting tea, smelting iron, and even over the marketing and exchanges of various commodities.

Marketing is the business of merchants and traders. In ancient times, the ruler having gained a surplus of commodities from the local tributes, it was not the practice of the state to seize control of the marketing of commodities. The latter practice began with the *ch'üan-fu*[ev] [control of money in public markets] system described in the *Chou-kuan*[ew] (Institutes of Chou). This was adopted by later rulers [and the practice] came to be known [variously under such systems] as *chün-shu*[ex] [price adjustment and transportation], *shih-i*[ey] [official markets and exchanges] and *ho-mai*[ez] [harmonious procurement], all based on the precedent of the *ch'üan-fu* system. Purchasing is the business of the common people. In ancient times, the ruler having gained a surplus of rice and grain by taxing one-tenth of the produce of the people, it was not the practice of the state to take control of grain purchasing. The practice of government grain procurement emanated from the *p'ing-ti*[fa] [price regulating] system devised by Duke Huan of Ch'i[fb] and Marquis Wen of Wei,[fc] and was adopted by later rulers under such systems as *ch'ang-p'ing*[fd] [ever-normal granary], *i-ts'ang*[fe] [relief granary] or *ho-ti*[ff] [harmonious purchase], all based on the precedent of the *p'ing-ti* system.

However, the establishment of the *ch'üan-fu* and *p'ing-ti* systems was designed for the convenience of the people. When the supply of commodities among the people had become excessive, the government would purchase them, and when they were in demand among the people, the government would dispose of them. . . . There was never the intention [of the state] to encroach upon the wealth [of the people] in order to profit the state, but as time wore on, the ancient ideal fell into oblivion. When the government took control of the marketing of commodities, it used the pretext of trying to thwart the designs of traders who were attempting to hoard the goods to wait for higher profits. With the passage of time, however, the officials adopted the practices of merchants and traders, and [sought to justify their way by] calling it a means to increase the wealth of the state. When they took over control of the procurement of grain, they gave the pretext that they were succoring the poor people who had suffered from the low price of grain and shortage of currency. As time wore on, however, the officials never thought of benefiting the common people and were concerned only with the profits accruing from the hoarding of grain through the control of procurement.[72]

Here Ma Tuan-lin gave a succinct account of the major sources of state levies and tolls accruing from the resources of the country and the major arguments advanced by scholar-officials to justify the collection of such revenue from the people. In discussing these developments, he meticulously traced the stages of evolution of these fiscal institutions from the feudal era to the imperial dynasties, paying special attention to the changes in the implementation of these systems and policies. He did not question the intention behind some of these fiscal systems and policies, but deplored the departure in practice from the ideal of benefiting the country, and the shift to that of profiting the state at the expense of the common people. These changes in actual practices through a manipulation of the ancient institutions, he pointed out, had enabled the rulers to concentrate the wealth of the country in their own hands and enhanced their absolute authority. [73]

In a different place, Ma Tuan-lin returned to the theme of "public welfare" versus "private interest" to illustrate how the imperial rulers purported to serve the common good of the people but were in fact pursuing personal gain. He had offered some revealing examples in his "General Preface," dealing with the development and changes of the imperial and state treasuries from the Ch'in and Han down to the Sung dynasty, as follows:

According to the "Six Statutes" of the *Chou-kuan*, there were [fiscal agencies in Chou times such as] the *t'ai-fu* [fg] [Grand Treasury], *wang-fu* [fh] [King's Treasury], and *nei-fu* [fi] [Inner Treasury]. There was also a tradition that the king would not monopolize [the wealth of the people], and all the later rulers followed suit. In the Han dynasty, there was the fiscal agency called *ta-nung* [fj] [Grand Chief of Agriculture]; it was the treasury of the state. There was the *shao-fu* [fk] [Privy Treasury] and *shui-heng* [fl] [Department of Waterworks and Parks]: they were the private treasuries of the ruler. The T'ang had [offices such as] the *chuan-yün* [fm] [Department of Transportation], *tu-chih* [fn] [Department of Public Revenue] [as public treasuries], and also the *ch'iung-lin* [fo] [Carnelian Grove], *ta-ying* [fp] [Great Affluence] [as private treasuries of the emperor]. The Sung had the *hu-pu* [fq] [Ministry of Finance], *san-ssu* [fr] [Three Finance Commissions] [as public treasuries], and also the *feng-chuang* [fs] [Sealed Chest], *nei-tsang* [ft] [Inner Storage] [as private treasuries of the emperor], Therefore, with all the wealth in the country which had gone to the emperor, there was yet the distinction between public [treasuries] and private [treasuries]. Virtuous rulers who were reverent and frugal often contributed money from their private treasuries for the need of the country and the army; therefore, people became prosperous and the dynasty flourished. However, wicked rulers who were licentious and extravagant would even spend the funds of the public treasuries for their sensual pleasure; therefore, the wealth of the country came to be exhausted and people held a grudge against their ruler. [74]

Here Ma showed clearly that, according to the established practices of government, although in theory the wealth of the country all went to the emperor, yet in practice there had been a distinction made since the earliest times between the public treasuries and the private treasuries. Later rulers all acknowledged the distinction between public and private funds, and there were separate fiscal agencies in charge of these treasuries. However, Ma Tuan-lin pointed out that this distinction was not always observed in practice, and only a virtuous ruler would refrain from encroaching upon the public treasuries, or might even appropriate funds

from his own coffers to meet the needs of the country. This violation of
the public welfare, which frequently occurred in later dynasties, he conceded, not only enhanced imperial absolutism, but also provided a major
source of disaffection among the population that in turn undermined the
strength of the dynasty.[75]

In recapitulating Ma Tuan-lin's appraisal of the postfeudal period
down to the end of the Sung, we have noted earlier that he did not
introduce a similar periodization scheme for these later dynasties. He
may have considered the Ch'in and Han as one outstanding period, and
the T'ang and Sung another, but unlike other historians, rather than
holding to a rigid formula of demarcation he preferred to apprehend the
dynamics of the historical process from an overall perspective. Thus he
focused his primary attention on significant stages of development in important institutions in order to illuminate continuity and change in this
long period of Chinese history.

In the political realm, we have taken note of Ma Tuan-lin's analysis
of the evolution of the prefectural system from the Ch'in to Han, and
the implications of this change for the growth of imperial absolutism in
subsequent periods. Mention has also been made of his attention to the
examinations and official appointments systems, where he placed emphasis on the changes that occurred in the Han and Chin periods which
enhanced the trend towards centralized imperial authority.[76] In addition,
Ma focused on the landmarks in the development of other institutions.
For instance, in the evolution of the military system, he attached great
importance to the *mu-ping*[fu] (hired soldiers) system of the T'ang and Sung
as the yardstick of the strength and weakness of the imperial rulers, and
in the development of administrative geography, he gave credit to the
prefectural and subprefectural systems introduced under the Sung as constituting the foundation of local administration in later dynasties.[77] Similarly, Ma gave special attention to key stages in the development of
economic institutions and policies, such as the land tax (wherein he
pointed to the major reform of Shang Yang of Ch'in, which sought to
tax people's land without putting restrictions on the size of their landholdings), and the two-tax system of Yang Yen of T'ang (which taxed
people on the land they held without considering whether they were adults
or minors).[78] As for the currency systems, he divided their evolution into
two distinct phases: the coined currency developed since the Chou kingdom and the paper money inaugurated in the late T'ang. In the latter,

he demarcated two major stages of development: the *fei-ch'ien*[fv] (flying cash) of the T'ang, and the *hui-tzu*[fw] (check medium) and *chiao-ch'ao*[fx] (exchange vouchers) of the Sung.[79] In regard to the salt and iron monopoly systems, he traced them to the Ch'i state of the Spring and Autumn period, the liquor monopoly to the Han, and the tea monopoly to the T'ang, and he gave a detailed account of the iron and salt monopolies under Emperor Wu of Han and their development under the T'ang and Sung. For the official markets and purchases, he attached great importance to the *chün-shu* (price adjustment and transportation) and *ch'ang-p'ing* (ever-normal granary) systems of the Han, the *i-ts'ang* (relief granary) system of Sui, the *ho-ti* (harmonious purchase) system of T'ang, and the *shih-i* (official markets and exchanges) system of the Sung.[80] Furthermore, Ma also paid attention to the development of the corvée labor service by identifying three distinctive systems. They were the appointment system presided over by the village elders of Chou and the community headmen of Han, the household service system (*hu-i*)[fy] from the post-Han through the T'ang, and the miscellaneous categories of corvée service such as *chai*[fz] (commissioned), *ku* (hired), and *i*[ga] (voluntary) labor of T'ang and Sung and others.[81]

In all these instances, Ma Tuan-lin traced the inception of these institutions and policies to the Ch'in and Han, and then stressed the changes that occurred in the T'ang period which he saw as heralding the transformation that would occur in the Sung dynasty. Not only did he carefully scrutinize the changes in institutions and practices, particularly in those areas that altered the relationship between ruler and subjects and that strengthened the state at the expense of the general population, but also he laboriously explained how these changes enhanced imperial absolutism and affected developments in later dynasties. In view of the extended discussions by modern historians on the T'ang and Sung as the "great divide" in the imperial era and the genesis of the "modern period," Ma Tuan-lin's observations and judgments on institutional developments during this important transitional period should warrant special consideration.[82]

Ma Tuan-lin was no less concerned with the development and changes in the institutions and policies under the Sung dynasty, and particularly the Southern Sung, against the backdrop of the Mongol conquest of China. He analyzed the state policies under the Sung rulers and made judicious observations on their performance. In various ways, he not only attempted to sum up the heritage of the defunct dynasty with which he inherited, but also reflected upon the lessons of the past and their meaning for his own time under the rule of an alien conqueror.

In his comments on the Sung dynasty, Ma again invoked the concepts "public welfare" and "private interest" as the criteria for his appraisal of the weaknesses and malpractices of government. For instance, he was critical of the military establishment of the Sung for its poor planning and leadership, its failure to ward off nomadic invasions, and its aggravating of the plight of the people. In this case, even though he hailed the *pao-chia*[gb] (mutual security) system under the Northern Sung, he found fault with its ineffective performance due to maladministration and official corruption.[83] In regard to the reforms of Wang An-shih, though he had a high opinion of the laudable intentions behind some of the programs, he took a negative view of those concerning the "Young Shoots Money" (*ch'ing-miao ch'ien*),[gc] "Price Adjustment and Transportation," and "Official Markets and Exchanges," since they served to promote the wealth of the state at the expense of the general population.[84] Similarly, much as he recognized the importance and desirability of state taxes and tolls and corvée service to meet the needs of government, he heavily criticized the multiple increases by the Sung rulers in these revenue collections and labor requisitions. He regarded these measures as principally responsible for increasing the burden on the people and sapping the economic well-being of the country; that in turn sowed the seeds of popular discontent and peasant uprisings, increasing the vulnerability of the dynasty under the threat of foreign invasions.[85] In these instances, Ma Tuan-lin evidently echoed some of the viewpoints of Sung scholar-officials, who had also invoked the same concept of "public welfare" versus "private interest" in criticizing Sung rulers for pursuing their own personal gain at the expense of the well-being of the common people.

We should note that Ma Tuan-lin had the advantage of a detached perspective in his criticisms of the Sung government, since he wrote his institutional encyclopedia under a new dynasty. He was not hamstrung by an orthodox ideology or inhibited in his criticisms of his former ruler, and thus he had a rare freedom to judge both past and recent times. In effect, some of his criticisms of the Sung government may also be construed as veiled and circumspect attacks on the corrupt administration of Mongol rulers. This was certainly one of the great advantages of Chinese scholar-officials under Mongol rule.

CONCLUSION

There are several points in the foregoing exposition of the *Survey* that merit special attention. First of all, Ma Tuan-lin was most distinguished for reviving and elaborating the concepts of "comprehensiveness" and "change" in Chinese historiography, harking back to the traditions of Confucius, Ssu-ma Ch'ien, and Cheng Ch'iao. In applying these ancient ideals and principles of historical writing, he devoted full attention to the documentation and analysis of traditional governmental institutions from legendary antiquity down to the end of the Sung dynasty. Ma, moreover, was not content simply to provide a topical summation of dead facts under conventional categories, as the Ch'ing historian Chang Hsüeh-ch'eng[gd] (1738–1801) has prejudicially charged, downgrading Ma Tuan-lin in favor of Cheng Ch'iao. He also did not resort to theories about the mystical Five Agents or to the moralistic principles of the *Spring and Autumn Annals* for the interpretation of history.[86] Instead, he tried to expound a rational evolutionary view of history by uncovering the reasons for changes in the historical process through a periodization based on the distinctive developments in governmental institutions, taking into account both subjective and objective factors. In this way, Ma broadened the critical methodologies of Tu Yu and Cheng Ch'iao to produce an institutional encyclopedia that elucidated the dynamics of continuity and change in history. His work thus provided an inspiring model for its sequels in the Ming and Ch'ing, such as the *Hsü Wen-hsien t'ung-k'ao*[ge] and *Huang(Ch'ing)-ch'ao Wen-hsien t'ung-k'ao*,[gf] although none of them lived up to his high scholarly standards or to his critical spirit of historical inquiry.[87]

Secondly, Ma Tuan-lin formulated his criteria of the subjective and objective factors in historical development by skillfully invoking certain key concepts in ancient Chinese thought. He developed, for instance, the notion of a concern for *kung* (public welfare) versus *ssu* (private interest) in the Confucian context as the criteria of the subjective factors, and distinguished between *kuang* and *yüeh* in cosmogonical theory as criteria for evaluating the objective factors that produced incremental changes in social and political organizations. It is true that he did not make a clearcut distinction as to the relative importance of subjective and objective factors, since he often emphasized the importance of the moral caliber of the rulers and the literati, rather than the cumulative development in institutions, as the principal mechanism of change in the historical process. It is also true that in his evaluation of the objective factors, Ma often failed to give a precise and analytical account of the evolution of some of the key institutions, such as land tenure, property rights, agricultural systems, or population registration, which are essential to a proper understanding of the social and economic transformation in traditional China. However, in stressing the importance of moral cultivation by the rulers and individuals for the improvement of the state and society, he also argued that when cumulative changes had altered the objective circumstances, even a sage could not turn against the times to reestablish archaic institutions and practices. This indicates that Ma Tuan-lin definitely attempted to strike a balance between the subjective and objective factors determining the course of history, exhibiting a pragmatic and rational approach that went well beyond the concerns of earlier historians.[88]

Thirdly, Ma Tuan-lin sought to draw attention to what he considered the darker side of the imperial dynasties through a meticulous investigation into governmental institutions and practices to convey the lessons and meaning of history to later rulers and scholar-officials. In this he depicted the praiseworthy achievements of the ancient sages, not just to exalt the past or expound his own idealistic version of history, but also to provide criteria for the evaluation of the more recent past and of present rulers. For instance, he extensively invoked the Confucian ideal of rulership and principles of government to criticize the concentration of imperial power from the Ch'in and Han through the end of the Sung dynasty. This shows that Ma was not simply concerned with documenting the rise and fall of the past dynasties. He also sought to inculcate in Mongol rulers and contemporary scholar-officials Confucian ideals of good government, a concern for moral principles and the welfare of the people, and the need to redress political, social, and economic inequities.

Finally, we may make some general observations on how Ma Tuan-lin's historical views and his historiographical contributions appear in the broad context of the intellectual development of the Sung and Yüan dynasties:

In the first place, Ma Tuan-lin clearly revealed the concern of the literati over the increasing centralization and bureaucratization of the Chinese empire in the later imperial era. In the realm of political thought, this was manifested in the tensions between the ideal of moral leadership in government and the need for well-structured and orderly mechanisms, based on laws and regulations, for the governance of the state and the protection of the population. The polarization of views on these issues during the era of reform under the Northern Sung, between the conservatism of Ssu-ma Kuang and the pragmatism of Wang An-shih, vividly illustrates the dilemma confronting Chinese scholar-officials.[89] There was no satisfactory way to resolve this tension in theory and in practice, and Ma Tuan-lin offered no conclusive answer. It seems, however, that he tried to steer a middle course between the two. While he focused on objective historical forces as molding the evolution of governmental institutions and practices, he also attached great importance to having rulers and officials of moral and upright character to monitor these developments and changes.

Furthermore, Ma Tuan-lin attests to a new view of history within the Neo-Confucian tradition. Following Cheng Ch'iao, he had questioned the applicability of the Five Agents theory and the moralistic principles of the *Spring and Autumn Annals* to history. Similarly, much as he was under the influence of the Sung Neo-Confucians, he did not espouse their cosmological views or their metaphysical interpretation of history. It appears that Ma, while being exposed to Chu Hsi's philosophy since his youth, had adopted an open-minded attitude towards the Neo-Confucian orthodoxy. He did not apply the categories of moralistic judgment formulated by Chu Hsi in the *Tzu-chih t'ung chien kang-mu*[gg] (*Outline and Digest of the Comprehensive Mirror for Aid in Government*).[90] Instead, he espoused those basic Confucian concerns such as the promotion of public welfare (*kung*) and suppression of private interest (*ssu*), and the importance of moral commitment to the highest order, which, as mentioned earlier, were also true to the spirit of Neo-Confucianism. It is equally significant, moreover, that he sought to uphold traditional values as criteria for improvement in dire situations created by constant changes in objective circumstances. These adjustments to the contemporary clearly put Ma Tuan-lin in a unique position in the historiographical and intellectual development of the Sung and Yüan, and they indicate that there was ample room for adaptation within the orthodox Neo-Confucian tradition.

Ma Tuan-lin, who did not seek an active official career in the Yüan government, made no specific reference to Mongol administration in his own work, no doubt in view of the possibly dangerous repercussions upon him. However, he repeatedly criticized imperial rulers for failing to take heed of the "public welfare" of the people, and for the proscription of frank remonstrance and public dissent in the process of tightening their control over scholar-officials and the general population. Could we then take these as expressing the indirect protest of the Chinese literati against Mongol rule? Were they a viable form of expression for an eremite who found it improper to serve in government under these difficult circumstances? Whatever the case, Ma Tuan-lin's persistent exhortation of the ruler to cherish lofty moral principles, promote the public welfare, and suppress his selfish interests could well have represented a plea to alien conquerors to pay heed to the lessons of history in order to achieve a benevolent government and harmonious society.[91]

Above all, Ma Tuan-lin distinguished himself as a learned and perceptive historian who sought to transmit basic Confucian principles and values through the study of traditional governmental institutions and practices. To later generations he left a richly documented encyclopedia for the study of the past and provided an exemplary model for imitation in later dynasties. He also imparted an evolutionary view and dynamic interpretation of history that has captured the attention of modern historians. Whether Ma merits acclaim as a "progressive" and "scientific" historian will depend on how one defines one's criteria.[92] He will certainly qualify if "progressive" means surpassing the achievements of past historians, and "scientific" means an objective, rational, and systematic interpretation of the historical records. But if these labels are to imply a departure from tradition, they do not apply. More fittingly, Ma Tuan-lin should be seen in the context of the new intellectual orientation of the Sung and Yüan, and of the political vicissitudes wrought by the Mongol conquest of China. This provides us with a proper understanding of his stature in the development of historical thought and the writing of institutional encyclopedias in imperial times. It shows as well the genuine concern of Confucian literati for reposssession and transmission of the great tradition when Chinese civilization was seriously imperiled by alien conquest.

NOTES

Footnotes here are intended only to identify sources and elucidate points in the discussion, not to provide extensive references to many of the governmental institutions mentioned in Ma Tuan-lin's work. In the following citations, the *Shih T'ung*[gh] ed. (Shanghai: Commercial Press, 1936), is used for *T'ung-tien* (TT), *T'ung-chih* (TC), and *Wen-hsien t'ung-k'ao* (WHTK), and the PN ed. for the dynastic histories.

1. For studies on the Chinese literati's response to Mongol rule and the Mongol rulers' attitudes towards the Chinese institutions and Confucian tradition, see, among others, Yao Ts'ung-wu, *Tung-pei shih lün-ts'ung*[gi] (Taipei: Cheng-chung shu-chü, 1959), vol. 2, pp. 376–401; Sun K'o-k'uan, *Yüan-tai Han wen-hua chih huo-t'ung*[gj] (Taipei: Chung-hua shu-chü, 1968), pp. 109–209; Abe Takeo, *Gendaishi no kenkyū*[gk] (Tokyo: Sōbunsha, 1972), pp. 9–29; F. W. Mote, "Confucian Eremitism in the Yüan Period," in *The Confucian Persuasion*, ed. A. F. Wright (Stanford: Stanford University Press, 1962), pp. 229–36; Hok-lam Chan, "Liu Ping-chung (1216–74): A Buddhist-Taoist Statesman at the Court of Khubilai Khan," *T'oung Pao* (1967), 53(1–3):98–146, and W. T. de Bary, "The Rise of Neo-Confucian Orthodoxy in Yüan China," in de Bary, *Neo-Confucian Orthodoxy and the Learning of the Mind-and-Heart* (New York: Columbia University Press, 1981), pp. 1–66.

2. For studies on Ma Tuan-lin's life and historical scholarship, see the references cited in notes 5 and 14.

3. For a general survey of Chinese historiography during the T'ang and Yüan periods, see, among others, Naitō Torajiro, *Shina shigaku shi*[gl] (Tokyo: Kō-bunko, 1949), chaps. 8–10; Chin Yü-fu, *Chung-kuo shih-hsüeh shih*[gm] rev. ed. (Shanghai: Commercial Press, 1957), chaps. 6–7; Yang Lien-sheng, "The Organization of Chinese Official Historiography . . . ," in *Historians of China and Japan*, eds. W. G. Beasley and E. G. Pulleyblank (London: Oxford University Press, 1961), pp. 44–59, and Hok-lam Chan, *The Historiography of the Chin Dynasty (1115–1234): Three Studies* (Wiesbaden: Franz Steiner, 1970), chap. 1.

4. For a bibliographical note of the TT, TC, and WHTK, see Chi Yün et al., eds., *Ssu-k'u ch'üan-shu tsung-mu t'i-yao*[gn] (Shanghai: Ta-tung shu-chü, 1930), 50:3b; 81:1a, 3b. See also Ssu-yü Teng and Knight Biggerstaff, *An Annotated Bibliography of Selected Chinese Reference Works*, 3d ed. (Cambridge, Mass.: Harvard University Press, 1971), pp. 108–110. In addition to the general surveys on Chinese historiography cited in note 1, there are several important studies on these three comprehensive institutional encyclopedias in modern scholarship. For the TT, see Cheng Ho-sheng, *Tu Yu nien-p'u*[go] (Shanghai: Commercial Press, 1934); Robert des Rotours, *Traité des fonctionnaires et traité de l'armee*, 2 vols. (Leiden: E. J. Brill, 1947), *passim*; and Ch'ien Mu, *Chung-kuo shih-hsüeh ming-chu*[gp] (Taipei: San-min

shu-chü, 1973), vol. 2, pp. 165–99. For the TC, see Ku Chieh-kang, [gq] "Cheng Ch'iao chu-shu k'ao" and "Cheng Ch'iao chuan," [gr] in *Kuo-hsüeh chi-k'an*[gs] (January–April 1923), 1(1–2):96–138, 309–32; Albert Mann, "Cheng Ch'iao: An Essay in Re-evaluation," in *Transition and Permanence in Chinese History and Culture: A Festschrift in Honour of Dr. Hsiao Kung-ch'üan*, ed. D. C. Bauxbaum and F. W. Mote (Hong Kong: Cathay Press, 1972), pp. 24–57, and Ch'ien Mu, vol. 2, pp. 249–66. For the WHTK, the most important study has been Pai Shou-i, "Ma Tuan-lin ti shih-hsüeh ssu-hsiang"[gt] in *Hsüeh-pu chi*[gu](Peking: San-lien shu-tien, 1961), pp. 210–52 [originally published in Hou Wai-lu et al., eds., *Chung-kuo ssu-hsiang t'ung-shih*[gv] (Peking: Jen-min ch'u-pan-she, 1960), bk. 4, pt. 1. pp. 832–74]. For a briefer account, see Ch'ien Mu, vol. 2, pp. 267–83. The only study of WHTK in a Western language is the French translation of the survey on "Foreign Peoples" (*ch.* 324–48) by Le Marquis d'Hervey de Saint-Denys, *Éthnographie des peuples étrangers à la Chine ouvrage composé au XIIᵉ siècle de notre ère par Ma-Touan-lin* (Paris: Ernest Leroux, 1876), 2 vols. For a brief comparative study of the TT, TC, and WHTK, see Chang Chün-mai (Carsun Chang), "San T'ung hsing-chih chin-chieh,"[gw] *Tzu-yu chung*[gx] (August–October 1966), 2(6–8):20–21, 22–25, 21–23; and Étienne Balazs, "History as a Guide to Bureaucratic Practice," in *Chinese Civilization and Bureaucracy*, tr. H. M. Wright (New Haven: Yale University Press, 1964), pp. 78–94 (originally published in French as "L'histoire comme guide de pratique bureaucratique" in *Historians of China and Japan*, pp. 129–49). It should be noted that these works provided the model for the compilation of institutional encyclopedias in later dynasties culminating in the compendia known as *Shih T'ung* ("ten comprehensive compendia"). For a list of the table of contents and subsection headings of the TT, TC, and WHTK, see *Shih T'ung so-yin*[gy] (Shanghai: Commercial Press, 1936), and also *Bunken tsu kō sōmokuroku, fu tsuten, tsushi,*[gz] comp. By Tōyōshi kenkyūkai[ha] (Kyoto: Kyoto University, 1954).

5. The word *t'ung* has various shades of meaning in ancient Chinese classical and philosophical texts. In one sense, it has the connotation of movement or penetration, and hence, thorough mastery of the subject. It is paired and often contrasted with *po*, [hb] which denotes breadth of knowledge or erudition. In another sense, *t'ung* also means generality and the ability to transmit one's knowledge of the field to others; hence, it gives rise to the term *t'ung-jen,* [hc] *t'ung-ts'ai,*[hd] or *t'ung-shih.*[he] For a sample of quotations in early Chinese literature including the terms *t'ung* and *pien*, see Chang Ch'i-yün et al., eds., *Chung-wen ta tz'u-tien*[hf] (Taipei: Institute for Advanced Chinese Studies, 1968), vol. 33, p. 61. The word *t'ung* as it was used in traditional historiography encompassed all these shades of meaning. For a detailed elaboration, see Chang Hsüeh-ch'eng, "Shih T'ung,"[hg] in *Chang-shih i-shu*[hh] (Wu-hsing: Liu-shih chia-yeh t'ang, 1922), 4:33b–40a. It has been conventionally translated as "general" in Western writings on Chinese historiography in general and on these three institutional encyclopedias in particular.

In this essay, I prefer to render it as "comprehensiveness" because the word connotes a continuous and encyclopedic coverage of historical records, and it therefore conveys a more accurate meaning of the original in this context.

6. There are several useful accounts on the ancient Chinese cosmogonical concept and the relations between nature and man in recent general surveys on Chinese thought in Western scholarship. See, for example, Fung Yu-lan, A History of Chinese Philosophy, tr. Derk Bodde, vol. 1 (Princeton University Press, 1952); Joseph Needham et al., Science and Civilization in China, vol. 2 (Cambridge: Cambridge University Press, 1954); W. T. de Bary et al., eds., Sources of Chinese Tradition, vol. 1 (New York: Columbia University Press, 1960); Kung-ch'üan Hsiao, A History of Chinese Political Thought, tr. F. W. Mote, vol. 1 (Princeton: Princeton University Press, 1979), relevant sections. In addition, see also H. G. Creel, "The Great Clod: A Taoist Conception of the Universe," in Wen-lin: Studies in the Chinese Humanities, ed. Tse-tsung Chow (Madison: University of Wisconsin Press, 1968), pp. 257–68; F. W. Mote, "The Cosmological Gulf between China and the West," in Transition and Permanence: Chinese History and Culture—A Festschrift in Honour of Dr. Hsiao Kung-ch'üan, pp. 1–21; Mitukuni Yoshida, "The Chinese Concept of Nature," in Chinese Science: Explorations of an Ancient Tradition, ed. Shigeru Nakayama and Nathan Sivin (Cambridge, Mass.: M. I. T. Press, 1973), pp. 71–89, and Hellmut Wilhelm, Heaven, Earth, and Man in the Book of Changes (Seattle: University of Washington Press, 1977), chaps. 1–3, 5.

7. Shih chi, 130:32a; Han shu, 62:21a. The translation here follows Burton Watson, Ssu-ma Ch'ien: Grand Historian of China (New York: Columbia University Press, 1958), p. 66, and de Bary, Sources, p. 235. For discussions on Ssu-ma Ch'ien's view of universal history and the impact of the Shih chi on later historical compilations, see, for example, Naitō Torajiro, chaps. 5, 7; Chin Yü-fu, chap. 3; Hsü Hao, Nien-wu shih lun-kang[hi] (Shanghai: Shih-chieh shu-chü, 1947), pp. 27–42, and Liu I-cheng, Kuo-shih yao-i[hj] (Shanghai: Chung-hua shu-chü, 1948), passim.

8. See, among others, Naitō Torajiro, chap. 6; Chin Yü-fu, chap. 3; Hsü Hao, pp. 168–86, and Liu I-cheng, passim.

9. Shih t'ung (SPTK ed.), 20 chüan, divided into the "Inner" and "Outer" sections. There are several important studies on this outstanding work; see, in particular, Fu Chen-lun, Liu Chih-chi nien-o'u[hk] (Shanghai: Commercial Press, 1934); Byongik Koh in Oriens Extremus (1967), 4:5–51, 125–81; E. G. Pulleyblank, "Chinese Historical Criticism: Liu Chih-chi and Ssu-ma Kuang," in Historians of China and Japan, pp. 135–66; William Hung, "A T'ang Historiographer's Letter of Resignation," Harvard Journal of Asiatic Studies (1969), 29:5–52, and Pai Shou-i in Hsüeh-pu chi, pp. 155–209.

10. TT, "Table of Contents," p. 7; author's "General Preface," p. 9. See also the references on this work cited in note 4.

11. TC, author's "General Preface," pp. 1–4. This has been fully annotated by Chang Hsü in T'ung-chih tsung-hsü chien[hl] (Shanghai: K'ai-ming shu-tien,

1933), and partially translated in de Bary, *Sources*, pp. 442–44. The *Chi* covers *ch.* 1–24; *Lüeh*, *ch.* 27–77; and *Chuan*, *ch.* 78–200.

12. For a succinct account of the Confucian views of history, see in addition to the general references cited in note 3 and note 6, Otto van der Sprenkel, "Chronologie et historiographie Chinoises," *Mélanges publiés par l'Institut des Hautes Études* (Paris: L'Institut des Hautes Études Chinoise, 1960), vol. 2, pp. 407–21; P. van der Loon, "The Ancient Chinese Chronicles and the Growth of Historical Ideals," in *Historians of China and Japan*, pp. 24–30, and D. Lancashire, "A Confucian Interpretation of History," *Journal of the Oriental Society of Australia* (January 1965), 3(1):76–87.

13. See Pai Shou-i's study cited in note 4. His work, a preliminary investigation into Ma Tuan-lin's thought and his WHTK drawing on the Marxist categories of analysis, provides the standard evaluation of Ma Tuan-lin in mainland Chinese historiography.

14. The basic sources for a study of Ma Tuan-lin's life and his WHTK are his "General Preface" and the prefatory material to this institutional encyclopedia. His "General Preface" has been fully annotated by Ch'en Chih-hsien in *T'ung-k'ao hsü chien*[hm] (Taipei: Commercial Press, 1967 rep.), and partially translated in de Bary, *Sources*, pp. 444–46. The prefatory material includes the memorial submitted by the Taoist emissary Wang Shou-yen in May 1319 for the presentation of WHTK to court, and the imperial edict of July 1322 to the authorities of Jao-chou for the publication of Ma Tuan-lin's work. There are several secondary biographical accounts of Ma Tuan-lin that draw upon these and other sources. They include: *Lo-p'ing-hsien chih*[hn] (1659), 7:5a, 8:6a; Huang Tsung-hsi and Ch'üan Tsu-wang,[ho] SYHA (SPPY ed.), 89:4a; Ch'ien Shih-sheng,[hp] *Nan-Sung shu* (1797), 37:7a; Shao Yüan-p'ing, *Yüan shih lei-pien*[hq] (1797), 34:8b; Tseng Lien, *Yüan shu*[hr] (1911), 89:7b; Wang Fen, *Jou-ch'iao wen-ch'ao*[hs] (1914), 14:1a; K'o Shao-min[ht] *Hsin Yüan shih* (Tientsin, 1930 ed.), 234:1a, and others. For a modern account of his life and works, see Pai Shou-i, *passim*, and the biography in German by Yamauchi Mashiro in *Sung Biographies*, ed. Herbert Franke (Wiesbaden: Franz Steiner Verlag GMBH, 1976), vol. 2, pp. 758–61.

15. For biographies of Ma T'ing-luan, see T'o-t'o[hu] et al., eds., *Sung shih*, 414:23a; K'o Wei-ch'i, *Shung-shih hsin-pien*[hv] (Shanghai: Ta-kuang shu-chü, 1936 ed.), 152:9b; *Nan-Sung shu*, 62:1a; and the modern account in German by Dietlinde Schlegel in *Sung Biographies*, vol. 2, pp. 756–58. For a fuller study of his life and writings, see Huang Hsiao-min, "Ma T'ing-luan chi ch'i i-wen,"[hw] *Shu-mu chi-k'an*[hx] (December 1970), 5(2):43–66.

16. *Sung shih*, 414:24b–27a; Huang Hsiao-min, pp. 47–48. The date of Ma T'ing-luan's death is based on *Yüan shu*, 89:7b, but the source cannot be identified.

17. For a brief appraisal of Ma T'ing-luan's writings, see *Ssu-k'u ch'üan-shu tsung-mu t'i-yao*, 165:2b, and the postscript to his *Pi-wu Wan-fang chi* by Hu Ssu-ching[hy] in the *Yü-chang ts'ung-shu* ed. (1915) of this collection. Several specimens of Ma T'ing-luan's writings not included in his extant

collected works have been retrieved; for a complete listing, see Huang Hsiao-min, pp. 55–66.

18. SYHA, 89:4a; *Nan-Sung shu*, 37:7a; *Hsin Yüan shih*, 234:11a; *Lo-p'ing-hsien chih*, 7:5a, 8:6a. See also Pai Shou-i, p. 210; Yamauchi Mashiro, pp. 758ff.

19. This is based on the imperial edit of July 1322 to the authorities of Jao-chou for the publication of Ma Tuan-lin's work. It is included in WHTK, p. 11.

20. WHTK, "General Preface," p. 3. Ma Tuan-lin frequently cited the opinion of his father in his comments. They are indicated by the opening remark in these quotations: "This is what my late father said . . ." ("hsien-kung yüeh[hz] . . .") For a listing of these quotations, see Huang Hsiao-min, pp. 57–62.

21. See WHTK, "General Preface," p. 3, and the imperial edict authorizing the publication of the WHTK cited in note 19.

22. See the memorial by the Taoist Wang Shou-yen for the submission of Ma Tuan-lin's work to Emperor Ayurbarwada (Jen-tsung) in May 1319. It is included in WHTK, p. 13. On the background of the Yüan emperor's search for talents for government services, see Sun K'o-k'uan, *Yüan-tai Han wen-hua*, pp. 345–63. Ma Tuan-lin served only briefly as Director of Studies in that local academy; see Chou Tsu-mo, "Sung wang hou shih Yüan chih ju-hsüeh chiao-shou,"[1a] *Fu-jen hsüeh-chih*[1b] (December 1946), 14(1–2):201.

23. Tho official Yüan edition of the WHTK published in 1322/23 in Jao-chou was reprinted in a block-print editions in 1324, 1339, 1521, 1524, and again in 1747. It was later included in the *Chiu T'ung ch'üan-shu*[ic] published by Che-chiang shu-chü[id] between 1882 and 1896. The *Shih T'ung* edition of WHTK is a photolithographic reproduction of the latter. See Ssu-yü Teng and Knight Biggerstaff, *Annotated Bibliography*, pp. 107, 110. The date of Ma Tuan-lin's death has not been ascertained. Pai Shou-i points out that he was already 68 years old when the WHTK was officially published, but it is not certain what year this was. Yamauchi, on the other hand, places his death in 1325 without citing the evidence. My own estimation is based on his biographical records cited in note 14.

24. For a list of these works, see *Lo-p'ing-hsien chih* 10:5a, and Pai Shou-i, p. 210.

25. *Analects*, 3. Translation follows James Legge, *The Chinese Classics* (Hong Kong: Hong Kong University Press, rpt. 1960), vol. 1, p. 158.

26. See Étienne Balazs, p. 146.

27. WHTK, "General Preface," p. 3; cf. de Bary, *Sources*, pp. 445–46. Italics mine.

28. *Ibid.*

29. Translation of the titles of these individual surveys follows Endymion Wilkinson, *The History of Imperial China: A Research Guide* (Cambridge, Mass.: Harvard University Press, 1973), with minor modifications.

30. WHTK, "General Preface," p. 3.

31. It should be noted that WHTK furnished one of the basic sources for the composition of the official *Sung shih*, in particular those sections on govern-

mental institutions under the auspices of the Yüan historiographical office
in 1344, along with the official Liao and Chin histories. For details, see
Teng Kung-san (Kuang-ming),[ie] "Sung shih chi-kuan chih chueh-yüan
kuang-miao,"[if] *Wen-shih tsa-chih*[ig] (April 1942), 2(4):27–38; Teng Kuang-
ming, "Sung shih chih-kuan chih k'ao-cheng" and "Sung shih hsing-fa chih
k'ao-cheng,[ih] in *Bulletin of the Institute of History and Philology, Academia
Sinica* (1948), 10:123–73, 433–593. For a brief account of the composition
of the *Sung shih*, see, among others, Hsü Hao, pp. 218–38, and Hok-lam
Chan, "Chinese Official Historiography at the Yüan Court . . . ," in *China
Under Mongol Rule*, John D. Langlois, Jr., ed. (Princeton: Princeton University Press, 1981), pp. 64–79.

32. TT, author's "General Preface," p. 9, and the references on this work cited
    in note 4.

33. TC, author's "General Preface," p. 1, and the references on this work cited
    in note 4.

34. WHTK, "General Preface," p. 1.

35. *Shih-t'ung, ch.* 13, 14, 16, 19. See also E. G. Pulleyblank, "Chinese His-
    torical Criticism . . . ," pp. 143, 145, and Pai Shou-i, pp. 178, 184.

36. Pai Shou-i, pp. 211–13.

37. For an account of the skeptical attitude and critical scholarship of the North-
    ern Sung scholars on the Confucian classics, see Liu Tzu-chien (James
    T. C. Liu), *Ou-yang Hsiu chih chih-hsüeh yü ts'ung-cheng*[ii] (Hong Kong:
    New Asia Research Institute, 1963), pp. 19–37; and Ch'ü Wan-li, "Sung-
    jen ti i ching feng-ch'i,"[ij] *Ta-lu tsa-chih*[ik] (August 1964), 29(3):23–25. There
    are numerous studies on the cosmological, metaphysical philosophy of Chou
    Tun-i and the numerological interpretation of historical causation of Shao
    Yung. For a useful introduction, see, among others, Fung Yu-lan, *Chinese
    Philosophy*, vol. 2, pp. 434–76; de Bary, *Sources*, pp. 455–64; and Mitukuni
    Yoshida, pp. 81–84.

38. TC, *ch.* 74: "Tsai-hsiang lüeh," preface, p. 853.

39. These refer to the *Tso chuan, Kung-yang chuan*, and *Ku-liang chuan*. For
    Cheng Ch'iao's further remarks on these commentaries of the *Ch'un-ch'iu*,
    see TC, 63:758–60.

40. TC, author's "General Preface," p. 1.

41. WHTK, "General Preface," p. 9(iii).

42. *Ibid.*; Pai Shou-i, pp. 213–16. For the surveys on "Prodigies of Nature," see
    WHTK, *ch.* 295–314.

43. WHTK 182:1564, comments on the *Ch'un-ch'iu*. For a detailed account of
    the career of Liu Hsiang and Liu Hsin and their attempt to establish them-
    selves as leaders of the "Old Text" School of the Confucian classics, see
    Ch'ien Mu, *Liang-Han ching-hsüeh chin-ku wen p'ing-i*[il] (Hong Kong: New
    Asia Research Institute, 1958), pp. 1–163.

44. Pai Shou-i, pp. 216ff.

45. *Ibid.*, p. 218. The *Ta T'ang K'ai-yüan li*, 150 *chüan*, was compiled by Hsiao
    Sung[im] (d. 749) and others under imperial auspices at the end of the K'ai-

yüan period. For a bibliographical note, see *Ssu-k'u ch'üan-shu tsung-mu t'i-yao*, 82:1a. The Ssu-k'u ch'üan-shu[in] edition has been reproduced photolithographically in SKCSCP, 8th ser. (Taipei: Commercial Press, 1978).

46. TT, preface by Li Han,[io] p. 3.

47. TC, author's "General Preface," p. 3; de Bary, *Sources*, pp. 443–44.

48. TC, *ch.* 71: "Chiao-ch'ou lüeh,"[ip] p. 831; *ch.* 72: "T'u-p'u lüeh,"[iq] p. 837.

49. For details, see TC, *ch.* 25–30, 30–35, 63–70.-

50. WHTK, "General Preface," p. 3; de Bary, *Sources*, pp. 445–46.

51. Pai Shou-i, pp. 224–25.

52. WHTK, "General Preface."

53. Pai Shou-i, pp. 226–27.

54. WHTK, "General Preface," p. 4(i); de Bary, *Sources*, p. 448. Ma Tuan-lin discussed further these land tax reforms in WHTK, *ch.* 1, 3. For a recent study of Shang Yang's reform, see Yang K'uan, *Shang Yang pien-fa*[ir] (Shanghai: Shanghai jen-min ch'u-pan she, 1974) (portions tr. by Li Yu-ning in *Shang Yang's Reforms and State Control in China* [White Plains, N.Y.: M. E. Sharpe, 1977]). For Yang Yen's two-tax system, see Denis Twitchett, *Financial Administration under the T'ang Dynasty*, 2d ed. (Cambridge: Cambridge University Press, 1970), pp. 39–48, 157–64.

55. WHTK, 3:49. Lu Chih was a distinguished statesman and fiscal expert during the middle reign of the T'ang dynasty. For an account of his career and his economic policies, see Denis Twitchett, "Lu Chih (754–805): Imperial Adviser and Court Official," in *Confucian Personalities*, ed. D. C. Twitchett and A. F. Wright (Stanford: Stanford University Press, 1962), pp. 84–122.

56. WHTK, 13:140(iii).

57. Pai Shou-i, pp. 228–35.

58. These concepts of *kung* and *ssu* in ancient political thought can be found in the *Odes, Book of Documents, Li chi, Analects, Mencius, Hsün Tzu, Lao Tzu, Chuang Tzu, Han Fei Tzu, Lü-shih ch'un-ch'iu*, and others. For an important study on this subject, see Sawada Takio, "Senshin ni okeru kōshi no kannen,"[is] *Tokai daigaku kiyo bungakupu*[it] (July 1976), 25:1–8.

59. For a sample of opinion on these concepts among the Neo-Confucian philosophers and statesmen under the Sung and Yüan, see Ch'eng Hao and Ch'eng I, *Erh-Ch'eng i-shu* (in *Erh-Ch'eng ch'üan-shu*)[iu] (SPPY ed.), 14:2a, 17:2b; Ch'eng Hao, *Ming-tao wen-chi*[iv] (in *Erh-Ch'eng ch'üan-shu*), 3:1a; Chu Hsi, *Hui-an hsien-sheng Chu Wen-kung wen-chi*[iw] (SPTK ed.), 11:9a–10a, 15b–16a; Hsü Heng, *Lu-chai i-shu*[ix] (SKCSCP, 4th ser., Taipei: Commercial Press, 1973), 7:2a, 8a, 10a, 13a, and others. For details, see de Bary, "The Rise of Neo-Confucian Orthodoxy," in *Neo-Confucian Orthodoxy and the Learning of the Mind-and-Heart*, pp. 34, 37, 38, and the paper by John W. Dardess included in this volume, *passim*.

60. The terms *kuang* and *yüeh* appeared in various contexts in early Chinese literature. *Kuang* is often mentioned in the context of *san-kuang*,[iy] i.e., "three brightness," referring to "sun, moon, and stars." It can be found in the *Odes, Book of Documents, Tso chuan, Ku-liang chuan, Li chi, Erh-ya*,

Kuo-yü, Huai-nan Tzu, and others. There is a sample collection of these sources in *Chung-wen ta-tz'u tien,* vol. 3 (1965), pp. 354–55. *Yüeh* is often used in the context of *wu-yüeh,*[iz] i.e., five lofty and sacred mountains in east, west, north, south, and central China. They refer to Mt. T'ai, Mt. Hua, Mt. Heng, and Mt. Sung.[ja] These references can be found in the *Odes, Book of Documents, Chou Li, Li chi, Erh-ya, Shih chi, Pai-hu t'ung, Feng-su t'ung-i,* and others. There is a sample collection of these sources in *Chung-wen ta-tz'u tien,* vol. 2 (1962), p. 221; and vol. 11 (1965), pp. 113–14. For a brief account of the development of the Chinese theories of cosmogony, see Joseph Needham et. at., *Science and Civilization in China* (Cambridge: Cambridge University Press, 1959), vol. 3, pp. 210–28; and Cheng Wen-kuang / Hsi Tse-tsung, *Chung-kuo li-shih shang ti yü-chou li-lun*[jb] (Peking: Jen-min ch'u-pan she, 1975), *passim.*

61. WHTK, "General Preface," pp. 8–9. For a general account of the development of the enfeoffment system in early China until its replacement by the prefectural system under the Ch'in regime, see Ch'ü T'ung-tsu, *Chung-kuo feng-chien she-hui*[jc] (Changsha: Commercial Press, 1937); and Derk Bodde, "Feudalism in China," *Feudalism in History,* ed. Ruston Coulborn (Princeton: Princeton University Press, 1956), pp. 49–92.

62. WHTK, 265:2095–96.

63. *Ibid.,* 265:2096.

64. *Ibid.,* 47:435.

65. *Ibid.,* "General Preface," p. 4.

66. There are numerous treatises on the merits and faults of the enfeoffment system among the T'ang and Sung scholars and statesmen in the light of its implications to contemporary political development. The most important of them were contributed by Li Pai-yao[jd] (565–648), Liu Tsung-yüan[je] (773–819), Su Hsün[jf] (1009–1066), Liao Ch'eng,[jg] Hu Yin[jh] (1098–1156), Chu Hsi, and others. For a selected anthology of writings on this subject, see Ch'en Meng-lei et al., eds., *Ku-chin t'u-shu chi-ch'eng*[ji] (1884 ed.), vol. 24 ch. 119–20.

67. Pai Shou-i, pp. 233, 237.

68. For an account of the growth of imperial absolutism in Chinese history, see F. W. Mote, "The Growth of Chinese Despotism: A Critique of Wittfogel's Theory of Oriental Despotism as Applied to China," *Oriens Extremus* (1961), 8(1):1–41, and Hok-lam Chan, "Monarchie und Regierung: Ideologien und Traditionen im kaiserzeitlichen China," *Saeculum* (1980), 31(1):15–17.

69. WHTK, "General Preface," p. 8(iii). For a general account of the political and institutional developments of the early Han and the rebellion of the seven feudal kingdoms, see T'ung-tsu Ch'ü, *Han Social Structure,* ed. Jack Dull (Seattle: University of Washington Press, 1972), chaps. 4, 5.

70. WHTK, "General Preface," p. 5. For a general account of the development of the examination and official appointment systems in early China, see Teng Ssu-yü, *Chung-kuo k'ao-shih chih-tu shih,*[jj] rev. ed. (Taipei: Hsüeh-sheng shu-tien, 1967), pp. 1–179.

71. WHTK, 49:450. For a general account of the development of the central government organizations from the Han through the Chin, see Lü Ssu-mien, *Ch'in-Han shih*[1k] (Shanghai: K'ai-ming shu-tien, 1947), chap. 18, and *id.*, *Liang-Chin Nan-pei ch'ao shih*[jl] (Shanghai: K'ai-ming shu-tien, 1948), chap. 22.

72. WHTK, "General Preface," pp. 4–5. For a general account of the development of the systems of "Customs and Tolls" and the "Official Markets and Purchases" adopted by the imperial rulers in the Ch'in and Han periods, see, among others, Nancy Lee Swann, *Food and Money in Ancient China* (Princeton: Princeton University Press, 1950), and Twitchett, *Financial Administration*, relevant sections.

73. Pai Shou-i, pp. 237–38.

74. WHTK, "General Preface," p. 5. For a general account of the development and changes of the imperial and state treasuries from the Ch'in and Han down to the Sung dynasty, see Nancy Lee Swann, *Food and Money*; D. C. Twitchett; *Financial Administration*; and Edward A. Kracke, Jr., *Civil Service in Early Sung China, 960–1067* (Cambridge, Mass.: Harvard University Press, 1953), relevant sections.

75. Pai Shou-i, pp. 238–39.

76. WHTK, "General Preface," pp. 5, 8. Cf. notes 61, 69, 70.

77. *Ibid.*, pp. 7, 10.

78. See note 54.

79. WHTK, p. 4. See also *ibid.*, ch. 8–9. For an account of the development and changes in these currency systems in imperial China, see Lien-sheng Yang, *Money and Credit in China* (Cambridge, Mass.: Harvard University Press, 1952), chaps. 1, 4, 5, and P'eng Hsin-wei, *Chung-kuo huo-pi shih*[jm] (Shanghai: Shang-hai jen-min ch'u-pan she, 1958), chaps. 3, 6.

80. WHTK, "General Preface," pp. 4–5. For a general survey of these systems and practices, see Nancy Lee Swann, *Food and Money*, D. C. Twitchett, *Financial Administration*, and Shiba Yoshinobu, *Commerce and Society in Sung China*, tr. Mark Elvin (Ann Arbor: The University of Michigan Center for Chinese Studies, 1970), relevant sections.

81. WHTK, "General Preface," p. 4. See also WHTK, ch. 12–13. For an account of the development and changes in the labor service systems in imperial China, see T'ung-tsu Ch'ü, *Han Social Structure*, pp. 144, 145, 149; D. C. Twitchett, *Financial Administration*, pp. 104–20, and Brian McKnight, *Village and Bureaucracy in Southern Sung China* (Chicago: University of Chicago Press, 1971), pp. 21, 98, 143, 152.

82. For different accounts of the modern historians' views on the significant changes in the T'ang-Sung period in reference to the periodization of Chinese history, see James T. C. Liu and Peter Golas, eds., *Change in Sung China: Innovation or Renovation?* (Boston: D. C. Heath, 1969), pp. vii–xiv, 1–20.

83. WHTK, 153:1337 and 154:1348. See Pai Shou-i, pp. 240–42, 246–47.

84. WHTK, 12:130; 20:196; 21:208. See Pai Shou-i, pp. 243–45, 249–50. For an interpretive account of Wang An-shih's reforms in recent Western schol-

arship, see James T. C. Liu, *Reform in Sung China: Wang An-shih (1021–1086) and His New Policies* (Cambridge, Mass.: Harvard University Press, 1959).

85. WHTK, *ch.* 10, 12, 13, 15, 19, 20; summarized in Pai Shou-i, pp. 243–46.

86. Chang Hsüeh-ch'eng greatly favored Cheng Ch'iao over Ma Tuan-lin. In his own mind, Cheng stood for true history concerned essentially with "meaning," whereas Ma stood for more encyclopedism concerned with dead facts. He also considered Cheng a superior scholar for his meticulous classification and investigation of the historical sources, and disparaged Ma as a typical example of the pointless and indiscriminate collector and cataloguer of facts. These criticisms, however, are excessively prejudicial, because, even though Ma Tuan-lin might have been less meticulous in his documentation and classification of historical data, he was equally concerned with the "meaning" of history, and went beyond Cheng Ch'iao in expounding the concepts of change in the historical process. For Chang Hsüeh-ch'eng's criticism of Ma Tuan-lin, see *Chang-shih i-shu, ch.* 4, and the summary in David S. Nivison, *The Life and Thought of Chang Hsüeh-ch'eng (1738–1801)* (Stanford: Stanford University Press, 1966), pp. 49, 51, 173, 196, 201, 219.

87. There are two different works entitled *Hsü Wen-hsien t'ung-k'ao.* The first was written by the Ming scholar Wang Ch'i[jn] (fl. 1565–1614) in 254 *chüan*, with a preface dated 1586, extending the coverage of the WHTK to the time of his compilation. The other was compiled by Ch'ing official historiographers in 250 *chüan* upon an imperial order issued in 1747. It supplements the former by covering the later Ming period to the end of the dynasty. The *Huang(Ch'ing)-ch'ao Wen-hsien t'ung-k'ao,* 300 *chüan*, was also compiled under imperial sponsorhip ordered in 1747. It covers the period from the beginning of the Ch'ing to 1785. It was followed by the *Huang(Ch'ing)-ch'ao Hsü Wen-hsien t'ung-k'ao,* 400 *chüan*, compiled by Liu Chin-tsao[jo] with a preface dated 1921. It deals with the period between 1786 and 1911. With the exception of Wang Ch'i's work, the rest have been included in the *Shih T'ung* edition. For a brief bibliographical note of these sequels to the WHTK, see Ssu-yü Teng and Knight Biggerstaff, *Annotated Bibliography*, pp. 111–14.

88. Pai Shou-i, pp. 228–40.

89. For a succinct account of these tensions in political thought since the Sung dynasty, see James T. C. Liu, "An Administrative Cycle in Chinese History: the Case of Northern Sung Emperors," *Journal of Asian Studies* (February 1962), 21(2):137–52, and *id.*, "Sung Roots of Chinese Political Conservatism: the Administrative Problems," *ibid.* (May 1967), 26(3):457–63.

90. For a useful study of Chu Hsi's view of history expounded in his *Tzu-chih t'ung-chien kang-mu* and other writings, see Nakayama Kyūshiro[jp] in *Shichō,*[jq] (October 1931), 1(3):33–60; *ibid.* (October 1932), 2(1):72–98; and more recently, Ch'ien Mu, *Chu Tzu hsin hsüeh-an*[jr] (Taipei: San-min shu-chü, 1971), vol. 5, pp. 1–150.

91. Pai Shou-i, pp. 250–52. For a vivid account of the attitude of the Chinese literati towards the Mongol rulers, see F. W. Mote, "Confucian Eremitism in the Yüan Period," in *The Confucian Persuasion*, ed. A. F. Wright (Stanford: Stanford University Press, 1960), pp. 202–40, and Lao Yen-hsüan (Yanshuan Lao), "Yüan-ch'u nan-fang chih-shih fen-tzu—shih chung so fan-ying ch'u ti pien-mien,"[js] *Journal of the Institute of Chinese Studies of the Chinese University of Hong Kong* (1979), 10(1):130–58.

92. This is the central thesis of Pai Shou-i's study couched in the Marxist dialectics of historical development. The argument, however, is not quite sound since Pai has not gone deep into the intellectual and historiographical traditions of the Sung and Yüan periods to place Ma Tuan-lin in a comparative perspective. I intend to pursue this theme in a larger study of Ma Tuan-lin's historiographical contributions in the near future.

GLOSSARY

a	陳學霖	ak	賈似道
b	通典	al	讀史旬編
c	杜佑	am	永樂大典
d	通志	an	碧梧玩芳集
e	鄭樵	ao	豫章叢書
f	文獻通考	ap	貴與
g	馬端臨	aq	朱熹
h	三通	ar	曹涇
i	通	as	休寧
j	變	at	承事郎
k	鄒衍	au	臨安
l	司馬遷	av	留夢炎
m	史記	aw	山長
n	班固	ax	慈湖書院
o	漢書	ay	仁宗
p	劉知幾	az	王壽衍
q	史通	ba	柯山書院
r	紀	bb	衢州
s	傳	bc	台州
t	略	bd	多識錄
u	尚書	be	義根守墨
v	春秋	bf	大學紀傳
w	樂平	bg	夏
x	饒州	bh	杞
y	宋史	bi	殷
z	元史	bj	司馬光
aa	南宋書	bk	資治通鑑
ab	宋元學案	bl	會要
ac	新元史	bm	天寶
ad	馬廷鸞	bn	寧宗
ae	理宗	bo	歐陽修
af	池州	bp	王安石
ag	丁大全	bq	周敦頤
ah	吳潛	br	邵雍
ai	度宗	bs	災祥
aj	端明殿	bt	欺人之學

bu 欺天之學

bv 左氏、公羊、穀梁

bw 寇

bx 僭

by 義

bz 逆

ca 反常

cb 物異

cc 經籍

cd 劉向

ce 劉歆

cf 食貨

cg 禮

ch 開元禮

ci 會通

cj 類

ck 故

cl 田賦

cm 商鞅

cn 楊炎

co 租、庸、調

cp 兩稅

cq 陸贄

cr 雇役

cs 職役

ct 公

cu 私

cv 光

cw 嶽

cx 義

cy 利

cz 天理

da 人慾

db 程顥

dc 程頤

dd 許衡

de 封建

df 禹

dg 郡縣

dh 堯

di 舜

dj 啓

dk 有扈氏

dl 仲康

dm 羲和

dn 姬

do 文、武、昭、穆

dp 唐

dq 虞

dr 伯夷

ds 伊尹

dt 職官

du 伏羲

dv 太皥

dw 炎帝（神農）

dx 少皥

dy 顓頊

dz 成

ea 三公

eb 三孤

ec 六官

ed 戶口

ee 士

ef 劉邦

eg 項羽

eh 高祖

el 韓、彭、英、盧、張、吳

ej 荊、吳、齊、楚、淮南

ek 賈誼

el 鼂錯

em 景

en 武

eo 選舉

ep 刺史

eq 九品中正

er 尚書

es	中書	ge	續文獻通考
et	征榷	gf	皇（清）朝文獻通考
eu	市糴	gg	資治通鑑綱目
ev	泉府	gh	十通
ew	周官	gi	姚從吾，東北史論叢
ex	均輸	gj	孫克寬，元代漢文化之活動
ey	市易	gk	安部健夫，元代史の研究
ez	和買	gl	內藤虎次郎，支那史学史
fa	平糴	gm	金毓黻，中國史學史
fb	齊桓公	gn	紀昀，四庫全書總目提要
fc	魏文侯	go	鄭鶴聲，杜佑年譜
fd	常平	gp	錢穆，中國史學名著
fe	義倉	gq	顧頡剛
ff	和糴	gr	鄭樵著述考；鄭樵傳
fg	太府	gs	國學季刊
fh	王府	gt	白壽彝，馬端臨的史學思想
fi	內府	gu	學步集
fj	大農	gv	侯外廬，中國思想通史
fk	少府	gw	張君勱，三通性質今解
fl	水衡	gx	自由鐘
fm	轉運	gy	十通索引
fn	度支	gz	文獻通考五種總目：附通
fo	瓊林		典、通志
fp	大盈	ha	東洋史研究會
fq	戶部	hb	博
fr	三司	hc	通人
fs	封樁	hd	通材
ft	內藏	he	通史
fu	募兵	hf	張其昀，中文大辭典
fv	飛錢	hg	釋通
fw	會子	hh	章氏遺書
fx	交鈔	hi	徐浩，廿五史論綱
fy	戶役	hj	柳詒徵，國史要義
fz	差	hk	傅振倫，劉知幾年譜
ga	義	hl	張須，通志總序箋
gb	保甲	hm	陳志憲，通考序箋
gc	青苗錢	hn	樂平縣志
gd	章學誠	ho	黃宗羲

hp 錢士升

hq 邵遠平，元史類編

hr 曾廉，元書

hs 王棻，柔橋文鈔

ht 柯劭忞

hu 脫脫

hv 柯維騏，宋史新編

hw 黃筱敏，馬廷鸞及其佚文

hx 書目季刊

hy 胡思敬

hz 先公曰

ia 周祖謨，宋亡後仕元之儒學教授

ib 輔仁學誌

ic 九通全書

id 浙江書局

ie 鄧恭三（廣銘）

if 宋史職官志抉原匡謬

ig 文史雜誌

ih 宋史職官志考證；宋史刑法志考證

ii 劉子健，歐陽修之治學與從政

ij 屈萬里，宋人的疑經風氣

ik 大陸雜誌

il 兩漢經學今古文平議

im 蕭蒿

in 四庫全書

io 李翰

ip 校讎略

iq 圖譜略

ir 楊寬，商鞅變法

is 澤田多喜男，先秦における公私の觀念

it 東海大学紀要文学部

iu 二程遺書（二程全書）

iv 明道文集

iw 晦菴先生朱文正公文集

ix 魯齋遺書

iy 三光

iz 五嶽

ja 泰、華、恆、衡、嵩

jb 鄭文光、席澤宗，中國歷史上的宇宙理論

jc 瞿同祖，中國封建社會

jd 李百藥

je 柳宗元

jf 蘇洵

jg 廖偁

jh 胡寅

ji 陳夢雷，古今圖書集成

jj 鄧嗣禹，中國考試制度史

jk 呂思勉，秦漢史

jl 兩晉南北朝史

jm 彭信威，中國貨幣史

jn 王圻

jo 劉錦藻

jp 中山久四郎

jq 史潮

jr 朱子新學案

js 勞延煊，元初南方知識份子——詩中所反映出的片面

John D. Langlois, Jr.

Law, Statecraft, and *The Spring and Autumn Annals* in Yüan Political Thought

INTRODUCTION

WHEN KHUBILAI KHAGHAN was making preparations for the conquest of the Southern Sung in the 1270s, one of his most important innovations was the adoption of the dynastic name "Yüan." The edict of 1272 which proclaimed the new name was written by a Jurchen named T'u-tan Kung-lü,[a] and was skillfully couched in allusions to the *Book of Changes* (*I ching*)[b] and to events in China's dynastic history.[1]

The announcement of the dynastic title was made in tandem with the abolition of the existing Chinese statutory code, the *T'ai-ho lü* (T'ai-ho Statutory Code).[c] This statutory code, or *lü* in Chinese, named after the T'ai-ho reign period (1201–1208), had been in effect since its enactment in 1201 by the Jurchen under the Chin Dynasty (1115–1234). When the Mongols conquered the Jurchen state in north China in 1234, the Chin *lü* continued to be efficacious despite the change in rulers. Khubilai abolished it finally in 1272, and no *lü* or statutory code was enacted again in China until the founding of the Ming Dynasty in 1368.[2] The Yüan is the only major dynasty in Chinese history to rule without a statutory code.

What was the importance of a *lü* or statutory code to political and legal institutions in China? How did the Mongols' failure to enact such a code affect political thought among Chinese literati? What responses were made by Chinese scholars and thinkers? These questions are the subject of this paper. Related questions are: How did the lack of a *lü* affect judicial behavior? Were law cases handled differently as a result of the absence of a *lü*? These questions, crucial in a study of legal history, will not be explored here. The main concern here is the history of political thought under the Mongols. The important area of judicial behavior and legal thought (jurisprudence) must be left for a future study.

Khubilai Khaghan's completion of the conquest of China in the 1270s brought about two immediate results that are important to the present study. First, it wove the entire land of the Middle Kingdom into the larger, multinational (or State) empire of the Mongols. From the point of view of the Mongols, the lands that had once been ruled by Han Chinese or by Jurchen and other ethnic peoples in what today we consider China proper were made part of the great Mongol empire. Although in fact Khubilai and his successors in Yüan China ruled the dynasty as though it were a separate fiefdom, and therefore a separate realm, in theory and in ideal the land of the Middle Kingdom was merely a part of the larger whole.

Second, the conquest reunited the land of the Han Chinese under one ruler. This reunification was important primarily to the Han Chinese, for their land had been disunited since the fall of the T'ang centuries earlier. The Sung at its peak had never established full control over the territories it felt it should dominate. Submersion in a larger world empire and reunification of the territory of the Middle Kingdom thus posed contradictory ways of looking at the same historical events surrounding the Mongol conquest.

In this light, the Chinese and the Mongol perspectives on the conquest of the Middle Kingdom naturally were different. Beyond these, many Han Chinese, loyal to the Sung, naturally felt a degree of animosity toward the conquerors. But as a recent study of the poetry of the intellectuals who endured the transition to Mongol rule shows, the animosity towards the conquerors eroded as the years went by, and the initial reluctance to cooperate with the conquerors was also gradually mitigated as intellectuals came to grips with the new state of things in the Middle Kingdom. One suspects that the reunification of the Middle Kingdom by Khubilai, among aother factors, was a convincing basis for his claim to be the legitimate ruler of the land.[3]

Yet nothing said so far suggests that the Mongols and their conquered peoples lost their different perspectives. Given these, it follows that in the realm of political thought the Chinese and the Mongols, not to mention the other ethnic groups in China at that time, held radically different views as to how the realm should be governed.

Herbert Franke has observed that the Mongols governed the land of the Middle Kingdom much as though it were a colony.[4] The chief aim of the Mongols was the extraction of booty from the rich, cultivated, and sedentary society of the Chinese. Initially they did not see the possibility for increasing their profits through orderly administration and taxation, but after they were advised in these matters by Yeh-lü Ch'u-ts'ai[d] (1189–1243) and others they began to alter their methods of rule.[5] In this way there ensued the possibility for some degree of convergence between the Chinese and their conquerors. The argument made by Yeh-lü was essentially that the best way to maximize one's profits from China was to utilize so-called "Han methods" (Han fa)[e] in administering the realm and removing its surpluses. This would ensure a peaceful and orderly rule in which the productivity of the native culture and economy would continue to thrive.

While the Mongols achieved considerable success in adapting themselves to "Han methods" in the administration of China, the basic conflict between these and the Mongols' own notions of what they were about remained. No amount of eloquent and subtle persuasion could have dissolved the basic rift between conqueror and conquered. This rift then formed the environment of Chinese political thought in the Mongol era.[6]

One of the unhappy concomitants of Mongol domination was the constant threat of rebellion by Mongol princes. The throne itself was the prize that was fought over at nearly every turn. Khubilai had sought to stabilize the succession by naming his son Chen-chin[f] (1244–1286) as the heir apparent.[7] But Chen-chin died before Khubilai, and the throne became an object of contention as soon as Khubilai died in 1294. None of the subsequent successions to the throne were entirely peaceful. Intrigue and assassination were the normal order of things throughout the Yüan Dynasty.[8]

If the center of authority was so unstable, it followed that the entire structure of authority in the Yüan political and military order was continually threatened with destablizing events. The facts bear this out, as the Mongol and other non-Han Chinese agents of the the khans were frequently independent of central authority. Corruption and maladministration were an ever-present problem in Yüan governance.

This is not to obscure the brighter side of Mongol rule. During the first forty years of their rule following reunification in 1279, the Mongols were relatively successful in maintaining peace. The economy was strong; trade and commerce were healthy, and the arts also flourished.[9]

But in terms of order, discipline, and authority, the Yüan administration was troubled by the problems mentioned above. These problems were the subject of grave concern by Chinese literati. In their view, judging from extant writings, the solution to these problems was chiefly a matter of reconstituting and strengthening the nature of central authority. As they analyzed the weaknesses of Yüan rule, the main cause of the constant acts of rebellion by Mongol princes was the lack of a central, authoritarian emperor. The tradition of Chinese imperial rule demanded that the emperor provide a locus of authority.[10] These scholars therefore put forth this view to the throne on numerous occasions.

Demanding that the throne fulfill its traditional Chinese obligation to provide a central and supreme—yet responsible—authority for the realm, these literati essentially argued for a realization of the theoretical autocracy that was part and parcel of the Chinese imperial institution. Furthermore, in arguing thus they were well within the mainstream of history, for during Sung times the trend had been in the direction of heightened authoritarianism.

Chinese literati who argued for increased central authority, to be exercised wisely by the Mongol rulers, certainly did not hope for despotism. Rather, they presumed that the responsible exercise of power by the Mongol rulers would result in greatly improved administration. They believed this because in their eyes the centralization of powers by the throne, based in part on the considered contributions of literati who advised the throne, would facilitate the stabilization of the imperial succession and promote discipline and order in the institutions of government. If the throne could occupy and be faithful to its rightful place—central, responsible, and supreme—then the lower-ranking persons who staffed the government would be less inclined to ignore the law through corruption, or to take the law into their own hands through arbitrary exercise of their powers in the bureaucracy.

Statutory codes (*lü*) had functioned as the permanent legal basis of punishments in earlier dynasties. In Ming and Ch'ing times, the dynasties that succeeded the Yüan, statutory codes continued to serve as the permanent bases of the legal systems. Although a statutory code did not create or limit imperial powers, it did a great deal to convey the impression of order and discipline in the exercise of those powers, and it served as an over-arching law for all personnel in the government. The Mongol refusal to proclaim such a code was seen as a refusal to be bound by the legal tradition of the Chinese world as well as a source of political weakness.

The abolition of the *T'ai-ho Code* spawned two related movements among the Chinese literati. The first was the call for the adoption of a statutory code. This movement proved futile, as already noted, for no such code was ever proclaimed, although various efforts to compile one did get underway.[11] The second movement was more complex. Recognizing that the Mongols were simply not going to enact a statutory code, many literati looked for sources of law that were in some ways analogous to a statutory code. Among the ancient classics associated with the Confucian tradition, the *Spring and Autumn Annals* (*Ch'un-ch'iu*) was the one that had a line of interpretation which was seen as serving some of the needs that would otherwise have been served by a statutory code.

The long tradition of *Annals* scholarship dating from the Han Kung-yang[g] School thinker Tung Chung-shu[h] (176–104 B.C.) became a vitally important school in Yüan times. This school viewed the *Spring and Autumn Annals* as a "penal code" (*hsing-shu*)[i] or, in other words, the record of Confucius' judgments against immoral behavior by feudal lords and kings during the Spring and Autumn period. The Kung-yang School had held that Confucius had compiled the *annals* in order to provide the standards or norms which, if applied by a true king, would "quell the righteous world and restore it to rectitude." In Yüan times the importance of this "penal code" lay here. This is because, in the absence of a formal statutory code, the *Spring and Autumn Annals* could provide a source of norms and laws and precedents which would assist the ruler in restoring order to the world, and provide the scholar-official with guidelines and support in the efforts to advise the rulers in statecraft.

Another facet of this second movement in political thought, as it related to the absence of a *lü* or statutory code, was the tendency to view various compilations of regulations and subsidiary legislation as being tantamount to a *lü*. It was argued in some instances that the many compilations of this nature virtually amounted to a statutory code since they largely followed the format and contents of the *T'ang lü*,[j] or the *T'ang Statutory Code*. Many such compilations had been made during the Yüan period. One of the earliest and most important was the *Chih-yüan hsin-ko*[k] or *New Regulations of the Chih-yüan Era*, promulgated in 1291.[12]

These compilations were generally made in order to serve as reference works for officials to use in the conduct of their duties. They were important in terms of the actual conduct of government, but none had the prestige or authority of a statutory code or *lü*. Yet some scholars were willing to entertain the notion that these compilations made the necessity for a statutory code less pressing.

It was plausible to advance this argument because in fact in Sung times the statutory code, known as the *Hsing-lü t'ung-lei*[1] (Classified Penal Statutes) or simply as *Hsing-t'ung*,[m] which was based closely on the *T'ang Code*, was out of date and outmoded.[13] Social and economic conditions had changed markedly since T'ang times, yet the formalistic statutory code did not reflect the changes. The statutory code was in many ways simply symbolic; for in the actual administration of justice it often took second place to the subsidiary legislation and regulations that were codified from time to time. The discrepancy between social and economic reality and the provisions of the statutory code were significant, and therefore it could be argued plausibly that a statutory code was not absolutely necessary to the orderly functioning of government.

This argument was ultimately less persuasive than the arguments in favor of the enactment of a body of laws or a source of law which would enable the ruler to establish an orderly, centralized administration. Although the latter arguments did not carry the day in Yüan times, they did carry the day in the following Ming. Thus we are forced to conclude that a statutory code bore a significance that transcended the ephemeral social and economic aspects of human life. We are compelled to think that a statutory code supplied an important and even a vital link in the legitimacy of Chinese imperial rule. In a sense, a *lü* served as a kind of constitution for the state. It embodied the basic Confucian belief in the importance of the rules of ceremonious behavior, known as the *li*[n] (.lit., "rites"); and it demonstrated the subordination of legal measures to Confucian values. In a word, the statutory code was the embodiment of the "Confucianization of the law" which lay at the heart of the traditional Chinese state system.[14]

All statutory codes in China after the T'ang period were based directly or indirectly on the *T'ang Statutory Code*, and particularly on the mature version of that code which was promulgated in the year 739 under the title *T'ang lü shu i*[o] (T'ang Statutory Code with Commentary).[15] The Chin *T'ai-ho Code* was based directly on the *T'ang Statutory Code with Commentary*, as was the code of the Sung, as already mentioned. The Ming code was based closely on the T'ang code, and the Ch'ing code in turn was based closely on that of the Ming. Other codes, such as that of the Khitan, were also based on or directly influenced by the T'ang code. Among all these codes, only one title is missing: the Yüan code.

Khubilai did not explain why he abolished the Chin code. As we shall see below, the sources contain the suggestion that the Chin code was abolished because it had been considered too harsh.[16] But this reason may not accurately reflect the Mongols' view of that code. It is of course possible that the Mongols simply wanted their "dynasty" to assume its own identity, and that the continued efficacy of the Chin code was seen as an obstacle to that. One is still, however, forced to explain why the Mongols did not want a Chinese-style code to be in force in the Yüan Dynasty. The modern scholar Iwamura Shinobu[p] has speculated that the Mongols did not want local or particular national forms of law to be formally recognized in parts of their great empire. That is, the Chinese law represented by the Chin code was essentially a local law, one that applied merely to Chinese sedentary culture. On that ground, therefore, it could not be adopted by the khans as a formal set of legal norms.[17] Iwamura argues that if any law had been adopted by the Mongols and promulgated for all or part of the empire, it would have had to incorporate the customary law and tradition of the Mongols themselves, as well as the law and tradition of the Chinese and the Western and Central Asians who lived under the Mongol regime. The latter, of course, were mostly Muslims, and therefore any general law for the Mongol empire would have had to accommodate itself to Islamic law. Such a general law was not possible, Iwamura argues, since no one code of law could have resolved the important differences among various local forms of law. Since local laws contravened the spirit of Mongol supremacy in their empire, and since no general law was possible, the Mongols simply abolished the indigenous laws—in this case the Chin statutory code— and ruled according to their own preferences.

It has been argued that the Yüan represented a new kind of state in Chinese history.[18] While the Sung had been a "national state," identified with the Han Chinese people, universal pretensions notwithstanding, the Yüan was a "world state" based on ethnic pluralism. Yet it was of course a state in which the Mongols enjoyed the superior position with regard to law and custom. Either ethnic pluralism or Mongol supremacy would suffice as grounds for rejecting the Chin *T'ai-ho Code*. As a code written in Chinese and designed to prevail in sedentary society, the *T'ai-ho Code* would have restrained, at least in principle, the power of the Mongol rulers vis-à-vis their Chinese subjects.

Ideological reasons undoubtedly lay behind Khubilai's decision to bolish the Chin code. The Mongols believed in *möngke tengri*, Eternal Heaven, which they believed conferred upon the Mongols the right to rule over the entire world.[19] As Igor de Rachewiltz put it, the Mongols believed that their empire was a divinely inspired social order. Beyond that, the Mongols had their own understanding of law, which was an outgrowth of their own tribal and customary relationships and interests. They called it the *jasagh*, and it was "a systematization and adaptation of tribal customary laws to the needs of the 'modern' state founded by Chingis Khan in 1206." In the Mongols' view, "the supreme authority proceeded from Eternal Heaven, whose power guided and protected the emperor."[20] If the Mongols perceived the Chin statutory code as a rival to their own *jasagh*, then they naturally would have abolished the former.

Whatever the reasons for the abolition of the code by Khubilai, the Chinese literati and their sinicized non-Han brethren were not stopped from raising the issue in their memorials to the throne. Many literati sorely bemoaned the abolition of the code, for in their eyes a statutory code had traditionally served as a constitutional bedrock for institutions and legal values of the realm.

A statutory code was considered permanent and unchanging, while other legal compilations were subject to periodic replacement. The word *lü*, translated here as statutory code, is glossed in the ancient *Erh-ya*[q] dictionary as *ch'ang*[r] (constant) and *fa*[s] (standard, norm, or law).[21] *Lü* also has the meaning of "discipline" in Buddhism, where it is used for the Sanskrit term *vinaya* in contrast to the Buddhist use of *fa* for *dharma*, the normative standards of all Buddhist behavior. Basic Chinese inconsistency in use of *fa* complicates the issue of definition here, although the word *lü* is used in a much less ambiguous manner. In classical music theory, *lü* refers to the pitch pipes which regulated the tones of music. In poetry *lü-shih*[t] or "regulated verse" is a genre in which the rules of prosody are precise and strict. In legal history, the word *lü* came to designate the permanent statutory code of a dynasty.

The *T'ang Code with Commentary* contains a preface outlining the authors' view of the importance of the *lü*. This is a complex and ultimately ambiguous exercise in semantics. But that is part of the problem of understanding law in Chinese civilization. The *T'ang Code with Commentary* preface sets the notion of law in terms of the *Book of Changes*, which in turn sets it in nature. The text asserts that the meaning of the word *lü* (statutory law) is *fa*, thus identifying statutory law with normative law. It further notes that it was Shang Yang,[u] chief minister of the ancient state of Ch'in, who changed the nomenclature of promulgated statutory law from *fa* to *lü*.[22] It then cites other texts to show that *fa* and *lü* are used as if identical in meaning.[23] The importance of identifying *lü* or statutory law with *fa*, a general term for law which also includes the concepts "model" and "norm," is that the *Book of Changes* gives a cosmogonic underpinning to the notion of *fa*. The identification of *lü* and *fa* thus ascribes to the former a similar cosmogonic importance.

These notions appear in the *Hsi-tz'u*[v] or "appended commentary" to the *Book of Changes*. The *T'ang Code with Commentary* notes that "at this [the ancient sage kings] made knotted cords and opened the roads, filling the abysses and unplugging the springs."[24] The *Commentary* observes that this means that "the *lü* and its existence in the empire is comparable to the dependability of the water that flows from the abysses." The allusion here is to the hexagram *K'an*[w] in the *Book of Changes*. *K'an* means "the abyss." In the standard translation, the text of this hexagram reads:

Commentary: The Abysmal repeated is twofold danger. Water flows on and nowhere piles up; it goes through dangerous places, never losing its dependability.[25]

The *k'an* hexagram thus conveys the idea of great danger. But it is also linked with the idea of *fa* or law. In short, the functions of *lü* are validated by their derivation from or identity with *fa*. The *T'ang Code with Commentary* points out that "the word *lü* is glossed as *ch'üan*[x] ['to weigh'] and *fa* ['law']." The commentary also notes that "*Lü* [statutory law] and *fa* differ in name but not in meaning."[26] The source for this gloss, quoted right in the text of the commentary on the *T'ang Code*, is the *Erh-ya*. The commentary then goes on to cite a famous commentary to the *Erh-ya* by Kuo P'u[y] (276–324), in which it is noted that "The *k'an* hexagram in the *Book of Changes* governs the law (*fa*). The law (*fa-lü*)[z] is in all instances that which is used to measure weights."[27] The unquoted yet implied and understood passage in the *Book of Changes* is the famous line from the *Hsi-tz'u*:

When in early antiquity Pao Hsi[aa] ruled the world, he looked upward and contemplated the images in the heavens; he looked downward and contemplated the patterns (*fa*) on earth.[28]

The word translated "patterns" is *fa*. Thus passage has frequently been associated with the discovery of laws by Pao Hsi, the ancient legendary culture-hero sage ruler. The laws or norms to which human beings must subscribe were observed in the very markings of the earth, and thus they have a natural origin.[29] The implication is that they are not man-made, and that they therefore have a validity and importance that is coeval with the earth itself.

These ideas are further linked together in the opening passages of the treatise on penal law in the official history of the Sui Dynasty:

The Sage Kings observed the firmament on high and took as a model [the regular course of] the stars; they observed [the earth] below and saw the danger of the abysses. Following the five primordial powers, taking as a rule the four seasons, none failed to give precedence to the vernal spring, which dispenses mercy, over the frost of autumn, which sets into action the laws (*tung hsien*)[ab][30]

Thus the natural order, symbolized in this text by the seasons, the primordial powers, and the stars in the sky, forms the basis of norms and punishments which are applied in the world of human beings.

In this essay, the notion of a form of statutory law (*lü*) embodies the ideas of permanence, natural legitimacy, danger, and "weighing" (*ch'üan*). A statutory code is seen as an important reservoir of norms which will assist the leaders of the human community to overcome the dangers inherent in life.

The notion of a statutory code as the permanent framework for the law and government of a dynasty became vitally important in later times. The Sung scholar Yeh Shih[ac] (1150–1223) observed that "the present dynasty takes the statutory code (*lü*) as the standard (*ching*[ad] [lit., 'woof']), whereas the edicts, commands, regulations, and ordinances are instituted in accordance with the moment (*sui shih hsiu li*)."[ae][31] This is a succinct statement of the relationship between a statutory code (*lü*) and the other forms of promulgated law in traditional China. The code was seen as the "standard" or the permanent framework, while the other forms of law (e.g. precedents, ordinances, commands, and so forth) were seen as provisional and expedient. Clearly, if this analysis is right, the absence of a "standard" in Yüan times must have been greatly regretted by Chinese literati officials.

The founder of the Ming Dynasty, T'ai-tsu[af] (r. 1368–1398) was keenly aware of the crucial importance of a statutory code, and he therefore took pains to see that one was proclaimed early in his reign, as has already been indicated. The *Ta Ming lü ling*[ag] (Statutes and Commands of the Great Ming) was compiled even before the dynasty was founded.[32] The emperor evidently knew well that the new *Ming Code* not only demarked his dynasty from that of the Mongols, but asserted his claim to traditional dynastic orthodoxy as well. The T'ang was his model, as the following passage reveals:

The T'ang and Sung dynasties both had written codes (*ch'eng-lü*)[ah] for use in judging criminal cases. The Yüan alone did not follow this ancient institution, but compiled its regulations (*t'iao-ko*)[ai] on the basis of matters that were current at particular times.[33]

Ming T'ai-tsu considered the compilation of a statutory code to be extremely important because, as he expressed it, a major cause of the defects of Yüan rule had been the lack of a statutory code. In order to avoid the continuation of the misrule that had occurred under the Mongols, the emperor was determined to enact a statutory code early in his reign. The lack of a code was seen as the cause of a lack of uniformity in legal judgments from place to place and over time. Penalties varied in unpredictable ways and judicial corruption was hard to check.

T'ai-tsu evidently was convinced that the *Ming Code* once fixed should never be changed. The head of the Ministry of Justice memorialized the throne to suggest that when the statutory code differed from subsidiary legislation (the *t'iao-li*),[aj] the articles of the code should be revised. T'ai-tsu's reply was that "law is the tool for guarding the people and the techniques that serve as the auxiliary in governing. There are both the 'standard' (*ching*) and the 'exigent' (*ch'üan*). The statutory code (*lü*) is the permanent standard (*ch'ang-ching*)[ak] and the subsidiary items of legislation are provisional expedients (*i-shih chih ch'üan-i*).[al] We have ruled the empire for nearly thirty years and have long since commanded the officers to fix the statutory code. What need is there to revise it?"[34] Thus both ruler and statesman in the Ming were committed to the central importance of the statutory code. That helps us to understand the dilemma so keenly felt by Yüan Confucian statesmen.

YÜAN REACTIONS TO THE LACK OF A STATUTORY CODE

Yüan literati officials themselves were very conscious of the fact that their dynasty had no statutory code. They often wrote memorials urging the swift adoption of a formal code, and at least twice the imperial court ordered work on a statutory code to begin. But none was ever completed. An edict of 1351, for example, ordered the compilation of a "Dynastic Statutory Code" (*kuo lü*), [am] and work was actually begun on it. But it was not completed. [35]

In the absence of a formal code, there was a tendency among some scholars to treat various legal compilations as though they were the longed-for code. Some compilations of subsidiary legislation (mostly regulations issued by various government agencies) were organized much like the *T'ang Code*. Therefore these works may be regarded as rough approximations of the *T'ang Code*, and to that extent they may have served to compensate for the lack of a formal statutory code. Thus the *Yüan shih*, [an] the official history of the Yüan Dynasty compiled early in the Ming period, observes in the Treatise on Penal Law:

The Yüan arose, and at its beginning [its officers] "lacked laws by which to keep themselves." [36] The officials settled legal cases and lawsuits in accordance with the *Chin Code* [i.e., the *T'ai-ho lü*], but they rather lamented its harshness. When Shih-tsu [Khubilai] pacified the Sung, he proceeded to simplify [the law] and to eliminate its harshness. Thereupon a new statutory code (*hsin lü*) [ao] was established, and it was promulgated to the authorities. It was called the *Chih-yüan hsin-ko*. [37]

This compilation had appeared in the year 1291. But it is important to note that these "new regulations" did not actually amount to a *lü* or statutory code. Perhaps this is the reason why an integral copy of the text has not been preserved. [38]

The *Yüan History* lists many other legal compilations, but none of them is a *lü* or statutory code. Despite what his historian-officials implied in the *Yüan History*, the Ming founder was correct when he asserted that the Yüan was unique in its lack of a statutory code. [39]

The *Yüan History* offered some penetrating observations, nevertheless, on the nature of Yüan law, particularly with respect to its failures. It calls one's attention to weaknesses that could well have stemmed directly from the dynasty's lack of a national statutory code. The history notes that "institutions were different in the north and the south, categories of matters were extremely numerous and trivial, and clerks manipulated the law for private pursuits. . . ."[40] Had a national statutory code been enacted by the dynasty, it is possible that the lack of regional integration in the legal system could have been overcome to some extent. Yet it must be recognized that the reunification of north and south China, while accomplished through military and administrative means, did not necessarily lead to the dissolution of the differences in custom, expectations, and other aspects of life that had emerged during the period of disunion. This was pointed out by Niida Noboru,[ap] the great historian of Chinese legal history, many years ago.[41]

One of the most informative discussions of the importance of statutory codes (*lü*) was provided by the Chinese scholar Wang Yün[aq] (1227–1304) in a memorial to the throne in 1268. The memorial listed thirty-five topics, each consisting of an area of government to which the emperor should give attention. At this time Khubilai Khaghan had still not proclaimed the dynastic title Yüan, and the Chin *T'ai-ho lü* was theoretically still in effect. Yet the first item on Wang Yün's list of suggestions was "enact law" (*li fa*),[ar] by which he primarily meant a statutory code.[42] In his memorial he argued that "Since antiquity rulers seeking to establish good government have always established a fixed law (*i ting chih fa*).[as] The rulers wield it above, making it an eternal, written set of regulations (*yung tso ch'eng-hsien*).[at]The clerks apply it below, treating it as a standard (*shih wei chun-shih*).[au] When the people know the law, it is easy for them to avoid [getting punished] and hard for them to commit wrongs." And he added, commenting on the permanence of such a law, "As in the cases of the 'three canons'[43] of the Chou and the 'nine articles'[44] of the Han, when fixed they did not change. That is why they were able to be sparing in the use of punishments and to perfect the way of good government." Finally, suggesting what should be done in his own day, Wang Yün concluded: "Now our dynasty (*kuo-chia*)[av] has existed for more than sixty years, yet we are still far away from defining our laws, whether major or minor. In the court the censorate wields the law on behalf of the son of heaven, and outside the court the surveillance officers (*lien-fang*)[aw] are the judicial officers in the local governments. This amounts to having officers to administer justice, but no law for them to uphold." As a consequence, he points out, there are many inconsistencies in the application of legal judgments, such that the same crime may be severely punished in one place and lightly in another. The thing to do, he suggests, is to compile a statutory code, for that would eliminate these problems. As he put it, "Would it not be appropriate to edit the edicts into a statutory code and commands (*lü ling*)[ax] and promulgate these as a new law of the Chih-yüan era (*Chih-yüan hsin fa*)[ay]? This would provide a renewal for the empire and serve as the eternal written law (*ch'eng-hsien*). Would that not be great indeed? If [among the edicts] there are some that are not currently applicable, then select some from the dynasty's *jasagh*, and in the manner of the Chin institutes issue them separately as edicts and regulations. . . . These laws and commands will serve as the bright test of the fixed law."[45]

Niida points out that one key element in Wang Yün's remarks is the idea of deterrence.[46] If the dynasty were to adopt a statutory code, he is suggesting, then the deterrent effect of the law would be heightened throughout the bureaucracy and populace. Desperately desiring stability and continuity in the legal system, Wang Yün saw that the adoption of a statutory code would be a significant step toward that end.

The Yüan abolition of the *lü* and the failure to enact a replacement for it struck a blow at the traditional authority of the scholar-official. Without a statutory code, there was no legislated basis for the predominance of Confucian values and institutions. What remained was merely the occasional and fortuitous support of traditional Chinese ideology and beliefs that the Mongol rulers offered. Often that support was superficial, or was directly contravened by actions that implied contempt or disregard for the traditional Chinese ideology and beliefs. Naturally there were among the Mongol rulers those who saw and appreciated the value of Confucian and Chinese traditional values and ways of doing things. But they did not have a stable basis of power at court.

All this did not mean that the traditional learning of the literati of China was universally devalued throughout Yüan society. By and large Chinese civilization maintained its traditional high regard for classical learning. But there was nonetheless a profound challenge to that learning brought on by the Mongol administration of the realm. Chinese literati developed a number of intellectual approaches to this challenge, one would assume, but among them the question that was addressed by many was one of how to erect a comprehensive and fundamental legal standard for the realm. As long as the rulers were unwilling to take that step, the scholars were strongly inclined, even impelled, to do that for them. Of course, their efforts could never be completely convincing, since nothing could take the place of a formal, statutory code promulgated under the endorsement of the founder of the dynasty. But their efforts were imaginative and to a great extent must have been persuasive, if only in a rough compensatory manner.

Chinese efforts to induce the Mongols to adopt what the Chinese considered a permanent moral law were continuous. Not only were the Mongol emperors considered fully legitimate by many Han Chinese subjects of the Yüan, but many of the scholars among the latter articulated the idea that the son of heaven and his law were supreme. Thus the well-known scholar official Chang Yang-hao[az] (1270–1329) stated in his widely circulated handbook *Mu-min chung-ku*[ba] (Frank Advice for the Magistrate) that, "Now the law is [the law of] the Son of Heaven. If the people should violate it, they violate the law of the Son of Heaven."[47]

The view that the emperor was the highest authority in the civilized world had long been the established view in China. The Mongol conquest, however, did nothing to undo that notion, for Chinese scholars continually urged their Mongol sovereigns to recognize their supreme place and to promulgate legal norms for the entire realm. The scholar Yao Shu[bb] (1203–1280) presented lengthy discussions on "the great craft of governing the state and pacifying the empire" in order to "cure the maladies of the time." He argued that the emperor should endeavor to establish institutional discipline and order, a concept expressed with the words *kang-chi*[bc] (or sometimes as *chi-kang*),[bd] by seeing that the emperor's commands were enforced, a statutory code was adopted, and criminal cases were carefully judged. If these things were done, he claimed, "then the powers of life and death will be held by the Court, the feudal lords will not arrogate power, great crimes will not be let off improperly, trivial errors will not be stricken with the ultimate punishment, and the innocently sentenced will have opportunities for appeal."[48]

Yao Shu's emphasis on the need for the Court or the throne to grasp firmly "the powers of life and death" is a plea for judicial and institutional rationality and centralism. The thrust of his argument is that in the absence of rationality and centralism, the legal order of the realm will be one of chaos, inconsistency, and unreasonable punishments.

A near contemporary of Yao's was Li Chih[be] (1192–1279), and it was Li who singled out the theme of institutional discipline and order for special attention. He linked it with specifically legal measures:

In general, if there are laws and standards of measurement (*fa-tu*),[bf] there will be good government. . . . Now, the way to make good government is merely to establish legal measures and to rectify institutional discipline and order (*cheng chi-kang*).[bg] Institutional discipline and order exist when those above and those below each maintain [their proper places]. By legal measures is meant the use of rewards and punishments to show [the meaning of] reprimands and exhortations (*shang fa shih ch'eng ch'üan*).[bh][49]

In Li's eyes, "legal measures" were the key to political order, for without them "it will be a matter of sheer luck if the empire is not thrown into chaos."[50]

Similar points were even more eloquently made by the scholar Sung Tzu-chen[bi] (1187–1266), a northerner who had served in the "brain trust" of Yen Shih[bj] (1182–1240) in Tung-p'ing[bk] (modern southwest Shantung).[51] In 1259, during Khubilai's wars against the Sung, Sung Tzu-chen was summoned to give advice to the rising general and future emperor. He impressed Khubilai so much that a year later he was appointed to a position in Khubilai's new government, after the latter's assumption of the throne. In Sung's new position he submitted a list of ten items which he considered essential for effective government. One of these dealt with the importance of a statutory code:

[The power to confer] office and court rank are the "handles" (*ping*)[bl][52] [of power which are wielded] by the ruler, whereas the official examination system should entirely be under the Board of Personnel. As for the statutory code and commands (*lü ling*), they are [the basis] of institutional discipline and order (*chi-kang*) in the dynasty and should be fixed as early as possible.[53]

The point that a statutory code would facilitate the ruler's exercise of supreme power and assist the maintenance of orderly administration was followed by a subsidiary point. This was that the often unruly bureaucracy would more easily be disciplined if a statutory code were adopted, for only such a code could serve as a general law for the entire dynastic era.

This point appears frequently in Yüan writings, and was most clearly stated by the northern scholar Ts'ui Yü,[bm] a Chinese with a Mongolian literary name. He was acting as head of the Ministry of Justice when he presented Khubilai in 1283 with a memorial detailing eighteen political and legal matters for the leader's attention. One of his points was that "The censorial officials (hsien-ts'ao)[bn] have no laws by which to keep themselves, and this is why treacherous people have no scruples. It would be best to determine a statutory code and commands (lü ling), which would serve as the legal norm (fa) for the entire era."[54]

Many other scholars pressed for the adoption of a statutory code for the dynasty.[55] Their arguments were couched in various terms, and many of them brought forth the criticism that contemporary law was unduly harsh. They attacked what they considered the excessive use of general amnesties by the Court, which led to the freeing of many criminals who deserved severe punishment. They felt that the rulers should not indulge the demands of the Buddhist monks, who often urged the proclamation of amnesties, and that instead the rulers should make an effort to see that criminals received their just punishments.[56]

It was the theme of the supreme power of the emperor, however, which received the greatest attention from the literati writers on statecraft. The security of the entire structure of the dynastic system hinged, in some writers' views, on the prestige and power of the throne. Su T'ien-chüeh[bo] (1294–1352), the famous compiler of Kuo-ch'ao wen-lei[bp] (Literature of Our Dynasty classified by Genre) and Kuo-ch'ao ming-ch'en shih-lüeh[bq] (Records of Eminent Officials of Our Dynasty), and a famous judge in his own right, held views of this nature.[57] As Su put it in a memorial:

Rewards and punishments are the great handles [of power exercised by the ruler] of the state. The institutional discipline and order (chi-kang) of the Court depends upon them [i.e., upon their proper use]. Thus, if in rewarding one does not overlook the meritorious, then devoted officials will be encouraged [to serve well]. If in punishing one does not overlook the guilty, then evil persons will be frightened. If there are lapses in these two, then the institutional discipline and order will inevitably be destroyed.[58]

There is a strong element of Legalism in this view, as it, like the others, borrows the idea of "handles" from Han Fei Tzu.[br] But this Legalist position is offset by the simultaneous adoption of the "Confucian" position, to the effect that law is merely an auxiliary measure in the administration of good government. Su T'ien-chüeh made this point quite clear in a memorial requesting the Court to order the compilation of a sequel to a code of regulations known as the *Ta Yüan t'ung-chih*[bs] (Comprehensive Institutes of the Great Yüan).[59] In his memorial Su wrote:

Law is the impartiality of the empire used to augment good government. A statutory code (*lü*) is the canon of an age which is used to put the law into practice. Therefore ever since ancient times the rulers of dynasties have always established the law for an age (*i-tai chih fa*).[bt] In enacting the law, it has always been necessary to institute a fixed statutory code (*i-ting chih lü*).[bu][60]

Su then went on to argue that as legal institutions and penalties were auxiliaries in the establishment of good government, it followed that it was necessary to provide formal instruction in the statutory code at schools known as *lü-hsüeh*[bv] (school for the study of the statutory code). He contended that the examination system should incorporate a *lü-k'o*,[bw] or a special category for candidates choosing to offer themselves for office on the basis of their mastery of legal studies. He thought this would be especially valuable as a way of examining the clerks (*li*)[bx] who staffed the government, but who were not ranked officials.[61] Since the *li* or clerks handled the bulk of the technical legal work, Su apparently felt that the dynasty should test them on their knowledge of the law.

Su T'ien-chüeh's position is that while law is merely an auxiliary arm in the service of the government, it is nevertheless a repository of "impartiality" (*kung*).[by] As such, it is the *lü* or the statutory code which bears the burden of articulating that impartiality and which makes it possible for the government to institute a just legal system.

Similarly, the scholar Chang Kuei[bz] (d. 1327) focussed on the importance of the ruler's authority in a memorial to Yesün Temür (the "T'ai-ting Emperor," r. 1323–1328). He asserted that the authority of the emperor must be jealously guarded and maintained, because upon it rested the security of the dynasty and its people. The notion of imperial authority which he promoted was rooted in the ancient *Shang shu*[ca] or *Book of Documents*. In his memorial, which he drafted with a colleague, he wrote:

In the *Book of Documents* it is written: "It is the ruler who dispenses rewards, and it is the ruler who dispenses punishments. As to the servitors (*ch'en*),[cb] it should never occur that they dispense rewards and punishments. . . . If it occurs that servitors dispense rewards and punishments, it is injurious to your house and baleful to your state."[62] This is because granting of life and death, bestowing or taking away, these are the "balances" (*ch'üan*)[cc] of the Son of Heaven, and they must not be stolen by the servitors below.[63]

The *Book of Documents* teaches the importance of the rewards and punishments which are employed by the all-powerful ruler to effect his orderly rule over the realm. Should these powers devolve upon persons below the ruler, the consequence for orderly rule will be disastrous.

The ancient Kung-yang school taught ideas similar to these. They taught that the ruler was the supreme power or judge in the empire and that he should exercise his discretionary power to make exceptions to the norms. This power was termed the "balance" (*ch'üan*), because it represented the power of the ruler to weigh the merits of unique cases and to formulate policy toward them accordingly even if it meant disregarding the standard policy applicable to usual situations. In Chinese, *ch'üan* also acquired the meaning "exigent," which applied to making an interim decision in the light of exigencies. It was often contrasted with the words *ching* ("standard") and *ch'ang* ("constant" or "abiding").[64] By Yüan times the word had acquired a range of meanings including "weighing," "evaluating," "judging," and "taking irregular action in accordance with exigencies," and even "temporary measures or appointments." In short, something close to the modern idea of "power" is meant by *ch'üan*, but only in the sense that it refers primarily to decision-making "under power," i.e., exigently, and to the "power" to authorize exceptions to the "standard" or the norm.

The earliest explanation of this notion, and the application of it to the "power" of the ruler, is found in the ancient *Kung-yang chuan*,[cd] the *Kung-yang Commentary* to the *Spring and Autumn Annals*:

> [Chi Chung] is to be considered as knowing how to weigh the exigencies (*chih ch'üan*)[ce]. . . . What is meant by weighing the exigencies? It is going counter to the standard (*ching*), such that good shall result [as a consequence].[65]

This same idea was reiterated clearly by Tung Chung-shu in his influential work *Ch'un-ch'iu fan-lu*[cf] (Luxuriant Gems from the *Spring and Autumn Annals*): "Although weighing the exigencies entails going counter to the standard (*ching*), it must nevertheless remain within the realm of the acceptable."[66] As will be noted below, Tung was a famous adjudicator who used the *Spring and Autumn Annals* in writing his decisions.

In their remarks to the emperor, Chang Kuei and his colleagues were urging him to "display the celestial (i.e., imperial) awe" (*chang t'ien-wei*)[cg] and to punish a particular Mongol noble who had usurped considerable power from the throne. Without entering into the facts, let it suffice to note that Chang felt that unless the emperor took steps to grasp power in his hands, the "institutional discipline and order of the dynasty" would deteriorate even further.[67]

Chang Kuei's demand that the emperor take steps to grasp the authority that institutional order and discipline required was echoed by his sinicized Arab contemporary Shan-ssu[ch] (Šams) (1278–1351). Šams was an extremely prolific writer, a scholar of the Chinese classics, and a student of imperial rule. He once submitted to Tugh Temür (Emperor Wen-tsung, r. October 1328 to February 1329 and September 1329 to September 1332) a text entitled *Ti-wang hsin-fa*[ci] (The Emperors' and Kings' System of the Mind). Šams urged the emperor to adopt several improvements in his administration, and among them a few have importance to the present discussion. He urged, above all, that the ruler should "grasp the balance and the rope" *(lan ch'üan kang)*,[cj] his metaphor for saying that the ruler should firmly hold in his own hands the means of power. Šams also urged the ruler to unify the penal statutes and to relax the web of prohibitions, so that genuine criminal behavior would be properly punished.[68]

From these examples, it would seem fair to conclude that many scholars in the Yüan period, including both Han Chinese and non-Han, believed that the ruler was the only legitimate seat of power and authority. They frequently alluded to something in the nature of a "constitution" of the dynasty, according to which the powers of life and death, rewards and punishments, were reserved exclusively for the Son of Heaven. A word sometimes used for this "constitution" *hsien*[ck] is also used in the modern Chinese for "constitution." Šams, for example, called on the ruler to uphold the *ch'eng-hsien* or "established laws" (elsewhere translated "written laws") of the dynasty. The word *hsien* appeared earlier in the text from the *T'ang Code with Commentary*, and it has a range of meanings including law, pattern, and the way of doing things. Thus the notion *ch'eng-hsien* means the "established laws" of the dynasty. The term dates all the way back to the *Book of Documents*.[69]

In the absence of a formal statutory code, which would have provided a solid footing for the "established laws" of the dynasty, at least in the eyes of those primarily concerned with China, scholars sought an alternative foundation for the "established laws" or constitution of the dynasty. Direct argumentation was one means by which this was done. Hence the marked tendency to attribute total power and authority to the Son of Heaven. It almost seems as if they were overcompensating for the lack of a legislated eternal norm (i.e. a *lü*) by devising one based one based purely on classical authority and reason. Thus we frequently find Chinese literati taking hard-line authoritarian positions with respect to the sentencing of offenders before the law. The Mongols, by comparison, appear indecisive and soft.[70]

An early instance of this, aside from ones already cited, involves the northern scholar Chang Hsiung-fei[cl] (d. 1286). When Li-chou[cm] in modern Hunan was taken by the Mongols, he was sent to restore order. Two rich merchants had violated laws against dodging taxes and committing assault, but because the local officials had been softened up with bribes the merchants were going to get off with light punishments. When Chang found out about it he insisted on having them punished with severity. The sources say that someone asked why he was taking such a trivial case with such seriousness, and he explained, "My purpose here is not to restrain those who would defraud on taxes or assault people, but to correct the misrule of the Sung and give a warning to those who do not fear the law" (*ch'eng pu wei fa che*).[cn][71]

Chang evidently felt that the Sung had been incapable of dealing with corrupt officials who flouted basic legal standards. As a consequence, people under the Sung did not fear the law. Chang undertook to rectify that. In his view, the stability and strength of the dynasty rested on the ability of the legal system to inspire fear in the minds of the people and the officials, because only fear would dissuade them from violating the law. The "fear" (*wei*) that he had in mind, of course, was the fear of prompt and just, if not even harsh, punishment. Chang evidently hoped to create a general fear of the law and of state power. He likely thought this would help establish an atmosphere of authority and intimidation on behalf of the Mongols. His ultimate goal was a state free of alleged Sung defects and leniency, one resting on a law-abiding populace and a stable social order.

FOUR YÜAN SCHOLARS ON LAW AND IMPERIAL AUTHORITY

Hu Chih-yü[co] (1227–1293) was a northerner who began service in government under Khubilai in 1260.[72] For the next thirty-three years he served in government as an influential official known for a deep concern for institutional discipline and order. Although he apparently never became a close personal advisor of Khubilai, he was highly regarded as a man of learning by his contemporaries. A prolific writer, he produced model essays notable for their clarity and boldness.

In his essay "Lun ting fa-lü"[cp] (On Determining the Statutory Laws), Hu Chih-yü confronts directly the radically different natures of Chinese and Mongol law and makes the startling proposal that these two systems be integrated. He evidently recognized the conflicting pulls of the indigenous Chinese legal tradition, which was regarded as a local phenomenon, and the law of the superimposed Mongol empire, which was in some respects transnational. A formal integration of the two legal systems or traditions would have been helpful as a measure to overcome the contradiction, at least in theory.

Elsewhere Hu had recognized that "to rule Han people one must employ Han law, and to rule the Northerners [i.e., the Mongols] one must employ northern law." He also recognized that "It is also permissible to select that which is appropriate [from both types of law] and employ them both together." The only caveat he insisted on was that "there has never been anyone who could accomplish something without instituting laws."[73]

In "On Determining the Statutory Laws" Hu observes that the entire bureaucracy suffered from the lack of a set of legal norms which they could enforce. "They dare not rely upon the old statutory code of the T'ai-ho era [i.e., the Chin *T'ai-ho lü*], and as for the Mongolian ancestral family law, the Han people cannot fully comprehend it."[74] Thus in principle even if one wanted to require the bureaucracy to apply the family law of the Mongols as the law for China, the bureaucracy would not be equipped to do that. Therefore, Hu proposed that scholars should get together to select one or two hundred articles in the Chinese laws that relate to matters of great importance, and that these articles should be set down and explained in Mongolian and Chinese. As he put it,

[These articles] should be placed in parallel to the established laws (*ch'eng-fa*)[cq] of the [Mongol] ancestors. When circumstances and intent are similar, then explain them in Mongolian letters. When they have been explained with approximate clarity, they should be presented to the throne so that they will then be enacted [as law]. "Above there will then be the Way to follow, and below there will be the laws to observe."[75] Then the empire will be fortunate indeed.[76]

The process which Hu proposed here would result, he evidently hoped, in the endorsement by the Mongol rulers of Chinese or Han law. But it would not, however, have been an unconditional endorsement. Only that part of the Han law which had parallels in Mongol clan law would be treated in the proposed manner. Thus the product of all this would have had a universality as far as the Mongol empire and its Chinese share were concerned.

Hu also wrote an essay entitled "Lu chih fa"[cr] ("On Ordering the Laws").[77] In this essay he outlined his view of imperial authority and proposed a further strengthening of the center of legitimate power represented by the throne. He noted that "law is the great balance (ch'üan) of the ruler of humanity and the impartial instrument (kung-ch'i)[cs] of the empire." From this supposition, he drew the inference that the establishment of an orderly legal system occurred when the ruler held firmly the "balance" and gave it weight in the handling of affairs. Lacking these conditions, no orderly legal system could be established.

He explains his thoughts as follows:

The establishment of laws by a dynasty means that a murderer deserves such and such a punishment, or someone who wounds a person or who is a robber deserves such and such a punishment. Henceforth, evil-doers are caused to fear the law and dare not to violate it; when a transgression occurs it is always dealt with by the law. Even though there may be dishonest officials and old [and crafty] clerks, they will not be able to distort the administration of justice. And when, in the course of applying the law against crime, error is committed either in the direction of lenience or severity, the officials will receive a proportionate punishment for their crime (ti tsui).[ct][78] In such a situation good people can rely upon the law; good clerks can have laws to which they shall adhere; and those devoted to evil will have the law to fear, to be terrified by, and to be executed by. The small and the large, the noble and the low, all will look only to the law, daring not to contravene it. They are awed (wei)[cu] without being angered, and they die without bitterness [because the executions are just]. Is this not truly the great "balance" (ch'üan) of the ruler of humanity and the impartial instrument of the empire?[79]

For Hu Chih-yü, an orderly legal system is one which deters people from committing crimes. It accomplishes this by enforcing punishments promptly and justly, serving as a deterrent to misconduct. Such a system is legitimate, Hu says, and as a consequence people of all walks of life will accept its judgments with equanimity. Only when the ruler takes into his own hands the supreme power and authority to reward and punish will the legal system function properly. Thus Hu calls for a realization of the proper and supreme power of the throne.

The opposite condition, when the ruler fails to grasp the power and authority, is one of judicial chaos and rampant corruption. This occurs when the "balance slips down to the ministers below." When that occurs, there are no general legal norms. As a consequence, legal judgments will be inconsistent, bribery and favors will pervert the administration of justice. Such was the situation in Hu's day, he claimed:

Nowadays, since there is no law, each town has a different administration, each county has different laws, each district (*chou*)[cv] has a different text (*wen*),[cw] each commandery (*chün*)[cx] has a different set of records (*an*),[cy] each of the Six Boards has a different policy (*i*),[cz], and each of the three chancelleries has a different viewpoint (*lun*).[da 80]

Under these chaotic circumstances, appeals are impossible, and the powers to grant life and death and rewards and punishments have shifted entirely to the clerks in government. Thus innocent people are being put to death, and officials of good conscience are unable to do anything about it. As a consequence, "the common people know to fear the clerks but not the law. They know of the country but not of the [imperial] Court." In this situation, standards of right and wrong are turned upside down. The risk to the community is grave, he claims, for in such a situation it is difficult to continue to behave as a human being. Thus, he asks, using an expression from Mencius, "If a person loses his original heart (*pen-hsin*),[db] then he is no better than a tiger or a wolf. How can good government be achieved?"[81]

The alternative Hu Chih-yü outlines for the ruler is a choice between taking and exercising prudently the powers that normally accrue to the throne, or leaving humanity to be reduced to the level of untamed maneating beasts.

Hu may have been a northerner, but his views were not representative of any known geographic uniqueness. The southern scholar Wu Ch'eng[dc] (1249–1333) had a similar interest in the establishment of a legal system based on a coherent set of laws and a throne that held and exercised authority. He also believed that a proper education demanded a thorough knowledge of statutory law.

Wu was a native of Lin-ch'uan,[dd] Kiangsi, the home of the Northern Sung reformer Wang An-shih[de] (1021–1086).[82] Kiangsi, on its part, had become by Yüan times well known for the customary litigiousness and contentiousness of its inhabitants.[83] It was a center of legal reformism and professionalism during the Yüan period, and there the publication of important legal texts was actively pursued.[84] Thus it should not be surprising that Wu Ch'eng revealed a deep concern for law and order in his works, in addition to his concerns with classical Confucian learning.

Wu Ch'eng's belief that a knowledge of statutory law was an essential part of learning is revealed in the curriculum he drew up for the Imperial College. Entitled *Hsüeh-t'ung*[df] (Tradition of Learning) the curriculum required the study of the Sung statutory code, the *Hsing-t'ung*.[85] Aside from this, Wu's intellectual interest in law is shown in two important writings. The earlier one, dated 1317, is a "policy question" (*ts'e wen*)[dg] for the provincial examination for that year. He drew up three such questions in his capacity of *ssu-yeh*[dh], or Director of Studies of the Imperial College.[86] The later essay is a preface to a private compilation of statutory law, a handbook to the *Ta Yüan t'ung-chih* of 1323.[87]

In his "policy question" Wu does not take a position on the use of law and the importance of a statutory code, for his purpose is to elicit carefully constructed arguments from the examinees. But from the way the question is constructed, it would seem that a particular attitude towards the law is implied.

Wu's question hinges on a very subtle point. He observes that while no statutory code was in effect to provide the legal norms for the realm, the many *ad hoc* subsidiary statutes known as *li*[di] and *tuan-li*,[dj] which serve as guides to judicial practice, in fact "accord with the principles of heaven" and "match the circumstances of human beings." In this light, then, it would be plausible to argue that a statutory code was not needed. But this is precisely the issue that Wu Ch'eng raises in his policy question.

The question begins by noting that "In antiquity, the sages employed punishments and administrative measures [i.e. laws] in the governing of the empire, and they established laws and institutions (*fa-chih*)[dk] to transmit to later generations." In subsequent times, there were a number of statutory codes which were prepared by various rulers. Continuing this trend, "the Han succeeded the Ch'in and compiled the first statutory code and commands (*lü ling*)."[88]

Wu then turns to the relationship between "the laws of a state" (*pang-hsien*),[dl] using an ancient term from the *Book of Odes*,[89] and the welfare of the people. He notes that such laws are essential if "treacherous and conniving clerks" are to be prevented from manipulating the penal system to enrich themselves. Clearly, the implication is that some standard basis for the laws is required if corruption of the legal system is to be averted. But he does not suggest that a formal statutory code is necessary in order to do this, for as already indicated one might plausibly argue that a code already existed in an informal or *de facto* manner.

To add an interesting intellectual dimension to the argument, Wu alludes to the Northern Sung scholars Wang An-shih, Ch'eng I[dm] (1033–1107), and Su Shih[dn] (1036–1101). The examinee was probably expected to recognize these allusions right off. Wu's question, with the allusions identified, reads as follows:

It was said [by Wang An-shih] that the statutory code [the *Hsing-t'ung*] was an example of "the clerkly style" (*pa-fen shu*[do]).[90] [Ch'eng I said that] he had his insight.[91] The great scholar of I-lo[dp] [i.e., Ch'eng I] deeply approved [of Wang's view]. Is one to suppose [from this] that scholars devoted to the Way and Virtue will find something of value in a statutory code? Someone [i.e., Su Shih] once said that he studied books but never the statutory code.[92] He had something to be sarcastic about, but when he explained the classics he cited the text of the statutory code. Is one to suppose that highly principled men of letters need not reject the statutory code?[93]

Concluding, Wu then asks the examinees to explain whether a statutory code was necessary. He notes that there are basically two current positions with respect to this question. One position held that the current substatutes and precedents should be combined with the ancient *T'ang Code* to yield a statutory code relevant to the present day. The other position was that the current substatutes were really no different from a statutory code and that therefore a new code was unnecessary. Wu asks simply, "are they right or are they wrong?"

Wu's questions cannot be answered merely by rote recitation of classical texts, for they require careful thought and analysis. Aside from the difficult question of the necessity for a statutory code at all, given the fact that there were many substatutes and precedents in use which seemed to serve the needs of the legal system, Wu also directs attention to another, equally interesting question. He points directly to the great irony of the position of legal thought and study within the larger Confucian intellectual tradition. Great Confucian scholars of the stature of Wang An-shih,

Ch'eng I, and Su Shih, who represented very different types of learning
within the Confucian school, seemed to agree reluctantly that the statutory code was extremely valuable to the well-being of the community.
And while Su Shih may have said he preferred not to study the code, he
in fact knew it very well and even cited it when elucidating the meaning
of the Confucian classical texts. Wu's challenge to the candidates for
degree is not only that they discuss the importance and relevance of a
formal statutory code that might be enacted in their era, but also that
they address the apparent irony and dilemma of the traditional Confucian
learning with respect to the importance of law.

One imagines that well-reasoned answers to the question could argue in support of the view that a statutory code was essential to legal and
political stability, or the precise opposite, without being automatically
failed by the examiner. Either possibility is implied in the question. The
real import of the question concerns the role of the man of learning vis-
á-vis the legal system and the importance of that role to the community
at large. The breadth of the question is thus extremely impressive and
demanding.

Wu's suggestion that some of his contemporaries believed the *T'ang
Code* actually enjoyed *de facto* efficacy in Yüan times is borne out by
another essay of Wu's. This is his preface to *Ta Yüan t'ung-chih t'iao-li
kang-mu*[dq] (Outline and Digest of the Classified Substatutes in the Comprehensive Institutes of the Great Yüan), compiled by his friend from
Lin-ch'uan, Chang Shao.[dr][94] Chang Shao had compiled his digest to
serve as a handbook or guide to the *Ta Yüan t'ung-chih*, a compilation
that had been promulgated by Shidebala (Emperor Ying-tsung, r. 1320–
1323). It was designed to serve as "the new statutory code (*hsin lü*) of the
Great Yüan," as Wu Ch'eng points out. Furthermore, while in itself the
Ta Yüan t'ung-chih was not a statutory code, it nevertheless closely resembled one: "If one place the former [T'ang] statutory code and the
new compilation [i.e., the *Ta Yüan t'ung-chih*] together, the language
and style would differ, but the meaning and principles would largely be
identical. [The *Ta Yüan t'ung-chih*] employs the ancient statutory code
indirectly [lit. "secretly"] and yet ostensibly does not employ it. It abol-
ishes it in name but not in substance."[95]

The original preface to the *Ta Yüan t'ung-chih* also makes the point
made by Wu Ch'eng. The preface is by the prominent scholar Po-chu-
lu Ch'ung[ds] (1279–1338), a man of Jurchen descent who served in po-

sitions of influence under the Mongols.[96] Po-chu-lu observed[97] that the
Ta Yüan t'ung-chih helped the dynasty to overcome the absence of an
official statutory code and served to guide officers and clerks in the conduct of their duties. The dynasty had acquired its ch'eng-hsien or "established laws" during the reigns of its emperors, but these were not anywhere set down in a coherent and accessible compilation. Thus Po-chu-
lu hoped the Ta Yüan t'ung-chih would serve that purpose.

Another scholar who expressed the view that only a firm set of legal
institutions could protect the integrity of the dynasty was Ou-yang Hsüan[dt]
(1283–1357),[98] descendant of the famous Northern Sung scholar Ou-
yang Hsiu[du] (1007–1072). Ou-yang Hsüan received the chin-shih[dv] in
1315, when the examination system was revived. His speciality was the
Book of Documents, a fact which is revealed in his view of law.[99]

Ou-yang wrote a preface for a compilation of regulations known
under the title Chih-cheng t'iao-ko[dw] (Regulations of the Chih-cheng Era
[1341–1368]).[100] In this preface he observed that in antiquity the officers
of a state at the beginning of the New Year would publicly post the laws
at the gate of the palace. The laws in question, according to Ou-yang,
were those that pertained to "administrative and educational measures,
and to the trying of criminal cases." The classic text on government, the
Chou li[dx] (Rites of Chou) preserved that regulation, Ou-yang notes. Furthermore, in the Book of Documents the officers of a state are charged
with the task of "examining clearly the penal code (hsing-shu) and mutually deliberating [on the punishments]."[101] Thus the classical texts endorse the importance of publicly proclaiming the laws and of critically
debating the punishments called for by those laws.

The Book of Changes is also invoked by Ou-yang Hsüan to illustrate
the importance of laws and their interpretation. He cites the text of two
hexagrams, Shih-k'o[dy] ("Biting Through") and Feng[dz] ("Abundance"). The
former states:

> Thunder and lightning:
> The image of Biting Through.
> Thus the kings of former times made firm the laws
> Through clearly defined penalties (hsien wang i ming fa ch'ih fa).[ea 102]

And the latter states:

> Both thunder and lightning come:
> The image of Abundance.
> Thus the superior man decides lawsuits
> And carries out punishments (chün-tzu i che yü chih hsing).[eb 103]

These images lead to Ou-yang's concluding remarks on the value of the compilation of regulations for which he wrote these remarks:

The images of the two hexagrams employ thunder and lightning to manifest the power of heaven (T'ien-wei)ec [i.e., the metaphor for the awesome power of the emperor]. From now on the officials in charge of criminal cases, and the scholars who enforce the laws, when they take up their posts and engage in governing they will have this compilation to rely upon. Do not be irreverent towards the laws of the dynasty (kuo-hsien);ed do not violate the norms of heaven (t'ien-ch'ang). ee "Punishments aim at the elimination of punishments," [as it is stated in the Book of Documents]. 104 It begins here indeed. It is also stated, "Be earnest. Be reverent." 105

Ou-yang Hsüan's belief in the law as the sine qua non of an orderly community was profound. This is demonstrated in his long, detailed, and expert history of the legal disputes over a piece of land in Fen-ief county, Kiangsi. 106 The case took many years to resolve, and its roots lay in the last years of the Southern Sung. The land in question had been bought by a Buddhist monk in 1273. He had assumed a lay person's name and bought the land for his temple, but in doing so he violated Sung law. According to Ou-yang, Sung law forbade temples from buying land from common people (min)eg if the temple already possessed "endowed lands" (ch'ang-chu t'ien).eh An initial legal ruling held that the land had to be turned over to the Fen-i School, and for some twenty-eight years the school had benefited from the revenue from this land. But in 1300, for various reasons the temple regained possession of the land. Furthermore, the income from the land had been used by the monks to finance their legal maneuverings to keep the land. After appeals, hearings, and other legal actions, the land was finally returned to the school by the authorities. At this Ou-yang observed: "The case of forty-odd years finally came to an end. . . . I remark that . . . things are one's own when the law is operating properly, and they are not one's own when it is not. The monks broke the law, and the land was returned to the government. The government gave the land to the school; the school received it from the government, not from the monks." 107 For Ou-yang, the law and the state were of fundamental importance to the institution of property. In his eyes, the case supports the view that there could hardly be an orderly civilization without government support of property rights through careful enforcement of the law. Ordinary human beings with limited resources were vulnerable to injury and therefore needed the protection of the law and the state. At the same time, that law was subject to abuse in the absence of careful supervision and study. Thus the case of Fen-i School illustrated the importance of laws that were accessible to the people and which were conscientiously administered by the state.

These views were articulated more precisely by Ou-yang Hsüan in an answer to a "policy question."[108] The question mentioned four major problems then current in political affairs, and it directed the examinee to take up each of them to propose solutions. One of the four was "the failure to establish a statutory law" *(fa-lü chih wei ting)*.[ei]

In his answer, Ou-yang pointed out that the dynasty had enacted the *Chih-yüan hsin-ko* (promulgated in 1291). But he also noted that actual legal decisions may not always correspond fully with the provisions in that compilation. Therefore it was necessary to consider the question of the compilation of a statutory code. He noted that the essential thing in an orderly legal system was the recruitment of the legal experts, the *fa-li*[ej] or clerks who specialized in legal matters. It was the clerks who actually applied the the regulations and laws to criminal matters. In Ou-yang's time, the legal system suffered from two main problems: the slipshod recruitment of the legal experts, and the absence of a statutory code. Although there was no code, there were a great number of subsidiary statutes and regulations. These were so numerous, in fact, that criminal cases were handled as though they were merely "routine matters" *(ch'ang-liu)*.[ek] The officials themselves did not even examine all the various laws in effect. Consequently, "judgments are made on the basis of their joy or anger, everything depends on their likes and dislikes." The solution to this problem is the compilation of a formal statutory code. As Ou-yang put it, "without a written code *(ch'eng shu)*,[el] we approach entrapment of the common people."[109] Such a code must be publicly promulgated to be effective, he said. Alluding to an ancient precedent, he wrote: "In antiquity Tzu-ch'an[em] cast the Penal Code *(hsing shu)*. Although it is said that Shu-hsiang[en] laughed at him, [the state of] Cheng had good government because it was able to stop crimes."[110]

In this passage, although Ou-yang does not use the word *lü*, it is apparent that he was referring to the problem of a statutory penal code. In the course of making his argument, Ou-yang challenges a part of the Confucian tradition. The story of Tzu-ch'an and the criticism of him is often cited as an example of early Chinese views of law. According to the traditional view, Tzu-ch'an's public display of the penal code in the state of Cheng opened a Pandora's Box of nasty litigiousness among the people and led ultimately to a nearly universal degradation of the political system and of public morality. The hostile view of Tzu-ch'an is recorded in the *Tso chuan*,[eo] the commentary to the *Spring and Autumn Annals* that enjoyed virtual "classic" status among the ancient books; the hostile view was in turn copied nearly verbatim into the *Han shu*[ep] (History of the [Former] Hans Dynasty) by the historian Pan Ku.[eq][111] Ou-yang's view is clearly diametrically opposed to the traditional view, for he claims that Tzu-ch'an was on the correct path when he made the law a matter of public record. Thus, he would argue, the Yüan should follow Tzu-ch'an's example. It should adopt a code and promulgate it throughout the land.

CH'UN-CH'IU STUDIES: (A) THE PRE-YÜAN DEVELOPMENT IN LEGAL CONCEPTS

The intellectual tradition proved to be extremely resilient during the era of Mongol rule, and one source of its resiliency was the tradition of classical studies, especially that concerning the *Ch'un-ch'iu*.[er] The *Ch'un-ch'iu* or *Spring and Autum Annals*, one of the Five Classics, is a chronicle of events in the ancient state of Lu during the period 722 to 481 B.C.[112] Tradition held that it was compiled by Confucius. Ever since Han times, this terse classic had provided grist for the mills of scholars who sought to uncover the hidden judgments of the sage. Since it was believed that those judgments could be determined by careful study of the text and its commentaries, the text and the commentaries were viewed as a potential source of eternal standards of right and wrong. The text in particular was regarded as a repository of moral law, couched in the "righteous decision" made by Confucius long ago.

During the Yüan period, the *Spring and Autumn Annals* took up some of the slack caused by the absence of a formally enacted *lü*. Since Chinese views of law demanded that there be a *ching* or standard against which deviations from the norms could be weighed and penalized, the importance of the *ching* (classic) known as the *Spring and Autumn Annals* drew much intellectual attention. So did other *ching* such as the *Book of Changes*. A recent survey has counted some 213 works on the *Book of Changes* in Yüan times, 149 on the Four Books, and 127 studies of the *Spring and Autumn Annals*.[113] To a noticeable degree, the *Spring and Autumn Annals* was looked to as a source of moral law, as it was considered a "penal code" consisting of precedents embodying Confucius' standard of right and wrong. This "penal code" could provide the proper foundation of a coherent legal order, or so it was hoped.

This approach to the *Spring and Autumn Annals* long antedated the Mongol conquest of China. In antiquity Mencius hsd provided clues to the meaning of the work. His insights challenged scholars to explain why Confucius would have devoted time to such an apparently meaningless collection of facts. The *Annals* is, at first glance, utterly without significance. The entry for the year 602 B.C., for example, consists of only twenty-one characters and informs us that so-and-so and so-and-so attacked the state of Ch'en; it was summer; it then was autumn and there were locusts; and finally it became winter.[114] What possible significance could these facts have had for Confucius, let alone later times? Nothing in Confucius' *Analects* tells us why the master bothered to transcribe such apparent drivel from the historical records of the state of Lu. Yet Mencius tells us that Confucius had stated that the work by which he wanted to be judged and remembered was the *Annals*. Mencius provides a clue to Confucius' reasoning:

When the world declined and the Way fell into obscurity, heresies and violence again arose. There were instances of regicides and parricides. Confucius was apprehensive and composed the *Spring and Autumn Annals*. Strictly speaking, this is the Emperor's prerogative. That is why Confucius said, "Those who understand me will do so through the *Spring and Autumn Annals*; those who condemn me will also do so because of the *Spring and Autumn Annals*". . . . Confucius completed the *Spring and Autumn Annals* and struck terror into the hearts of rebellious subjects and undutiful sons.[115]

As if this were not clear enough, the Han interpretor of *Mencius* Chao Ch'i[es] (d. A.D. 201) explained that Confucius "set forth the law [or norms] of the uncrowned king" (*su-wang chih fa*)[et] in the *Spring and Autumn Annals*.[116]

Thus the *Annals* helps to accomplish the task which properly belongs to the Son of Heaven, namely the provision of a moral law for the human community. It may be held to constitute an alternative source of authority and law in the event the Son of Heaven fails to uphold his expected task. For this reason, the *Spring and Autumn Annals* remained and intensely important subject of study throughout the millennia of Chinese history.

A difficult passage in the ancient *Chuang Tzu*[eu] text, in the chapter entitled "On the Equalization of Things," supplies another early lead to this approach towards the *Annals*. Translators disagree sharply on its interpretation, so the one given here can only be tentative. Chuang Tzu said, "The *Spring and Autumn Annals* supplies the standard for the world (*ching-shih*)[ev] and is the record of [the governing of] the former sage kings. The Sage [Confucius] passed judgments [in recording the facts] but he did not argue."[117]

Chuang Tzu says elsewhere that "the *Spring and Autumn Annals* defines names and duties."[118] In this respect, K. C. Hsiao's observation is very useful. He pointed out that the *Annals* was compiled in order to help "straighten out real situations" through the application of the doctrine of "the rectification of names."[119] Realizing that he had no direct means of altering the ways of the world, Confucius chose the *Annals* as a vehicle for preserving his principles in the hope that ultimately they would come to bear.

As a chronicle of deeds and judgments, then, the *Annals* verges on history.[120] As Mencius said, "the style is that of the official historian."[121] Yet like most Chinese historiography, the *Annals* was meant to be didactic. Thus Mencius quotes Confucius as saying, "I have appropriated the didactic principles therein."[122] If the *Annals* is history, it is history with an overt political and moral aim. The *Kung-yang Commentary* explained that aim clearly: "to quell the rebellious world and return it to rectitude."[123]

Han scholars were deeply intrigued by the *Spring and Autumn Annals* and saw in it valuable lessons. Ssu-ma Ch'ien,[ew] the great Han historian, conceived of himself as a historian in a manner that was built on his interpretation of the *Spring and Autumn Annals*. This is clear from his autobiographical remarks appended to the *Shih chi*[ex] (*Records of the Historian*):

The *Spring and Autumn Annals* distinguishes right and wrong, and is therefore the strongest [of the Six Classics] in the governing of human beings. . . . The *Spring and Autumn Annals* defines righteousness. For quelling the rebellious world and returning it to rectitude, nothing comes close to the *Spring and Autumn Annals*. . . . Therefore the ruler of a state must know the *Spring and Autumn Annals*, for otherwise he will not recognize slander when it appears in front of him, or a villain when one is behind him. The official must know the *Spring and Autumn Annals*, for otherwise in managing affairs he will not know what is proper, and in dealing with changing circumstances he will not know how to weigh the exigencies (*ch'üan*).[124]

Ssu-ma Ch'ien must have hoped that his *Shih chi* would also serve as a *ching* or permanent repository of information for later people and thus help them to make correct decisions in the face of changing circumstances (*ch'üan*).

During Han times the importance of the judgments in the *Spring and Autumn Annals* was equal to that of the statutory code. In fact, it is possible to argue that the *Annals* served as a code, for it was cited in criminal cases as support for judgments. Tung Chung-shu is said to have left records of some 232 cases in which the *Annals* provided all or part of the rationale for the legal disposition of the cases.[125] Tung, of course, was not the only Han scholar to refer to this work in legal cases.[126] In post-Han times, the practice of referring to the *Annals* as though it were a legal code continued in some dynasties. The Chin[ey] (265–420) and the Northern Ch'i[ez] (550–577) both left records indicating that the *Annals* was cited in criminal cases.[127] Thus Tung Chung-shu's approach to the *Annals* was not idiosyncratic, but rather general.

Among the early commentaries to the *Spring and Autumn Annals* we also find evidence of this legalistic interpretation of the text. The great Chin dynasty commentator Tu Yü[fa] (222–284), author of the commentary *Ch'un-ch'iu Tso-shih ching-chuan chi-chieh*[fb] (Collected Explanations of the Text of the *Spring and Autumn Annals* and the Commentary by Tso), marks an important milestone in the history of *Annals* studies.[128] Tu Yü was not only a classical scholar, for he served as the principal compiler of the Chin statutory code, and he wrote a commentary to that code.[129] Beyond these scholarly endeavors, Tu Yü served as a general in the Chin defeat of the state of Wu.

Tu tended to view the *Annals* as a quasi-legal document or as a repository of law. He revealed this in his preface to the commentary mentioned above:

All the precedents (*li*) that it adduces in order to present its major point are the eternal institutions for administering a state, the laws that were handed down by the Duke of Chou, and the old statutes (*chiu lü*)[fc] of the historical records.[130]

As we have seen, this approach to the *Annals* did not end in Tu Yü's time. Not only did it extend into Northern Ch'i times, but there is evidence that the *Annals* was cited in legal contexts well into Sung times.[131]

In Northern Sung times the *Spring and Autumn Annals* was the subject of intense interest on the part of scholars. The main approach of Sung scholarship tended to follow that set by the T'ang scholar Tan Chu[fd] and his student Lu Ch'un.[fe][132] The early Neo-Confucian scholar Sun Fu[ff] (992–1057) carried on their work, but in doing so he nevertheless continued as a subtheme the legalistic interpretation of the text. He was even criticized for being a "Legalist" by other scholars. One person wrote, "Sun Fu treated the *Spring and Autumn Annals* the way Shang Yang did law. [According to the measures instituted by Shang Yang], if one dropped ashes in the street, he was punished, and if one's stride exceeded six *ch'ih* in length he was to be executed. One would say his defect lay in harshness."[133]

Shao Yung[fg] (1011–1077) had similar ideas to those of Sun Fu, and he stated them even more clearly. He said simply, "The *Spring and Autumn Annals* is Confucius' penal code (*hsing-shu*)."[134] Shao's contemporary Ch'eng I also viewed the text in this way, and since his ideas were incorporated into the Neo-Confucian anthology *Chin-ssu lu*[fh] (Reflections on Things at Hand) by Chu Hsi[fi] (1130–1200) and Lü Tsu-ch'ien[fj] (1137–1181), they became very influential in later times, certainly during the Yüan. Ch'eng I said that Confucius "wrote the *Spring and Autumn Annals* as the unchanging great law for kings of the next hundred generations."[135] He criticized scholars of his day for failing to recognize "the great law for governing the world" (*ching shih chih ta fa*)[fk] which is set forth in the *Annals*.[136] Ch'eng I's idea here may well have taken its inspiration from the statement by Chuang Tzu, quoted above, to the effect that the *Annals* "supplies the standard for the world" (*ching shih*, or "governs the world").

To make his point even clearer, Ch'eng I noted that, "The place of the *Spring and Autumn Annals* in the Five Classics is like that of the substatutes (*tuan-li*, lit. "decisional precedents") in the sphere of law."[137] Thus the *Annals* should be read as an explication of the law code and an exemplification of how it should be applied.

The "law" of the *Annals* was a universal one in Ch'eng I's view. An aphorism of his, reported by a student, makes this evident: "The laws (*fa*) of the Three Sage Kings were laws of individual kings, but the law of the *Spring and Autumn Annals* is the unchanging, universal law (*pu i chih t'ung fa*)[fl] for the kings of the next hundred generations."[138]

A further example and amplification of this legalistic interpretation of the *Annals* in Sung times is found in a poem by Han Ch'i[fm] (1008–

1075), the Sung prime minister,[139] about a friend's exegesis of the text.
Part of the poem reads as follows:

> What Confucius' *Spring and Autumn Annals* records is 242 years.
> His strict laws must not be violated.
> He sought to show the eternal balance (*ch'üan*) of the Son of Heaven.
> Rules of ceremonious behavior, music, punitive expeditions, and chastise-
> ments must issue from the emperor.
> The feudal lords, although strong, must not arrogate [power].
> King P'ing of the Chou moved [the capital] east, and the ruler of Lu was
> Duke Yin, [the first duke in the *Annals*].
> The rope (*kang*)[fm] [i.e. the authority] of the true king was broken and could
> not be rejoined.
> All that the Celestial King had left were his throne and his title.
> The states were autonomous, passing down their titles of duke on their
> own [without authorization from the sovereign].[140]

Han Ch'i's poem records the history of the fate of the Chou Dynasty. Its
message is that when the "balance" (*ch'üan*) of the ruler, which is to say
the ruler's capacity to make decisions about life and death, rewards and
punishments, and so forth, slips out of the ruler's hands, the dynasty will
lose its unity and will dissolve into disreputable autonomous states. In
that situation, the ruling house will lose its actual control and the dynasty
will eventually crumble. For Han Ch'i, a man whose political career
involved him intimately in questions of authority and punishment, the
Spring and Autumn Annals addressed both these matters and offered a
blueprint for all time.

In Sung times the theme of "revering the king" (*tsun wang*)[fo] was
perhaps the dominant overt theme in *Annals* scholarship.[141] But this was
a label, in effect, for the broader question of the authority and power of
the sovereign. Related to it was of course the notion of a universal law
or norm which made possible the existence of the organized community
of human beings. A second major theme in Sung *Annals* scholarship
was the theme of "repelling the barbarians" (*jang i*)[fp] and revenge against
them for the damage they had caused to the empire after the fall of the
north to the Jurchens in the twelfth century. This theme, too, can be
reduced to the question of imperial authority.

One of the studies of the *Annals* which was most explicit on the
question of imperial authority was *Ch'un-ch'iu huang-kang lun*[fq] by Wang
Che.[fr 142] This title might be rendered *On Imperial Authority in the Spring
and Autumn Annals*. Wang noted that "if the institutes of statecraft (*ching*

chih)^{fs} can settle the empire, then those in the *Spring and Autumn Annals* are all that are needed."[143] Thus in Wang's view, the *Annals* contained all the knowledge necessary for the task of administering the empire. Not only were the technical matters contained therein, but so were the spiritual and moral matters: "If perfect sincerity can assist the moral transformation [of the empire], then the perfect sincerity of the *Spring and Autumn Annals* is profound." So long as the ruler "grasped the institutes of statecraft and extended perfect sincerity," he could bring about the establishment of a united and orderly civilization. Summing up his argument, Wang wrote:

Embodying the Way and Virtue, and thus to maintain them with the rules of ceremonious behavior and the law, setting roots in benevolence and righteousness, thereby to reinvigorate the balance and the rope (*ch'üan kang*) [i.e. the power and authority], revering superior persons and worthy men, honoring the good and condemning the evil—these are the balance (*ch'üan*) of the Way of the True King and the task of the Great Peace.[144]

Wang's careful study of the "imperial authority" and its presentation in the *Spring and Autumn Annals* was not wholly legalistic. That is, he did not argue that the *Annals* should be viewed as a legal code which set forth the laws of a well-functioning community. Yet he clearly drew on the long tradition of *Annals* studies which stressed the nature of the imperial institution and the powers and authority that should be exercised by it. In this sense, then, his work falls well within the trend of *Annals* studies which became most useful to scholars living under Mongol rule.

CH'UN-CH'IU STUDIES: (B) CH'UN-CH'IU AND LAW IN YÜAN THOUGHT AND STATECRAFT

The Mongol conquest put many of the ideas outlined above to a severe test. The idea that the ruler should be the sole locus of legitimate power and authority in the realm lent itself to borrowing by authoritarian rulers. The trend in Sung times had been one of increasing authoritarianism. The ruler of the Mongols, which had replaced that of the Jurchens and the Han Chinese in the north and south, respectively, was by nature authoritarian, especially with regard to the conquered peoples. Under the Mongols, scholars continued to espouse the authoritarian theories which had earlier been brought forth in connection with the *Spring and Au-*

tumn Annals. But Mongol rule, while inherently authoritarian, was not therefore efficient. That is, from the Chinese point of view, Mongol statecraft was unsophisticated if not even nonexistent. Responding to this situation, scholars found in the *Annals* a tradition of statecraft which they thought or hoped would help improve the nature of Mongol rule for their own benefit. This tradition emphasized centralism and autocracy, and at the same time it implied the notion of responsible authority. The autocracy and authoritarianism of these theories pointed not to tyranny or despotism, but rather to enlightened authoritarianism.

Hu Chih-yü, whom we have discussed above, was a devoted student of the *Spring and Autumn Annals*. His writings on the *Annals* lucidly convey the theme of centralized power and authority. One of his most emphatic statements is his essay "Tu Ch'un-ch'iu"[ft] (Studying the *Spring and Autumn Annals*).[145] In this essay he argues that the *Annals* teaches the way to "reinvigorate the authority of the king" (*chen wang kang*),[fu] and that it does so by providing negative examples as warnings to rulers. Hu takes off from Mencius' point that "in the *Spring and Autumn Annals* there are no righteous wars."[146] The reason why this is so, Hu claims, is simply that all the wars mentioned in that work were conducted by "hegemons" (*pa*)[fv] who engaged in military actions without proper authorization from the Son of Heaven. Thus their crime, in Hu's eyes, is their arrogation of authority. Arrogation cuts at the heart of the political order of the empire and therefore is something to be sharply deplored. As Hu put it, had the hegemons truly aimed to "reinvigorate the authority of the king and to reverence the house of Chou, then as [proper] ministers who do not presume to act arbitrarily [i.e., without authorization from the throne], they would in each instance have requested orders from the capital [i.e., from the throne]."[147] They never made any such requests, and hence the Chou order collapsed.

Hu Chih-yü explains:

The Sage [Confucius] lamented the fact that the authority of the king (*wang kang*, lit. "the king's rope") had grown loose, that rebellious subjects and undutiful sons had destroyed both the rules of ceremonious behavior and the sense of righteousness, and that brutal punishments and mass murders [were occurring]. That is why he clearly recorded these crimes to show to people of later times. They are so clear that when studying [the *Annals*] even an ox-boy or a horse attendant[148] would be able to distinguish the nature of the crimes, as though a balance and a mirror were hanging [right there in the text].[149] The severity [of evil] can be distinguished by people without having to wait for explanations. One hopes that those who are evil will suddenly know fear [as a consequence].[150]

Hu Chih-yü's point relates to the overall purpose of the *Annals*, which was in his eyes a design to discourage deviance from certain norms. Such deviance was discouraged by recording for all time the examples of those whose deviation caused evil things to occur in the world.

Hu Chih-y'ü subscribed to the view which considered the *Annals* a law code. He made this point when he wrote, "A breach of the rules of ceremonial behavior is a crime (*tsui*).[fw] For a crime, one receives a punishment. The *Spring and Autumn Annals* is a penal code (*hsing-shu*)." [151]

The scholar Wu Ch'eng also held this view, and stated it in nearly the same terms employed by Hu Chih-yü: "According to the principles of the *Spring and Autumn Annals*, if one breaches the rules of ceremonial behavior, it is recorded. When one departs from the rules of ceremonial behavior, one then becomes subject to the law. Therefore it [i.e., the *Annals*] is called a penal code (*hsing-shu*)." [152]

Wu Ch'eng made this important point in the preface to his influential study of the commentaries to the *Annals*, his *Ch'un-ch'iu tsuan-yen*[fx] (Collected Commentaries on the *Spring and Autumn Annals*). [153] The work itself is arranged conventionally according to the original text of the *Annals*. Each line of text is followed by the relevant passages from the major commentaries, as viewed by Wu Ch'eng, and by observations of his own. But it is prefaced by an original analysis of "general principles" of the *Annals*. This work, called *Tsung-li*,[fy] takes an analytical approach to the *Annals* as a "penal code," and divides the "principles" into seven categories. These become the headings for eighty-one entries. [154] The first five categories are the traditional five areas of rituals. These have been described by F. W. Mote as follows:

Chi-li,[fz] or the auspicious rites, meaning sacrifices (of the state and the imperial shrines, of family ancestral shrines, to local deities patronized by the state, etc.); *Hsiung-li*,[ga] or the rites for inauspicious events (funerals, national disasters, etc.); *Pin-li*,[gb] or the rites for ceremonial visits (of the state and in high royal and official circles, both public and private); *Chün-li*,[gc] or the rites for martial occasions (in conjunction with wars, field exercises, and to standardize relations within the military); and *Chia-li*,[gd] or the rites for festive occasions (especially weddings, but also betrothals, births, capping ceremonies, feastings and rejoicings, congratulations and celebrations, etc.). [155]

Wu Ch'eng added to these five areas of rituals two more categories, and these he termed *T'ien tao*[ge] or "the Way of Heaven," and *Jen-chi*,[gf] "the bonds that hold people together." [156] This division of the material in the *Annals* is an original contribution of Wu Ch'eng's. [157] Its significance lies in the fact that as a "penal code," the *Annals* embraces the totality of human existence and thus provides a set of all-encompassing principles upon which an orderly structure of human relationships may be constructed and maintained.

Elsewhere Wu Ch'eng observed that the purpose behind the compilation of the *Spring and Autumn Annals* had to do with the "downward slippage of the handles (*ping*) [i.e., the levers of imperial power] afforded by the rituals, music, military expeditions, and punishments, to the feudal lords" in Chou times. As a consequence, "[individual] states made their own government, the hegemons blocked the true king, and the *i-ti*[gg] [barbarians] disturbed the Chinese (*Hsia*)."[gh] In such a situation all order is lost, for "the norms of Heaven are chaotic (*t'ien ching wen*)[gi] and the principles of humanity are perverted (*jen li kuai*)."[gj][158] Confucius wanted to rectify this bad situation, but lacking the position from which he could achieve reform he was incapable of doing it. "So he transcribed [the events] in the classic [i.e., the *Annals*] as a legacy for a later sage. Thus it is said, 'The *Spring and Autumn Annals* [deals with] the affairs which pertain to the Son of Heaven.' It is also said, 'The *Spring and Autumn Annals* is Confucius' penal code.' "[159]

The last *Annals* scholar who needs mention here is Wu Lai[gk] (1297–1340), a native of P'u-chiang[gl] county, Chekiang. He never served in government, but not for lack of trying. He took the palace examination in the *Spring and Autumn Annals* field, but was not passed. He then became a teacher in his native locale, although he never gave up his ambition to effect a constructive influence on politics in the capital city of Ta-tu[gm] (modern Peking). His father, in fact, spent over fifty years in the Yüan capital and became extremely close to a number of influential Mongol leaders.[160]

Wu Lai's own original writings on the *Annals* are not extant. But we do have a number of prefaces by him that deal directly with the *Annals*. Among these prefaces, the one he wrote for his contemporary Wu Shih-tao[gn] (1283–1344) is most revealing.[161] Wu Shih-tao was the author of a study of the then-standard commentary to the *Annals* by Hu An-kuo[go] (1074–1138). It had been made the official interpretation for the purposes of the examination system in 1313. Wu Lai wrote a preface to Wu Shih-tao's study which contains some important ideas relevant to the present inquiry.[162]

It should be noted first that Hu An-kuo's commentary fell well within the tradition of *Annals* studies here considered, to wit the tradition of viewing the *Annals* as a penal code. As Hu put it in his own preface: "Thus the gentleman [i.e., Ch'eng I] held that 'the place of the *Spring and Autumn Annals* in the Five Classics is like that of the substatutes in the sphere of law.'[163] No one who is ignorant of the *Spring and Autumn Annals* can decide difficult cases without confusion."[164] For Hu An-kuo, the *Annals* was "the great canon for governing the world" (*ching-shih ta-tien*), a term which evoked a central concern of Yüan period scholars and became the title of an enormous compilation of documents and laws in 1332, known as *Huang-ch'ao ching-shih ta-tien*,[gp] under Emperor Wen-tsung.[165]

In his preface Wu Lai takes note of the shifting importance of Hu's study of the *Annals*. That is, he neatly disposes of what by Yüan times had become an awkward emphasis of the Sung dynasty scholars' writings: he observes that Hu was extreme in his interpretation in stressing the theme of "repelling the barbarians," primarily because of the insecure conditions of his dynasty. Following the debacle of 1126, when the Jurchens captured the Sung ruler Hui-tsung and many members of the court, Emperor Kao-tsung never succeeded in avenging the death of his father. Hu An-kuo was deeply affected and embittered by that, and so his study of the *Annals* devotes an inordinate (but for him quite natural) amount of attention to the theme of "repelling the barbarians." By Wu Lai's time, however, that theme was no longer a crucial one, for the obvious reason that the "barbarians" could no longer harm the empire. (Clearly, the Mongols could not be considered "barbarians," for the Son of Heaven was a Mongol.) For Wu Lai, then, other themes were now more crucial.

The primary question for Wu Lai was that of standards of judgment which would or should be set by the ruler. These are interpreted in the judicial manner, in keeping with the tradition of *Annals* study to which he was heir. For Wu Lai, the unstated problem was the one caused by the failure of the Yüan to proclaim a code, or by the underlying legal uncertainties that were the by-product of the lack of a statutory code. Thus in his comments he observes the historical importance of such codes and the difficulties caused when available codes were not fully applied.

Wu Lai suggests that in antiquity, during the reigns of the Sage Emperors Yao and Yü, the empire enjoyed the benefits of strict and disciplined, yet eminently humane rule. Rewards and punishments were applied properly by those rulers, and the rulers performed their tasks of warning people against misbehavior. Government was good then because the rulers gave proper stress to moral transformation and because rewards and punishments were strictly applied. Helping to make possible this era of enlightened rule were the penal codes of Po I[gq] and Kao Yao.[gr] As Wu Lai expressed it, "As for the regulations sent down by Po I and the penal laws which he distributed, and as for Kao Yao's enlightened penal laws which assisted [the task of] moral instruction, these all [followed] the Way."[166]

Kao Yao is the subject of various legends in early China which link him with law-giving and judicial functions.[167] The Po I mentioned by Wu Lai was also an ancient law-giver, although he does not seem to have become the subject of popular legend the way Kao Yao did. Pursuing these references, Wu Lai goes on to observe that during the early years of the Chou dynasty there also had been an era of enlightened rule based on codified law. In Wu's words, this was because "the ancient statutes and ceremonial codes of Emperors Wen and Wu and the Duke of Chou" were effectively administered. Yet by Spring and Autumn times these ancient legal norms were no longer in force.

As Wu Lai saw it, this decline in the efficacy of the ancient legal codes lay at the heart of Confucius' attempt to offer his *Spring and Autumn Annals* as a substitute for the codes. By filling the vacuum left by the decline of the old standard legal norms, the *Annals* helped make it possible for humanity to regain its moral and political excellence.

As for the techniques by which this restoration might be accomplished, Wu Lai makes it apparent that the keys to them are found in the *Annals*. Since the fundamental difficulty faced by rulers and ministers alike is the exercise of the power to make judgments, it is here that the *Annals* offers the most precious insights. The *Annals* teaches two basic doctrines or approaches in the judgment-making process. Wu describes them as *ching-chih*[gs] or laying down a permanent set of standard institutions and norms, and *ch'üan-i*[gt] or weighing the principles of unique cases and making appropriate exceptions to the norms in order to achieve good ends. Wu Lai wrote of these two as follows:

Our Sage [Confucius] had the virtue appropriate to great intelligence and wisdom, but not the appropriate position. [That is, he did not have the position of king.] So alone he grasped the brush that rewards virtue and punishes guilt [by writing the history of good and bad men] and sought to establish [the difference between] right and wrong in the empire. One rewards, but in rewarding one must not be selfish or perverse. One punishes, but in punishing one must not act out of selfish anger. Between comfort in the sun and misery in the shade, between being straight and tall and being cut off and bent, there is a proper order, all things have their essential aspects. This is called *ching-chih*: to grasp and uphold a standard objective and not to permit even a small irregularity. The relative weights of human passions vary, and the amount of order or confusion in the world's events also varies. This is called *ch'üan-i*: constantly shifting forwards and backwards, to be bound to reach the appropriate point.[168]

The *Annals* thus offers a methodology for dealing with difficult problems as a ruler or as an individual in one's own life. It contains within it the "permanent norms" to which one should be fully committed; and it contains also the "making of exceptions," the recognition that eternal norms can only serve as guidelines when unanticipated situations are encountered. The *Annals* teaches both rigidity and flexibility. The ruler must have a firm and unwavering commitment to a standard (*ching*); at the same time, he must be able to cope with and respond effectively to the infinite variations that occur in real life (*ch'üan*).

In short, the ruler and the scholar must become a judge, and for the judge the *Annals* serves as a code:

Truly it is the great law of timeliness[169] of the Sage [Confucius]. Hence the *Spring and Autumn Annals* is the law code (*fa-shu*)[gu][170] of the Sage. A scholar of the world is comparable to the legal clerk [whose job it is to] interpret the law (*i-fa chih li*).[gv] Only when he has understood the Sage's principles [by which the ruler] examines [his administration] and houses his mind in loyalty and altruism, can he then comprehend the Sage's laws [by which the minister] keeps [himself in the discharge of his duties] so as to make decisions that are fair.[171]

THE QUESTION OF "LEGALISM" IN YÜAN THOUGHT

Many of the analyses presented here have a distant flavor of ancient "Legalism." The discussion of "weighing" (*ch'üan*) as an expression of the ruler's power is found in the *Kung-yang Commentary*, but the notion is also developed by certain early Legalist thinkers. In the Legalist work *Shang-chün shu*[gw] (The Book of Lord Shang) a full chapter is devoted to *hsiu-ch'üan*,[gx] "the cultivation of the balance," or in other words the cultivation of the ruler's power. Shang Yang reprotedly taught that "there are three [methods] for ruling a state: law, trust, and the balance (*ch'üan*)." [172] He explained that "law is that which ruler and subject observe together; trust is that which is established by ruler and subject together. The balance is that which the ruler alone controls." [173] Thus for Shang Yang, while the ruler was expected to join with those over whom he ruled in observing the law and in establishing a relationship of trust, he had autocratic power over the "balance." Maintaining this autocratic control over the "balance" was essential to the security of the state. "If the ruler loses [control over it], then danger." The reason why this is so, Shang Yang held, was that the ruler's wielding of the "balance" gave him *wei*[gy] or an air of authority. [174]

Shang Yang argued principally against the ruler's exercise of arbitrary, "private" judgment in administering the rule. For Shang Yang, it was essential that the ruler uphold the law, which in turn would ensure that the state would be well governed. Shang Yang noted, "the kings of old suspended the balance, erected measures, and they are copied until today. This is because their measurers were precise. . . . Thus the law is the balance (*ch'üan-heng*)[gz] of the state. . . ." [175]

The notion of *ch'üan* is also explored a bit in *Hsün Tzu*, [ha] although not in the same way as in *Shang-chün shu*. Hsün Tzu taught that the intelligent person cultivates his ability to "weigh" and draw appropriate conclusions through careful thought. [176] In this respect, as Fung Yu-lan pointed out, Hsün Tzu and the Later Mohists shared a common mode of analysis. [177] *Ch'üan* or "balance" also occurs as a metaphor in two of the fragments attributed to Shen Pu-hai[hb] and discussed by H. G. Creel. [178] The ancient Legalist text *Kuan Tzu*[hc] contains an entire chapter devoted to the topic *ch'üan hsiu*, [hd] or "the cultivation of the balance." [179] A better rendering, without the metaphor, would be "the cultivation of [the ruler's] power."

In respect to the common use of the term *chüan* or "balance" by the early Legalists and also by many of the Yüan thinkers here considered, the mere fact that the term is used in both eras does not necessarily mean that the Yüan thinkers were Legalists. Whatever similarities there may have been between these Yüan thinkers and the ancient Legalists, they do not make up for the single most important issue that divides them. [180] Legalists were concerned above all with building up the power of the ruler, so that he became a supreme autocrat whose rule rested on harsh and swift punishments to those who violated his commands and prompt rewards to those who served him well. The Yüan thinkers did not stress the harshness of punishments as a remedy for perceived weaknesses in administration. Rather, their writings stressed the importance of "grasping" firmly the "handles" of rewards and punishments. The point was not that criminals would be severely punished, but rather that the empire would be stabilized by the maintenance at the center of a "standard" upon which the legal system rested.

The Yüan thinkers advised the ruler to grasp firmly the powers that the traditional imperial institution afforded him. They did this not because they wanted their Mongol rulers to become despots. Instead, they wanted their Mongol rulers to become more humane and concerned, and to see the importance of a "standard" legal norm which would contribute to orderly enforcement of humane laws. Their aim was the improvement of the craft of administering the state. Their analysis of Mongol rule was that the Mongols did not sufficiently guard their authority. The rulers often permitted their subordinate "lords" without authorization to carry out idiosyncratic policies, thus in effect replacing the Son of Heaven as the source of law. In principle the power of the throne was supreme. But the nature of Mongol rule, despite the Mongols' belief in *möngke tengri* or Eternal Heaven, was such that the emperor permitted lower ranking lords to acquire booty and wealth on their own initiative, so long as they met certain minimal demands of reciprocity placed upon them by the emperor. This was because the conquest of China was accomplished not in order to establish a regular bureaucratic empire but instead as a means of extracting booty for the people whom the spirits and heaven above had supposedly blessed. Military conquest and what Joseph Fletcher has termed "bloody tanistry" were part and parcel of Mongol life.[181] Therefore, one way in which a ruler could increase his prestige in the Mongol world order was by permitting his lower-ranking subordinates to obtain booty as best they could. Naturally there were limits to this, as the ruler's prestige and dignity could not permit a subordinate to transgress on the ruler's own territory. But in principle, Mongol rule was contrabureaucratic. It was personal arbitrary, and, from the standpoint of the Chinese, capricious and unpredictable. There was, in short, too much *ch'üan* and not enough *ching*.

The Yüan thinkers here considered addressed precisely these issues. They aimed to persuade the rulers to adopt essentially Chinese methods of rule; these were bureaucratic, regular, and authoritarian. In their writings these thinkers stressed the importance of the ruler's authority because as they viewed things the Mongols were not sufficiently authoritarian in the sense that the emperor kept a firm grip on the levers of state power. These rulers may have been arbitrary and personal, and occasionally despotic; but they were not effectively authoritarian. Important actions were frequently taken by lower-ranking subordinates without prior authorization from the throne. To the Mongols a certain amount of delegation and discretion were necessary. To the Chinese it caused havoc. In the view of the Chinese, havoc could be averted only if the ruler would exercise all power himself. For then his subordinates would not be permitted to run rampant at the expense of Chinese treasure and harmony.

The metaphor of the "balance" (*ch'üan*) was one which served two ideological ends. On the one hand, it supported the idea of supreme power in the hands of one man, the emperor. Thus it could hardly be considered a threat to imperial power or prestige. On the other hand, it contained within it the idea of reasonableness. It is the very opposite of unaccountable, arbitrary power, for it implies that power will be exercised by an enlightened autocrat. Perhaps the best description of the virtues of the "balance" is that put forth in the ancient text *Huai-nan Tzu*.[he] The passage reads:

The balance as a measure acts quickly but not excessively, killing but not afflicting. It [presides over] the full, the real, the solid, wide and profound yet not dispersed. It destroys things without diminishing [the totality of the world] and executes the guilty without [possibility of] pardon. Its sincerity and trustworthiness give certainty, its firmness and genuineness give reliability. In its sweeping away of hidden evils it cannot but be straightforward. Thus when the administration of winter is about to take charge, it must weaken in order to make strong, and soften that which is about to be made hard. It weighs correctly and without error, so that the ten thousand things return into the treasuries of the earth.[182]

And of course Mencius also referred to the "balance" as a metaphor for the exercise of power by the autocrat:

It is by weighing a thing that its weight can be known, and by measuring it that its length can be ascertained. It is so with all things, but perhaps particularly so with the heart. Your Majesty should measure his own heart.[183]

Mencius' point of view, of course, is that the ruler should watch over himself and guard against inhumane conduct. The same metaphor is used elsewhere in the *Mencius* to suggest discretion.[184] Occasionally circumstances may require that one discard the strict rules of ceremonial behavior; such cases require careful discretion on the part of the individual to prevent abuses. It suggests the Confucian ideal of "suspended judgment," showing that circumstances alter cases, but that basic principles keep exceptions from becoming arbitrary and disruptive of good order.

One may make the case that the Yüan thinkers here considered were influenced by Legalist categories of analysis. The arguments they made echoed strongly of Legalist thought about the nature of the imperial institution. But it is not necessary to characterize the thinking of these people as either Legalist or Confucian, for by Yüan times the two schools of thought about government were thoroughly intertwined.

NOTES

This essay has benefitted greatly by suggestions and corrections from the organizers of the conference at which it was first presented, Professors Wm. Theodore de Bary and Hok-lam Chan. I am especially grateful to Professor F. W. Mote, Dr. Karl Bünger, and Dr. Wm. S. Atwell for their thoughtful suggestions regarding many matters raised in the essay.

1. For a translation of this text see my introduction to *China under Mongol Rule* (Princeton: Princeton University Press, 1981), pp. 3–4. For the text of the edict, the best version appears in *Ta Yüan sheng-cheng kuo-ch'ao tien-chang*[hf] (facsimile reproduction of Yüan edition, Taipei: National Palace Museum, 1976), 1:2b. See Sung Lien[hg] et al., eds., YS (Peking: Chung-hua shu-chü,[hh] 1976), 7:138. See also Su T'ien-chüeh, ed., *Kuo-ch'ao wen-lei* (SPTK ed.), 9:4a. (It is in the *Kuo-ch'ao wen-lei* that the author's name is provided.) The edict was promulgated in the last month (lunar month) of the eighth year of the Chih-yüan reign. The date is often given as 1271, but actually in the Western calendar the correct date was January 18, 1272. The edict is discussed in Herbert Franke, *From Tribal Chieftain to Universal Emperor and God: The Legitimation of the Yüan Dynasty* (Munich: Bayerische Akademie der Wissenschaften, 1978), pp. 22–29.

2. On the abolition of the *T'ai-ho lü*, see YS, 7:138. The edict announcing the dynastic title was promulgated on the same day. For studies of the Chin code, based on extant fragments, see Yeh Ch'ien-chao,[hi] *Chin-lü chih yen-chiu*[hj] (Taipei: Commercial Press, 1972). See also Niida Noboru,[hk] *Chūgoku hōseishi kenkyū: keihō*[hl] (Tokyo: Tokyo University, 1959), pp. 453–524, "Kindai keihō ko."[hm] For a study of codification under the Yüan, see Paul H. C. Ch'en, *Chinese Legal Tradition under the Mongols: The Code of 1291 as Reconstructed* (Princeton: Princeton University Press, 1979), pp. 3–40.

3. Lao Yen-hsüan[hn] (Yan-shuan Lao), "Yüan-ch'u nan-fang chih-shih fen-tzu—shih chung suo fan-ying ch'u ti p'ien-mien,"[ho] *Hsiang-kang Chung-wen ta-hsüeh Chung-kuo wen-hua yen-chiu-so hsüeh-pao*[hp] (1979) 10(1):129–158. For a discussion of anti-Mongol behavior by early Yüan literati, see Wai-kam Ho, "Chinese under the Mongols," in Sherman Lee and Wai-kam Ho, eds., *Chinese Art under the Mongols: The Yüan Dynasty (1279–1368)* (Cleveland: Cleveland Museum of Art, 1968), pp. 73–112. See also F. W. Mote, "Confucian Eremitism in the Yüan Period," in Arthur F. Wright, ed., *The Confucian Persuasion* (Standford: Stanford University Press, 1960), pp. 202–40. The unification of the Middle Kingdom was indeed a reason behind the theory of legitimacy proposed by the Yüan scholar Yang Wei-chen[hq] (1296–1370) in his "Cheng-t'ung pien"[hr] ["Debate on the Orthodox Succession of Dynastic Regimes]. For a biography of Yang, see Edmund H. Worthy in L. C. Goodrich and Chaoying Fang, ed., *Dictionary of Ming Biography* (New York: Columbia University Press, 1976), pp. 1547–53. For

a discussion of the *cheng-t'ung* issue in Yüan times, see Hok-lam Chan, "Chinese Official Historiography at the Yüan Court: The Composition of the Liao, Chin and Sung Histories," in Langlois, *China under Mongol Rule*, pp. 68–77.

4. Personal Remarks delivered at the American Council of Learned Societies Research Conference on the Impact of Mongol Domination of Chinese Civilization, at the Breckinridge Public Affairs Center of Bowdoin College, York, Maine, July 1976.

5. See Igor de Rachewiltz, "Yen-lü Ch'u-ts'ai (1189–1243): Buddhist Idealist and Confucian Statesman," in Arthur F. Wright and Denis Twitchett, ed., *Confucian Personalities* (Stanford: Stanford University Press, 1962), pp. 189–216. de Rachewiltz observes that Yeh-lü's advice in this regard often fell on deaf ears owing to the Mongols' "insatiable cupidity" (p. 211).

6. See Yao Ts'ung-wu,[hs] "Ch'eng Chü-fu yü Hu-pi-lieh han p'ing Sung i-hou ti an-ting nan-jen wen-t'i,"[ht] (*Kuo-li T'ai-wan ta-hsüeh*) *Wen-shih-che hsüeh-pao*,[hu] (June 1968), 17:353–79, for a discussion of related issues.

7. The name Chen-chin was of Chinese origin and should not be transcribed as though it were of Mongolian origin. (It often is mistakenly transcribed as Jinggim.) I am indebted to Professor Joseph Fletcher for this information.

8. For a standard survey see René Grousset, *The Empire of the Steppes: A History of Central Asia*, trans. by Naomi Walford (New Brunswick, New Jersey: Rutgets University Press, 1970). See also John W. Dardess, *Conquerors and Confucians: Aspects of Political Change in Late Yüan China* (New York: Columbia University Press, 1973). See also J. Langlois, "Yü Chi and His Mongol Sovereign: The Scholar as Apologist," *Journal of Asian Studies* (November 1978), 38(1):99–116.

9. See the articles in Langlois, *China under Mongol Rule*, for materials bearing on several of these topics.

10. See K. C. Hsiao, "Legalism and Autocracy in Traditional China," *Tsing-hua Journal of Chinese Studies*, N.S. (February 1964), 4(2):108–121; and F. W. Mote, tr., K. C. Hsiao, A *History of Chinese Political Thought*, vol. 1 (Princeton: Princeton University Press, 1979), pp. 446–65.

11. Ch'en, *Chinese Legal Tradition*, pp. 3ff.

12. This compilation has been studied by Uematsu Tadashi,[hv] who collected ninety-five fragments of the original code, in "Ishu 'Shigen shinkō' narabi ni kaisetsu,"[hw] *Tōyōshi kenkyū*[hx] (March 1972), 30(4):272–325; and by Paul Ch'en, who established ninety-six articles and translated them into English in *Chinese Legal Tradition*. pt. 2.

13. The Sung *Hsing-t'ung* was considered a *lü*. Chu Hsi said of it, "The *lü* is the *Hsing-t'ung*." Similarly, Lü Tsu-ch'ien, Chu Hsi's associate, stated, "Of the *lü*, *ling*, *ko*, and *shih* [the four main categories of legislation], starting with the present dynasty the *lü* has been separated out and called the *Hsing-t'ung*." The historian Li Hsin-ch'uan[hy] also made a similar observation. For these references, see Sogabe Shizuo,[hz] *Chūgoku ritsuryōshi no kenkyū*[ia] (Tokyo: Yoshikawa kōbunkan, 1971), p. 36. For a discussion of the outmod-

edness of the *Hsing-t'ung*, see Miyazaki Ichisada,[1b] "Sō Gen jidai no hōsei to saiban kikō,"[1e] rpt. in *Ajiashi kenkyū,*[1d] vol. 4 (Kyoto: Tōyōshi kenkyūkai, 1964), pp. 170–305, esp. pp. 170–185.

14. See T'ung-tsu Ch'ü, *Law and Society in Traditional China* (Paris: Mouton, 1965), pp. 267–79.

15. This work is now being translated into English for the first time. See Wallace Johnson, *The T'ang Code, Volume 1, General Principles* (Princeton: Princeton University Press, 1979).

16. See also Ch'en, *Chinese Legal Tradition*, p. 13

17. Iwamura Shinobu, *Mongoru shakai keizaishi no kenkyū*[1e] (Kyoto: Jimbun kagaku kenkyūjō, 1968), p. 277.

18. Mitamura Taisuke,[1f] *Kōdo o hiraita hitobito*[1g] (Tokyo: Kawade shobō shinsha, 1976), pp. 38–40.

19. See Igor de Rachewiltz, "Some Remarks on the Ideological Foundations of Chingis Khan's Empire," *Papers on Far Eastern History* (March 1973), 7:21–36.

20. de Rachewiltz, "Some Remarks," pp. 25–26. On the *jasagh* see the remarks in Ch'en, *Chinese Legal Tradition*, pp. 5–10. See also Tamura Jitsuzō's[1h] summary of the various views on the *jasagh* in *Ajia rekishi jiten*[1i] (1959; rpt. Tokyo: Heibonsha, 1975), vol. 4, p. 234. The *Yüan shih* glosses the *jasa[gh]* as *fa-ling,*[1j] "laws." See YS, 2:29. See also P. Ratchnevsky, *Un code des Yuan*, vol. 1 (Paris: Ernest Leroux, 1937), p. vii. Khubilai cited the *jasagh* in 1260 when he proclaimed a new reign-title. See YS, 5:99. Francis W. Cleaves translates the word *jasagh* as "code" in "The 'Fifteen "Palace Poems" ' by K'o Chiu-ssu," *Harvard Journal of Asiatic Studies* (December 1957) 20(3–4):429, note 14. Cleaves also lists a number of important studies bearing on the *jasagh*. To these one should add David Ayalon, "The Great Yāsa of Chingiz Khān, A Reexamination," *Studia Islamica* (1971), 33:97–140; (1971) 34:151–80; (1972) 36:113–158; and (1973) 38:107–56. Note that the Yüan handbook for clerks, the *Li-hsüeh chih-nan,*[1k] defined the meaning of the words *ta cha-sa*[1l] ("great *jasa[gh]*") as "to follow the classified articles and measures." See Hsü Yüan-jui,[1m] ed., *Li-hsüeh chih-nan* (Taipei: Ta-hua yin-shu-kuan, 1969), p. 53.

21. Cited in Sogabe, *Chūgoku ritsuryōshi no kenkyū*, p. 1.

22. *T'ang lü shu i* (rpt. Taipei: Commercial Press, 1969), vol. 1, p. 8. See Johnson, *T'ang Code*, p. 52.

23. E.g., the *Shang-shu ta-chuan*[1n] (SPTK ed.), 3:3a, where the text states: "Receive the great *lü* of Heaven." The commentary states: "[This means:] Receive the great *fa* of Heaven." Hence *fa* and *lü* are identical.

24. *T'ang lü shu i*, vol. 1, p. 2. See Johnson, *The T'ang Code*, p. 49.

25. Richard Wilhelm and Cary Baynes, *The I Ching or Book of Changes* (New York: Pantheon Books, 1950), vol. 2, p. 174.

26. *T'ang lü shu i*, vol. 1, p. 6.

27. *Ibid.*; *Erh-ya* (SPTK ed.), *shang*, 8b.

28. Wilhelm and Baynes, *The I Ching*, vol. 1, p. 353.

29. See Étienne Balazs, *Le traité juridique du "Souei-chou"* (Leiden: E. J. Brill, 1954), p. 96.
30. Tr. from Balazs, "Souei-chou", p. 26. I have changed the rendering of the words *tung-hsien*.
31. Yeh Shih, *Shui-hsin hsien-sheng wen-chi*[io] (SPTK ed.), 3:21b; quoted in Sogabe, *Chūgoku ritsuryōshi no kenkyū*, p. 45.
32. It was compiled in the twelfth month of the first year of Wu (1367). See *Ming T'ai-tsu shih-lu*[ip] (Taipei: Academia Sinica, 1962), 28:422. The emperor's intense interest in this work, or that of his literati advisers, is reflected in his command that a simple explanation of the crucial portions of the code be made available to the populace. This was the *Lü-ling chih-chieh*[iq] (Straightforward Explanation of the Lü-ling), and the emperor ordered its compilation in the same month of the first year of Wu. (The actual date would have been January 1368.) See *Ming T'ai-tsu shih-lu*, 28:431. The earliest extant version of the code dates from 1395, a Korean edition. See Wolfgang Franke, *An Introduction to the Sources of Ming History* (Kuala Lumpur: University of Malaya Press, 1968), p. 185. For a study of the Ming *lü* promulgations, see Huang Chang-chien,[ir] "Ta Ming lü kao k'ao,"[is] rpt. in his *Ming Ch'ing shih yen-chiu ts'ung-kao*[it] (Taipei: Commercial Press, 1977), pp. 155–207.
33. *Ming T'ai-tsu shih-lu*, 26:388. The date was the tenth lunar month of 1367.
34. *Ibid.*, 236:3456; the date was the second lunar month of 1395.
35. YS, 184:4620. For a discussion of this effort see Abe Takeo,[iu] "Genshi Keihōshi to Genritsu to sono kankei ni tsuite,"[iv] rpt. in *Gendaishi no kenkyū*[iw] (Tokyo: Sōbunsha, 1972), pp. 255–60. The Yüan scholar Ou-yang Hsüan also indicated that the last Mongol emperor of China had ordered work begun on a code. See his *Kuei-chai wen-chi*[ix] (SPTK ed.), 7:8b. See also Ch'en, *Chinese Legal Tradition*, pp. 38–39.
36. These words come from the *Meng Tzu*,[iy] 4A:1/8. See James Legge, tr., *The Chinese Classics* (Hong Kong: University of Hong Kong Press, rpt. 1961), vol. 2, p. 290.
37. YS, 102:2603.
38. Just fragments survive. See note 12.
39. Furthermore, the Ming was extremely concerned about preserving the inviolability of the *lü*. See *Ming shih*[iz] (Peking: Chung-hua shu-chü, 1974), 93:2284, 2285–86, 2287, and 2289. Distinguishing the *lü* (statutory code) and the *li* (subsidiary legislation or substatutes), the Treatise of Penal Law in the *Ming Shih* states "The *lü* articles on redemption one dares not to alter, but the *li* articles on the payment of redemption are changed over time in accordance with exigencies. . . ." *Ming shih*, 93:2293.
40. YS, 102:2604.
41. See *Chūgoku hōseishi kenkyū: keihō*, pp. 531–32.
42. Wang Yün, *Ch'iu-chien hsien-sheng ta ch'üan wen-chi*[ja] (SPTK ed.), 90:3a–3b. Quoted in Niida Noboru, *Chūgoku hōseishi kenkyū: keihō*, p. 538, note 10; see partial translation in Ch'en, *Chinese Legal Tradition*, pp. 8–9.

43. The "three canons" (*san tien*)[jb] refers to the *Chou li*,[jc] according to which light punishments were used in a newly founded state, medium punishments in a peaceful state, and severe punishments in a rebelling state. These three were the "three canons." See *Chou li*, "Ch'iu kuan,"[jd] under "Ta-ssu-k'ou."[je]

44. The "nine articles" (*chiu chang*)[jf] refers to the Han statutory code compiled by Hsiao Ho[jg], often known as the *chiu chang lü*, "the nine article code." For a translation from the *Han shu* with this reference, see A. F. P. Hulsewé, *Remnants of Han Law*, vol. 1 (Leiden: E. J. Brill, 1955), p. 333.

45. *Ch'iu-chien hsien-sheng ta ch'üan wen-chi*, 90:3b. See Ch'en, *Chinese Legal Tradition*, pp. 8–9.

46. *Chūgoku hōseishi kenkyū: keihō*, p. 540.

47. *Mu-min chung-ku*, pt. 1 of *Wei-cheng chung-ku*[jh] (Loyal Advice for the Conduct of Government (*Ssu-k'u ch'üan-shu*[ji] ed., Taipei: Yeewen Press rpt., n.d.), *hsia*, 4b–5a.

48. Biography of Yao Shu in YS 158:3712. See Hok-lam Chan, in *Papers on Far Eastern History* (September 1980), 22:32–33.

49. YS, 160:3760. Li Chih served the Chin as a minor official and withdrew from official affairs after the Mongol conquest of his locale in 1232. The points made here were presented by him to Khubilai when the latter had summoned Li and had inquired of him about the T'ang minister Wei Cheng[jj] (580–643) and about the Tao or Way of good government.

50. YS, 160:3760.

51. YS, 159:3737. For this group of reformers see Yüan Kuo-fan,[jk] "Tung-p'ing Yen Shih mu-fu jen-wu yü hsing-hsüeh ch'u-k'ao,"[jl] *Ta-lu tsa-chih*[jm] (December 1961), 23(12):11–14; and Sun K'o-k'uan,[jn] *Yüan-tai Han wen-hua chih huo-tung*[jo] (Taipei: Chung-hua shu-chü, 1968), pp. 109–38. Other materials on this topic are cited by Herbert Franke in his article in this volume.

52. The metaphor of the "handle" appears in the *Tso chuan* under the year 534 B.C. It was made famous by Han Fei Tzu, who held that the two "handles" that should be manipulated by a powerful ruler were rewards and punishments. *Han Fei tzu* (SPTK ed.), 2:4a; Burton Watson, tr., *Han Fei Tzu: Basic Writings* (New York: Columbia University Press, 1964), p. 30.

53. YS, 159:3737.

54. Biography of Ts'ui Yü in YS, 173:4040. The words "no laws by which to keep themselves" come from Mencius. See note 36.

55. Ch'en, *Chinese Legal Tradition*, pp. 3–40, outlines some of the arguments. See also P. Ratchnevsky, *Un code des Yuan*, vol. 1, introduction, for a brief summary. The examples of Li Ch'ien[jp] (1234–1312), YS, 160:3768; and Yen Fu[jq] (1236–1312), YS, 160:3773, are pertinent.

56. On this point see the example of Ch'en T'ien-hsiang[jr] (1237–1316) in YS 168:3947. See also Ch'en, *Chinese Legal Tradition*, p. 46.

57. The *Kuo-ch'ao wen-lei* was first published in 1334, while *Kuo-ch'ao ming-ch'en shih-lüeh* first appeared in 1335 (rpt. Taipei: Hsüeh-sheng shu-chü, n.d.). The SPTK ed. of *Kuo-ch'ao wen-lei* is a reproduction of an edition of 1342. Su T'ien-chüeh was known for his judicial expertise and for his rever-

sal of incorrect verdicts. See "Su yü-shih chih-yü chi"[js] (Trials by the Censor Su), in Huang Chin[jt] (1227–1357), *Chin-hua Huang hsien-sheng wen-chi*[ju] (SPTK ed.), 15:1b–3b. For Su's biography see YS, 183:4224.

58. Su T'ien-chüeh, *Tzu-ch'i wen-kao*[jv] (*Shih-yüan ts'ung-shu*[jw] ed. [1916]), 26:9b.

59. Now only partially extant, this work was promulgated in 1323. For a thorough study, see Abe Takeo, "Dai Gen tsūsei kaisetsu,"[jx] in *Gendaishi no kenkyū*, pp. 277–318. The extant portions, known under the title T'ung-chih *t'iao-ko*,[jy] have been annotated and translated into Japanese. See Kobayashi Takashiro[jz] and Okamoto Keiji,[ka] *Tsūsei jōkō no kenkyū yakuchū*,[kb] vol. 1 (Tokyo: Kokusho kankōkai, 1964, 2d printing 1975); Okamoto Keiji, *Tsūsei jōkō no kenkyū yakuchū*, vols. 2 and 3 (Tokyo: Kokusho kankōkai, 1975 and 1976).

60. *Tzu-ch'i wen-kao*, 26:7b.

61. *Ibid.*

62. Bernhard Karlgren, tr., *The Book of Documents* (Stockholm: Museum of Far Eastern Antiquities, 1950), p. 32, modified slightly. The passage is from the *Hung-fan*[kc] chapter (chap. 32).

63. YS, 175:4076.

64. See the statement by Ming T'ai-tsu quoted above, and other materials cited below. See also Antonio S. Cua, "The Concept of Paradigmatic Individuals in the Ethics of Confucius," in Arne Ness and Alastair Hannay, ed., *Invitation to Chinese Philosophy* (Oslo: Universitetsforlaget, 1972), pp. 50–57. For the ideas *ching* and *ch'üan* in Kung-yang School thought see Hentona Tomokuni,[hd] "Shunjū kuyō gakuha no 'ken' setsu ni tsuite,"[ke] *Kyūshū Chūgoku gakkaihō*[kf] (May 1975), 20:1–10. See also Hihara Toshikuni,[kg] *Shunjū kuyōden no kenkyū*[kh] (Tokyo: Sōbunsha, 1976), pp. 216–34.

65. The eleventh year of Duke Huan. See Legge, *The Chinese Classics*, vol. 5, prolegomena, pp. 56–57; modifed slightly. This is also quoted in Hihara Toshikuni, *Shunjū kuyōden no kenkyū*, p. 219.

66. *Ch'un-ch'iu fan-lu* (SPTK ed.), 3:4a; quoted in Hihara, *Shunjū kuyōden no kenkyū*, p. 220.

67. YS, 175:4076.

68. Šams was a native of Ta-shih[ki] (Arabia). For his biography, see YS, 190:4351. It was partially translated by Ch'ien Hsing-hai and L. C. Goodrich in Ch'en Yüan, *Western and Central Asians in China under the Mongols* (Los Angeles: Monumenta Serica, 1966), pp. 60–62, 174–76. For a brief discussion of Šam's *Ti-wang hsin-fa*, see Wm. T. de Bary *Neo-Confucian Orthodoxy and Philosophy of the Heart-and-Mind* (New York: Columbia University Press, 1981), p. 152.

69. See *T'ang lü shu i*, vol. 1, p. 4, where the word *hsien* is glossed simply as *fa*, "law." On the term *ch'eng-hsien*, see YS, 190:4352. Chang Kuei, who has been cited above, also used it. See YS, 175:4078, 4079. On the origin of this term in the *Book of Documents*, see Legge, *The Chinese Classics*, vol. 3, p. 382.

70. This point is made also in Ch'en, *Chinese Legal Tradition*, pt. 1, chap. 3 and *passim*.

71. YS, 163:3821.
72. For Hu's biography, see YS, 170:3992.
73. Hu Chih-yü, *Tzu-shan ta ch'üan chi*[kj] (1924 woodblock ed.), 21:19a.
74. "Lun ting fa-lü," in *Tzu-shan ta ch'üan chi*, 22:27a. "Ting fa" is also the title of a section in *Han Fei Tzu*, the ancient Legalist text. See *Han Fei Tzu* (SPTK ed.), 17:4b.
75. This line is from *Mencius*. See note 36.
76. *Tzu-shan ta ch'üan chi*, 22:27a–b.
77. *Ibid.*
78. The legal doctrine represented by *ti-tsui* first appeared in Han Kao-tsu's "three article statute." See *Shih chi* (Peking: Chung-hua shu-chü, 1959), 8:362; and Hulsewé, *Han Law*, vol. 1, p. 33.
79. *Tzu-shan ta ch'üan chi*, 21:4b–5a.
80. *Ibid.* 21:5a.
81. *Ibid.* 21:5a–b. For the expression *pen-hsin*, see *Meng Tzu*, 6A/10; Legge, *The Chinese Classics*, vol. 2, p. 414.
82. For Wu Ch'eng's biography, see YS, 171:4011. See also the paper by David Gedalecia in this volume.
83. On Kiangsi, see Miyazaki, "Sō Gen jidai no hōsei to saiban kikō" pp. 276–77. The Yüan scholar Chih Hsi-ssu[kk] (1274–1344), a native of Kiangsi, said: "Kiangsi is difficult to govern." He was referring to the propensity to litigate. See *Chieh Wen-an kung ch'üan-chi*[kl] (SPTK ed.), 9:2b–3a.
84. The *T'ang lü shu i* was reprinted in Kiangsi in Yüan times. See the preface by Liu Kuan[km] (1279–1342) to that edition, in *Kuo-ch'ao wen-lei* (SPTK ed.), 36:10a–12a. Miyazaki discusses the *Yüan tien chang*[kn] and its heavy concentration of Kiangsi materials in the article "Sō Gen jidai no hōsei to saiban kikō" (cited in note 13), pp. 265–77.
85. *Hsüeh-t'ung* (Tradition of Learning) is part of Wu's *Tao-hsüeh chi-t'ing*[ko] (Foundation and Tradition of Learning of the Way). appended after *ch.* 49 to *Ts'ao-lu Wu Wen-cheng kung chi*[kp] (1756 ed.); the reference to the Sung *Hsing-t'ung* appears on 8b. *Tao-hsüeh chi-t'ung* is discussed by David Gedalecia in a paper included in Langlois, *China Under Mongol Rule*, pp. 199–204. One should note also that Wu Ch'eng had a deep interest in Taoism. For this, see Sun K'o-k'uan, "Yü Chi and Southern Taoism During the Yüan" in *China under Mongol Rule*, pp. 212–53, *passim*.
86. For the *ts'e-wen* text, see *Ts'ao-lu Wu Wen-cheng kung chi*, 2:7a–b.
87 For the preface, see *Ts'ao-lu Wu Wen-cheng kung chi*, 11:25a–26b. This is discussed in Abe Takeo, *Gendaishi no kenkyū*, p. 294.
88. See Hulsewé, *Han Law*, pp. 26–70, for a discussion of the Han code.
89. See Legge, *The Chinese Classics*, vol. 4, p. 283.
90. This alludes to *Chin-ssu lu*, ch. 9. See Wing-tsit Chan, tr., *Reflections on Things at Hand* (New York: Columbia University Press, 1967), p. 233. I have translated the expression *pa-fen-shu* to follow L. C. Goodrich, who described it as follows: "A kind of *li* style used on the wooden and bamboo tablets of early times, much in fashion during the Later Han." See Ch'ien

Hsing-hai and Goodrich, *Western and Central Asians in China under the Mongols,* p. 202, note 94.

91. It was Ch'eng I who said, "This is his insight." See Chan, *Reflections on Things at Hand,* p. 233.

92. The poem to which this alludes is discussed in Hsü Tao-lin,[kq] "Fa-hsüeh-chia Su Tung-p'o,"[kr] in Hsü's *Chung-kuo fa-chih-shih lun-chi*[ks] (Taipei: Chih-wen ch'u-pan-she, 1975), pp. 309–26. Hsü discusses other materials, including memorials and letters by Su, to show that Su Shih had an expert knowledge of the statutory code.

93. *Ts'ao-lu Wu Wen-cheng kung chi,* 2:7b.

94. *Ibid.,* 11:25a–26b.

95. *Ibid.,* 11:26a. See also Ch'en, *Chinese Legal Tradition,* p. 29.

96. For Po-chu-lu's biography, see YS, 183:4219. (The incorrect transcription Po-chu-lu Chung is given in Ch'en, *Chinese Legal Tradition,* pp. 26ff.)

97. For the preface, see *Kuo-ch'ao wen-lei,* 36:6a–7b. For an annotated translation in Japanese, see Kōbayashi and Okamoto, *Tsūsei jōkō no kenkyū yaku-chū,* vol. 1, pp. 2–8. The preface is also discussed in Abe Takeo, *Gendaishi no kenkyū,* pp. 278ff.

98. For Ou-yang's biography, see YS, 182:4196.

99. See Ch'en, *Chinese Legal Tradition,* p. 38, on the orders to Ou-yang to compile a code.

100. The *Chih-cheng t'iao-ko* was completed in 1345. See Abe Takeo, *Gendaishi no kenkyū,* p. 312, note 3. For Ou-yang's preface, see *Kuei-chai wen-chi* (SPTK ed.), 7:8b–9a.

101. For this citation from the *Chou li,* see *Chou li* (SPTK ed.), 1:16b and 9:11b; for the citation from the *Book of Documents,* see Legge, *The Chinese Classics,* vol. 3, p. 608.

102. Wilhelm and Baynes, *The I Ching,* vol. 1, p. 92.

103. *Ibid.,* vol. 1, p. 228.

104. For this line from the *Book of Documents,* see Legge, *The Chinese Classics,* vol. 3, pp. 58–59.

105. *Kuei-chai wen-chi,* 7:8b–9a. The closing words in quotation marks are from the *Book of Documents.* See Legge, *The Chinese Classics,* vol. 3, p. 74.

106. See the essay "Fen-i hsien hsüeh fu-t'ien chi,"[kt] in *Kuei-chai wen-chi,* 6:1b–3b.

107. *Ibid.,* 6:3a–b.

108. The text of this "ts'e" question appears in *Kuei-chai wen-chi,* 12:4b–7b.

109. The expression *wang-min*[ku] ("to entrap the people") appears in *Meng Tzu,* 1A:7; see Legge, *The Chinese Classics,* vol. 2, p. 148.

110. *Kuei-chai wen-chi,* 12:7a.

111. See Hulsewé, *Han Law,* pp. 331–32; *Tso chuan,* under the year 535 B.C. For a translation of the latter entry, see Legge, *The Chinese Classics,* vol. 5, p. 609.

112. Burton Watson discusses the nature of this text in *Early Chinese Literature* (New York: Columbia University Press, 1962), pp. 37–40.

113. Li Tse-fen,[kv] *Yüan shih hsin chiang*[kw] (Taipei: Chung-hua shu-chü, 1978), vol. 1, preface, p. 6.

114. See Legge, *The Chinese Classics*, vol. 5, p. 299.

115. *Meng Tzu*, 3B:9; D. C. Lau, tr., *Mencius* (Middlesex: Penguin Books, 1970), pp. 114–15.

116. Chao Ch'i's commentary to *Meng Tzu* (SPTK ed.), 6:13a.

117. *Chiao-cheng Chuang-tzu chi-shih*[kx] (Taipei: Shih-chieh shu-chü, 1962), p. 83. The text reads: "Ch'un-ch'iu ching shih hsien wang chih chih, sheng-jen i erh pu pien."[ky] For the translation of the second clause, I follow Wing-tsit Chan, *A Source Book in Chinese Philosophy* (Princeton: Princeton University Press, 1963), p. 186. Cf. Lin Yutang, *The Wisdom of China and India* (New York: Random House, 1942), p. 639: "With regard to the wisdom of the ancients, as embodies in the canon of *Spring and Autumn*, the Sage comments, but does not expound." Burton Watson, *The Complete Works of Chuang Tzu* (New York: Columbia University Press, 1968), p. 44: "In the case of the *Spring and Autumn*, the record of the former kings of past ages, the sage debates but does not discriminate."

118. In *Chuang Tzu* (SPTK ed.) *ch.* 33; cited in Hsiao/Mote *Chinese Political Thought*, vol. 1, p. 132.

119. Hsiao/Mote, *Chinese Political Thought*, p. 134.

120. But see Legge's unwillingness to let the *Annals* pass as a work of history in *The Chinese Classics*, vol. 5, prolegomena, pp. 50–51.

121. *Meng Tzu*, 4B:21; Lau, *Mencius*, pp. 131–32.

122. *Meng Tzu*, 4B:21; Lau, *Mencius*, p. 132.

123. "Po luan shih, fan chu cheng."[kz] See Ho Hsiu[la] (A.D. 129–182), *Ch'un-ch'iu Kung-yang ching-chuan chieh-ku*[lb] (SPTK ed.), 12:9b (under the fourteenth year of Duke A.I). For study of the Kung-yang school, and the important difference between it and the approach later taken by Tu Yü, see Ch'ien Mu,[lc] "K'ung-tzu yü *Ch'un-ch'iu*,"[ld] (1952), reprinted in *Liang-Han ching-hsüeh chin-ku-wen p'ing-i*[le] (Taipei: San-min shu-chü, 1971), pp. 235–83.

124. *Shih chi*, 130:3297–3298. *Cf.* Burton Watson, *Ssu-ma Ch'ien: Grand Historian of China* (New York: Columbia University Press, 1958), pp. 51–52. For the point that Ssu-ma Ch'ien modelled his historiography on that of Confucius, see Ch'ien Mu, "K'ung-tzu yü *Ch'un-ch'iu*."

125. For one translation of an entry from Tung Chung-shu's *Ch'un-ch'iu chüeh-shih pi*[lf] (*The Spring and Autumn Annals* as Reference in Deciding Lawsuits), see Hsiao/Mote, *Chinese Political Thought*, p. 468.

126. For Tung's and other scholars' citations of the *Annals* in legal cases, see Ch'eng Shu-te,[lg] *Chiu-ch'ao lü k'ao*[lh] (Taipei: Commercial Press, rpt. 1973), pp. 197–212.

127. Ch'eng Shu-te, *Chiu-ch'ao lü k'ao*, pp. 218–19, 480.

128. For praise of this work by Legge, see *The Chinese Classics*, vol. 5, prolegomena, p. 26. For Tu Yü, see Miyakawa Shōji's entry in *Ajia rekishi jiten*, vol. 7, p. 148.

129. Tu's preface to this commentary is preserved in a Japanese text. See Sogabe Shizuo, *Chūgoku ritsuryōshi no kenkyū*, p. 12.
130. Quoted in Chu I-tsun,[li] comp., *Ching-i k'ao*[lj] (SPPY ed.), 173:4a.
131. The Sung record of cases known as *Ming-kung shu-p'an ch'ing-ming chi*[lk] (rpt. Tokyo: Koten kenkyūkai, 1964), 1:3b–4a (pp. 18–19), preserves an instance when the *Ch'un-ch'iu* was cited in a legal case.
132. See Morohashi Tetsuji,[ll] *Jugaku no mokuteki to Sō ju no katsudō*[lm] (rpt. as vol. 1, *Morohashi Tetsuji choshakushū*[ln] [Tokyo: Daishūkan shōten, 1975]), pp. 202–4.
133. The author of this statement was Ch'ang Chih[lo] (1019–1077). See Chu I-tsun, *Ching-i k'ao*, 179:3a.
134. *Ibid.*, 168:3b.
135. Adapted from Chan, *Reflections on Things at Hand*, p. 116.
136. Chu I-tsun, *Ching-i k'ao*, 182:5a; *cf.* Chan, *Reflections on Things at Hand*, p. 116.
137. Chu I-tsun, *Ching-i k'ao*, 168:3b; *cf.* Chan, *Reflections on Things at Hand*, p. 117.
138. This was quoted by Lo Ts'ung-yen[lp] (1072–1135). See Chu I-tsun, *Ching-i k'ao*, 184:3a, for Lo's preface to *Ch'un-ch'iu chih-kuei*.[lq] For Lo Ts'ung-yen, see K. Schirokauer's entry in Herbert Franke, ed., *Sung Biographies* (Wiesbaden: Franz Steiner, 1976), p. 667.
139. For Han Ch'i biography see *Sung shih*[lr] (Peking: Chung-hua shu-chü, 1977), 312:10221–10230.
140. Chu I-tsun, *Ching-i k'ao*, 181:4a.
141. On Sung *Ch'un-ch'iu* studies, see Mou Jun-shu,[ls] "Liang Sung *Ch'un-ch'iu* hsüeh chih chu-liu,"[lt] *Ta-lu tsa-chih* (August 1952), 5(4):113–16; reprinted in *Chu-shih chai ts'ung-kao*[lu] (Hong Kong: New Asia Research Institute, 1959), pp. 141–61. See also Ch'en Ch'ing-hsin,[lv] "Sung ju *Ch'un-ch'iu* tsun-wang yao-i fa-wei yü ch'i cheng-chih ssu-hsiang"[lw] (pt. 1), *Hsin-ya hsüeh-pao*[lx] (1971), 10(1):269–368; and Morohasi Tetsuji, *Jugaku no mokuteki to Sō ju no katsudō*, pp. 204–46.
142. For the little that is known about Wang Che's life, see *Sung-Yüan hsüeh-an pu-i*[ly] (Taipei: Shih-chieh shu-chü, rpt. 1962), 10:92b. For a note on *Ch'un-ch'iu huang-kang lun*, see *Ssu-k'u ch'üan-shu tsung-mu*[lz] (Taipei: Yeewen Press, 1969 [3rd. printing]), 26:22b–24a.
143. From Wang's essay "K'ung-tzu hsiu *Ch'un-ch'iu*"[ma] (Confucius Compiled the *Spring and Autumn Annals*), in *Ch'un-ch'iu huang-kang lun* (T'ung-chih t'ang ching-chieh[mb] ed.), 1:1b–2a.
144. *Ch'un-ch'iu huang-kang lun*, 1:1b–2a.
145. *Tzu-shan ta ch'üan chi*, 20:16b–23a.
146. *Meng Tzu*, 7B:2; following James Legge, trans., *The Chinese Classics*, vol. 2, ;. 478.
147. *Tzu-shan ta ch'üan chi*, 20:17a.
148. "Niu t'ung ma tsou."[mc]
149. "Ju ch'üan chien chih tsai hsüan."[md]

150. *Tzu-shan ta ch'üan chi,* 20:18a.

151. *Ibid.*

152. Chu I-tsun, *Ching-i k'ao,* 194:6b.

153. This work was reprinted by the Commerical Press, Taipei, in the SKCSCP series.

154. The *Tsung-li* is included in the SKCSCP edition.

155. Frederick W. Mote, "Yüan and Ming," in K. C. Chang, ed., *Food in Chinese Culture: Anthropological and Historical Perspectives* (New Haven: Yale University Presss, 1977), pp. 193–257, esp. p. 204.

156. The term *jen-chi* appears in *Shang shu,* book 13; see James Legge, *The Chinese Classics,* vol. 3, p. 195.

157. *Ssu-k'u ch'üan-shu tsung-mu,* 28:3a.

158. See Wu's "*Ch'un-ch'iu pei-wang* hsü,"[me] a preface to a work by the late-Chin early-Yüan scholar Ching Hsüan,[mf] in *Ts'ao-lu Wu Wen-cheng kung chi,* 11:7b–9a. Ching's work was printed at the command of Emperor Jen-tsung (r. 1311–1320). He was a northerner who won the *chin-shih* in 1220 and served both the Jurchens and the Mongols. See YS, 175:4096.

159. *Ts'ao-lu Wu Wen-cheng kung chi,* 11:8a.

160. For Wu Lai's biography, see YS, 181:4189. See also Sun K'o-k'uan, *Yüan-tai Chin-hua hsüeh shu*[mg] (Taichung: Tung-hai University, 1976), pp. 75–106; and my essay, "Chin-hua Confucianism and the Mongol Conquest," in *China under Mongol Rule,* pp. 168–71, 173–78. Wu Lai's father Wu Chih-fang[mh] (d. 1356) is discussed in some detail in my`unpublished dissertation, "Chin-hua Confucianism under the Mongols (1279–1368)" (Princeton University, 1974).

161. For Wu Shih-tao's biography, see YS, 190:4344. See also Sun K'o-k'uan, *Yüan-tai Chin-hua hsüeh shu,* pp. 45–48.

162. This preface, entitled "*Ch'un-ch'iu Hu-chuan pu-shuo* hsü,"[mi] is found in Wu Lai, *Yüan-ying Wu hsien-sheng wen-chi* (SPTK ed., rpt. of 1353 ed. [there are two versions in the SPTK]), 10:9b–11a.

163. For this statement, see note 137.

164. Chu I-tsu, *Ching-i k'ao,* 185:1b.

165. The *Huang-ch'ao ching-shih ta-tien* is discussed briefly in my "Yü Chi and His Mongol Sovereign," pp. 108–10.

166. Wu Lai, *Yüan-ying Wu hsien-sheng wen-chi,*[mj] 10:10a. The allusions are to the *Book of Documents.* For the reference to Po I, see Legge, *The Chinese Classics,* vol. 3, pp. 595 and 598; and for Kao Yao see p. 58. Cf. Karlgren, *The Book of Documents,* pp. 74–76, for the Po I reference. (Karlgren does not translate the chapter containing the Kao Yao reference.)

167. These are discussed by Derk Bodde in Derk Bodde and Clarence Morris, *Law in Imperial China, Exemplified by 190 Ch'ing Dynasty Cases Translated from the "Hsing-an hui-lan"* (Cambridge: Harvard University Press, 1967), pp. 559–60.

168. *Yüan-ying Wu hsien-sheng wen-chi,* 10:12a.

169. *Shih chung,*[mk] or "always maintaining the mean." See *Chung-yung;*[ml] Legge, *The Chinese Classics,* vol. 1, p. 386.
170. In some contexts the expression *fa-shu* may mean "handwriting" or "calligraphy." For other uses with the meaning "law book" or "law code," see Ou-yang Hsüan, *Kuei-chai wen-chi,* 12:7b (this is the "ts'e" essay discussed above); and the preface to *Huang-ch'ao ching-shih ta-tien,* reprinted in *Kuoch'ao wen-lei,* 42:1b.
171. *Yüan-ying Wu hsien-sheng wen-chi,* 10:12a–b.
172. Kao Heng,[mm] ed., *Shang-chün shu chü-i*[mn] (Peking: Chung-hua shu-chü, 1974), p. 110. See J.J.L. Duyvendak, trans., *The Book of Lord Shang* (1928; Chicago: University of Chicago Press, rpt. 1963), p. 260: "Good standards" is Duyvendak's rendering of the word *ch'üan* ("balance"). He comments in a note that *ch'üan* refers to the weight of a steelyard.
179. See Duyvendak, *Lord Shang,* p. 260.
174. See Duyvendak's "prestige," *Lord Shang,* p. 260.
175. Kao Heng, ed., *Shang-chün shu chu-i,* p. 112. Duyvendak does not translate this sentence as it has been restored to the text by Kao Heng from another source.
176. See Derk Bodde, tr., Fung Yu-lan, *A History of Chinese Philosophy* (Princeton: Princeton University Press, 1952), vol. 1, p. 292.
177. *Ibid.*
178. H. G. Creel, *Shen Pu-hai: A Chinese Political Philosopher of the Fourth Century B.C.* (Chicago: University of Chicago Press, 1974), pp. 353, 391.
179. *Kuan Tzu* (SPTK ed.), 1:7b–10b. This is chapter 3 in the text. It is not translated in W. Allyn Rickett, Kuan Tzu: *A Repository of Chinese Thought* (Hong Kong: University of Hong Kong Press, 1965).
180. For a useful discussion of Legalism, see Vitali Rubin, "Shen Tao and Fachia," *Journal of the Americal Oriental Society* (July–September 1974), 94(3):337–46. See Hsiao/Mote, *Chinese Political Thought,* chaps. 7 and 8 for a valuable analysis of early Legalism.
181. The expression "bloody tanistry" describes the warlike resolution of succession disputes among the Mongols. See Joseph Fletcher, "Bloody Tanistry: Authority and Succession in the Ottoman, Indian Muslim, and Later Chinese Empires," paper presented at the Conference on the Theory of Democracy and Popular Participation, Bellagio, Italy, September 1978. (Cited with the author's permission.)
182. Tr. in Joseph Needham, *Science and Civilisation in China,* vol. 4, pt. 1 (Cambridge: Cambridge University Press, 1976), p. 17.
183. *Meng Tzu,* 1A:7; Lau, *Mencius,* p. 57.
184. *Meng Tzu,* 4A:17; Lau, *Mencius,* p. 124: "in stretching out a helping hand to the drowning sister-in-law, [thereby violating the rites,] one uses one's discretion [*ch'üan*]."

GLOSSARY

a 徒單公履
b 易經
c 泰和律
d 耶律楚材
e 漢法
f 眞金
g 公羊
h 董仲舒
i 刑書
j 唐律
k 至元新格
l 刑律統類
m 刑統
n 禮
o 唐律疏議
p 岩村忍
q 爾雅
r 常
s 法
t 律詩
u 商鞅
v 繫辭
w 坎
x 權
y 郭璞
z 法律
aa 疱犧
ab 動憲
ac 葉適
ad 經
ae 隨時修立
af 明太祖
ag 大明律令
ah 成律
ai 條格
aj 條例

ak 常經
al 一時之權宜
am 國律
an 元史
ao 新律
ap 仁井田陞
aq 王惲
ar 立法
as 一定之法
at 永作成憲
au 視爲準式
av 國家
aw 廉訪
ax 律令
ay 至元新法
az 張養浩
ba 牧民忠告
bb 姚樞
bc 綱紀
bd 紀綱
be 李治
bf 法度
bg 正紀綱
bh 賞罰示懲勸
bi 宋子貞
bj 嚴實
bk 東平
bl 柄
bm 崔彧
bn 憲曹
bo 蘇天爵
bp 國朝文類
bq 國朝名臣事略
br 韓非子
bs 大元通制
bt 一代之法

bu	一定之律	dg	策問
bv	律學	dh	司業
bw	律科	di	例
bx	吏	dj	斷例
by	公	dk	法制
bz	張珪	dl	邦憲
ca	尚書	dm	程頤
cb	臣	dn	蘇軾
cc	權	do	八分書
cd	公羊傳	dp	伊洛
ce	知權	dq	大元通制條例綱目
cf	春秋繁露	dr	張紹
cg	彰天威	ds	孛尤魯狖
ch	瞻思	dt	歐陽玄
ci	帝王心法	du	歐陽修
cj	攬權綱	dv	進士
ck	憲	dw	至正條格
cl	張雄飛	dx	周禮
cm	澧州	dy	噬嗑
cn	懲不畏法者	dz	豐
co	胡祇遹	ea	先王以明罰勅法
cp	論定法律	eb	君子以折獄致刑
cq	成法	ec	天威
cr	論治法	ed	國憲
cs	公器	ee	天常
ct	抵罪	ef	分宜
cu	威	eg	民
cv	州	eh	常住田
cw	文	el	法律之未定
cx	郡	ej	法吏
cy	案	ek	常流
cz	議	el	成書
da	論	em	子產
db	本心	en	叔向
dc	吳澄	eo	左傳
dd	臨川	ep	漢書
de	王安石	eq	班固
df	學統	er	春秋

es	趙岐	ge	天道
et	素王之法	gf	人紀
eu	莊子	gg	夷狄
ev	經世	gh	夏
ew	司馬遷	gi	天經紊
ex	史記	gj	人理乖
ey	晉	gk	吳萊
ez	北齊	gl	浦江
fa	杜預	gm	大都
fb	春秋左氏經傳集解	gn	吳師道
fc	舊律	go	胡安國
fd	啖助	gp	皇朝經世大典
fe	陸淳	gq	伯夷
ff	孫復	gr	皐陶
fg	邵雍	gs	經制
fh	近思錄	gt	權宜
fi	朱熹	gu	法書
fj	呂祖謙	gv	議法之吏
fk	經世之大法	gw	商君書
fl	不易之通法	gx	修權
fm	韓琦	gy	威
fn	綱	gz	權衡
fo	尊王	ha	荀子
fp	攘夷	hb	申不害
fq	春秋皇綱論	hc	管子
fr	王哲	hd	權修
fs	經制	he	淮南子
ft	讀春秋	hf	大元聖政國朝典章
fu	振王綱	hg	宋濂
fv	霸	hh	中華書局
fw	罪	hi	葉潛昭
fx	春秋纂言	hj	金律之研究
fy	總例	hk	仁井田陞
fz	吉禮	hl	中國法制史：刑法
ga	凶禮	hm	金代刑法考
gb	賓禮	hn	勞延煊
gc	軍禮	ho	元初南方知識份子—詩中所
gd	嘉禮		反映出的片面

hp 香港中文大學中國文化研究所學報

hq 楊維楨

hr 正統辨

hs 姚從吾

ht 程鉅夫與忽必烈汗平宋以後的安定南人問題

hu 國立台灣大學文史哲學報

hv 植松正

hw 彙輯「至元新格」並びに解説

hx 東洋史研究

hy 李心傳

hz 曽我部静雄

ia 中国律令史の研究

ib 宮崎市定

ic 宋元時代の法制と裁判機構

id アジア史研究

ie モンゴル社会経済史の研究

if 三田村泰助

ig 拓土を廣いた人人

ih 田村実造

ii アジア歴史事典

ij 法令

ik 吏學指南

il 大札撒

im 徐元瑞

in 尚書大傳

io 水心先生文集

ip 明太祖實錄

iq 律令直解

ir 黃彰健

is 大明律詰考

it 明清史研究叢稿

iu 安部健夫

iv 元史刑法志と元律とその関係に就いて

iw 元代史の研究

ix 圭齋文集

iy 孟子

iz 明史

ja 秋澗先生大全文集

jb 三典

jc 周禮

jd 秋官

je 大司寇

jf 九章

jg 蕭何

jh 為政忠告

ji 四庫全書

jj 魏徵

jk 袁國藩

jl 東平嚴實幕府人物與興學初考

jm 大陸雜誌

jn 孫克寬

jo 元代漢文化之活動

jp 李謙

jq 閻復

jr 陳天祥

js 蘇御史治獄記

jt 黃溍

ju 金華黃先生文集

jv 滋溪文稿

jw 適園叢書

jx 大元通制解說

jy 通制條格

jz 小林高四郎

ka 岡本敬二

kb 通制条格の研究訳註

kc 洪範

kd 辺土名朝邦

ke 春秋公羊学派の「権」説について

kf 九州中国学会報

kg 日原利国

kh	春秋公羊伝の研究	ll	諸橋轍次
ki	大食	lm	儒学の目的と宋儒の活動
kj	紫山大全集	ln	諸橋轍次著作集
kk	揭傒斯	lo	常秩
kl	揭文安公全集	lp	羅從彥
km	柳貫	lq	春秋指歸
kn	元典章	lr	宋史
ko	道學基統	ls	牟潤孫
kp	草廬吳文正公集	lt	兩宋春秋學之主流
kq	徐道鄰	lu	注史齋叢稿
kr	法學家蘇東坡	lv	陳慶新
ks	中國法制史論集	lw	宋儒春秋尊王要義發微與其
kt	分宜縣學復田記		政治思想
ku	罔民	lx	新亞學報
kv	李則芬	ly	宋元學案補遺
kw	元史新講	lz	四庫全書總目
kx	校正莊子集釋	ma	孔子修春秋
ky	春秋經世先王之志，聖人議	mb	通志堂經解
	而不辯	mc	牛童馬走
kz	撥亂世，反諸正	md	如權鑑之在懸
la	何休	me	春秋備忘序
lb	春秋公羊經傳解詁	mf	敬鉉
lc	錢穆	mg	元代金華學述
ld	孔子與春秋	mh	吳直方
le	兩漢經學今古文平議	mi	春秋胡傳補說序
lf	春秋決事比	mj	淵穎吳先生文集
lg	程樹德	mk	時中
lh	九朝律考	ml	中庸
li	朱彝尊	mm	高亨
lj	經義考	mn	商君書注譯
lk	名公書判清明集		

Herbert Franke

Wang Yün (1227–1304): A Transmitter of Chinese Values

WANG YÜN[a] is not counted among the outstanding thinkers of the Yüan dynasty. The brief biographical handbook of Yüan Confucians, the *Yüan-ju k'ao-lüeh* by the late Ming scholar Feng Ts'ung-wu[b] (1556–1627), has no entry for Wang Yün,[1] and no traditional history of Chinese philosophy seems to mention him, nor does the compendium *Sung-Yüan hsüeh-an*. Only the supplement (*pu-i*) to the latter work compiled in the early nineteenth century lists him among the followers of Wang P'an[c] (1202–1293), and has a short notice based chiefly on his biography in the *Yüan shih*.[2] But even if Wang Yün can by no means be ranked as a major philosophical or intellectual figure he should not *a priori* be considered unworthy of a closer study. Transmission and transfusion of ideas is never channeled through a few original thinkers alone, but depends on a multiplicity of humble writers and teachers. Wang Yün seems to belong to this latter category. But another reason justifies a study of Wang Yün as well. Two of his works were translated into Mongolian under the Yüan, a distinction never achieved by any other of his contemporaries. This shows that his work must have had an appeal which other perhaps more sophisticated productions did not have in the eyes of the Mongols.

Apart from Buddhist texts, not many Chinese works were translated into Mongolian under the Yüan; some were printed but the majority remained in the manuscript stage.[3] The printed Mongolian translations included the Confucian classic *Hsiao ching*, the compendium *Ta-hsüeh yen-i*,[d] the annalistic history *Tzu-chih t'ung-chien*, the administrative handbooks *Ta-Yüan t'ung-chih*[e] and *Lieh-sheng chih-chao*,[f] the T'ang political and ethical analects *Chen-kuan cheng-yao*,[g] and the collection of edicts and admonitions of the Mongol emperors, chiefly those of Khubilai Khaghan (r. 1260–1294), *Huang-t'u ta-hsün*.[h] Manuscript translations are recorded to have been made of the *Shu ching*, of Hsün Yüeh's *Shen-chien*,[i] of the *Ti fan*[j] ascribed to emperor T'ang T'ai-sung (r. 627–649), the "Holy Injunctions" of Khubilai, *Shih-tsu sheng-hsün*,[k] the *Veritable Records* (*Shih-lu*) of Ögödei (r. 1229–1241), Möngke (r. 1251–1259), and Khubilai, the medical work *Nan ching*,[l] and a materia medica, *Pen-ts'ao*.[m] And, of particular concern to us here, Wang Yün's *Ch'eng-hua shih lüeh*,[n] was also translated into Mongolian.[4]

With the exception of the Mongolian *Hsiao ching*, the translations listed above are all lost.[5] A fragment of a printed Mongolian page discovered in Khara Khoto and preserved in Leningrad might belong to the Mongolian *Ta-Yüan t'ung-chih*.[6] But the list given above is not complete because the data assembled by Walter Fuchs are based exclusively on the *Yüan shih* and the collected works of Chinese authors of the Yüan period. More data on translations into Mongolian can be found in Korean sources. The existence of Mongolian translations in Korea for the use of language students was first made known by Maurice Courant.[7] A detailed study of Mongolian, Jurchen, and Manchu translations used in Korea over the centuries as language textbooks has been made by the Japanese scholar Ogura Shimpei whose researches have been summarized in a recent work on Manchu studies in Korea.[8] Some of the titles of the Mongolian translation can be identified. One of these is a treatise which in Sino-Korean reads *Su-sŏng sa gam*, i.e. (*Yüan-chen*) *Shou-ch'eng shih-chien*,[o] also by Wang Yüan.[9] The Mongolian translation of this work was used for the examination in Mongolian in the fifteenth century (1469). It was reedited by several Korean scholars in 1690 but had fallen into disuse by 1737 because the language of the text was considered obsolete (which, incidentally, indicates an early date of the translation, probably into preclassical Mongolian of the thirteenth and fourteenth centuries).[10] No copy has come to light so far although it is possible that the text is still preserved somewhere in Korea.

We can see, therefore, that not less than two treatises by Wang Yün were translated into the language of his Mongol overlords and that at least one of them served as a language textbook in Korea into the seventeenth century. It seems also that the collection of edicts, *Huang-t'u ta-hsün*, which was translated in 1326 and printed in 1330 with a preface by the famous scholar Yü Chi[p] (1272–1348), goes back in part to a previous collection of imperial admonitions compiled by Wang Yün (see below).[11] Thus Wang Yün must be considered a key figure in the process of transmitting Chinese political thought to the Mongols. It is also evident that the translation of secular, non-Buddhist works into Mongolian centered on books which were thought to be of immediate practical use in government and administration, and that Wang Yün's treaties rank there on a par with the T'ang dynasty classics of statecraft such as *Ti fan* or *Chen-kuan cheng-yao*. This heavy emphasis on the T'ang as a model for not only the Mongols but also other foreigners is in itself significant. The only Chinese work which we know to have been translated into Khitan, Tangut, Jurchen, and Mongolian was the *Chen-kuan cheng-yao*. [12] Those responsible for the selection of works to be translated, that is, Chinese scholars under foreign rulers or sinicized foreigners, apparently wanted their emperors to model thsmselves on T'ang T'ai-tsung, and thus to establish a continuity from the T'ang to the new regimes, bypassing the Sung. Leaving the *Tzu-chih t'ung-chien* aside as an historical work, we find only two Sung texts translated into Mongolian, namely, the *Ta-hsüeh yen-i* by Chen Te-hsiu[q] (1178–1235) and the earlier short essay "Tai-lou yüan chi" by Wang Yü-ch'eng[r] (954–1001). The latter describes the principles of good government and was quite popular in China, to judge from its inclusion in many anthologies. The Mongolian translation was used in language teaching in Korea along with the *Shou-ch'eng shih-chien* of Wang Yün and, like the latter, was reedited in 1690. [13] This neglect of Sung thought in translated literature is, of course, plausible if we take the political situation into account. The Sung state had succumbed to the Mongols, after having been halved by the Jurchen after 1126, so that Sung politics and statecraft were certainly regarded as inferior and unpractical, whereas the glory and splendor of T'ang were sufficiently far removed in time to become an idealized model for statecraft that could be imitated by the Mongols. We shall see later that Wang Yün also concentrated heavily on this image of the T'ang.

Wang was a very prolific writer who apparently never threw a piece of paper away. His collected works, *Ch'iu-ch'ien hsien-sheng ta-ch'üan wen-chi*[s] (henceforth abbreviated as CW), fill not less than one hundred *chüan*, and contain a great number of texts which elucidate his family background and his career. [14] The appendix (*fu-lu*) to the collected works of Wang Yün contains a long funeral text written by his son Wang Kung-ju,[t] which has served as the basic source for Wang Yün's biography in the Yüan history. From all these sources we can obtain the following picture of Wang Yün's descent. [15]

The Wang clan had been living in Honan for a long time. The original family seat was in Yang-wu[u] county where the family owned landed property close to the dams of the Yellow River. During the Jurchen invasions in 1126 the family moved to Chi[v] county in Wei[w] prefecture. It does not seem that any ancestor of Wang Yün held an office under the Sung. The gradual rise from a family of peasants to a family of officials seems to be linked with the establishment of Jurchen rule in Honan. Another element which seems to be typical for Chinese society under the Chin (1115–1234) is the fact that the Wang family made their way up on the social ladder by serving first as local clerks (*li*).[x] The first ancestor of Wang who held public office was a police chief (*wei*)[y] in Chi county in the T'ien-hui period (1123–1138). Wang Yün's grandfather Wang Yü[z] (1174–1224) was also a police clerk in Wei prefecture. He became a favorite of the local Jurchen commander and must have distinguished himself in office because it is reported that the greater number of the clerks in Wei prefecture were his pupils and that he taught the craft of clerkdom (*li-hsüeh*)[aa] to his own son, Wang Yün's father. This was Wang T'ien-to[ab] (1202–1257), a studious youth who soon found favor with powerful officials, and was even recommended by an imperial Jurchen clan member, Marshal Wan-yen E-k'o.[ac][16] As a result of this patronage, Wang T'ien-to found himself in 1228 attached to the household of the ruling emperor's elder brother, and in 1229 he became a scribe in the Ministry of Revenue. The collapse of the Chin state in early 1234, however, prevented him from pursuing a metropolitan career and he returned to his home in the following year and lived in retirement thereafter.

Like so many Chinese in the past who found their career thwarted by political events, Wang T'ien-to turned to scholarship and devoted himself to classical studies. He became an expert on the *Book of Changes*, which he used "to purify his heart," and also compiled a book with collected explanations of the *Changes* by previous scholars. This book was apparently never printed; in 1228 his son Wang Yün wrote a preface to it.[17] Wang T'ien-to had numerous intellectual friends, many of whom were former Chin officials living in retirement like himself.[18] Wang Yün's father was the first in the family to study the Confucian classics seriously, in contrast to his ancestors who had for over a century concentrated on practical affairs and served as local bureaucrats in legal, police, and clerkly matters. If the Chin state had lasted longer, Wang T'ien-to would perhaps have become a prominent official but his enforced retirement led him to more intellectual pursuits. He seems to have been an uncompromising man who laughed and spoke rarely. Aided by a strong sense of discipline, he wrote ten thousand characters in standard script every day and transcribed several thousand *chüan* of literature in ten years' time.[19] His wife is also described as a stern lady who managed the household, practiced female crafts and took part in the sacrifices for Confucius. After her death in 1248 Wang T'ien-to declined to remarry. The eldest of his two sons was Wang Yün; the younger, about whom not much is known except that he was some sort of commissioner in the capital, was Wang Shen.[ad]

If we try to summarize Wang Yün's family background we must come to the conclusion that he came from an upstart family which achieved some local prominence only after the Jurchen conquest, having repeatedly married rich daughters. All of Wang Yün's ancestors, if they were employed at all by the state, served as clerks and in similar positions. None of them ever passed a literary examination. They all were loyal subjects of the Chin whom they served up to the last days of the regime. The first person in the family to study more than just legal documents was Wang Yün's father, and he took up literary pursuits only after he had lost his employment and lived in retirement in his home country. Intellectually, Wang Yün's father must be ranked as a conservative who confined his studies to the standard classics and had no artistic leanings. We may visualize Wang the father as a somewhat wooden and humorless person, but he seems to have been prominent enough to associate with many former Chin officials who lived privately as *i-min*[ae] in Honan after 1234. Among his friends were such prominent literary figures as Yüan Hao-wen[af] (1190–1257), Liu Ch'i[ag] (1203-1250), Yang Huan[ah] (1186–1255),[20] and Wang P'an. Of these, Wang P'an became young Wang Yün's teacher in poetry, and Wang Yün is expressly mentioned in the *Sung-Yüan hsüeh-an* supplement as having been tutored by Yüan Hao-wen, Yang Huan, and Liu Ch'i.[21] This school of affiliation must, of course, be understood more as a sort of general education in literary skills than as referring to a distinct philosophical school of thought. Other contemporaries who communicated with Wang Yün and his father were Yang Kuo[ai] (1197–1269), Hao Ching[aj] (1223–1275), and Hu Chih-yü[ak] (1227–1293),[22] not to mention other minor literati some of whom we cannot identify. But all persons who were related in some way or other to Wang Yün in his early years seem to belong to the category of *i-min*, former Chin officials who tried to perpetuate Chinese cultural values throughout the formative period of Mongol rule over Northern China. In the following we shall give a brief account of Wang Yün's political career based chiefly on his biography in the Yüan History.

In those days when no examination system existed, the only way for an educated Chinese to obtain an office was to attract the attention of a powerful person, preferably someone who had been sent out by the Mongol court to recruit talented personnel. This was indeed the way through which Wang Yün entered an official career. When the distinguished myriarch of the Han army, Shih T'ien-tse[al] (1202–1275),[23] passed through Wei prefecture on his campaign against the Sung for the Mongols some time prior to 1260, he met Wang Yün and treated him as a guest. This favor is reflected in the fact that Wang Yün later wrote a family history for Shih T'ien-tse.[24] And when Yao Shu[am] (1203–1280), another important political figure, who was sent to Tung-p'ing District[an] in the fall of 1260 as Pacification Commissioner, met Wang Yün, he appointed him as advisor. This occurred soon after Khubilai Khaghan had ascended the throne and began to build up a Chinese-style administration.[25] In 1260 Wang Yün was made a *hsiang-ting kuan*[ao] in the Central Secretariat (*chung-shu sheng*)[ap] in the capital Ta-tu (Peking) together with Chou Cheng,[aq] a man from Po-hai.[26] This appointment resulted in Wang Yün's compilation of a very detailed diary of the initial period of Khubilai's reign, the *Chung-t'ang shih-chi*[ar] (in CW, *ch.* 80–82). It is by far the best source on the beginning of the new emperor's reign and it includes summaries of important documents (and, incidentally, a report on the first visit of European travellers in Yüan China).[27] But Wang Yün did not serve for long in the Central Secretariat. In 1261, Wang O[as] (1190–1273) persuaded the emperor to reestablish the Hanlin Academy and the National History Office. Among the ex-Chin officals and men of letters whom he recommended was also Wang Yün, who was made Redactor-Compiler (*hsiu-chuan*)[at] concurrently with an office in the Central Secretariat. He also took a very active interest in the compilation of the Chin history on the initiative of Wang O.[28]

For the time from 1261 until 1268 all biographical sources on Wang Yün remain silent. His career must have been interrupted for some reason. Lao Yan-shuan has discovered in Wang Yün's writings evidence that he had been accused and dismissed from his offices and was even in danger of losing his life. It is very probable, as Lao has pointed out, that

Wang's temporary disgrace was connected with the fall of Wang Wen-t'ung,[au] the powerful Administrator of Political Affairs (*p'ing-chang cheng-shih*) [av] in the Central Secretariat, who was executed in early 1262 for alleged collusion with his son-in-law Li T'an[aw] during the latter's rebellion in Shantung.[29] Wang Wen-t'ung, a native of Shantung of obscure origin, was employed by Khubilai and rose to prominence because of his expertise in fiscal affairs, and must be regarded as one of the patrons of the so-called Tung-p'ing school (see below). It is significant that in Wang Yün's works not a word of blame for Wang Wen-t'ung can be found, and indeed some oblique references point to a strong attachment between the two.[30] It was only after a lapse of six years that we find Wang Yün back in office, this time in the newly established Censorate, where he held the office of Inspecting Censor. During his term of office in the Censorate Wang Yün wrote many impeachments (CW, *ch.* 83–91) from which we obtain a realistic picture of how the administration in Khubilai's empire functioned, or rather, malfunctioned.

This metropolitan employment was followed in 1272 by transfer to a provincial post, that of Judge (*p'an-kuan*)[ax] in the General Administration (*tsung-kuan fu*)[ay] of the Ping-yang District[az] (Shansi). The biographical texts on Wang Yün do not fail to praise his achievements in solving criminal cases and deciding lawsuits which had been protracted over many years. In 1276 he was sent on a recruiting tour to five districts in Honan in order to test Confucian scholars who might be employed by the government. In 1277 he was promoted to Hanlin Academician-in-waiting (*tai-chih*)[ba] and in 1278 became a Commissioner of the Inspection Bureau (*t'i-hsing an-ch'a chih*)[bb] in the Ho-pei and Honan Regions.

In 1282 he presented his *Ch'eng-hua shih-lüeh* to crown prince Chen-chin[bc] (Jingim, 1244–1286), the second son of Khubilai (see below). In the spring of 1282 Wang Yün again received a provincial appointment as Commissioner of the Inspection Bureau in the Eastern and Western Regions of Shantung, but after one year in this office he asked to be allowed to return to his native prefecture on grounds of illness. In the spring of 1285 he was again promoted and became the First Secretary (*lang-chung*)[bd] of a bureau in the Central Secretariat. This was when Lu Shih-yung[be] (d. 1285) was in power at the court. Lu is ranked by Chinese historiographers as one of the most corrupt officials under Khubilai, along with Ahmed and Sengge.[31] Lu wished to promote Wang Yün but Wang declined because he had his doubts that a person like Lu would stay in power. Soon thereafter Lu indeed fell into disgrace and was executed, so that people at the court admired Wang's insight. It seems that he had learned from his previous involvement with Wang Wen-t'ung to stay away from powerful but controversial figures.

There followed another provincial appointment in 1289. This time Wang Yün was sent, for the first time in his career, into the newly conquered territories of the former Sung state as Judge in the Min-hai[bf] Region (modern Fukien), where greedy officials and general instability had caused repeated local rebellions. Wang Yün eliminated some of the most notorious officials and impeached members of the provincial administration on grounds of mismanagement. He also forbade soldiers to be billeted in the homes of the people and ordered barracks built for them. In addition, as during his previous assignments, he decided lawsuits which had been lingering on for years and released suspects who had been in jail without sufficient reasons. His chief concern was to build up an efficient local administration and to obtain the right people for the offices. A major problem was the local rebellion started by a man called Chung Ming-liang,[bg] a native of Kiangsi. Chung had managed to attract a great number of followers, and a punitive campaign under Ötmish (Yüeh-ti-mi-shih)[bh] was started early in 1289. In June Chung surrendered with 18,573 men. Ötmish asked the court to appoint Chung as prefect as a reward for his surrender but the emperor refused and ordered Chung to come to the capital. Thereupon Chung rebelled again in late November and invaded with his forces several counties in Fukien. A new punitive campaign was started under Ötmish, and again Chung surrendered in March 1290. This time the orders issued by the court were more severe; the gang leaders should be taken to the court in fetters, whereas the innocent followers of the rebel should be given grain. Although the sources are not very clear, it seems that Wang Yün took an active part in suppressing the revolt, not only by assisting Ötmish's campaign but also by trying to resettle the population which had initially joined the revolt.[32]

This service in China's deep south seems to have affected Wang Yün's health, because he was allowed to return to the north in 1290 for reasons of ill health. But he did not stay for long in his native town and was summoned to the court again in the following year. In 1292, he was given the privilege of an audience with Khubilai Khaghan. Earlier, the emperor had been reluctant to grant an audience to Hanlin scholars and had deferred it for some time but eventually consented to meet them.

The person who had suggested the meeting was the Chief Censor Örlük (Yüeh-erh-lu).[bi] Finally, the audience took place in the hunting residence of Liu-lin,[bj] southeast of Ta-tu (Peking).[33] On that occasion Wang Yün presented a long memorial of ten thousand characters on contemporary affairs, arranged under sixteen headings.[34] The emperor was not displeased, and Wang Yün was promoted to a Hanlin Academician (*hsüeh-shih*).[bk]

Another occasion for Wang to propagate his ideas on politics arrived after the accession of Temür (Ch'eng-tsung) in 1294. He composed the *Yüan-chen Shou-ch'eng shih-chien* mentioned above and presented it to the emperor. Then he was ordered to compile the *Veritable Records* of Khubilai's reign, which he completed and presented to the court in July 1295. The *Records* consisted of 210 chapters of text, 54 chapters of classified tables of contents (*shih-mu*)[bl] and 6 chapters containing basic edicts and orders of the late emperor (*Shih-tsu sheng-hsün*), altogether 270 chapters.[35] His labors were rewarded by promotion to the titular rank of *Chung-feng ta-fu*[bm] in 1279, and in 1298 by a gift of 10,000 strings (*min*) of paper money. He was not the only one to be given money; over a dozen other Hanlin scholars and officials who had distinguished themselves as incorruptible and virtous servants of the dynasty were so rewarded, the total sum spent being 105,000 strings.[36] At that time Wang was over 70 years old, but his request for retirement was not granted. Finally, in 1301, he was allowed to retire. At the same time, in order to make his old age more comfortable, his son Wang Kung-ju was given the post of Judge in Wei prefecture and his grandson Wang Ko[bn] was appointed as Imperial Librarian. Wang Yün enjoyed a few peaceful years of retirement and died of an illness in the "Spring Dew Hall"[bo] of his home on July 23, 1304, at the age of 77. This hall had been built in 1285 and was dedicated to the memory of his father.[37] When he was buried at the side of his wife in the fall of the next year, an enormous crowd followed his coffin. The tomb was situated in the village known as Ho-shi li.[bp] Wang Yün received the usual posthumous rank by being proclaimed Hanlin Executive Academician (*ch'eng-chih*)[bq] with the title of *Tzu-shan ta-fu*.[br] He was also enfeoffed as T'ai-yüan chün kung[bs] (perhaps alluding to his term of office in Shansi) and was canonized as Wen-ting[bt] (Cultured and Steadfast) by Emperor Ayurbarwada (Jen-tsung, r. 1311–1320) in 1312.

Wang Yün had married into a respectable but not very prominent family. His wife *née* T'ui[bu] came from a family of physicians in Honan province. She died in 1286, having given birth to Wang Kung-ju, the same son who later, c. 1312, wrote the "Spirit-way Stele" for his father and was at that time a prefect of Ying. Wang Yün's grandson Wang Ko had been born in 1275 and was, c. 1312, a Director (*lang*) in the Ministry of Justice. Wang had two more sons from a concubine. One son, Wang Kung-i,[bv] had become through the *yin* privilege accorded to descendants of meritorious officials Vice Prefect of Tz'u[bw] (modern Hopei), and the other, Wang Kung-yüeh,[bx] was Inspector of Confucian Studies in Wei-hui[by] District (Honan). One of Wang Yün's granddaughters married Yeh-lü K'ai,[bz] the eldest son of Yeh-lü Yu-shang[ca] (1246–1320). Yu-shang was a great nephew of the famous Yeh-lü Ch'u-ts'ai[cb] (1189–1243), so that through his granddaughter's marriage the Wang clan had allied itself with a very ancient and prominent family of Khitan descent.

All the extant writings of Wang Yün can be found in his collected works, and none of them has been transmitted outside that corpus.[38] Two works of his which were translated into Mongolian also form part of the collected works. His biography, however, mentions two more works which must be considered lost. One of them is the *Hsiang-chien*[cc] in 50 *chüan* which, to judge from its title, must have been a "Mirror for Prime Ministers." The preface alone, dated 1283, is extant.[39] The other work is a gazetteer of his home county *Chi-chün t'u chih*[cd] in 15 *chüan*. This gazetteer had originally been begun by Wang Yün's father and was completed by the son. The title implies that this work included maps and diagrams. The preface was composed in 1266, that is, during the time when Wang Yün had lost his metropolitan office and lived at home in temporary retirement.[40]

From the abundant data on Wang Yün's background and family traditions he appears a man with a practical mind and considerable experience in practical administration, above all in the field of justice. He mastered all the customary skills of a Chinese literatus without, it seems, creating works of genius. Wang Yün's practical talents are also praised in the biography written by his son, who uses the word *ching-chi*[ce] which, in modern usage, means economy but originally had a much wider connotation and could be translated as "statecraft."

It remains a question to what degree Wang Yün was influenced by Sung Neo-Confucianism and metaphysics. He certainly was not unaware of Sung thought and thinkers, and indeed not a few references to them can be found in his collected works. The idea, formulated by Chou Tun-i[cf] (1017–1073), that literature has to serve as a vehicle for the True Way, permeates the entire life and works of Wang Yün. He once praised the *T'ai-chi t'u*[cg] for its diagrammatical clarity.[41] And when he wrote a preface to his teacher Yüan Hao-wen's *Ti-wang ching lüeh*[ch] he quotes in the beginning "Tung-lai," that is, Lü Tsu-ch'ien[ci] (1137–1181) to the effect that next to the classics the histories should be the basis for serious studies.[42] This preface, like so many other of his works, was written during his retirement in 1267. Wang Yün was also familiar with Chu Hsi (1130–1200), whose works gradually became known in Northern China after the fall of the Chin state. He wrote several colophons to autographs by Chu Hsi and advocated the establishment of a hall for the worship of Chu Hsi in Hangchow.[43] From these texts he appears to have had some reverence for Chu Hsi as an intellectual figure but a deeper influence of Chu Hsi on his own ideas seems to be absent from his works.

Modern scholars have ranked Wang Yün as a member of the so-called Tung-p'ing school. This school is named after the county town of Tung-p'ing in southwestern Shantung, a region not very far from Wang Yün's family home. Tung-p'ing had been a sort of hereditary fief of Yen Shih[cj] (1182–1240), who had in time surrendered to the Mongol general Mukhali (1170–1223) and had become a myriarch. The myriarchy remained also in the hands of Yen Shih's sons.[44] Another patron of the "literary" faction, an alternative name for the Tung-p'ing school, was Wang Wen-t'ung, a Shantung man, who, as mentioned earlier, had risen from humble background to the rank of a senior administrator at Khubilai's court and played a prominent role in introducing Chin government structures to the early Mongol rule in North China. His influence, however, was short-lived, since he was put to death as an accomplice of his son-in-law Li T'an in plotting the rebellion in Shantung in 1262. In spite of this handicap, the Chinese scholars who had become protégés of these grandees continued to exert influence at court, and the Hanlin Academy had become one of their strongholds. Their ideological position has been aptly described as "vaguely Confucian"[45] and concentrating on Chinese art forms in literature, at the same time trying to introduce traditional Chinese ideas of statecraft into the nascent Sino-Mongol state in Northern China.[46] This made them natural antagonists of the hereditary fief-holders and appanage owners, and of the Mongol nobility in general, but also of the people from Western Asia who were active in financial economy. Wang Yün's general intellectual tendencies seem to fit well into what has been said about the Tung-p'ing school. Statecraft was what he had in mind and not so much Neo-Confucian metaphysical speculation or theorizing.

In this context we must also view his *Ch'eng-hua shih-lüeh*. This title could be translated as *Summaries of Actions of a Crown Prince*. The work had originally 20 paragraphs (*p'ien*) in 6 chapters (*chüan*). At present it fills *ch*. 78 and 9 folios of *ch*. 79 of Wang's collected works. The table of contents and the text itself have retained the original division into 6 chapters.[47] But there has occurred a minor confusion. In the collected works of Wang Yün, chapter 6 of the *Ch'eng-hua shih-lüeh* consists of the *Shou-ch'eng shih-chien*, which seems rather misplaced since it is a much later work and has nothing to do with the former. This is certainly a mistake of the editor of Wang Yün's works and inconsistent with the original table of contents. The accompanying letter with which Wang presented the *Ch'eng-hua shih-lüeh* to the crown prince Chen-chin is dated the twelfth month, eighteenth year of Chih-yüan (CW 78, 1a–b). This was early in 1282 because the first day of this month was January 12, 1282. The letter itself shows a mixture of self-depreciation and adulation customary for such documents. There follows a preface (CW 78, 2a–3b) in which Wang Yün tries to give a logical reason for the sequence of the 20 paragraphs. He says that in his opinion filial obedience is the root of virtue, therefore he has put the paragraph on "Broaden Filial Obedience" at the beginning of the book. Love is what is born from obedience, and therefore the paragraph "Set up Love," should logically follow. Following this, he goes on to the last paragraph, "Investigate Officals." We also learn from the preface that each paragraph was accompanied by a picture (*t'u*) "so that one may see the greatness of the recorded actions of the men of old in their times."[48] The pictures have certainly been added by way of explanation in order to appeal to those who could not read the classical Chinese of the text itself. It is not mentioned whether the pictures have been drawn expressly for the book or whether they were taken from another moralistic treatise on an ideal heir apparent's behavior, nor is it said by whom they were originally painted.

We have two accounts by Wang Yün of the presentation of his work to the crown prince. One follows immediately the text proper and has been incorporated in Wang's biography in the Yüan History.[49] The text is interesting enough to be translated here.

In the beginning, when Yü-huang[ck] [i.e., Chen-chin] "read" [the passage] where emperor Ch'eng of Han did not cross the imperial pathway and T'ang Su-tsung changed the garments from red gauze to summer clothing, he was pleased in the heart and said: "If I had encountered such rites I would also have acted like them. I did not realize that the men of antiquity already practiced these."

When he came to [the passage where] Hsing Ch'ih[el] stopped the crown prince of Ch'i from eating the "evil artemisia," he turned to the palace officials and said: "How can the name of one vegetable, even if one eats it, suddenly corrupt people?" The Assistant in the Princely Household [chan-ch'eng[cm]] Chang Chiu-ssu,[cn] answered: "A correct man should guard himself even in the smallest matters. This principle is unquestionable. Let us take the hare for comparison: even if thirsty he would not drink from a dirty source, and if tired, not rest in the shadow of a poisonous tree!" The sovereign was pleased by this explanation and praised it.

The word used by Wang Yün for "to read" is *tu*.[co] Indeed, Chen-chin had taken lessons in Chinese and was able to read—he studied, for example, the *Hsiao ching* in the Chinese original version.[50] Chen-chin also ordered his sons, the grandsons of Khubilai, to look at (*kuan*[cp]) the book,[51] presumably at the pictures. The use of the word *kuan* seems to imply that they could not read the text itself. Chang Chiu-ssu (1242–1302) was involved in the plot against the notorious Uighur financial administrator Ahmed (d. 1282) and was afterwards appointed as an assistant in the heir apparent's household administration and eventually rose to the office of Administrator of Political Affairs in 1298.[52]

The meeting between Chen-chin and Wang Yün did not take place immediately after the latter had submitted his work to the crown prince, but many months later. This we know from the other account which Wang Yün has written of his audience with Chen-chin—the preface to a poem captioned: "A Favored Meeting at the Western Pond.[cq]" The poem as such is without deeper interest but the preface contains some additional details, above all the exact date of the audience: the twelfth day of the tenth month in the *jen-wu* year, (i.e., November 13, 1282).[53] There Wang recalled that at the *ssu* hour (9–11 A.M.) he was introduced by Chang Chiu-ssu, then Minister of Works, to the crown prince, who was just practicing archery west of his palace. After being presented, Chen-chin asked him what sort of ruler Ch'in Shih-huang-ti (r.221–210 B.C.) had been, and Wang answered that his actions had been cruel. The rest of Wang Yün's account in the preface to the poem tallies more or less with the text translated above. Chen-chin interrupted his archery, and after having "read" through the book, asked for an explanation of the general meaning of each chapter. His questions were answered by Chang Chiu-ssu and Chu-hu-nai,[cr] who was perhaps, like Chang, a member of Chen-chin's household administration. After Chen-chin had finished "reading," the book was given to Tung Pa-ko[cs][54] so that Chen-chin might hear more about it in a quiet moment later. At the end of the hour *wei* (1–3 P.M.), wine was served and Wang Yün left the palace slightly drunk.

These, then, were the circumstances of Wang Yün's meeting with Chen-chin—a brief encounter late in the fall of 1282. We do not know if Chen-chin showed more than a polite interest in Wang Yün's work. The book itself shows clearly the educational purpose that its author had in mind. It has a simple structure. Each of the 20 paragraphs has a title in two characters which summarizes the virtues of an exemplary crown prince. The texts under each heading are first quotations from history, either actions or words of model princes, and are followed by an explanatory comment by Wang Yün. In truly scholarly fashion he keeps his sources apart from his own exposition of the themes. In most cases, it is possible to identify the sources for the various quotations. Given below is a summary of the 20 paragraphs, with identification of the sources wherever possible, showing which virtues Wang thought to be most important for a future Son of Heaven, and also from which category of books he selected his examples. It should be noted that Wang has sometimes altered slightly the original text by adapting certain characters, or by replacing unusual characters with the current ones. He might also not have quoted directly from the source (except in the case of Confucian classics) but from some intermediate texts, such as an encyclopedia or compendium.

1. *Kuang-hsiao.*[ct] Broaden Filial Obedience.
    a. Wen-wang's filial behavior as crown prince. Source: *Li chi.*[55]
    b. T'ang Hsüan-tsung (r. 712–756) gave in the second year of K'ai-yüan (714) a banquet honoring aged palace officials. Source: *Hsin T'ang shu.*[56]
    c. Hsüan-tsung ordered by edict in the third year of T'ien-pao (744) that all households in the empire should have a copy of the *Hsiao ching.* Source: *T'ang shu; Hsin T'ang shu.*[57]
2. *Li-ai.*[cu] Set up Love.
    a. "Now your majesty is entering on the inheritance of virtue; everything depends on how you commence your reign. To set up love,

it is for you to love your elders; to set up respect, it is for you to respect your relatives." Source: *Shu ching, I-hsün* (a spurious chapter).[58]

b. Ho Ti of the Later Han dynasty (r. 88–106) as crown prince loved dearly his elder brother, the Prince of Ch'ing-ho, Liu Ch'ing,[cv] with whom he shared the same room and the same chariot. After he became emperor he was even more friendly toward the brother. Source: *Hou-Han shu.*[59]

c. T'ang Hsüan-tsung as crown prince treated his brothers in a very friendly manner. Source: *T'ang shu; Hsin T'ang shu.*[60]

3. *Tuan-pen.*[cw] Make the Basis Proper.

a. "Let the one man be greatly good, and the myriad regions will be rectified by him." Source: *Shu ching, T'ai-chia* (a spurious chapter).[61]

b. Hsü Ching-tsung[cx] (592–672), the teacher of the T'ang prince of Yen, Li Chung,[cy] said: "If the basis is correct all affairs will be in order. The crown prince is the basis for the state." Source: *Hsin T'ang shu.*[62]

c. The teacher of Wei Yüan-chung,[cz] Yüan Ch'u-k'o[da] said: "If one wants to make the state safe, one must first make the basis proper. If this is done, the empire will be stable. The rise and fall of the state depend on this." Source: *Hsin T'ang shu.*[63]

4. *Chin-hsüeh.*[db] Advance Learning.

a. Learning is necessary for a ruler. Source: *Shu ching, Yüeh-ming* (a spurious chapter).[64]

b. On Erudite Scholar Huan Jung[dc] and his excellence as a tutor of the crown prince, the future Han emperor Hsien-tsung (Ming Ti, r. 57–75). Source: *Hou-Han shu.*[65]

5. *Tse-shu.*[dd] Selection of Methods.

Yü Liang[de] (289–340) under Chin Yüan Ti (r. 317–323) warns the crown prince (the future emperor Ming Ti, r. 323–325) against the extreme methods of government of Shen and Han, i.e., Shen Pu-hai and Han Fei Tzu, the legalist authors par excellence. Source: *Chin shu.*[66]

6. *Ch'in-hsi.*[df] Attention to Studies.

a. Han Ching Ti (r. 157–141 B.C.) paid great attention to the studies of the crown prince, future emperor Wu, who was an attentive and assiduous pupil and did not share the predilection of the Empress Dowager *née* Tou for Taoism. Source: *Han shu.*[67]

   b. The eulogy for emperor Yüan of Han (r. 48–33 B.C.) praises the
      literary and artistic pursuits of the emperor. Source: *Han shu*.[68]

7. *T'ing-cheng*.[dg] Participation in Government.
      On the activities of the emperor T'ai-wu (r. 424–452) of the Yüan-
      Wei (Toba) when he was crown prince and the good advice given
      by Ts'ui Hao[dh] (d. 450). Source: *Wei shu*.[69]

8. *Ta-ts'ung*[di] Perfecting Intelligence.
      T'ang T'ai-tsung asked Wei Cheng[dj] (580–643) about the proper
      way of a ruler. Source: *Chen-kuan cheng-yao*.[70]

9. *Fu-Chün*.[dk] Handling the Army.
   a. On a crown prince of the state of Chin during the Spring and
      Autumn period who led the army into battle. Source: *Tso chuan*.[71]
   b. In 196 B.C. Han Kao-tsu (r. 202–195 B.C.) gave his crown prince
      a military command. Source: *Han shu*.[72]
   c. The military valor of T'ang Shun-tsung (r. 805) as a crown prince
      during the flight of emperor Te-tsung. Source: *Hsin T'ang shu*.[73]

10. *Ming-fen*.[dl] Understanding Status.
      For a full translation, see below.

11. *Ch'ung-ju*.[dm] Honoring Confucians.
   a. When Han Ming Ti was a crown prince he treated his teacher
      Huan Jung very well. Source: a patchwork, chiefly from *Hou-
      Han shu*.[74]
   b. T'ang Hsüan-tsung as crown prince personally performed liba-
      tions in the imperial college in the first year of T'ai-chi (711).
      Ch'u Wu-liang[dn] (645–719) explained to him the *Hsiao ching*
      and the *Li chi*. He and other scholars were amply rewarded.
      Source: *T'ang shu; Hsin T'ang shu*.[75]
   c. As a crown prince Shun-tsung of T'ang always bowed first to his
      teacher. Source: *Hsin T'ang shu*.[76]

12. *Ch'in-hsien*.[do] Befriend the Virtuous.
   a. The episode of the Four Old Men (*ssu-hao*[dp]) who dissuaded Han
      Kao-tsu from appointing somebody else as heir apparent.
      Source: *Shih chi*.[77]
   b. The way of T'ang T'ai-tsung in associating with worthy people.
      Source: Yüan Chen (779–831), *Chiao-pen shu*.[dq][78]

13. *Ch'ü-hsieh*.[dr] Eliminating Evil.
      For a full translation, see below.

14. *Na-hui*.[ds] Accept Criticism.
      Emperor Ming Ti of the Chin Dynasty had as his tutor Wen

Ch'iao[dt] (288–329) who enjoyed great favors and could even criticize the prince. Source: *Chin shu*.[79] Wen Ch'iao also presented a memorial warning against favoritism, the "Shih-ch'en chien."[du 80]

15. *Chi-chien*.[dv] Gentle Remonstrations.

The term *chi-chien* is taken from *Lun-yü* IV, 18. "In serving his parents, a son may remonstrate with them, but gently."[81]

a. Emperor Kuang-wu of the Eastern Han (r. 25–57) held audiences from morning to night and went to bed at midnight. He also had scholars explain the classics to him. His crown prince thought he overworked himself and asked him to take more care of himself. The emperor replied that all this did not tire him. Source: *Hou-Han shu*.[82]

b. T'ang Shun-tsung as crown prince could persuade his father not to employ P'ei Yen-ling[dw] (d.796) and Wei Ch'ü-mou.[dx] Source: *Hsin T'ang shu*.[83]

16. *Ts'ung-chien*.[dy] Follow Admonitions.

a. An adult crown prince should follow the instructions of his tutor. Source: Chia I (201–169 B.C.), *Hsin-shu*.[dz 84]

b. Chin Ming Ti as crown prince heeded Wen Ch'iao who criticized him for an extravagant building project. Source: *Chin shu*.[85]

17. *T'ui-en*.[ea] Share Kindness.

a. The story about the frightened sacrificial bull to be exchanged for a sheep and about kindness to people. Source: *Meng Tzu*.[86]

b. Several examples showing the kindheartedness of prince Hsiao T'ung[eb] of the Liang dynasty (501–531). Source: *Liang shu* and *Nan shih*.[87]

18. *Shang-chien*.[ec] Esteem Frugality.

a. Anecdotes showing the frugality of Hsiao T'ung. Source: *Liang shu* and *Nan shih*.[88]

b. T'ang T'ai-tsung composed the *Ti fan* and gave a copy of the chapter on frugality to his crown prince. A summary of the text is given. Source: *Ti fan*.[89]

19. *Chieh-i*.[ed] Abstain from Idleness.

a. "Do not be arrogant like Chu of Tan; negligence and pleasure, only these he loved." Source: *Shu ching*.[90]

b. "Oh what the noble man aims at is to have no pleasurable ease," with expatiations on this subject. Source: *Shu ching*.[91]

20. *Shen-kuan*.[ee] Investigate Officials.

Shen-kuan is also the title of a paragraph in the *Ti fan*. The necessity of appointing the right kind of tutor for a crown prince and to treat him with great respect and honor. Source: Yüan Chen, *Chiao-pen shu.* [92]

Already this brief survey of anecdotes and quotations shows the moralistic approach of Wang Yün, and also his preoccupation with ritual and ceremonial. At the same time he has made use of historical, or pseudohistorical, subject matter. Historical figures are used as examples, instead of just showering maxims on Chen-chin. One cannot help feeling some sympathy for Chen-chin, who was throughout his life flooded with Lamaist treatises and sanctified as Prince Bodhisattva by the Sa-skya-pa lamas. He was, from that side, expected to become a second Aśoka, and now here was Wang Yün, a Chinese Hanlin scholar, piously hoping he might develop into a second exemplary emperor of China like all those heir apparents from whose lives Wang had selected colorful anecdotes. Altogether Wang Yün compiled 40 examples. Of these, 9 are taken from the Confucian classics and 5 from authors or works of the Han and T'ang (2 Han, 3 T'ang). Most are, however, taken from histories, 26 altogether. Of these, 10 are from T'ang history, 9 from the two Han dynasties, the rest from the period of the Northern and Southern dynasties. There is a heavy emphasis on the T'ang, the last dynasty which had imperial splendor as a world power. If we were to label the ideology of Wang Yün's work we could perhaps call it a moderate version of practical Confucianism, devoid of any metaphysical implications.

It is of some interest which authors or works are expressly quoted by Wang Yün in his personal comments to the 20 paragraphs. There are 8 quotations, 5 of which are taken from the Confucian classics, and one each from Yang Hsiung's (53 B.C.–A.D. 18) *Yang-tzu fa-yen*[ef93] and Chia I's *Hsin-shu.* In addition, Ssu-ma Kuang (1019–1086) is quoted once (see the full translation of No. 13 below). But Wang Yün's comments are not only historical. He frequently alludes to government actions taken by Khubilai Khaghan or even the crown prince himself. In his comment to No. 4 he says Chen-chin had once summoned Confucian scholars to explain to him the classics and histories and he refers to the fact that in 1260 Chen-chin allowed scholars to make proposals for good government. [94] And in No. 9 on military actions, Wang Yün mentions that Chen-chin has directed the Bureau of Military Affairs (*shu-mi yüan*) as

ordered by the emperor. In his comment to No. 17, "Share Kindness,"
Wang praises the emperor for reducing the military and corvée services
and increasing relief for the population in Shantung which had suffered
from natural disasters.[95] Another comment seems to be a little exaggerated, however. When speaking of frugality (No. 18), Wang Yün says of
Kubilai Khaghan that "after he ascended the throne, he looked into the
ancient ways and practiced frugality. For example, he forbade alcoholic
drinks, had coarse silk manufactured, and did away with parasols inlaid
with gold. Thus he showed that simplicity was his main concern" (CW
79:7b). It is somewhat surprising to learn that anti-alcoholism should
have been practiced at Khubilai's court. In addition to these references
to contemporary events Wang Yün also adverts to what was for him recent history. When explaining paragraph No. 20, on officals, he reminds
the crown prince that under the Chin dynasty officials serving the heir
apparent got preferential treatment—a not very subtle self-advertise-
ment.[96] The analysis of the text therefore shows that Wang Yün tried to
set forth historical anecdotes which had practical applications, either already carried out by Khubilai or expected from his heir apparent.

We have seen above from Wang Yün's account of his encounter
with Chen-chin which paragraphs chiefly attracted the heir apparent's
curiosity, namely the chapters on "Understanding Status" and on "Eliminating Evil." It seems therefore appropriate to give below a full translation of these two paragraphs. A translation will also show the mode of
argumentation adopted by Wang Yün in his personal comment, which
follows the quotations from the sources.

10. *Ming-fen.* Understanding Status.
   In the annals of Emperor Ch'eng [r. 33–7 B.C.] of the Western Han, it is
said: "When the emperor was a crown prince, he was broad-minded and generous, circumspect and attentive. Previously, when he lived in the Kuei Palace,
the emperor [i.e., Yüan Ti] once summoned the crown prince to come in haste.
He went out of the Lung-lou Gate to his palace, but did not dare to cross the
imperial pathway. The emperor said that he had noticed his diffidence, and asked
the reason for it. The crown prince replied by explaining the circumstances, and
the emperor was greatly pleased. Thereupon he issued an ordinance, ordering
that a crown prince should be allowed to cross the imperial pathway."[97]
   In the annals of T'ang Su-tsung [r. 756–762], it is said: "When he was first
appointed as crown prince, the office-holders carried out the investiture ceremony. The ceremonial had the solemnity of the central [imperial] palace and the
distinctions proper for outside the palace. Their clothes were of red gauze. The

crown prince said: 'This is the ritual for the Son of Heaven!' and then ordered the high officials to deliberate. Hsiao Sung[eg] and others petitioned to change the outer distinctions and to replace the red gauze clothes prepared for them outside [the palace] with summer garments. This was followed."[98]

Your servant Yün comments: "Great indeed is the necessity for clarifying names and statuses. What does 'name' mean? This refers to [the relation] of ruler above and servant below. If even once they are not correct, what is there to stop something regrettable from developing? Moreover, there will be the mistake of nonconformity between actions and speech. This applies in particular to the rectification of names and the status of a crown prince. If the whole empire knows clearly that the heir apparent has the virtue of honoring the ruler and treating the servant as inferior; then in future, when he comes to handle the myriad territories, how could there be any interference with names, violations of status, or irreverent actions and speech? Thus [Emperor] Ch'eng of Han who left by the Lou-lou Gate and did not dare to cross the imperial pathway, or Su-tsung who had red gauze changed for summer garments, can indeed be taken as models for later rulers."

13. *Ch'ü-hsieh.* Eliminating Evil.

Hsing Ch'ih served the Ch'i [dynasty of] Kao as Erudite Scholar of the Four Gates [*ssu-men po-shih*][eh] and taught the classics to the imperial crown prince. When the kitchen steward brought in vegetables which included Evil Artemisia [*hsieh-hao*],[ei] Ch'ih ordered him to take it away and said: "This vegetable has an improper name and is not fit to be eaten by Your Highness." When [Emperor] Wen-hsüan [r. 550–559] heard this, he praised Ch'ih and presented him with a blanket, cushion, and fine silk.[99]

Chia I, [*Hsin*]-*shu* says: "Wen-wang of Chou ordered T'ai-kung Wang[ej] to be tutor of the crown prince. Once [the prince] was keen on having dried fish [*pao-yü*,[ek] abalone?], but T'ai-kung would not give it to him and said: 'It is ritual that *pao*-fish should not be allowed on dishes. How is it possible that one could feed the crown prince with something that is not in accord with ritual?' "[100]

Your servant Yün comments: "To judge from these two cases the nourishment might be trivial but the men of antiquity when bringing up a crown prince eliminated [such food] and did not serve it. Such was their strictness. How much more does this apply to having relationships with crooked and improper persons: Therefore, Ssu-ma Kuang has said: 'In the education of a crown prince, even the menial servants in the retinue over the years must be scholars of filial obedience, brotherly love, and moral principles.'[101] This is indeed excellent!"

The early death of Chen-chin in January 1286 prevented Wang Yün, like all his contemporaries, from finding out what profit the contact with Chinese civilization had brought to the heir of Khubilai Khaghan. A new chance for Wang to propagate his ideas on how to rule the state came when the new ruler Temür (Ch'eng-tsung, r. 1294–1307), the third son of Chen-chin, ascended the throne. Immediately after Temür's accession

Wang Yün presented to the emperor his *Yüan-chen Shou-ch'eng shih-chien*. This title could be translated as *Mirror of Actions for Preserving the Achievements in the Yüan-chen Era*.[102] As pointed out earlier, it now forms *ch*. 6 of the *Ch'eng-hua shih-lüeh*, although originally the two works had nothing to do with each other, being separated by more than 13 years. It consists of 15 actions (*shih*)[el] expected from a model ruler.[103] Wang Yün's introduction mentions the favors which he has received from the late emperor, including the interview with him, and hopes that he can repay his moral debt by compiling this work. We shall give here a summary of the contents.

1. *Ching-t'ien*.[em] Revere Heaven.

    Government actions must conform to the principles of Heaven. Wang refers to historical rulers who did this in an exemplary way: the King of Yin Wu-ting, Wen, and the Duke of Chou. He quotes from a *Commentary* (*chuan*[en]): "Men are aroused by actions and not by words; one answers Heaven with solidity and not with ornaments (*wen*)."[eo][104]

2. *Fa-tsu*.[ep] Take Ancestors as Models.

    The state was never before as big as now and never was there a ruler as holy as Shih-tsu (Khubilai). Temür should continue his exemplary actions and statutes, as King Wu followed Wen of Chou, and Han Wen Ti followed Kao-tsu. The *Shu ching* says: "Survey the perfect pattern of the former king so may you forever be preserved from error."[105]

3. *Ai-min*.[eq] Love the People.

    Heaven in his benevolence (*jen*) produces the myriad beings and the ruler governs them as the viceroy of Heaven. His priorities should be benevolence and love. Shih-tsu (Khubilai) completed the conquest of All-under-Heaven which T'ai-tsu (Chinggis Khan, 1167–1227) had begun. Now the emperor should act like the kings Ch'eng and K'ang of Chou to stabilize the empire, or like emperors Wen and Ching of the Han. Love can be realized by letting the army rest, decreasing punishments and reducing taxes. No war in distant countries should be undertaken. The people should be treated so that they will not commit crimes. Be militarily prepared but be lenient with those who live afar. Practice frugality and economy, and reduce expenditure. The poor people in Chiang-nan (i.e., South of the

Yangtze) live at a great distance from the court. They could easily make trouble and should be treated by the officials with love, then there will be no disturbances. Think of the old saying "Ten sheep and nine shepherds" as a warning.[106]

4. *Hsü-ping.*[er] Care for the Soldiers.

The soldiers and the people are the two great fundaments of the state. Much has been done for the people, and similar actions should be taken with regard to the army, including care for the veterans. Conscription should be reformed, and the legislation of 1271 be reintroduced.[107] Military policies should be flexible and adapted to the current situation.

5. *Shou-ch'eng.*[es] Preservation of Achievements.

Preservation of achievements is tantamount to holding a full vessel (*ch'ih-ying*[et]): One must be careful [not to spill it]. This can be achieved by honoring ancestors, treating officials according to the rites, avoiding war, loving the people, paying attention to officials, and reducing expenditure. A conversation to that effect between Wei Cheng and T'ang T'ai-tsung is quoted,[108] and also Ssu-ma Kuang: "A man who owns a property of ten pieces of gold still bears in mind that it has taken previous generations hard work to achieve this. Thus he diligently preserves and fears losing it."[109] This applies also to the empire. In politics the civilian virtues (*wen-te*)[eu] and a yielding approach (*jou-tao*)[ev] are important, and so are the implementation through benevolence and righteousness, rites and music.

6. *Ch'ing-hsin.*[ew] Purify the Mind.

All good comes from the mind. Therefore rulers of old could maintain equilibrium. Good balance and impartiality come from a purified mind.

7. *Ch'in-cheng.*[ex] Diligence in Government.

The ruler should govern continuously like Heaven which produces the four seasons. Reference to the Great Yü who toiled incessantly. Also T'ang T'ai-tsung had the spirit of antiquity. He should be the model. The ruler must listen to memorials and attend audiences. It is most important to regulate the audiences, as has been done for the congratulatory audiences which already have a fixed ceremonial.

8. *Shang-chien.*[ey] Esteem Frugality.

When superiors practice economy and restraint, inferiors will have plenty. If superiors are wasteful and extravagant, inferiors will be exhausted and in distress. Your predecessor preferred simple textiles, did away with gold, and had unadorned saddles, shoes, and garments. He also issued regulations for marriages. Now things are different because officials and commoners dress like nobles, and marry with greater sumptuosity than dukes and ministers. Under the Han emperors Wen and Ching the empire was peaceful and the customs were good. Today the income of the state is plentiful. Nevertheless, the policy should be to reduce military actions and cut down expenditures, and adapt spending to revenues. Emperor Chin Shih-tsung (r. 1161–1189) can be taken as a model. Once somebody came and petitioned because he had not been given presents. The Chin emperor said: "You all should know that the riches in the treasury are really those of the people. I am only their manager. How could I dare to spend them recklessly?"[110]

9. *Chin-ling.*[ez] Be Careful with Ordinances.

Ordinances proclaim virtues and warnings. They should take Heaven as a model and conform to the people. They should be issued with care; once Heaven has thundered it cannot be concealed anymore. The *Shu ching* is quoted to this effect, and also T'ang T'ai-tsung: "When issuing commands they should be considered as eternal models and not issued lightheartedly."[111] It is important that the ruler and his government remain credible in the eyes of the people. Precedents should be changed only after due deliberation.

10. *Li-fa.*[fa] Establish Laws.

Laws are a tool of orderly government and therefore indispensable. Now our state has existed for over 60 years and yet does not have fixed laws. At the court law is handled by the emperor, in the provinces by the legal-officials (*fa-li*).[fb] We have officials but no laws for them to apply. This is like a physician who has no medicine. Therefore, decisions are biased and without discrimination or balance. Take the statutes and ordinances of former dynasties and proclaim them as "New Laws of the First Year" (*yüan-nien hsin-fa*).[fc] [112]

11. *Chung t'ai-chien.*[fd] Respect the Censorate's Criticism.

Censors are the eyes and ears of the Son of Heaven. When they are sharp, nothing remains hidden. They are important for the guidelines of the court. Criticism is sometimes disliked. This became clear when recently some persons wished to conceal their crimes.

There should be no groundless accusations. Take Yü-tsung (Chen-chin) as a model who always investigated properly.[113]

12. *Hsüan-shih.*[fe] Selection of Scholars.

Khubilai Khaghan had, both as heir apparent and as emperor, continuously summoned worthy men to his court, and found a great number of them. Formerly there existed examinations with fixed rules, which was a good policy. The recent decrees on local recommendations (*kung-chü*)[ff] were a good start. Through regularized examinations the state can obtain genuine talents. Both Khubilai Khaghan and Chen-chin had such ideas but did not put them into effect. The new emperor should carry out what they had in mind. This will be the basis for preserving the achievements.

13. *Shen ming-chüeh.*[fg] Be Careful with Titles and Ranks.

According to the *Shu ching* a ruler should not confer ranks just for private reasons, but only to the virtuous and capable. If ranks are given indiscriminately they will attract only inferior people. Rules should be introduced. One should by no means take as a model the policies of the late Chin dynasty after the transfer to the south (1215). The good models are the Han and T'ang; achievements and labors were rewarded by ranks, capability and virtue by offices. Never should the office of minister be used as a means for rewarding past merits. We must have clear regulations for all this.

14. *Ming shang-fa.*[fh] Clarify Rewards and Punishments.

Rewards and punishments are a great instrument of government. They must be regularized. This can only be done when properly appointed officials exist. In antiquity people were selected because of the special nature of the office, but later offices were created because of people. This resulted in too many officials. Therefore T'ang T'ai-tsung in the first year of Chen-kuan (627) regulated the civil and military offices, eliminated the useless and appointed the virtuous. Also Chin Shih-tsung after his accession to the throne concentrated on this problem. He clarified promotions and demotions, and introduced the classification into three grades of provincial officials. For the court, one should imitate T'ang T'ai-tsung, for the provinces, Chin Shih-tsung.[114]

15. *Yüan-lü.*[fi] Think of the Distant Future.

Your majesty has inherited a prosperous empire and therefore should have no worries. But an enlightened ruler should also pay attention to seemingly insignificant details which may contain the germ for future developments. Trouble may come from small things which have been neglected. The main concerns for the future should be (1) guard the frontiers, improve the horse administration, feed the soldiers, and store for the future. Pacify the recently annexed regions by appointing good officials, and there will be no robbers. (2) Prepare against natural disasters. Improve water-control and store provisions. (3) Make the customs sincere. Encourage learning and skills, honor the filial and honest, virtuous and right people. Attack extravagance and forbid waste. (4) Purify officials and clerks. Promote the honest and able, throw out the petitioners, forbid clerks to engage in trade, eliminate the greedy. When all this is observed there will be no need to worry. "Make far-reaching your plans and intentions."[115] "Thus the superior man takes thought of misfortune and arms himself against it in advance."[116] You should not rely on the present peaceful conditions but see that peace will be preserved in the future. I think this was also the intention of your imperial ancestor." "I have heard that among the thousand ideas of a wise man there must be one error and that among the thousand ideas of a fool there must be one inspiration. Hence it is said that the sages chose even from the sayings of a madman."[117] This may apply also to my words, but they are certainly sincere.

This ends our summary of the *Yüan-chen Shou-ch'eng shih-chien*. It was intended as a guide for the new ruler and voices the concern of a Chinese scholar with a strong predilection for history and historical precedents. At the same time we can see what Wang Yün considered to be the greatest problems of the empire that Khubilai Khaghan had left to his successor: a lack of procedural guidelines and of regularized rules for the state, chiefly in recruiting officials. It is obvious that Wang Yün's proposals are of a pragmatic nature throughout, and one may even feel that the quotations from or allusions to the Confucian classics are merely ornamental. This distinguishes the *Mirror* from the *Ch'eng-hua shih-lüeh*, which is mainly educational and moralistic. Here we can see not only the great role of T'ang T'ai-tsung as an exemplary emperor,[118] but also to what degree the Jurchen emperor Chin Shih-tsung was regarded as a model. Shih-tsung had lived well over 100 years back in time from 1295 and was thus sufficiently far removed to become idealized. The remnants

of the Chin state had been annexed by the Mongols in 1234, which again
was over half a century before, but the extinction of the Sung was perhaps too recent to allow an author like Wang Yün to select his examples
from Sung history. Here again we have a case of continuity from T'ang
to Chin and Yüan, bypassing the Sung dynasty. The funeral text for
Wang Yün says of the *Mirror* that it was based on classical scriptures and
that it had the spirit of Wei Wen-chen⁶ and Ssu-ma Tuan-ming.ᶠᵏ ¹¹⁹
Wei Wen-chen is Wei Cheng, who had been canonized as Wen-chen,
so that Wang Yün is thereby compared with this famous statesman of the
T'ang. Ssu-ma Tuan-ming is Ssu-ma Kuang, who was indeed a Sung
scholar. His fame in the early Yüan, however, seems to rest chiefly on
the *Tzu-chih t'ung-chien*, a work which had been partly translated into
Mongolian under the Yüan. He was praised as an historian, but not as a
statesman or a thinker.

It is not easy to define the place of Wang Yün in early Yüan intellectual history. We have seen that perhaps much of his pragmatic and
practice-oriented approach can be attributed to his education in a family
where service as a clerk had almost been hereditary. But it is clear that
he also belonged to the intellectuality of the Chin dynasty literati. Persons like Yüan Hao-wen and many others had concentrated on literary
pursuits because literature and the arts had come to be regarded as an
integral part of the Confucian way. In Wang Yün's case we can also
distinguish a complementary element, namely, that service in official
functions embodied a commitment to cultural values. In all this Wang
Yün follows the tradition of the Chin literati. This applies also to Wang's
insistence on T'ang models for statecraft, a tradition which he certainly
inherited from the Chin intellectuals.

In Chin times, too, we find a tendency to praise the T'ang at the
expense of Sung. This tendency found its expression during the discussions over which "agent" or "power" should be associated with Chin in
the later reigns of the dynasty. Some discussants proposed that the Chin
should adopt the agent Metal in cosmological succession to the agent
Earth of the T'ang, thus building up the Chin state as a legitimate successor to T'ang, bypassing the Sung. This extreme anti-Sung theory was,
however, discarded and eventually the agent Earth was assigned to the
Chin dynasty. The adoption of Earth by Emperor Chang-tsung (r. 1189–
1208) in November 1202, succeeding the Sung whose agent had been
Fire, amounted to a recognition of Sung as a legitimate dynasty, but it

was an overt political move designed to enhance the Chin against the
Southern Sung, which still claimed legitimacy as continuation of the
Sung house.[120] Nevertheless, pro-T'ang sentiments and nostalgic remi-
niscences still played an important role in Chin thought. The statecraft
of Sung was considered inferior, and under the Chin as well as the early
Yüan, although some references had been made to Sung authors like
Ou-yang Hsiu (1007–1072), Ssu-ma Kuang, the Ch'eng brothers (Ch'eng
Hao, 1032–1085 and Ch'eng I, 1033–1107), Su Shih (1036–1101) and
Chu Hsi, they are quoted as classicists, historians, and belle letterists, not
as statesmen, and their philosophy received only passing attention.[121]
The fact that the Hsin T'ang shu was translated into Jurchen must also
be seen in this context.

A perusal of the works of some eminent Chin authors shows indeed
that Wang Yün's works on statecraft and princely education must be seen
as a continuation of tendencies prevalent among Chin writers. Already
Wang Jo-hsü[fl] (1174–1243) had given the T'ang a prominent place in
his historical essay on the duties of a ruler.[122] He devotes not less than
ten examples to the T'ang in this work. A more pronounced emphasis
on T'ang models can be found in the works of Chao Ping-wen[fm] (1159–
1232). He composed a digest of the Chen-kuan cheng-yao for the Chin
emperor under the title Chen-kuan cheng-yao shen-chien.[fn] The work itself is lost but the preface is preserved. There Chao praises the early
reigns of T'ang. In his opinion T'ai-tsung was the most enlightened ruler
in later history.[123] Also in his essay on the T'ang, Chao Ping-wen considers the reign of T'ai-tsung as the culmination of the ideas of antiquity,
and attributes the later decay of the T'ang to a neglect of the original
foundations laid by T'ai-tsung.[124] Another effort of Chao Ping-wen to
present the Chin court with an educational book was his treatise, Essence
of Government for Ruler and Servant (Chün-ch'en cheng-yao),[fo] which he
wrote in collaboration with Yang Yün-i[fp] (1170–1228). This was a book
on statecraft arranged according to topics.[125] Although the book itself is
no longer extant, the title is modelled after that of the Chen-kuan cheng-
yao and hence suggests a conscious imitation of the T'ang work on the
art of government. Chao's leading disciple Yüan Hao-wen also wrote a
similar handbook, the Concise Mirror for Emperors and Kings (Ti-wang
ching-lüeh), which is known only through the preface Wang Yün wrote
in 1267 for a printed edition.[126] It was a florilegium covering several
thousand years of history, consisting of condensed four-character maxims

arranged according to rhymes, and serving as an introduction to a deeper understanding of the Confucian exemplary rulers.

The examples given here will suffice to show the extent to which scholars of the Chin tried to preserve T'ang ideas of statecraft and how much Wang Yün must be seen as continuing this tradition. Both he and the Chin scholars found themselves in the same position: they wished to improve and educate the alien rulers by putting before them time-honored Chinese traditions which they thought would be appreciated and perhaps put into practice. But a more direct influence of T'ang political ideas on Wang Yün can be seen in his conscious imitation of the *Examples of the Emperor (Ti fan)*, which are attributed to T'ang T'ai-tsung himself. In its extant versions the book has four chapters and is subdivided into twelve subchapters, each with a two-character title, a formal arrangement which Wang Yün also adopted for his *Ch'eng-hua shih-lüeh* and *Yüan-chen Shou-ch'eng shih-chien*. Such subchapter headings are "Searching for the Virtuous" (*ch'iu-hsien*), "Investigate Officials" (*shen-kuan*), "Accept Admonitions" (*na-chien*), and "Esteem Frugality" (*ch'ung-chien*) (*Ti fan, ch.* 1, no. 2; *ch.* 2, nos. 4, 5; *ch.* 3, no. 8). These occur also in Wang Yün's two works as titles of chapters. There can be no doubt that Wang's aim was to produce a second *Ti fan*, and it is significant that both Wang's treatises and the *Ti fan* were translated into Mongolian. Another point of resemblance is that the *Ti fan* was written in A.D. 648 for the heir apparent who later became Emperor Kao-tsung (r. 650–694) of the T'ang. All this indicates Wang's strong preoccupation with T'ang models of statecraft. His own works show the same mixture of generalized exhortation and historical examples as the *Ti fan*. T'ang T'ai-tsung's work suffered some eclipse under the Sung and it seems that some parts of the original text were lost during that period, although it is listed in Sung bibliographies.[127] Another work of the T'ang which can be seen as a companion of the *Ti fan* was the *Ch'en kuei*,[fq] (*Rules for the Subject*,) attributed to Empress Wu Tse-t'ien (r. 684–705). This book, however, remained unknown to Wang Yün and his contemporaries, probably because it was lost already under the Southern Sung and survived only in Japan.[128]

The high praise T'ang T'ai-tsung received as an exemplary emperor was, of course, not an invention or innovation of the Chin and early Yüan periods. We can find it under the Northern Sung, for example, in the works of Ou-yang Hsiu, who also saw in T'ai-tsung a ruler of the same excellence as that of the legendary emperors of antiquity. The important contribution of thinkers like Ou-yang Hsiu and Ssu-ma Kuang was perhaps their insistence that not only the Confucian classics could serve as the basis for political thought and statecraft, but the histories as well.[129] It is equally significant that under the early reigns of the Chin dynasty, the Northern Sung intellectuals belonging to the "conservative" faction in the eleventh century enjoyed high prestige at the expense of the "reformist" school of Wang An-shih and his followers, which was held responsible for the collapse of the Northern Sung.[130] In this respect, Wang Yün must also be seen as belonging to the traditionalists of the Chin and early Yüan for whom the Northern Sung achievements in many fields remained a model, whereas artistic and intellectual developments under the Southern Sung had not yet made a deep impact.[131]

In closing, a few words should be said on the *Huang-t'u ta-hsün* which, as we have noted above, also was translated into Mongolian and even printed. This work contained the edicts and admonitions of the early Yüan emperors, and this was also the case for the *Shih-tsu sheng-hsün*, the "Holy Injunctions" of Khubilai Khaghan, a work of which a manuscript Mongolian translation existed after 1326.[132] Wang Yün had after Khubilai's death compiled not only the *Veritable Records* of his reign but also the *Sheng-hsün* in 6 *chüan*. It seems to be almost certain that the scholars who, a generation later, in 1325 and 1326, compiled a book of admonitions, followed the earlier work of Wang Yün, a copy of which would have been preserved in the Hanlin Academy or the Office of Historiography. If this assumption is correct, Wang Yün would come into play three times in the process of translating Chinese non-Buddhist texts into Mongolian: as author of the *Ch'eng-hua shih-lüeh* and the *Yüan-chen Shou-ch'eng shih-chien*, and as compiler of Khubilai's fundamental edicts.

Wang Yün did not live to see this eventual though limited success of his endeavors. He would certainly have been proud to see at last some result of his lifelong work, even if he had not become a second Wei Cheng, trusted minister of state under a powerful ruler. His intellectual approach must be called conservative and pragmatic, but this was just what the empire needed in his eyes and what seems to be a feature common to the Tung-p'ing school. He was no intellectual innovator, and certainly did not see himself as such. During his life he had witnessed the all too slow and gradual transformation of the Mongol state from a primitive exploitative phase into a more regularized and stable common-wealth. He looked back to the empires of Han and T'ang, which had both lasted for several centuries, and sought his inspiration from them in his attempt to transmit to the Mongol rulers the elements which he believed were responsible for the long duration and stability of these dynasties. He believed that daring innovation was not what the world needed, but a return to trusted and proven values.

APPENDIX: WANG YÜN'S FAMILY

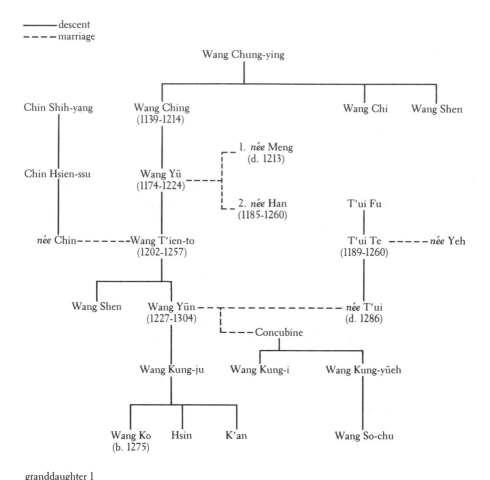

———— descent
– – – – marriage

granddaughter 1
m. Yeh-lü K'ai

granddaughter 2
m. Ning

great-grandsons: Han-chang, Te-chang, Jun-chang
two great-granddaughters

The names of two of the grandchildren of Wang T'ien-to are given as Chen-sun[hn] and I-sun,[ho] and of one great-grandchild as Chien-lang[hp] (CW, 49:10a-10b). Chien-lang is the childhood name of Wang Ko (CW, 46:12b-13a). Chen-sun and I-sun could perhaps be the alternative names of sons of Wang Yün and Wang Shen.

NOTES

1. There is an 1892 edition of this work. It contains 4 *chüan* and includes one hundred Yüan Confucians.
2. See *Sung-Yüan hsüeh-an pu-i* (*Ssu-ming ts'ung-shu* ed., 1932), 78:40a–42a. Wang P'an has a biography in YS (PN ed.), 160:1a. For Wang Yün's biographies, see notes 14, 15 below.
3. Walter Fuchs, "Analecta zur mongolischen Übersetzungsliteratur der Yüan-Zeit," *Monumenta Serica* (1946), 11 (1):33–64. See also Herbert Franke, "Chinese Historiography under Mongol Rule," *Mongolian Studies: Journal of the Mongolian Society* (1974), 1:15–26.
4. YS, 143:3a. See also Fuchs, "Analecta," 52.
5. Walter Fuchs/Antoine Mosteart, "Ein Ming-Druck einer chinesisch-mongolischen Ausgabe des Hsiao-ching," *Monumenta Serica* (1939–1940), 4:326. The Mongolian text has been romanized by Louis Ligeti, *Monumenta Linguae Mongolicae Collecta Monuments Préclassiques* (Budapest: Akadémiai Kiadó, 1972), pp. 76–104.
6. N. Ts. Munkuev, "Two Mongolian Printed Fragments from Khara-Khoto," in Louis Ligeti ed., *Mongolian Studies* (Budapest: Akadémiai Kiadó, 1970), pp. 341–57.
7. Maurice Courant, *Bibliographie Coréenne* (Paris: Ernest Leroux, 1894), vol. 1, pp. 93ff.
8. Ogura Shimpei, *Chōsengo gakushi*[fr], 2d ed. (Tokyo: Tōkōshoin, 1940); Hiu Lie, *Die Mandschu-Sprachkunde in Korea* (Bloomington: Indiana University Press, 1972), pp. 22–30.
9. Herbert Franke, review of Hiu Lie, in *Zeitschrift der Deutschen Morgenländischen Gesellschaft* (ZDMG) (1975), pp. 125, 464. Maurice Courant misinterpreted the title of this book as "Le miroir de la défense de la ville," reading the character *ch'eng* for *ch'eng* ("ville" = "town"). See *Bibliographie Coréenne* vol. 1, p. 93.
10. Hiu Lie, *Mandschu-Sprachkunde*, p. 26.
11. Yü Chi, *Tao-yüan hsüeh-ku lu*[fs] (SPTK ed.), 22:6b–7b; see also Fuchs, "Analecta," pp. 51–52.
12. Franke, "Chinese Historiography," p. 23.
13. Hiu Lie, *Mandschu-Sprachkunde*, p. 29; Herbert Franke in ZDMG (1975), pp. 125, 464.
14. The SPTK edition of Wang Yün's collected works is used throughout this paper. It is a facsimile reproduction of a Ming edition printed in 1498. A copy of the original Yüan edition printed in the early fourteenth century in Chia-hsing is preserved in the National Central Library in Taipei: *Kuo-li chung-yang t'u-shu kuan shan-pen shu-mu*,[ft] rev. ed. (Taipei: National Central Library, 1967), p. 479. A very useful topical index to the SPTK edition has been compiled by Wang Te-i and P'an Po-ch'eng[fu] in the journal *Shih-*

yüan[fv] (1976), 1:145–216. I wish to thank Mr. Wang for presenting me with a copy of this index. In addition to the funeral text on Wang Yün in CW, *fu-lu*, 11a–18a, the following texts written by Wang Yün on his family should be mentioned: a detailed family history (CW, 49:4a–10b), the tomb inscriptions for his father (CW, 49:13a–16b) and his great grandfather (CW, 59:8b–10a), the funeral texts for his mother (CW, 49:17b–19a) and his father-in-law (CW, 59:10a–12a). For a detailed bibliographical note on Wang Yün's collected works, see Sun K'o-kuan, *Yüan-tai Han wen-hua chih huo-tung*[fw] (Taipei: Chung-hua shu-chü, 1968), pp. 445–55.

15. Wang Yün's biography in YS, 167:19a–22a has been translated in Lao Yan-shuan, *The Chung-t'ang shih-chi of Wang Yün: An Annotated Translation with an Introduction* (Ph.D. diss., Harvard University, 1962), pp. 283–93. I am grateful to Professor Lao for allowing me to quote from his valuable work. Although the funeral text on Wang Yün is much more detailed, the biography in the YS is clearer and easier to consult. It also contains several passages which are not to be found in the funeral text, see Lao Yan-shuan, p. iv. For a family tree of Wang Yün see below, *Appendix* (p. 183).

16. Wan-yen E-k'o has a short biography in *Chin shih* (PN ed., hereafter abbreviated CS), 111:7a–9b.

17. CW, 42:3a–4a.

18. A list of Wang T'ien-to's friends and intellectual partners, altogether 43 persons, is given in CW, 59:5b–8b. This list includes one Buddhist monk and four Jurchen.

19. Wang Yün collected his father's works of calligraphy in 1267 together with his son Wang Kung-ju and wrote a preface; CW, 41:4a–5a.

20. On Yüan Hao-wen and Liu Ch'i, see Hok-lam Chan, *The Historiography of the Chin Dynasty: Three Studies* (Wiesbaden: Franz Steiner, 1970), pp. 67ff, 121ff. On Yang Huan, see Hok-lam Chan in *Papers on Far Eastern History* (Canberra), (September 1976), 14:37–59.

21. *Sung-Yüan hsüeh-an pu-i*, 78:40a (Wang P'an); 14:42b (Yüan Hao-wen); 90:130a (Yang Huan); 100:44a (Liu Ch'i).

22. For their biographies, see YS, 164:15a, 157:12b, 179:8b.

23. Shih T'ien-tse's biography is in YS, 155:10a–18a. For a detailed account of his career, see also Sun, *Yüan-tai Han wen-hua*, pp. 250–70.

24. CW, 48:11a–21b.

25. For Yao Shu's biography, see YS, 158:1a, and Hok-lam Chan in *Papers on Far Eastern History* (September 1980), 22:17–50. For a detailed account of the Chinese administration set up by Khubilai Khaghan since 1260, see Hok-lam Chan, "Liu Ping-chung (1216): A Buddhist-Taoist Statesman at the Court of Khubilai Khaghan," *T'oung Pao* (1967), 53 (1–3):98–146.

26. YS, 167:19b; CW, 80:6a. The office of the *hsiang-ting kuan* had originally been created under the Chin for the codification of laws and ritual (CS, 28:1b and 45:8b–9a). Also the Yüan government has an office of the same name, established formally in 1280 for the screening and handling of me-

morials which should be presented to the emperor (YS, 92:4a–4b). Wang
Yün's appointment in 1260 shows, however, that the office existed already
at this time.

27. For a fully annotated translation of this important historical source see Lao
Yan-shuan (note 15). The report on the first visit of European travellers in
Yüan China has been discussed in Herbert Franke, Review of Leonardo
Olschki, *Marco Polo's Asia*, in ZDMG (1962), 112:229–32.

28. See Wang O's biography (YS, 160:6a–8a); cf. Hok-lam Chan in *Papers on
Far Eastern History* (September 1975), 12:54–57.

29. On Wang Wen-t'ung and Li T'an, see their biographies in YS, 206:4a–7a,
1a–4a. For details of Wang's downfall and Li's rebellion, see Otagi Masao[fx]
in *Tōyō gakuhō* (1931), 6(4):1–26; Sun K'o-k'uan, in *Ta-lu tsa-chih* (October
1956), 13(8):7–15, and Hsiao Ch'i-ch'ing, *Hsi-yü jen yü Yüan-ch'u cheng-
chih[ty]* (Taipei: Faculty of Letters, National Taiwan University, 1966), pp.
56–61.

30. For a detailed discussion of the relations between Wang Yün and his patron
Wang Wen-t'ung who, as Administrator of Political Affairs, was Wang Yün's
chief, see Lao, *Chung-t'ang shih-chi*, pp. iv–viii.

31. Lu Shih-yung's biography in YS, 205:9a–16b is translated in Herbert Franke,
Geld und Wirtschaft in China unter der Mongolenherrschaft (Leipzig: Otto
Harrassowitz, 1949), pp. 60–76. This translation needs revision.

32. See YS, 15:15b; 15:19b–20b; 15:24a; 16:2b and 4a for the details of Chung's
revolt and its extinction.

33. YS, 17:5b, 172:3a.

34. The text of this memorial is preserved in CW, 35:1a–13a.

35. The address with which Wang Yün presented his compilation to the court is
in CW, 67:10b–12b.

36. YS, 19:19b.

37. See the Ch'un-lu t'ang inscription in CW, 38:5b–6b and the ceremonial text
for the completion of the building in CW, 70:16a–17a.

38. Several of Wang Yün's longer writings in his collected works have been reprinted at various times and published separately. This applies, for example,
to the miscellanea collection *Yü-t'ang chia-hua[tz]* in 8 *chüan*, which contains
much important information on Yüan history and civilization. The *Ssu-k'u
ch'üan-shu tsung-mu t'i-yao* catalog (Shanghai: Commercial Press, 1933),
vol. 3, p. 2558 devotes a separate entry to this text. It should be warned here
that the reprint of the *Yü-t'ang chia-hua* in the TSCC series is useless because the non-Chinese names and terms have been changed out of recognition through the orthographic "reforms" of the Ch'ien-lung period (1736–
1796). Also the catalog of calligraphers and paintings in the imperial Yüan
collection (mostly works that had been brought to Peking from Hangchow
after 1276) has been reprinted separately (*Mei-shu ts'ung-shu*, 3d ed. [Shang-
hai: Shen-chou kuo-kuang she, 1936], vol. 4, p. 6). This catalog, which
gives evidence of Wang Yün's artistic interests, is hidden in the *Yü-t'ang
chia-hua*, CW, 94:11b–15a and 95:1a–4b. The preface can also be found in

CW, 41:13b–14b. The anonymous Ch'ing editor of the anthology of popular short stories, *Wu-ch'ao hsiao-shuo (ta-kuan)*[ga] attributes to Wang Yün a story on supernatural events, the *P'eng-li hsiao-lung chi*,[gb] identifying him as a Sung author. It concerns the miraculous apparition of a dragon in the Po-yang Lake in 1076 during a Sung campaign against Annam. This is included in the modern edition of the anthology reprinted by Hsin-hsing shu-chü, Taipei (1960), vol. 3, p. 247. Internal evidence shows, however, that the Yüan intellectual Wang Yün cannot be the author of this story, which must therefore have been written by a Sung author of the same name. The Yüan official Wang Yün would never have referred to the Sung armies as "royal."

39. CW, 41:18b–19b, where, however, the title is given in a different form, using the archaic term *t'iao-yüan*[gc] instead of the more usual *hsiang* for "prime minister."

40. CW, 41:5a–6b.

41. CW, 44:1b–2b.

42. CW, 41:3b–4a.

43. CW, 72:13a, 15a–15b (dated 1290), 16a–16b; 70 8a–8b.

44. For Yen Shih's biography see YS, 148:16b–19a; for his sons', *ibid.*, 19a–20b. For details, see the article by Inosaki Takaoki[gd] on Chinese hereditary feudal lords in Ho-pei and Shan-tung, *Shirin* (1954), 37(6):27–48, and also Sun, *Yüan-tai Han wen-hua*, pp. 109–38.

45. See John W. Dardess, *Conquerors and Confucians: Aspects of Political Change in Late Yüan China* (New York: Columbia University Press, 1973), pp. 32–34.

46. The first study to have brought the Tung-p'ing school into relief was, as it seems, Sun K'o-k'uan, *Yüan-ch'u ju-hsüeh*[ge] (Taipei: I-wen yin-shu kuan, 1952), pp. 1–25; rpt. in *Yüan-tai Han wen-hua*, pp. 109–38: also see Abe Takeo, "Gendai chishiki jin to kakyo,"[gf] *Shirin* (1959), 42:885–924; Igor de Rachewiltz, "Personnel and Personalities in North China in the Early Mongol Period," *Journal of the Social and Economic History of the Orient* (1966), 9:88–144, and John W. Dardess, *Conquerors and Confucians*, pp. 33–36, 183. For an older study, see Otto Franke, "Khublai Khan und seine chinesischen Berater," *Forschungen und Fortschritte* (1942), 18:29–30, 283–85. It is not at all clear that the Yüan court consistently favored Neo-Confucianism over the Tung-p'ing tendency (Dardess, p. 34). Under Khubilai Khaghan Neo-Confucianism did not play a great role. Certainly Wang Yün cannot be termed a Neo-Confucian.

47. For the table of contents see CW, 78:4a–4b.

48. CW, 78:2b.

49. CW, 79:9a; YS, 167 20b. Throughout this passage, Wang Yün addressed the crown prince as if he were a reigning emperor. This is because Chen-chin was posthumously elevated to imperial status with the temple-title Yü-tsung[gg] (Resourceful Ancestor) by his third son Temür (Ch'eng-tsung) in April 1295 following his accession. See YS, 18:3a and 115:10a (Chen-chin's biography). The quotations on these historical episodes are in CW, 78:3a.

50. The parallel text in YS, 167:20b, line 5 has *lan*[gh] "to look at, inspect" instead of *tu*. For Chen-chin's knowledge of Chinese, see Herbert Franke, "Could the Mongol Emperors read and write Chinese?" *Asia Major*, N.S. (1952–53), 3(1):30–31.

51. YS, 167:20b.

52. For Chang Chiu-ssu's biography, see YS, 169:14b–16a. His name in the PN ed. of YS, 167:20b is misprinted as K'ung Chiu-ssu.[gi] Ahmed has a biography in YS, 205:1a. For an account of his rise and fall, see Herbert Franke in *Oriens*, (December 1948), 1(2):222–236, and Hsiao Ch'i-ch'ing, *Hsi-yüeh jen*, pp. 61–69.

53. CW, 23:17b–18a.

54. Chu-hu-nai is mentioned in YS, 2:6b as being sent by Ögödei in September 1237 to preside over the examination of the scholars summoned from the various districts in North China. The name Tung Pa-ko ("Tung the Eighth Elder Brother") seems to refer to Tung Wen-chung[gj] (1231–1281), another eminent myriarch of the Han army, who was usually addressed by Khubilai as "Tung Eight" according to his biography in YS, 148:3b–16a. Tung was the eighth son of Tung Chün[gk] (1185–1232), who had distinguished himself in military services under the early Mongol rulers. But according to his biography, Tung Wen-chung died on the 25th day of the tenth month in 1281, which would contradict the unequivocal dating of Wang Yün's audience. For details of Tung Wen-chung's career, see also Sun, *Yüan-tai Han wen-hua*, pp. 296–330.

55. *Li chi*, *Wen-wang shih-tzu* 8. See James Legge, tr., *The Book of Rites* (New York: Paragon rpt., 1967), vol. 1, pp. 343–45.

56. *Hsin T'ang shu* (hereafter abbreviated: HTS, PN ed.), 5:5a (9th month, *ting-yu* day).

57. *T'ang shu* (PN ed.), 9:7a; HTS, 5:13b (Wang Yün gives the wrong date of T'ien-pao thirteenth year instead of the correct date T'ien-pao third year).

58. Tr. Legge, *The Chinese Classics* (Hong Kong: Hong Kong University Press, rpt. 1960), vol. 3, *The Shoo King*, p. 195.

59. *Hou-Han shu* (hereafter abbreviated: HHS, PN ed.), 45:5a.

60. *T'ang shu*, 95:2a; HTS, 81:7b.

61. Tr. Legge, *The Shoo King*, p. 211.

62. HTS, 81:1a.

63. HTS, 122:5a.

64. Tr. Legge, *The Shoo King*, pp. 259–60.

65. HHS, 37:3b.

66. *Chin shu* (PN ed.), 73:1a.

67. A part of the quotation in Wang Yün's text goes back to the *Han shu* (PN ed.), 6:31b–32a (eulogy for Emperor Wu); tr. Homer H. Dubs, *History of the Former Han Dynasty* (Baltimore: Waverly Press, 1944), vol. 2, pp. 119–20. The Taoist inclinations of Empress Tou are mentioned several times in the *Shih chi* and the *Han shu*.

68. Dubs, vol. 2, pp. 337–38.

69. *Wei shu* (PN ed.), 44:1a.

70. *Chen-kuan cheng-yao* (hereafter abbreviated CKCY, SPPY ed.) 1:2b–3a. According to this passage, the conversation took place in the second year of Chen-kuan (A.D. 628).

71. *Tso chuan*, Duke of Min 2; tr. Legge, *Chinese Classics*, vol. 5, *The Ch'un Ts'ew with the Tso Chuen*, pp. 127, 130. Legge translates the term *fu-chün* as "soother of the host."

72. *Han shu*, 18:16b; tr. Homer H. Dubs, *History of the Former Han Dynasty* (Baltimore: Waverly Press, 1938), vol. 1, p. 135.

73. HTS, 7:10b. See also Bernhard S. Solomon, *The Veritable Record of the T'ang Emperor Shun-tsung* (Cambridge, Mass.: Harvard University Press, 1955), p. 1.

74. HHS, 37:3a–4b.

75. *T'ang shu*, 102:3a; HTS, 200:2a. See also Wang P'u, *T'ang hui-yao*[gl] (Shanghai: Commercial Press, 1935 ed.), vol. 2, *ch.* 35:642.

76. HTS, 7:10b. See also Solomon (note 73).

77. *Shih chi* (PN ed.), 55:11a–11b (biography of Chang Liang[gm]), tr. in Burton Watson, *Records of the Grand Historian of China: Ssu-ma Ch'ien* (New York: Columbia University Press, 1961), vol. 1, pp. 148–49. For a German annotated translation, see also Wolfgang Bauer, "Der Fürst von Liu," ZDMG (1956), vol. 106, p. 197.

78. Yüan Chen, *Yüan-shih Ch'ang-ch'ing chi*[gn] (SPTK ed.), 29:2a.

79. *Chin shu*, 67:1b.

80. This text is preserved and can be found in Yen K'o-chün, *Ch'üan Shang-ku San-tai Ch'in-Han San-kuo Liu-ch'ao wen*[go] (Kuang-ya shu-chü, ed. 1887–1893), *Chin-wen*, 80:11a. Yen K'o-chün has exerpted this text from the T'ang encyclopedia *I-wen lei-chü*[gp] (Taipei: Hsin-hsing shu-chü, 1969 ed.), 16:3b–4b.

81. Tr. Legge, *Chinese Classics*, vol. 1, *Confucian Analects*, p. 170.

82. HHS, 1B:31b.

83. HTS, 7:10b.

84. *Hsin shu* (SPPY ed.), 5:4a–4b.

85. *Chin shu*, 67:1b.

86. *Meng Tzu*, tr. James Legge, *Chinese Classics*, vol. 2, *The Works of Mencius*, pp. 139–41.

87. The text as given by Wang Yün is a patchwork from *Liang shu* (PN ed.), 8:4b–6b, and *Nan shih* (PN ed.), 53:3b–5b.

88. *Liang shu*, 8:4b–5a, and *Nan shih*, 53:4a–4b.

89. *Ti fan* (Wu-ying tien chü-chen pan ts'ung-shu, ed., 1895), 3:4a–5b.

90. *Shu ching*, I-chi; tr. Bernhard Karlgren, *The Book of Documents* (Stockholm: Museum of Far Eastern Antiquities, 1950), p. 11, para. 16.

91. *Shu ching*, Wu-i; tr. Karlgren, *ibid.*, pp. 56 and 58, paras. 1, 5, and 5, 7.

92. Yüan Chen, *Yüan-shih Ch'ang-ch'ing chi*, 29:2a–2b.

93. Yang Hsiung, *Yang-tzu fa-yen* (SPPY ed.), 13:8a. This is quoted in CW, 78:5b, Wang Yün's postscript to no. 1: "Kuang-hsiao."
94. CW, 78:8b, 11a.
95. CW, 78:13a; 79:6a.
96. CW, 79:8b–9a.
97. *Han shu*, 10:1a–1b. The translation follows that of Dubs, vol. 2, pp. 373–74.
98. HTS, 6:1a. *Wai-pien* [gq] "outer distinctions" might perhaps be read as "outer managers," *wai-pang*, [gr] cf. *Dai Kanwa jitan* (Tokyo: Taishukan shōten, 1955–1960), vol. 3, p. 336, section IV for references. *Chu-ming*, [gs] "red and clear," is a term for "summer." According to the HTS text this took place in the twenty-sixth year of K'ai-yüan (738).
99. *Pei-Ch'i shu* (PN ed.), 44:11b; *Pei shih* (PN ed.), 81:25b.
100. *Hsin-shu*, 6:1a. Dried fish (abalone?) had a strong smell, hence perhaps the taboo.
101. This quotation is adapted from Ssu-ma Kuang, *Wen-kuo Wen-cheng Ssu-ma kung chi* (SPTK ed.), 26:2a–2b.
102. Lao Yan-shuan, *Chung-t'ang shih-chi* p. xxxi, note 40, translates the title as "Mirror for Keeping the Patrimony."
103. CW, 79:9b–19b.
104. I have not been able to identify the source of this quotation.
105. *Shu ching, Yüeh-ming*; tr. Legge, *The Shoo King*, p. 261.
106. This proverbial phrase seems first to be attested in the biography of Yang Shang-hsi, [gt] *Sui shu* (PN ed.), 46:5a, but it occurs in many other passages of Chinese literature. For the T'ang see, e.g., biography of Wei Yüan-chung, HTS, 122:6a.
107. This probably refers to the decree of 1271 exempting the remaining adults of the wealthy traders from the various households in the Tung-p'ing District, who had already contributed one soldier, from induction into the army. See YS, 99:12a–12b; tr. in Ch'i-ch'ing Hsiao, *The Military Establishment of the Yüan Dynasty* (Cambridge, Mass.: Harvard University Press, 1978), p. 85.
108. CKCY, 1:3b–4a, a conversation held in the tenth year of Chen-kuan, i.e., A.D. 636.
109. This quotation is adapted from Ssu-ma Kuang's collected works, 18:11a–11b.
110. CW, 79:15a. This quotation attributed to Chin Shih-tsung is not found in the CS. It may have been included in his *Veritable Records* (*Shih-lu*), now lost, which Wang Yün gained access to in the Office of National Historiography for the composition of the official Chin history. Cf. Hok-lam Chan, *The Historiography of the Chin Dynasty*, pp. 5, 10. Shih-tsung was one of the most sinicized alien rulers in Chinese history; he presided over the so-called "golden era" of the Chin dynasty and earned the epithet of a "small Yao and Shun" [gu] from traditional historians for his distinguished achieve-

ment. He was highly praised not only for his frugality, uprightness, and extreme devotion to state affairs, but also for his effort to rejuvenate the Jurchen culture and native spirit under the onslaught of the intensified sinicization of his predecessors. See CS, *ch.* 6–8. For a modern appraisal of his reign, see Yao Ts'ung-wu, *Chin-ch'ao shih*,[gv] in *Yao Ts'ung-wu hsien-sheng ch'üan-chi* (Taipei: Cheng-chung shu-chü, 1973), vol. 3, pp. 155–201 and Jing-shen Tao, The *Jurchen in Twelfth-century China: A Study of Sinicization* (Seattle: University of Washington Press, 1976), pp. 68–83.

111. CKCY, 8:13b–14a, from a conversation held in A.D. 636.

112. Wang Yün has repeatedly applied to codify the laws, see Paul Ratchnevsky, *Un Code des Yuan* (Paris: Ernst Leroux, 1937), vol. 1, p. xii, and Paul Ch'en *Chinese Legal Tradition under the Mongols* (Princeton: Princeton University Press, 1979), pp. 8–10.

113. Here Wang Yün seems to refer to the "villains" Ahmed, Lu Shih-yung, and Sengge (d. 1241), three of the notorious financial administrators at Khubilai's court. Chen-chin had indeed been the motivating force behind the eventual plot against Ahmed. See the references cited in notes 31, 52 above.

114. For the Chin, Wang Yün refers to an edict issued on December 12, 1162. See CS, 6:10a.

115. *Shu ching, K'ang-kao*; tr. Karlgren, p. 43.

116. *I ching*, hexagram *Chi-chi*, tr. Richard Wilhelm, tr. into English by Cary F. Baynes, *The I-ching or Book of Changes*, 3d ed. (Princeton: Princeton University Press, 1967), p. 245.

117. *Shih chi*, 92:8b (Biography of Han Hsin),[gw] tr. John de Francis, "Biography of the Marquis of Huai-yin," *Harvard Journal of Asiatic Studies* (1947), 10:194.

118. For the fascination which T'ang T'ai-tsung and his councillor Wei Cheng had for Khubilai Khaghan, see Hok-lam Chan, "Liu Ping-chung," p. 123 and the article by Yanai Wataru quoted *ibid.*, note 48.

119. CW, *fu-lu*, 4b–5a.

120. A very detailed record of the discussions on cosmological speculations about the legitimate succession of dynasties is preserved in the *Ta Chin te-yün t'u shuo*[gx] (in SKCSCP 4th ser.; Taipei: Commercial Press, 1975). On this work and its content see the forthcoming study of Hok-lam Chan, *Theories of Legitimacy in Imperial China: Discussions on "Legitimate Succession" under the Jurchen-Chin Dynasty (1115–1234)* (Seattle: University of Washington Press, 1982), pts. 1 and 2. I am grateful to Professor Chan for providing me with a manuscript of his important study. For the eventual adoption of the agent Earth in late 1202, see CS, 11:12b.

121. For some of these examples, see Hsü Wen-yü, "Chin-yüan ti wen-yu,"[gy] in Cheng Chen-to, ed., *Chung-kuo wen-hsüeh yen-chiu*[gz] (Hong Kong: Li-sheng shu-tien, 1963 rpt.), pp. 677–714, and Tao, *The Jurchen in Twelfth-century China*, pp. 99–110.

122. Wang Jo-hsü, *Hu-nan i-lao chi*[ha] (SPTK ed.), 26:4a–8b. A useful survey of Chin literature including works known only from prefaces or quotations is Yang Chia-lo, "Hsin-pu Chin-shih i-wen-chih"[hb] ("Newly supplemented monograph on the literature of the Chin dynasty") in the edition of *Chin shih* published in 1970 by the National War College (Taipei) under the editorship of Dr. Chang Chi-yün, vol. 2, pp. 1–214.

123. Chao Ping-wen, *Hsien-hsien lao-jen Fu-shui wen-chi*[hc] (SPTK ed.), 15:7a–8a.

124. Chao Ping-wen, 14:12b–14b.

125. CS, 110:8b. See Yang (note 122), p. 32.

126. See note 44 above.

127. The *Ti fan* was also introduced to Japan at an early date and remained for a long time a textbook of statecraft. For a recent study, see Fumoto Yasutaka,[hd] "On the *Ti-fan* and the *Ch'en-kuei*: The Theory of the Principles that Existed between Sovereign and his Subjects in China," in A. R. Davis, ed., *Proceedings of the 28th International Congress of Orientalists* (Wiesbaden: Otto Harrassowitz, 1976), pp. 207–8, and the Japanese annotated version of Fumoto's article in *Bōei daigakkō kiyō*,[he] (1972), 24:57–62.

128. The *Ch'en kuei* was reintroduced into China from Japan in the eighteenth century, see Juan Yüan, *Ssu-k'u wei-shou shu-mu t'i-yao*[hf] (Shanghai: Commercial Press, 1939 ed.), *ch.* 2:27. Like the *Ti fan*, the *Ch'en kuei* enjoyed favor among Japanese Confucians, and several studies on these books and their transmission have been published in Japan, e.g., Abe Ryūichi, in "Teihan Shinki genryūko,"[hg] *Shidō bunko ronshū*[hh] (1969), 7:171–289. See also Fumoto, pp. 207–8. We could also mention here another work on T'ang statecraft, namely, the *Chin ching*[hi] (Golden Mirror) written by T'ang T'ai-tsung as a sort of political testament for his successor. The text has been preserved in the Sung anthology *Wen-yüan ying-hua*[hj] (Taipei: Hua-lien ch'u-pan she, 1965 ed.), 360:1b–5b and also in *Ch'üan T'ang-wen*[hk] (Taipei: Hua-lien ch'u-pan she, 1965 ed.), 10:24a–29a. The latter version is better insofar as it has filled out some lacunae of the *Wen-yüan ying-hua* text. On the *Golden Mirror* see also the Sung encyclopedia *Yü-hai*[hl] (Taipei: Hua-wen shu-chü, rpt. 1964), 32:17a–17b. This work, however, does not seem to have been known to Wang Yün at all.

129. See, for example, James C. T. Liu, *Ou-yang Hsiu, An Eleventh-century Neo-Confucianist* (Stanford: Stanford University Press, 1967), p. 95.

130. For the attitude of the early Chin toward the two Sung factions, see Toyama Gunji, *Kinchōshi kenkyū*[hm] (Kyoto: Tōyōshi kenkyūkai, 1964), pp. 594–618.

131. It is significant that when Wang Yün wrote a eulogy on "Twenty-four Great Confucians," he did not include a Sung Neo-Confucianist. The last Confucian listed is the T'ang scholar Han Yü (768–824); see CW, 66:16a–20a. On the other hand, Wang Yün wrote in 1298 the inscription for a shrine in Lo-yang in honor of five worthy Confucians of the Northern Sung. However, he sees them not so much as important innovators, but rather as

traditionalists who continued the orthodox Confucian heritage of Confucius and Mencius. See CW, 40:11b–13a.

132. YS, 30:3a, 6a. See also Yü Chi's preface to this work cited in Fuchs, "Analects," pp. 51–52.

GLOSSARY

a 王惲

b 馮從吾，元儒考略

c 王磐

d 大學衍義

e 大元通制

f 列聖制誥

g 貞觀政要

h 皇圖大訓

i 荀悅，申鑑

j 帝範

k 世祖聖訓

l 難經

m 本草

n 承華事略

o 元貞守成事鑑

p 虞集

q 眞德秀

r 王禹偁，待漏院記

s 秋澗先生大全文集

t 王公孺

u 陽武

v 汲

w 衞

x 吏

y 尉

z 王宇

aa 吏學

ab 王天鐸

ac 完顏訛可

ad 王忱

ae 遺民

af 元好問

ag 劉祁

ah 楊奐

ai 楊果

aj 郝經

ak 胡祗遹

al 史天澤

am 姚樞

an 東平路

ao 詳定官

ap 中書省

aq 周正

ar 中堂事記

as 王鶚

at 修撰

au 王文統

av 平章政事

aw 李璮

ax 判官

ay 總官府

az 平陽路

ba 待制

bb 提刑按察使

bc 眞金

bd 郎中

be 盧世榮

bf 閭海

bg 鍾明亮

bh 月的迷失

bi 月兒魯

bj 柳林

bk 學士

bl 事目

bm 中奉大夫

bn 王筍

bo 春露堂

bp 河西里

bq 承旨

br 資善大夫

bs 太原郡公

bt 文定

bu 推

bv 王公儀

bw 磁

bx 王公說

by 衞輝

bz 耶律楷

ca 耶律有尙

cb 耶律楚材

cc 相鑑

cd 汲郡圖志

ce 經濟

cf 周敦頤

cg 太極圖

ch 帝王鏡略

ci 呂祖謙（東萊）

cj 嚴實

ck 裕皇

cl 邢峙

cm 詹丞

cn 張九思

co 讀

cp 觀

cq 西池幸遇詩

cr 尤忽乃

cs 董八哥

ct 廣孝

cu 立愛

cv 劉慶

cw 端本

cx 許敬宗

cy 李忠

cz 魏元忠

da 袁楚客

db 進學

dc 桓榮

dd 擇術

de 庾亮

df 勤習

dg 聽政

dh 崔浩

di 達聰

dj 魏徵

dk 撫軍

dl 明分

dm 崇儒

dn 褚無量

do 親賢

dp 四皓

dq 元積，教本書

dr 去邪

ds 納誨

dt 溫嶠

du 侍臣箴

dv 幾諫

dw 裴延齡

dx 韋渠牟

dy 從諫

dz 賈誼，新書

ea 推恩

eb 簫統

ec 尙儉

ed 戒逸

ee 審官

ef 揚雄，揚子法言

eg 蕭蒿

eh 四門博士

el 邪蒿

ej 太公望

ek 鮑魚

el 事

em 敬天

en 傳

eo 文

ep 法祖

eq 愛民

er 恤兵

es 守成

et 持盈

eu 文德

ev 柔道

ew	清心	gg	裕宗
ex	勤政	gh	覽
ey	尚儉	gi	孔九思
ez	謹令	gj	董文忠
fa	立法	gk	董俊
fb	法吏	gl	王溥，唐會要
fc	元年新法	gm	張戾
fd	重臺諫	gn	元氏長慶集
fe	選士	go	嚴可均，全上古三代秦漢三
ff	貢舉		國六朝文
fg	愼名爵	gp	藝文類聚
fh	明賞罰	gq	外辦
fi	遠慮	gr	外辦
fj	魏文貞	gs	朱明
fk	司馬端明	gt	楊尚希
fl	王若虛	gu	小堯舜
fm	趙秉文	gv	姚從吾，金朝史
fn	貞觀政要申鑑	gw	韓信
fo	君臣政要	gx	大金德運圖說
fp	楊雲翼	gy	許文玉，金源的文囿
fq	臣軌	gz	鄭振鐸，中國文學研究
fr	小倉進平，朝鮮語学史	ha	滹南遺老集
fs	道園學古錄	hb	楊家駱，新補金史藝文志
ft	國立中央圖書館善本書目	hc	閑閑老人滏水文集
	（增訂本）	hd	麓保孝
fu	王德毅、潘柏澄	he	防衛大學校紀要
fv	史原	hf	阮元，四庫未收書目提要
fw	孫克寬，元代漢文化之活動	hg	阿部隆一，帝範臣軌源流考
fx	愛宕松男	hh	斯道文庫論集
fy	蕭啟慶，西域人與元初政治	hi	金鏡
fz	玉堂嘉話	hj	文苑英華
ga	五朝小說（大觀）	hk	全唐文
gb	彭蠡小龍記	hl	玉海
gc	調元	hm	外山軍治，金朝史研究
gd	井崎隆興	hn	振孫
ge	元初儒學	ho	宜孫
gf	安部健夫，元代知識人と科	hp	韃郎
	舉		

Wing-tsit Chan[a]

Chu Hsi and Yüan Neo-Confucianism

THE NEO-CONFUCIANISM of the Yüan period is mainly the Neo-Confucianism of Chu Hsi[b] (1130–1200). Chu Hsi's philosophy dominated the Yüan from beginning to end. Its growth and spread took two main courses and a minor one. One main course arose from an unpredictable event and the other as a direct transmission from the philosopher himself.

The unpredictable event involves an obscure Confucian scholar whose dates of birth and death are unknown and whose name seldom appears in accounts of Chinese philosophy. In early 1235 the Mongol ruler Ögödei Khan (T'ai-tsung,[c] r. 1229–1241) ordered a prince to lead an expedition against the Southern Sung. When the Mongol forces captured Te-an[d] prefecture (modern An-lu,[e] Hupei) in the tenth month,[1] hundreds of thousands of inhabitants were made captives. The Chinese commander Yang Wei-chung[f] (1205/6–1260), who was highly regarded by Ögödei and later rose to become chief of the Central Secretariat, was ordered by imperial command to seek out from among the prisoners Confucian scholars, Taoists, medical practictioners, and diviners and bring them to the Mongol headquarters at Yen-ching[g] (modern Peking). Yang assigned this task to his chief of staff, Yao Shu[h] (1203–1280), a noted Confucian scholar who joined the Mongol service a few years earlier; he rounded up dozens of well-known scholars, and Chao Fu[i] (c.1206–c.1299) was one of them.[2]

According to Chao's biography,[3] he refused to go north because most of his clan had perished. Fearing that Chao might take his own life, Yao Shu invited him to retire in his tent so as to watch him. When Yao woke up during the night and saw only Chao's pajamas, he rushed to the waterfront and discovered that Chao was about to jump into the river. He was able to persuade Chao to change his mind and follow him to Yen-ching. Chao gave Yao Shu his notes on readings from the commentaries of Ch'eng I[j] (1033–1107) and Chu Hsi on Confucian Classics and some of their own works. In Yen-ching, more than a hundred scholars came to study with Chao. Yang Wei-chung heard his discussions and came to like him very much. In 1238, in collaboration with Yao Shu, he established the T'ai-chi[k] (Great Ultimate) Academy and built a memorial hall in honor of Chou Tun-i[l] (1017–1073) in which Ch'eng I, his elder brother Ch'eng Hao[m] (1032–1085), Chang Tsai[n] (1020–1077), the Ch'engs' pupils Yang Shih[o] (1053–1135) and Yu Tso[p] (1053–1123), and Chu Hsi were also enshrined. More than 8,000 *chüan* of their works were collected. Chao Fu and others[4] were invited to lecture there.

In order to help scholars understand the doctrines of Chou Tun-i and Ch'eng I, Chao drew the *Ch'uan-tao t'u*[q] (Diagram of the Transmission of the Way) to show the continuation of the sacred doctrines from Emperors Fu-hsi,[r] Shen-nung,[s] Yao,[t] and Shun[u] to Confucius (551–479 B.C.), his pupil Yen Hui[v] (521–490? B.C.), Mencius (372–289? B.C.) and then on to Chou Tun-i, the Ch'eng brothers, and Chu Hsi. To this drawing he appended a list of their works. To expound the Neo-Confucian doctrine, he wrote the *I-Lo fa-hui*[w] (Exposition of the Doctrines of the Ch'engs and Chu Hsi). At that time, Chu Hsi's followers scattered all over the country. From what he read and what he heard, he found fifty-three names and made a chart of them called *Shih-yu t'u*[x] (Chart of Teacher and Friends). Thus he indicated that Chu Hsi was his teacher and the fifty-three were fellow pupils. In other words, he suggested that he was an indirect pupil (*ssu-shu*)[y] of Chu Hsi's. He further collected the words and deeds of I Yin[z] (eighteenth cen. B.C.) and Yen Hui in his *Hsi-hsien lu*[aa] (Records of Aspiring to Become a Worthy) so the students may know which direction to follow and what method of self-cultivation to adopt.[5]

In the meantime (1241), Yao Shu had retired from government service because he refused to accept bribes.[6] He went on to live in the Su-men[ab] mountain in Hui-chou[ac] (modern Hui county, Honan). He built a private temple and installed in it the images of Confucius and six Sung Neo-Confucians, namely, Chou Tun-i, Ch'eng Hao, Ch'eng I, Chang Tsai, Shao Yung[ad] (1011–1077), and Ssu-ma Kuang[ae] (1019–1086).[7] It was a family temple and the Sage and Worthies were enshrined in a special room.[8] Yao also personally published in Yen-ching the *Hsiao-hsüeh*[af] (Elementary Learning), the *Lun-yü huo-wen*[ag] (Questions and Answers on the *Analects*), the *Meng Tzu huo-wen*[ah] (Questions and Answers on the *Book of Mencius*), and the *Chia li*[ai] (Family Rites), all by Chu Hsi, and had Yang Wei-chung publish the Four Books (the *Analects*, the *Book of Mencius*, the *Great Learning*, and the *Doctrine of the Mean*) and another official publish Ch'eng I's *I chuan*[aj] (Commentary on the *Book of Changes*), Ts'ai Ch'en's[ak] (1167–1230) *Shu chuan*[al] (Commentary on the *Book of Documents*), and Hu An-kuo's[am] (1074–1138) *Ch'un-ch'un chuan*[an] (Commentary on the *Spring and Autumn Annals*), among others.[9] Hsü Heng[ao] (1209–1281), who lived in nearby Wei[ap] prefecture (modern Wei county, Hopei), came to Hui to copy the commentaries by Ch'eng I and Chu Hsi. When he returned home, he is said to have told his pupils that all he had learned and taught before was wrong. Only from now on did he know the procedure of learning.[10] According to his tomb tablet inscription, besides Ch'eng I's and Chu Hsi's works on nature and principle (*hsing-li*),[aq] he obtained Ch'eng I's commentary on the *Book of Changes*, Chu Hsi's *Ssu-shu chang-chü chi-chu*[ar] (Commentaries on the Four Books), his *Huo-wen*[as] (Questions and Answers on the *Great Learning* and the *Doctrine of the Mean*), and the *Hsiao-hsüeh*.[11] To this the supplement to the *Sung-Yüan hsüeh-an*,[at] *Sung-Yüan hsüeh-an pu-i*,[au] has added Hu An-kuo's *Commentary on the Spring and Autumn Annals*, Ts'ai Ch'en's *Commentary on the Book of Documents*, and Chu Hsi's *Commentary on the Book of Odes*, probably a conjecture but a reasonable one.[12] Not only Hsü Heng, but Hao Ching[av] (1223–1275) and Liu Yin[aw] (1249–1293) also, obtained the Neo-Confucian works from Yao Shu. Thus, as the *Yüan shih* (Yüan History) has alleged, the North first knew of the Ch'eng-Chu learning through Chao Fu.[13] This is the dramatic story of how the Chu Hsi philosophy was introduced to north China.

The point made by *Yüan shih* has been disputed by, among others, Professor Jao Tsung-i.[ax] According to him, the Chin scholar Li Ch'un-fu[ay] (1185–1231) had severely criticized Ch'eng I and Chu Hsi and other Sung Neo-Confucianists for their attack on Buddhism. Jao gave Chao Fu credit for spreading Neo-Confucian works and for building a basis for Neo-Confucianism in the Yüan to become pure Confucianism devoid of Buddhist and Taoist elements.[14] Jing-shen Tao has also pointed out that the Chin scholar Wang Jo-hsü[az] (1174–1243) had criticized Sung Neo-Confucianists, and particularly Chu Hsi for his commentaries on the Four Books.[15] Technically Professor Jao is correct, for Chu Hsi was certainly known in the Chin. However, if we are to follow the *Yüan History* and emphasize "the learning of Ch'eng-Chu," that is, the Ch'eng-Chu teaching as a systematic school of thought and an intellectual lineage, this did not exist in the Chin. In this respect, the Yüan almost began in a vacuum, which Chao Fu filled.

The other course of development was less exciting but more direct. It centered in the Chin-hua[ba] area (modern Chekiang) in the South and went directly back to Chu Hsi. His teachings were first passed on to his pupil Huang Kan[bb] (1152–1221) and then successively to Ho Chi[bc] (1188–1268) and Wang Po[bd] (1197–1274) in late Sung, and Chin Lü-hsiang[be] (1232–1303) and Hsü Ch'ien[bf] (1270–1337) in the Yüan.

Ho Chi was a native of Chin-hua. His father was assistant magistrate of Lin-ch'uan[bg] (modern Hangchow) when Huang Kan was magistrate there. He was told by his father to study with Huang Kan. Huang urged him to be earnest at heart and work hard.[16] Wang Po's grandfather was a pupil of Ch'eng I's disciple Yang Shih and also a friend of both Chu Hsi and Lü Tsu-ch'ien[bh] (1137–1181). Both his father and uncle were followers of Chu Hsi and Lü. When he heard that Ho Chi had learned from Huang Kan the doctrines handed down by Chu Hsi, he went to study with Ho right away. Ho cited Hu Hung's[bi] (1105–1155) words, "Make up the mind to affirm the foundation and abide in seriousness in order to hold on to the will" (*li-chih chü-ching*,[bj] *ching* meaning to be serious or reverent).[17] Chin Lü-hsiang came from the same prefecture as Wang Po. When he served under Wang Po, he had already developed an interest in Neo-Confucianism. Following Wang Po, he went to study with Ho Chi.[18] When he asked Wang Po about the method of study, Wang cited the same words of Hu Hung, and when he asked Ho Chi, Ho told him about the distinction between Heavenly principle and human desires.[19] Hsü Ch'ien, a student of Chin's, was also from Chin-hua.[20] Thus the Chu Hsi doctrines were transmitted by Huang Kan to four generations of followers in Chin-hua, in the persons of what historians have called the Four Masters of Chin-hua. As the *Yüan History* has noted, after Ho Chi, Wang Po, and Chin Lü-hsiang died, their doctrines had not prevailed. Hsü Ch'ien, however, made them prominent. "Therefore," says the *Yüan History*, "scholars, tracing the source and the generations of heritage, have considered the period as the time of Chu Hsi."[21]

The third source of the Chu Hsi philosophy in the Yüan, like the Chin-hua tradition, was also derived from Huang Kan. Jao Lu[bk] (fl. 1256) of Kiangsi was his student. His line was continued by Ch'eng Jo-yung[bl] (fl. 1268) and finally by Wu Ch'eng[bm] (1249–1333). Although philosophically speaking this line did not play as great a role as the other two, it does underline the tremendous influence Huang Kan exerted on Yüan thought.

From the above accounts, it is clear that both the Neo-Confucianism in the North and the Neo-Confucianism in the South converged on Chu Hsi. More precisely, it converged on Chu Hsi's teachings as transmitted by Huang Kan. Both the Chekiang (Chin-hua) line and the Kiangsi line originated with him. The Neo-Confucianism brought to the North by Chao Fu was that of Ch'eng-Chu. No mention was made of Huang Kan. However, as it will become clear, the Ch'eng-Chu philosophy was practically that of Chu Hsi and the Chu Hsi philosophy that came to prevail in the Yüan was that interpreted by Huang Kan. It is now necessary to examine Huang Kan's teachings to see how they reflect the teachings of the Master.

After Chu Hsi died, his followers spread over modern Fukien, Kiangsi, Chekiang, and Kiangsu. Their interests and their understanding of the Master differed. It is generally agreed, however, that Huang Kan correctly understood the Master's ideas and handed down to others accordingly. As the *Sung-Yüan hsüeh-an* has said, "Huang Kan inherited the orthodox tradition from Chu Hsi." [22] He was the most intimate and most trusted of all pupils. He was Chu Hsi's son-in-law. Chu Hsi provided him with a residence, urged him to apply for government service, and asked him to take over some of his lectures. When Chu Hsi was compiling the *Chia li*, he entrusted Huang Kan with the chapters on funerals and sacrifices, undoubtedly the two most serious chapters in Chu Hsi's mind. On his death bed, he gave Huang Kan his informal robe and his works, and in a written farewell note, said that he would have no more regret because his doctrines were now in safe hands. [23] Until Huang Kan died, Chu Hsi's disciples dared not circulate their records of the Master's sayings for fear that they might not represent the Teacher accurately.

Huang Kan did not write any major philosophical work. His philosophical ideas are found in his letters and essays. [24] His ideas cannot be said to form any system. However, certain doctrines do stand out. They reflect the central teachings of Chu Hsi and have greatly influenced the development of Yüan Neo-Confucian thought. We shall discuss some of these ideas and see how they have served as the connecting link between Chu Hsi and Yüan thinkers. We shall begin with the doctrine of the *tao-t'ung*[bn] (Tradition of the Way).

Huang Kan concluded his biographical account of Chu Hsi by saying:

The transmission of the correct orthodox tradition of the Way required the proper men. From the Chou Dynasty [1111–249 B.C.] on, there have been only several people capable of inheriting the correct tradition and transmitting the Way and only one or two could enable the Way to become prominent. After Confucius, Tseng Tzu[bo] [505–c. 436 B.C.] and Tzu-ssu[bp] [492–431 B.C.] perpetuated it in its subtlety but it was not prominent until Mencius. After Mencius, Master Chou, the Masters Ch'eng, and Master Chang continued the interrupted tradition, but only with our Master did it become prominent. . . . With the appearance of the Masters, the Way transmitted from the Chou through sages and worthies suddenly became vastly clear like the sun shining in the sky.[25]

In Huang Kan's mind, one of the greatest accomplishments of Chu Hsi was his perpetuation of the orthodox tradition. For decades Chu Hsi had concerned himself with the tradition of the Way. He was the first to use the term *tao-t'ung*, in his preface to the *Chung-yung chang-chü*[bq] (Commentary on the *Doctrine of the Mean*) in 1189, where he outlines the transmission from Yao, Shun, and other sages to Confucius and through his pupils to Mencius and then on to the Ch'eng brothers. As early as 1172, his follower, Li Yüan-kang,[br] had drawn up a diagram called *ch'uan-tao cheng-t'ung*[bs] (Orthodox transmission of the Way) in his *Sheng-men shih-yeh t'u*[bt] (Chart of Achievements of the Confucian School) to show the line of transmission. The line starts with Fu-hsi and Shen-nung and goes on to Yao and Shun and others, on to the Duke of Chou[bu] (d. 1094? B.C.) and Confucius, his pupils, and Mencius, and further on to Sung Neo-Confucians and ends with Chu Hsi. In a previous study I have traced the development of the *tao-t'ung* from Mencius to Han Yü[bv] (768–824) and Li Ao[bw] (fl. 798), then to Ch'eng Hao and Ch'eng I, and finally to Chu Hsi.[26] I have explained the philosophical reasons why Chu Hsi eliminated the Han (206 B.C.–A.D. 220) and T'ang (618–907) Confucians, why he selected the Ch'eng brothers as the main line instead of the other Sung Neo-Confucians, and why he put Chou Tun-i ahead of the Ch'engs. In his own essay on the transmission, Huang Kan traced the philosophical development from one generation to the next, explaining what particular doctrines each one developed so as to continue the tradition. In the case of Chu Hsi, Huang said that "The learning of the Master is found in the Four Books but more importantly in the *Great Learning,* which is the procedure for entering into the Way."[27] All the three elements present here—the *tao-t'ung,* the Four Books, and the *Great Learning*—had a great impact on Yüan thinkers, as we shall see. By the end of Sung, the *tao-t'ung* concept was so strongly entrenched that Wang Po went as far as to say that before the *tao-t'ung* of the sages there had already been the *tao-t'ung* of Heaven and Earth, as is evidenced by the continuous production of things.[28]

The inauguration of Neo-Confucianism in the North practically started with the reaffirmation of the *tao-t'ung.* It will be recalled that Chao Fu drew the *Ch'uan-tao t'u.* His order is this: Fu-hsi, Shen-nung, Yao, Shun, Confucius, Yen Hui, Mencius, Chou Tun-i, the Ch'eng brothers, Chang Tsai, and Chu Hsi. This is of course strictly the line established by Chu Hsi and his followers. By way of explanation, Chao Fu said that Fu-hsi, Shen-nung, Yao, and Shun, carrying on the task of Heaven, founded the ultimate standards; Confucius, Yen Hui, and Mencius founded the teachings to hand down to later generations; and Chou, the Ch'eng brothers, Chang, and Chu developed and continued them. He thus conceived the transmission in three successive stages. Although the philosophical importance of this historical interpretation is little, it does show that the *tao-t'ung* was widely accepted. It is to be expected that Chu Hsi's own followers in the South would have welcomed the *tao-t'ung* which culminated in their Master, but it is quite amazing to find that the tradition had become entrenched in the Hupei area within three or four decades after Chu Hsi's death and now was brought to the North. Although Chao Fu's chart was drawn after he arrived in Yen-ching, there can be no doubt that he had embraced the *tao-t'ung* long before. Evidently Chu Hsi's doctrines had prevailed in the Te-an area before it was captured by the Mongol forces. Huang Kan had been prefect there some two decades before. When Tou Mo[bx] (1196–1280), another northern Chinese scholar, got to Te-an fleeing from the Mongol invaders, a magistrate gave him books on nature and principle by the Ch'engs and Chu Hsi.[29]

Practically all Yüan thinkers followed the *tao-t'ung* without question. Three examples will suffice. In attacking the Buddhists, Hsü Ch'ien said that only after the appearance of Neo-Confucians Chou, the Ch'engs, Chang, and Chu could the 1,500 years of the evil influence of Buddhism be removed.[30] Hsü Heng had nothing to say about the *tao-t'ung* himself, probably avoiding the subject because the Mongol rulers had reservations about Neo-Confucianism, but it is said in his tomb tablet inscription that he inherited the *tao-t'ung* from the Duke of Chou, Confucius, and Mencius, etc.,[31] that Heaven assigned the *tao-t'ung* to him, and that a good discussion of him must begin with the *tao-t'ung*. It was also said that he gathered and synthesized all doctrines in a grand concord in the Yüan as Chu Hsi did in the Sung[32] and that in the transmission from Chu Hsi to Hsü Heng we know the true story of the *tao-t'ung*.[33] In the case of Wu Ch'eng, when he talked about the importance of thinking, he showed how Confucius passed the teaching to Tzu-ssu, who transmitted it on to Mencius and thence from Mencius to Chou, Chang, and the Ch'engs.[34] Likewise, on the subject of the mind, he said this had been the central subject that came from Yao and Shun through the Duke of Chou, etc., to Confucius and Mencius and then to Chou, the Ch'engs, Chang, and Shao Yung.[35] In neither case did he mention Chu Hsi. However, in at least one other place he did mention him.[36] We shall take up the question whether Wu Ch'eng was for or against Chu Hsi. It is noteworthy that he accepted the *tao-t'ung* as conceived by Chu Hsi.

Note that the three examples represent the three lines of the development of Neo-Confucian thought, Hsü Ch'ien representing the Chinhua line in the South, Hsü Heng the Chao Fu line in the North, and Wu Ch'eng the Jao Lu line of Kiangsi. Note also that Wu Ch'eng did not include Chu Hsi. Because he was more inclined to the philosophy of mind of Lu Hsiang-shan (Lu Chiu-yüan,[by] 1139–1193), he probably thought that Lu, rather than Chu, represented the correct transmission. But our present concern is with the *tao-t'ung* developed by Chu Hsi, and Wu Ch'eng embraced it.

In connection with the *tao-t'ung*, special attention must be paid to Chou Tun-i. The fact that a temple was built in his honor is intriguing but not easy to explain. There is no evidence .that his teachings were widespread in the Te-an area in particular or in the South in general at the end of the Sung. His home was in Tao-chou[bz] (modern Tao county, Honan), far from Te-an. Yet we have noticed that Yao Shu built a memorial in his honor and established the T'ai-chi Academy, and Chao Fu wrote the *Hsi-hsien lu* for the guidance of moral cultivation. In his *T'ung-shu*[ca] (Penetrating the *Book of Changes*), Chou wrote, "The sage aspires to become Heaven, the worthy aspires to become a sage, and the gentle-

man aspires to become a worthy. I Yin and Yen Hui were great worthies.
. . . [We should] desire what I Yin desired and learn what Yen Hui
learned."[37] This teaching exercised a considerable influence on Ch'eng
I. When he was at the Imperial College, he wrote the famous essay, "A
Treatise on What Yen Tzu[cb] (Yen Hui) Loved to Learn."[38] I Yin and
Yen Hui remained idols for Yüan thinkers. Hsü Heng, for example, referring to I Yin's desires and Yen Hui's learning, said that all men of
honor should follow their examples.[39] The T'ung-shu, too, was by no
means ignored. Ho Chi wrote the T'ung-shu fa-hui[cc] (Exposition of the
T'ung-shu).[40] Besides telling his readers to read Ho Chi's T'ung-shu fa-
hui, Wang Po wrote the Chou Tzu fa-ch'ien[cd] (Exposition of Master
Chou's Philosophy) himself.[41] He also wrote the T'ai-chi T'ung-shu
chiang[ce] (Discussions on the Great Ultimate and the T'ung-shu).[42] Chin
Lü-hsiang was interested in Chou's philosophy even before he became a
pupil of Wang Po.[43] Chou's works are valuable in their own right, but
he did not have much of a following. The Ch'eng brothers hardly referred to his philosophy. It was Chu Hsi who put Chou ahead of all Sung
Neo-Confucians in the line of transmission. I believe much of the attention paid to Chou in the Yüan was due to his position in the tao-t'ung
established by Chu Hsi.

In Chu Hsi's concept of the tao-t'ung, the T'ai-chi stands out as the
primary concept in Neo-Confucian philosophy. Chu Hsi took Chou's
T'ai-chi-t'u shuo[cf] (Diagram of the Great Ultimate Explained) out of the
T'ung-shu and put it at the head of the Neo-Confucian system. In his
explanation of the diagram, Chou says that the wu-chi[cg] (the Ultimate of
Non-being) is also the T'ai-chi. Through movement and tranquility, the
T'ai-chi generates yin[ch] (weak force or element) and yang[ci] (strong force
or element). As a result of their interaction, all things are generated and
transformed.[44] This theory had little impact on his pupils or contemporaries. The Ch'eng brothers never mentioned the T'ai-chi.[45] Instead, they
advocated li[cj] (principle, reason, order) as the source, the basic law, and
the reason of being. But the two Ch'engs had little to say about ch'i[ck]
(material force), that is, the forces of yin and yang which actualize li and
give rise to the material world. Chu Hsi had to clarify their relationship
and to resolve their apparent conflict. To do so, he equated li with the
T'ai-chi and ch'i with yin-yang. In a recent study, I have explained more
in detail how Chu Hsi accomplished this by bringing to the fore Chou
Tun-i's concept of the T'ai-chi.[46] For the present, we shall examine how

Yüan Neo-Confucians reacted to the theory of the *T'ai-chi*. To do so we shall have to return to Huang Kan.

Huang Kan wrote little on the subject, and in what he wrote, he strictly adhered to Chu Hsi's interpretation, especially from the point of view of substance and function. In his own words:

The way in the universe consists only of substance and function. In substance it is one but in its functioning it is manifested in the many. . . . "If one speaks of its greatness, nothing in the world can contain it."[47] This means that the myriad things are united in substance. "If one speaks of its smallness, nothing in the world can split it."[48] This means that everything has its own *T'ai-chi* in its completeness. As the myriad things are united in substance in the *T'ai-chi*, there can be nothing outside the nature (*hsing*), and as everything possesses its own *T'ai-chi*, the nature is everywhere. . . . The *T'ai-chi* is both substance and function. In the final analysis, however, the *T'ai-chi* in each thing is derived from the *T'ai-chi* that unites all substance as one.[49]

In his *Chung-yung tsung-lun*[cl] (Summary Discussion of the *Doctrine of the Mean*), he reiterates the theme that "The *T'ai-chi* is the substance of Tao . . . [but] substance and function are never separate from each other."[50] In all this, Huang Kan is but repeating Chu Hsi.[51]

However, although he carried the concept of the *T'ai-chi* no further than Chu Hsi, he kept the concept in a central position, and thus aroused considerable interest among Yüan thinkers. This can be seen in the works written by major late Sung and Yüan philosophers on it. From the Te-an sources, aside from the T'ai-chi Academy, there was Hao Ching, who wrote the *T'ai-chi yen-yüan*[cm] (Exposition on the Origin of the Great Ultimate).[52] In the Chin-hua group, Ho Chi's *T'ung-shu fa-hui* may be presumed to include a discussion on the Great Ultimate because the *T'ai-chi-t'u shuo* was originally a part of it. Wang Po wrote the *T'ai-chi T'ung-shu chiang* and also the *T'ai-chi yen-i*[cn] (Elaborations on the Great Ultimate).[53] Hsü Ch'ien discussed the *T'ai-chi* in his "Ta huo-jen wen"[co] (Response to Someone's Question).[54] In the Kiangsi line, Jao Lu, Ch'eng Jo-yung, and Wu Ch'eng all had something to say. Jao Lu drew three charts for the *T'ai-chi*.[55] In his answer to someone's question on the *wu-chi*, he practically paraphrased Chu Hsi in saying that the Ultimate of Non-being is not an entity but simply the *T'ai-chi* without shape or sound.[56] Ch'eng Jo-yung was the author of *T'ai-chi Hung-fan-t'u shuo*[cp] (Diagram and Explanation of the Great Ultimate and the Grand Plan [of the *Book of Documents*]).[57] And Wu Ch'eng wrote the *Wu-chi T'ai-chi shuo*[cq] (Discussion on the Ultimate of Non-being and the Great Ultimate).[58] To these three lines we may add Liu Yin, who also wrote a postscript to Chou Tun-i's *T'ai-chi-t'u shuo* (Chi *T'ai-chi-t'u shuo* hou).[cr 59] In *chüan* 12 of the *Sung-Yüan hsüeh-an* on Chou Tun-i, following the debate between Chu Hsi and Lu Hsiang-shan on the *T'ai-chi*, there are four selections on the subject. A very short one is by Wang Po of late Sung, but the remaining three are all by Yüan writers, namely, Liu Yin, Wu Ch'eng, and Hsü Ch'ien.

A brief examination of the three pieces will throw some interesting light on the concept of the *T'ai-chi* in Yüan times. Liu Yin deals with the question whether Chou Tun-i obtained his diagram from a Taoist priest. He emphasized the point that, regardless whether this was the case, the principle is the same as that of Confucianism, for, in Liu's view, the *T'ai-chi* is identical with Tao and the mind.[60] In his letter in answer to T'ien Chün-tse,[cs] Wu Ch'eng also equated the *T'ai-chi* with Tao. As such, he said, it is not a thing but is shapeless and soundless and therefore is also the *wu-chi*.[61] He wrote the *Wu-chi T'ai-chi shuo*, he said, in order to clarify Chu Hsi's ideas.[62] Hsü Ch'ien basically defends Chu Hsi's position against the criticism of Lu Hsiang-shan that the term *wu-chi* is superfluous, for, as Chu Hsi had contended, it is necessary to show the realm of principle before yin and yang take shape.[63] Thus Liu Yin deals mainly with the historical question of the diagram, Wu Ch'eng with the *T'ai-chi*, and Hsü Ch'ien with the *wu-chi*. But none of them has said anything really new.

These selections were made by Huang Tsung-hsi[ct] (1610–1695) in his original draft of the *Sung-Yüan hsüeh-an*,[64] but a later editor, Wang Tzu-ts'ai[cu] (1752–1851), shifted them to *chüan* 12 on Chou Tun-i. He could have also shifted what Ch'eng Jo-yung had to say on the *T'ai-chi*. In a lecture on Tao, Ch'eng said that *T'ai-chi* is Tao according to which all things are created and operate. All things are unified in substance in the *T'ai-chi*. However, the mind is the basis of the *T'ai-chi*'s differentiation and classification of things. In this way each thing unifies its substance as a *T'ai-chi*. . . . Only with the totality of the human mind can there be the totality of the universe."[65] In terms of intellectual history, Ch'eng Jo-yung's theory is of greater significance than those of the other three writers, because while the others have hardly added anything new,

Ch'eng identified the *T'ai-chi* with the mind. It should be noted that Ch'eng came from Jao Lu's Kiangsi line, which reached its peak in Wu Ch'eng, who was inclined to Lu Hsiang-shan's philosophy of mind.

Unfortunately, the doctrine of *T'ai-chi* as the mind did not develop. The question of the historicity of the diagram of the *T'ai-chi* was not pursued in depth either. It had to wait for several hundred years until Huang Tsung-hsi's brother, Huang Tsung-yen[cv] (1616–1686), who established the fact of how one person passed the diagram to another.[66] No new dimension was added by Yüan thinkers as to the real nature of the *T'ai-chi* or *wu-chi* or their relationship.

Perhaps the most meaningful discussion on the *T'ai-chi* was by Wu Ch'eng. As already noted, he conceived of the *T'ai-chi* as Tao. He sharply distinguished the *T'ai-chi* of the Neo-Confucians and that of early Taoists. In Taoist cosmology, Tao is originally one but splits into two, namely, yin and yang. In contrast, the Neo-Confucian Tao is indivisible.[67] Thus *T'ai-chi* involves both yin and yang or activity and tranquility. In this sense, the *T'ai-chi* is both substance and function. He also strongly criticized the view held by some that shapeless and soundless tranquility is the substance of the *T'ai-chi* whereas the activity of the process of universal operation is the function of *T'ai-chi*, thus splitting *T'ai-chi*, and substance and function, into two stages. He argues that activity and tranquility are inherent in each other and there is no division between them.[68] We can scarcely miss the familiar ring of Huang Kan here. Huang Kan was echoing Chu Hsi, and Wu Ch'eng was echoing them both.[69] As to how *T'ai-chi* gives rise to the operation of yin-yang, Wu Ch'eng cites Chu Hsi's analogy of the crossbow in the passage just referred to.[70] The passage was deemed so important that both the *Hsing-li ta-ch'üan*[cw] (Compendium of Commentaries on Human Nature and Principle)[71] and the *Hsing-li ching-i*[cx] (Essential Ideas of Nature and Principle)[72] have included it. Chu Hsi had compared *T'ai-chi* and yin-yang with a crossbow and an arrow and also a man and a horse.[73] As the crossbow is triggered, the arrow flies, and as the horse moves, the man also moves. These analogies, however, have led to two misunderstandings. One was that the *T'ai-chi* and *ch'i* are two different things like the crossbow and the arrow, and the other was that *T'ai-chi* is passive and depends on the material force for its activity just as man depends on the horse for his movement. Wu Ch'eng's deliberation is to make clear that *T'ai-chi* is substance while *ch'i* is function, but there is essentially no dichotomy between the two. He is reaffirming Chu Hsi's view that substance and function are one. He does make clear, however, that there is a difference between the identity of substance and function in the universal process and the separate states of substance and function in the human mind. The mind, he says, is not as constant as the operation of the universe and therefore can remain tranquil as substance or aroused and active as function.[74] This point has not been developed, but it does help to remove the ambiguity about substance and function. However, by retaining Chu Hsi's analogies of the crossbow and the horse, it may lead to the suspicion that a dead person is riding on the horse. But as Ts'ao Tuan[cy] (1376–1434) has reminded us, the man riding on the horse is very much alive indeed.[75] From the very start, Chu Hsi had maintained that *T'ai-chi* involves the principles of activity and tranquility. Rather than principle riding on material force passively, the principle of activity in *T'ai-chi* is the source of power of material force.[76]

I believe the lack of development on the subject of *T'ai-chi* was in line with Hsü Heng's thought and is attributable to his influence. He showed almost no interest in the subject at all. He accepted the traditional view that the *T'ai-chi* evolves into all things.[77] In talking about substance and function, these ideas lay behind all of their moral teachings.[78] He did say that everything has its own *T'ai-chi* but again he reverts to the moral self by saying that "All things are already complete in oneself,"[79] that is, the *T'ai-chi* in oneself.[80]

Because of their almost exclusive concern with practical matters, Yüan thinkers did not go into speculative, metaphysical matters or "things on the higher level." Confucius had taught "studying things on the lower level in order to understand things on the higher level."[81] Chu Hsi was careful in maintaining the balance of the study of both levels. That was why, in addition to self-cultivation and human relations, he also discussed at length such subtle subjects as *li, ch'i,* nature, mind, *kuei-shen*[cz] (negative and positive spiritual forces), what is with form and what is above form (*hsing-shang hsing-hsia*),[da] principle being one while its manifestations are many (*li-i fen-shu*),[db] and investigation of things. Huang Kan tried his best to maintain the balance, as in his discussions on the *Doctrine of the Mean*. In his *Chung-yung tsung-lun*, already quoted, he deals with the metaphysical aspects of substance and function, while in his *Chung-yung hsü-shuo*[dc] (Further Explanation of the *Doctrine of the Mean*), he deals with the moral aspects of substance and function in

terms of wisdom, humanity, and courage.[82] But he was more interested
in moral cultivation than philosophical speculation. He had practically
nothing to say about such matters of "higher understanding" as principle,
material force, or investigation of things. As he said, "In the matter of
learning, the ancients first of all devoted their efforts to their bodies and
minds." To him, this means "cultivating body and mind so as to preserve
Heavenly principle and eliminate evil human desires."[83] Under his impact, his follower, Ho Chi, stressed moral effect in his teaching.[84] The
influence of this late Sung philosopher on Yüan thinkers can readily be
seen. We have already referred to Chin Lü-hsiang's receiving the teaching of making up the mind and abiding in seriousness from Ho Chi's
pupil, Wang Po. In Wang's teaching, we are told, he always began with
the Great Learning, which sets forth the principles of and procedure for
personal cultivation, family regulation, ordering the state, and bringing
peace to the world.[85] Chin himself strongly emphasized abiding in seriousness and earnest practice.[86]

The one who made the study of things on the lower level the chief
and almost the exclusive goal of learning, however, was Hsü Heng. Since
he dominated the Yüan philosophical scene, he virtually determined the
color and shape of the landscape especially in the north. His sayings and
writings are almost entirely on moral cultivation and human relations,
although a few remarks are made on the investigation of things and principle,[87] on what is with or above form,[88] and on principle being one and
manifestations being many.[89] It is interesting that a note is attached to
his saying on principle being one and manifestations being many that
there might be an error. If anything, Hsü Heng's position on this matter
was not clearly enunciated or clearly understood. At any rate, his primary
interest lies in matters on the lower level.

He said, "in ancient times, the rise of order and peace necessarily
depended on elementary education and great learning."[90] By elementary
education is meant daily duties such as cleaning up the floor, and by
great learning is the teaching contained in the Great Learning. As his
tomb tablet inscription says of him, "In his learning, the chief object was
to clarify substance and function. In self-cultivation, the essential was to
preserve the mind and nourish the nature. In serving the ruler, his business was to admonish against what is wrong and tell what is good. And
in teaching people, he started with performing elementary duties such as
cleaning up the floor, answering questions, and learning to advance or

withdraw, and aimed at excellent principles to the point of being spirit-like."[91]

The elementary duties and correct behavior in conducting oneself and in dealing with people are best explained in the *Hsiao-hsüeh* compiled by Chu Hsi in 1189. In his preface, he said the ancients considered the moral education of the young as the foundation of self-cultivation, regulation of the family, ordering of the state, and bringing peace to the world. For this purpose, he selected sayings from Confucius and Mencius, the *Book of Rites*, and some twenty-eight other works including works of fiction, dynastic histories, and Sung Neo-Confucian works. These are divided into six *chüan*. The four "Inner Chapters" are on principles of education, the Five Human Relations,[92] personal cultivation, and historical examples, and the two "Outer Chapters" consist of wise sayings and meritorious deeds. In each case, instructions and examples are provided with little discussion on ethical theories.[93] He said, "The fundamentals of personal cultivation are completely covered in the *Hsiao-hsüeh*."[94] Still it does not rank with Chu Hsi's major works. The work was largely that of a pupil, and it is not without oversight. When someone asked why in section 2 of *chüan* 6 on concrete demonstrations in human relations the relationship of friends is omitted, he said that the material was gathered from various groups of material and somehow no item had been included.[95] But because of the emphasis on lower-level studies, Yüan thinkers gave the *Hsiao-hsüeh* first priority in moral training.

Three people were responsible for this remarkable development. One was Yao Shu. We have already noted that he printed the book among other works. Finding that the *Hsiao-hsüeh* was not widely read, he had a pupil print it for circulation in the country.[96] Later, Liu Yin wrote "recorded sayings" on the *Hsiao-hsüeh*, showing that he must have discussed the primer often.[97] But the one who contributed the most to its eminence was Hsü Heng. Since he was the most influential thinker in the Yüan period, the impact of the *Hsiao-hsüeh* can be imagined. We have noted that he copied Chu Hsi's works when he was with Yao Shu. After he returned to Hui, he told his students that all his former teaching was a waste of time. Only now did he learn the procedure for the advancement of learning. If the pupils wanted to continue to study with him, they should all discard what they had learned before and devote themselves to the duties of cleaning the floor and answering questions as taught in the

Hsiao-hsüeh. Otherwise they should seek another teacher. According to the account, they all agreed and burned their notes and would now only engage their attention in the *Hsiao-hsüeh*. Hsü Heng himself carefully read it day and night and earnestly put the teachings into practice to set an example for the students.[98]

At the age of 47, he wrote the *Hsiao-hsüeh ta-i*[dd] (General Meanings of the *Hsiao-hsüeh*) for the purpose of explaining the goal and structure of Chu Hsi's work. In teaching pupils, he always began with the *Hsiao-hsüeh*.[99] When students asked him, he would send them to the *Hsiao-hsüeh* rather than the *Book of Documents* or the *Book of Changes*.[100] The *Hsiao-hsüeh* was the first book he taught students at the Imperial College.[101] According to one account, at the Imperial College, "He honored the *Hsiao-hsüeh* above all others. . . . Many great officials and scholars became his pupils."[102] He honored the *Hsiao-hsüeh* as the gate to enter the virtue.[103] He said, "The *Hsiao-hsüeh* and the Four Books of Wen-kung[de] (Chu Hsi) are complete in procedure and priority. When one rises to become a wise king, he will have to follow their patterns."[104] He wrote his son that he "reverently believes in the *Hsiao-hsüeh* and the Four Books as gods," and added, "I have taught you these from childhood with the hope that you achieve something from them. Even if other books are not studied, there would be no regret."[105]

From the above, it is clear that Hsü Heng honestly believed in the importance of the *Hsiao-hsüeh* for moral cultivation and daily conduct. Perhaps he was teaching Mongols and Central Asians for whom the simple and plain text of the *Hsiao-hsüeh* was the most practical. Perhaps he preferred to confine himself to practical matters to avoid any possible ideological controversy or political complication. Or perhaps he sought to reestablish the *tao-t'ung* through the simple and plain teachings of the *Hsiao-hsüeh*. All these speculations aside, for himself, for his son, and for his students, there is no doubt that he looked to the *Hsiao-hsüeh* as the moral guide. The upshot was that the *Hsiao-hsüeh* became the basic text for moral cultivation. Wu Ch'eng, for example, said that one should practice what the *Hsiao-hsüeh* taught about self-cultivation and human relations in order to support the foundation of the *Great Learning* which itself should precede reading books and investigating principle.[106]

Hsü Heng mentioned the *Hsiao-hsüeh* and the Four Books together and in that order. More than once in the present study, the *Great Learning* is mentioned along with the *Hsiao-hsüeh*. The simple reason is that while the *Hsiao-hsüeh* gives specific instructions and examples, the Four Books explain the moral principles behind them. Consequently Hsü Heng held that the way to enter the gate of virtue must begin with the *Hsiao-hsüeh* and then proceed to the Four Books.[107]

In 1190 Chu Hsi published the Four Books as the Four Masters, grouping them together for the first time. This arrangement may seem to be trivial, but it represents some very important developments. It means, first of all, the removal of the authority of the Five Classics[108] as the authority of Confucian thought. Further, it signals the direct return to Confucius and Mencius for their teachings. And finally, the Four Books, especially the *Great Learning*, offer a new methodology in moral training and intellectual pursuit.[109] For some thirty years Chu Hsi had been working on them. In 1163, when he was 34, he wrote the *Lun-yü yao-i*[df] (Essential Meanings of the *Analects*). In 1172, evidently not satisfied with the commentary, he wrote another one, namely, the *Lun-yü cheng-i*[dg] (Correct Meanings of the *Analects*). Five years later, he produced the *Lun-yü chi-chu*[dh] (Collected Commentaries on the *Analects*) and the *Meng Tzu chi-chu*[di] (Collected Commentaries on the Book of *Mencius*), in which he selected comments from outstanding Sung Neo-Confucians and added his own. In 1189, at the age of 60, he finished the *Ta-hsüeh chang-chü*[dj] (Commentary on the *Great Learning*) and the *Chung-yung chang-chü*[dk] (Commentary on the *Doctrine of the Mean*). In addition to these, in order to explain his interpretation and his selections of comments, he wrote the *Huo-wen* (Answers to Questions) on all the Four Books. On his death bed he was still revising his comment on *chüan* 6 of the Great Learning on sincerity of the will.

By the end of the Sung, the Four Books and Chu Hsi's commentaries had become basic source materials for Confucian studies. Ho Chi looked upon the Four Books as of primary importance. According to him, Chu Hsi's commentaries should be the standard interpretation of the Four Books, to be supported by Chu Hsi's recorded sayings[110] later collected in the *Chu Tzu yü-lei*[dl] (Classified Conversations of Master Chu). He wrote the *Ta-hsüeh fa-hui*[dm] (Exposition of the *Great Learning*) and the *Chung-yang fa-hui*[dn] (Exposition of the *Doctrine of the Mean*).[111] He attached so much importance to the Four Books that Huang Tsung-hsi described his goal as "merely reading the Four Books thoroughly."[112] Wang Po read the Four Books with a friend and marked with red ink Chu Hsi's comments to show how the Master had made his selections.[113]

As we have related, Chao Fu brought the Neo-Confucian works to the North, which surely included the Four Books. We have related that Yao Shu had Yang Wei-chung publish them for circulation. Chin Lü-hsiang and Liu Yin wrote extensively on the Four Books.[114] Hsü Ch'ien wrote a series of comments on Chu Hsi's collected commentaries on the Four Books.[115] How highly he regarded the Four Books can be seen in his enthusiastic statement, "The mind of the Sage is complete in the Four Books."[116]

It was Hsü Heng, however, who made the Four Books the "main current" of Yüan thought.[117] As already noted, he copied all of Chu Hsi's commentaries at Yao Shu's place and he believed in the Four Books as gods. He wrote the *Ta-hsüeh chih-chieh*[do] (Straightforward Explanations of the *Great Learning*),[118] the *Ta-hsüeh yao-lüeh*[dp] (Essentials of the Great Learning in Brief),[119] the *Chung-yung chih-chieh*[dq] (Plain Explanations of the *Doctrine of the Mean*),[120] the *Chung-yung shuo*[dr] (Explanations of the *Doctrine of the Mean*) (now lost), and the *Meng Tzu piao-t'i*[ds] (Exposition of the *Book of Mencius*) (also not extant). In teaching others, he confined himself to the *Hsiao-hsüeh* and the Four Books.[121] To him, these works are the gateway to enter virtue[122] and the way for his own self-cultivation and teaching others.[123] After he obtained these works, he changed all his old habits.[124] Since he presided over the Imperial College, the Four Books became prevalent throughout the country.

There is no doubt that the universal presence of the Four Books contributed to the imperial decree in the second year of the Huang-ch'ing[dt] period (1313) to make the Four Books and the Five Classics the basic required texts for the civil service examinations, and in the following year to reaffirm Chu Hsi's commentaries as their official interpretations.[125] Needless to say, this led to the imperial order to compile the *Ssu-shu ta-ch'üan*[du] (Great Compendium of Commentaries on the Four Books) in 1414. For hundreds of years, the Four Books were the primary texts for elementary education and the commentaries for higher education.

Among the Four Books, the *Great Learning* comes first. As Chu Hsi said, "In the pursuit of learning, one should begin with the *Great Learning*."[126] Wang Po wrote two treatises on it, namely, the *Ta-haüeh yen-ko lun*[dv] (Treatise on the Successive Changes of the *Great Learning*) and the *Ta-hsüeh yen-ko hou-lun*[dw] (A Further Treatise on the Successive Changes of the *Great Learning*).[127] So did Hsü Heng, as we have noted. In teaching, Wang Po started with the *Great Learning*.[128] Wu Ch'eng,

too, said, "In reading Confucian works, one should begin with the Four
Books, and in reading the Four Books, one should begin with the *Great
Learning*."[129] Hsü Heng also said that it is the starting point of Confu-
cian teaching.[130]

According to the *Hsin Yüan shih*[dx] (New Yüan History), not only
Chu Hsi's commentaries on the Four Books and the *Hsiao-hsüeh*, but
the *Chin-ssu lu*[dy] (Reflections on Things at Hand) also, circulated widely
in the country.[131] If this was the case, I have found no evidence to
support it. Nevertheless, one would expect it to be so because Chu Hsi
regarded it as "the ladder to the Four Books."[132] In his own eyes and in
the eyes of Chinese thinkers, the *Chin-ssu lu* is a far more important
work than the *Hsiao-hsüeh*. In collaboration with Lü Tsu-ch'ien, he selected 622 passages and sayings from Chou Tun-i, Ch'eng Hao, Ch'eng
I, and Chang Tsai on the substance of Tao, personal cultivation, the
family, education, government, and criticism of Buddhism and Taoism
in fourteen *chüan*.[133] Chu Hsi and Lü Tsu-ch'ien worked together very
carefully, and Chu Hsi and his pupils discussed it often. Two of his
pupils and two of pupils' pupils wrote commentaries on it.[134] We know
that Ho Chi wrote a commentary too.[135] But there is not enough evidence to show that it spread as widely as did the *Hsiao-hsüeh*. It is true
that Yao Shu had it printed for circulation in the country along with the
Hsiao-hsüeh.[136] It is also true that there was one commentary on it during the Yüan, by Liu Kuan[dz] (1270–1342).[137] It is no longer extant. Mao
Hsing-lai[ea] (1678–1748) mentioned Huang Chin[eb] (1277–1357) as the
author of a commentary recorded in *chüan* 181 of the *Yüan shih*.[138] It is
true that the commentary is mentioned in this chapter, which is the
biography of Huang Chin. But Mao Hsing-lai has overlooked the facts
that appended to the biography of Huang Chin is the biography of Liu
Kuan and that the commentary is mentioned here as Liu Kuan's work.[139]
None of the major Yüan thinkers wrote on the *Chin-ssu lu* or discussed
it at any length if at all. We have no basis on which to judge the quality
of the two Yüan commentaries. Quantitatively, they do not compare favorably with those of the Sung or the Ch'ing (1644–1912). In the Southern Sung, there were six commentaries and in the Ch'ing, eight.[140] It
compares only with the Ming period, of which we know of only two,
those by Chou Kung-shu[ec] (fl. 1420) and Wang Tao-k'un[ed] (1525–1593).
But the former is definitely poor and the latter most likely a forgery.[141]
This poor showing in the Ming is of course due to the overshadowing of

the Ch'eng-Chu tradition by the Wang Yang-ming (Wang Shou-jen,[ee] 1472–1529) school, but the lack of interest in the anthology in the Yüan most probably contributed to it.

The main reason for the Four Books and *Hsiao-hsüeh* eclipsing the *Chin-ssu lu* is not difficult to see. Chu Hsi said, "Refined and subtle principles are fully treated in the *Chin-ssu lu*."[142] By and large Yüan thinkers were not much inclined to refined and subtle principles. It has been pointed out that the doctrine of the *T'ai-chi* did not develop. The more important reason for the obscurity of the *Chin-ssu lu* is that while the *Hsiao-hsüeh* and the commentaries on the Four Books are works of Chu Hsi himself, the *Chin-ssu lu* contains the doctrines of Northern Sung Neo-Confucians instead, and Chu Hsi, but not the Sung philosophers, was the idol of Yüan thinkers. The most outstanding philosopher of Yüan was Hsü Heng, and the greatest idol for Hsü Heng was Master Chu. In his works, there is not a single reference to the *Chin-ssu lu!*

Reference has been made to Chao Fu's assuming the discipleship of Chu Hsi and his transmission of Chu Hsi's works to Yao Shu, and Yao Shu's printing and distributing of them. We have seen how Yüan scholars were attracted to Chu Hsi's followers and how religiously they took his works. The one who elevated Chu Hsi to the position of the highest honor among the Sung philosophers, however, was Hsü Heng. If he regarded his works as gods, how much more would he regard the Master himself? But it is ironic that Hsü Heng rarely mentioned Chu Hsi in his conversations or writings. Rather, it was the spirit of Chu Hsi that saturated his life and teaching. As his chronological biography says of him, "Throughout his life, his desire for Master Chu was like that of a hungry or thirsty person. His teaching was entirely based on Master Chu. When he was asked about other philosophers' works, he would tell the student to concentrate for the time on one person only," and that meant Chu Hsi.[143] It has also been said, "From the beginning to the end, Hsü Heng believed and honored Chu Hsi."[144] According to another source, "In his teaching, Hsü Heng always took the works of Master Chu as his teacher."[145] In conducting himself, in serving the ruler, and in teaching the rising generation, he always relied on Master Chu.[146] Because he strongly believed and honored Chu Hsi, he has been considered as being able to reveal the deep meanings of Chu Hsi's teachings.[147] It was claimed that since Chu Hsi's death, Hsü Heng alone was able to obtain Chu Hsi's learning of the mind.[148] In other words, in the eyes of the later Confucians, after Chu Hsi, it was Hsü Heng who continued the true transmission of the *tao-t'ung*.[149] That is to say, just as Chu Hsi continued the tradition from Ch'eng I and Ch'eng Hao, so did Hsü Heng continue it from Chu Hsi.[150] "When Wen-cheng Kung[ef] (Hsü Heng) appeared," it was said, "scholars all followed him with one accord. In his learning, he honored and believed in Master Chu. Consequently, the Way of Chou Tun-i and the Ch'eng brothers became more brilliant. It was his effort that enabled the people in the country to know and read the books of Ch'eng and Chu."[151] Momentarily approaching death, he sang a short poem composed by Chu Hsi.[152]

Since Hsü Heng put Chu Hsi in such an overwhelming position, it is almost anticlimactic to quote what later Neo-Confucianists did for or said of the Master. Still, it is worthy of note that Huang Chen[eg] (1213–1280), who traced his heritage to Chu Hsi's pupil Fu Kuang[eh] (fl. 1208) rather than Huang Kan, restored the memorial hall to Chu Hsi.[153] To Liu Yin, "Shao Yung was the greatest, Chou Tun-i the most refined, and Ch'eng Hao and Ch'eng I the most correct, but Master Chu was great to the highest degree and refined to the limit, and penetrated all with correctness."[154] Hsü Ch'ien thought "the mind of the Sage and worthies are complete in the Four Books, and the principles of the Four Books are complete in Master Chu."[155] When Wu Ch'eng was nineteen, he wrote about Tao, saying, "Master Chou is its Origination, the Ch'engs and Chang its Flourish, and Master Chu its Advantage, but who is its Firmness today?"[156] He was referring to the four stages of Change in the *Book of Changes*.[157] There is no doubt that he aspired to play the role of the Firmness of Tao himself. Nevertheless, his admiration for Chu Hsi is unmistakable. Drawing a general picture of the Chu Hsi landscape in the Yüan, the *Hsin Yüan shih* says:

After Chao Fu arrived at the Central Plain, scholars in the North began to read books by Chu Hsi. Hsü Heng and Hsiao K'u[ei] [1241–1318], lecturers and great teachers, both religiously followed Master Chu as the standard. Chin Lü-hsiang was an indirect pupil of Master Chu's pupil, and Hsü Ch'ien studied with Chin. Because of them, the learning of Chu Hsi became even more honored. When the North and the South were united, Hsü Heng became Chancellor of the Imperial College. Although Hsü Ch'ien repeatedly refused the invitation to serve in the government, he was highly respected by the Court. Under their influence, scholars looking forward to learning were aroused and came forward. Master Chu's commentaries on the Four Books, the *Chin-ssu lu*, and the *Hsiao-hsüeh* prevailed throughout the country. Consequently, in the Yen-yu[ej] period [1314–1320], Chu Hsi's books became the official texts for the civil service examinations. The system remained unchanged throughout the Yüan.[158]

This account, however, contains two doubious statements. It inaccurately asserts that only after Chao Fu's arrival scholars in the north began to read books by Chu Hsi, for, as indicated above, Chu Hsi's works were already known by several scholars under the Chin, although the north did not know the Ch'eng-Chu learning as an intellectual system until after the arrival of Chao Fu. It also quibbles on Hsü Heng's tenure of office as Chancellor of the Imperial College; the latter, according to his biographical records, assumed this office in 1267, eight years before the Mongol conquest of Southern Sung.

Although Chu Hsi's domination of Yüan thought was almost total, there were some excursions, nevertheless, to the thoughts of his opponent, Lu Hsiang-shan. It is often stated that perhaps the most important intellectual development in the Yüan period was the harmonizing of Chu Hsi's and Lu's teachings. Sometimes the word "synthesis" is used. This, all agree, was done by Wu Ch'eng and Cheng Yü[ek] (1298–1358). Surely this was a very significant development. It not only showed that there was some dissent from Chu Hsi's ideas but also offered an opportunity for Neo-Confucianism to unfold in a new direction. What did the movement actually accomplish?

After Lu died, his doctrine spread eastward to Chekiang. Before long, his home district, Kiangsi, came under the influence of Chu Hsi's followers. As a result, the Lu school eventually declined. This was due to several factors. The erratic behavior of Lu's followers did not attract people to them. Lu did not write any book which could serve as a rallying point for his movement. His philosophy that "The universe is my mind and my mind is the universe"[159] was too close to that of the Buddhist meditation school to suit the Confucianists. Most important of all, Chu Hsi's works were the required texts for the civil service examinations and his philosophy was the orthodoxy of the time. Since Hsü Heng promoted the doctrines of Chu Hsi, scholars flocked to Chu instead of Lu. Consequently, there was simply no Lu school to speak of in the Yüan. Historians of Chinese philosophy usually mention Chao Chieh[el] (fl. 1271) and Ch'en Yüan[em] (1256–1330) as Yüan followers of the Lu philosophy, but they were only trickles in the Yüan intellectual current.

Although a Lu school as such did not exist, the Lu Hsiang-shan philosophy of mind enjoyed some local loyalty in Kiangsi, especially in the Kuang-hsin[en] prefecture area, the site of the famous debate between Chu and Lu at the Goose Lake (O-hu[eo]) Grove in 1175. Historians have oversimplified the debate by saying that Lu favored "following the path of inquiry and study,"[160] for Chu honored the moral nature too, but the divergent tendencies were to some extent real. Quite early in the thirteenth century, Kuang-hsin had become a Chu Hsi sphere of influence. Whatever Lu influence remained was minor. There was a family of three brothers, T'ang Chung, T'ang Chin, and T'ang Ch'ien[ep] (1172–1226), with T'ang Chin following Lu while his elder and younger brothers followed Chu. As a reaction to the partisan recrimination of the followers of the two schools against each other after the debate, the tendency in Kuang-hsin was to compromise rather than to confront. T'ang Chung was probably the first one to do so.[161] His friend, Ch'eng Shao-k'ai[eq] (1212–1280) built an academy and called it the Tao-i[er] (The Way is One) Academy to show that the Tao of Chu and Lu was identical.[162] The idea found an eloquent expression in his student Wu Ch'eng.[163]

Wu argues that the doctrine of the mind had been handed down from Yao and Shun, etc., to Confucius and Mencius. This is where Lu's philosophy of mind came from. But it is not his own; Chou, the Ch'eng brothers, Chang, and Shao all taught it. It is therefore wrong to consider only Lu's philosophy as the philosophy of mind.[164] The omission of Chu Hsi's name here is conspicious. In a letter answering T'ien Chün-tse, Wu insisted on honoring the moral nature as the first priority for moral cultivation, but he added that this should be followed by following the path of inquiry and study.[165] As he said in a farewell essay for Ch'en Hung-fan,[es]

In teaching people, Master Chu always began with reading books and discussion, while Master Lu always told people to know truly and practice concretely. Reading and discussion of course provide true knowledge and concrete practice with a foundation, and true knowledge and concrete practice must be attained through reading and discussion. The two teachers are the same in their teaching. Only inferior pupils in the two schools set up slogans and slander each other. . . . For your sake, you should untiringly devote yourself to the Four Books as explained by Master Chu.[166]

In his essay on honoring the moral nature and following the path of inquiry and study, he blames Chu Hsi's followers for overemphasizing book learning and literary studies.[167] Wu Ch'eng was definitely more inclined to Lu's philosophy of mind, but he seems to be more concerned with the partisan spirit of the followers of the two schools. As his most famous pupil, Yü Chi[et] (1272–1348) understood it, because his many students were "unequal in their capacities, each seeking according to his desire and each receiving according to his ability, he wrote the essay "Hsüeh-chi"eu (Foundation of Learning) so they would know that the moral nature should be honored and the "Hsüeh-t'ung"ev (Tradition of Learning) so they would know that the path of inquiry and study should be followed." In other words, in Wu Ch'eng's view, the different Chu and Lu formulae were meant for people of different capacities.[168] At any rate, his total orientation was still toward Chu. Ch'üan Tsu-wangew (1705–1755) is not mistaken in saying that "Wu Ch'eng, coming from the Jao Lu line, was of course a pursuer of the learning of Chu Hsi. Later he also held certain doctrines taught by Lu. . . . But in his writings he was in the final analysis close to Chu."[169] Surely in his ideas on the *T'ai-chi* and nature and principle, he remained solidly in the Ch'eng-Chu tradition.[170]

In the case of Cheng Yü, his preference for Chu Hsi is even more clear-cut. He said,

Master Lu's endowment was high and brilliant and therefore he loved to be simple and easy. Master Chu's endowment was earnest and solid and therefore he preferred to be obstruse and full. Because of their natural inclination, they travelled on different paths. But as they arrived at their destination, was there any difference in moral principles and virtue? Both of them honored the Duke of Chou and Confucius and both of them rejected Buddhism and Taoism. . . . When people in the east of the River [Chekiang] point to the west of the River [Kiangsi] and say, "Queer doctrines are operating there," and when people in the west of the River point to the east of the River and say, "Theirs is a doctrine of isolated details," is that a good way to learn? Master Chu's doctrines are regular ways to teach people to learn, while Master Lu's doctrines are an excellence achieved by one's own great ability. The two schools are not free from defects. The defect of Lu's learning is similar to that of the Buddhists talking about emptiness and mystery. They excell in abruptness and carelessness and cannot devote themselves to the effort of extending knowledge. The defect of Chu's learning is like vulgar scholars tracing lines and counting words. They will end up downhearted and wearied, and cannot accomplish any result in earnest practice. Are these the faults of the teaching of the Masters? They are only the defects of their followers.[171]

Cheng Yü also considered Lu as making insufficient effort and lacking a procedure. His learning was all right for his own cultivation, Cheng thought, but bad for others to practice. Therefore, students should follow Chu Hsi instead but at the same time should not slander Lu.[172]

Both Wu Ch'eng and Cheng Yü aimed at reconciling the opposite approaches and attitudes with respect to learning and cultivation, but neither made any attempt at philosophical synthesis. There was no attempt, for example, to combine Chu's philosophy of principle as identical with nature with Lu's philosophy of principle as identical with the mind. Nor was there any effort to resolve the supposed dichotomy of honoring the moral nature and following the path of inquiry and study. Even in the discussions on the *T'ai-chi*, there was no inquiry as to the compatibility between the positions held by Chu and Lu. We cannot help feeling that a golden opportunity for synthesis was lost.

An excellent synthesis would be that of the two wings of cultivation summed up in Chu Hsi's celebrated phrase, *chü-ching ch'iung-li*ex (abide in seriousness and investigation of principle to the utmost) which became the standard formula for the Confucian search for sagehood. The idea goes back to Ch'eng I, who said, "Self-cultivation requires seriousness and the pursuit of learning depends on the extension of knowledge."[173] Chu Hsi elaborated on it and said, "To hold seriousness as fundamental is the essential way to preserve the mind, and to extend knowledge is the effort to advance learning. The two promote each other."[174] To him, "Abiding in seriousness and investigating principle to the utmost cannot be followed onesidedly or ignored."[175] "Although they are two," he said, "in reality they are of one foundation."[176]

The theme runs through Huang Kan's writings.[177] He quoted Chu Hsi as saying, "Abide in seriousness in order to establish the foundation and investigate principle in order to extend knowledge."[178] Their words have appeared in numerous Neo-Confucian works ever since. But strange to say, with all their loyalty to Chu Hsi, Yüan thinkers did not give any attention to this cardinal doctrine. Chin Lü-hsiang stressed both holding on to seriousness and extensive study,[179] and Hsü Ch'ien quoted Ch'eng I's saying,[180] but the latter's concern was with the doctrine of principle being one and its manifestations being many. In so far as Hsü Heng taught earnest practice and careful study of the *Hsiao-hsüeh* and the Four Books, he may be presumed to advocate both abiding in seriousness and investigating principle. He has been described as following Chu Hsi's words completely, namely, "Investigate principle to extend knowledge and return to oneself for concrete practice."[181] Here, too, we may assume that the spirit of seriousness and investigation of principle permeated his personality as well as his teaching. He discussed investigation of things on several occasions,[182] but to him investigation of things mean to make moral choices.[183] He was practically silent on the subject of ching. We do not see any deliberate effort on the part of this towering figure to advance the Ch'eng-Chu teaching of chü-ching ch'iung-li.

Nor do we find any attempt on the part of the other towering figure, Wu Ch'eng. It is amazing that when he discussed Shao Yung's philosophy of form and number (hsiang-shu),[ey] instead of talking about investigation of things as one would expect, he said that all form and number are complete in oneself.[184] To him, investigation of things to the utmost means such things as being cautious when alone.[185] "Seriousness," he said, "is the controlling factor in book reading and investigation of principle."[186] He was definitely one-sided in exclusively favoring ching. In his way of thinking, ching is the "essence of Confucian learning,"[187] "the step to sagehood,"[188] "the master of the mind and the foundation of Confucian learning."[189] Therefore, one's duty is to "be serious in order to preserve the mind," that is, "the humanity in one's mind."[190] To the extent that he strongly strengthened the tendency towards seriousness and the mind, he paved the way for further development in the Ming. Eventually the doctrine of chü-ching ch'iung-li was revived and advanced by such Ming philosophers as Hu Chü-jen[ez] (1434–1484), and the doctrine of the mind ultimately culminated in the philosophy of Wang Yang-ming. In this sense, Yüan philosophers performed a constructive service.

NOTES

1. YS (PN ed.), 2:6b.
2. Yao Sui,[fa] *Mu-an chi*[fb] (SPTK ed.), 15:3a-b; YS, 146:14a. See Hok-lam Chan, "Yao Shu (1203–1280), *"Papers on Far Eastern History* (September 1980), 22:19–22.
3. YS, 189:1b–3a.
4. *Mu-an chi*, 15:4a: YS, 146:14a.
5. YS, 189:2b.
6. YS, 158:1b, biography of Yao Shu.
7. *Mu-an chi*, 15:4a; K'o Shao-min,[fc] *Hsin Yüan shih* (Peking: Peking University Research Institute, 1933), 157:13b, "Ju-lin chuan"[fd] (biographies of Confucianists); YS, 189:2a. Chu Hsi wrote poems in praise of portraits of these Six Masters. See *Chu Wen-kung wen-chi*[fe] (SPPY ed.) entitled *Chu Tzu ta-ch'üan*,[ff] 85:9a–b.
8. Huang Tsung-hsi, comp., SYHA (SPPY ed.), 90:7a.
9. According to *Mu-an chi*, 15:4b.
10. See note 6 above.
11. Ou-yang Hsüan,[fg] *Kuei-chai wen-chi*[fh] (SPTK ed.), 9:2b; *Hsü Wen-cheng kung i-shu*[fi] (hereafter IS) (1790 ed.), concluding *chüan*, 8a.
12. Wang Tzu-ts'ai and Feng Yün-hao,[fj] comp. (Taipei: World Book Co., 1962), 90:28a. They misunderstood the statement in IS, beginning *chüan*, 8a, that "Yao Shu transmitted the Ch'eng-Chu learning of Chao Fu" to mean that Yao Shu transmitted the Ch'eng-Chu learning to Chao Fu." For Hsü Heng, see YS, 158:6b; SYHA, 90:1b; and also Yüan Kuo-fan (Chi),[fk] *Yüan Hsü Lu-chai p'ing-shu*[fl] (Taipei: Commercial Press, 1972).
13. YS, 189:2b, biography of Chao Fu.
14. Jao Tsung-i, "San-chiao lun yü Sung-Chin hsüeh-shu"[fm] (Harmony of the Three Religions and the Learning of Sung and Chin), *Tung-hsi wen-hua*[fn] (Eastern and Western Cultures), (May 1968), 11:28–32. For Li Ch'un-fu's criticisms of Sung Neo-Confucianists, see his *Ming-tao chi-shuo*[fo] (undated Ming ms.; microfilm from the rare book collection of the former Peiping Library, no. 178) 5:4b–5b, 12b–13b. Cf. Jan Yün-hua, "Li Ping-shan and His Refutation of Neo-Confucian Criticism of Buddhism," in *Developments in Buddhist Thought: Canadian Contributions to Buddhist Studies*, ed. Roy C. Amore (Waterloo, Ontario: Wilfrid Laurier University Press, 1979), pp. 162–93.
15. Jing-shen Tao, *The Jurchen in Twelfth-century China: A Study of Siniciza-tion* (Seattle: University of Washington Press, 1976), pp. 105, 109, 151 note 3. For Wang Jo-hsü, see his *Hu-nan i-lao chi*[fp] (SPTK ed.), ch. 3–8. Yosh-ikawa Kōjirō[fq] has discussed more thoroughly the transmission of Chu Hsi's philosophy to North China under the Chin in his "Shushigaku no hokuden zenshi,"[fr] in *Uno Tetsujin sensei hakuju shukuga kinen Tōyōgaku ronsō*[fs] (Tokyo: Tōhō Gakkai, 1974), pp. 1237–58. See also briefly, Wm. Theodore

de Bary, "The Rise of Neo-Confucian Orthodoxy in Yüan China," in *Neo-Confucian Orthodoxy and the Learning of the Mind-and-Heart* (New York: Columbia University Press, 1981), pp. 18–20.

16. *Sung shih*[ft] (PN ed.), 438:5a–b. For Ho Chi, see SYHA, 82:1a.

17. *Sung shih*, 438:8a; SYHA, 82:1a. Hu's saying, Professor Conrad Schirokauer has informed me, is found in Hu's *Wu-feng chi*[fu] (SKCSCP 1st ser.; Shanghai: Commercial Press, 1935).

18. YS, 189:4a.

19. YS, 189:6a; SYHA, 82:1a.

20. YS, 189:6b. For Hsü Ch'ien, see SYHA, 82:18b.

21. YS, 189:6b. For an informative account of the Chin-hua group, see John D. Langlois, Jr., "The Chin-hua Tradition and the Mongol Conquest," in *id.*, ed., *China Under Mongol Rule* (Princeton: Princeton University Press, 1981), pp. 137–85.

22. SYHA, 83:1b.

23. *Sung shih*, 430:1b–2a.

24. See *Mien-chai chi*[fv] (SKCSCP, 2d ser.; Taipei: Commercial Press, 1971), *ch.* 4–18. See also SYHA, 63:1a.

25. *Mien-chai chi*, 36:48a–b; *Huang Mien-chai chi*[fw] (*Cheng-i t'ang ch'üan-shu*[fx] ed.) 8:37a–b. See also *Sung shih*, 429:20b.

26. See my "Chu Hsi's Completion of Neo-Confucianisn," in Françoise Aubin, ed., *Études Song in memoriam Étienne Balazs* (Paris: Mouton Co., 1973), ser. 2, no. 1, pp. 73–81.

27. *Mien-chai chi*, 3:19a; SYHA, 63:2a–3b.

28. *Lu-chai chi*[fy], 11:1a, "Pa Tao-t'ung lu"[fz] (Postscript to *Records of the Transmission of the Way*).

29. YS, 158:22b. For Tou Mo, see SYHA, 90:7a.

30. SYHA, 82:19b.

31. *Kuei-chai wen-chi*, 9:1a, 6a, 1b, respectively; IS, concluding *chüan*, 6a.

32. Supplement to concluding *chüan*, 3b.

33. *Ibid.*, 3b.

34. *Wu Wen-cheng chi*[ga] (SKCSCP, 2d ser.), 8:1b.

35. *Ibid.*, 48:13b.

36. *Ibid.*, 37:12b.

37. *T'ung-shu*, ch. 10. For a translation, see Wing-tsit Chan, A *Source Book in Chinese Philosophy* (Princeton: Princeton University Press, 1963), p. 470.

38. *I-ch'uan wen-chi*[gb] (SPPY ed.), 4:1a–2b. For a translation, see Chan, *Source Book*, pp. 547–50.

39. IS, 1:20a.

40. *Sung shih*, 438:6b.

41. *Ibid.*, 438:8b.

42. In the *Chou Tzu ch'üan-shu*[gc] (*Wan-yu wen-k'u*[gd] ed.), 5:74–76.

43. YS, 189:4a.

44. See *Sung shih*, ch. 463, and *Chou Tzu ch'üan-shu* 1:5–14.

45. The *T'ai-chi* is mentioned in Ch'eng I's preface to the *I-chuan*, but most scholars have considered the preface a forgery.

46. See my "Chu Hsi's Completion of Neo-Confucianism," pp. 67–72.
47. *Doctrine of the Mean*, ch. 12.
48. *Ibid.*
49. *Huang Mien-chai chi*, 1:27a–28b, "Ta Yeh Wei-tao"ge (Letter in Answer to Yeh Wei-tao).
50. *Mien-chai chi*, 3:31a; SYHA, 63:3a–4a.
51. For Chu Hsi on the *T'ai-chi* and substance and function, see *Chu Tzu yü-lei* (Taipei: Cheng-chung Book Co., 1970), ch. 94.
52. YS, 157:24b.
53. *Lu-chai chi*, 8:6a–7b; *Sung shih*, 438:8a.
54. SYHA, 12:10b–12a.
55. *Ibid.*, 83:1a.
56. Quoted in the *Hsing-li ta-ch'üan*, comp. Hu Kuang,gf et al., in 1415, 1:22b.
57. SYHA, 83:4a.
58. *Wu Wen-cheng chi*, 4:1a–3a.
59. SYHA, 12:9a–10a.
60. *Ibid.*
61. *Wu Wen-cheng chi*, 4:1a–3a.
62. *Ibid.*, 3:2b, 6b–7a. For Chu Hsi, see *Chu Tzu yü-lei*, 94:3756.
63. For the debates between Chu and Lu, see *Hsiang-shan ch'üan-chi*gg (SPPY ed.), 2:4b–11b; *Chu Wen-kung wen-chi*, 36:7a–16b; SYHA, 12:3a–8b.
64. SYHA, 91:2a, 82:20b, 92:8a.
65. *Ibid.*, 83:5a.
66. *Ibid.*, 12:12b–15a.
67. *Wu Wen-cheng chi*, 3:1b–2a: "Letter in Reply to T'ien Chün-tse."
68. *Ibid.*, 2:12b–14b, "Letter in Reply to Wang I-po."gh For a translation, see D. Gedalecia, *Wu Ch'eng: A Neo-Confucian of the Yüan* (Ann Arbor: University Microfilms, 1975), pp. 98–103.
69. See *Chu Tzu yü-lei*, 94:3766.
70. See note 68.
71. *Hsing-li ta-ch'üan*, 1:46b–47a.
72. Compiled by Li Kuang-ti,gi SPPY ed., 1:4b.
73. *Chu Tzu yü-lei*, 94:3773.
74. *Wu Wen-cheng chi*, 2:13b.
75. *Yüeh-ch'uan i-shu*gj (1832 ed.), 1:17b–18a; *Chou Tzu ch'üan-shu*, 5:86.
76. *Chu Tzu yü-lei*, 1:1.
77. IS, 10:1a.
78. *Ibid.*, 1:4b.
79. *Mencius* 7A:4.
80. IS, 6:12b.
81. *Analects* 14:37.
82. SYHA, 63:4b–5a; *Mien-chai chi*, 3:14b–17a.
83. *Mien-chai chi*, 17:10b–1a, "Letter in Reply to Jao Po-yü";gk *Huang Mien-chai chi*, 4:20b.
84. SYHA, 82:1a.
85. *Sung shih*, 438:7a.

86. SYHA, 82:9b.
87. IS, 1:6a–b, 2:16b.
88. *Ibid.*, 2:12b.
89. *Ibid.*, 2:13a, 2:16a.
90. *Ibid.*, 3:17a.
91. *Kuei-chai wen-chi*, 9:5b; IS, concluding *chüan*, 11a.
92. Ruler and minister, father and son, brothers, husband and wife, and friends.
93. Translations: *Seaou Heo or Primary Learning*, tr. by E. C. Bridgeman, *Chinese Repository*, vol. 5 (1836), pp. 81–87, 305–16; vol. 6 (1837), pp. 185–88, 393–96, 562–68; *La Siao Hio, ou morale de la jeunesse, avec le commentaire de Tschen-Siuen*[gl] (1430–1487) (Paris, 1889): *Annales du Musée Guimet*, vol. 15, 366 pp.
94. *Chu Tzu yü-lei*, 105:4179.
95. *Ibid.*, p. 4178.
96. *Mien-chai chi*, 15:10a.
97. YS, 171:5a.
98. IS, beginning *chüan*, 8a–b; *Mu-an chi*, 15:4b–5a; *Hsin Yüan shih*, 170:1b.
99. IS, supplement to concluding *chüan*, 13a, 17b.
100. *Ibid.*, beginning *chüan*, 8b–9a; *Hsin Yüan shih*, 170:1b–2a.
101. YS, 171:6a; *Hsin Yüan shih*, 170:15a.
102. Yü Chi, *Tao-yüan hsüeh-ku lu*[gm] (SPPY ed.), 5:10a: "Sung Li K'uo hsü"[gn] (Farewell to Li K'uo).
103. IS, supplement to concluding *chüan*, 5b.
104. *Ibid.*, 2:8a.
105. *Ibid.*, 9:6b.
106. *Wu Wen-cheng chi*, 2:11b–12a.
107. IS, supplement to concluding *chüan*, 2a.
108. The *Book of Odes*, the *Book of Documents*, the *Book of Changes*, the *Book of Rites*, and the *Spring and Autumn Annals*.
109. See my "Chu Hsi's Completion of Neo-Confucianism," pp. 82–87.
110. SYHA, 82:2a.
111. *Sung shih*, 438:6b.
112. SYHA, 82:2b.
113. SYHA, 82:3a.
114. YS, 189:5b, 171:5a, respectively.
115. YS, 189:7a.
116. *Ibid.*
117. See Shimizu Nobuyoshi,[go] *Kinsai chūgoku shisō shi*[gp] (History of Modern Chinese Thought) (Tokyo: Meiji Book Co., 1950), pp. 272–73; Morohashi Tetsuji,[gq] *Jukyō no shomondai*[gr] (Certain Problems of Confucianism) (Tokyo: Shimizu shōten,[gs] 1948), p. 197.
118. IS, *ch.* 4.
119. *Ibid.*, 3:4a–17a.
120. *Ibid.*, *ch.* 5.
121. IS, preface, 9a.

122. IS, supplement to concluding *chüan*, 2a.
123. *Ibid.*, 4a.
124. *Ibid.*, 13b.
125. YS, 81:5a.
126. *Chu Tzu yü-lei*, 105:397.
127. *Lu-chai chi*, 9:10b–13b, 10:1a–4a.
128. *Sung shih*, 438:7a.
129. *Wu Wen-cheng chi*, 9:19a.
130. IS, 3:4b.
131. *Hsin Yüan-shih*, 234:1a, "Ju-lin chuan."
132. *Chu Tzu yü-lei*, 105:4179.
133. See Chu Hsi and Lü Tsu-ch'ien, *Reflections on Things at Hand, the Neo-Confucian Anthology*, tr. Wing-tsit Chan (New York: Columbia University Press, 1967). Also *Djin-silu*, tr. into German by Olaf Graf, 3 vols. (Tokyo: Sophia University Press, 1953).
134. *Reflections on Things at Hand*, p. 338, nos. 1–4.
135. *Sung shih*, 438:6b.
136. *Mu-an chi*, 15:4b.
137. YS, 181:21a. See *Reflections on Things at Hand*, p. 340, note 7.
138. *Chin-ssu lu chi-chu*[gt] (SKCSCP, 1st ser.), 66a.
139. See note 137.
140. See *Reflections on Things at Hand*, pp. 338–39 and 341–45 respectively. There was also one commentary by Jao Lu. See SYHA, 181:21a.
141. See *ibid.*, pp. 340–41.
142. See note 132.
143. IS, beginning *chüan*, 8b.
144. Supplement to concluding *chüan*, 5a.
145. *Ibid.*, 2a.
146. *Ibid.*, 13b.
147. Old preface, 2b.
148. Supplement to concluding *chüan*, 4b.
149. *Ibid.*, 5b.
150. *Ibid.*, 4a.
151. *Ibid.*, 3a.
152. Beginning *chüan*, 19a. I cannot find the poem in *Chu Wen-kung wen-chi*.
153. *Sung shih*, 438:19b.
154. YS, 171:1b–2a.
155. SYHA, 89:3a.
156. *Tao-yüan hsüeh-ku lu*, 44:3a; YS, 171:8a; *Hsin Yüan shih*, 170:14b.
157. I.e., explanation of the hexagram Ch'ien.[gu]
158. YS, introduction to *ch.* 234, "Ju-lin chuan."
159. *Hsiang-shan ch'üan-chi*, 22:5a.
160. *Doctrine of the Mean*, ch. 27.
161. Yüan Chüeh,[gv] *Ch'ing-jung chü-shih chi*[gw] (SPPY ed.), 21:4b; Ch'üan Tsu-wang, *Chi-i-t'ing chi*[gx] (*Kuo-hsüeh chi-pen ts'ung-shu*[gy] ed.), 34:430–31,

"Letter in Reply to Master Lin-ch'uan." See SYHA, 84:1a–2b. For a discussion, see Gedalecia (note 68), pp. 93–97.

162. SYHA, 84:6a–b, 9a:1a.
163. *Ibid.*, 92:1a.
164. *Wu Wen-cheng chi*, 48:12b–14a, "Hsien-ch'eng pen-hsin-lou chi"[gz] (Essay on the Pen-hsin Tower at Hsien-ch'eng), tr. in Gedalecia, pp. 235–38.
165. *Ibid.*, 3:28a.
166. *Ibid.*, 27:18b–19a, tr. in Gedalecia, pp. 254–56.
167. *Ibid.*, 40:1b–2a, "Tsun-te-hsing tao-wen-hsüeh chi"[ha] (Essay on Honoring the Moral Nature and Following the Path of Inquiry and Study), tr. in Gedalecia, pp. 203–7. Cf. also the paper by Gedalecia in this volume.
168. *Tao-yüan hsüeh-ku lu*, 44:13b; *Wu Wen-cheng chi*, supplement, 42b; the "Hsüeh-chi" and "Hsüeh-t'ung" are found in the 1756 ed. of the *Wu Wen-cheng chi*, suppl. *chüan*, 1:1b–8b.
169. SYHA, 92:1a.
170. *Wu Wen-cheng chi*, 2:18a–20b, "Ta jen wen *hsing-li*"[hb] (Answering Someone's Question on Nature and Principle), tr. in Gedalecia, pp. 137–45.
171. *Shih-shan chi*[hc] (SKCSCP, 4th ser.; Taipei: Commercial Press, 1973), 3:19a–20b, "Sung Ko Tzu-hsi hsü"[hd] (Farewell to Ko Tzu-hsi).
172. *Ibid.*, 3:8a, "Letter to Wang Chen-ch'ing."[he]
173. Ch'eng Hao and Ch'eng I, *I-shu*,[hf] in the *Erh-Ch'eng ch'üan-shu*[hg] (SPPY ed.), 18:5b.
174. *Chu Wen-kung wen-chi*, 38:49a.
175. *Ibid.*, 41:1b.
176. *Chu Tzu yü-lei*, 9:239.
177. *Mien-chai chi*, 5:24a, "Letter to Li Ching-tzu,"[hh] 8:5a, "Letter to Hu Po-liang";[hi] 17:5a, "Letter in Reply to Assistant Magistrate Wang";[hj] 17:12a, "Letter in Reply to Jao Po-yü," respectively.
178. *Ibid.*, 18:19a, "Letter in Reply to Li Kung-hui"[hk] (*Huang Mien-chai chi*, 2:3a).
179. SYHA, 82:10a.
180. *Ibid.*, 82:20b.
181. IS., supplement to concluding *chüan*, 2a, quoting *Mien-chai chi*, 36:39b (*Huang Mien-chai chi*, 8:30b).
182. IS, 1:5a, 2:6a–b, 2:16b.
183. *Ibid.*, 3:7b.
184. *Wu Wen-cheng chi*, 1:30b–31a.
185. *Ibid.*, 30:17a.
186. *Ibid.*, 4:4b.
187. *Ibid.*, 4:4b, 5:2b.
188. *Ibid.*, 5:2b.
189. *Ibid.*, 5:5a.
190. *Ibid.*, 45:18a–b.

GLOSSARY

a	陳榮捷	ak	蔡沈
b	朱熹	al	書傳
c	太宗	am	胡安國
d	德安	an	春秋傳
e	安陸	ao	許衡
f	楊惟中	ap	魏
g	燕京	aq	性理
h	姚樞	ar	四書章句集註
i	趙復	as	或問
j	程頤	at	宋元學案
k	太極	au	宋元學案補遺
l	周敦頤	av	郝經
m	程灝	aw	劉因
n	張載	ax	饒宗頤
o	楊時	ay	李純甫
p	游酢	az	王若虛
q	傳道圖	ba	金華
r	伏羲	bb	黃榦
s	神農	bc	何基
t	堯	bd	王柏
u	舜	be	金履祥
v	顏回	bf	許謙
w	伊洛發揮	bg	臨川
x	師友圖	bh	呂祖謙
y	私淑	bi	胡宏
z	伊尹	bj	立志居敬
aa	希賢錄	bk	饒魯
ab	蘇門	bl	程若庸
ac	輝州	bm	吳澄
ad	邵雍	bn	道統
ae	司馬光	bo	曾子
af	小學	bp	子思
ag	論語或問	bq	中庸章句
ah	孟子或問	br	李元綱
ai	家禮	bs	傳道正統
aj	易傳	bt	聖門事業圖

bu	周公	dg	論語正義
bv	韓愈	dh	論語集註
bw	李翶	di	孟子集註
bx	竇默	dj	大學章句
by	陸象山（九淵）	dk	中庸章句
bz	道州	dl	朱子語類
ca	通書	dm	大學發揮
cb	顏子	dn	中庸發揮
cc	通書發揮	do	大學直解
cd	周子發遣	dp	大學要略
ce	太極通書講	dq	中庸直解
cf	太極圖說	dr	中庸說
cg	無極	ds	孟子標題
ch	陰	dt	皇慶
ci	陽	du	四書大全
cj	理	dv	大學沿革論
ck	氣	dw	大學沿革後論
cl	中庸總論	dx	新元史
cm	太極演原	dy	近思錄
cn	太極衍義	dz	柳貫
co	答或人問	ea	茅星來
cp	太極洪範圖說	eb	黃溍
cq	無極太極說	ec	周公恕
cr	記太極圖說後	ed	汪道昆
cs	田君澤	ee	王陽明（守仁）
ct	黃宗羲	ef	文正公
cu	王梓材	eg	黃震
cv	黃宗炎	eh	輔廣
cw	性理大全	ei	蕭㪍
cx	性理精義	ej	延祐
cy	曹端	ek	鄭玉
cz	鬼神	el	趙偕
da	形上形下	em	陳苑
db	理一分殊	en	廣信
dc	中庸續說	eo	鵝湖
dd	小學大義	ep	湯中、湯巾、湯千
de	文公	eq	程紹開
df	論語要義	er	道一

es	陳洪範	gb	伊川文集
et	虞集	gc	周子全書
eu	學基	gd	萬有文庫
ev	學統	ge	答葉味道
ew	全祖望	gf	胡廣
ex	居敬窮理	gg	象山全集
ey	象數	gh	王儀伯
ez	胡居仁	gi	李光地
fa	姚燧	gj	月川遺書
fb	牧庵集	gk	饒伯輿
fc	柯劭忞	gl	錢選
fd	儒林傳	gm	道園學古錄
fe	朱文公文集	gn	送李擴序
ff	朱子大全	go	清水信良
fg	歐陽玄	gp	近世中国思想史
fh	圭齋文集	gq	諸橋轍次
fi	許文正公遺書	gr	儒教の諸問題
fj	王梓材，馮雲濠	gs	清水書店
fk	袁國藩（冀）	gt	近思錄集註
fl	元許魯齋評述	gu	乾
fm	三教論與宋金學術	gv	袁桷
fn	東西文化	gw	清容居士集
fo	鳴道集說	gx	鮎埼亭集
fp	潭南遺老集	gy	國學基本叢書
fq	吉川幸次郎	gz	仙城本心樓記
fr	朱子学の北伝前史	ha	尊德性道問學記
fs	宇野哲人先生白寿祝賀紀念 東洋学論叢	hb	答人問性理
		hc	師山集
ft	宋史	hd	送葛子熙序
fu	五峰集	he	汪眞卿
fv	勉齋集	hf	遺書
fw	黃勉齋集	hg	二程全書
fx	正誼堂全書	hh	李敬子
fy	魯齋集	hi	胡伯量
fz	跋道統錄	hj	王
ga	吳文正集	hk	李公晦

Tu Wei-ming[a]

Towards an Understanding of Liu Yin's Confucian Eremitism

IN A paraphrase of a delightful image in Plato's *Republic*, Thomas More explains in the *Utopia* "why a sensible person is right to steer clear of politics":

He sees everyone else rushing into the street and getting soaked in the pouring rain. He can't persuade them to go indoors and keep dry. He knows if he went out too, he'd merely get equally wet. So he just stays indoors himself, and, as he can't do anything about other people's stupidity, comforts himself with the thought: "Well, I'm all right, anyway."[1]

On the surface, this seems to have been the main reason, according to general historical accounts at least, why Liu Yin (Ching-hsiu)[b] (1249–1293) repeatedly resisted pressure to take office under Mongol rule. Not unlike the sensible Raphael, who, having come across a mixture of conceit, stupidity, and stubbornness in the leadership throughout sixteenth-century Europe, refused to become a member of any privy council,[2] Liu found the world of politics in his lifetime too harsh and humiliating to merit his service. Liu's repeated defiance of the summons of the Yüan court may have been significantly different from Raphael's philosophical aloofness. But it seems that they both cherished a sense of personal integrity and were determined to retain their purity as thinkers and scholars.

However, Raphael, the student of philosophy who tried to open people's eyes to the causes of social evils, was by and large a generic type created by More to occasion the discussion of a world that was "no place" (*Utopia*). By contrast, Liu Yin, one of the two most highly regarded Confucian masters of Khubilai's reign,[3] was a historical figure with all the specificities of birth, education, and vocation. Although our knowledge of his life history is extremely scanty, we have a twelve-*chüan* collection of his writings and some supporting information from contemporary official documents and miscellaneous notes.[4] We learn that Liu was born into a scholar-official family of Jung-ch'eng[c] in Pao-ting[d] (modern Hopei). For generations, the family had been known for its Confucian studies and distinguished government services. As Professor Sun K'o-k'uan[e] notes in his informative research on Yüan Confucianism, the Liu clan can be characterized as a "gentry family" (*shih-chu*) of the Jurchen Chin dynasty (1115–1234).[5] In fact, Yin's grandfather (Ping-shan)[f] moved the whole family to the south in the Chen-yu[g] period (1213–1217), obviously as a result of the decision of the Chin government, under Mongol pressure, to move its capital from Yen-ching[h] (modern Peking) to Pien[i] (Kaifeng) by 1215. Not until 1232, two years before the Mongols extinguished the Chin dynasty, did Yin's father (Shu)[j] manage to have the family returned to Hopei.[6]

SPIRITUAL SELF-DEFINITION

At the time of Yin's birth in 1249, his father was already in his forties. According to Yin's biography in the dynastic history, the aging patriarch of the Liu clan had actually offered a pledge to Heaven, promising that if he should be blessed with a son, he would give him a fine education. Since Shu himself is said to have dedicated much of his life to scholarship (*wen-hsüeh*)[k] and, in particular, to the study of Confucian moral philosophy (*hsing-li chih shuo*),[l] his personal commitment in this regard is quite understandable. The seeming hyperbole in the description of Yin's intellectual precociousness may, against this background, appear credible: he acquired an ability to read books at three, learned to remember several hundred words per day as a young boy, began to compose poems at six and essays at seven and, when he was "yet to be capped" (*jo-kuan*)[m] at twenty, had already earned a wide reputation as a promising scholar. Indeed, he was soon recognized as the best student of Yen Mi-chien[n] (1212–1289), a reputable teacher from the South.[7] And as he became more deeply immersed in classical scholarship, he began to raise serious questions about the then prevalent mathods of philology and exergetics. He strongly suspected that the "essential meanings" (*ching-i*)[o] of the sages must be more than what the standard commentaries purported to convey. This intense concern for self-development as a scholar impelled him to search for other interpretations of the Confucian Way.[8]

The kind of scholarship that Liu Yin had been exposed to, we may surmise, consisted of standard works such as the *Correct Meanings of the Five Classics* (*Wu-ching cheng-i*)[p] with commentaries and subcommentaries by Han-T'ang textual analysts who were particularly concerned about philological and exegetical matters. It was unlikely that in his formative years he had ready access to the writings of the Sung Neo-Confucian masters, and especially to the philosophical essays and conversations of Chu Hsi[q] (1130–1200). It is commonly believed that Sung Learning was first introduced to the North when Mongol armies took the famed scholar Chao Fu[r] (c. 1206–c. 1299) and brought him, against his will, from Te-an[s] of modern Hupei to the Mongol capital in 1235. Even assuming that the cultural enthusiast Yao Shu[t] (1203–1280), who was instrumental in arranging this unusual feat of upgrading Confucian studies in the North, succeeded only a few years after his arrival in persuading Chao to lead the T'ai-chi[u] (Great Ultimate) Academy, the newly created center of learning, the initial instructions on Sung Learning to the students of the North would have had to wait until the 1240s. Liu Yin must have gained a considerable mastery over the classics before he first learned about the great Sung Masters.[9]

An essay entitled, "On Aspiring to Become a Sage" ("Hsi-sheng chieh"),[v] dramatically and poetically constructed, provides us with a rare opportunity to see how, in Liu Yin's spiritual self-definition, the Sung masters actually guided him to pursue the Way of the Sages. Historically it may also be taken as Liu's "rite of passage" into the Confucian world. Since the main part of the essay has been admirably translated by Professor F. W. Mote,[10] we shall quote only the most relevant passages in our analysis. The essay begins with a vivid description of a full-moon night in autumn. As the word *wang*,[w] indicating the fifteenth day of the lunar month, also a sense of longing and hoping, it immediately imparts a mood of anticipation to the reader. Liu tells us that as he sits in the central court, a melancholy feeling arises. Wine becomes tasteless and the lute tuneless. He is now both so puzzled and so fascinated by the lofty ideas in Master Chou Tun-i's[x] (1017–1073) *Penetrating the Book of Change*[11] (*T'ung-shu*)[y] that he takes it out again to read it in the moonlight. When he encounters the line, "the scholar aspires to become a worthy, the worthy aspires to become a sage, and the sage aspires to become Heaven," he cannot but sigh and feel terribly perplexed. How can anyone really aspire to become Heaven, he asks. This kind of absurdity may have been intended to take an unfair advantage of unsophisticated students like himself, he ponders. Then, in a spirit of complete release, he "hums a poem to the pure breezes, fondles the bright moon, raps on the big earth, drinks the 'Great Harmony' (*t'ai-ho*)^z and chants the line, 'How vast and empty the primordial beginnings.' " This trance-like experience evokes in him a song of the *Ch'u-tz'u*[aa] style, which is reminiscent of Ch'ü Yüan's[ab] (338–277 B.C.) helpless appeal to the Supreme Being for meaning and direction. Just then, he reports, three divine elders appear.

One of them, with an untrammelled demeanor like a "pure breeze and clear moon,"[12] identifies himself as the Plain Old Man (Cho-weng).[ac] The others introduce themselves as the Nameless Elder (Wu-ming kung)[ad] and the Master of Sincerity, Brilliance, and Centrality (Ch'eng-ming-chung tzu).[ae] In an awe-inspired mixture of joy and fear, Liu Yin asks their reasons for such an unexpected visit. He wonders why he is honored with their majestic presence. Surely the humble abode of a self-imposed meditator is not the vast space for them to roam freely with the spirit of the universe. The Nameless Elder remarks first that he comes in response to the song of the "Great Void" and the chant of the "primordial beginnings." Is it possible that Liu's selfish desires have now so beclouded his Heavenly Principle that he has already forgotten what he called out for just a moment ago? The Master of Sincerity, Brilliance, and Centrality joins in, noting that he cannot bear to see Liu, as a younger brother of his fellow human beings, fail to realize the "superior talents" (*ying-ts'ai*)[af] and fall into the moral snares of the unworthy. "I wish that you should be nourished to fruition," the Master continues, "How can you forsake me and forget all about it?"

However, the most pertinent and extensive instructions come from the Plain Old Man, who, after a long pause, enters into a dialogue with Liu:

"The scholar aspires to become a worthy, the worthy aspires to become a sage, and the sage aspires to become Heaven—these are my words that you have doubted, haven't you, my young friend?"
"Can one really become a sage?
"Yes."

"Is there any essential way?"
"Yes."
"Please explain it to me."
"The essential way is singleness."
"What is singleness?"
"No desire."
"Who can [attain the sate of] 'no desire'?"
"All people under Heaven can [attain the state of] 'no desire.' "
"Does this mean that all people under Heaven can become sages?"
"Yes."[13]
"If so, then I am absolutely confused. I really don't understand this."
"Please sit down. I will explain it to you. Listen carefully."

With this rhetorical device, Liu introduces the Plain Old Man's metaphysical justification for universal sagehood. There is only one Principle (li)[ag] in the universe. Although the Principle manifests itself in the myriad things, it is the ultimate source to which all of them eventually return. Therefore, in the perspective of the Principle, Heaven and Earth are human beings and human beings are Heaven and Earth. Similarly, the sages and worthies are myself and I am the sages and worthies. However, what human beings have gathered from the Principle is complete and all-pervading, whereas what the myriad things have obtained are partial and blocked. Surely that which is partial and blocked cannot be transformed, but that which is complete and pervasive, once communicated, can reach everywhere. The sage aims to become Heaven. If he can attain that, he will be Heaven; if not, he will still be a great sage. The worthy aims to become a sage. If he can go beyond that, he will be Heaven; if not, he will still be a great worthy. Similarly, the scholar aims to become a worthy. If he can go beyond that, he will be a sage or if he just reaches that, he will be a worthy; if not, he will still preserve his good reputation as a scholar. Based upon this general observation, the Plain Old Man then focuses his attention on Liu himself:

You have received the centrality [the highest excellence] of Heaven and Earth and have been endowed with the wholesome and harmonious material forces (ch'i)[ah] of the Five Constancies (Wu-ch'ang).[ai] Your talents are the essence of the sages and your learning is the achievements of the sages. You are like the sages and the sages are like you. Now you have offended yourself and yet you consider me [my words] absurd. Are you absurd, or am I, your teacher, absurd? If you cultivate (hsiu)[aj] yourself and dwell in tranquillity (ching),[ak] encourage yourself and take comfort in doing so, realize your design, fully develop your nature, improve from thought to wisdom, and progress from brilliance to sincerity, then will you really aspire to become a sage, or the sages aspire to become you? Now you have forsaken yourself and yet you think that I have taken mean advantage of you. Is it you who have cheated your teacher, or I, your teacher, who have cheated you?

The essay ends with a line revealing Liu Yin's self-image. He fully acknowledges his narrow-mindedness and accepts the instructions of the Plain Old Man. The Nameless Elder and the Master of Sincerity, Brilliance, and Centrality then pat him on the back and urge him to live up to their expectations. Thereupon they express the wish: "Some day if we hear about 'an exemplar of purity' in the world, it will be you!"

There are a few salient features of this deceptively simple essay that merit some further discussion. Philosophically the argument in it mainly consists of digested statements from Chou Tun-i's *Penetrating the Book of Change* and *Diagram of the Great Ultimate Explained (Tai-chi-t'u shuo).*[al] Indeed, virtually all of the instructions of the Plain Old Man are from the writings of Master Chou. But it is vitally important to note that since there is internal evidence to show that the Nameless Elder refers to Shao Yung[am] (1011–1077) and the Master of Sincerity, Brilliance, and Centrality refers to Chang Tsai[an] (1020–1077), Liu Yin seems to have constructed his thesis on a general appreciation of Northern Sung Confucian moral metaphysics rather than on a limited exposure to the works of one master.[14] This is particularly significant in view of the fact that Sung Learning was still in a preliminary stage of development among Yüan scholars of Liu's generation. Especially noteworthy in this regard is the date of the essay. The *ting-mao*[ao] year in traditional Chinese chronology that appears in the first line of the essay corresponds to either the third year of Hsien-ch'un[ap] of the Sung or the fourth year of Chih-yüan[aq] of the Yüan (1267) when Liu was only 18 years old. This seems to substantiate the claim of Liu's biographer in the dynastic history that he had established himself as a significant interpreter of Sung Learning prior to his capping ceremony. Indeed, according to the same account, after he had read extensively the writings of Chou Tun-i, Ch'eng Hao[ar] (1032–1085), Ch'eng I[as] (1033–1107), Chang Tsai, Shao Yung, Chu Hsi, and Lü Tsu-ch'ien[at] (1137–1181), he confidently remarked that he had long suspected that such a tradition ought to have existed.

Liu Yin's acceptance and promulgation of Sung Learning, recognized and appreciated by quite a few of his contemporaries, amounted to an ultimate commitment to an ethicoreligious tradition, a phenomenon believed to have become more prevalent among late Ming students of Confucian thought. This, however, must not give the impression that Liu uncritically surrendered himself to the authority of the Sung masters. On the contrary, since his dissatisfaction with the philological and exegetical approaches to the classics preceded his discovery and confirmation of the "essential meanings" of Sung Learning, he was predisposed to the spiritual directions of the Sung masters by his own intellectual struggle. "On Aspiring to Become a Sage," in this connection, is as much a statement of his own faith in self-perfectibility as an acknowledgement of his indebtedness to the three Northern Sung Confucian teachers. Indeed, he is said to have been able to elucidate the subtleties of their teachings as soon as he was exposed to their writings. Liu's independence of mind is further shown by his succinct characterizations of the strengths of the philosophies of each of the three Northern Sung masters: the encompassing nature of Shao, the refined quality of Chou, and the authenticity of Ch'eng. Only Chu Hsi, he further observed, was capable of reaching a great synthesis.[15]

In the light of Liu Yin's spiritual self-definition, it seems that Liu's decision not to accept an official position to serve the Yüan court was not an outright rejection of politics. It may have been a commitment to something else which was, to him, more meaningful in a deep, personal way. Yet, it is difficult to believe that the idea of "purity," as he used it, did not imply a negative attitude toward the politics of his time. His contemporaries certainly read political significance into his actions. Even the ruler is alleged to have interpreted them in this way. It may not be farfetched to suggest that Liu Yin could, to a certain extent, subscribe to Raphael's reasons why a sensible person is right to steer clear of politics. Yet the *Problematik* involved is more complex. For one thing, how can Liu Yin's apparent eremitism be justified in terms of his faith in Confucian teachings?

PUBLIC IMAGE AND PERSONAL CHOICE

Liu Yin's official biography, which provides extremely limited information about his life history, tells us that his father died when Liu was young, probably in his early teens. For quite a while, he was not able to perform proper burial rites for either his grandfather or for his father because of poverty. Only with the financial help of an influential friend did he finally manage to fulfill his wishes and obligations as a filial son. We learn from his poems that his mother died when he was only six years old;[16] he was probably raised by a stepmother. His biography also tells us that he earned a meager living for his family, including his stepmother, by teaching. Although his seriousness of purpose attracted several outstanding students, he did not have a large following. And his strong sense of propriety also inhibited him from meeting influential scholar-officials. Even after he had gained a considerable reputation as one of the foremost Confucian masters of his time, he still declined to receive admirers of high official status. Thus those who were disappointed by his refusal to grant an audience criticized him as being "arrogant" (*ao*).[au] This was perhaps the reason that the power elite by and large ignored him.

Nevertheless, it is not entirely true that Liu never accepted any official appointment. In 1282, when he was 33 years old, he was unexpectedly recommended for a respectable position and served briefly as a tutor for the imperial clan in the capital, Yen-ching (modern Peking). But within a month or so he resigned and returned home to attend his ailing stepmother who died the following year. In 1291, he turned down a summons from the court, inviting him to become an academician of the Imperial College. It was this event that attracted a great deal of attention in the scholar-official circle. Probably as an attempt to silence the further spread of rumors about his alleged "arrogance," which could easily anger the court, he wrote a famous letter to the highest authority in the government, giving poor health as the real reason for his inability to accept the invitation.[17] This, on the surface at least, seems credible, for he died only two years afterwards. But the significance of the letter as a clue to his self-description cannot be overestimated. Indeed, almost half of his biography in the dynastic history consists of the letter in its entirety.

Liu died on the sixteenth day of the fourth month of the thirtieth year of Khubilai's reign (1293). He had no male progeny. Nor did he have enough of a discipleship to carry on his mode of scholarship. However, he is recorded to have composed a thirty-*chüan* study of the "essential points" (*ching-yao*)[av] of the Four Books and five *chüan* of poems. His students and friends compiled another collection of his articles and conversations in more than ten *chüan*, which includes an essay on the "Great Commentary" of the *Book of Change*; it was completed after he had become gravely ill.[18] Most of his writings are probably no longer extant, but an anthology of his works in twelve *chüan* is still readily available. It includes eight miscellaneous articles, ten essays, seventeen prefaces, twelve memoirs, ten epilogues, fifteen letters, four memorials, two biographical sketches, fifteen obituaries, eight funeral odes, eleven inscriptions, and over eight hundred poems.[19]

During the Yen-yu[aw] reign (1314–1320) of Emperor Ayurbarwada (Jen-tsung,[ax] r. 1311–1320), more than a decade after Liu's death, he was posthumously enfeoffed as the Duke of Jung-ch'eng and given the honorific name of Wen-ching[ay] (Cultured Tranquility). He also received the title of Academician of the Imperial College. Although it was not unusual for the court to recognize outstanding scholars in this way, its belated action in this case seems to have been taken in response to Liu's growing reputation among a select group of influential scholar-officials. The great literary figure Yü Chi[az] (1272-1348), for example, unequivocally characterized Liu as the foremost scholar in the North in terms of "loftiness, brilliance, steadfastness, and courage." He also contended that Liu was the authentic transmitter of Sung Learning, for he had learned the teachings of Chu Hsi from Chao Fu and, through them, fully understood the philosophies of the Northern Sung masters.[20] Yüan Chüeh[ba] (1266-1327), another eminent literatus, praised Liu's writings as "refined and profound" and his ideas as "single-minded and truthful." He particularly noted Liu's serious commitment to the Confucian Way and his independence of mind in arriving at a critical appreciation of Chu Hsi.[21] In the same spirit, Ou-yang Hsüan[bb] (1283–1357), the director-general of the dynastic histories of Sung, Liao, and Chin, depicted Liu as the embodiment of the best in two of Confucius' esteemed disciples: the freedom of Tseng Tien[bc] without its wildness and the courage of Tzu-lu[bd] without its militancy.[22]

The public image of Liu Yin, as it was formed in the literary world of the time, presents us with several intriguing questions. Why did a Confucian eremite, such as Liu was, emerge as a culture hero for the generation of the 1310s? Since the aforementioned Yü, Yüan, and Ou-yang were all southerners, what could have been their motivation for lavishing such high praise on this particular northern scholar? Was Liu's reputation used for some political end? These questions seem to have prompted Professor Sun K'o-k'uan to offer his "conspiracy" thesis. A simplified version of it, for our purpose, goes somewhat like this: The intellectual circle of the North was at the time dominated by the followers of another highly regarded Confucian master, Hsü Heng[be] (1209–1281). When the great southern classicist Wu Ch'eng[bf] (1249–1333), who later received critical acclaim as the most distinguished Confucian scholar of the Yüan dynasty as a whole, visited the capital, he was poorly treated with much discrimination by the northern scholars. As the rivalry between the North and the South intensified, Wu's students, such as Yü Chi, decided to launch a campaign to elevate the status of Liu Yin in the Confucian legacy as a challenge to the overpowering influence of the Hsü school.[23]

In addition to the "conspiracy" thesis, Professor Sun also offers us a "promotion" thesis. The principal actor in this connection was Su T'ien-chüeh[bg] (1294–1352), famous for his systematic attempt to compile anthologies of representative writings of the Yüan era. As the compiler of a voluminous collection of Yüan literary works, Su created early in his career an ever-widening circle of literary talents around him. His close friends, Yü Chi and Yüan Chüeh, were among the examiners who ranked him number one in the 1316 provincial examination. Ou-yang Hsüan was for some time his colleague in the Hanlin Academy. This partly explains his ability to influence the climate of opinion in which Liu's reputation soared. The immediate occasion for his promotional efforts, however, came from a different connection. Su, it should be mentioned, was a northern scholar with long and extensive associations with many prominent literati in the North, mainly because he himself came from a scholarly family with an impressive tradition of Confucian studies. Su was also a disciple of the Neo-Confucian master An Hsi[bh] (1270–1311), whose admiration for Liu Yin led him to a self-identification as Liu's "privately cultivated" (*ssu-shu*)[bi] student.[24] Even though An Hsi never met Master Liu, he is listed in the *Sung-Yüan hsüeh-an*[bj] as one of Liu's students, which, by association, makes Su a follower of Liu's Ching-hsiu School also. It seems reasonable then for Su to have advocated the significance of Liu and to have rallied his influential literary friends to Liu's support. The very fact that both Yü and Yüan's laudatory remarks on Liu are found in their writings honoring Su's teacher, An Hsi, seems to give further weight to this line of reasoning.[25]

We encounter in either the "conspiracy" or the "promotion" thesis an implicit assertion that Liu Yin was not only different from but adversary to Hsü Heng. A most revealing story about this is found in T'ao

Tsung-i's[bk] *Cho-keng lu.*[bl] When Hsü was summoned to the court by Khubilai in 1260, the story tells us, he paid a special visit to Liu. As he was criticized by Liu for his apparent alacrity in serving the Mongol ruler, Hsü replied that if scholars like themselves did not respond with eagerness to the imperial calls, the Confucian "Way could not prevail" (*tao pu-hsing*).[bm] More than two decades later, in 1283, the story continues, when Liu first resigned a respectable official position after an extremely short tenure and then declined to accept an even more prestigious position, he was asked for an explanation. Liu stated that if scholars like themselves did not decline such offers, the Confucian "Way would not be respected" (*tao pu-tsun*).[bn][26] It is true, as Professor Sun has pointed out, that T'ao was also a southerner. But in the *Cho-ken lu* story there is no indication that Liu's attempt to dignify the Way was necessarily superior to Hsü's attempt to put it into effect. The moral seems to suggest that, given the circumstances and the personal sense of involvement in them, both choices were righteous and fitting. The gap between the North and the South notwithstanding, both the effectiveness and the respectability of the Way were vitally important to all concerned Confucian scholars.

To be sure, the likelihood of Hsü's having met with Liu in 1260 seems slim. For one thing, it is highly improbable that the already well-known Hsü would have consulted an 11-year-old boy about his new appointment.[27] However, the story does symbolize a real existential conflict between two radically different, if equally acceptable, modes of life faced by virtually all eminent Confucians under the Mongol conquest. Paradoxically, during the Yen-yu years, when Liu Yin's dignity as a scholar was formally recognized by the court, the reopening of the examination system actually attracted quite a few Confucian literati to government service. In fact, those who were instrumental in formulating a powerful public image for Liu were themselves officials and thus, more or less, emulated Hsü's approach to politics. In 1349, an imperial dispatch was issued, instructing local educational authorities throughout the country to make the writings of Liu Yin readily available for students. The rationale behind this unusual action is instructive. It is true that Liu only served the government briefly, the dispatch states, but his "purity and integrity" (*ch'ing-chieh*)[bo] had exerted such a remarkable influence upon the country that the circulation of his works would "assist in the moral transformation of the government above and provide a model for the students below."[28] When the court failed to recruit Liu in 1291, Khubilai is alleged to have said that there had been "unsummonable ministers" (*pu-chao chih ch'en*)[bp] and that Liu must have been a follower of them.[29] He would have been pleased to know that Liu inadvertently performed a good service to the government after all.

The exemplariness of Liu's life and thought assumes a new shape of meaning in the light of his own justification for his existential choice. The letter that he submitted to the highest authority in the government is particularly relevant here. As already mentioned, he gave poor health as the reason. But it is his strategy of presentation and the manner in which he presented himself to the court that merit a more focused investigation. Needless to say, he was critically aware of the gravity of the situation when he decided that he was not able to respond to the imperial summons. Especially noteworthy was his reference to mounting rumors that he was actually motivated by a desire to fish for fame. He must have known well that any indication that his choice was intended to defy the authority of the court could easily infuriate the emperor and bring disasterous consequences to him and his family. Furthermore, since the power of a newly founded dynasty to attract the services of hermits had long been considered in traditional Chinese historiography as an important index of the spread of its legitimacy, he could not argue his case simply in terms of a personal preference.[30]

Thus, in the very beginning of the letter, Liu states that even as a young boy he learned and understood from his father and his teacher the meaning of the "righteous relationship between ruler and minister" (*chün-chen chih i*).[bq] Since the security and livelihood of the people are direct concerns of the ruler which the people themselves share in, they must exert themselves in this service either with their physical labor or with their mental strength. This is the inevitable course of history for thousands of years and what Chuang Tzu[br] called "that which is inescapable between heaven and earth."[31] With this introductory statement, Liu explains that in forty-three years he has not yet contributed a modicum of energy to the service of the country (*kuo-chia*)[bs] that has protected and reared him. Now with this extraordinary opportunity at hand, how can he continue to betray his country by indulging in self-imposed isolation? If he does, it will amount to committing a serious transgression against the teachings of "centrality and commonality" (*chung-yung*)[bt] in the tradition of the sages. Liu then makes it clear that he has never entertained the thought of becoming a hermit or a recluse, for, we may add, he has always set his heart on the Confucian Way. This is why, he further states, he immediately responded to the imperial summons of 1282. Although his service was abruptly cut short because of his stepmother's illness and death, it was not at all an excuse to go into seclusion. The letter concludes with a detailed description of his deteriorating health and his inability, rather than unwillingness, to accept the new appointment.

There is no reason for us to believe that the letter was written in bad faith. But it also seems that, given the circumstances, it could not have been composed otherwise. This sense of inevitability implies a twofold meaning. On the surface, Liu admitted that he was to blame for his failure to serve. He was probably aware that he might have appeared unreasonably arrogant to his contemporaries when he turned down an offer from the mighty ruler, Khubilai. Therefore self-criticism seems to have been the only way out. Once he made his philosophy of life clear, it seems that he had to resort to poor health as the real reason. Actually, he promised in the letter that he would embark on the journey to the capital as soon as he became well. On the other hand, he may have had something else in mind. To be sure, the first appointment had ended briefly and the second offer could not be honored. Yet almost ten years had elapsed in between 1282–1291. The government could have enlisted his service after he had fulfilled his mourning rite and before his health deteriorated. This interpretation seems compelling in light of his plea toward the end of the letter. After all, he argues, unlike the central figures in the court, he is but a remote and lowly official. It in fact matters very little whether he enters into or withdraws from the government. Indeed, the court can afford to "allow him to complete what he is from beginning to end." [32]

The expression "allow him to complete what he is from beginning to end" is most suggestive. It may simply refer to an earlier statement in which he requested that the highest authority of the government find a way to protect and save him. Since the letter was sent to the government (*cheng-fu*)[bu] and was specifically addressed to the prime minister (*tsai-hsiang*),[bv] Liu was gingerly trying to win the sympathy of the leadership of the scholar-official class so that his case would not be misinterpreted by the court (*ch'ao-t'ing*).[bw] The fact that he was not further pressured to accept the appointment indicates that the strategy worked. Thus Liu subtly conveyed his wish to lead an alternative way of life. To be sure, it was not that of a hermit or of a recluse. But neither was it "political" in the sense that the lives of all scholar-officials who joined the government inescapably were. It seems that Liu opted for a way to "complete" himself which was neither a conscious design to escape from official service nor an unquestioned attachment to it. It was in many respects a solitary struggle of an independent mind. And yet undeniably, by his profound sense of purity and integrity, he not only developed enough inner strength to make this particular form of the Confucian Way meaningful to him and to his small group of students but also symbolically opened the way for later scholars who wished to cultivate their sense of dignity without any direct reference to politics.[33]

We may say that, to a certain extent, Liu sincerely regretted that as a Confucian he had failed to fulfill one of the five basic human relationships, the righteous relationship between ruler and minister. By analogy, he must have suffered even more intensely at the death of his only son in 1290.[34] The experience must have been extremely painful, as his father and mother had died when he was very young. And so far as we know, he did not have any brothers or sister. Thus, at the time he wrote the letter, he could have maintained at most only one of the five basic human relationships defined in Confucian teachings. We are not even sure that even this relationship existed because there is virtually no reference to Liu's wife that has been preserved in the sources extant. Therefore, his wish to face death alone, also alluded to in the letter, should have conveyed a sense of tragedy to those who had any idea of the brute realities of life that he had experienced.

Liu's conscious choice not to participate directly in governmental service and his ineluctable fate not to be blessed with familial ties in the last years of his life may appear diametrically opposed to the ideal image of a Confucian. Furthermore, since most of his students also emulated him in refusing to take an active political role, the direct influence he had upon his times was relatively small. As a result, the school of thought that he is alleged to have founded has often been labeled as a form of "quietism." His style name, Ching-hsiu (Quiescent Cultivation), which has been widely used to designate his teachings, may also give the impression that there is a strong Taoist element in his Confucianism. It is perhaps in this sense that his Confucian eremitism has sometimes been interpreted as a kind of Confucian-Taoist syncretism.[35]

POLITICS, POETRY, AND INTELLECTUAL IDENTITY

We noted earlier that Liu might have cherished the hope of serving the state in an offical capacity in the intervening years between the first and secod summons from the court. A poem written by him in 1278 to record a dream that he had on the twenty-fourth day of the eleventh month of that year is of particular interest in this connection.[36] Liu states vividly that in the dream he has been recommended to the court by a joint memorial sponsored by a group of more than ten elderly persons all formally dressed in magnificent attire. In the memorial, he is addressed as "Chin-wen shan-jen"[bx] (the mountain man of "golden" literature). Among many of the laudatory phrases that the elders lavish on him, he remembers two in particular. One obviously refers to a statement by Confucius in the *Analects*, "Only when the year grows cold do we see that the pine and cypress are the last to fade."[37] And the other, taken at its face value, does not convey a sense of praise at all: "The evening scene of the mulberry-tree," which ordinarily means the fading years of old age because the dying rays of the sun often light up the tops of these trees. It is not difficult to surmise that in the dream Liu was recommended by those dignified senior statesmen as a person who has proven his incorruptibility and whose service must be sought immediately, lest a rare chance be missed. Since the dream actually preceded his first appointment by three years, it seems to convey a persistent concern rather than simply an isolated occurrence.

Even his choice of a style name, Ching-hsiu, reflects a similar concern. It is not true, as one would suspect, that by "Quiescent Cultivation" he meant to convey a Taoist preference for quietism. The evidence shows that it was in fact based on Chu-ko Liang's[by] (181–234) famous statement, "Quiescence wherewith to cultivate the self" (*ching i hsiushen*).[bz][38] The delicate difference lies partly in divergent motivations. Of course, Taoist quietism is also a form of self-cultivation, but what Chu-ko had in mind was primarily a spiritual preparation for a great political task. As the legend goes, only after the ruler of the State of Shu[ca] had visited him in person three times at his thatched-straw hut did Chu-ko consent to reemerge from his self-imposed moratorium to serve as the prime minister of Shu. Recalling Liu's alleged criticism of Hsü Heng, it was not governmental service itself but the manner in which it was requested and rendered that made all the difference. Far from being a kind of ritualism, what was involved had far-reaching political implications. The scholar must maintain his dignity not only as an advisor but more importantly as a critic. And in order to maintain his critical judgment, he must be able to distance himself from the center of power. Only then could he really perceive and influence politics from a broad cultural base. The scholar-official, by implication, must subscribe to a set of value priorities significantly different from the status quo. "Quiescence wherewith to cultivate the self" as Chu-ko, and for that matter Liu, would have it, was a political as well as a personal dictum.

Liu Yin's relationship to and perception of the existing structure of power under the domination of the Mongol court were further complicated by what may be called his loyalist sentiments toward the extinguished Chin dynasty. The rise of the Jurchen in northeastern Manchuria and their rebellion against the state of Liao (947–1125) in 1114, which resulted in the establishment of the Chin ("Golden") dynasty in the following year, is a story widely known to students of Chinese history. Also known is the military expansion of the Chin in northern China: the capture of the Sung capital of Kaifeng, together with its emperor and the abdicated former emperor Hui-tsung[cb] (r. 1100–1125) in 1126, the consolidation of its power base in the North by moving the capital from Manchuria to Yen-ching in 1153, and the maintenance of a large mobile nomad cavalry that presented a continuous threat to the survival of the Southern Sung (1127–1279). Less known, however, is the whole story of Chin's development into an increasingly sinicized state and the Confucian influences, including the examination system and the court rituals, that were exerted upon it.[39]

It is vitally important to note that when the Mongols conquered the Chin capital in 1215 and destroyed the Chin state in 1234, the North had already developed its own style of learning independent of the flowering of Neo-Confucian thought in the South, for it had been cut off from the South for almost a century. A synoptic view of Yüan Hao-wen's[cc] (1190–1257) biographical sketches of some of the eminent ministers of the Chin[40] gives us an indication of the range of cultural activities that the Chin political elite had been engaged in. Yüan himself had profound knowledge of Chinese culture, and his literary works made him one of the great writers of all time in Chinese poetry and prose. Yeh-lü Ch'u-ts'ai[cd] (1189–1243), from a highly cultured ruling house of the Khitan Liao, may have been unique as an influential advisor in the court of Chinggis Khan. But his literary competence seems to reflect the norm of cultural attainments among the Chin political elite. It was people of Yeh-lü's background, such as the Yeh-lü A-hai-t'u-hua[ce] brothers, Marshal P'u-ch'a,[cf] Wang Chi,[cg] Li Pang-jui,[ch] and Kuo Pao-yü,[ci] who were instrumental in introducing "Confucian consciousness" as a way of government to the Mongol ruler.[41] Liu Yin, as we have already mentioned, came from such a tradition.

To be sure, classical scholarship in the Chin was limited in scope and, by comparison with that of Southern Sung, lacked sophistication. This was the reason that Chao Fu's arrival in the North marked the beginning of a new era for the northern scholars. And this was also the reason that Liu Yin's initiation into Sung Learning was through Chao. But the Chin intellectual world was so rich in literary and artistic expression that the warfare accompanying the Mongol conquest can easily be interpreted as the annihilation of a superior civilization by a brutal force of destruction. This was certainly Liu's view of what happened to the culture in which he was raised. His great admiration for Yüan Hao-wen,[42] his emotional response to the paintings of the Chin prince Wan-yen Yün-kung[cj] (1146–1185),[43] and his frequent references to words and ideas associated with the character "chin"[44] in his writings seem to show a nostalgic identification with a faded cultural world that still remained meaningful to him. Indeed, he claims in one of his poems that "literary brilliance does not perish together with scorched earth."[45] This reminds us of the honorific title by which the elderly statesmen referred to him in his dream. Although Chin-wen has been rendered as "golden literature," it is not unlikely that it may have also been intended to suggest "the literature of the Chin." Liu's "loyalist sentiments" had little to do with the Chin state. Although the Liu clan of his grandfather's generation had figured prominently in politics, his father had only served briefly as a local official. There certainly was no impelling reason for Yin to feel obligated to the conquered dynasty. However, the Mongol takeover had been so devastating to the general population and the Mongol government so harsh on the literati, we can easily surmise, that he felt utterly disgusted with the conquerors. These sentiments pervade his poems.

It is difficult to summarize Liu's poetic production in terms of themes and subjects. The quantity alone prevents us from generalizing about such matters. We can of course acquire a sense of the mood pervading the majority of his poems. Even a limited exposure should call to our attention a deep feeling of melancholy which underlies both the tranquility of his five-line poems and the virility of his seven-line poems. Against the background of a traumatic experience, the T'ao Yüan-ming[ck] (365–427), Liu Yin[46] expressed himself not in a soaring spirit of detachment and transcendence but in a sad awareness of fateful inevitability. Similarly the knightliness in his poems, reminiscent of the works of the frontier poets in the T'ang (618–907), such as Ts'en Ts'an[cl] (715–770) and Kao Shih[cm] (d. 765),[47] far from being an expression of romantic heroism, also seems to signify a lament for the deaths of many strong and courageous men. Indeed, several of his powerful historical accounts, including the funerary inscriptions, give us a vivid, sometimes even graphic, picture of the horrible last decade of the Chin dynasty.[48] Liu's proficiency and sensitivity in other highly refined cultural activities, such as painting and calligraphy, must have made the dehumanizing effects on all forms of cultural life under the Mongol conquests unbearable.

We therefore encounter in Liu's poems a fascinating paradox. At first it appears that he wished to lead a way of life reminiscent of the carefree spirit of T'ao Yüan-ming, but upon closer examination we discover that his "withdrawal" was also meant to deliver a political message. Undeniably, when T'ao decided to retire to his country cottage where he cultivated his own vegetable garden, enjoyed wine, and read books for pure pleasure, he too delivered a political message: "Never to bow for a mere five pecks of rice."[49] Yet although T'ao had several times been forced to take office in order to provide a minimum livelihood for his family, once he left the political arena (so the legend goes), his heart never again returned to the mundane world. Instead it found a permanent home in the Taoist Arcadia. What Liu found in T'ao, however, was not only a personality ideal but also poetic inspiration. Quite a few of Liu's poems are modelled on the style of T'ao. Time and time again, T'ao's celebrated themes, such as chrysanthemums and "the Peach-blossoms Source," struck a sympathetic chord in Liu's imagination. One entire category of Liu's poetry consists of some eighty elegantly constructed poems devoted to the single task of rhyming with some of Tao's well-known verses ("Ho T'ao").[cn][50] However, it would be a mistake to assume that Liu's fascination with the aesthetic world of perhaps the greatest master of Taoist lyric poetry reflects his personal identification with the Taoist view of life.

Liu Yin's attitude toward Taoism has been well documented by Professor Mote. Evidently he was "clear-minded about Taoist thought and its implications," rejecting the teachings of Chuang Tzu and Lao Tzu[co] on grounds of illusory escapism and manipulative distortion. What Liu found most objectionable in the Taoist tradition was not the original philosophical intention but the manner in which lofty ideas were put into effect. His subtle discussion of the "butterfly-metaphor" in the chapter "Ch'i-wu lun"[cp] ("Equalization of Things") in the *Chuang Tzu* is a case in point.[51] By asking, "Am I Chuang Chou who dreamed I was a butterfly, or am I really a butterfly dreaming I am Chuang Chou?" after he has awakened from a dream in which he was a butterfly, Chuang Tzu poses a fundamental question about our perception of reality. In principle, Liu accepts Chuang's idea of "equalizing" (*ch'i*)[cq] and his desire to "move freely without constraint" (*wu shih er pu-k'o*,[cr] which literally means "no end that cannot be reached" or "nothing will not do"). But he argues that the creation of a world of fantasy (*huan*)[cs] would not get us very far. The problem with Chuang is his inability to see through that fantasy as a tactic, a psychological device, to lessen the painful realization that one is "adrift among all the innumerable and motley things of this world for but a brief moment of time." The equalizing ideal of being human, Liu seems to contend, must not be sought in the escapist illusion of being transformed into a different being. Real freedom lies in the courage to face up to the actual conditions of one's life.

The real existential choice, then, is to opt for Mencius' idea of a "profound person" (*chün-tzu*)[ct]: "[What he] follows as his nature is not added to when he holds sway over the Empire, nor is it detracted from when he is reduced to straitened circumstances."[52] The self-sufficiency of what the profound person follows as his nature is, according to Mencius, "rooted in his heart, and manifests itself in his face, giving it a sleek appearance. It also shows in his back and extends to his limbs, rendering their message intelligible without words."[53] Liu identifies this inner strength as "righteous destiny" (*i-ming*).[cu] Following the Neo-Confucian, in particular the Ch'eng-Chu, teachings on the matter, Liu insists that a step-by-step effort of "exhaustively appropriating the Principle inherent in things" (*ch'iung-li*)[cv] is absolutely necessary for its acquisition. The difficulty of accomplishing the task is obvious. Even among the leading Confucians there are those who, on suffering extreme hardships, fall back on Taoist fantasies for solace and diversion. To cultivate a true sense of one's own "righteous destiny" is thus a great challenge.[54]

This line of thinking reminds us of Liu's essay "Aspiring to Become a Sage." His initial uneasiness with Chou Tun-i's assertion in *Penetrating the Book of Change* is comparable to what he believes to be the trouble with Taoists: "They see how vast the world is, and how great the span of time from the past to the present. They observe how comprehensive and how abundant are the achievements of the Sages and Worthies, and how tiny and insignificant they themselves are."[55] The belittling of one's true self and, by implication, one's humanity, accounts for much of the escapism in Taoist thought. This may seem to be a failure of nerve, but if Liu's own experience is any guide, it also results from narrow-mindedness. One's limited perception or understanding of reality in its fullest manifestation often ends in failure to act in accordance with one's "righteous destiny." Paradoxically this is not simply an epistemological question, because the actual application of what one really knows ultimately determines the quality and the correctness of one's knowledge. His essay explaining the name of "The Studio of Withdrawal" is most instructive in this connection.[56]

The essay begins with an observation. If read out of context, it could easily be taken as unqualified support for the Taoist point of view:

The substance of the Tao is originally tranquil. It produces things but is not produced by things and governs things but is not governed by things; it governs the myriad with singleness and it transforms but is never transformed. If this is perceived from the mutuality of the Principle (*li*), the interaction of the Power (*shih*)[cw] and the circulation of the Number (*shu*),[cx] all those that emulate the substance of the Tao are free from constraints with an inexhaustible potential for creative adaptation.[57]

Yet, Liu is quick to point out that Lao Tzu does not really understand the substance of the Tao because what he describes as the Tao is, according to Liu, a perversion, a self-serving tactic. Liu then gives us a long list of examples enumerating how this is so. For example, humility becomes a means to gain and weakness to conquer; selflessness turns out to be an insidious form of egoism and withdrawal a camouflage for aggression. Lao Tzu's manipulative intentions are further shown in his practices of disguising cleverness behind the facade of dullness and hiding eloquence under the appearance of inarticulation. The image of a Taoist in Liu's depiction is therefore the embodiment of a calculating mind who places himself in a strategic position so that he can advance or retreat at will, "anticipate the end as he begins, plan the exit as he enters, occupy the center in order to seek for profitable returns and read the incipient signs of conflict so as to benefit from it."[58] He takes advantage of others without leaving a discernible trace. Since for him personal gains and losses outweigh all other considerations, his action is detrimental to the state and harmful to the people, although he himself manages to remain aloof and beyond reproach.

A critic may argue that Lao Tzu's great ability to manipulate the world should also be considered a reflection of his profound knowledge of the Tao. Ironically it seems that Liu himself has, to a certain extent, advanced such a thesis. He admits that the Taoist "strategy" (shu)[cy] fully exploits natural as well as human forces. And it is extremely difficult to comprehend the mysterious pivot from which he turns the world around his fingers. What Liu has in mind here comes close to a political appropriation of Taoist values and symbols. By characterizing Lao Tzu in this fashion, he seems to suggest that unlike Chuang Tzu's Taoists who prefer to dwell in fantasies, Lao Tzu's Taoists are really skillful strategists in the government who manipulated politics for selfish ends. We have no way of determining historically what group of individuals his criticism is directed against. It seems likely, however, that he has in mind influential politicians in the court who have long forsaken their ethical principles for personal expediency, as he suggests in his brief remarks toward the end of the essay to the effect that these manipulators now style themselves champions of the Righteousness of Confucius and Mencius and of the Principle of Ch'eng I and Chu Hsi. Nevertheless, it is difficult to substantiate the Ch'ing historian Ch'üan Tsu-wang's[cz] (1705–1755) claim that this essay contains an implicit critique of Hsü Heng.[59]

We encounter here another fascinating paradox. Liu finds in Lao Tzu's manipulative perversion of the Tao a deliberate attempt to exercise a kind of deceitful cunningness. It is not the choice of "withdrawal" itself but the insincere psychology behind it that really bothers him. By contrast, Chuang Tzu's philosophy of life seems more acceptable. At least his quest for inner spirituality points to a realm of value where the standards of this world are no longer applicable. What the Taoist manipulators effect in the court, on the other hand, is a total relativization of ethical norms which leads to great confusion in moral conduct. The isolated individuals who set high standards of personal integrity in the wilderness can still have a salutary influence on society and indirectly contribute to the respectability of the Tao. On the other hand, those who corrupt the government from within can never put the Tao into effect because they have perverted it from the very beginning. The distinction between Confucianism and Taoism assumes a different shape of meaning in the light of this. The genuine Taoist can have a wholesome influence on society that the Confucian ought to appreciate, but the false Confucian, who distorts and manipulates Taoist ideas in politics, is destructive on all accounts.

Liu is understandably appreciative of some of the outstanding Taoist personalities in history, although he clearly does not subscribe to their modes of life. In addition to the aforementioned T'ao Yüan-ming, who seems to have inspired unreserved admiration from scholars of all kinds of philosophical persuasions, Liu, in two poems and several references, praises the famous Former Han recluses known as the "four white-haired ones" (*ssu hao*).[da][60] We also find in his poetry a highly laudatory comment on the cordial relationship between Emperor Kuang-wu[db] (r. A.D. 25–57) of the Later Han and the much honored hermit Yen Kuang[dc] (37 B.C.–A.D. 43).[61] In addition, he asserts that the accommodating Hui[dd] of Liu-hsia[de] was narrow-minded and that Po I,[df] the "pure sage" who was absolutely uncompromising in his sense of personal integrity, was really receptive to the "populist" idea of human equality.[62] This rather unconventional judgment further contributes to the impression that for Liu self-respect, as an overarching concern, is a precondition for social service. This thesis can of course be taken as a consistent and sophisticated argument for morality and culture over politics.

SELF-DEVELOPMENT AS A CALLING

Another central concern in Liu Yin's life and thought was the demonstration that morality and culture are essential to politics because they are the prerequisites of responsible service in the government. Obviously Liu was not simply making a general comment on politics. He understood well that the Mongol conquerors styled their rulership on entirely different principles. He knew that the majority of the people were victims of the most ruthless imposition of military and economic controls China had ever experienced. And he could also see the necessity for virtually all scholar-officials to muddle through an extremely dangerous situation. His sense of purity was definitely not what Mencius took the purity of

Po-i to have been. This was perhaps the reason that he reversed the Mencian critique of Po I as "narrow-minded," and used it to characterize the seemingly flexible Hui of Liu-hsia. In what sense, then, could Liu justify his sense of purity as a universal value rather than merely as a personal preference?

Undeniably Liu was painfully aware that the audience to whom his message was delivered constituted a small coterie of like-minded friends and students in the intellectual world, in other words the tiny minority of a tiny minority. From the viewpoint of the sociology of knowledge, Liu seems to have been inescapably caught in a kind of moral and cultural elitism. By setting up an extremely high standard in personal conduct, Liu had already excluded himself from the "main stream" of scholar-official activities. His feeling of alienation, not unlike the solitariness in Ch'ü Yüan's "Encountering Sorrow" (Li-sao),[dg] is captured in a poem probably occasioned by insomnia on a spring night:

> People are all soundly asleep as I sit alone
> And peruse the spring in the cosmic tranquility.
> If perchance for a moment everyone rests,
> Who will tell the time and count the watches?[63]

Many other poems of similar spirit are found in his collection. Among them, several earlier ones focused on the heroic personality of Ching K'o,[dh] whose abortive attempt to assassinate the First Emperor of the Ch'in dynasty (r. 221–210 B.C.) made him a paradigmatic example of the impassioned knightly figure from the state of Yen.[di][64] As a native of the same region, Liu, in his youth, sometimes styled himself as the man from the I[dj] River,[65] obviously referring to the place where Ching K'o said an emotional farewell to his best friends before he embarked on the fateful journey. Liu's youthful fascination with Ching K'o even brought him to the I River in the tenth month of 1266 to deliver a funeral ode in memory of the pre-Ch'in hero.[66] Liu's enthusiasm for unusually courageous persons was more than a reflection of his adventurist spirit as a young man. His poems and essays clearly indicate that he was continuously impressed by them, and that he believed their idiosyncratic modes of behavior have a universal appeal.

Consistent with this line of thinking was his choice of exemplary teachers in the Confucian tradition as a whole. Among Confucius' disciples, he singled out Yen Hui[dk] and Tseng Tien.[67] Philosophically he was indebted to Mencius for his view on human nature and his attitude towards politics. He was not very much impressed by Han-T'ang thinkers. Prior to the emergence of Neo-Confucianism in the Sung, he mentions prominently only Tung Chung-shu[dl] (176–104 B.C.) and Han Yu[dm] (768–824).[68] The Northern Sung Confucian master that inspired him most was Shao Yung,[69] but he seems to have learned more from Chou Tun-i and Chang Tsai. He had a great admiration for the Ch'eng brothers, whom he describes in a poem as instrumental in helping us to understand the Heavenly truth and to appropriate fully the meaning of the principle in things by examining the minuteness of one hair.[70]

Liu's veneration for Ch'eng Hao is further shown in a poem where he praises the Elder Ch'eng as "propitious sun and auspicious clouds."[71] This may have prompted Professor Sun K'o-kuan to contend, in response to the eminent Ming thinker Liu Tsung-chou's[dn] (1578–1645) claim that Liu Yin reminded him of Shao Yung, that Yin's style of life was closer to Ming-tao[do] [Ch'eng Hao]. And it suggests that he would have been sympathetic to Lu Hsiang-shan[dp] (1139–1193), if he had heard of him.[72] In fact, we know that although Liu may not have read Lu Hsiang-shan's collected works, he was certainly knowledgeable about Lu's philosophical challenge to Chu Hsi. Yet, Liu completely identified himself with the Chu Hsi school;[73] he even characterizes Chu's teacher Li T'ung[dq] (1093–1163) in one of his poems as "iced pot and autumn moon" (*p'ing-hu ch'iu-yüeh*),[dr][74] a conventional way of describing an exemplar of clarity and purity. This is not difficult to understand, however, because the real controversy between Chu and Lu as a recognizable philosophical issue occurred much later. In fact, even in the first century of the Ming dynasty (1368–1644), Confucians were still overwhelmingly in favor of the Chu Hsi school. Nevertheless, despite Liu's whole-hearted devotion to Chu Hsi and, for that matter, to Sung Learning in general, he was absolutely serious about maintaining an independent mind as the ultimate judge of relevance and value. He not only confidently remarked that a thousand years of "divinational wisdom" really resides in the human mind,[75] but insisted that one's "innate knowledge" (*liang-chih*)[ds] must not be swayed by opinions from outside, even if they are as authoritative as the teachings of the Sung masters.[76]

Again, we encounter here an obvious conflict. The historical personages to whom Liu attached great cultural and moral significance were well-known "loners." All of them remained marginal to the center of power and some, by deliberate choice, detached themselves from it. Their source of strength did not come from political participation but from learning and self-cultivation. With the exception of Ching K'o, they all made their reputation as scholars and teachers. And even Ching K'o evoked sympathy in literary minds mainly because of his poetlike passion. Ironically, his clumsiness in handling an assassin's dagger enhanced his reputation as a tragic loner who inevitably met his death by confronting the most powerful tyrant of his times. However, unlike the Taoists who preferred either to create a realm of value completely outside politics or to develop a personal sanctuary within it by subtle manipulations, Liu's heroes were serious about improving the political situation to the extent that their critical judgments on it never allowed them to become totally independent of it. Instead of seeing this as a failure to differentiate morality and culture from politics, it is possible to view the dilemma in which virtually all of them were caught as the result of a conscious decision to transform politics through morality and culture. Undeniably, the language of the whole conceptual scheme employed here is foreign to Liu Yin's linguistic world, but its validity as a heuristic device can be shown by focusing on Liu's perception of scholarship.

It is not at all difficult to see that Liu himself was critically aware of the distinction between culture and politics. His refusal to serve in a manner deemed perfectly acceptable by the scholar-officials of his time can also be understood as a personal means of demonstrating that the respectability of the Tao, a cultural idea to be sure, could not be preserved simply by political participation. A clear indication that Liu knew what he was talking about is found in his essay on a Confucian temple located near his home town. He emphatically argues that since what Confucius was to "establish the Way to be human" (li jen-tao),[dt] the right to honor him is open to all villagers and cannot be monopolized by authorized educational officials.[77] A poem dedicated to a Taoist hermit gives us another indication: with a touch of irony, he says that while in officialdom rats are all taken as tigers, in the life that certain people (Taoist hermits) lead dragons are taught to become fish.[78] If it is deplorable that courageous tigers are really timid rats and that talented dragons merely learn to disguise themselves as evasive fish, what is the way Liu himself recommends? Rather than a delicate balance of the two, he offers a different approach: "Strenuous efforts at the classics, philosophy, and history for ten years. Then allow one's painting, poetry, and calligraphy to flourish forever." This sense of immortality through cultural activities is a common motif in Liu's writings. We shall later examine in some detail his "ten-year plan" of learning for his students because, in his view, access to the possibility of exerting the most profound and lasting influence on the human community lies in culture rather than in politics.

It would be wrong to suppose, however, that Liu's commitment to culture was apolitical in the sense that he saw in what he did little political relevance and only a general sort of human relevance. His deliberate disclaimer in one poem is revealing: "There are real Confucians in the court. Please do not say that this culture (*ssu-wen*)[du] would depend on me for support!"[79] His critical awareness that "this culture" would have to depend upon people like him for survival was probably the main reason that he often referred to his vocation metaphorically as putting the fragmented texts in order.[80] He also discussed frequently in his poetry the difficulty of the task and the loneliness one had to bear in order to fulfill it.

> Broken slips and fragmented texts interrupted the appreciated sound
> Who would manifest the genuine gold through a hundredfold of smelting?
> Now after the Dragon Gate has lost its song for a thousand years,
> More so do we feel the great lonely pains of the fine artisan.[81]

But Liu's single-minded attempt to rescue the culture from oblivion was much more than the scholarly ambition of a private citizen. It was also intended to be a challenge to those who presumed to be cultural transmitters as well as political participants, namely the scholar-officials who were actively in support of the Mongol government.

Liu seems to have been perfectly capable of sarcastic remarks when it came to his perceived or real competition with the gentlemen in the court. In an obvious attempt to silence those who still thought that he could be won over, he says in a poem, "As for the great peace, there are you gentlemen to take care of it/ Who would have need of turning to the direction of Nan-yang[dv] and asking K'ung-ming[dw] [Chu-ko Liang] for advice?"[82] Sarcasm it was, especially in the light of his remark about rats in officialdom, but Liu's main concern was not so much to humiliate those whom he despised as to perfect his own studio. Although he deeply regretted that he had no teachers and friends and that his students were few,[83] a sense of self-possession, suggesting inner repose and tranquility, underlies many of his poems. For example, he meditates on a winter day that Chu Hsi hardly enjoyed any earthly comfort and that Confucius came to realize the Mandate of Heaven as he went around in mufti.[84] As neither of them had necessarily been better off than he was, the idea that he too was personally responsible for the continuity of the cultural tradition must have crossed his mind numerous times.[85] A poem written in the first month of 1279 when he had just turned 30 shows the intensity of this concern:

> As I silently sit in the autumn breeze of the Confucian Temple,
> A thousand years of antiquity overwhelmingly enter into my deep meditation
> I offer myself totally [to the great task], noticing still the presence of the primordial mind
> Nowadays who will truly continue the Tao?[86]

This seemingly unbridled subjective assertion would have been no more than hubris, had Liu Yin refused to divulge the actual process by which he intended to complete his self-assigned task. The "presence of the primordial mind" may refer to his existential decision at the age of 18 to "aspire to become a sage." However, the attempt to continue the Tao required a long and strenuous process of learning. He entertained as a possibility no shortcut such as "sudden enlightenment." The key phrase in the title of what was probably his last essay, composed in 1292, is particularly apt in this connection, "planting virtue" (shu-te).[dx][87] The development of oneself, the purpose of Confucian learning, is like the growth of a tree. It has to be planted, watered, and nourished. The persistence with which one must work at one's learning may have prompted Liu to confess that since he dared not emulate Shao Yung in the sky, he might as well follow Ssu-ma Kuang[dy] (1019–1086) on the solid ground.[88]

Liu Yin's recommendations for learning "on the solid ground" are detailed in a long essay.[89] Although we do not know when it was written, internal evidence shows that it must have been composed after he had been teaching for several years. It thus reflects his mature thought on the subject. Entitled, "On Learning" ("Hsü-hsüeh"),[dz] the essay consists of a short introductory note and four main parts. Fitting well into the balanced style of examination prose, the material is introduced, explained, developed, and eventually concluded with a summary statement. The thematic approach involves two contrasting sets of ideas along with some secondary thoughts. One major theme is developed by Liu's constant return to the main structure of the presentation, which is a rather formal

instruction on the exact sequence by which one masters the basic literature in the Confucian tradition. At the same time, another set of ideas
seems to argue that at every juncture of this learning process there is
infinite possibility for creative adaptation. The primary concern here is
to develop a sense of direction. The interplay between self-discipline and
self-discovery gives the essay a dynamism which distinguishes it from ordinary manuals for book-learning.

At the beginning, Liu asserts that inherent in the nature (*hsing*),[ea]
mind (*hsin*),[eb] and material force (*ch'i*) of every human being is an irreducible potential for self-completion. Learning means the process by which
this potential is realized. Since each person is originally endowed with
the capacity to learn, it is inconceivable that the task of self-completion
is not open to all people. However, the present state of scholarship (*hsüeh-
shu*)[ec] has deviated much from the norm, its pattern (*p'in-chieh*)[ed] is confusing, and it has suffered a great deal from the attacks of heterodox
traditions (*i-tuan*).[ee] This is the reason that learning to be fully human
requires a systematic inquiry into the best of the cultural heritage.

I. *Six Classics, Confucian Analects, and Mencius.* Clearly intended
as a departure from Chu Hsi's pedagogy, Liu insists that learning should
commence with the Six Classics.[90] Only after the student has been extensively exposed to classical scholarship, he argues, can he really appreciate the refined expressions of the *Analects* and *Mencius*. Since the wisdom in these two books symbolizes the crystallization of many years of
sagely efforts, the student ought to be well prepared before a fruitful encounter is possible. Among the classics, the *Odes* should be on top of the
list because it not only properly channels basic human feelings but also
opens up new areas of human sensitivity. The *Odes* and the *Documents*,
alleged to be a written account of sagely sentiments, are said to have
established the great foundation. The *Rites*, both the *Book of Rites* and
the *Rites of the Chou*, can thus be seen as social and political applications
of the great foundation. The *Spring and Autumn Annals* are then studied
for their historical judgments, which we may consider a concrete manifestation of the aforementioned classics.

Only after these classics have been carefully learned can one begin
to understand the subtle meanings of the *Book of Change*, a task which
leads to the culminating point of classical scholarship. Following the Sung
thinkers, Liu notes that an exhaustive appropriation of the principle in
things and a full appreciation of human nature can eventually lead to a

comprehension of the Mandate of Heaven. All these, he believes, must precede the study of the *Change*. He also instructs that a balanced classical education must involve intensive work on the Han commentaries, the T'ang subcommentaries, and the Sung interpretations. However, he urges his students to maintain the independence of their own "innate knowledge" (*liang-chih*)[91] in the whole process.

II. *History*. Quoting from *Mencius*, Liu says that to master classical education is to "establish that which is great,"[92] suggesting a center of gravity and a sense of priority. With the established standards of conduct in the classics as a guide, the student should proceed to the study of history. Liu states that in ancient times there was no distinction between classics and history and that "the *Odes*, the *Documents*, and the *Spring and Autumn Annals* were [originally] all history." It is interesting to note that this perceptive observation, which is commonly attributed to the Ch'ing scholar Chang Hsüeh-ch'eng[ef] (1738–1801) as a bold attempt to see history as on a par with classics, is here formulated and presented as a matter of fact by Liu several centuries earlier.[93] Liu's recommendation for the study of history itself is again a remarkable demonstration of his balanced approach to scholarship. As expected, he puts a great deal of emphasis on Ssu-ma Ch'ien's[eg] (145–86? B.C.) *Records of the Historian* (*Shih chi*)[eh] as the major source of inspiration for all subsequent Chinese historians in terms of organization, style, and narrative art. Liu also singles out the *History of the (Former) Han* (*Han shu*)[ei] and the *History of the Later Han* (*Hou-Han shu*)[ej] for praise. Although he makes some scathing criticisms on Ch'en Shou's[ek] (233–297) biased approach in the *Chronicles of the Three Kingdoms* (*San-kuo chih*),[el] he believes that P'ei Sung-chih's[em] (372–451) commentaries serve as useful correctives.[94]

He feels that the *History of the Chin* (*Chin shu*)[en] under the compilation of a group of famous high scholar-officials in T'ang T'ai-tsung's[eo] (r. 627–649) court is unduly complex. He observes, too, the shortcomings of the *History of the Southern Dynasties* (*Nan shih*),[ep] *History of the Northern Dynasties* (*Pei shih*),[eq] and *History of the Sui* (*Sui shu*),[er] all completed in the first few decades of the T'ang dynasty. He then compares the two versions each of the *History of the T'ang* (*T'ang shu*)[es] and the *History of the Five Dynasties* (*Wu-tai shih*).[et] His admiration for Ou-yang Hsiu[eu] (1007–1072), who was responsible for both new versions, does not lead him to conclude that the old ones are outdated. In fact, he argues that precisely because Ou-yang and his colleagues had a particular viewpoint to convey, their interpretations may have significantly departed from the factual basis. Thus the old versions should still be read for countervailing effect. Since the Sung and Chin histories have not yet been compiled, he further observes, the student should take advantage of the *Veritable Records* (*Shih-lu*)[ev] and miscellaneous notes of informed literati.[95] His general recommendation is to obtain an overview of Chinese history first, to sharpen one's judgment by a continuous application of the principles in the classics as a second step, and finally to compare what one has learned from the primary sources with the opinions expressed in Ssu-ma Kuang's *Comprehensive Mirror for Aid in Government* (*Tzu-chih t'ung-chien*)[ew] and in the writings of Sung Confucians. In short, Liu considers it imperative that the student confront history as a holistic structure rather than as isolated events.

III. *Philosophy*. Liu's open-mindedness is best seen in his approach to the philosophical schools in early China. He recommends that, after studying history, the student should read *Lao Tzu*, *Chuang Tzu*, the late Han Taoist classic *Lieh Tzu*,[ex] and the T'ang religious Taoist work *Yin-fu Chinq*[ey] because they contain many remarkable insights into principle. Furthermore, he recommends for careful reading books in medicine and military sciences, such as *Su-wen*[ez] for the former and the treatises attributed to Sun Pin,[fa] Wu Ch'i,[fb] Chiang Tzu-ya,[fc] and Huang Ti[fd] for the latter.[96] He criticizes Hsün Tzu's[fe] theory of human nature but praises it for its sophistication in argumentation. Although he regards the *Kuan Tzu*[ff] as a book advocating the way of the hegemon, he still thinks that it should be studied. Among the Han Confucians, he mentions Yang Hsiung,[fg] (53 B.C.–A.D. 18), Chia I[fh] (201–169 B.C.), Tung Chung-shu, and Liu Hsiang[fi] (77–6 B.C.) in particular; he asserts that Tung's celebrated views on the mutuality of Heaven and man are second only to the thought of Mencius. During the eight-century interval between the Han and the Sung, he only mentions Wang T'ung (Wen-chung Tzu,[fj] 584–618), the famed Confucian teacher of the Sui dynasty who is alleged to have trained a generation of outstanding scholar-officials for the T'ang, and Han Yü. Among the Sung thinkers, he groups together Chou Tun-i, Ch'eng Hao, Ch'eng I, and Chang Tsai as philosophers of "human nature and principle" (*hsing-li*).[fk] Shao Yung is singled out as the founder of the school of "form and number" (*hsiang-shu*).[fl] And Ou-yang Hsiu, Su Shih,[fm] (1036–1101) and Ssu-ma Kuang are characterized as exponents of "statecraft" (*ching-chi*).[fn] Nevertheless, he does not even mention

Buddhism, and he refuses to recognize Mohist and Legalist texts as legitimate subjects in this highly selective list of basic philosophical readings for the confirmed Confucian.

IV. *Poetry, Prose, Calligraphy, and Painting.* Liu begins his discussion of the arts with a quote from the *Analects:* "Set your will on the Way, have a firm grasp on virtue, rely on humanity, and roam among the arts."[97] He admits that the meaning of "arts" (*i*)[fo] has undergone a fundamental change since the time of Confucius: while the Master used it to refer to the practices of rituals, music, archery, charioteering, calligraphy, and arithmetic,[98] nowadays the arts mainly include poetry, prose, calligraphy, and painting. Since these cultural activities are essential for furthering self-completion, Liu continues, the student ought to study them in a systematic way. He then offers precise suggestions for undertaking a comprehensive program of learning. In the area of poetry, Liu gives a six-point instruction, identifying his choices in practically all the major genres available to a Yüan scholar: (1) an understanding of the "six meanings" (*liu-i*)[fp] in the *Book of Odes;* (2) an exposure to the *Ch'u-tz'u* style, especially the "Encountering Sorrow" of Ch'ü Yüan; (3) an awareness of the rhymed prose of the Han, in particular of pieces such as the "Three Cities" and the "Two Capitals"; (4) an acquaintance with the Wei-Chin tradition, notably the writings of the Ts'aos (Ts'ao Ts'ao[fq] [155–220] and Ts'ao Chih,[fr] [192–232]), Liu Chen[fs] (d. 217), T'ao Yüan-ming and Hsieh Ling-yün[ft] (385–433); (5) a knowledge of the Sui-T'ang poetic transformation, with emphasis on the works of Li Po[fu] (699–762), Tu Fu[fv] (712–770), and Han Yü; and (6) a familiarity with the Sung poets such as Ou-yang Hsiu, Su Shih, and Huang T'ing-chien[fw] (1045–1105). This seemingly comprehensive list is, again, highly selective. For one thing, Liu has deliberately deleted virtually all of the romantic poets. His "classicism" is also reflected in his choices for other arts. He recommends a similar procedure for the study of prose, and, although his instructions for calligraphy and painting are much briefer, they are basically in the same spirit.

Toward the end of the essay, Liu Yin remarks confidently that if his students learn to educate themselves in this way, they will be ready either for the most active roles in the government or for a complete withdrawal to the wilderness. Indeed, all three well-known paths to immortality will be open to them: morality, politics, and scholarship. In the case of Liu Yin himself, we may surmise, his self-development or, more specifically, his quest for "purity" was not simply an attempt to steer clear of politics. Yet not unlike the "sensible person" in More's *Utopia,* he wisely decided to work on the Confucian texts indoors rather than to get soaked in the pouring rain.

In retrospect, Liu Yin's Confucian eremitism seems to symbolize more than a rejection of and a protest against the Yüan dynasty. Nor did Liu's decision not to serve the Mongol government have much to do with loyalism either, despite some nostalgic sentiments expressed by him over the collapse of the Chin state. Professor Mote has noted that Liu was not engaged in any "compulsory" eremitism which was theoretically binding on all servitors of a fallen dynasty.[99] But in what sense can Liu's refusal to serve be understood as a kind of "voluntary" eremitism? Of course, his decision signified "clearly an expression of protest against impossible conditions of service, and more or less directed against the ruler and his government,"[100] but the grounds on which the decision was made were not exclusively political, for the Confucian demand that a man serve society is primarily an ethicoreligious one. Moreover, the basic Confucian commitment is to morality and culture rather than to any particular structure of power.

It is therefore quite understandable that Liu Yin should not have been particularly interested in what is alleged to have been Confucian historiography in the writings of Ou-yang Hsiu. Although Liu praised Ou-yang for his *New Histories* of the T'ang and the Five Dynasties, it seems that Ou-yang's highly politicized attempt to rally ideological support for the threatened Sung state was to Liu no more than a personal historical judgment.[101] Furthermore, despite Liu's admiration for Ssu-ma Kuang as a historian, there is no indication that he subscribed to Ssu-ma's view on political legitimacy. Liu's decision to withdraw from politics was surely not imposed on him as a moral duty in the name of what Ou-yang and Ssu-ma characterized as "loyalty."[102] Nor, in a deeper sense, was it what Nemoto Makoto[fx] refers to as a kind of "subjectively determined"[103] loyalism because he was impelled to choose morality and culture over politics by a profound sense of mission, an ultimate concern for personal purity and dignity out of respect for the Confucian Tao. Since his purpose in life was to become an exemplary teacher and a cultural transmitter through the effort of self-realization, Liu Yin's eremitism not only challenged a well-established convention of identifying Confucian service with political participation but also reenacted a powerful Confucian practice, inspired by the example of Mencius: The great man carries out the Way alone, when the time does not permit him to join the government. "He cannot be led into excesses when wealthy and honored or deflected from his purpose when poor and obscure, nor can he be made to bow before superior force." [104]

NOTES

1. Thomas More, *Utopia*, tr. Paul Turner (Middlesex, England: Penguin Books, 1975), p. 65. It is evident that, as Turner notes, "More's simile is a very free paraphrase of *Republic* 6:496d–e," see *ibid.*, p. 140, note 41.
2. *Ibid.*, pp. 57–63.
3. The other Confucian master who seems to have exerted a much wider influence on Yüan politics than Liu Yin did was Hsü Heng. For an anthology of Hsü's writings, see *Lu-chai i-shu,*[fy] 14 *ch.*, various editions. For a recent study on Hsü Heng, see Yüan Chi,[fz] *Yüan Hsü Lu-chai p'ing-shu*[ga] (Taipei: Commercial Press, 1972).
4. See *Ching-hsiu hsien-sheng wen-chi*[gb] (hereafter abbreviated as *Wen-chi*; 1879 ed.); YS (Peking: Chung-hua shu-chü, 1976), 171:4007–10. *Hsin Yüan shih*[gc] (Tientsin, 1930 ed.), 170:13a; SYHA (1846 ed.), 91:1a–11b and T'ao Tsung-i, *Cho-keng lu* (TSCC ed.) 2:37. For a recent addition to scholarship on Liu Yin, see Yüan Chi, "Yüan ming-ju Liu Ching-hsiu hsing-shih pien-nien,"[gd] in *id.*, *Yüan shih lun-ts' ung*[ge] (Taipei: Lien-ching Publishers, 1978), pp. 19–76. Also, see his interpretive essay on Liu's literature and personality and his annotation on and addition to Liu's biography in the SYHA, in *Ibid.*, pp. 77–105, 107–127.
5. Sun K'o-k'uan, "Yüan-ju Liu Ching-hsiu hsüeh-hsing shu-p'ing,"[gf] in his *Meng-ku Han-chün yü Han wen-hua yen-chiu*[gg] (Taipei: Wen-hsing Book Co., 1958), p. 75.
6. YS, 171:4007.
7. For an account of Yen Mi-chien's biography, see Su Tïen-chüeh, *Tzu-hsi wen-kao*[gh] (Taipei: National Central Library, 1970), 7:287–93, and SYHA, 90:14b–15a. Since he is classified as a "t'ung-tiao"[gi] (similar tune) of the Chiang-han[gj] School in SYHA, his philosophical ideas were viewed as compatible with those of the more famous Confucian master from the South, Chao Fu.
8. YS, 171:4008.
9. For Chao Fu's life and thought as well as the development of the so-called Chiang-han School alleged to have been founded by him, see SYHA, 90:1a–23b. It should be noted, however, that although Liu Yin was indebted to Chao for his exposure to Sung Learning, he was not, in a strict sense, a follower of Chao Fu. Sun K'o-k'uan argues against the supposed claim in SYHA that Liu belonged to the Chiang-han School. But a careful reading of the SYHA interpretation seems to show that the authors are critically aware of this. Although they note that Hsü Heng was a follower of Chao Fu, they actually put Liu Yin in a different category. The subtle difference between "Chiang-han so-ch'uan" in the case of Hsü and "Chiang-han pieh-ch'uan,"[gk] in the case of Liu is particularly relevant here. See SYHA, 90:1a and 3a. For Sun's observation, see "Yüan-ch'u ju-hsüeh,"[gl] in his *Yüan-tai Han wen-hua chih huo-tung*[gm] (Taipei: Chung-hua shu-chü, 1968), p. 185. See also the paper by Professor W. T. Chan included in this volume.

10. Frederick W. Mote, "Confucian Eremitism in the Yüan Period," in *The Confucian Persuasion*, ed. A. F. Wright (Stanford: Stanford University Press, 1960), pp. 213–15. The conclusions Professor Mote arrived at almost two decades ago concerning the salient features of Confucian eremitism in the Yüan period provide an excellent background for the present inquiry.

11. For a translation of this important Confucian document, see Wing-tsit Chan, tr., *A Source Book in Chinese Philosophy* (Princeton: Princeton University Press, 1973), pp. 465–80. I would like to acknowledge my indebtedness to Professor Chao Tzu-ch'iang[gn] for translating *I ching*[go] as the *Book of Change* rather than as the *Book of Changes*.

12. The phrase was originally coined by the well-known Northern Sung poet Huang T'ing-chien in characterizing the lofty personality of Chou Tun-i. Chu Hsi's teacher Li T'ung was particularly fond of this expression. It seems that by Chu Hsi's time, it had already been widely recognized among Confucian literati as a sort of poetic reference to Master Chou. For a brief discussion on this, see Ch'ien Mu,[gp] *Chu Tzu hsin hsüeh-an*[gq] (Taipei: San-min Book Co., 1971), vol. 3, pp. 49. See also Chu Hsi, "Shu Lien-hsi Kuang-feng chi-yüeh t'ing,"[gr] in *Chu Wen-kung wen-chi* (i.e. *Chu Tzu ta-chüan*)[gs] (SPPY ed.), 84:29b–30a.

13. The conversation is quoted verbatim from two sources in Chou Tun-i's *Penetrating the Book of Change*. The first statement is from *ch*. 10, "The Will to Learn" and the rest are from *ch*. 20, "Learning to Be a Sage." Cf. Chan, *Source Book*, pp. 470 and 473.

14. It is not difficult to figure out that the "Nameless Elder" refers to Shao Yung and the "Master of Sincerity, Brilliance, and Centrality" refers to Chang Tsai. For one thing, all the references to the former are from Shao's work, such as the *Huang-chi ching-shih shu*[gt] (Supreme Principles Governing the World) and *I-ch'uan chi-jang chi*[gu] (A Collection of [Poems] Striking the Earth at the I River) and the latter from Chang's *Hsi-ming*[gv] (Western Inscription) and *Cheng-meng*[gw] (Correcting Youthful Ignorance). In fact, Shao Yung's autobiography is called "Wu-ming kung chuan,"[gx] the biography of a nameless elder. See Michael D. Freeman's unpublished essay, "From Adept to Sage: The Philosophical Career of Shao Yung," p. 18. For a survey of philosophies of Shao and Chang, see Chan, *Source Book*, pp. 481–517. Actually, in one of Liu Yin's poems, he specifically notes that Shao Yung styled himself as the "Nameless Elder." See *Wen chi*, 9:1a.

15. YS, 171:4008.

16. See his poem, which was obviously inspired by a dream he reports to have taken place on the twenty-eighth day of the ninth month of 1279. He notes in the poem that his mother has been dead for twenty years; see *Wen-chi*, 11:9a–b. Based upon evidence of this kind, Yüan Chi also arrives at the same conclusion, see his *Yüan shih lun-ts'ung*, p. 25.

17. The letter entitled "Yü cheng-fu shu" is found in *Wen-chi*, 3:7b–9b.

18. Although we have only limited evidence for Liu's scholarship on the *Book of Change*, he was recognized by his contemporaries as an expert on the Book. See YS, 171:4010; see also Sun K'o-k'uan, "Yüan-ch'u ju-hsüeh," p. 185.

Professor Sun claims that precisely because of Liu's profound knowledge of *Lao Tzu* and the *Book of Change*, his spiritual orientation was significantly different from that of the so-called Chiang-han scholars.

19. For a readily available edition of Liu's literary works, see *Ching-hsiu hsien-sheng wen-chi* (TSCC ed.), *mu-lu* (Table of Contents).

20. See Yü Chi, "An Ching-chung wen-chi hsü,"[gy] in his *Tao yüan hsüeh-ku lu*[gz] (1730 ed.), 6:4b–6b.

21. See Yüan Chüeh, "Chen-ting An Ching-chung mu-piao,"[ha] in *Ching-jung chü-shih chi*[hb] (SPTK ed.) 30:22a.

22. See Ou-yang Hsüan, "Ching-hsiu hsien-sheng hua-hsiang tsan,"[hc] in his *Kuei-chai wen-chi*[hd] (SPTK ed.), 15:3b–4a. Also see his "An hsien-sheng ssu-t'ang chi,"[he] *ibid.*, 5:11b–12a.

23. Sun, "Yüan-ju Liu Ching-hsiu . . . ," p. 77.

24. The expression is found in *Mencius* 7A:40. Mencius claims that one of the five ways by which the "profound person" (*chün-tzu*) instructs is to set an example so that those who have no direct access to education can emulate the mode of life he exemplifies. By implication, the "privately cultivated" student is one who follows the example of the teacher, even though he does not have any immediate contact with him.

25. It is interesting to note that as an obvious recognition of An Hsi's intellectual self-identification, the authors of SYHA list him as a follower of Liu Yin and qualify the description with the term *ssu-shu*. For a short anthology of An Hsi's surviving works, see *An Mo-an hsien-sheng chi,*[hf] (TSCC ed.). An account of An's philosophical ideas is found in "Chai-chü tui-wen,"[hg] *ibid.*, 3:15–17. For An's commitment to Liu Yin, see "Chi Ching-hsiu hsien-sheng wen,"[hh] in *ibid.*, 4:26. A very informative account of Liu Yin's life history is found in Su T'ien-chüeh, "Ching-hsiu hsien-sheng Liu-kung mu-piao,"[hi] in *Tzu-hsi wen-kao*, 8:295–305. According to Su, the great southern scholar Wu Ch'eng singled out Liu Yin as the only Yüan Confucian master of the previous generation whom he truly respected, see *ibid.*, 8:304–305.

26. This often-quoted statement is found in T'ao Tsung-i's *Cho-keng lu*, 2:37.

27. For a persuasive argument on this issue, see Sun, "Yüan-ju Liu Ching-hsiu . . . ," pp. 77–78.

28. See "Yüan Chih-cheng chiu-nien chiu-yüeh shih-i-jih tieh,"[hj] in *Wen-chi*, *tieh-wen,*[hk] 1b.

29. YS, 171:4010.

30. The idea of "voluntary eremitism of protest" as developed by Professor Mote should perhaps be understood as a subtle way of mobilizing the symbolic resources available to the Confucian eremite, not as bases for a "free" choice but as the necessary condition for asserting one's personal integrity on grounds different from political loyalty while yet necessarily endorsed by the imperial authority. See Mote, "Confucianism Eremitism," pp. 209–12. For contrasting the Confucian eremites with those Confucians who chose to transform politics from within, see John W. Dardess, *Conquerors and Confucians: Aspects of Political Change in Late Yüan China* (New York: Columbia University Press, 1973), pp. 53–94.

31. *Chuang Tzu* (SPPY ed.), *ch.* 4.

32. See "Yü cheng-fu shu,"[hl] *Wen-chi,* 3:8b–9b.

33. This may have been the main reason that scholars such as Yü Chi, Yüan Chüeh, and Su T'ien-chüeh wholeheartedly supported him in the first decades of the fourteenth century.

34. His intense feelings of great joy mixed with a realistic sense of doubt at the birth of his son when he was already forty *sui* are vividly captured in his poem entitled "Sheng-jih,"[hm] *Wen-chi,* 8:2b. It seems that his son died an infant of no more than two years. According to Su Ti'en-chüeh's biographical account, Liu had three daughters and all of them were married to prominent scholar-official families. See Su's "Ching-hsiu hsien-sheng Liu-kung mu-piao," in his *Tzu-hsi wen-kao,* 8:301.

35. Needless to say, his profound knowledge of the *Book of Change* further gives the impression that his mode of thought was somewhat in conflict with the Confucian learning of Yao Shu and Hsü Heng. For an example of Liu's interpretive position on the *Book of Change,* see his discussions of the hexagrams *Chieh*[hn] (no. 60) and *Chung-fu*[ho] (no. 61), in *Wen-chi* 1:16b–18a. For a brief reference to this, see Sun K'o-k'uan, "Yüan-ch'u ju-hsüeh," p. 185. This was probably also the reason that Ou-yang Hsüan characterized him as an exemplar of the spirit of Tseng Tien, see "Ching-hsiu hsien-sheng hua-hsiang tsan," in his *Kuei-chai wen-chi,* 15:3b–4a.

36. See "Chi-meng,"[hp] *Wen-chi,* 9:9a–b. The preface to the poem is very informative.

37. *Analects* 9:27.

38. Liu notes in one of his poems that he was so fond of Chu-ko Liang's phrase "Quiescence wherewith to cultivate the self" that he named his studio "Quiescent Cultivation." See the eighth verse in his "Ho tsa-shih," *Wen-chi,* 12:10a. It seems that this was the main reason that his students later referred to him as Ching-hsiu hsien-sheng (the Master of Quiescent Cultivation). See also Mote, "Confucian Eremitism," p. 213.

39. For one of the most comprehensive studies of the history of the Chin dynasty in modern scholarship, see Toyama Genji,[hq] *Kinchōshi kenkyū*[hr] (Kyoto: Society of Oriental Researches, 1964). However, even in such a broad coverage, the cultural history of the Chin is not adequately discussed. For a welcome monograph on this issue in English, see Jing-sheng Tao, *The Jurchen in Twelfth Century China: A Study of Sinification* (Seattle: University of Washington Press, 1976).

40. See Yüan Hao-wen, *I-shan hsien-sheng wen-chi*[hs] (SPTK ed.), *ch.* 16–30.

41. See Sun K'o-k'uan, "Yüan-ch'u ju-hsüeh," p. 143. For an informative discussion on the sinicized Western Asians in the Yüan, see Ch'en Yüan,[ht] *Yüan Hsi-yü jen Hua-hua k'ao*[hu] (Taipei: Chiu-ssu Publishers rpt., 1977), *ch.* 2. See also English tr. by Ch'en Hsing-hai and L. C. Goodrich, *Western and Central Asians in China under the Mongols* (Los Angeles: Monumenta Serica at U.C.L.A., 1966), pp. 18–80. For a useful background reading on this subject, see Hsiao Ch'i-ch'ing,[hv] *Hsi-yü-jen yü Yüan-ch'u cheng-chih*[hw] (Taipei: Faculty of Arts, National Taiwan University, 1966).

42. See his poem "Chin t'ai-tzu Yün-kung mo-chu,"[hx] in *Wen-chi*, 7:10b–11a, especially the last six lines. However, Professor Sun's claim that Liu's literary style was consciously modeled on that of Yüan Hao-wen needs further exploration. To be sure, as Sun notes, Liu seems to have established a friendly relationship with Hao Ch'ung-ch'ang,[hy] whose brother Hao Ching[hz] (1223–1275), a well-known literatus and an important Confucian master, was an influential disciple of Yüan Hao-wen. But the evidence seems to show that Liu was not particularly impressed by Hao Ch'ung-ch'ang's literary talents. See Liu's preface entitled "Sung Hao Chi-ch'ang hsü,[ia] in *Wen-chi*, 7b–8a. For Sun's contention, see his "Yüan-ju Liu Ching-hsiu . . . ," pp. 79–80. Yet it should be reiterated that it is beyond doubt that Liu himself greatly admired Yüan Hao-wen. See Liu's poem lamenting the fact that he had not had the fortune of meeting the literary giant, "Pa I-shan mo-chi," in *Wen-chi*, 7:27b.

43. See "Chin t'ai-tzu Yün-kung mo-chu," *Wen-chi*, 7:10b–11a. The other two seven-line verses bearing the same title are equally informative, see *Wen-chi*, 11:13a–b. Also see his poem "Chin t'ai-tzu Yün-kung T'ang-jen ma,"[ib] in *Wen-chi*, 7:7a–b.

44. A most revealing case is, of course, the one mentioned in note 36 where he identified himself as Chin-wen shan-jen. However, there are several cases in his poems where the use of the word *chin* seems to convey special meanings. For example, see his poem "Kan-shih,"[ic] *Wen-chi*, 11:8b. For his emotional response to a copy of the *Veritable Record* of the Chin, (*Chin-ch'ao shih-lu*),[id] see the aforementioned poem "Chin t'ai-tzu Yün-kung mo-chu," in *Wen-chi*, 7:11b.

45. See "Chin t'ai-tzu Yün-kung mo-chu," *Wen-chi*, 7:11b. A preliminary study of three outstanding literary figures of the Chin period clearly indicates that the "literary brilliance" of the Jurchen dynasty has yet to be fully explored in Chinese cultural history. It is interesting too that classical scholarship and historical learning were particularly emphasized by these literati. See Wang Jo-hsü,[ie] *Hu-nan i-lao chi*[if] (SPTK ed.), ch. 11–29. Chao Ping-wen,[ig] *Hsien-hsien lao-jen Hu-shui wen-chi*[ih] (SPTK ed.), *ch.* 1 and 14, and Yüan Hao-wen, *I-shan hsien-sheng wen-chi*, ch. 32–37. For an overview of numerous Chin studies on T'ang historical and literary studies, see Yang Chia-lo,[ii] "Hsin-pu Chin shih i-wen shih,"[ij] in *Chin shih* (Taipei: National War College, 1970), vol. 2 and Hsü Wen-yü,[ik] "Chin-yüan ti wen-yu,"[il] in Cheng Chen-to,[im] ed., *Chung-kuo wen-hsüeh yen-chiu*[in] (Hong Kong: Li-sheng Book Co., rep. 1963), pp. 677–714. See also, Hok-lam Chan, *The Historiography of the Chin Dynasty: Three Studies* (Wiesbaden: Franz Steiner, 1970), chap. 2. For a brief survey of art history in the Chin, see Susan Bush, "Literati Culture under the Chin (1122–1234)," *Oriental Art* (1969), 15:103–12.

46. As an example of this, see his nine poems after the style of T'ao Yüan-ming entitled "Ho i-ku,"[io] in *Wen-chi*, 12:7a–8b.

47. Sun K'o-k'uan, "Yüan-ju Liu Ching-hsiu . . . ," p. 81. For a historical account of the frontier poets in the T'ang, see Liu Ta-chieh,[ip] *Chung-kuo*

wen-hsüeh fa-chan shih[iq] (Taipei: Chung-hua shu-chü, rep. 1957) vol. 1, pp. 347–53.

48. For example, see "Hsiao-tzu T'ien-chün mu-piao,"[ir] in *Wen-chi*, 4:22a–24a. Also see his poems "Chai chieh-fu shih,"[is] *Wen-chi*, 6:10b–11b and "Wang I-ching,"[it] *Wen-chi*, 9:17a.

49. See Hsiao T'ung,[iu] "T'ao Yüan-ming chuan," [iv] in *Ching-chieh hsien-sheng chi*[iw] (1840 ed.), preface, 5b. The same reference is found in T'ao's biographies in both *Chin shu* and *Nan shih*.

50. *Wen-chi*, 12:1a–14b.

51. "Chuang Chou meng-tien-t'u hsü," [ix] *Wen-chi*, 2:4a–5b.

52. *Mencius* 7A:21. For this translation, see D. C. Lau, tr., *Mencius* (Middlesex, England: Penguin Classics, 1976), p. 185.

53. *Mencius* 7A:21. See Lau, *Mencius*, p. 186.

54. For references to "i-ming," see *Wen-chi*, 2:4a and 5a.

55. *Ibid.*, 2:4a.

56. See his "T'ui-chai chi," [iy] in *Wen-chi*, 2:22b–24b. The essay was composed in the eighth month of 1276.

57. *Wen-chi*, 2:22b.

58. *Wen-chi*, 2:23b.

59. For Ch'üan's interpretation, see SYHA, 91:3b–4a. It seems also possible that Liu's critique was directed against scholar-officials such as Liu Ping-chung.[iz] See Hok-lam Chan, "Liu Ping-chung (1216–74): A Buddhist-Taoist Statesman at the Court of Khubilai Khan," *Toung Pao* (1967), 53(1–3):98–146.

60. See the two poems entitled "Ssu-hao," in *Wen-chi*, 6:10a–b. Also, see his poem inspired by an artistic imagining of the portraits of the "four white-haired ones," entitled "Ssu-hao t'u," [ja] *Wen-chi*, 10:2a.

61. See his poem "Yen Kuang," *Wen-chi*, 6:10b.

62. See the fourth of his seven poems entitled "Ho yung p'in-shih," [jb] *Wen-chi*, 12:11a–b. For a perceptive analysis of this, see Mote, "Confucian Eremitism," pp. 225–27.

63. See his poem "Ch'un-yeh pu-mei," [jc] *Wen-chi*, 11:32b.

64. See his poem "Teng Ching K'o shan," [jd] *Wen-chi*, 7:3b.

65. For example, in the aforementioned essay "Hsi sheng-chieh," Liu refers to himself as the Liu of I River, see *Wen-chi*, 1:1a. Also see his poem "Tz'u-yün ta Liu Chung-tse," [je] *Wen-chi*, 9:41a.

66. See his essay "Tiao Ching K'o wen," [jf] in *Wen-chi*, 5:1a–2b.

67. See his two poems entitled "Yen Tseng," [jg] *Wen-chi*, 11:13b–14a. Also, see his two poems probably written on his personal fan, "Tseng Tien shan-t'ou," [jh] in *Wen-chi*, 11:18b.

68. See his essay "Hsü-hsüeh," in *Wen-chi*, 1:8a. Also see the ninth of his nine poems entitled "Kuei-yu hsin-chü tsa-shih," [ji] *Wen-chi*, 11:15b.

69. The following poems from the *Wen-chi* are particularly revealing in this connection: "Chou Shao," [jj] 8:6a, "Kan-shih," 8:11a, "Shui-pei tao-kuan," [jk] 9:21b, and "Hsin-chü," [jl] 11:22a. It should be mentioned that I take the expression "Yü-ch'iao" [jm] (fisherman and woodcutter) in the latter two poems

as a reference to Shao Yung's celebrated essay on the conversation between a fisherman and a woodcutter.

70. See the first of his three poems entitled "Hsieh-chen shih,"[jn] *Wen-chi*, 11:18a.
71. See his poem "Yu-huai,"[jo] *Wen-chi*, 9:9a.
72. Actually Su T'ien-chüeh also thought that Liu's personality was most compatible with that of Shao Yung. See Su's "Ching-hsiu hsien-sheng Liu-kung mu-piao," in *Tzu-hsi wen-kao*, 8:296–98. For Sun's observation, see "Yüan-ju Lin Ching-hsi . . . ," pp. 85–86.
73. See Liu's essay on "Ho-t'u pien,"[jp] *Wen-chi*, 1:10b–16b and his essay on "T'ai-chi-t'u hou-chi,"[jq] *Wen-chi*, 1:18a–20a.
74. See his poem "Yu-huai," *Wen-chi*, 9:9a.
75. See his poem commenting on a line from the *Analects*, "Man is born with uprightness" (6:17), *Wen-chi*, 11:4b.
76. See his essay on "Hsü-hsüeh," *Wen-chi*, 1:5b.
77. "Kao-lin ch'ung-hsiu K'ung Tzu miao chi,"[jr] *Wen-chi*, 2:21b–22b.
78. "Shou T'ien ch'u-shih,"[js] *Wen-chi*, 9:40a.
79. "Tz'u-yün ta Shih Shu-kao,"[jt] *Wen-chi*, 9:40b–41a.
80. See his poem "Min han,"[ju] *Wen-chi*, 9:23b–24a. Also, see his poem "P'ing-hsi,"[jv] *Wen-chi*, 9:12b–13a.
81. The sixth of his seven poems entitled "Kan-hsing,"[jw] in *Wen-chi*, 11:16b.
82. "Tz'u-yün k'ou p'an-kung,"[jx] *Wen-chi*, 9:41b.
83. See his poem "Chih ts'ai-lin,"[jy] *Wen-chi*, 9:29a.
84. See his poem "Tung-jih,"[jz] *Wen-chi*, 9:12a–b.
85. For example, see his poem "Tz'u-yün ta Shih Shu-kao" cited in note 79.
86. The second of the two poems entitled "Chi-mo yüan-jih," in *Wen-chi*, 11:9a. It should be noted that "chi-mo yüan-jih"[ka] means the new year's day of the "chi-mo" year (1279).
87. "Chung-te t'ing chi,"[kb] in *Wen-chi*, 2:25b–26b.
88. See the first of a group of nine poems entitled "Kuei-yu hsin-chü tsa-shih," in *Wen-chi*, 11:14b. It should be noted that these poems were composed in the "kuei-yu" year (1273).
89. "Hsü-hsüeh," in *Wen-chi*, 1:3b–10b.
90. *Ibid.*, 4a–b.
91. *Ibid.*, 5a–b.
92. *Ibid.*, 6a. Also see *Mencius* 6A:15.
93. As a matter of fact, Wang Yang-ming[kc] (1472–1529) also made it clear that he believed that the Five Classics are history (*shih*)[kd] as well as classics (*ching*). See his *Ch'uan-hsi lu* in *Yang-ming ch'üan-shu*[ke] (Taipei: Cheng-chung Book Co., rep. 1955), vol. 1, p. 8. It is important to note, however, it was Chang Hsüeh-ch'eng who for the first time offered persuasive arguments to show that the Six Classics should indeed be taken as historical records. See Chang Hsüeh-ch'eng, *Wen-shih t'ung-i*[kf] (Hongkong: T'ai-p'ing Book Co. rep., 1973), vol. 1, pp. 1–33. For a stimulating interpretation of this see Yü Ying-shih,[kg] *Lun Tai Chen yü Chang Hsüeh-ch'eng*[kh] (Hongkong: Lung-men Book Co., 1976), pp. 45–53.

94. "Hsü-hsüeh," in *Wen-chi*, 1:6b.

95. *Ibid.*, 7b.

96. *Ibid.*, 7b. For his interest in and knowledge of medicine, see *"Nei-ching lei-pien* hsü,[ki] *Wen-chi*, 2:5b–6b, "Shu shih yang-i,"[kj] *ibid.*, 3:11b–12b and "Ta i-che Lo Ch'ien-fu,"[kk] *ibid.*, 3:16b–17a.

97. *Analects* 7:6. For this translation, see Chan, *Source Book*, p. 31.

98. For a brief account of the "six arts" (*liu-i*) in Confucian learning, see Tu Wei-ming, "The Confucian Perception of Adulthood," *Daedalus* (Spring 1976), 105(2):115.

99. Mote, "Confucian Eremitism," pp. 229–32.

100. *Ibid.*, p. 209. For a survey of the political thought of this important scholar, see James T. C. Liu, *Ou-yang Hsiu, An Eleventh-Century Neo-Confucianist* (Stanford: Stanford University Press, 1967).

101. See Liu Yin, "Hsü-hsüeh," *Wen-chi*, 1:7a–b; Mote, "Confucian Eremitism," pp. 209–12.

102. For a critical examination of interpretive positions on the Classics, such as Ssu-ma Kuang's attack on Mencius, see Hsiung Shih-li,[kl] *Tu-ching shih-yao*[km] (Taipei: Kuang-wen Book Co. rep. 1960), vol. 2, pp. 1–22. It is interesting to note that Hsiung's own sense of "loyalty" led him to a severe criticism of Wu Ch'eng and Liu Yin. See *ibid.*, p. 25.

103. Nemoto Makoto, *Sensei shakai ni okeru teiko seishin*[kn] (Tokyo: Sogen sha, 1952), pp. 51–54, quoted in Mote, "Confucian Eremitism," p. 209.

104. *Mencius* 3B:2. See D. C. Lau, *Mencius*, p. 107.

GLOSSARY

a 杜維明
b 劉因（靜修）
c 容城
d 保定
e 孫克寬
f 秉善
g 貞祐
h 燕京
i 汴
j 述
k 問學
l 性理之說
m 弱冠
n 硯彌堅
o 精義
p 五經正義
q 朱熹
r 趙復
s 德安
t 姚樞
u 太極
v 希聖解
w 望
x 周敦頤
y 通書
z 太和
aa 楚辭
ab 屈原
ac 拙翁
ad 無名公
ae 誠明中子
af 英才
ag 理
ah 氣
ai 五常
aj 修

ak 靜
al 太極圖說
am 邵雍
an 張載
ao 丁卯
ap 咸淳
aq 至元
ar 程灝
as 程頤
at 呂祖謙
au 傲
av 精要
aw 延祐
ax 仁宗
ay 文靖
az 虞集
ba 袁桷
bb 歐陽玄
bc 曾點
bd 子路
be 許衡
bf 吳澄
bg 蘇天爵
bh 安熙
bi 私淑
bj 宋元學案
bk 陶宗儀
bl 輟耕錄
bm 道不行
bn 道不尊
bo 清節
bp 不召之臣
bq 君臣之義
br 莊子
bs 國家
bt 中庸

bu 政府

bv 宰相

bw 朝廷

bx 金山文人

by 諸葛亮

bz 靜以修身

ca 蜀

cb 徽宗

cc 元好問

cd 耶律楚材

ce 耶律阿海禿花

cf 蒲察

cg 王檝

ch 李邦瑞

ci 郭寶玉

cj 完顏允恭

ck 陶淵明

cl 岑參

cm 高適

cn 和陶

co 老子

cp 齊物論

cq 齊

cr 無適而不可

cs 幻

ct 君子

cu 義命

cv 窮理

cw 勢

cx 數

cy 術

cz 全祖望

da 四皓

db 光武

dc 嚴光

dd 惠

de 柳下

df 伯夷

dg 離騷

dh 荊軻

di 燕

dj 易

dk 顏回

dl 董仲舒

dm 韓愈

dn 劉宗周

do 明道

dp 陸象山

dq 李侗

dr 冰壺秋月

ds 良知

dt 立人道

du 斯文

dv 南陽

dw 孔明

dx 樹德

dy 司馬光

dz 叙學

ea 性

eb 心

ec 學術

ed 品節

ee 異端

ef 章學誠

eg 司馬遷

eh 史記

ei 漢書

ej 後漢書

ek 陳壽

el 三國志

em 裴松之

en 晉書

eo 唐太宗

ep 南史

eq 北史

er 隋書

es	唐書	ge	元史論叢
et	五代史	gf	元儒劉靜修先生述評
eu	歐陽修	gg	蒙古漢軍與漢文化研究
ev	實錄	gh	滋溪文稿
ew	資治通鑑	gi	同調
ex	列子	gj	江漢
ey	陰符經	gk	江漢所（別）傳
ez	素問	gl	元初儒學
fa	孫臏	gm	元代漢文化之活動
fb	吳起	gn	趙自强
fc	姜子牙	go	易經
fd	黃帝	gp	錢穆
fe	荀子	gq	朱子新學案
ff	管子	gr	書濂溪光風霽月亭
fg	揚雄	gs	朱文公文集（朱子大全）
fh	賈誼	gt	皇極經世書
fi	劉向	gu	伊川擊壤集
fj	王通（文中子）	gv	西銘
fk	性理	gw	正蒙
fl	象數	gx	無名公傳
fm	蘇軾	gy	安敬仲文集序
fn	經濟	gz	道園學古錄
fo	藝	ha	眞定安敬仲墓表
fp	六義	hb	清容居士集
fq	曹操	hc	靜修先生畫像贊
fr	曹植	hd	圭齋文集
fs	劉楨	he	安先生祠堂記
ft	謝靈運	hf	安默庵先生集
fu	李白	hg	齋居對問
fv	杜甫	hh	祭靜修先生文
fw	黃庭堅	hi	靜修先生劉公墓表
fx	根本誠	hj	元至正九年九月十一日牒
fy	魯齋遺書	hk	牒文
fz	袁冀	hl	與政府書
ga	元許魯齋評述	hm	生日
gb	靜修先生文集	hn	節
gc	新元史	ho	中孚
gd	元名儒劉靜修編年	hp	記夢

hq 外山軍治

hr 金朝史研究

hs 遺山先生文集

ht 陳垣

hu 元西域人華化考

hv 蕭啓慶

hw 西域人與元初政治

hx 金太子允恭墨竹

hy 郝仲常

hz 郝經

ia 送郝季常序

ib 金太子允恭唐人馬

ic 感事

id 金朝實錄

ie 王若虛

if 滹南遺老集

ig 趙秉文

ih 閑閑老人滏水文集

ii 楊家駱

ij 新補金史藝文志

ik 許文玉

il 金源的文圃

im 鄭振鐸

in 中國文學研究

io 和擬古

ip 劉大杰

iq 中國文學發展史

ir 孝子田君墓表

is 翟節婦詩

it 望易京

iu 蕭統

iv 陶淵明傳

iw 靖節先生集

ix 莊周夢蝶圖序

iy 退齋記

iz 劉秉忠

ja 四皓圖

jb 和詠貧士

jc 春夜不寐

jd 登荊軻山

je 次韻答劉仲澤

jf 弔荊軻文

jg 顏曾

jh 曾點扇頭

ji 癸酉新居雜詩

jj 周邵

jk 水北道館

jl 新居

jm 漁樵

jn 寫眞詩

jo 有懷

jp 河圖辨

jq 太極圖後記

jr 高林重修孔子廟記

js 壽田處士

jt 次韻答石叔高

ju 憫旱

jv 平昔

jw 感興

jx 次韻叩泮宮

jy 示彩鱗

jz 冬日

ka 己卯元日

kb 種德亭記

kc 王陽明

kd 傳習錄

ke 陽明全書

kf 文史通義

kg 余英時

kh 論戴震與章學誠

ki 內經類編序

kj 書示瘍醫

kk 答醫者羅謙父

kl 熊十力

km 讀經示要

kn 專制社会における抵抗精神

David Gedalecia

Wu Ch'eng's Approach to Internal Self-cultivation and External Knowledge-seeking

I. THE PROBLEM OF INTERNAL SELF-CULTIVATION AND EXTERNAL KNOWLEDGE-SEEKING IN WU CH'ENG AND HIS FORBEARS

A. *Introduction*

WU CH'ENG[a] (1249–1333), who was born into a poor but scholarly family in Lin-ch'uan[b] in southeastern Kiangsi, spent the first thirty years of his life during the Southern Sung, up to its demise in 1279. In the 1260s he received his education at the Lin-ju[c] Academy under Ch'eng Jo-yung[d] (fl. 1268), whose philosophic lineage traces back to the son-in-law of Chu Hsi[e] (1130–1200), Huang Kan[f] (1152–1221). It was also around this time that Wu studied at the Tao-i[g] Academy under Ch'eng Shao-k'ai[h] (1212–1280), who, in his attempts to harmonize the teachings of Chu Hsi and Lu Hsiang-shan[i] (1139–1193), had an impact on Wu's later philosophical development.[1]

Although Wu failed the *chin-shih* in 1271, he had apparently tired of the pursuit of an official career several years earlier, in the context of dynastic decline. When the Sung fell, Wu took refuge in the mountains southwest of his home and pursued editing and revision of the Classics which, about a decade later, during the Yüan, led to the propagation of his established textual versions by his fellow student from the Lin-ju Academy, Ch'eng Chü-fu[j] (1249–1318). With the establishment of Mongol control in China, however, Wu was at first reluctant to serve in either the Imperial College or the Hanlin Academy, to which he had been recommended at the turn of the fourteenth century.

Even though he served in official positions for less than five of his eighty-five years, he was not an archetypal eremite: he did serve as Proctor and Director of Studies in the Imperial College between 1309 and 1312 and as Chancellor of the Hanlin Academy between 1323 and 1325. In the first case, however, he retired from the post after conflict with his colleagues over curriculum and, in the second, assumed a diminishing role in a project to compile the *Veritable Record* of the recently assassinated Ying-tsung[k] emperor (Shidebala, r. 1320–1323). For the last decade of his life, he wrote his well-known exhaustive commentaries on the Classics.[2]

It can be said that Wu's intellectual predilections were to a great degree shaped by his foundation in the Chu Hsi tradition, with added input from Ch'eng Shao-k'ai. Not only did this latter aspect allow Wu to become more familiar with the philosophical approach of Lu Hsiangshan; it also made him aware of the growing disparity between the followers of Chu and Lu from late Sung times, as well as the need to bridge the philosophical gap. In addition, since Wu lived during the Yüan, he was faced with the problem of whether or not, or to what extent, he should serve the alien dynasty. As his classical studies put him in the forefront of Confucian intellectual activity in the South, the throne sought to recognize and recruit him. Since his was a scholarly mission, Wu eventually did feel that he could serve in educational posts; in light of bias against southerners among northern scholars and the related intellectual conflicts he experienced while in the capital, however, the nature of this mission was tempered by the political climate.

In order to see more clearly how Wu Ch'eng's intellectual development was affected by late Sung traditions and early Yüan developments, it is necessary to focus initially on Wu's feelings about service before he went to the capital for the first time, as well as on his experience in the Imperial College between 1309 and 1312. It is also desirable to relate them to his ideas on philosophical approach, as set down in an important essay which was most likely written around the time of his first period of service.

We thus return to the years 1286–1287, when the Yüan official Ch'eng Chü-fu was in the process of enlisting Confucian scholars from the South for service at the court of Khubilai.[3] Ch'eng's boyhood friendship with Wu Ch'eng made the latter a likely candidate but Ch'eng, sensing Wu's reluctance to serve, used the argument that one should see "the central plain" (North China) at least once. This form of persuasion must have produced some curiosity in Wu for he readily complied with the request but soon returned home, mindful of the fact that Ch'eng was still intent on recommending him for an official post.[4]

In a philosophical essay from a later period, Wu speaks of the necessity of gaining knowledge through experience and makes reference to the sights and sounds of the capital, Yen-ching (Ta-tu, modern Peking), as follows:

For example, if one wants to go to Yen-ching, he then looks into the means for the journey, on the same day charters a boat, buys a horse, and sets out. In two months time he can reach Yen-ching and observe what all these things are like: the palace and the gates, the thoroughfares and avenues, the winds and dust, and the customs. Moreover, he will understand them clearly without inquiring of anyone else. Now if one does not seek to go to Yen-ching and only relies on the records of someone who has already gone there, then as soon as he goes and makes a close investigation, he will observe that the records do not agree with one another and he will be much more in doubt and confused. Thus, if one does not personally go to a place and only relies on another's words, then the more he seeks, the more he will be unable to get at the truth.[5]

When Wu ultimately did go to serve in the post in the Imperial College in 1309, it was as a sexagenarian who experienced the nature of government under Mongol rule for the first time. In the post, Wu perceived that instruction had deteriorated into frivolous practices and entrenched self-interest under the disciples of Hsü Heng[l] (1209–1281), who had been Chancellor there some forty years before.[6] Wu concentrated on a more personal, as well as a more broad-minded, approach to instruction. Using ideas on educational reform from the Sung Confucian Hu Yüan[m] (993–1059) (some of which had appeared in the reform program of Fan Chung-yen[n] [989–1052]),[7] memorials on the schools by Ch'eng Hao[o] (1032–1085),[8] as well as Chu Hsi's criticisms of examination practices in his day,[9] Wu developed a four-part curriculum incorporating classical study, daily conduct, literary skill and practical administration; apparently Wu also wished to place less emphasis than did his colleagues on competitive examiniations, and friction with them led him to resign before he had consolidated his instructional program.[10]

Thus, within two years, Wu's practical experience in educational policy-making had been played out, and, before departing from his post (probably in 1310 or 1311), he raised the problem of how one should

relate study and self-cultivation, chiding his colleagues for their ignorance of the contributions of Lu Hsiang-shan as follows:

Master Chu was preeminent in the practice of "maintaining constant inquiry and
study," while Lu Tzu-ching [Hsiang-shan] looked upon the "honoring of the
virtuous nature" as the main occupation. If inquiry and study are not based on
virtuous nature, then their faults will become apparent in the trivia of exegetical
remarks on textual language. Surely this is comparable to what Lu Tzu-ching has
said. Now the scholars should take virtuous nature as the basis; only then may
one succeed.[11]

This statement of contrast is important in terms of the sequence of
events during Wu's service in the Imperial College. We have first the
built-in differences in educational approach between Wu and his new
northern colleagues and the apparent challenge Wu proposed once he
began to suggest policy. Obviously, Wu's opinions about the state of
scholarship in the Imperial College, while perhaps not virulently expressed, were demonstrated by his actions. His frustrations, then, led him
to criticize his colleagues for encouraging a too formalistic approach to
study which ignored application to personal cultivation.

When Wu invoked Lu's thought as a methodological corrective, it
led to his being branded as a Lu man who opposed the prevailing version
of Chu school teaching among the followers of Hsü Heng, and who was
thus unfit for a higher position in the Imperial College. Because he was
a southerner who hailed from the same place as Lu Hsiang-shan, his
colleagues may have harbored suspicions about him from the outset.[12]

Wu's challenge to the educational establishment, in which he accorded legitimacy to the ideas of Lu, was based on a deeply felt philosophical predilection arising from his own intellectual roots and versatile
intellectual outlook. The political situation surrounding scholarship in
the North, bound up as it was in discussions concerning the reinstitution
of the examination system, set off Wu's predilections in high relief. We
might conjecture as well that his defense of Lu, besides being a personal
inclination, was a way of opting out of an uncomfortable situation. Had
he not, like Lu, tired of the pursuit of learning designed to pass the
examination[13] and found this attitude being reawakened while in the
capital? Certainly Wu was willing to be relieved of an obligation toward
which he had become diffident, but the retiring temperament must also
be viewed in a Lu-ist Neo-Confucian context.

Wu's statement also indicates that the tensions which had arisen in

Neo-Confucianism from the late Sung were still prevalent in Yüan. Issues concerning self-cultivation and knowledge-seeking, arising from the debates between Chu Hsi and Lu Hsiang-shan in 1175, were still vibrant, although they were resolved institutionally once the commentaries of Chu Hsi on the Four Books were officially adopted for the civil service examination in 1313.[14]

Thus while Wu had cautioned fellow southerners against going northward to serve in government in 1287,[15] within fifteen years, as his fame as a premier classicist increased,[16] he had nevertheless decided at least to "run the gauntlet." In doing so, Wu was forced by his anti-Lu colleagues into rethinking his intellectual position. Moreover, it appears that at about this time, or soon after, Wu had a kind of intellectual illumination regarding the scholarly path and his own formal training, which helps to explain the rather terse, cryptic remarks on his departure.[17]

Wu's intellectual awakening and evaluation of his past are related in his essay "Tsun te-hsing tao wen-hsüeh chai chi"[p] ("In Commemoration of the Studio to Honor the Virtuous Nature and Maintain Constant Inquiry and Study"), written in commemoration of the adoption of a new studio name by one of Wu's disciples.[18] Dating this piece presents a problem since if, as many commentators point out,[19] it was a product of Wu's later years, it may reflect a transition in his thought away from a Chu-ist, of "rationalist" position, and toward a Lu-ist, or "idealist" one. The essay presents Wu's *reflections* on his career, which would indicate that what he says about the changes in his thinking occurred sometime before the composition of the essay.

By Wu's own admission, he only began to question the role of exegesis in scholarly work after more than forty years in the mold of the Chu school thinkers Ch'en Ch'un[q] (1153–1217) and Jao Lu[r] (fl. 1256). Since Wu began his studies of Neo-Confucianism with Ch'eng Jo-yung, a follower of Jao Lu and a relative of his friend Ch'eng Chü-fu, at the Lin-ju Academy in Kiangsi around 1265,[20] his doubts probably surfaced in the first decade of the fourteenth century. This would be around the time of his departure from the Imperial College, when he uttered the statement of methodological contrast between Chu and Lu, but still some twenty years before his death.

Thus do we confront the first problem posed by the essay in terms of Wu's career: that is, is there a chronological basis for intellectual evolution in the thought of Wu Ch'eng? Did he, in other words, show a profound shift toward the idealistic position in the last two decades of his life? A secondary, but perhaps more difficult, problem concerns the definition of the polarities in question: what kinds of distinctions and reconciliations can one find in regard to internal self-cultivation and external knowledge-seeking in Chu Hsi, his followers, and Wu Ch'eng? We know, for example, that Wu wrote his *Li-chi tsuan-yen*[s] (Observations on the Book of Rites), a very precise but imaginative exegetical work, only two years before his death;[21] on the other hand, however, this text was highly praised by Wang Yang-ming[t] (1472–1529), who was hardly enamored of rote textual commentaries.[22]

As will be shown in this paper, the vitality of the thought of Wu Ch'eng lay in the fact that he viewed as harmonious those divisive elements in the Neo-Confucian tradition which others, including those scholars in the capital to whom he addressed himself around 1310–1311, saw as irreconcilable. At different periods in his life, Wu came to view one or the other as valuable, without opting for exclusiveness. Such reconciliations reflected the combined wisdom of political experience and philosophic introspection and became significant for thinkers of later times.

B. The Polarities of Internal Self-Cultivation and External Knowledge-Seeking in the Neo-Confucian Tradition

Hard and fast divisions between the ideas of *tsun te-hsing*,[u] honoring the virtuous nature (or internal self-cultivation), and *tao wen-hsüeh*,[v] maintaining constant inquiry and study (or external knowledge-seeking), as first contrasted in the *Doctrine of the Mean* (*Chung-yung*),[w] chapter 27, are no doubt only provisionally useful.[23] As with other apparent polarities in Chinese thought, they are inextricably conjoined since both address the issue of ethical realization; distinguishing between them, however, serves to clarify the range of approaches to it which are available to the scholar. It is only when the synergistic spirit is lost and provisional commitment made permanent that petulant controversy may arise.

As Wu Ch'eng puts it:

In Master Chu's teachings of others, one must first study and investigate; in Master Lu's teaching of others, he caused them genuinely to know and truly to practice. Study and investigation surely are the foundations of real knowledge and true practice, just as real knowledge and true practice must also be attained through study and investigation. What the two teachers taught is one, yet the run-of-the-mill followers of the two schools in each case set up slogans according to which they defamed and reviled each other. Even scholars today are as though deluded.[24]

Thus instead of there being a pragmatic approach to particular intellectual problems within a continuum embracing internal self-cultivation and external knowledge-seeking, dogmatism arises and a controversy develops between the two approaches.[25] Let us now attempt to examine the view of Sung Neo-Confucians on the polarities from the *Mean* in order to see how such a controversy could have taken shape.

Chang Tsai[x] (1020–1077), the uncle of the Ch'eng brothers, states:

If one does not honor the virtuous nature, then inquiry and study will not be in proper accord.[26]

In similar fashion, Ch'eng I[y] (1033–1107), the younger of the Ch'eng brothers, declares:

To have the highest virtue is how one consolidates *tao*. Even if one has inquiry and study, should he not honor his own virtuous nature, then inquiry and study will be of no avail. . . . All this refers to the uniting of virtue with *tao*.[27]

Here, as in Chang Tsai, the approach is based on virtuous nature, even though inquiry and study are the initial elements mentioned.

It is important to qualify Chang's definition of nature in the context of the contrast between internal self-cultivation and external knowledge-seeking. Chang viewed the physical nature as basic, with the proviso that man should return to his original nature through denial of the physical; in doing so, the nature of heaven and earth (the metaphysical nature) would be preserved.[28]

On this score, Wu Ch'eng desired to clarify possible confusion resulting from dichotomizing the physical and metaphysical natures; these are two terms which essentially describe an ethical continuum:

The nature of heaven and earth and the physical nature . . . are of one grade, despite the two usages of the term. Hence, when it is said: "to differentiate these into two separate entities is wrong," this refers to the fact that man's nature is the acquisition of the principle (*li*) of heaven and earth. . . . As for the physical component, although there is diversity, the goodness of the original nature is unitary. It is only because the physical part is either pure or not excellent that the original nature cannot escape having that which defiles it.[29]

Thus the physical nature, being essentially *ch'i*,[z] material force, is heterogeneous and can accommodate *li*,[aa] principle, which, being ho-

mogeneous, provides order and direction. The physical nature is suscep-
tible to defiling influences which obstruct the full realization of virtue.
As in Chang Tsai, Wu Ch'eng shows that the return to original nature
involves an active process of deep personal transformation. This process
also implies a return to the study of oneself, or internal self-cultivation:

Now if one does not effect study in relation to himself but desires to penetrate
into the textual language, stating that so-and-so speaks of nature in this way and
another in that way, it is not skillful scholarship.[30]

Knowledge-seeking *per se* is not sufficient for self-examination, especially when it concerns itself with textual superficialities. The emphasis
on original thought is reminiscent of Lu Hsiang-shan:

Students of today only pay attention to details and do not search for what is
concrete. . . . When scholars read today, they only try to understand words and
do not go further to find out what is vital. If you pay attention to what is concrete
to yourself, you will eventually understand.[31]

Presently we shall see how Wu developed the antitextualist theme further.

Chu Hsi himself finds the passage in chapter 27 of the *Mean*, dealing with the polarities in question, to be the main point of the whole
chapter.[32] Still, he feels that some reduction is necessary:

When asked about the section [from the *Mean*] concerning the "honoring of the
virtuous nature" and the "maintaining of constant inquiry and study," he [Chu
Hsi] said: "These are two things to begin with. If we divide [them up] finely, we
will then arrive at ten.[33] In reality, there are only two and the two, moreover,
only one. There is only the honoring of the virtuous nature. Nevertheless, one
uses the honoring of the virtuous nature in order to maintain constant inquiry
and study. This is why we speak of them in conjunction."[34]

Here Chu Hsi is explaining the sentence from the *Mean*, in which
the two ideas are linked by the word *er*.[ab] This word forms a conjunction
between them because, in Chu's view, one would use *tsun te-hsing* to
achieve *tao wen-hsüeh*. The latter would be achieved under the conditions of the former (A *er* B: B occurring under A conditions, or *tao wen-
hsüeh* occurring under *tsun te-hsing* conditions), since Chu replaces *er*
with *lai*[ac] (in order to) in his explanation.

Thus while the two can be analyzed as separate items, ethical
achievement itself implies fundamental linkage, or conjunction, in the

preceding sense. The fact that one engages in internal self-cultivation *in order to* pursue external knowledge seems to indicate that *tsun te-hsing* takes precedence over *tao wen-hsüeh*. Actually, since the former is engaged in "for the sake of" the latter goal, external knowledge-seeking could conceivably overshadow internal self-cultivation, since it is the desired end.

Chu Hsi also likens *tsun te-hsing* to another of Ch'eng I's ideas, namely his definition of *ching*,[ad] reverence, as the unifying principle:

The method for "honoring the virtuous nature" is quite easy to summarize. It is rather like I-ch'uan's [Ch'eng I's] explanation of reverence as the unifying principle and the unity as meaning undifferentiated.[35]

Indeed, Chu likens *tsun te-hsing* to Ch'eng I's *han-yang*,[ae] the nourishing of virtue, and *tao wen-hsüeh* to *chih-chih*,[af] the extension of knowledge, the latter being one of Chu's central ideas.[36]

It is clear from the discussion of the Neo-Confucians up to this point that both approaches mentioned in the *Mean* must be accounted for. We see that Chu Hsi clearly inherited the ideas of his predecessors on the problem and especially stressed their ideas on internal self-cultivation. As he says:

If one is able to "honor the virtuous nature," then he will be able to "maintain constant inquiry and study" and this means that once the root is obtained, the branches will naturally follow.[37]

In another place, however, he looks to *tsun te-hsing* for the general method and *tao wen-hsüeh* for the details.[38] Which one, then, does he favor? He certainly agrees with Chang and Ch'eng on the root-quality of virtuous nature, yet, even though it may be primary in a temporal sense, he looks toward the detailed end result teleologically.

Thus the answer to the above question is revealed in actual practice, for when we look at Chu's reordering of chapters in the *Great Learning*, in order to place *ko-wu chih-chih*,[ag] the extension of knowledge through the investigation of things, before *ch'eng-i*,[ah] making the will sincere, we can see why Wang Yang-ming sought to return to the original order in the *Book of Rites* (*Li chi*),[ai] which found these two items reversed.[39]

In a reply to Hsiang P'ing-fu,[aj] Chu apparently realized that sides were being taken on this issue and that those followers who supported him had tended to value external knowledge-seeking over self-cultivation.[40] Thus methodology was an important consideration for Chu Hsi and the reliance on extending knowledge through broad investigation was reflected in his textual commentaries.

One comes next to Huang Kan, who had significant influence on thinkers of the late Sung.[41] Kusumoto Masatsugu points out that in Huang's thought, the extension of knowledge was the means to engage in external knowledge-seeking, whereas *ts'un-hsin,*[ak] the preservation of mind, was the means to pursue internal self-cultivation; to him, these two were inseparable, indicating a unity of knowledge and action. This view is close to that of Chu Hsi yet amplifies things somewhat. Since the Chu tradition came down to Wu Ch'eng through the thinkers Jao Lu and Ch'eng Jo-yung, it is not surprising, as we shall see, that Wu could stress the preservation of mind well within the Chu framework.[42]

It is also to be noted that Ch'en Ch'un was a harsh critic of the Lu school,[43] whereas Kusumoto feels that Huang Kan, who was Ch'en's contemporary, represented a unifying spirit which can be traced through Wu Ch'eng and into the early Ming thinker Wu Yü-pi[al] (1391–1469).[44] Ch'ien Mu supports Kusumoto on this last point in expressing the following opinion on Huang:

He had already completely harmonized Chu and Lu, therefore, during his lifetime, his followers did not dare to pit one school against the other by necessarily rejecting Lu in order to put forth Chu. Furthermore, in accordance with his view, it seemed as if they did not have to argue definitely over whether or not principle was prior to material force.[45]

Yü Ying-shih, on the other hand, points out that there was a confrontation between Chu Hsi and Lu Hsiang-shan at the Goose Lake Grove in 1175 in which they discussed their respective methods of instruction: Lu and his brother wished first to develop the original mind, *pen-hsin,*[am] while Chu wanted extensive examination and learning in the initial stage. Chu considered the Lus' method too facile and they thought Chu's too complicated. Yü believes that this was the basis for the later contrast of *tsun te-hsing* and *tao wen-hsüeh.*[46]

The methodological differences between Chu and Lu are presented in relief in the following selection from Lu's collected works:

Chu Yüan-hui [Chu Hsi] once wrote to one of his students saying, "Lu Tzu-ching [Lu Hsiang-shan] primarily taught people the doctrine of honoring the moral nature. Therefore those who studied under him are mostly scholars who put their beliefs into practice. But he neglected to follow the path of study and inquiry. In my teaching is it not true that I have put somewhat more emphasis on following the path of study and inquiry? As a consequence, my pupils often do not measure up to his in putting beliefs into practice." From this it is clear that Yüan-hui wanted to avoid two defects [failure to honor the moral nature and failure to practice] and combine the two merits [following the path of inquiry and study, and practicing one's own beliefs]. I do not believe this to be possible. If one does not know how to honor his moral nature, how can he talk about following the path of study and inquiry? [47]

In this passage we see that Chu Hsi readily conceded that he *did* emphasize the *tao wen-hsüeh* aspect more than the other, and that this made his students less likely to make applications with their knowledge than Lu's. By the same token, Lu did not disallow *tao wen-hsüeh*, even though he opted for *tsun te-hsing* quite clearly. He was compelled to frame the argument in Chu's terms, as if to say: "Although I will not comment on inquiry and study, should you want these, this would require that cultivation of the virtuous nature be made first and foremost." In Lu, the methodological scale is tipped undeniably toward the side of internal self-cultivation.

T'ang Chün-i points out that the concept of mind in Chu Hsi was such that he required a special kind of moral cultivation for the expressed, or *i-fa*[an] part, namely *ko-wu*,[ao] and another for the unexpressed, or *wei-fa*[ap] part, namely *han-yang* (the nourishing of virtue) or *ts'un-yang*,[aq] the preservation of virtue.[48] As suggested in discussing Chu's interpretation of Ch'eng I, the extension of knowledge was likened to *tao wen-hsüeh* and the nourishing of virtue to *tsun te-hsing*. One could also say, in light of the above, that the *ko-wu* and *han-yang* categories have the same association in his thinking.

In Lu's system, however, no distinction was made between *i-fa* and *wei-fa* with respect to the mind and he relied solely on the notion of original mind, *pen-hsin*, from Mencius.[49] For Lu, the original mind has self-illumination, or self-awakening, *tzu-ming*,[ar] or *tzu-ch'eng*,[as] so that the different kinds of moral cultivation we find in Chu Hsi become merely natural stages in the process of self-awakening for Lu. Thus *ko-wu* never has to go beyond the domain of self-consciousness of the original mind.[50] As T'ang says:

The different ways of moral cultivation as taught by Chu Hsi were all united into one teaching of self-awakening of mind as taught by Lu Hsiang-shan. The original mind is what is greatest in the universe and man.[51]

No wonder, then, that Lu would abide solely in the remark of Mencius that one first had to establish his mind, the nobler part of his nature, before anything else.[52]

Lu's concept of mind, which integrated the expressed and unexpressed aspects, naturally led him to unite *tsun te-hsing* and *tao wen-hsüeh* when he confronted the larger issue of internal self-cultivation versus external knowledge-seeking. Thus a transition occurred as *ko-wu* became *ko-hsin*,[at] the investigation of mind, reminding one of Wang Yang-ming. One type of cultivation was required and it was internally oriented; any grounding in the *i-fa/wei-fa* matrix became irrelevant as identification superseded teleological interaction between the two modes.

In the same vein, the concept of mind and coordinate methods of moral cultivation (internal and external) in Chu Hsi put him in a rather ambiguous philosophical position regarding these polarities, a position highlighted in Lu's comments on it (in the extended quotation above) and only resolved in his knowledge-oriented methodology.

Yü Ying-shih feels, however, that differences between Chu and Lu on the issue of internal self-cultivation versus external knowledge-seeking are only superficial, though he admits that for later thinkers it was quite a significant problem with sides more sharply drawn.[53] While there was not the same furor over it as arose with the clash of faith and reason (scholarship) in Western medieval thought, it did represent a similar struggle between what Yü provisionally calls intellectualism and antiintellectualism in Yüan and Ming times.[54] The roots of this struggle will be taken up in more detail in the third section of this paper.

If, in fact, the problem between intellectualism and antiintellectualism is ultimately irreconcilable, we may say that Wu Ch'eng recognized the difficulty by presenting a modified solution in which the two trends could intertwine and complement each other. Yet in his solution he does seem to favor the virtuous nature as the base, perhaps not as much as Augustine and Tertullian favored faith over reason, but more in the spirit of either Peter Abélard, who said: "I do not wish to be a philosopher to the point of resisting Paul; I do not wish to be an Aristotelian to the point of being separated from Christ,"[55] or Saint Bonaventure, who said: "Philosophical knowledge is a road toward other knowledge; he who would stop there falls into darkness."[56]

In short, the roots of a compromise between internal self-cultivation and external knowledge-seeking are latent in the controversy itself and, as we shall discuss, Wu Ch'eng consciously sought to reconcile, or harmonize, the two, even if a Thomist-scale synthesis was not achieved. It was his concern not to drift toward either pole to the extent that the other might be neutralized. As we shall see, this elicited a dual-purpose methodology and epistemology.

C. Sketching the Problem of Evolution in the Thought of Wu Ch'eng

There are two essays by Wu Ch'eng which deal directly with the issue of relating the polarities in question. The first is entitled "In Commemoration of the Mountain Studio to Consolidate Tao,"[57] which, according to the commentator Li Tsu-t'ao[au] (fl. c. 1808),was composed in Wu's early years,[58] and thus indicated a partiality toward the *tao wen-hsüeh* approach. Su T'ien-chüeh[av] (1294–1352), however, dates this essay in the year 1317, only some sixteen years before Wu's death.[59] The essay translated in the following section of this paper, "In Commemoration of the Studio to Honor the Virtuous Nature and Maintain Constant Inquiry and Study," which indicates Wu's break with his Chu school forbears, is said by Li to date from Wu's later years, or decidedly after the composition of the previous essay.[60] If we accept Su's dating of the first, the second would have to have been written very near the end of Wu's life; of course, the problem of Wu's sixty-ninth year being one of his "early years" still remains in the case of the first.

In terms of content, the first essay mentioned above is certainly less iconoclastic than the second, in that it does not show Wu ideologically breaking with his mentors. The approach to the polarities is balanced and in fact details the *tao wen-hsüeh* aspect rather thoroughly in stressing the need for knowledge and action:

The "honoring of the virtuous nature" finds its unity in reverence (*ching*) and the "maintaining of constant inquiry and study" is united in knowledge and action. The one is to establish the root and the several items serve to complement each other. If the efficacy of inquiry and study is deep, then the substance of the virtuous nature is complete and the function extensive. This is the means by which *tao* is consolidated. Nevertheless, this may not be spoken of with empty words. It lies in actually accomplishing it and that is all.[61]

The emphasis on reverence in aimed at the purification of the self via internal self-cultivation involving the expanding of the virtuous nature. This aspect has been emphasized previously in discussing the nature in Chang Tsai and Ch'eng I.[62] Inquiry and study, when directed inward, lead to a kind of moral cultivation described as reverence; areas of imperfection can thus be rectified. There is a certain introspective quality to this which comes out in other writings by Wu.[63] Perhaps Li Tsu-t'ao was aware of this when he commented that the approach to *tsun te-hsing* in the first and, in his view, earlier essay on the mountain study differed somewhat from Chu Hsi.[64]

This also explains why Li Tsu-t'ao determined the chronology for these two essays the way he did, since in the second the introspective mode is used in a polemical sense to admonish those who pursue mere textual exegesis so that external knowledge-seeking has no relevance to self-perfection. Li was apparently influenced in his view of the development of Wu Ch'eng's thought by the Ming Neo-Confucian Lo Ch'in-shun[aw] (1466–1547), who also attributed the second essay to Wu's later years.[65] Of course, Lo was aware of Wang Yang-ming's use of material from the second essay to bolster Wang's case for evolution toward idealism in the later thought of Chu Hsi. Thus he considered the possibility that Wu had strayed from the Chu Hsi fold, as had Wang. It is interesting to note that while Lo could have denied evolution in the case of Wu, he chose instead to criticize it, apparently accepting such evolution, or transition, as a fact.[66]

It is difficult to remove the cloud of Ming controversy which hovers over the interpretation of Wu Ch'eng's thought. Huang Tsung-hsi[ax] (1610–1695) and Ch'üan Tsu-wang[ay] (1705–1755) maintain that Wu merely sought to blend, or harmonize, the Chu and Lu strains,[67] in contrast to the Lo-Li idea of a definite shift. Li, of course, qualified the latter evolutionary view somewhat in stating that although Wu's thought did evolve, he never repudiated Chu.[68] Conceivably, Wu sought to refresh the ideas of the former, as they had been handed down, with those of the latter. The Huang-Ch'üan view, of course, looks at the total picture, whereas the Lo-Li searches for a precise point of transition.

Both views must be taken into account. On the one hand, it is difficult to compartmentalize stages in someone's thought, but, on the other hand, one cannot exclude the possibility of a shift. If, in light of the political situation c. 1310–1311, Wu increasingly came to reevaluate philosophic methodology, this could have had an impact on his later work. Certainly if Su T'ien-chüeh is correct in his dating, there was not much time for a marked change to occur between 1317 and 1333, although this cannot be entirely ruled out. Nevertheless the 1317, or supposedly earlier, essay does not betray the kind of methodological shift one might expect in light of the events and remarks of some six or seven years before. It is possible, however, that Wu's reflections late in life uncovered a philosophical turning point in the teens which he brought out explicitly in an essay written in his waning years.

Thus the impact of political frustration may have led him not so much to deny his earlier rationalist background in the teens as to broaden gradually, over the years, the importance of internal self-cultivation in his philosophy. The translated essay which follows is, in any case, pivotal regardless of which hypothesis is followed. It suggests, at the very least, a personal awakening on Wu's part about the philosophical enterprise.

II. AN ESSAY ON INTERNAL SELF-CULTIVATION AND EXTERNAL KNOWLEDGE-SEEKING

A. *Translation*

"In Commemoration of the Studio to Honor the Virtuous Nature
and Maintain Constant Inquiry and Study" [69]

That by which heaven gives birth to man, and that by which a man is a man, is the virtuous nature. After Mencius, however, the sagely tradition was not continued and scholars had no mentor to follow, so who could know about this? [70]

For more than a thousand years from the Han and T'ang, the Confucian scholars each made the most of their own strong points, plunging headlong into their own pursuits, without being aware of their own shortcomings. The two masters Tung [Chung-shu] and Han [Yü] came close to the sagely teaching in some of the things they said but failed to grasp the fundamentals, so they were little better than the other Confucians of Han and T'ang.

In the early Sung we have Hu [Yüan] and Sun [Fu], who first established the model for instruction through elucidating the classics of the sages. At that time, they were known for their learning, which embraced both substance and function. A large number of scholars, lofty in conduct and unusual in their abilities, came out of their schools. They certainly made some contributions to correcting men's minds and the way of the world; but if we look carefully into what they did best, [we see that] they still just barely surpassed Tung and Han. Why was this so? It was because they had not yet comprehended how to apply their efforts to [cultivating] the virtuous nature.

It was not until Chou [Tun-i], Ch'eng [Hao and I], Chang [Tsai], and Shao [Yung] arose that, for the first time, there were those who could reach up to Mencius and be united with him. The teachings of the Ch'eng brothers passed down after four generations to Chu Hsi, who, in terms of the fine points of meaning [in the Classics], discussed each sentence and word with a precision not achieved by anyone else since Mencius. Chu's disciples, however, often got mired in these exegetics and their minds became obscured. Therefore, even though they looked down upon the memorization and literary composition of the Confucian scholars of the day as vulgar scholarship, their own method of learning was not far removed from the trivia of words and compositions.[71] They went so far as only to specialize in a single classic text, paying no attention to other writings; they gathered together stale and lifeless sayings, without being able to contribute anything of their own. Ironically, this only made it possible for those who indulged in literary composition to ridicule their ineptitude. These, then, were the defects of the superficial scholarship of the Chu school after the Chia-ting period [1208–1224] and there was no one capable of curing them.[72]

That which is of value in the learning of the sages in the ability to preserve what heaven has conferred upon us. What heaven has conferred upon us is the virtuous nature.[73] This is the basis of humanity, righteousness, propriety, and wisdom, the directing agent[74] of corporeal form. If one sets this aside and looks elsewhere to learn, in the final analysis, what does he have to study?

Even in the case of those whose conduct was comparable to the venerable Ssu-ma Wen-cheng [Kuang][75] and abilities comparable to Marquis Chu-ko Chung-wu [Liang],[76] it was still not possible for them to avoid acting without understanding and doing so habitually without reflection.[77] It was just that their natural endowment surpassed that of others, and we cannot say that they had achieved the learning of the sages. How much less [can one say it of] those who only attained the subtleties of textual criticism and refinement in deliberation, such as Ch'en Pei-hsi [Ch'un] and Jao Shuang-feng [Lu], Such attainments, when compared with the said vulgar scholarship of memorization and literary composition, are no more than inches apart. The Confucians of Han and T'ang could hardly be blamed for the latter, but once the learning of the sages had been set forth with such clarity in the Sung [period], there was no excuse for their later followers becoming like this.[78]

The venerable P'i of Ch'ing-chiang gave the courtesy name Shao-te [Brilliant Virtue] to his son.[79] His teacher named the studio where he studied "Learning." After he came to study with me, he requested that I change the tablet of his studio to "Honor the Virtuous Nature and Maintain Constant Inquiry and Study," so that he could unite what his father and teacher had decreed. Oh, that which one's father decrees is what heaven decrees! A scholar studies this and that is all. When it comes to your learning, in terms of literary composition, it can be said to have reached a pinnacle, and in terms of memorization, can be said to be rich. Nevertheless, if it has nothing to do with the virtuous nature, it would be best set aside.

I have myself investigated into textual meanings, analyzing them in great detail, and consider that Ch'en was still not subtle enough nor Jao minute enough. I fell into this mold for forty years and then, for the first time, realized that it was wrong. In responding to your inquiry, I am troubled that I have wasted so much time. Thus, in speaking to you, how could I mislead you with that by which I misled myself in the past![80]

As it is now, every day from the first hour (*tzu*) to the last (*hai*);[81] every month, from the first day to the last of the lunar month; every year, from spring to winter, I constantly witness the illumination of my virtuous nature,[82] which is comparable to the rotation of the heavens, like the going and coming of the sun and moon, not allowing for a break of even an instant. Thus it closely approximates the way of honoring [the virtuous nature]. If in this [process] there is some deficiency noted, one should then inquire of others, learn from himself, and seek to achieve the highest [good for oneself].

As to the method one uses to apply one's efforts, words cannot suffice to explain it, but one should become familiar with the first chapter of the *Doctrine of the Mean*[83] and the final section of *Resolving Dullness*,[84] so as to realize it for oneself. If one does this, he will be able to be on a par with the worthies and raise himself [to the level of] the sages, as surely as the harvest is reaped from the sowing.

I should like for us to work together. However, if you make a lot of noise about it and call it a new and good-sounding name, without exerting yourself in pursuit of the actuality, this will then be like the hypocrisy and deception of the recent scholars. This is what does harm to the world, to the state, and to oneself, and gives those who hold a different opinion a pretext to criticize [our endeavors] as false learning. The defect will be worse than superficial scholarship and you should not do this.

B. Analysis of the essay

Despite Wu's emphasis on the personal application of inquiry and study, the primacy of the virtuous nature is very much evident in this essay. Wu regrets the decay of scholarship in his own time, just as Chu Hsi spoke of the decline of the learning of the sages after Mencius. Wu is critical of Han and T'ang Confucians especially. Along this line, in another essay, it is interesting to note that Wu criticized Cheng Hsüan[az] (127–200), because his learning was based on memorization, and Han Yü[ba] (768–824), because his was based on words and composition,[85] which echoes the charges he makes in the present essay in finding fault with post-Chu Hsi scholars and in reflecting back on the Han and T'ang.

As for the early Sung Confucians, Wu is still quite negative. Even though, as we have seen, in his tenure at the Imperial College he used some of the ideas of Hu Yüan in developing an educational curriculum,[86] he feels that Hu did not emphasize internal self-cultivation sufficiently. Perhaps, in fact, his experience with educational policy in the capital left him disillusioned enough to produce a change in spirit by the time he announced his departure.

Wu's immediate targets in this essay, however, are the scholars in the Ch'eng-Chu tradition who carried investigations into textual meaning, begun so auspiciously by the Ch'eng brothers and Chu Hsi in their classical commentaries, to trivial and hair-splitting excess. There is a narrowness and an inability to express the essence of the material in terms of internal self-cultivation. Doctrines are accumulated but there is a failure to convey an understanding of the essentials.

Wu's criticism of exegesis is expressed in his attack here on *chi-t'ung tz'u-chang,* [bb] memorization and literary composition, which he equates with *yen-yü wen-tzu chih mo,* [bc] the trivia of textual language and phraseology. This attack parallels his criticism of the Sung historian Cheng Ch'iao [bd] (1104-1162), the author of the *Comprehensive Treatises* (*T'ung-chih*). [be] [87] In Cheng's case, Wu felt that the approach to historical writing was based on *wen-chien,* [bf] external knowledge, which neglected to get down to fundamentals. [88] Elsewhere, Wu states that the approach to scholarship through memorization and literary composition is identifiable with *hua-hsüeh,* [bg] ornamental learning, not *shih-hsüeh,* [bh] real learning. [89]

Wu becomes more pointed in his attack on the later Chu school in stating that virtuous nature should have been the goal but that the emphasis was lost, the mind is obscured. The reason for this was an overemphasis on exegesis beginning after the second decade of the thirteenth century (the post-Chia-ting [bi] era). He then openly criticizes Ch'en Ch'un and Jao Lu, whose fine-grained explanations in the subtleties of textual analysis were hardly more worthwhile than the vulgar scholarly traits previously criticized.

This view of Ch'en and Jao is consistent with the biographical treatment of Wu Ch'eng by his disciple Yü Chi [bj] (1272–1348), wherein we find an account of Wu's criticism of the northern scholars upon his departure from the Imperial College. In that passage, Wu used the term *yen-yü shun-shih chih mo,* [bk] the trivia of exegetical remarks on textual language, which is quite similar to the words used to describe the work of Ch'en and Jao in this essay. This similarity may provide a textual clue as to the time when Wu's intellectual awakening occurred, even though this would not ultimately solve the problem of dating the essay itself, which has the tone of later reflection upon the experience.

At this point in the essay, Wu tips the balance toward internal self-cultivation, rather than external knowledge-seeking. The purpose of learning is to understand one's inner potentiality for ethical self-realization, not merely careful textual analysis. In another essay we find further support for such a priority:

In general, we may say that true knowledge is knowledge of the virtuous nature and that extensive knowledge is knowledge [acquired] through the senses.[90]

As Yü Ying-shih shows in citing Ch'eng I, there is a distinction in Neo-Confucianism between moral and intellectual knowledge, the latter relating to the *wen-chien*, or perceptual, approach[91] which Wu criticized in the case of Cheng Ch'iao. Thus, applying Yü's thesis, Wu may be seen as one of the "Neo-Confucianists who repudiated . . . intellectual knowledge on the ground that it can shed no light on our knowledge of the moral nature."[92]

Above all, Wu Ch'eng accuses his mentors Ch'en and Jao of falling into the trap of scholarship for its own sake, thereby disregarding the real purpose of philosophy, and renounces his dependence on them. As he says, internal self-cultivation has nothing to do with literary style; it must be accomplished personally and on an intuitive basis. Since Wu has experienced this himself, he is compelled not to mislead the disciple to whom he relates his remarks in the essay. Elsewhere, he says:

"Extensiveness in learning and restraint in propriety" were the methods of study passed down by the sages and worthies. For fifteen hundred or more years after the Chou this tradition continued. Since the Masters Chou [Tun-i], Ch'eng [Hao and I], and Chang [Tsai], and the demise of Master Chu, this learning was lost so that scholars of the present age amass the works of Master Chu and people repeat from memory his theories . . .[93]

This was a bold step to break with his past and the enlightenment he relates foreshadows that of Wang Yang-ming some two centuries later. Thus when Wu speaks of the "illumination of the virtuous nature" (next to the last paragraph), he means this in terms of mental experience, as well as figuratively, in the sense of "brilliance."

In terms of targets, it is interesting to note that Wu casts a wide net, that is to say, thinkers after the year 1224. In a postscript to this essay by Li Tsu-t'ao, Chu school thinkers in the Yüan are also referred to.[94] Wu is circumspect on this score, for he only mentions the Sung figures. If Li is correct, the criticism might extend to early Yüan Confucians as well, which is possible, as we shall see, in looking at Wu's final advice to the young scholar in the essay.

Thus while we should question Li's opinion, we may at least say that Wu also had in mind the Hsü Heng school, as it had devolved upon those whom he confronted in the capital between 1309 and 1311. It is also well to remember that Wu was balanced in his incorporation of the ideas of Lu Hsiang-shan into his thinking in that he also criticized followers of Lu who, in the Yüan, failed to embody an independent spirit in cultivating the mind.[95]

In order to indicate the centrality of the concept of virtuous nature in his thought at this stage, Wu likens it to heavenly process, implying constancy of a similar order in cultivation. Here Wu identifies it as *chu-tsai*,[b1] the directing agent within corporeal form and the basis for the four virtues. Study must focus on oneself; inquiry of others can only serve as an objective means for self-correction. The aim is inward and although there is no mention of the role of mind *per se*, the current is flowing in that direction; in another essay, Wu does equate virtuous nature with mind.[96] There is, therefore, a strongly personalistic role for knowledge in that one must experience it first-hand. Whereas the metaphor of a trip to Yen-ching (mentioned in the introduction to section one) can be applied to the method of external knowledge-seeking in general, here we find the individualistic approach in terms of internal self-cultivation.

We note also how the change that the younger P'i wanted for the name of his studio (from "Learning" to "Honor the Virtuous Nature and Maintain Constant Inquiry and Study") was designed to combine the original name Pi's teacher had given the studio and the courtesy name P'i's father gave to him ("brilliant," or "illuminating virtue": Shao-te). Thus when Wu tells the younger P'i to stick with his father's decree, he is advancing the characterization he gives later on ("illumination of my virtuous nature"). Wu feels that P'i is skillful in terms of learning but that this has little to do with internal self-cultivation.

In advising him to actualize sage-learning on a personal basis through self-illumination, Wu cautions him not to publicize his efforts with catchy phrases. He feels that this was the fate of recent scholarship as it drifted into divisiveness, with one school labeling the other as heterodox, a theme exemplified in Wu's earlier quotation concerning rivalry between the Chu and Lu schools. One can also surmise that the criticism of Wu by northern scholars in the Imperial College demonstrated this defect. Superficiality in philosophical understanding resulted in a kind of intellectual petulance.

In moving toward the side of internal self-cultivation, Wu Ch'eng can still be considered to be within the Chu school mold since, as Li Tsu-t'ao points out in his postscript to this essay, Wu did not desert Chu Hsi himself but only the approach of some of his followers.[97] Those who viewed Wu as favoring Lu were thus too hasty in their judgments, yet in Li's postscript to the essay on the mountain studio he does suggest that Wu was partial to the approach favoring internal self-cultivation in the essay translated here.[98]

As mentioned in section one, in this second instance Li was following the ideas of the Ming thinker Lo Ch'in-shun, who had his own axe to grind in his controversy with Wang Yang-ming (see section III, parts D and E). Thus even though Li's postscript may reflect the personal bias of either Li or Lo, the latter is quoted as saying that Wu became more heterodox merely to make learning more consistent with its goal,[99] a defense which conveniently fits Wu's maverick approach into a Chu Hsi framework.

Despite the theory that the present essay is from a time late in Wu's career, when he had turned more Lu-ist, we know that Wu did not desert erudition in his later years, as pointed out by Huang Tsung-hsi and Ch'üan Tsu-wang in the Ch'ing era, and as borne out in the rather late completion of his *Observations on the Book of Rites* in 1331. The issue was to direct external knowledge-seeking toward legitimate ends, and the idea of an ideological blend, as first presented by Huang and Ch'üan and in one instance admitted even by Lo, seems increasingly more cogent as chronology becomes harder to establish with certainty.

This synthetic treatment of Wu Ch'eng's thought is all the more intriguing for the very fact that it disturbs the categorizations one encounters in discussions of the rationalist and idealist schools in Neo-Confucianism. It implies that the enlightenment which Wu relates in this essay had more the flavor of a reappraisal than a conversion.

As will be discussed in the next section, Wang Yang-ming was much interested in this essay and quoted it almost in its entirety in his *Chu Tzu wan-nien ting-lun*[bm] (The Final Doctrine of Master Chu in His Later Years). Wang did so for at least two reasons. The first was that Wu Ch'eng manifested an intellectual compulsion to break out of the bonds of superficial study, an independent spirit which was in tune with the attitudes of Wang. Here we are reminded of Wang's realization of the unity of knowledge and action in 1509, in which he came to seek for truth solely within his own mind. The second reason was that Wu realized that the virtuous nature must be sought first and foremost and, to this end, external knowledge-seeking was largely secondary.

The difference, and it is significant, was the extent to which each broke with the Ch'eng-Chu tradition: in Wang's case, the split was fundamental; external knowledge-seeking was largely superfluous and the tension between the polarities could be abandoned. In Wu's case, we are brought up to a stage somewhere before such a crucial split, where the scale is tipped heavily on the side of internal self-cultivation without the apparatus itself (the framework of internal self-cultivation and external knowledge-seeking) being abandoned.

III. INTERPRETING THE PHILOSOPHICAL POSITION AND INFLUENCE OF WU CH'ENG

A. *The Yüan: Elements of Similarity*

As for the impact of Wu Ch'eng's thought in his own time, the situation is far from clear. Contemporary with Wu were the thinkers Ch'en Yüan[bn] (1256–1330) in Kiangsi and Chao Hsieh[bo] in East Chekiang, who are both considered to be direct followers of the Lu school in Yüan times.[100] Wu does not appear to have had contact with either, even though he was acquainted with a certain Hu Shih-t'ang,[bp] who is said to have veered away from the Lu school toward the Chu.[101] Neither Chao nor Ch'en is mentioned in Wu's preface to the Yü-lu,[bq] the *Collected Conversations*, of Lu Hsiang-shan;[102] perhaps, however, they represent the Lu school figures of whom he was critical. As he says:

That one should not seek to find it [*tao*] in oneself but seek to discover it in the words of others is what the Master [Lu] deeply grieved about. Now those who converse about the Master and express admiration for him are numerous. However, is there really a single person who is able to know the teachings of the Master? Is there a single person who is capable of putting them into practice?[103]

Kusumoto Masatsugu feels that Wu's disciple, Liu Ts'ung-lung,[br] who stressed quiescence, *ching*,[bs] and vacuity, *hsü*,[bt][104] was similar in this regard to some of the disciples of Ch'en and Chao and that Wu, therefore, represented a broad philosophical influence in his era.[105] This association is rather diffuse, even though implied criticism of Ch'en and Chao would not be out of character for Wu, in that he tried to break down sectarian barriers created by disciples of different schools.

The Yüan thinker Cheng Yü[bu] (1298–1358) was very much the junior of Wu Ch'eng. Ch'üan Tsu-wang mentions that Cheng continued the synthetic blending of Chu and Lu which had been initiated by Wu, though there appears to have been little connection between the two.[106] Ch'üan points out that whereas Wu leaned toward Lu, Cheng Yü veered toward Chu, and that therein lay the difference.[107] As we have noted, such inclinations mostly describe points of emphasis which often have only a vague chronological basis. As Cheng Yü says:

Master Lu, being lofty and intelligent in character, loved the simple and easy. Master Chu, being sturdy and straightforward by nature, therefore loved subtle refinement. Each pursued a different course to attain his object, in accordance with his own inclinations. . . . Since the essential thing was to realize tao, how could they differ? Later scholars did not seek to discover similarities, only the differences.[108]

This passage reflects some points of similarity between Cheng and Wu, especially when elsewhere the former criticizes the followers of Chu who merely count the words of a given text, without original analysis.[109] Much of the spirit of Wu's essay on internal self-cultivation and external knowledge-seeking is present. Even though direct influence is problematical, there is an affinity between the two Yüan thinkers in carrying forth similar synthetic ideals.

B. The Ming: Hu Chü-jen contra Ch'en Hsien-chang

While there is some controversy over whether or not Wu Yü-pi represents a middle ground between the Chu and Lu schools,[110] Wing-tsit Chan nevertheless believes that he typifies early Ming Neo-Confucianism as

it grew less and less interested in such aspects as metaphysical speculation and the doctrine of the investigation of things and more and more concerned with mind, its cultivation and preservation . . . remind[ing] us of Lu Hsiang-shan, the greatest philosopher of mind in Sung times.[111]

Certainly the problem of relating knowledge-seeking and self-cultivation became quite prominent in two of Wu Yü-pi's disciples, Hu Chü-jen[bv] (1434–1484) and Ch'en Hsien-chang[bw] (1428–1500), who figure respectively in delineating these two approaches. It is also the case that both had strong opinions about Wu Ch'eng, which must be considered in evaluating his thought and its impact. In other words, it is through them that Wu Ch'eng is drawn into philosophical controversy in the Ming.

Yü Ying-shih places Hu Chü-jen in the knowledge-seeking, or in his view the "intellectualist," camp in this era. The major thinker in the opposing self-cultivation, or "anti-intellectualist," camp, Ch'en Hsien-chang, was criticized by Hu for not engaging in *ch'iung-li*, [bx] exhausting principle, a favorite idea in the knowledge-seeking of the Ch'eng-Chu school. Ch'en seems to have taken a subjective approach to the learning of the sages. [112] As has been suggested, this independent investigative strain was strong in Wu Ch'eng as well; thus it comes as no surprise that he was an object of debate within the Ch'ung-jen [by] school of Wu Yü-pi.

Hu Chü-jen says of Wu Ch'eng:

In his early years, Wu Ts'ao-lu [Ch'eng] was very intelligent. In his later years, what he accomplished was not very important. In discussing the learning of Chu and Lu, he took Master Chu as [representing] the "maintaining of constant inquiry and study" and Master Lu as [representing] the "honoring of the virtuous nature" and this explanation was incorrect. I think that in the application of honoring the virtuous nature one can do no better than Master Chu. [113]

This passage suggests an evolution in Wu Ch'eng's thought and dubiously assumes that Wu slighted Chu Hsi. In any case, it is obvious that Hu was criticizing Wu Ch'eng directly and Ch'en Hsien-chang by implication. The quotation contained in a letter to Lo Lun [bz] (1431–1478), an associate of Ch'en with a mind-oriented philosophy, and curiously, Hu is critical in it of the exegetical emphasis of the late Chu school followers such as Ch'en Ch'un and Jao Lu as well. As in the case of the translated essay of Wu Ch'eng in this paper, Hu regrets the loss of understanding of Chu's fundamental ideas, yet instead of Wu, he praises Hsü Heng in the Yüan. [114]

Hu has reservations about Wu's "later" theories, feeling that in Wu's criticism of exegesis he went too far in the direction of Lu. Elsewhere, Hu states that the ideas of his teacher, Wu Yü-pi, reflect the sage-learning in exhausting principle, *ch'iung-li*, and in preserving the mind, *ts'un-hsin*. [115]

If Hu had been able to see through the bias surrounding Wu's statement on Chu and Lu, c. 1310–1311, and noted Wu's idea that both should be praised, he would not have had second thoughts about Wu's commitment to Chu Hsi. His criticisms of Wu, therefore, may be based on his view of Ch'en Hsien-chang, who was partial to Wu, and on Hu's assumption of the position as defender of the intellectual tradition of the orthodox Chu school in early Ming. In the developing polemic on philosophic method, Wu's thought was playing a useful role.

Whereas Hu Chü-jen disliked Lu Hsiang-shan, Ch'en Hsien-chang, like Wu Ch'eng before him, moved in the direction of the "method of simplification"[116] espoused by Lu and away from the Ch'eng-Chu stress on *ko-wu*, the investigation of things, on the knowledge-seeking side. Thus it is easy to see how Ch'en had strong disagreements with Hu.[117]

Ch'en *did* approach Lu via the Mencian concepts of "seeking for the lost mind"[118] and "establishing the nobler part of oneself"[119] (the mind), which were also stressed quite prominently in Wu Ch'eng's thought. Again, the methodological approach favors Lu, as in Wu Ch'eng. Furthermore, we can say that Ch'en was less hesitant in acknowledging Lu than was Hu Chü-jen, though perhaps not to the extent that Wu was. Even so, neither Hu nor Ch'en quote Lu very much in their writings.

Ch'en Hsien-chang was apparently conversant with the writings of Wu Ch'eng, for he is in agreement with a statement attributed to the latter, which reads in the version quoted by Ch'en as follows:

By lifting his ears and instructing him, one can make even an ordinary man who does not know a single character arrive right away at the realm of spirit and wonder.[120]

This passage does not appear in Wu's writings yet Chou Ju-teng[ca] (1547–1629) quotes it in his section on Wu in his *Sheng-hsüeh tsung-ch'uan*[cb] (The Orthodox Transmission of the Learning of the Sages), capping off a selection of the more Lu-oriented quotations from Wu, and thus betraying Chou's own philosophical inclinations. Chou was an admirer of Wang Chi[cc] (1498–1585), one of the major figures of the T'ai-chou[cd] school of the late Ming.[121] Wang Chi himself stressed direct enlightenment even more strongly than did Wang Yang-ming and thus it is not surprising that his disciple, Chou, should emphasize the Lu side of Wu Ch'eng.

The idea of *pu-shih i-tzu*,[ce] not knowing a single character, was a popular one which can be found in the works of Lu Hsiang-shan[122] and it should be noted that Ch'en Hsien-chang's pupil, Chan Jo-shui[cf] (1466–1560), also attributed the above passage, beginning with the second clause, to Wu Ch'eng.[123]

Wu did not elaborate on the antitextual approach implied in the passage but characterized it as the method of the Ch'an Buddhist patriarch Hui Neng[cg] (638–713):

> Among those who studied Buddhism in the past, Shen Hsiu [605?–706] of the northern school comprehensively synthesized the various texts and Hui Neng of the southern school did not even know a single character.[124]

Wu states, however, that in geomancy there is a difference between those who would use texts and those who would not. He asked a geomancer from Kiangsi about this and received the following reply:

> You are an accomplished scholar of wide learning and I but a dumb fellow who does not even know a single character. If you ask me about my art, I will not have a single word to transmit nor a single phrase of explanation, and I will not be able to answer in a letter. As for geomancy taking the two approaches of Shen Hsiu and Hui Neng, not knowing my art, how can I weigh the relative superiority of these two approaches.[125]

Since the tone of even the shorter phrase used by Lu was tinged with Ch'anism, we can see why Hu Chü-jen might have taken a dim view of both Lu and Wu, feeling that their ideas were too much inspired by heterodox doctrine. For Ch'en Hsien-chang, however, the approach was justified in that it took one away from the purely textual to the introspective, vis-à-vis the learning of the sages, and he defends it, Lu, and Wu against charges of making things too easy or coming too close to Ch'an.[126] We might speculate that Ch'en's use of the passage to characterize Wu in this antitextual framework probably foreshadowed the use of the passage in Chan Jo-shui and Chou Ju-teng.

With the above assumptions in mind, Ch'en mentions the dissipation into textualism after the Chia-ting period in Sung, as did Hu, and Wu's resultant break with Ch'en Ch'un and Jao Lu.[127] He does not mention outright the essay translated in this paper, in which Wu disavows them, yet because he fairly summarizes Wu's reasons for the break, we have evidence that he was conversant with the piece. This is the earliest reference to this essay. It is also notable that while Hu Chü-jen emphasized evolution in a negative sense in criticizing Wu Ch'eng, Ch'en did not feel compelled to stress it in praising Wu's philosophical approach.

C. Ch'eng Min-cheng and Wang Yang-ming

Ch'eng Min-cheng[ch] (1445–1499) wrote a well-known treatise called *Tao-i pien*[ci] (Compendium on the Unity of Tao) which foreshadowed Wang Yang-ming's *Final Doctrine of Master Chu in His Later Years* in its contention that in his waning years Chu Hsi emphasized teachings akin to those of Lu.[128] Ch'eng thus continued the synthetic trend toward internal self-cultivation and external knowledge-seeking, which we have noted in Wu Ch'eng, on a somewhat different basis. As he says:

The "honoring of the virtuous nature" centers around abiding in reverence, whereas the "maintaining of constant inquiry and study" has the effort of exhausting principle. The two are mutually nourished and develop together. One cannot dispense with either.[129]

While it is certainly the case that Chu Hsi did not ignore the necessity for the kind of balance stressed here,[130] by the time of Wu and Ch'eng it had to be stated quite emphatically. In Wu's case, for example, the relationship between *chü-ching,*[cj] abiding in reverence, and *ch'iung-li,* exhausting principle, is stated as follows:

To investigate first prescribes making reverence the primary consideration in order to honor the virtuous nature, and afterwards exhausting principle through the study of books in order to maintain constant inquiry and study. . . .[131]

Ch'eng also made additions to a rather cryptic compilation of the sayings written by Chen Te-hsiu[ck] (1178–1235) called *Hsin-ching*[cl] (*The Heart Classic*). In it Ch'eng quotes from the essay translated in this paper.[132] In the preface to the work by Li Huang[cm] (fl. c. 1566) there are doubts expressed that Wu Ch'eng was of the Lu school; it is only later disputants who said that this was the case. Li furthermore states that it was Ch'eng's task to rectify the matter, which he does clearly in a letter discussing the 1310–1311 statement by Wu Ch'eng.[133] Li also mentions that Ch'eng's *Compendium on the Unity of Tao* was criticized by Ch'en Chien[cn] (1497–1567) in his *Hsüeh-pu t'ung-pien*[co] (*Comprehensive Critique on Obscure Learning*), where he accused Ch'eng and Wang Yang-ming of legitimizing the Lu school.[134]

Li Huang feels, despite Ch'en Chien's criticisms, that Ch'eng Min-cheng merely wished to unite the two schools and that the unification was based on the ideas of Wu Ch'eng.[135] Kusumoto Masatsugu, in mentioning the inclusion of Wu's essay in *The Heart Classic*, also notes the influence of Wu on the synthetic spirit in Ch'eng Min-cheng, which surfaced again later in Wang Yang-ming's essay on Chu Hsi's later thought.[136] In terms of a continuity of interest in the thought of Wu Ch'eng, Kusumoto sees Ch'eng Min-cheng inheriting Wu's dislike of Ch'en Ch'un because of the latter's overspeculative tendencies and rejection of the Lu school.[137]

Wing-tsit Chan points out that Wang Yang-ming in his time had aroused much criticism because of his independent ideas, in opposition to those of Chu Hsi, whose commentaries were then orthodox in the examination system. Sometime between 1514 and 1518, Wang attempted to put his own theories into the mouth of Chu Hsi, selecting passages from Chu's supposedly later letters, as well as an extended one from the essay by Wu Ch'eng translated in this paper. This latter selection matches up exactly with the portion chosen by Ch'eng Min-cheng for *The Heart Classic* and Wang's thesis was also foreshadowed by Ch'eng, who believed that Chu came close to Lu philosophically in his later years. Wang's tract was published in 1518 and his purpose was to illustrate a shift in Chu Hsi: Chu had arrived at positions which Wang eventually espoused.[138]

In introducing Wu Ch'eng's essay, Wang says:

After Master Chu, Chen Hsi-shan [Te-hsiu], Hsü Lu-chai [Heng], and Wu Ts'ao-lu [Ch'eng] all understood this yet Ts'ao-lu saw it especially clearly and his regret was especially trenchant. I am not now able to set it down in full so I will select one theory of his and append it.[139]

It is significant that Wang singles out Wu Ch'eng as a thinker after Chu Hsi, whose thought was most like his own. Wu's regret over following Ch'en Ch'un and Jao Lu for so long made an impression on Wang, doubtless because it was brought on by a kind of intellectual awakening to the primacy of internal self-cultivation.[140]

D. *The Views of Lo Ch'in-shun*

Upon publication of his treatise on Chu Hsi, Wang Yang-ming submitted it and his *Ta-hsüeh wen*[cp] (Inquiry on the *Great Learning*) to Lo Ch'in-shun, the chief supporter of the Chu school at this time and a noted rival of Wang. Around 1520, Lo wrote a letter to him about the two works in which he gave his own analysis of the thought of Wu Ch'eng, based on the essay quoted by Wang.

This letter[141] presents ideas which indicate the Chu school predilection of Lo Ch'in-shun for study over reliance on the mind and the cultivation of the virtuous nature. In mentioning how the ideas of Neo-Confucians often can be put into the mouths of Buddhists, we find a pointed attack on Wang Yang-ming. Since Wang was apparently attracted not only to Wu's break with his predecessors but also to his stress on internal self-cultivation, Lo had to consider Wu Ch'eng in this context as well. Lo allows Wu to escape the charge of being Buddhist-tinged only if the period of tutelage in the Ch'en-Jao tradition is considered instrumental for his refined evaluations of his past. He thus subtly criticizes Wang for *his* break with the past as well.

Lo mentions that in being fond of the Ch'eng brothers and Chou Tun-i, Wu approached the idea of "singing in the breeze under the full moon"[142] yet was ultimately a classicist. Lu Hsiang-shan had felt that this carefree spirit related to the ideals of Tseng Tien, as expressed in the *Analects*.[143] Lo overstates Wu's embodiment of this quality so that he can then have free rein to chide him for his repudiation of Ch'en and Jao. In a sense, however, it is perhaps a valuable insight into Wu's political temperament, for his career does reflect a penchant for withdrawal.

Lo, above all, criticizes Wu for being hypocritical: one should not criticize the means (that is to say, the Ch'en-Jao heritage) which allow you to reach a given goal once you arrive there.[144] In fact, the need to value the gradual, step-by-step approach is similar to Lo's opinion as represented in Li Tsu-t'ao's postscript to Wu's essay on the mountain studio: one requires wide learning in the acquisition of knowledge.[145]

As to the matter of Wu's emphasis on *tsun te-hsing*, Lo cannot but agree on the need to scrupulously guard one's inner virtue. Yet he emphasizes Wu's idea on the necessity of learning when gaps in the continuity of the inner life are sensed. Such exaggeration of Wu's position toward the Chu side[146] was criticized in the Ch'ing era by Li Fu[cq] (1675–1756), as we shall see later.

Yü Ying-shih points out that for Lo, *tao wen-hsüeh* really became the basis for *tsun te-hsing*. To this extent, Lo Ch'in-shun was much closer to Chu's methodology than Hu Chü-jen, who was more Chu-oriented than Ch'en Hsien-chang. Thus the controversy between the methodological approaches reached a peak in the contrasting views of Wang and Lo. Lo placed the blame on Lu for this split, especially reviling the latter's idea that the Six Classics were footnotes to his own ideas.[147] As we have mentioned, such a division was not as harshly drawn during the Southern Sung as it was at this time.

E. The Role of the Thought of Wu Ch'eng in the Wang-Lo Controversy

Where does the thought of Wu Ch'eng truly fall in terms of the controversy between Wang Yang-ming and Lo Ch'in-shun? Wang picked up the lead from Ch'eng Min-cheng in attempting to synthesize the thought of the later Chu Hsi with that of Lu, transforming it so that he and Chu would agree. He gave the idea of synthesis a new direction yet it is clear that he had an intellectual debt to Ch'eng Min-cheng. He used Wu Ch'eng as a transitional figure in his attempts to harmonize two methodological possibilities and thus Lo's letter was a reaction, a response to Wang. Lo's critique of Wu, of course, was qualified in certain respects in that he felt that Wu veered off the proper track in his later years by abandoning Chu Hsi and *tao wen-hsüeh*. Yet he overstated the case regarding Wu Ch'eng no doubt to chide Wang.

All this goes to show how much the two sides were polarized at this time. We have already noted how Wu Ch'eng came into disfavor in educational circles in the north because he was considered too much of a Lu man and an opponent of Hsü Heng. By the time of Ch'eng Min-cheng, this was quite a strong, if perhaps mistaken, belief in some quarters and Ch'eng sought to rectify this. In Ch'eng's time, Ch'en Chien was a strong adversary on the other side, indicating polarization on the issue.

In the controversy between Wang and Lo, the latter again defended the mistaken impression of Wu Ch'eng for two reasons. The first was that Wang took the initiative in finding a "tradition" for his latest theory; the second was that for Lo not to attack any synthetic tendency of the Wu Ch'eng variety would play into Wang's hands. Lo added reinforcement to his opinion that Wu was a Lu man by linking him with Buddhism as well. It was to Lo's advantage to emphasize one side of Wu's philosophy.

Wu's philosophy seemed flexible enough so that Wang and Lo could grind their own axes to good advantage in the heat of controversy over methodology in Ming times. They both defended a chronological interpretation of his thought, Wang feeling that later developments were the most valid and Lo that the earlier ones were, as was the case with Hu

Chü-jen. Thus Wang felt that the thrust of Wu's synthesis was toward Lu and his own ideas, as was the thought of the later Chu Hsi. Lo felt that Wu was misguided when he moved toward Lu and discounted the synthetic disposition of his thought.

The Lu-oriented approach of Wu Ch'eng, rather than being a final, culminating stage, was used to provide for intellectual vitality within a Chu-oriented framework. It is not surprising, then, that the controversy in Ming thought over methodology (what Yü Ying-shih terms intellectualism versus antiintellectualism) should in one respect center around the transitional thought of Wu Ch'eng, wherein the possibilities for polarization are considered. Wang was most definitely in sympathy with the independent spirit of the essay translated here[148] and used it to his own good advantage.

F. The Ch'ing: The Views of Li Fu

In considering Li Fu, we find a Ch'ing thinker who strongly reflected the influence of Wu Ch'eng via the more famous thinkers Ch'eng Min-cheng and Wang Yang-ming. Li was the author of the *Lu Tzu hsüeh-p'u*[cr] (*An Intellectual Biography of Master Lu*), a book exclusively concerned with the writings of Lu Hsiang-shan and his school and one which contains many passages from Wu Ch'eng. Li, like Lu and Wu before him, hailed from Lin-ch'uan, his father having married into a family named Wu. While familial connections are dubious, it is interesting that Li was one of several people who were instrumental in having Wu's tablet restored in the Confucian temple (it had originally been placed there in 1443, removed in 1530, and finally reinstated in 1737).[149] Li was also the teacher of Ch'üan Tsu-wang, whose opinions on Wu Ch'eng and others supplemented the work of Huang Tsung-hsi in *Sung-Yüan hsüeh-an*.[cs] Ch'üan was also the author of the funeral tablet of Li Fu.[150]

As has been previously mentioned, Ch'üan Tsu-wang stressed the idea that Wu Ch'eng harmonized the ideas of Chu and Lu, even though he came closer to Chu in terms of scholarship.[151] Ch'üan probably obtained some of his ideas on this from Huang Tsung-hsi, yet, as the student of Li Fu, his opinions were no doubt influenced by him. Thus Li says:

His excellency Wu Wen-cheng throughout his life trusted in Master Chu. In his later years, he began somewhat to pose a theory by which the "honoring of the virtuous nature" and the "maintaining of constant inquiry and study" could be reconciled. His remarks basically emanate from Master Chu yet the disputants created quite a fuss in attacking him.[152]

This passage recognizes Wu's leanings toward Lu, while maintaining that he was still quite faithful to Chu, which of course adds some legitimacy to Lu's thought.

Li Fu mentions, in discussing Ch'eng Min-cheng's *Compendium on the Unity of Tao*, that Chu and Lu were of the same mind in their later years. Li was also the author of the *Chu Tzu wan-nien ch'üan-lun*[ct] (*The Complete Theory of Master Chu in His Later Years*), a work which is no longer extant but which is purported to have reinforced Wang Yang-ming's work on this subject and which defended the endeavors of Wang and Ch'eng against the criticisms of Sun Ch'eng-tse[eu] (1592–1676), who fell chronologically between Wang and Li.[153]

In the preface to the work, which is still extant, Li writes:

The teachings of Master Chu and Master Lu in their early years were half similar and half different. In their middle years, the differences were fewer and the similarities greater. In their later years, they were in perfect agreement.[154]

Li then goes on to criticize Lo Ch'in-shun and Ch'en Chien for their attacks of Wang's *Final Theory* on the grounds of shallowness and recklessness.[155]

In another preface, Li Fu declares that in the last ten years of Chu Hsi's life the following applied: "Both in how he studied and how he taught others, he relied on the theories of Master Lu in 'honoring the virtuous nature' and in seeking for the lost mind."[156] Wu Ch'eng himself did not mention the similarities and differences between Chu and Lu in terms of chronology. It is interesting, however, that he arrived at a reconciliation by emphasizing the same ideas with which Chu is said to have been concerned, according to Li Fu. This provides added support to the *Final Theory* or *Complete Theory* idea and helps to link Ch'eng Min-cheng, Wang Yang-ming and Li Fu.

Li Fu stresses that Chu Hsi moved toward the pole of internal self-cultivation and emphasis on the mind in his later years. As we have noted, Lo Ch'in-shun, and even Hu Chü-jen, saw a development of Wu's thought along chronological lines so that in his later years Wu was seen to be inclined toward Lu, an inclination decried by both, even though Ch'üan Tsu-wang and Li Fu question the characterization itself. By the same token, Li feels that Sung Lien[cv] (1310–1381) and Wang Wei[cw]

(1323–1374), the probably authors of the biography of Wu Ch'eng in the *Yüan shih*, wought to emphasize Wu's Chu affiliation too much and that this was insufficient to fully account for the diversity of Wu's thought.[157]

IV. CONCLUSIONS

A. *The Pivotal Role of the Thought of Wu Ch'eng*

It seems to be the case that Wu Ch'eng wrestled with the polarities of *tsun te-hsing* and *tao wen-hsüeh* throughout his intellectual career. His textual work, which continued throughout his life, was enlivened by an approach emphasizing internal self-cultivation. Naturally, since Wu sought to balance, or harmonize, the two polarities, with shifting emphasis, the issue of whether or not he established a true philosophic synthesis between the Chu and Lu strains arises.

Huang Tsung-hsi and Ch'üan Tsu-wang both feel that Wu was given his orientation toward Lu Hsiang-shan through the influence of Ch'eng Shao-k'ai, who built the Tao-i Academy, the Academy on the Unity of Tao,[158] for the purpose of uniting the teachings of Chu and Lu.[159] In the case of Ch'eng, the term used for his endeavor is *ho-hui*.[cx] Huang also mentions that Ch'eng's lineage traces back to the late twelfth-century thinker T'ang Chin,[cy] who is said to have shifted from a Chu to a Lu emphasis in his thinking and may have, according to Ch'üan, expressed a tendency toward synthesizing, *hui-t'ung*,[cz] Chu and Lu, which is sometimes credited to his younger brother T'ang Chung.[da] T'ang Chin is said to have begun the "indirect tradition" (*ssu-shu*)[db][160] of Lu, which was later represented by Ch'eng Shao-k'ai and Wu Ch'eng.[161]

Ch'eng Shao-k'ai was also known as Ch'eng Shao-k'uei[dc] and was born in 1212. He attained the *chin-shih* degree in 1268 and was appointed as an instructor in the prefectural school in Lin-ch'uan. He died in 1280, shortly after leaving that post.[162] Wu Ch'eng mentions these points in speaking about Ch'eng's official career but more importantly stresses that Ch'eng was his master.[163] Wu does not, however, delve into Ch'eng's philosophical position, yet because of the indirect Lu tradition (traceable to the T'ang Chin line)—the possibility of synthetic tendencies in the T'ang school, and the alleged purpose of Ch'eng's academy—we can conjecture that Wu was likely to have been touched by these elements, which were part of the Kiangsi intellectual scene.[164] It is also important to note that the harmonizing appeal of Huang Kan is part of this picture in the matter of influences on Wu Ch'eng.

The terms *ho-hui* and *hui-t'ung* (and another used in the case of the T'angs, *ho-ho*[dd]), all point to the idea of "convergence" or "accommodation." Perhaps the term synthesis is also appropriate in terms of a reconciliation between external knowledge-seeking and internal self-cultivation precisely because there was a latent potential for harmony from the outset. This would serve to explain why, although we see convergence and accommodation of ideas cropping up in many different eras by way of different spokesmen, there is a feeling that they are tapping an existing source of harmony.

The divisions on the Chu-Lu, and thus the knowledge-seeking versus self-cultivation, positions, then, took on the tenor of a genuine controversy in the Ming era as a trend toward the philosophy of mind, *hsin-hsüeh*,[de] emerged. Yet those on the side of the former were less inclined to desire a synthesis; it was to their disadvantage to dilute what they considered to be the main thrust of the thought of Chu Hsi. For those on the side of the latter, there was an appeal to tradition, which was legitimized by utilizing the thought of Wu Ch'eng: two hundred years earlier a thinker had arrived at conclusions similar to their own concerning the inadequacy of a philosophy dominated by external knowledge-seeking to the detriment of internal self-cultivation.

If a chronological interpretation concerning Wu is at all valid, or even if Wu moved as close to Lu as Chu was said to have moved, we might speculate on two possibilities. The first is that Wu Ch'eng suspected that Chu moved in the direction of Lu and that some of this was reflected in his own philosophical development. The second is that within the Chu school there may have been a natural inclination toward reconciliation with the allegedly opposite trend. In this latter regard, we might consider that during Wu's lifetime the possibility for reconciliation was more acceptable than it came to be by the time of Wang Yang-ming.

In the main, however, strict chronological interpretation of evolution in Wu Ch'eng's thought is dubious. He renounced neither imaginative classical exegesis nor the ideas of Chu Hsi himself. He was devoted, however, to the reassertion of Neo-Confucian values in a broad sense in his own time. He saw contentiousness among the followers of Chu and Lu and felt that the best way to preserve the traditions of Sung in the Yüan was to combine consciously two apparently rival schools in terms of establishing his own ideological authority. Wu felt that the Neo-Confucian tradition had devolved on him and that in picking up the mantle of Chu Hsi [165] and legitimizing the thought of Lu [166] in the Yüan, he was posing a challenge to prevailing inflexible orthodox viewpoints.

B. Wu Ch'eng and Neo-Confucianism in the Mongol era

To what extent can we view the thought of Wu Ch'eng as a response to Mongol rule? We know that upon the demise of Southern Sung, Wu went into retreat and worked assiduously on emendations of the classics, only visiting the Mongol capital briefly in 1287 and 1302. [167] In fact, he served in the post in the Imperial College at the age of 60, and then for about two and a half years (his second period of service, in the Hanlin Academy, 1323–1325, lasted about two and one-quarter years). Certainly, for a man who lived eighty-five years, his actual service in government was quite brief.

Wu Ch'eng's dedication to classical scholarship and a creative accommodation of the divisive trends in late Sung thought relate to his desire to strike a balance in preserving the Sung intellectual heritage. The problem of exegesis for its own sake, as he perceived it in scholars of the early thirteenth century, was addressed in both these ways. His role as an eminent private scholar was reinforced by the uncongenial atmosphere he encountered during his brief periods of service. Hellmut Wilhelm's characterization of the scholars of the Sung learning in Ch'ing times might well apply to Wu, since the former were thinkers "whose center of gravity rested with the intellectual tradition and not with political institutions for which this was exploited." [168]

In the case of Wu Ch'eng, as evidenced in the essay translated here, the stress on personal mental insight made him one who was unlikely to accept the prevailing ideological orthodoxy. For him, the intellectual tradition at its best encouraged intellectual independence. Thus in the Yüan he did not become aligned with the intellectual establishment in the North. The Ch'ing scholar Wei Yüan[df] (1794–1857), in fact, finds a basis for Wu's attitude c.1310–1311 in the political situation with which he was confronted, [169] namely, hostility to his background and proposals and his challenge to what he perceived as a narrow educational and scholarly outlook in the Imperial College. If there is veiled polemic, however, it is very much built upon a foundation in self-inquiry and philosophical freedom.

Wu Ch'eng was quite well known in private scholarly circles as a teacher of great skill and patience, one who could bring out the best in his students. Yü Chi comments on this as follows:

The Master was very earnest and encouraging. His remarks were very clear and trenchant and he guided and helped them [his students] along, each according to the degree of talent and character, as well as differences in experience. . . . Often this would last until midnight and whether it was winter or summer he did not give it up.

On this same theme, Yü Chi also observes:

His disciples were so numerous that they could not be restrained. Each sought after what he desired and received what he was able to because they were unequal in endowment. He composed the "Hsüeh-chi"^{dg} ["Foundation of Learning"] in one chapter so that they would know the necessity of "honoring the virtuous nature" and the "Hsüeh-t'ung"^{dh} ["Tradition of Learning"] in one chapter so that they would know the necessity of "maintaining constant inquiry and study." [170]

The "Foundation of Learning," combines important quotations from early Confucians and Neo-Confucians which express basic ethical ideas, while the "Tradition of Learning" lists the basic classical texts and significant commentaries for study, and outlines the instructional methods Wu Ch'eng attempted to implement (but never, in fact, put into practice) while serving in the Imperial College. In a sense, this was an attempt by Wu to establish a practical scholastic program for which he would be the primary spokesman.

As to Wu's disagreements with his colleagues' desires to standardize educational procedures through competitive examinations (ultimately accomplished in 1315), one might conjecture that, meeting such opposition to his *tao wen-hsüeh* approach, Wu might have sought to emphasize the *tsun te-hsing* aspect to his colleagues, to wit his parting statement. The intellectual climate, as well as the specific conflict, touched off the reevaluation of the late Chu Hsi school, as in the essay here.

In addition, Wu's mention of Lu Hsiang-shan in his parting statement is significant. The disenchantment he felt while serving in the Imperial College occurred within the context of Mongol rule and thus we cannot disregard the possibility that his syncretic philosophical approach, incorporating the Lu spirit, was in part a response to it.

On the other hand, by definition, the philosophical approach of Wu Ch'eng, which incorporated the ideas of two Sung intellectual giants, was

creatively conceived through a personal vision which enlivened philosophic speculation and substantive classical learning. The directional ambiguity in his thought was very much a product of reflective analysis in a
unique historical context. Nevertheless, in looking at Wu's thought on
its own terms, one must say that it embraced the kind of flexibility which
allowed for adherents on both sides of a vibrant controversy, in which
Wu Ch'eng was a significant factor, throughout three eras.

NOTES

1. The biographical material of Wu Ch'eng on these first two pages is based on the author's article "The Life and Career of Wu Ch'eng: A Biography and Introduction," *Journal of the American Oriental Society* (October–December 1979), 99(4):601–41. It incorporates a translation of the family biography composed by Yü Chi in 1335 (original text in *Tao-yüan hsüeh ku-lu*)[di] (SPTK ed.; hereafter TYHKL, 44:2b–14b). Other sources include the funeral tablet and chronological biography found in Wu's collected works, the *Wu Wen-cheng kung ch'üan-chi*[dj] (1756 ed., hereafter WWC), *ts'e* 1 and the biography found in YS (PN ed.), 171:5a–9a.

2. For a general discussion of Wu's classical commentaries in the context of his thought see the author's "Neo-Confucian Classicism in the Thought of Wu Ch'eng," *The Bulletin of Sung and Yüan Studies* (1978), 14:12–21.

3. YS, 171:5b; 172:2a, 4a; TYHKL, 44:5b.

4. TYHKL, 44:5b.

5. WWC, 2:17a.

6. TYHKL, 5:14b-15b, 44:7a; Su T'ien-chüeh, *Kuo-ch'ao wen-lei*[dk] (SPTK ed.), 35:17b.

7. Wang Chien-ch'iu, *Sung-tai t'ai-hsüeh yü t'ai-hsüeh-sheng*[dl] (Taipei: Chung-kuo hsüeh-hsü chu-tso chiang-chu wei-yüan-hui, 1965).

8. Ch'eng Hao, *Ming-tao wen-chi*[dm] (SPPY ed.), 2:6a–7b.

9. Chu's "Private Opinion on the Schools and Civil Service" is found in *Hui-an hsien-sheng Chu Wen-kung wen-chi*[dn] (SPTK ed.), 69:20a–28b. It was discussed in David Nivison, "Protest Against Conventions and Conventions of Protest," in A. F. Wright, ed., *The Confucian Persuasion* (Stanford: Stanford University Press, 1960), pp. 189–190.

10. WWC, *shou:* 16b, 34a–b (chronological biography); YS, 171:6a.

11. TYHKL, 44:7b–8a; YS, 171:6a. The internal quotations are from the *Doctrine of the Mean*, ch. 27, as found in James Legge, tr., *The Chinese Classics* (Hong Kong: Hong Kong University Press, rpt., 1960) vol. 1, pp. 422–23.

12. TYHKL, 44:8a, 5:15b (also in *Kuo-ch'ao wen-lei*, 35:19a); Sun K'o-k'uan, *Yüan-ch'u ju-hsüeh*[do] (Taipei: I-wen yin-shu kuan, 1953), p. 84; Ch'eng Min-cheng of the Ming also takes note of this characterization, as mentioned in section III, part C of this paper.

13. *Hsiang-shan hsien-sheng ch'üan-chi*[dp] (SPTK ed.), 34:18b–19a; SYHA (Shanghai: Commercial Press, 1933), 58:16.

14. YS, 81:4a; *Ta Yüan sheng-cheng kuo-ch'ao tien-chang*[dq] (1908 ed.), 31:11b–12a. For background on the Chu-Lu debates, see Julia Ching, "The Goose Lake Monastery Debate (1175), "*Journal of Chinese Philosophy* (1974), 1:161–78 and cf. Yü Ying-shih, "Some Preliminary Observations on the Rise of Ch'ing Confucian Intellectualism," *Tsing Hua Journal of Chinese Studies*, N. S. (1975), 11:123.

15. *Wu Wen-cheng chi*[dr] (SKCSCP, 2d ser.; Taipei: Commercial Press, 1971; hereafter WWC, *chen-pen*), 36:14b–16a.

16. In 1288, Ch'eng Chü-fu propagated editions of the *Book of Changes, Book of Odes, Book of History*, the *Spring and Autumn Annals*, the *Rites and Ceremonies*, and the *Ritual Texts of the Elder and Younger Tai* in the Imperial College. See TYHKL, 44:5b; YS, 171:5b.
17. See section II, p. 297.
18. This is found in WWC, 22:1a–3a; *Chin Yüan Ming pa-ta-chia wen-hsüan*[ds] (hereafter CYMWH), Li Tsu-t'ao ed. (1845), 4:21a–23a and in *Sheng-hsüeh tsung-ch'uan*, Chou Ju-teng ed., (1606), 11:42b–44a.
19. See part C of this section and section III, parts B through F, in this paper.
20. TYHKL, 44:3b–4a.
21. *Ibid.*, 44:11a, 13a–13b.
22. WWC, 7:27a–28a; Julia Ching, *To Acquire Wisdom* (New York: Columbia University Press, 1976), pp. 95–96, 204.
23. James Legge, vol. 1, pp. 422–23. See also Yü, "Some Preliminary Observations," pp. 108–9: here Yü defines them simply as "morality" and "knowledge."
24. WWC, 15:31b.
25. Yü, "Some Preliminary Observations," pp. 109–10.
26. *Chang Tzu ch'üan-shu*[dt] (Shanghai: Chung-hua shu-chü, 1935), 2:49.
27. *Erh-Ch'eng ch'üan-shu*[du] (1908 ed.), 8:11a.
28. *Chang Tzu ch'üan-shu*, 2:42; for translation, see W. T. Chan, *A Source Book in Chinese Philosophy* (Princeton: Princeton University Press, 1963), p. 511.
29. WWC, 2:16a. According to Wing-tsit Chan, the internal quotation is most likely from Ch'eng I (see *Source Book*, p. 536, note 92, for discussion of this attribution).
30. WWC, 2:17a; Kano Naoki in *Chūgoku tetsugaku shi*[dv] (Tokyo: Iwanami shōten, 1953), p. 453 quotes this passage as an example of Wu's criticism of the vulgar scholarship of the day, a theme emphasized in the essay translated in section II of this paper.
31. *Hsiang-shan hsien-sheng ch'üan-chi*, 35:17b–18b; tr. in Chan, *Source Book*, p. 585.
32. *Chu Tzu yü-lei*[dw] (hereafter CTYL), (Taipei: Cheng-chung shu-chü, rpt. of 1473 ed., 1970), 64:25a (p. 2525).
33. There are eight themes enumerated in *ch.* 27 of the *Mean* (Legge, vol. 1, p. 423), immediately following the contrast between self-cultivation and knowledge-seeking. Chu Hsi broke these down under the two contrasting headings (*Yü-tsuan Chu-Tzu ch'üan-shu*,[dx] 1713 ed., 25:36a-b; CTYL, 64:23b, p. 2522), whereas Wu Ch'eng broke them down under the headings of knowledge and action (WWC, 23:28b), a breakdown he ascribes to Jao Lu (*ibid.*, 23:14b–5a).
34. *Yü-tsuan Chu Tzu ch'üan-shu*, 25:36b; CTYL, 64:24b (p. 2524).
35. CTYL, 64:23b (p. 2522).
36. *Ibid.*
37. *Ibid.*, 64:24a (p. 2523).
38. *Ibid.*, 64:25a (p. 2525).
39. W. T. Chan, *Instructions for Practical Living* (New York: Columbia Uni-

versity Press, 1963), p. xxv and *Wang Wen-ch'eng kung ch'üan-shu*[dy] (SPTK ed.), 2:58a-b (tr. in Chan, *Instructions*, pp. 159–60).

40. *Hui-an hsien-sheng Chu Wen-kung wen-chi*, 54:6a-b; Yü Ying-shih, "Some Preliminary Observations," p. 108.

41. Kusumoto Masatsugu, *Sō-Min jidai jugaku shisō no kenkyū*[dz] (Hiroike ga-kuen: Chiba ken, 1962), p. 396.

42. *Ibid.*, p. 287.

43. SYHA, 58:37; cf. Kusumoto, p. 396 and Ching, *To Acquire Wisdom*, p. 281, note 5.

44. Kusumoto, p. 289.

45. Ch'ien Mu, *Sung Ming li-hsüeh kai-shu*[ea] (Taipei: Chung-hua wen-hua shih-yeh wei-yüan-hui, 1953), vol. 1, p. 166.

46. *Hsiang-shan hsien-sheng ch'üan-chi*, 34:44b; Yü Ying-shih, "Ts'ung Sung-Ming ju-hsüeh ti fa-chan lun Ch'ing-tai ssu-hsiang shih"[eb] (Ch'ing Thought as Seen Through the Development of Sung Ming Confucianism), *Chung-kuo hsüeh-jen*[ec] (1970), 2:21–22.

47. *Hsiang-shan hsien-sheng ch'üan-chi*, 34:8a; tr. in Chan, *Source Book*, p. 582.

48. For the *i-fa/wei-fa* distinction, see *Doctrine of the Mean*, 1:4, in James Legge, vol. 1, p. 384. Cf. pp. 289–90 of this book.

49. *Mencius* 6A:10, Legge, vol. 2, pp. 413–414.

50. T'ang Chün-i, "The Devlopment of the Concept of Moral Mind from Wang Yang-ming to Wang Chi," in W. T. deBary, ed., *Self and Society in Ming Thought*, (New York: Columbia University Press, 1970), pp. 94–100.

51. *Ibid.*, p. 100.

52. *Mencius* 6A:15, Legge, Vol. 2, p. 418; quoted in *Hsiang-shan hsien-sheng ch'üan-chi*, 11:1a, 34:8a.

53. Yü, "Ch'ing Thought," pp. 21–22.

54. *Ibid.*, and Yü, "Some Preliminary Observations," pp. 106, 123–24.

55. This is quoted in Paul Vignaux, *Philosophy in the Middle Ages: An Intro-duction*, tr. E. C. Hall (New York: Meridian Books, 1959), p. 52. Abélard lived 1079–1142.

56. *Ibid.*, p. 110. Bonaventure lived 1221–1274.

57. WWC, 23:27a–28b; CYMWH, 4:28a–29b; *Kuo-ch'ao wen-lei*, 29:1a–2b. An abbreviated version appears in Feng Yün-hao and Wang Tzu-ts'ai, eds., *Sung Yüan hsüeh-an pu-i*[ed] (Ssu-ming ts'ung-shu ed., Shanghai, 1937), 92:15b–16b.

58. CYMWH, 4:22b–23a, 29b.

59. *Kuo-ch'ao wen-lei*, 29:1a–2b.

60. CYMWH, 4:29b.

61. WWC, 23:28b.

62. See part B of this section.

63. WWC, 15:31a–32a, 10:26b–27b, 26:9b–11a (this last piece deals expressly with the issue of original mind, *pen-hsin*).

64. CYMWH, 4:29b.

65. *Ibid.*

66. For more on the Wang-Lo controversy, see section III, parts D and E of this paper.
67. SYHA, 92:5; also see section IV, the conclusion to this paper, part A.
68. CYMWH, 4:22b; cf. SYHA, 92:5.
69. The text used for the translation is found in WWC, 22:1a–3a. For other sources, see note 18 above.
70. Wu was concerned about the legitimate line of succession in Confucianism, *tao-t'ung*,[ee] in his early years (TYHKL, 44:4a–5a, c. A.D. 1267).
71. This criticism was voiced when Wu was about to depart from his post in the Imperial College as well.
72. This last sentence is quoted by the late Ming scholar Chiao Hung[ef] (1541–1620) in *Chiao-shih pi-ch'eng*[eg] (*Yüeh-ya-t'ang ts'ung-shu* ed., 1850), 4:34a.
73. As a point of comparison, in another essay, found in WWC, 5:25b–26a, virtuous nature is replaced by mind, in terms of what heaven confers.
74. In the essay referred to in the previous note, the directing agent, *chu-tsai*, is said to be mind.
75. In SYHA, 92:12, a passage from Wu Ch'eng refers to the idea of daily renovation, *jih-hsin*,[eh] in Ssu-ma Kuang[ei] (1019–1086); the *locus classicus* for this is the *Great Learning*, 2:1 (see James Legge, vol. 1, p. 361).
76. Chu-ko Liang[ej] (181–234): Having wearied of the pursuit of study geared toward securing official position in the 1260s, and failing to pass the *chin-shih* in 1271, Wu built several thatched huts, on the lattice windows of which he superscribed phrases associated with Chu-ko. Ch'eng Chü-fu and others realized Wu's intentions and from this point on Wu was known as *ts'ao-lu*,[ek] "thatched hut" (TYHKL, 44:5a), a reference to Chu-ko's "First Memorial on the Occasion of Initiating a Campaign," found in Ch'en Shou, *San-kuo chih*[el] (PN ed.), 35:8b–10a (translation by Achilles Fang, *The Chronicle of the Three Kingdoms* [Cambridge, Mass.: Harvard University Press, 1962], vol. 2, p. 225).
77. *Mencius* 7A:5; Legge, vol. 2, p. 45.
78. The last four paragraphs are also translated in Carsun Chang, *The Development of Neo-Confucian Thought* (New York: Bookman Associates, 1957), vol. 1, pp. 342–43. As regards Ch'en Ch'un, Wu may have in mind his lexicon of Neo-Confucian words and expressions called *Pei-hsi tzu-i*.
79. P'i Chin,[em] the son mentioned here, is referred to in SYHA, 92:43; essays written to him can be found in WWC, 9:22b–23a and 19:14b–15a. The name Shao-te,[en] brilliant or illuminating virtue, is referred to two paragraphs hence in the context of Wu's stress on the cultivation of virtue (cf. note 82).
80. This paragraph is translated in Carsun Chang, p. 343.
81. *Tzu*: the hours from eleven to one A.M., *Hai*: the hours from nine to eleven P.M.
82. The expression *shao-shao*,[eo] bright and shining, is found in the *Doctrine of the Mean*, 26:9, in Legge, vol. 1, p. 420. The words could also be read *chao-chao*, in the sense of illumination, which embodies both literal and figurative meanings.

83. That chapter begins: "What Heaven has conferred is called THE NATURE" (Legge, vol. 1, p. 383), which parallels the first sentence in this essay; also cf. note 73 above.

84. Later on this was called the "Western Inscription," as contained in *Chang Tzu ch'üan-shu*, 1:1–8 and praised by Wu Ch'eng in WWC, 10:10b.

·85. WWC (*chen-pen*), 2:4a.

86. YS, 171:6a; WWC, *shou:* 34a–b; cf. p. 281 of this book.

87. WWC (*chen-pen*), 2:4a–5a. For an account of Cheng Ch'iao's criticism of traditional historical scholarship, see his "General Preface" to *T'ung-chih*, tr. in W. T. de Bary et al., eds., *Sources of Chinese Tradition* (New York: Columbia University Press, 1960), pp. 497–99.

88. WWC (*chen-pen*), 5a–6a.

89. WWC, 5:25b.

90. WWC, 2:2b–4a.

91. Yü, "Some Preliminary Observations," p. 110.

92. *Ibid.*

93. WWC, 7:18a-b; cf. pp. 293–94. The internal quotation is from the *Analects* 6:25, in Legge, vol. 1, p. 193.

94. CYMWH. 4:22b; cf. p. 294 above.

95. WWC. 10:27a-b, 26:10b.

96. See notes 73 and 74 above.

97. CYMWH, 4:23a. Wu in one case was mildly critical of Chu's exegetical approach in suggesting how refinement and detail may result in mere skill-fulness and excess, which resembles his criticism of the late Chu school. While he generally lauded Chu's commentaries, he also felt that he had some differences. See WWC (*chen-pen*), 20:5a-b.

98. CYMWH, 4:29b.

99. *Ibid.* In this vein, Lo stresses Wu's dedication to extensiveness in learning and restraint in propriety. See section III, parts D and E.

100. SYHA, 93:61-62; Mishima Fuku, *Riku Shōzan no tetsugaku*[ep] (Tokyo: Kyōhō bunkan, 1926), pp. 156–57.

101. SYHA, 93:61.

102. WWC, 10:26b–27b.

103. *Ibid.*, 10:27a-b. Wu remarks elsewhere that the Lu school was not perpet-uated in the closing years of Sung because of a failure on the part of even his best disciples to grasp the essence of Lu's theory of mind (WWC, 42:14b, also found in *Sung-Yüan hsüeh-an pu-i*, 92:16b–17a).

104. WWC, 24:28b–30a: This essay is dedicated to Liu's hut, which was titled "Quiescence and Vacuity."

105. Kusumoto, pp. 392–94.

106. SYHA, 94:87. Cheng was an acquaintance, however, of Chieh Hsi-ssu[eq] (1274–1344), the author of Wu Ch'eng's funeral tablet (cf. note 1 above). See Cheng Yü, *Shih-shan chi*[er] (SKCSCP, 4th ser., Taipei: Commercial Press, 1973), *fu-lu*, 10a; WWC, *shou:* 14a–18b.

107. SYHA, 94:87.

108. *Shih-shan chi*, 3:19ab, and SYHA, 94:90 (cf. trans. in Chang Yü-ch'üan, "Wang Shou-jen as a Statesman," *The Chinese Social and Political Science Review* [April 1939], 23:158–59; on pp. 157–58, Chang translates Wu Ch'eng's 1310–1311 statement contrasting Chu and Lu); elsewhere in Cheng Yü's work he stresses the essential unity between Chu and Lu (45:7b).

109. SYHA, 94:90.

110. Wing-tsit Chan is critical of the placement of Wu Yü-pi's thought between Chu and Lu by the compilers of the *Ssu-k'u ch'üan-shu tsung-mu*[es] (See Chan, "The Ch'eng-Chu School of Early Ming," in *Self and Society in Ming Thought*, p. 44), a categorization with which Kusumoto might agree (p. 289).

111. Chan, "The Ch'eng-Chu School," p. 42.

112. Yü, "Ch'ing Thought," p. 27.

113. Hu Chü-jen, *Hu Ching-chai chi*,[et] in *Cheng-i-t'ang ch'üan-shu*[eu] (1868 ed.), 1:2b.

114. *Ibid.*, 1:17b–18a; *Hsü Lu-chai chi*[ev] (TSCC ed. [Shanghai: Commercial Press, 1936], 6:73).

115. *Hu Ching-chai chi*, 1:11b.

116. *Hsiang-shan hsien-sheng ch'üan-chi*, 34:44b.

117. Yü, "Ch'ing Thought," p. 27.

118. *Mencius* 6A:11: Legge, vol. 2, p. 414.

119. *Ibid.*, 6A:15: Legge, vol. 2, p. 418; cf. *Hsiang-shan hsien-sheng ch'üan-chi*, 34:8a, 11:1a.

120. Ch'en Hsien-chang, *Po-sha-tzu ch'üan-chi*[ew] (1771 ed.), 3:30a.

121. W. T. de Bary, "Individualism and Humanitarianism in Late Ming Thought," in *Self and society in Ming Thought*, p. 174.

122. *Hsiang-shan hsien-sheng ch'üan-chi*, 35:21b; SYHA, 58:9.

123. Chan Jo-shui, "Fu-chou hsin-ch'uang san-hsien-tz'u chi,"[ex] in *Fou-chou fu chih*[ey] (1876 ed.), 16:25a.

124. WWC, 13:24a; cf. *Sung Kao-seng chuan*,[ez] ch. 8 (biography of Hui Neng) in *Taishō shinshū daizōkyō*[fa] (Tokyo, 1922–1932), vol. 50, pp. 754–55; *Ching-te ch'uan-teng lu*[fb] (SPTK ed.), 5:1b; and *Liu-tsu ta-shih fa-pao t'an-ching*[fc] in *Taishō*, vol. 48, p. 355.

125. WWC, 13:24b.

126. *Po-sha Tzu ch'üan-chi*, shou:14b.

127. *Ibid.*, shou:15a.

128. Ch'eng Min-cheng, *Huang-tun wen-chi*[fd] (SKCSCP, 3d ser.; Taipei: Commercial Press), 16:22a, 28:27b, 38:7a.

129. *Ibid.*, 29:32a.

130. CTYL, 9:2b (p. 238).

131. WWC, 3:22b-23a and SYHA, 92:9.

132. Ch'eng Min-cheng, *Hsin-ching* (Korean ed., 1794?), 4:38b–40a.

133. *Huang-tun wen-chi*, 38:15a-b.

134. *Hsin-ching*, 1:2b; Ch'en Chien's criticism is found in *Hsüeh-pu t'ung-pien* (*Cheng-i-t'ang ch'üan-shu* ed.), 1:4a. For more on this see Fung Yu-lan, A

History of Chinese Philosophy, tr. Derk Bodde (Princeton: Princeton University Press, 1953), vol. 2, p. 622.

135. *Hsin-ching*, 1:4a–5a. Ch'eng, in fact, felt that Lu's thought was in some respects too tinged with Ch'an, while Wu's was more orthodox in the sense that he seldom strayed from the Confucian norms (*Huang-tun wen-chi*, supplementary selections: 6b–7a).

136. Kusumoto, p. 391.

137. *Ibid.*, p. 289.

138. The preface to it is found in *Wang Wen-ch'eng kung ch'üan-shu*, 7:21a–22b and the text itself, with the preface, in 3:63a–82b. The selection from Wu occurs in 3:80a–81b; also see Chan, *Instructions*, pp. 263–65 and Ching, *To Acquire Wisdom*, pp. 79–80.

139. *Wang Wen-ch'eng kung ch'üan-shu*, 3:80a-b.

140. Cf. Ching, *To Acquire Wisdom*, p. 79.

141. The text itself, upon which the summation in the following three paragraphs is based, can be found in *Lo Cheng-an chi ts'un-kao*[fe] (*Cheng-i-t'ang ch'üan-shu* ed.), 1:9b–10b.

142. *Hsiang-shan hsien-sheng ch'üan-chi*, 34:8b–9a; cf. *Erh-Ch'eng ch'üan-shu*, 3:1b.

143. *Analects* 11:25; Legge, vol. 1, p. 248.

144. Cf. Ching, *To Acquire Wisdom*, p. 92.

145. CYMWH, 4:29b.

146. See p. 302 of this book.

147. Yü Ying-shih, "Ch'ing Thought," pp. 27–30; *Hsiang-shan hsien-sheng ch'üan-chi*, 34:1b.

148. Wang also expressed profound admiration for Wu Ch'eng's 1331 work *Li-chi tsuan-yen* for which he wrote a preface in 1520; cf. Ching, *To Acquire Wisdom*, pp. 95–96, 202–5 (where Wang's preface is translated).

149. Thomas Watters, *A Guide to the Tablets in a Temple of Confucius* (Shanghai: American Presbyterian Mission Press, 1879), p. 189; Ling Ti-chih, (*Ku-chin*) *Wan-hsing t'ung-p'u*[ff] (undated Ming ed.), 10:20b; WWC, *shou* (third series):1a–5b.

150. Ch'üan Tsu-wang, *Chi-ch'i-t'ing chi*[fg] (SPTK ed.), 17:12a–15a.

151. SYHA, 92:5.

152. *Mu-t'ang ch'u-kao*,[fh] 43:12b; cf. passage by Wu at the beginning of part B of the first section of this paper. Li mentions that at first Wu was close to Chu and later on to Lu in *Lu Tzu hsüeh-p'u* (1732 ed.), 18:1a-b. In a memorial to Jen Lan-chih,[fi] however, in defense of Wu so that his tablet could be replaced, it is pointed out that Wu was mistakenly thought to be of the Lu school (WWC, *shou*:6a).

153. *Mu-t'ang ch'u-kao*, 45:13a–15a.

154. *Ibid.*, 32:2a.

155. *Ibid.*, 32:3a.

156. *Ibid.*, 32:4b; repeated in 32:6b–7a.

157. *Lu Tzu hsüeh-p'u*, 18:4b.

158. For the idea of *Tao-i*, the Wyy is one, see *Mencius* 3A:1, James Legge, vol. 2, p. 234. Cf. section III, part C of this paper.

159. SYHA, 94:1, 84:120.

160. This term appears in *Mencius* 4b:22; James Legge, vol. 2, p. 328. Li Fu speaks of Wu's embodiment of this tradition as well (*Lu Tzu hsüeh-p'u*, 18:1a-b; also cf. SYHA, 92:1).

161. SYHA, 79:55, 84:110–120; also see Ch'üan Tsu-wang, *Chi-ch'i-t'ing chi*, 34:7a-8b and Mishima Fuku, pp. 156–57.

162. *Kuang-hsin-fu chih*,[fj] (1783 ed.), 17:48a, 16:45b–46a. The laudatory farewell piece to Ch'eng by Wu is not found in WWC.

163. *Ibid.*, and WWC, 19:16a-b.

164. A synthetic spirit may have been noticeable among thinkers in the Shang-jao area of Kiangsi, the place from which Ch'eng Shao-k'ai hailed. Thus a pupil of T'ang Han[fk] (a thinker in the T'ang Chin lineage), Kung T'ing-sung,[fl] wrote a treatise on the Four Books in this vein entitled *Ssu-shu Chu Lu hui-t'ung chü-shih*[fm] (*Kuang-hsin-fu chih*, 16:46a-b).

165. TYHKL, 44:4a-b.

166. WWC, 26:11a.

167. In the first instance, see note 15. In the second, Wu's desire to be freed from a post in the Hanlin Academy, to which he had been appointed, led to him comparing himself with the ancient recluses Ch'ao Fu[fn] and Hsü Yu;[fo] ultimately his hesitancy led to the position being filled by someone else (TYHKL, 44:6b).

168. Hellmut Wilhelm, "Chinese Confucianism on the Eve of the Great Encounter," in Marius Jansen, ed., *Changing Japanese Attitudes Toward Modernization* (Princeton: Princeton University Press, 1965), p. 290.

169. *Yüan shih hsin-pien*[fp] (1905 ed.), 46:7b; cf. note 133 above.

170. TYHKL, 44:7a; 44:13b. Both pieces are found in WWC (supplementary *chüan*), 1:1b–8b.

GLOSSARY

a 吳澄
b 臨川
c 臨汝
d 程若庸
e 朱熹
f 黃榦
g 道一
h 程紹開
i 陸象山
j 程鉅夫
k 英宗
l 許衡
m 胡瑗
n 范仲淹
o 程顥
p 尊德性道問學齋記
q 陳淳
r 饒魯
s 禮記纂言
t 王陽明
u 尊德性
v 道問學
w 中庸
x 張載
y 程頤
z 氣
aa 理
ab 而
ac 來
ad 敬
ae 涵養
af 致知
ag 格物致知
ah 誠意
ai 禮記
aj 項平夫

ak 存心
al 吳與弼
am 本心
an 己發
ao 格物
ap 未發
aq 存養
ar 自明
as 自呈
at 格心
au 李祖陶
av 蘇天爵
aw 羅欽順
ax 黃宗羲
ay 全祖望
az 鄭玄
ba 韓愈
bb 記誦詞章
bc 言語文字之末
bd 鄭樵
be 通志
bf 聞見
bg 華學
bh 實學
bi 嘉定
bj 虞集
bk 言語訓釋之末
bl 主宰
bm 朱子晚年定論
bn 陳苑
bo 趙偕
bp 胡石塘
bq 語錄
br 柳從龍
bs 靜
bt 虛

bu 鄭玉
bv 胡居仁
bw 陳獻章
bx 窮理
by 崇仁
bz 羅倫
ca 周汝登
cb 聖學宗傳
cc 王畿
cd 泰州
ce 不識一字
cf 湛若水
cg 慧能
ch 程敏政
ci 道一編
cj 居敬
ck 眞德秀
cl 心經
cm 李滉
cn 陳建
co 學蔀通辯
cp 大學問
cq 李紱
cr 陸子學譜
cs 宋元學案
ct 朱子晚年全論
cu 孫承澤
cv 宋濂
cw 王禕
cx 和會
cy 湯巾
cz 會同
da 湯中
db 私淑
dc 程紹魁
dd 和合
de 心學
df 魏源

dg 學基
dh 學統
di 道園學古錄
dj 吳文正公全集
dk 國朝文類
dl 王建秋，宋代太學與太學生
dm 明道文集
dn 惠安先生朱文公文集
do 孫克寬，元初儒學
dp 象山先生全集
dq 大元聖政國朝典章
dr 吳文正集
ds 金元明八大家文選
dt 張子全書
du 二程全書
dv 狩野直喜，中国哲学史
dw 朱子語類
dx 御纂朱子全書
dy 王文成公全書
dz 楠本正継，宋明時代儒学思
　　想の研究
ea 錢穆，宋明理學概述
eb 余英時，從宋明儒學的發展
　　論清代思想史
ec 中國學人
ed 宋元學案補遺
ee 道統
ef 焦竑
eg 焦氏筆乘
eh 日新
el 司馬光
ej 諸葛亮
ek 草廬
el 陳壽，三國志
em 皮晉
en 昭德
eo 昭昭
ep 三島復，陸九淵の哲学

eq 揭傒斯

er 師山集

es 四庫全書總目

et 胡敬齋集

eu 正誼堂全書

ev 續魯齋集

ew 白沙子全集

ex 撫州新創三先賢祠記

ey 撫州府志

ez 宋高僧傳

fa 大正新修大藏經

fb 景德傳燈錄

fc 六祖大士發寶壇經

fd 篁墩文集

fe 羅整庵集存稿

ff 凌迪知，（古今）萬姓統譜

fg 鮚鯖亭集

fh 穆堂初稿

fi 任蘭枝

fj 廣信府志

fk 湯漢

fl 龔霆松

fm 四書朱陸會同注釋

fn 巢父

fo 許由

fp 元史新編

John W. Dardess

Confucianism, Local Reform, and Centralization in Late Yüan Chekiang, 1342–1359

IN THE LATE Yüan period, some significant instances of the development and implementation of Confucian doctrine took place at the prefectural and country level in parts of what is now Chekiang province. The actors are many and the story complex, but the matter merits attention because through it one can see how Confucian doctrine was actually applied by Confucians (men whose visible interests were centered upon the development and explication of Confucian doctrine and its implementation for public ends) in order to bring about a certain kind of social change at the popular level. The change in question was socio-moral reform in general, centered about a campaign for the proportional redistribution of unpaid state service obligations among the local landowning households.

I here take Confucianism as constituting, in the sociological sense of the word, a "profession." That is, Confucianism consisted in a specially recruited community of men who were dedicated to and expertly commanded an abstract, systematized, and generalized body of knowledge or doctrine. This doctrine, though abstract and general, was cultivated not mainly for its own sake, but for the explicit purpose that it must be applied by those learned in it to remedy or alleviate certain categories of ills or malfunctions that afflict the general public. As a profession, Confucianism took upon itself the ideal of social service, the obligation to use its knowledge in a disinterested way for the public benefit. As a profession, the Confucian community normally placed its qualified members in, or at least cooperated closely with, organized public authority (the imperial bureaucracy) in supplying its services. In the final analysis, however, Confucian doctrine was applicable only in the form of advice, not sanctions; and Confucianism's collegial ethic demanded loyalty to the norms of the profession whenever these might come into conflict with the requirements of bureaucratic organization or the coercive power of the state.[1]

In late Yüan Chekiang, Confucian doctrine was translated into action through the cooperation of at least two distinct groups: (1) local communities of professionally oriented Confucian elites, and (2) some favorably disposed personnel in Yüan bureaucracy at the regional, prefectural, or county level. The function of the first group was mainly advisory; that of the second, executory. As will be discussed later, the carrying out of local reform in the light of Confucian principles must be understood as the work of very small action groups whose own stake in such reforms cannot very easily be calculated in the coin of immediate material benefits. Ethnic origins, family social backgrounds, or personal career prospects also seem to offer no more than feeble clues to the motivations of the reformers, to the reasons why they willingly took such hard tasks upon themselves. The interest of the reformers in reform must perforce be calculated differently. Reform being inherently a conspicuous process, then for the reformers the rewards may well have had some clear link to visibility, i.e., for the Confucian advisors, enhanced professional prestige; for the reform bureaucrats, celebrity, reputation, or the overt exercise of power.

The elements of Confucian doctrine relevant to the reforms under review refer to the idea of the state as preeminently an instrument through which certain generalized benefits are delivered to the public *as a collectivity*. That is, the state may not extend its benefits to some and arbitrarily deny them to others. The main benefit extended by the state to the public collectivity is order *(chih)*[a] or security *(an)*.[b] In the detailed study that follows, the guiding theory appears to be that when the state (the bureaucracy) begins covertly to market its services to the highest bidders, then it has begun, by that very fact, to create and to foster the growth of insecurity and disorder within the public as a whole. The remedy is reform, and the duty of working for reform falls to dedicated and "impartial" Confucian elites, who know doctrine and are both personally and professionally committed to applying it to alleviate perceived social ills. As professionals, however, they offer advice and, unless they are themselves responsible officials, cannot normally issue orders or apply coercion. Thus there was a need for "clients" within the bureaucracy who, psychologically or otherwise, were inclined to take the advice and act upon it. The principal Confucian contribution to reform was that of articulating the goals and suggesting the methods through which reform in the public interest might best be effected. Invariably the methods they suggested involved a significant centralization of official power and responsibility at the relevant level of political organization.

In its broad outlines, local fiscal reform was hardly a new story in the long history of China. James T. C. Liu and Brian E. McKnight have described various reforms of the kind undertaken in Sung times. Reform attempts were also made, with little success, earlier in the Yüan.[2] All these had the endorsement of the central government. As for the reforms undertaken in the late Yüan, two things appear noteworthy in a historical sense. First, they were set in motion in only a few South China prefectures that yielded relatively little in tax revenues to the central government. Second, while the reforms were confined to a few locales, they featured the involvement of the local Confucian elites as an important intermediary between the landowning households and the reform-minded regional and local officials. This structural feature clearly distinguishes these from earlier service reforms. It also indicates that by the 1340s some Confucian elites found that the prefecture and county could also serve as a worthy theater of endeavor, and were no longer as strategically preoccupied with the imperial center as they had been earlier in the Yüan.

It admits of no simple answer why, out of all the vast reaches of China, only a handful of prefectures and counties in a largely marginal part of Chekiang in the south undertook fiscal reforms over the years 1342–1350. Nor is it easy to explain the reasons for the striking differences in the way in which the reforms were implemented in one place as compared to another. I have attempted elsewhere historical and geographical analyses of some of these questions.[3] For present purposes, it may suffice to emphasize that the reformers certainly intended that their efforts should be emulated elsewhere and ultimately become national policy. The immediate reform localities appear to have been "chosen" as starting points for reform in the light of at least three criteria. They were in obvious need of reform; they happened to have strong resident Confucian communities which would eagerly participate in reform; and whether the reforms succeeded or failed, these particular places were poor enough in resources that the total flow of vital imperial revenues would in no way be threatened.

The late Yüan local reform movements under consideration here fall into two broad phases, punctuated by the nationwide upheavals of 1351–1354 known as the "Red Turban" rebellions. The first phase was centered about fiscal reform, while the second involved the further organization of local military defense. The problems engendered in the first phase impinged heavily upon the difficulties encountered in the second. The main themes to be pointed up in this account include (1) the social backgrounds and personal proclivities of the principal actors; (2) the aims and methods of the reforms; and (3) the interconnections among dedicated Confucian professionalism, local reform, and the local-level centralization of political control.

While "professionalism," "reform," and "centralization" are modern concepts largely alien to the world to which I apply them, they are nevertheless implicit in the structure of events to be related. With due caution, they can be used as explanatory devices without doing violence to the Confucian sense of mission as the Confucians themselves perceived it.

Under the aegis of the censors of Che-tung[c] Circuit, fiscal reform was initiated in Shao-hsing[d] prefecture in 1342. The coordinator of the reform was Tai Bukha[e] (1304–1352), general administrator of the prefecture. A Mongol born in South China, Tai Bukha had taken instruction from a prominent Confucian teacher, attained the *chin-shih* degree, and besides having given zealous service in the Censorate, had also busied himself with caligraphy and philolgy, compiling a treatise on miswritten characters in the Chinese classics and histories. He took up his post in 1341, and at once applied himself to the task of acting as field marshal for the reforms.[4]

The most detailed information about these reforms centers upon Yü-yao,[f] a dependency of Shao-hsing. The survival of this information has everything to do with the fact that celebrated Confucian writers happened to provide it. Tai Bukha personally selected one Liu Hui[g] (1292–1352) to direct the reform in Yü-yao.

It is related of Liu Hui that he was a northern Chinese, and that several of his forebears had served the Yüan state in an official capacity. His epitaph states that, rather than take part in an inheritance fight among his brothers, Liu Hui moved away and supported himself by teaching.

He was especially fond of a Confucian primer compiled by Chu Hsi (1130–1200) entitled the *Hsiao-hsüeh*[h] (Elementary Learning), for what seemed to him its immediate relevance to social action. He believed it better to put to use the teaching in this one book than it was to read ten thousand books. Accordingly, he gave up teaching to become a government clerk. He was recommended by Tai Bukha to handle the Yü-yao reform on the basis of a principle he is said to have enunciated: "if we are lenient but careful of details, the people will sympathize and cooperate honestly; but if we are harsh and oppressive, people will fear indictment and become treacherous." Appointed assistant magistrate, Liu Hui worked day and night for two years on the reform, exhausting himself to the point that his "beard and hair turned white." But the effort succeeded, and its procedures were subsequently adopted as a model by the censorial authorities for fiscal reform in Chin-hua[i] and other parts of Che-tung.[5]

The aim of the reform was not to increase revenues for the sake of the state. Rather, it was to effect a just reapportionment of the state service levy for the sake of the public as a whole. These levies had been reapportioned earlier, in 1298, but later the records were destroyed in a fire, and "those in charge of matters in the rural districts willfully falsified their accounts of the fields, benefitting the rich and strong at the expense of the poor and weak."[6] This misregistry of fields underlay the misallocation of service levies, because the levies were assigned in proportion to the land the registers showed a household owned. As Chu Te-jun (1294–1365) wrote, "[Tai Bukha] began renovating government by reassigning services according to the fields, so that the largeholders might not escape [services] and the smallholders might survive. This was the pressing issue of the moment."[7] In Yü-yao, consequently, there first took place the laborious process of verifying all land titles for the 553,700 *mou* under cultivation. After appropriate investigation, there were then issued 463,000 stamped certificates (*wu-yu*)[j] to local landowners as proof of title. On the basis of this mass of new data, Liu Hui and his aides drew up several interrelated sets of registers and equitably reapportioned local service obligations.[8]

Fiscal reapportionment was not simply a technical problem made soluble by the application of expertise in fiscal accountancy. In Yü-yao, it was also a moral problem made soluble by the application of Confucian doctrine. Mainly this was because the reregistration drive depended for its success on the ability of those in charge to mobilize the population. Land titles were ascertained not by having investigators go out into the countryside, but by having the landowners themselves come voluntarily to the yamen to declare their holdings. In effect this meant that the poorer landowners who were disadvantaged by the older registers (presumably the majority), would, by voluntarily stating their holdings, put heavy social pressure upon the rest, who stood to lose by the equitable reallocation of obligations. Some hint of the tensions resulting from this mobilization is conveyed in an inscription written by Wei Su (1303–1372). It relates that the Yü-yao "rich" opposed the reform while the "poor" eagerly supported it. Liu Hui and his aides were determined to resolve this tension in favor of the poor, and when divination produced negative indications, they went ahead with the reform anyway. Liu finally planted an evergreen in front of his yamen and vowed to Heaven that if the tree died, he would cancel the program. Despite a drought the tree lived, and so the reform was pressed to a conclusion. In celebration of this portent, a shrine was built beside the tree.[9]

In conjunction with public mobilization for the self-declaration of property holdings, a series of other reforms were instituted with an eye toward local moral improvement. These included the establishment of a charity granary, an endowment whose purpose was to finance marriage and funeral rites for indigent *shih*,[k] i.e., the local Confucians. According to Chu Te-jun, these *shih* had been following "uncanonical" local custom, a matter he found detrimental to the maintenance of professional standards and public order.[10] Ch'eng Tuan-li (1271–1345), a retired government teacher of some note, was brought in by Tai Bukha to manage this granary, as well as to direct the revival of the antique rite known as the "Village Drinking Ceremony" (*hsiang yin-chiu li*).[1] As Ch'eng described it, this community rite, when performed conscientiously, aided in the task of popular mobilization in that it formally and visibly ranked the participants in a hierarchy of age and moral virtue, such that seniors preceded juniors and men of virtue took precedence over those less worthy. When badly performed, wrote Ch'eng. "seniors lose precedence over juniors and litigious strife increases."[11] Those honored in this ceremony were those who cooperated in the fiscal reform; those publicly disgraced were those who for selfish reasons struggled to keep the service load inequitably distributed. Thus, in the minds of its directors, fiscal reform was a problem that could not be disentangled from the local moral environment. The unequal allocation of service obligations was but a tangible symptom of a deeper-lying moral disarray. Such was the assumption in Yü-yao.

In 1350, fiscal reform was carried out in Chin-hua prefecture, the seat of the Che-tung Censorial Circuit, along much the same lines that had been followed in Yü-hao earlier. A subordinate official of that circuit, a man of Tangut ancestry named Yü Ch'üeh (1303–1358), was the principal director of the effort. Again, as social background and career variables are part of the analytical problem at hand, Yü Ch'üeh's credentials as a reformer should be looked into briefly.

The son of a local official, Yü Ch'üeh was an avid student and later a commentator on the classics, as well as a poet of some note. After his father died, he supported himself and his mother by teaching while he prepared himself for the civil service examinations, achieving his *chin-shih* in 1333. His career from that point included service in central, provincial, and local government; in the Censorate; and in the literary academies at the national capital. His behavior in office featured stern suppression of the clerical subbureaucracy; daring outspokenness; willingness to resign rather than "truckle to the powerful and noble"; and in one crisis situation, readiness to act on his own authority rather than observe the standard bureaucratic procedures.[12] It appears that Yü Ch'üeh possessed a strong commitment to the observance of professional Confucian norms, consistently observing them whenever they happened to conflict with bureaucratic demands or careerist pressures.

As in Yü-yao, fiscal reform in Chin-hua could not be conducted entirely through the existing corps of officials. Some special appointees had to be brought in from outside. One of these was Yeh Ch'en (Yeh Bayan,[m] d. 1362), magistrate of Ch'ing-t'ien[n] county in neighboring Ch'u-chou[o] prefecture. Yeh was chosen by Yü Ch'üeh to assist in the reform on the basis of his outstanding career record, one that showed an active concern with the relief of tax abuses, the suppression of banditry and villainry, and the question of local moral improvement. Yeh's family was one in which Confucian study was traditional, but the biographical accounts emphasize his official activities rather than his learning. As magistrate in Ch'ing-t'ien, a place "known to be hard to rule," he "realized that government could not transform the people unless enlightened studies were cultivated," and as soon as he took up his post he built a "Hall for Discriminating Social Relationships" (*Ming-lun t'ang*)[p] and a "Studio for Achieving Lofty Enlightenment" (*Chi-kao-ming hsüan*).[q] "Ceremoniously he engaged outstanding *shih* as expositors of the Six Classics, and set aside thirty more *mou* of fields for student stipends. Twice a month, when the students visited the Confucian temple, Yeh would put on formal wear and join them in the obeisances. Then he would go to the lecture hall and expound earnestly upon the doctrine of the five cardinal relationships."[13] Yeh Ch'en's task in the 1350 reform was to supervise operations in two Chin-hua counties. His further career will be noted below; he was one of the prominent local men who joined the rising Ming movement in 1359-1360.[14]

In an inscription commemorating the reform, Yü Ch'üeh wrote that the Che-tung region

> lacks either extremely rich or extremely poor families. Those who live in its hills and valleys typically own one *mou* of residential property and ten *mou* of fields which have passed down from father to son over many generations. The soil is poor, so the little people are conscientious and hard-working while the gentlemen are simple and frugal and devoted to the classics. It is nothing like the Yangtze Delta region, where people build large estates and act dictatorially, where the great families have a yearly income of millions of *hu* of grain while the little people have nothing at all.[15]

The misallocation of service levies in Chin-hua was attributed by Wang Wei (1323–1374) to the failure of the local governments to keep their registers abreast of changes in the patterns of landowning. Land in the prefecture was fiscally divided into units called *tu*.[r] The unreformed system assessed taxes on the *tu*, but allocated service levies by household, such that each landowning household within a *tu* bore a service assessment roughly equal to its holdings. By contriving to own parcels of land scattered over a number of *tu*, the rich (*fu-min*)[s] benefited unfairly, as their services were assessed only on the basis of their holdings in one *tu*, presumably the one where their homes were located. Further, the rich also reduced their service obligations (within the one *tu*) by falsely dividing their holdings among their kin, or by paying nominal rent to persons in the city or in another county, thus in effect claiming tenant status. As a result of this, poor or marginal landowners, with all their holdings in a single *tu*, were suffering ruin from having to bear a disproportionate share of the service burden.[16] According to Yü Ch'üeh,

> those who rendered services to the government were invariably marginal (*lü-tso*)[t] people. The rich owned fields but did not render services. In the worst cases,

they did not even pay taxes. At the end of each year, many [on service duty as] rural tax collectors (*pao-cheng*)ᵘ had to borrow to make up the deficit, and so went bankrupt. Thus although the fields were nearly equal [as to tax assessment], the service levies were unequal.[17]

The reformers remedied this problem by having all landowners present statements of the property they owned. Then the rural tax collector and his assistants in each *tu* made a separate investigation of the ownership of each land parcel. Data from these two sources were then compared with the information on the old registers. Finally, three new sets of registers were drawn up: (1) the "running water" or "fish-scale" maps of owned land and assessed tax; (2) a name list of taxpayers with their assessments; and (3) the "rat-tail" registers, listing taxpayers in descending order of assessed taxes, on the basis of which the service levies were proportionally reallocated. Triplicate copies were made of each register, one each for the circuit, prefecture, and county. Certificates of verified ownership (*wu-yu*) were issued to the landowners, and henceforth service obligations had to accompany any sale or transfer of land. Officially, the heaviest services were police duties; the medium were tax-collecting duties, and the easiest duties were porters and orderlies. Those too poor to serve in any of these functions were to pay a tax in cash. A final prefectural total of 2.6 million *mou* of land was thus assessed, with 12,668 individuals listed for service duties. Formerly obligated individuals who were relieved of obligations numbered 4,300; newly obligated individuals numbered 3,460. Service levies were imposed on all owned land regardless of location, except that the duties of rural tax collection (the *pao-cheng*, and his two aides, or *chu-shou*)ᵛ were imposed upon the largest landowners in each *tu* whose holdings were confined there. This arrangement in effect placed rural tax-collection as a medium-level service duty upon the shoulders of the middle-income landowners. As a result of the reform, "the rich were not harmed and the poor gained some respite. From this, there was no more distress over the unequal distribution of service obligations."[18]

The Chin-hua reform was by all indications fully supported by the local Confucian elites. Wang Wei, a local writer, composed one of the inscriptions describing the reform. Lü P'u, a Confucian teacher in his native Yung-k'ang county, wrote to the official who had been dispatched to Yung-k'ang to supervise the reform, urging him to carry out his task thoroughly and conscientiously. Lü P'u indicated that when registers were allowed to fall out of date, the newly rich gained an unfair advantage over the newly impoverished, who continued to be liable for the heavy service duties calculated upon the landholdings of their more prosperous days.[19] The reformers also undertook a few measures designed to please ·the local Confucians. In P'u-chiang county, for example, the officials restored the local Confucian schools and temples, and contributed funds toward the publication of the works of Liu Kuan (1270–1342),[w] an outstanding writer and native son.[20]

However, in contrast to what is known of Yü-yao, the fiscal reform in Chin-hua appears for some reason to have depended more upon coercion than popular enthusiasm. When local landowners were asked to submit declarations of their holdings, they were grouped by the authorities into mutual security units (*pao-chia*),[x] with unit members held collectively punishable for any false statement.[21] "The common people and the Taoist and Buddhist clergies were given a month in which to make their property declarations. If they failed to declare or declared falsely, then their fields were to be confiscated."[22] But by forcing the landowners to police each other, the reform bureaucrats were able to grant them one important concession: the yamen clerks and runners were henceforth confined to their urban locations, and were forbidden to enter the rural areas and disturb the population as they had done previously. Communications between the county yamens and the rural people were henceforth to be conducted solely through the rural tax collectors.[23]

Agitation for fiscal equalization in Lung-ch'üan[y] county (Ch'u-chou prefecture) makes an extraordinary appendix to the story of reform in Chin-hua. It is extraordinary because Ch'u-chou prefecture was not an official target of reform, and Lung-ch'üan county did not border directly upon any part of Chin-hua. It was geographically isolated, and its reform experience was more dependent upon Confucian voluntary action than reform elsewhere.

The principal Confucian reform leader in Lung-ch'üan was a private teacher by the name of Wang I (1303–1354), a man of humble origins and strong convictions. Halting in speech and physically small, Wang I was born into a Lung-ch'üan peasant family. He first began studying the classics while tending his family's oxen. It is related that one day his father sent him to grind rice at a mill, and Wang I, absorbed in reading, forgot his task and ruined all the rice. When his father threatened to evict him, an understanding uncle explained that the boy was not suited for farmwork and should be encouraged to study instead. The uncle moved Wang I into town and there funded his education. Wang I eventually came to earn his living as a private tutor in the classics.[24]

The nature of Wang I's professed commitment to the Confucian body of knowledge and service ideal may be detected in some statements made by and about him. He rejected the *T'ai-chi-t'u shuo* (Diagram of the Supreme Ultimate Explained), a seminal but controversial Neo-Confucian tract by Chou Tun-i (1017-1073),[z] as too constrictive. "The human mind," he wrote, "is of equal size with Heaven and Earth. How can it be confined within this one book?" Yet for the most part, Wang I clung fast to the core concepts of Chu Hsi Neo-Confucianism. Thus he wrote that meditative practice, by "preserving the mind and nourishing the nature," brought one into wordless union with the cosmos and facilitated the absorption of its eternal principles. He demanded of his students that they actualize these principles in their everyday behavior (*kung-hsing shih-chien*).[aa] When the nature of the "original mind" is made clear, then "self-interest and desire disappear," and one can act on the basis of what is right and not merely advantageous.[25] Wang I came to be so revered a figure that "even the stupid men and women of the mountain areas feared and admired him, and reformed their minds so as to follow the good." His belief that the "rich," unless instructed by forceful Confucian teachers, would inevitably ruin themselves through excess and arrogance, is an interesting clue to the socio-moral aspects of reform in Lung-ch'üan.[26]

Around 1335, Wang I and his student Hu Ch'en (see later; he was prominent in the Ming founding) journeyed to the Yüan capital. There Wang I met with and secured the personal endorsements of the high Confucian literati of the day. One of them wrote an inscription for Wang I's private studio. Later on, Wang I never hesitated to make use of extralocal connections such as these to pressure Yüan officials in the directions he desired.[27] Without such evidence of close informal relations with the leaders of his profession, it is doubtful whether Wang I could have succeeded as well as he seems to have done with his local reform work.

This work began with a food shortage, probably in the late 1340s. To solve it, Wang I persuaded the local officials of Lung-ch'üan to assess the incomes of the rich and impose graded demands for grain loans upon them. In essence this was a question of distributive justice, exactly the issue at the heart of the fiscal reform undertaken in Chin-hua in 1350. Owing largely to Wang I's voluntary efforts, fiscal reform was also launched in Lung-ch'üan in 1350. Wang made personal contact with Yü Ch'üeh about the matter, and at length Yeh Ch'en was dispatched to Lung-ch'üan to supervise the equitable reassignment of the service levy. No statistics about this are available. That such a reform was attempted is, however, evident from Wang I's own later complaint that owing to their anger at the fiscal reapportionments, the "rich" refused to contribute to a fund-raising drive whose purpose was to build a personal library for him.[28]

In the reform, Yeh Ch'en and Wang I gained needed cooperation from the Lung-ch'üan assistant magistrate, a Central Asian named Chiu-chu.[ab] When Chiu-chu left Lung-ch'üan for reassignment, Wang wrote him a memorandum which detailed the highlights of his recent service. The memorandum shows that Wang tended to view local politics in polarized extremes. He stated that through much of the Yüan period, Lung-ch'üan had suffered iniquity and oppression. Though a small county, it had swarmed with yamen underlings—lictors who, "holding their cudgels, massed themselves like a forest in front of the country offices"; and foot runners who, with their official tallies, "spread out like chesspieces through the countryside." He related how litigation had increased, right and wrong were obscured, with accusers and accused unequal in their ability to pay legal costs. Thanks to outdated or false assessments, powerful families escaped their service obligations and unloaded the burden upon the poor.

In Wang's view, the polarization of Lung-ch'üan politics featured on one side an "evil and devious clique" of the rich and powerful, the yamen underlings, and many of the local officials. The officials looked on the public at large as so much "fish and meat." They "sucked the people's fat and blood," the milder ones going about this business like "mosquitoes," the harsher ones like "ravenous beasts." On the other side, victims of this awful alliance, were the "people" (*min*).[ac] "The people," wrote Wang, "looked on the officials as enemies. They cursed them in their homes and in the streets, only fearing that they might not act fast enough to gather a mob and drive them out. This mutual hatred between government and people was most regrettable."

Prompted by Wang, Chiu-chu took action. He dismissed the excess yamen underlings, straightened out the litigation, and imposed a new regime of fiscal equalization. Then the evil party, "hating the fact that they were unable to prevail," brought suit against Chiu-chu. Yet in the trial that was held, "tens and hundreds of people, from the literati elite down to peasants and artisans, from merchants to Buddhist and Taoist clergy, came long distances to testify on Chiu-chu's behalf." As a result, the censorial authorities who heard the case dismissed the suit and arrested the plaintiffs for having brought false charges. Through the ordeal, Chiu-chu showed he had "won the people's minds," and the "people," for their part, exhibited an admirable impartiality in their "love of good and hatred of evil," Chiu-chu had acted not for selfish ends, but on the basis of principle, owing to the "excellence of his natural endowments."[29]

In sum, fiscal reforms over the years 1342–1350, involving three South China prefectures in whole or in part, were in no immediate sense advantageous to the Yüan state. They certainly did not result in increased tax revenues, and in Chin-hua prefecture, they even led to a net loss in the total population subject to the service levy. The fatiguing, nerve-wracking efforts devoted to reform by its principals were in no way commensurate with the fiscal returns to the state that the reform yielded. Local Confucians joined with Confucian-minded officials to bring about a fiscal change whose aim and result, remote from any idea of profiting the state or even ensuring a more efficient method of collection, instead reflected an ideal that obligations must be justly apportioned among the people according to their ability to render them, as ascertained by precise, objective, and up-to-date statistical investigations. Aside from the smaller landowners, the main beneficiaries of these reforms appear to have been the same activist Confucian elements who directed or assisted in them. Their rewards were collected at least in the coin of enhanced professional prestige. They were otherwise obscure men whose meritorious acts were publicized by themselves and by other Confucian writers, and as a result they became more widely known and respected, and, ultimately, more influential as Confucian professionals. This was clearly the case with Wang I.

The problem now turns to an assessment of the effects of the late Yüan popular rebellions and dynastic breakdown of 1352 and after upon conditions in the same three contiguous prefectures of Shao-hsing, Chin-hua, and Ch'u-chou, this time also including in the discussion the county of Tz'u-ch'i, administratively subordinate to Ning-po but sharing a boundary on the west with Yü-yao. From this discussion there should emerge some important conclusions about Confucian professionalism, popular mobilization, and local-level political centralization.

Shao-hsing prefecture lay along the south shore of Hangchow Bay, close to the main line of attack taken by the rampaging Red Turban rebels, whose main objective was the provincial capital to the northwest. On August 19, 1352, some of the rebels stormed the undefended city of Shao-hsing and set fire to the government offices and the homes of the wealthy. Some 15,000 familes were reported to have fled, only to find the countryside full of lawless elements and even more dangerous than the city. The Che-tung Branch Surveillance Office, a censorial body with headquarters in the city, put Assistant Surveillance Commissioner Tuman Temür[ad] in charge of restoring order. Tuman Temür hurriedly recruited an army of "people's braves" (*i-yung min-ting*)[ae] and resettled the refugees. He built a fifteen-mile defense wall around the city, laying costs on the local households according to their income, and hiring landless men as laborers.[30] Shao-hsing remained secure until 1355, when mercenaries of the Miao tribe, nominally under the command of the Kiangche provincial governor, raided the city for reasons of their own. The Shaohsing urban administrator, Mai-li-ku-ssu, organized a posse and discouraged further incursions from the unruly Miao tribesmen.

By 1355, the main cast of characters involved in the 1342 fiscal reforms had departed from the scene. Some new faces must be introduced. Mai-li-ku-ssu (Marcus?), known *more sinico* as Mai (or Wu) Shan-ch'ing,[af] a man of Tangut ancestry, was one of these.[31] His family lived in the Yangtze Delta area, and is described as so "poor" that he had to make a living as a tutor in order to support his mother. In 1354 he passed the civil service examinations at the *chin-shih* level, and was then assigned to his post as Shao-hsing urban administrator.

It is not irrelevant to an understanding of professionalization and centralization to relate what contemporary writers have to say about Mai Shan-ch'ing, a man who soon became a hero and martyr to the cause. He is described as a skiller fighter, a kind of bravo to whom classical learning came late, something he undertook when he realized that while expert fighting merely created more opponents, the "study of the sages and worthies" had no opposition and was thus a more certain route to success in life.[32] He was no captive to organizational routine. "Though by nature very filial, he was unrestrained and fond of raillery, and many famous men consorted with him" wrote T'ao Tsung-i (c.1316–c.1402). He was given to loud feasting and banqueting, and "when his official superiors happened to arrive at his gate on such occasions, he would completely ignore them." On duty, he courted popular sympathy at the expense of smooth relations with his official superiors. "He opposed his superiors straightforwardly and won the minds of the masses," wrote Tai Liang (1317–1383).[33]

When Nanking fell to the rebel forces of the future Ming founder in 1356, the offices of the Kiangnan Branch Censorate, with jurisdiction over all of South China, were removed from that city to Shao-hsing. Mai Shan-ch'ing was taken on as an official by the Branch Censorate, and he proceeded to recruit and train a force of 2,000 braves whom he styled the "Resolutes" (kuo-i chün).[ag] These men were used mainly for defense, although on one occasion they helped the Ch'u-chou forces of Shih-mo I-sum (d.1360) in an attack on "bandits" in neighboring Chin-hua prefecture.[34] Mai's growing reputation as a loyalist defender drew numbers of aspiring shih into his service as staff men and advisors, and his efforts are said by Tai Liang to have inspired further antiregionalist, pro-Yüan movements in Yü-yao and Tz'u-ch'i[ah] directly to the east.[35]

Detailed information bearing on the problem of professionalism reform, and centralization in Tz'u-ch'i county is available, and the case deserves some close scrutiny. It may be noted that, unlike the earlier reform localities, Tz'u-ch'i was a rather affluent place. This fact may in part explain why its reform history began only later, in 1356, when the integrity of the Yüan realm had been severely shattered in the aftermath of the Red Turban rebellions.

The reform in administration Tz'u-ch'i was headed by its magistrate, Ch'en Lin (1312–1368).[ai] Ch'en's origins were obscure. His ancestors had achieved modest official prominence in the tenth century, but his immediate forebears held no office, and his father simply served as a clerk in the Maritime Trade Superintendency in Ch'üan-chou (modern Fukien). Though non-Chinese, Mai Shan-ch'ing was of similar background in that his father too was the first of his line to hold even some kind of low official position. Like Mai, Ch'en Lin is also described as filially pious, even to the extent of cutting his flesh to feed his ailing father. After his father died, Ch'en yielded his share of the estate to his brothers and sisters and as a result became "extremely poor." He took a job as a county clerk, where despite his low status he dared to argue with his superiors. In 1354 he achieved the *chin-shih* degree, not on the basis of learning or literary talent, but explicitly in recognition of his willingness to express forthright opinions. Thus both he and Mai Shan-ch'ing shared a distaste for acquisitiveness and an impatience with the deferential observances usually performed by those in organizations who seek above all to protect their careers and enhance their incomes.

Appointed magistrate in Tz'u-ch'i after winning his degree, Ch'en Lin carried out an important series of reforms. These included a fiscal reform that followed generally the guidelines laid down in Shao-hsing and Yü-yao in 1342, and ended in an "equitable" reassessment of burdens. However, he achieved this reform by suppressing the yamen clerks and the powerful landowners (*hao-yu*)[aj] who opposed it. "To put an end to the abuses of the clerks, he visited the worthy resident sojourners (*yü-kung*)[ak] and the native elite (*shih ta-fu*)[al] for consultations. He also set up an empty cylinder at the local school, urging any commoner who had anything to say to write it and put it in anonymously. Thus he came to know all about the large and small affairs of the county, and the clerks were completely overawed."[36] To outflank the *hao-yu*, he recruited a team of twenty local *shih* of "talent" to check and rank all property holdings and post lists of these on the main roads. On this basis all obligations were reallocated, and "not the smallest fraction was finessed." Ch'en Lin also delegated the task of adjudicating disputes to the rural officers (*hsiang-cheng*),[am] a move that is said to have produced greater social solidarity than had ever existed before in the Yüan period. "Because a cooperative hierarchy of rural officers was established, matters had to come into the open, with the result that the rural thieves all returned what they had stolen. Those who had seized the women and property of others confessed and renovated themselves. All kinfolk who had been unable to get along with each other repented and reformed their behavior. The elders asserted that since the founding of the dynasty, no one else had been able to achieve anything like this."[37] Ch'en also rebuilt the county Confucian school, and imported two well-known teachers especially for it.[38]

Yet it is important to note that reform in Tz'u-ch'i was not something simply imposed by Ch'en Lin. Rather, the main thrust for reform, together with its centralizing implications that will be discussed momentarily, came from within Tz'u-ch'i society itself. Ch'en Lin depended heavily upon the advice of the local Confucian community, and served as the executor of a systematic reform program that was not actually of his own devising.

Ch'en Lin's advisors consisted of a small group of local Confucians who shared a strong belief in the "idealist" philosophy originally developed by Lu Hsiang-shan (Lu Chiu-yüan 1139–1193).[an] The group actively cultivated the Lu shcool's combination of sudden mystic illumination and everyday experience in practical affairs. Wu Ssu-tao listed himself and eight others as members.[39] Wu acknowledged that the group's activities generated controversy in Tz'u-ch'i. Several of its members later became enthusiastic supporters of the Ming founder. Its membership and outlook deserve some inspection.

The group included Chao Chieh, Wang Yüeh, Hsiang Shou, Wang Huan, Yang Jui, Chou Chien (1307–1363), together with Wu Ssu-tao and his older brother Wu Pen-liang (d. 1372).[ao] The first two were related by marriage. Yang Jui was a descendant of Yang Chien (c. 1169),[ap] a famous disciple of Lu Hsiang-shan, and the first to propagate the Lu teachings in Tz'u-ch'i. Chao Chieh was a descendant of the Sung imperial lineage; a forebear, Chao Te-yüan (d. 1260),[aq] had been a convert of Yang Chien's.[40] Thus some of the members enjoyed a distinguished ancestry. However, the Wu brothers were not so well favored and were poor as well, while Chou Chien's family, though rich, was otherwise undistinguished. Whatever common economic or social characteristics may have lent cohension to this circle, they cannot be rigidly specific. Primarily it was a set of shared attitudes that contributed to the group's formation.

An important point of agreement among them was an "elitist" sense of mission and an undisguised disdain for the vulgar materialism of the common run of mankind. Thus it is related that Hsiang Shou refused to take the civil service examinations, mainly on the grounds that because his ancestors had been Sung officials, it would be "shameful" for him to want to serve the Yüan.[41] Chou Chien refused the examination or commercial paths to success, not out of loyalism, but rather as an act of personal preference.[42] Chao Chieh, the informal leader of the group, began but later abandoned his study for the examinations. "This ladder to wealth and status is of no benefit to body and mind," he is reported as having said. 'I would like to serve in office, but as a descendant of the Sung imperial house I should not. Besides, the times are not right for carrying out the Way." [43] Wu Pen-liang refused a "rich" lineage's offer to adopt him as its principal heir. A former clerk and later a struggling private teacher, he renonuced his intent to try the examinations after having been accepted into Chao Chieh's circle. [44]

Admittance to the circle required an apparently genuine act of "conversion" to the Lu-Yang mystical philosophy. Chao Chieh, as leader, seems to have been the first to achieve the breakthrough to transcendence. "After having read the works of Yang Chien, he examined himself in reverent silence and came to the insight that the myraid phenomena, despite their complexity, converged into a single substance. This was the meaning [of Confucius' maxim that] there was but a single [thread] that bound together the Way." [45] After a period of instruction under Chao and Wang Yüeh and others, Wu Pen-liang "suddenly saw that Heaven, Earth, and the Myriad Things, and being and nonbeing were one substance ($t'i$), [ar] and that the clouds, the rain, and the dew were all the self. His joy was inexpressible." [46] Wang Yüeh and Chao Chieh also guided Chou Chien to the mystic vision. Acting on Chao's advice that the Way was to be found by "looking inward" (*fan-kuan*), [as] Chou sat silently until his thoughts and intentions dissolved, and he suddenly saw that "Heaven, Earth, and the Myriad Things constituted one substance; he was unaware that his self was his self, and there was brightness all over the room." As evidence of his new-found insight, Chou replied to his teachers in a way that signalled his grasp of the interpenetration of all phenomena. Asked who caused the red blossoms in a vase to appear alongside green leaves and twigs, Chou answered: "I did." Asked whether candlelight was caused by the candle or the flame, Chou stated that it was neither of those, but rather the "transformation" (*pien-hua*)[at] of the flowers in the vase. These responses satisfied Chao and Wang that Chou Chien had indeed achieved the "end result of looking inward." [47]

The mystical substance was not without its practical applications (*yung*). [au] In the words of Wu Ssu-tao, "the lessons of the Way lie in what is common and everyday." Applied in the world, the mystic vision came out as "true experience" (*chen-shih chien-lü*), [av] encompassing honesty, charity, and material self-denial. [48] Thus Yang Jui was "very frank and open by nature; he was so fond of giving that he had barely enough to feed and clothe himself. Any surplus he would donate for the relief of the poor. But he would never give or take anything unless it was completely right to so do." [49] Owing to his wealth, Chou Chien had to handle such unpaid service obligations as weapons manufacture and the shipping of grain taxes. These duties he reportedly carried out faithfully; and, unlike many, he ignored opportunities for making illicit profits. He also rescued dying beggars, paid bribes to release the innocent from prison, and persuaded his older brother to issue the family's grain reserves to the starving. "Grain is Heaven's commodity" and it should, he said, be given to "Heaven's famished people."[50]

The mysticism and charity cultivated by the group also had certain connections to Confucian political theory. Chao Chieh "once said that Confucius based his doctrines on the Way, and never once let his mind forget the realm. And although Chao lived in retirement, from time to time he showed by his demeanor how he grieved for the world." Just after his mystical enlightenment, Chao resolved all his doubts and affirmed that "the rule of the Three Dynasties [of antiquity] could be restored, and the theories of the Hundred Schools unified."[51] The restoration of antiquity did not mean decentralization. Wu Ssu-tao maintained that there was only one bureaucratic system in antiquity, not several; it was the Son of Heaven who appointed all the officials, and no regional lord could consider himself in any way independent of the Son of Heaven.[52] Hsiang Shou is known to have composed a treatise on government that was "based in the Three Dynasties and ignored the Han and T'ang [as models]." He especially emphasized the principle: "If a man in office is disloyal to his ruler and fails to offer his life in time of peril, then he has learned nothing worth learning."[53]

These universalistic moral and political concerns (of the Neo-Confucians, not limited to the Lu school) were put into effect in the limited milieu of Tz'u-ch'i county with the appointment of Ch'en Lin as magistrate in 1356. The biography of Chao Chieh has it that Ch'en submitted to him as a pupil to his master, and by receiving Chao's instructions, "won the minds of the people of Tz'u-ch'i."[54] Chao drew up written guidelines for Ch'en to observe in his official capacity. He explained that in "an age of decline" it was impossible for a magistrate to rule effectively unless he consulted daily with "those men in retirement who thoroughly understand past and present." They should meet in the county Confucian school and there "discuss successes and failure in policy, and good and evil in personalities; verify all the data that appear in the registers, and make all decisions on the basis of impartial opinion (kung-i)."[aw]

The notion of impartiality was absolutely crucial to the whole approach of Chao Chieh's group to political action. The implementation of administrative impartiality began with the leading official himself, in this case Ch'en Lin. According to Chao Chieh, there were mechanisms the official might use in order to develop impartiality, but the efficacy of these mechanisms depended upon the official's *psychological* capacity to listen to advice and publicly acknowledge his errors. "What you should do now," advised Chao, "is set up a register for the recording of your errors. You should place a sealed wooden box at the school and ask all your aides and functionaries plus the rural headmen and the Confucians (*ju*),[ax] Buddhists, and Taoists who have impartial opinions to state, to write these down, seal them confidentially, and put them in the box. Every five days open the box, and have the most impartial and least selfish people check through [the statements]. Where real errors [have been uncovered], you must resolutely correct them. Face the crowd, blame yourself, and apologize. Then go ahead and prosecute the crimes of the functionaries [named in the statements]."[55]

Chao Chieh went on to insist that the magistrate must disentangle himself from his clerks because these men were either underpaid or not paid at all, and thus had no choice but to use fraud and corruption in order to survive. To get around these men, the magistrate had to open channels of communication with the "loyal and upright" in the general population. Even here, however, the magistrate had to be careful to consult widely and not restrict his communications to any single individual. "Even a loyal and upright man may not speak fully, out of a desire to avoid suspicion or possibly harmful consequences. So you must consult among the many and not get everything from one source."[56] In addition, the magistrate should bring outsiders directly into the governing process. Rural headmen who "know decorum and can read characters" must be courteously invited to the yamen by half-monthly rota, be provided with lodgings, and be assembled daily for their opinions on pending decisions. If the decisions concerned matters the headmen didn't understand, then the magistrate should have them consult with others who were knowledgeable. Other problems arose in connection with impartiality in policy enforcement. The clerks, again owing to their inadequate incomes, would of course "outwardly conform to impartial opinion while inwardly harboring selfish desires." It was all too easy for the magistrate to hear them assent to orders and simply assume their subsequent compliance. He had in every case to check to see that they in fact did what they were told to do.

All this would go more smoothly if magistrate Ch'en Lin wore his cap and gown straight and put on a stern facial expression. Not only would the clerks fear and respect him, but such a posture would also affect favorably his own mentailty, making it "calm and bright" (*ching-ming*),[ay] and "able to discern right and wrong." Likewise noise and confusion should be banished from the yamen, and punishment applied to clerks and litigants who failed to observe decorum. As to his relationships above and below, Chao Chieh warned Ch'en that "if you follow superiors and go along with custom the Way is ruined; while if you disobey superiors and offend custom you put yourself in peril. To be disloyal and yet ingratiating is definitely wrong, but to be disrespectful and arrogant is also wrong."[57]

The scale of values implied here seems clear. Given the current "age of decline," Chao Chieh would have Ch'en Lin become, if necessary, an autonomous political actor, at war against both the official hierarchy and local "custom," even if this jeopardized his own safety. Rather that, than have the Way perish. Disrespect for superiors and arrogance toward inferiors were preferable to self-serving ingratiation. The magistrate's autonomy was of course not absolute, but contingent upon the persistence of improper external constraints.

The aim of this political reorientation in Tz'u-ch'i was to mobilize the public behind fiscal, social, and moral reform. Fiscal reform has been mentioned. The purpose of socio-moral reform was to erase the particularism and selfishness that led to fiscal inequity. Chao advised that socio-moral reform was possible because "the Heavenly order is imperishable in men's minds." Local government must "investigate every rural district and find out who maintains correct human relations and who does not," and draw up lists of names. The refractory were to be reprimanded first by district headmen, then by higher-level township headmen, and if necessary, finally by the school officials. "Those who fail to be influenced by this will be shamed by being put on forced labor, and if they persist in their errors, they will be given the extreme penalty, on the idea that the excution of one is a lesson to the many." The names of the good were to be recorded in a special "Register for Extolling the Good." Through this means, the public could be mobilized in the cause of its own ethical regeneration and physical security. "If we are really successful in bringing about a revival of the natural affections," concluded Chao, "[the repercussions] will hardly be confined to this one country. Because all this is where the good conscience (liang-hsin)[az] has its origin, there will be those elsewhere in the world who will react similarly. This is of the essence of the Way."[58]

In sum, Chao Chieh and Ch'en Lin tried to develop in Tz'u-ch'i what might be termed a "centralized" order at the local level, which is less a contradiction in terms than it may appear. According to the thinking of the Tz'u-ch'i reformers, political order in a country-level unit of government might take either of two opposing forms. One form was made up of a passive magistracy and an active clerical corps, which dealt with the public through informal, covert, and dyadic (noncollective) relationships. This form was corrupt, in that administration was conducted in particularistic ways, whereby certain individuals or families offered bribes or other considerations in return for governmental decisions favorable to them.[59] In its informal, uninstitutionalized mode of operation, this form may be styled "decentralized." It not only offended professional Confucian values, but it also violated the formal norms of bureaucratic office. (It may have conferred latent economic or other benefits on Tz'u-ch'i society, but this factor, if operative, was ignored in the contemporary argument).

The "centralized" form of local government, by contrast, placed initiative, control, and responsibility in the hands of its leading official, the magistrate. Following "impartial" professional advice at every step, the magistrate moved to curtail the independence of the clerical apparatus, holding it strictly accountable for its every act (without, however, providing adequate pay or any other material incentive for good behavior). The magistrate and his advisors then identified a collective public, which was that presumed majority of the population that for moral or financial reasons did not enjoy furtive and corrupt relations with the yamen clerks, or that had such relations but could be weaned from them. In order to mobilize this hitherto latent public, the magistrate set up channels of communication with it, established within it a system of anonymous spying and reporting, set up over it a controlling hierarchy of rural officers, and demanded that these officers take a formal consultative role in the making of country-level decisions. (An attempt was made to implement many of these devices on a national scale in the early Ming).

The centralization of local political control was in turn directly related to the exigencies of socio-moral reform. The rehabilitation or suppression of greedy or criminal elements in the local environment could only occur with the help of publicity, exposure, and open accountability. A crucial attribute of political centralization, in the sense used here, is precisely its relative openness and visibility, and its abhorrence of the clandestine mode that characterizes its unreformed opposite. One great weakness in the position of an entrenched antireform opposition is the inability of its goals and procedures to withstand the full light of public disclosure. Reformers, by contrast, thrive on publicity and can easily make use of the national value system as a weapon in their fight against "selfish" local interests. If reform in fourteenth-century rural China and twentieth-century urban America may be compared, then one can see that local reformers move against the opposition by (1) making political power publicly accountable; (2) placing that power in the hands of one or a few visible public officials; and (3) using some sort of "populist" device to validate the power centralization that has taken place, with the understanding that the "people" as a collectivity will not develop interests contrary to those of the reformers.[60]

While centralization and reform as complementary developments may stay confined to some particular locale in fact, in theory they must always transcend any such limitation and try to encourage similar events on a larger national scale. The universalistic values that sustain reform inevitably demand this. Local reform can never be *simply* local. Although a modern general theory of reform seems to be lacking, it may be suggested that the more local reform in one place proceeds apace with local reform in other places, the easier it becomes for reform leaders to assert supralocal values, and assert them convincingly. Communication among reforming elites in different locations also makes it easier to discover and implement the relevant elements of the supralocal value system. If local efforts at reform somehow succeed in encouraging national efforts at the same, then it further becomes possible for reformers at the national level to intervene in those localities whose continued refusal or failure to reform threatens the reform gains made elsewhere. (Something close to this logic seems to have worked itself out with the establishment of the Ming Dynasty in 1368).

At any rate, it is clear that the Tz'u-ch'i reformers never intended that their work should stay confined within the country boundaries. First, several writers point out that Ch'en Lin in Tz'u-ch'i and Tügel [ba] (a pro-reform assistant magistrate in neighboring Yü-yao) were inspired by the example Mai Shan-ch'ing was setting in Shao-hsing. Tai Liang observed that "these three men formed the three corners of a strategic envelopment that greatly lifted spirits in the Southeast."[61] Second, the Tz'u-ch'i reformers never appealed to Tz'u-ch'i customs or traditions, but to a universalistic ideal of political organization (the Three Dynasties of antiquity) and to a brand of Confucian thought that at the psychological level insisted upon the mutual unboundedness of phenomena. As was noted above, Chao Chieh stated that the Tz'u-ch'i reforms would inevitably inspire emulation elsewhere, because they were rooted in and appealed to that uniformity in the human psychic makeup known as the "good conscience." Everywhere, those of "good conscience" were asked to struggle against the particularistic interests that, far from being swallowed forgivingly into the undifferentiated cosmic unity, were taken to be the greatest enemies of that unity. Ming T'ai-tsu (r. 1368–1398) is later said to have asked Wang Huan, one of the members of the circle, what it was he "liked and hated in his local area." Wang Huan replied: "In my local area it is the good that I like and the evil that I hate."[62] The circle allowed no compromise here.

The fate of the reforming localities of Shao-hsing, Yü-yao, and Tz'u-ch'i was not a happy one in the short run. From 1356, the loyalist regional satraps Chang Shih-ch'eng (1321–1367)[bb] and Fan Kuo-chen (1319/20–1374)[bc] gradually absorbed more and more Kiangche territory. By 1359, the Che-tung region was partitioned among Chang, Fang, and the future Ming founder Chu Yüan-chang (T'ai-tsu, 1328–1398), and no more "centralizing" localities loyal to the Yüan remained in existence. The collapse of the reform movements yeilds, however, some further insights into the processes at work.

When the former salt-smuggler Chang Shih-ch'eng and his army entered the Yangtze Delta from the north in 1356, he was still in rebellion against the Yüan Dynasty. Accordingly, the court ordered that local defense militias be organized to resist him. In Shao-hsing, Mai Shan-ch'ing raised his army of "Resolutes," as was mentioned. In Tz'u-ch'i, Chao Chieh advised Ch'en Lin in the raising and training of a people's militia (i-min).[bd] Ch'en performed animal sacrifice to the gods, and assembled the militia leaders at a banquet at the Confucian school, where he "made a tearful oath to Heaven" and everyone pledged to serve loyally. Ch'en established a regular supply system and a network of personal operatives who saw to the "impartial" maintenance of discipline. The militia gave security to the countryside, eradicating a thieving gang of "evil youths" within the county limits, and capturing the chief of a band of raiders based outside. Ch'en's epitaph notes that "with this, the violent were destoryed and those wronged were avenged, and not a single stupid commoner broke the law anymore."[63] Ch'en used the militia against recalcitrant local elements who had eluded him before. "Two powerful and villainous lineages, the Su and the Ko, had used their advantage to seize the people's wealth. The Ch'en lineage had also acted in a very domineering way. These were all arrested and imprisoned."[64] Although the chronology is unclear, it may be that Ch'en Lin's fiscal and other reforms were implemented more or less concurrently with the formation of the militia. At any rate it is apparent that the level of popular mobilization represented by the formation of the militia afforded him a high degree of control over the countryside.

Not long after the beleaguered Yüan court ordered the formation of local militias, the possibility arose that Chang Shih-ch'eng and Fang Kuo-chen might accept accommodation into the existing dynastic order as regional governors. If they did, then the prospect of a long and difficult resistance could be avoided. Certain organs within the Yüan government backed the policy of accommodation. The Censorate, notably, broke with its earlier stance of support for local reform, and initiated contacts with Chang and Fang. As the Censorate swung in that direction, the local reformers found a new bureaucratic sponsor in the Branch Military Secretariat, a body under the control of the Kiangche provincial governor. Accordingly, Mai Shan-ch'ing (and other reform proponents, such as Shih-mo I-sun[be] in Ch'u-chou), formerly associated with the Censorate, were reassigned by the governor to the Branch Military Secretariat.

Because Shao-hsing remained the seat of the Kiangnan Branch Censorate, Mai's transfer to the Branch Military Secretariat, also with headquarters in that city, made Shao-hsing the arena of the sharpest possible conflict between the forces of "reform" and "accommodation" in South China. The Censorate with its army of 3,000 men made friendly overtures to Fang Kuo-chen and was ready to help him establish his power in the city. The Branch Military Secretariat, meanwhile, deployed its own army at Mai's direction on the Shao-hsing border and there skirmished with Fang's forces. On November 24, 1358, Mai was murdered by his bureaucratic opponent, the Censor-in-Chief. Shortly after that, Mai's army, in an act of revenge, dispersed the Censorate's army, and, rather than let the city fall to Fang, they invited Chang Shih-ch'eng to come occupy Shao-hsing instead. Thus one main center of reform fell under regionalist control.[65]

As for Yü-yao, another reforming locality, Tügel persisted until finally his opponents killed him. By 1358, Fang Kuo-chen took over and fortified the city against his rival Chang.[66] In Tz'u-ch'i, magistrate Ch'en Lin decided to avoid bloodshed and surrender peacefully to Fang Kuo-chen. Though urged otherwise by Wu Ssu-tao, he began to back away from the reforms he had so ardently pressed earlier, disbanding the militia and giving the clerks their freedom again. Tai Liang noted that while Mai Shan-ch'ing and Tügel were "careless" of superiors and so met violent deaths, Ch'en Lin proved adept at handling "powerful villains" and so escaped personal harm.[67] Wu Ssu-tao later became a Ming local official.

Upon the death of Fang Kuo-chen in 1374, the Ming government issued a retrospective indictment of his regime. Whatever its accuracy as to facts, it does provide a useful summation of what the "reformers" believed to be the essence of the antireform position. Here one had a nepotist, kin-based regime led by the "illiterate" Fang family, with Kuo-chen's brothers and nephew ruling various prefectures. "Adjudication and taxation were simply handled at whim. While in Wen-chou his nephew acted more or less legally, in T'ai-chou his brother just bought fields, built boats, and invested funds to enrich their families." Fang's advisors were one-time "local government clerks who had advanced through bribery and self-promotion, and had no deep thoughts or far-reaching plans."[68] Though nominally loyalist, the regime was committed to regional autonomy, and failed to devote itself to the welfare of the public collectivity.

Reactions in Chin-hua prefecture to the turmoil of the 1350s were different from those in Shao-hsing or Tz'u-ch'i. As was noted, the fiscal reform carried out there in 1350 did not provoke anything like the opposition that similar reform had done in Yü-yao. Moreover, the local officials who cooperated with Yü Ch'üeh in that reform were for the most part still serving in their positions at the time of the Red Turban uprising of 1352, and they had enough control of the situation to move rapidly and organize mutual security groups in the villages and so forestall rebel activity.[69] Officials rewalled the Chin-hua prefectural capital and expanded law-enforcement facilities; and, as Sung Lien (1310–1318) relates, in 1353 local officials built cells for the "mind-washing" (cho-hsin)[bf] of miscreants alongside the P'u-chiang[bg] county police station.[70] Looting and arson in the counties of I-wu, Wu-i, and P'u-chiang were swiftly stopped and failed to provoke serious anarchy.[71] With the exception of Yung-k'ang[bh] county, the landowners of Chin-hua for some reason did not organize themselves into militant armed camps (as happened almost everywhere in neighboring Ch'u-chou prefecture), and the influence of the loyalist warlord Fang Kuo-chen, which bore heavily on events in Tz'u-ch'i, Shao-hsing, and Ch'u-chou, never penetrated Chin-hua territory.

The relatively high level of social order in Chin-hua was complemented by a relatively high degree of solidarity among its officials. Unlike the case in Shao-hsing and Ch'u-chou, prefectural, county, and censorial officials cooperated fairly well in Chin-hua. Since formal government was able to play a dominating role, no "maverick" officials in the style of Mai Shan-ch'ing or Ch'en Lin emerged in Chin-hua, and likewise no voluntary leaders like Chao Chieh or Wang I arose from within the Confucian community to guide and influence the conduct of affairs. However, Chin-hua Confucian writers actively recorded local and regional events, and fervently supported the "reform" elements in Shao-hsing, Tz'u-ch'i, and Ch'u-chou. In fact it is to a great extent in the epitaphs and other commemorative pieces written by Chin-hua literati that one reads about affairs in those places. The Chin-hua literati did value such writing as one of the more important public services that the Confucian profession might perform.

To the south of Chin-hua lay Ch'u-chou prefecture, a scene of intense local conflict in the 1350s. It will be recalled that the fiscal reform of 1350 carried out in Lung-ch'üan county was socially divisive. In 1352, attacks by the Red Turban rebels upon Ch'u-chou exacerbated divisions, and once again the local Confucian teacher had a major part to play.

In 1352, the Che-tung censorial authorities sent Shih-mo I-sun, a hereditary military officer of Khitan ancestry, to Ch'u-chou to establish a military headquarters and coordinate local defenses against the Red Turbans. This task Shih-mo accomplished fairly rapidly. By early 1353, he stopped a rebel attack upon Lung-ch'üan and drove the rebels out of the countries on the Fukien side of the Ch'u-chou border. Shih-mo and the local notables who aided him celebrated their successful collaboration in

poems; and about a year later, Shih-mo returned east to his original post
to handle a new crisis there.

It so happened, however, that there had existed much friction between Shih-mo and his supporters and the regular local officials, who
were also responsible for local defense. This friction was serious enough
that Wang I, who sided with Shih-mo, saw at the root of it the same
cleavage between good and evil that had exhibited itself at the time of
the 1350 reform.

In the view of Wang I, the prefectural and county officials, the
yamen clerks, some landowners, and various *i-ping* [bi] or hired militia
constituted the side of evil. The Lung-ch'üan county officials hired un-
desirables as militia. These soldiers were "superfluous parasites," costly to
maintain, and requiring excessive economic and service support from the
public. The militia, wrote Wang, "scatter and flee when there is trouble,
and idly consume rations when things are quiet." He noted that a regiment of these men, commanded by the Ch'u-chou prefectural judge, was
shamefully routed when it tried to stop a rebel advance upon Lung-ch'üan,
and yet this regiment still put heavy demands on the officials, who in
turn made demands upon the people. He complained that the small villagers were angry at these high costs, and also at the fact that a court-
ordered tax reduction, designed to win support for the Yüan in the troubled conditions of the time, was being ignored by "stubborn and ignorant" rich landowners and local officials who continued to collect as usual.
These abuses, he concluded, ended only in forcing the people to become
rebels. [72]

The forces of good were made up of the censorial authorities, commander Shih-mo I-sun, other landowners (some of them Wan I's students), and their *hsiang-ping* [bj] (somtimes also termed *i-ping*) or "district"
troops. When Shih-mo came to Ch'u-chou in 1352, he ignored the local
officials and their militia and refused to cooperate with them. Instead he
listened attentively to Wang I's opinions on defense matters, and took
into his staff two students whom Wan I recommended to him: Chang I
(1314-1369) and Hu Ch'en (1314–1365). [bk] Chang and Hu were scions
of old and well-known lineages, but it is unknown whether they were in
fact poorer than the "rich commoners" on the opposite side that Wang I
so despised. However, an investigation of their family backgrounds and
those of other known adherents of their group does shed some light on
the nature of the moral-political division in Ch'u-chou.

The Chang were a very large lineage based in P'u-ch'eng county in Fukien. The main P'u-ch'eng lineage came into prominence in the tenth century and produced large numbers of officials and degree-holders in the Sung period. Chang I stemmed from a minor branch of this lineage, which was settled in Lung-ch'üan county. This branch became very wealthy in the Sung, but it produced very few officials, and none at all in Chang I's direct line of descent. The branch thus appears to have been dominated by "rich commoners." Chang I himself, under the guidance of his teacher Wang I, seems to have been the first to Confucianize the branch. As an organizer and commander of local militia under Shih-mo I-sun in 1352, Chang I achieved a level of influence unprecedented in his branch of the lineage. As soon as the early phase of fighting was over, he at once edited and published a genealogy, built and financed a charity school (which Shih-mo exempted from fiscal obligations), rebuilt and endowed the ancestral temple, established a charity graveyard, and joined his brothers in organizing a family commune with written rules for its operation. For himself, he built a hillside retreat.[73]

Hu Ch'en's lineage was, like Chang I's, established in Lung-ch'üan since early Northern Sung times, and produced several minor officials in the Sung and Yüan periods. None, however, ever achieved the *chin-shih* degree. After he and his teacher Wang I returned from their trip to the national capital in 1335, he set up a drug business in Lung-ch'üan. This he did on the grounds that he was too "poor and lowly" to have much influence, but could serve others through the medical arts. Wang I predicted of Hu Ch'en that because his "desires were shallow and his inclination to act upon principle deep," he might in future reach great eminence, provided that he worked to concentrate and unify his aims. Hu Ch'en gathered a loyal clientele through his drug business; and when the Red Turbans threatened Lung-ch'üan, he recruited "district troops" and built a hilltop stockade. Through Wang I's intercession, he attached himself and his men to Shih-mo.[74]

Among the other lineages who members sided with Shih-mo were the T'ang and the Chi. The T'ang were collateral descendants of the unpopular T'ang Ssu-t'ui,[bl] a high adherent of the notorious prime minister Ch'in Kuei (1090–1155)[bm] in the early Southern Sung period. In the early Yüan, one of his descendants established a "charitable estate" after the model of Fan Chung-yen (989–1052).[bn] His son, T'ang Ching (1299–1348),[bo] further expanded his family's activities into the field of

social philanthropy, providing free medical services, burial facilities, a
charity school, and local grain price equalization. He acted also as an
advocate for local interests before the state authorities. This legacy of
charity was said to account for the estate's escaping damage in the civil
troubles of the 1350s. T'ang Ching's nephew T'ang K'ai (1313–1365)[bp]
was friendly with Chang I and Hu Ch'en, and was made government
Confucian teacher in Lung-ch'üan by Shih-mo I-sun.[75]

The Chi family, descended from high-ranking Sung officials, was
mainly settled in Lung-ch'üan, but one branch of it lived in the Ch'u-
chou prefectural capital. A scion of this latter branch was Chi Jen-shou
(1302–1362),[bq] a failed *chin-shih* candidate, but nonetheless a locally
esteemed scholar and classics commentator. He was known and admired
by the fiscal reformer Yü Ch'üeh and, like T'ang K'ai, was friendly with
Liu Chi (1311–1375). During the civil troubles he served as a preceptor
in the charity school founded by T'ang Ching, and he joined the literary
circle that formed itself around Shih-mo I-sun. Chi Wen (1318–1377),[br]
a kinsman from Lung-ch'üan, was a militia organizer and an adherent of
Shih-mo's of equal status (according to Sung Lien) with Yeh Ch'en, Liu
Chi, and Chang I.[76]

What distinguished this group (which later abandoned the Yüan and
Shih-mo and joined the rising Ming state) from its local opposition? We
can never have the full story, because the opposition can be learned
about only through what their enemies said about them. As for Shih-
mo's adherents, there is some congruity of background in that the Liu of
Ch'ing-t'ien (Liu Chi's lineage) and the T'ang of Lung-ch'üan were both
descended from high dignitaries of the early Southern Sung who followed
the retrospectively condemned line of appeasement with the Jurchen invaders in the north. These unpleasant ancestral facts were widely publicized when the long-awaited Sung dynastic history was issued by the
Yüan court in 1345. As for the Chang and Chi, two representatives of
those lineages were officially branded as bandits and mutineers for their
attempt to rebel against the newly established Yüan authority in Ch'u-
chou in 1277, facts which were reemphasized many years later when a
temple to the local god who helped in their suppression was refurbished
and a commemorative inscription by Wei Su was emplaced upon it.[77]
The "conversion" of the leading representatives of these lineages to Confucian righteousness, to a new outlook of moral purism and zeal, was in
all cases of fairly recent origin. The "reform" group in Ch'u-chou thus

seems to have been composed in part of upwardly mobile lineages, possessing considerable wealth and long but blemished genealogies, and eager to acquire respectability and prestige through professionally guided action.

Wang I likened his cause to the righteous causes once championed by the Sung Confucian heroes Ssu-ma Kuang (1019–1086) and Chu Hsi; both were set upon by evil-minded detractors, who accused them of villainous cliquism and heterodoxy, but history in the long run had vindicated them.[78] In a letter to his student Chang I, Wang indicated that what the opposition lacked was a proper sense of hierarchy and what he elsewhere termed "principled motivations" (*t'ien-chi*).[bs] The local officials made petty calculations of private advantage and looked to their own safety; having gathered gangs of youths as militiamen, they took full control in the counties they held and ignored the orders of their superiors at the provincial level. To act thus, he said, was to deny the ruler-father, and to fail to behave as ministers and sons should. "If the local officials can treat their provincial superiors this way," he asked, "then why can't the ignorant masses treat the local officials in the same way?"[79]

Events in 1354 make clearer the nature of the ongoing internal conflict in Ch'u-chou. "Bandits" from Ch'ing-t'ien county, having burned and plundered two counties across the border in Fukien, destroyed Chi Jen-shou's market-town residence, and then marched upon Lung-ch'üan at the behest of the local people, who wanted to be rid of a local official by the name of Bawh ad-Din.[bt] The "bandit" leaders, P'an Wei-hsien and Yeh Chung-hsien,[bu] routed the government troops and took over the county headquarters on July 10. Bawh ad-Din fled to safety. P'an and Yeh held Lung-ch'üan until July 17, when a force of 8,000 "district troops" recruited by Wang I, Chang I, and Chi Wen under the authorization of Shih-mo's headquarters forced them to retreat. As a result, Wang I and his students and friends found themselves in complete control at the county seat. But they could not feed their army nor issue the cash rewards they had promised, and in consequence about half their men turned outlaw and ran away to forage for themselves. In November of the same year, Shih-mo's headquarters launched an investigation into Bawh ad-Din's conduct. Bawh ad-Din and the county clerks gathered a gang of "evil youths" and, presumably to frighten off the investigators, forced an entry into Wang I's home and murdered him there. Right after this sensational act, "bandits" in all seven counties of Ch'u-chou broke out in revolt.[80] This disturbance drove Liu Chi, who had been at home in Ch'ing-t'ien, away with his family toward the sea coast for safety.[81]

It is clear that the "bandits" in question were not Red Turbans. Wang I saw the Red Turbans as outsiders, a random collection of "insects and crows" from the mid-Yangtze who were ineptly led and, whatever the initial attraction of their messianism for the local poor, posed no great military threat at all.[82] The Red Turban threat to Ch'u-chou was foiled in 1352, and no more is heard of them there. Rather, by the loose term "bandits" seems to have been meant various rival leagues of local elites that were not easily distinguishable in kind from the circle around Shih-mo I-sun, and were moreover in competition with it for the adherence of the "people," as the case of P'an and Yeh indicates. We do not know who P'an and Yeh were, but there was an elite P'an lineage in Ch'ing-t'ien to which the "bandit" P'an Wei-hsien may have been related. The Yeh were too common a surname in the Ch'u-chou area to attempt to pinpoint any precise relationships.

Though conclusive evidence is lacking, it may be that this "bandit" activity, based in Ch'ing-t'ien since around 1348, continued to have the support of the former pirate Fang Kuo-chen, whom the Yüan court had "accommodated" and who was officially a Yüan loyalist. This supposition would help explain why the "bandits" voiced no anti-dynastic political aims, and why Liu Chi should have feared and hated Fang Kuo-chen so much.

In his *Yü-li tzu*[bv] (a work that in part blended Mencius' idealism with Hsün Tzu's realism), Liu Chi discussed the implications of the Yüan court's decision to appease Fang. He pointed out that central government may never relinquish control over any part of China, because as soon as even one county successfully defies the center, the disease and rot will inevitably spread further.[83] This will happen all the faster when government rewards such rebels; the people will rush to become rebels and bandits because this obviously is the way to profit and power.[84] He wrote,

The masses Heaven has produced are incapable of self-rule (*tzu-chih*),[bw] so Heaven sets up rulers for them. It gives the ruler powers of life and death so that he may stop violence and anarchy, suppress villainy, and succor the weak and the good. . . . It is no way at all to honor villains with the gifts of rank, salary, preference, and power so that the innocent people who cannot abide them have to swallow their rage and yield to them. Then the righteous people of the realm lose spirit, the brave seethe in anger, while greedy and violent elements roll up their sleeves and act as rebels in order to seek profitable advantages. Thus the idea of accommodation (*chao-an*)[bx] is really one of encouraging the realm to rebel. If the rulers don't see this, it is unfortunate.[85]

A parable in the *Yü-li tzu* appears directed specifically to an explanation of landlord "rebellion" in the Ch'u-chou area, at least insofar as it argues that a mindless ungovernability inheres in the masses especially when they are idle and well off.

The nature of people (*min-ch'ing*)[by] is such that after a long time of contentment they begin to think of disorder. . . . When the realm enjoys peace and prosperity, people do not experience hardship and do not anticipate that they cannot survive in rebellion. They are quick to resent superiors. As soon as their desires are frustrated, their anger is aroused and they think of revolt, and rebellion begins whenever leaders emerge. . . . The people are like horses. Stabled, pastured, and fed beans and grain, horses are placid and full. But once given freedom, they shake their manes and run with the wind, stallions bellowing to mares, snorting and bucking, doing just what they please, and impossible to recapture. But when these same horses are made to haul salt wagons over long and winding roads, sweating and stumbling, hungry and tired, then they can hardly return to their troughs fast enough and drool at the groom. . . . They could not even be whipped into freedom. At this point they will all submit to regulation.[86]

The talk of unruly, well-fed horses seems to be an allusion to the Ch'u-chou elites who opposed the Shih-mo I-sun circle. That this may be the case becomes more likely when the rest of the same story is taken into consideration. The rest of the story discusses the feasibility of restoring the "well-fields," in Yüan times a common metaphor for fiscal equalization, and in this instance almost certainly a reference to the divisive fiscal equalization sponsored by Yü Ch'üeh and Wang I in Lung-ch'üan in 1350. Liu Chi went on to state that after a long period of contentment when the people are beginning to think of disorder is precisely the worst time in which to institute "disruptive reform" (*fen-keng*),[bz] because the people will take it as a provocation to revolt. "It is impetuous to do something like this before the time has come, and narrow not to impose it when the time has arrived. The people's customs are now impure; half want the ancient way restored and half do not. The well-fields may be restored after great virtue has vanquished great disorder."[87] The apparent message, then, is that the late Yüan fiscal reform, though well-intended, was badly timed and provoked in Ch'u-chou society the militant polarization of the well-fed landlords (no question of destitution here) into pro- and antireform leagues. However, a future ruler will have imposed a peace of exhaustion and need not fear similar results from the same policy.

Late in 1354, after Wang I's murder, Shih-mo I-sun returned to Ch'u-chou to remedy the disarray of his adherents in that prefecture. The "bandits" were at this point based in elaborate hilltop encampments. They maintained communications with each other, and began to engage in an intricate game of negotiation and maneuver with Shih-mo's group. Neutral landlords could not stay clear of the struggle; charges that they were really in covert league with one side or the other compelled them to declare themselves openly.[88] Bribes were given and taken on both sides. Yeh Ch'en, active in the earlier fiscal reform, was appointed by the censorial authorities to the post of acting vice prefect in Ch'u-chou in 1355. He marched an army to Ch'ing-t'ien, where he accepted the banquets and operas of one of the leading "bandit" groups and for a while refrained from attacking them.[89]

Liu Chi also followed this conciliatory line for a while. In April 1356, Liu was sent by the Kiangche provincial authorities to serve as an advisor to Shih-mo I-sun. However, owing to the fall of Nanking to the future Ming founder, the transfer of the Kiangnan Branch Censorate to Shao-hsing, and its adoption of a policy favoring Fang Kuo-chen, Shih-mo's bureaucratic tie was soon shifted from the Censorate to the Military Commission, and Liu Chi was reassigned to the same body as a registry supervisor.[90] While the coastal regions were falling more firmly into the hands of Fang and Chang Shih-ch'eng, Liu Chi composed a notification to the "elders" of Ou-k'uo (i.e., Ch'u-chou and the Fukien border area) urging them on behalf of the emperor and the provincial authorities to cease their "rebellion" and surrender themselves.[91] He managed to coax a "mountain bandit," one Wu Ch'eng or Wu Ch'eng-ch'i,[ca] to come out and join him. However, Wu soon changed his mond. He bribed some of the members of Shih-mo's staff, but failed in an attempt to foment a mutiny in Shih-mo's army and seize the prefectural capital.[92] It was evidently in consequence of this clear failure of their conciliatory policy that Shih-mo and his group went on the offensive in 1356–1357. Yeh Ch'en, Chang I, and Hu Ch'en carried out a series of coordinated field operations and overran some of the chief enemy encampments.[93]

For a brief moment, a mood of euphoria and hope infected Shih-mo's circle, as the spirited interchange of poems within the group attests.[94] Some sixty poems that Liu Chi addressed to Shih-mo have survived, and from these it is possible to discern some of the reasons for the mood of optimism. There were two auspicious omens: the quashing of Wu Ch'eng's attempted mutiny; and Shih-mo's successful incantations for a drought-breaking rain.[95] The Yüan Dynasty, Liu felt, was worth restoring; the emperor was well-meaning and virtuous and the present troubles were not his fault, but stemmed rather from defects in the bureaucracy.[96] Liu Chi's intended role for Shih-mo was that of a hegemonic hero who righteously saves a falling dynasty. "Dark ice has frozen the axle of the world," he wrote, "who except you can make it spin again?" "Though the Chou order indeed went slack; its full rectification was accomplished by Duke Huan of Ch'i."[97] In a later preface to these poems, most of which were written in 1356, Liu Chi recalled, somewhat more ambivalently, a mixed feeling of world-saving zeal and hopeless futility about the real chances for achieving it.[98]

For Liu Chi, the whole point of the offensive thrust of the Shih-mo circle in Ch'u-chou was its intent to make of itself a pilot project in dynastic revival. It would lead, he believed, to the kind of sociopolitical reconstruction the Yüan Dynasty would have to agree to undertake on a much larger scale if it seriously expected to restore itself as a government once again in control of all of China. Liu Chi never considered Ch'u-chou and its politics as an ultimate focal point for his thought and effort, nor did he work to establish an independent regional state with Shih-mo as its chief. Quite the opposite, what made Shih-mo's movement significant was its commitment to the impartial politics of principle, not the "bandit" politics of regional self-interest as pursued by Chang and Fang.

In practice, this was an extremist, almost Manichean political line that everywhere demanded militant partisanship at the local level and the polarization of all society into irreconcilable armed camps, as was happening in Ch'u-chou itself. There was not the slightest chance, at least after 1355, that the Yüan central government might adopt such a pose. The post-1355 imperial administrations were resigned to the existence of loyalist regional autonomy in South China, and were in no position to do anything other than cooperate with Fang and Chang. Though the Shih-mo line was perhaps workable in the economically unimportant hinterland where Ch'u-chou was located, the court would not generally endorse a policy of vast and divisive struggle from below against the entrenched regional forces. This attitude became clear in 1357, when the

Yüan court offered Shih-mo and his group promotions to a higher grade within Ch'u-chou, but refused to raise them to a higher and more influential level in the national bureaucracy.

It was in these circumstances that Liu Chi gave up on the Yüan, quit his position, and went home. "It is not that I dare disobey the dynasty," he allegedly said, "but there is at present no way for me to exert myself."[99] Morale declined in Shih-mo's camp. Shih-mo himself began to ignore his superiors and appoint his own friends to local positions. Some of his staff made contact with the "bandits"; others left his service altogether. Hu Ch'en, Yeh Ch'en, and Chang I and their armies defected to the future Ming founder in the winter of 1359–1360; Shih-mo I-sun loyally continued to resist and was killed in an attempt to recover Ch'u-chou in August 1360.[100]

The time has come to offer a reprise of the rather complicated material offered thus far. In considering fiscal reform, local self-defense, and antiregionalism over the years 1342–1359, four variables have been given attention: Confucianism, reform, centralization, and coercion. In what way does the material serve to elucidate these terms and point up their interrelationships?

Confucian doctrine and reform appear to be linked as follows. It is evident from the various concrete contexts discussed that Confucian doctrine did not in any practical sense consist in a comprehensively detailed ordering of individual and social goals, nor did it specify any rigid set of methods or institutions through which such goals might be reached. Yet even while individual Confucian writers and activists varied widely in their specific ideas and approaches, the body of Confucian doctrine formed an ultimate unity, and among themselves, despite individual or local differences, the Confucian elite constituted a unified community of dedicated professionals that considered itself quite distinct from the lay society that surrounded it. The collective goals it tried to achieve for the public were simply the generalized goals of order and security. For the responsible individual, the goal it sought was no more than the resolute eradication of selfishness and particularism (*ssu*)[cb] and the conscientious cultivation of impartiality (*kung*).[cc] The doctrine insisted that the collective goal could only be approached to the extent that impartiality dominated the minds and behavior of responsible public and other authority. This was the irreducible ethical core of Confucianism, and it was around exactly these imperatives that the Confucian community mobilized its human energies and passions. Beyond this core, there clearly existed within the body of received doctrine a fairly generous range of permissible choices and variations. The specific disciplines through which impartiality might be cultivated; the specific instrumentalities through which impartial minds might best foster order and security in the public as a whole—in these matters, it was up to Confucian experience and expertise to make the choices and recommendations most appropriate in a given situation.

Confucian doctrine was related to reform in the same way that any professional body of knowledge or doctrine implies a service ideal, an obligation on the part of the professional community to apply that knowledge on an impartial basis for the public good. Professional wisdom will be doubted unless it can be shown that at least occasionally it can produce visible results. If now and then it manages to soften, neutralize, or remove from the public environment the kinds of crises, threats, or harms it claims exclusive competence in dealing with, then it proves its enduring value. Local fiscal reform, for late Yüan Confucianism, was just such an opportunity. Local reform, aimed at the equitable redistribution of service and other obligations, was a critical kind of social task in which professional Confucian guidance could make a demonstrable impact upon the public client at a relatively high level of interaction—that is, at a level above that of the family or the corporate kin group.

It was in the general Confucian interest to strive thus in the public behalf, because the survival of the profession as a whole was surely contingent upon its ability to demonstrate in certain critical situations its practical efficacy. But was it also in the *individual* interest of Confucians to undertake such efforts? The answer would seem to be that men such as Wang I and Chao Chieh stood to gain at least added stature as Confucians, if not an increase in income, by contributing their knowledge and energy to the cause of fiscal reform in their home communities. They were not nationally known men already at the top of their profession, but men lower in informal status who, whether they consciously intended it or not, certainly did win wider fame through their participation. Given the extremely strong commitment to professional norms expressed earlier by Wang and Chao, they may have stood to lose standing if they failed to do anything. If they were registered *ju* (Confucians) and thus officially exempt from service levies themselves, they would probably have had no personal financial stake in the reallocation of those levies. In the absence of contrary indications, the *prima facie* evidence does suggest that their actions were motivated by the Confucian principles they professed.

There were two main ways in which fiscal reform was implemented at the basic level. In Tz'u-ch'i, Shao-hsing, and Chin-hua, the population was mobilized and reform carried out through the official creation and sponsorship of artificial rural hierarchies, such as the village officer systems and the mutual security groups. In Ch'u-chou this method was not used, probably because local government in that prefecture remained largely in the control of officials and clerks who opposed the reforms. Consequently, reform mobilization in Ch'u-chou placed heavy demands upon the voluntary cooperation of a number of heads of large lineages, who were able to mobilize men and resources on their own initiative. Why did these figures (Hu Ch'en, Chang I, Chi Wen, etc.) rally to Wang I and the reform side, rather than bargain individually with local government as the other elite lineages appear to have done? This question cannot yield any satisfactory answer without some fuller knowledge of the history of local land tenure and intra-elite conflict. On the face of it, however, it is evident that the proreform side did include upwardly mobile elements, men eager to rise from obscurity (or perhaps remove the stigma of ancestral disgrace). For all its risks, association with reform did bring immediate benefits in the form of prestige, favorable literary publicity, and the power to take action. By identifying themselves as the forces of righteousness, the reformers definitely achieved a high degree of purpose and cohesion among themselves, and this, while not decisive, was certainly advantageous to them as strategy against a larger but possible more inchoate opposition. No doubt it was also personally rewarding to join a movement whose aims lent themselves to open and forthright statement, and whose sentimental ties could be advertised in joint efforts at poetry.

In each case considered here, local reform did require the support of some part of Yüan bureaucracy. Invariably those Yüan officials who busied themselves with reform work were, from the point of view of the organizational hierarchy, nonconformists. Despite their varied ethnic and regional backgrounds, virtually all the reform-minded officials—Tai Bukha, Liu Hui, Yü Ch'üeh, Yeh Ch'en, Mai Shan-ch'ing, Ch'en Lin, Shih-mo I-sun—were alike in chafing against organizational constraints and preferring to function as autonomous political actors. While few of them (with the exceptions of Tai Bukha and Yü Ch'üeh) could be taken to be full-fledged members of the Confucian professional community itself, all were to some degree guided by Confucian norms in their behavior, and where local professional advice was forthcoming, they were "clients" who were willing to heed it.

Connections between reform and centralization have been remarked upon earlier. It may suffice, then, to emphasize that by centralization is meant the visible and intentional concentration of decision-making power and responsibility in the hands of an official at any level of formal organization. Local reform went hand-in-hand with local-level centralization because (1) the Yüan Dynasty was not at the time eager to coordinate such reform at higher levels of organization; and (2) the previous distribution of power at the local level was both diffuse and covert, with a number of clerks and officials negotiating separate arrangements with individual local elites wishing to reduce their fiscal burdens. Obviously, the reform-minded official who took advice from Confucian professionals had to have wide discretionary powers if he were to act upon the advice he received. Since reform involved redirecting all the work routine of government in order to achieve a very difficult task in a rather short period of time, it would have been impossible to effect it without a centralized command structure.

A reform aimed at an equitable reallocation of burdensome obligations (a reallocation proportionate to the carefully assessed resource capacity of each obligated unit) is a reform designed to provide a collective public with a collective good or benefit. In Mancur Olson's definition, a collective good is one "such that if any person . . . in a group . . . consumes it, it cannot feasibly be withheld from the others in that group."[101] The good provided by the reforms was economic security for the largest possible number of landowning households. The leadership and organization necessary for providing that collective good could not have stemmed spontaneously from the public beneficiary itself, because, again following Olson's reasoning, a public as a large "latent group" is unable to reward any member who might make any contribution in its behalf, or punish any member who declines to make one.[102] A large public, in other words, cannot moblilze itself, no matter how valuable the collective benefit it might gain in so doing.

In the late Yüan, the delivery to some localized segments of the public of a collective benefit in the form of an equitable reassessment of service obligations was accomplished through the cooperation of parts of the bureaucracy and special *small* action groups within the public, that is, the local Confucian communities. The members of these small groups could provide themselves with incentives for bearing the heavy costs of action in the public behalf. These incentives included (but were not necessarily confined to) reputation, esteem, and the opportunity for fulfilling some world-saving sense of purpose. The Confucians were important agents for mobilizing the taxpaying public in the interest of providing it with a collective benefit that it could never have provided for itself. They were indispensible agents only to the extent that the bureaucracy itself was unable or unwilling to initiate and dominate the reforms.

Fiscal reform, however, was not exactly an end in itself. It did not occur simply because some elites were uncomfortable with statistical disarray in the registers. Rather, the belief was that the ultimate issue had to do with the maintenance of public security and order. Fiscal inequity was simply a tangible symptom of the erosion of order. If public order or security may be described as a general condition that varies according to the total amount of collective goods available, then disorder and insecurity occur to the extent that there is perceived to be a shortage in the provision of collective goods. Whether or not a shortage is perceived depends in turn upon the value system a society may have. In the present instance, the Confucian guardians of the public value system did perceive in the skewed distribution of service burdens powerful evidence of a dangerous situation where selfish, greedy, and unprincipled elements visibly thrived at the expense of the weaker, law-abiding citizenry. The danger in this to public security lay in the Confucian belief that a social or political system that rewarded greed and penalized virtue was a system destined to collapse into anarchy. It destroyed any incentive for maintaining the moral hierarchy of kin or the functional hierarchy of occupation, the twin structures on which the whole public order theoretically rested. (It may bear repeating that the moral hierarchy of kin recognized by Confucian doctrine was a "public" [*kung*] institution designed to eradicate particularistic greed, not augment it).

In these circumstances, coercion was necessarily linked to reform and centralization. Enough disincentive had to be applied so that the "selfish" elements who benefited from noncollective arrangements with the local yamens might be caused to terminate those arrangements. Since most of those who benefited from these special private arrangements stood to suffer materially from the provision of the collective good of fiscal equalization, the act of reform could not but engender a hostile opposition. The measures used by the reformers against this opposition were quite harsh, ranging from counterthreat, humiliation, and imprisonment to property confiscation, flogging, and death.

However, the writers were careful to insist that these coercive methods, suitable for suppressing the opposition, could not be used to mobilize the rest of the public. There was no great problem about this in the case of fiscal reform, since enough of the "latent" public figured to benefit, or at least not lose, from its imposition. In the civil troubles of the early 1350s, the public again had to be mobilized over an issue of collective security, but one where the costs of mobilization were much higher, as they involved the building of fortifications, the exaction of grain and weapons supplies, and the formation of local militias and security organs. In order not to anger the people, the leaders of these efforts had to use coercion as sparingly as possible. They had to use material incentives sparingly too, lest the people suffer from the extra exactions necessary to pay for them. (The writers asserted that the unreformed local governments followed either or both of these procedures to a ruinous extreme.) Therefore, the professionally approved path to mobilization for local self-defense demanded (1) the utilization of the reformed statistical base for apportioning material costs; (2) the use of the reformed rural hierarchies for mobilizing militia recruits and mutual security groups; and (3) the application of mainly psychological incentives (through ritual ceremony or moral propaganda) to rally the people against rebels or bandits. However, these measures were inadequate to prevent takeover by larger extraneous forces, and by 1359-1360 the "reform" locales fell either to anitreform loyalist warlords (Fang Kuo-chen and Chang Shih-ch'eng) or proreform rebels (the future Ming founder).

When the Yüan central administration chose after 1355 to confer legitimacy upon the unreformed and regionally autonomous governments of Chang and Fang, and ignored the counterdemonstration being mounted in Ch'u-chou, most of the Confucian community remained loyal to the dynasty. Those willing to heighten indefinitely the level of violence for the sake of preserving the principles of reform and centralization (e.g., Liu Chi) were decidedly a minority, yet it is this minority of die-hard Confucian activists whose professional stature was secured, and who later played an important role in the Ming founding.

Finally, it may be noted again how far Confucian activism in the late Yüan transcended ethnic, local, or sectarian ties. The seriousness of the reformers' dedication to the application of *general* principles may be gauged by the fact that they included among themselves Mongols and Central Asians as well as Northern and Southern Chinese; and by the fact that they were variously Chu Hsi followers, or Lu-Yang followers, or "independent" and eclectic formulators of doctrine. The very hard dividing lines that existed did not follow these considerations but cut in quite different directions, separating the corrupt from the upright, the selfish from the impartial, the particularizing from the universalizing.

From its beginnings, Yüan Confucianism was devoted more to practical implementation than to doctrinal development; perhaps the stormy reform episodes in a few South China prefectures in the 1340s and 1350s were its appropriate denouement. Yet its contributions were hardly ephemeral. It turned out that the terminal manifestations of Yüan Confucianism came to constitute in a very direct way the prehistory of the Confucianism of the early Ming.

370 *John W. Dardess*

27. *Ibid.*, 3:11b. The high literati were those Confucians serving in mainly advisory positions at court; Huang Chin, Wei Su, and Ou-yang Hsüan were among them.
28. Wang I, 3:4b–5a, 9b–10a; Sung Lien, 43:4a–7a.
29. Wang I, 1:8b–10a.
30. Huang Chin, *Chin-hua Huang hsien-sheng wen-chi*[cv] (*Hsü Chin-hua ts'ung-shu* ed.), 9:12a–13b; Yang Wei-chen, *Tung-wei tzu wen-chi*[cw] (SPTK ed.), 12:11a–13a.
31. I am indebted to Prof. Herbert Franke for the suggestion that Mai-li-ku-ssu may render in transliteration some form of "Marcus."
32. Yang Wei-chen, 24:6a–7b.
33. T'ao Tsung-i, *Nan-ts'un cho-keng lu*[cx] (SPTK ed., 3d ser.), 10:8a; Tai Liang, 8:8b—9b.
34. T'ao Tsung-i, 10:8a; YS, 188:11b–13a.
35. Tai Liang, 8:1a–2a, 8b–9b.
36. *Ibid.*, 15:2a–5b. Probably about this time the Tz'u-ch'i assistant magistrate humiliated the clerks; during a drought, he made them wear signs reading: "The lack of rain is caused by clerkly abuses." See Tai Liang, 11:6b–8b.
37. *Ibid.*, 15:4a.
38. Wang Wei, *Wang Chung-wen kung chi* (*Ch'ien-k'un cheng-ch'i-chi* ed.), 8:2a–3a.
39. Wu Ssu-tao, *Ch'un-ts'ao-chai chi*[cy] (*Ssu-ming ts'ung-shu* ed., 1935), 10:14a–18a. SYHA (Shanghai: World Book Co.,[cz] 1936), vol. 3, chaps. 74 and 93 cover this movement.
40. *Sung shih*[da] (PN ed.), 423:18b–19b also states that "wherever [Chao Te-yüan] went, he was eager to collect taxes and was near to being a fiscalist."
41. SYHA, Vol. 3, p. 1758.
42. Wu Ssu-tao, 10:14a–18a.
43. SYHA, Vol. 3, p. 1751.
44. Wu Ssu-tao, 10:24a–26b.
45. SYHA, Vol. 3, p. 1751.
46. Wu Ssu-tao, 10:24a–26b.
47. *Ibid.*, 10:14a–18a.
48. *Ibid.*,
49. SYHA, Vol. 3, p. 1425.
50. Wu Ssu-tao, 10:14a–18a.
51. SYHA, Vol. 3, p. 1751.
52. Wu Ssu-tao, 11:12ab.
53. SYHA, Vol. 3, p. 1758.
54. *Ibid.*, p. 1751.
55. *Ibid.*, p. 1752.
56. *Ibid.*
57. *Ibid.*
58. SYHA, Vol. 3, p. 1753.

NOTES

1. The concept of Confucianism as a profession is developed at much greater length in my *Confucianism and Autocracy, Professional Elites in the Founding of the Ming Dynasty* (in manuscript), chap. 1.
2. James T.C. Liu, *Reform in Sung China* (Cambridge, Mass.: Harvard University Press, 1959); Brian E. McKnight, *Village and Buraurcracy in Southern Sung China* (Chicago: University of Chicago Press, 1971); H. Franz Schurmann, *Economic Structure of the Yüan Dynasty* (Cambridge, Mass.: Harvard University Press, 1956).
3. *Confucianism and Autocracy*, chap. 2.
4. YS (PN ed.), 143:14a–17b.
5. Kung Shih-t'ai, *Kung li-pu wan-chai chi*[cd] (1535 ed.), 10:1a–6b.
6. Wei Su, *Wei T'ai-p'u chi*[ce] (Shanghai, 1913), Bl:3a–4b.
7. Chu Te-jun, *Ts'un fu-chai chi*[cf] (*Han-fen-lou mi-chi* ed.,[cg] Shanghai: Commerical Press, 1923), 4:4b.
8. Kung Shih-t'ai, 10:3b.
9. Wei Su, Bl:10ab.
10. Chu Te-jun, 4:4a–5a.
11. Ch'eng Tuan-li, *Wei-chai chi*[ch] (*Ssu-ming ts'ung-shu* ed.,[ci] Ssu-ming, 1932), 3:4b-5b, and the biographical preface to this edition.
12. YS, 143:17b–21b; Sung Lien, *Sung Wen-hsien ch'üan chi*[cj] (SPPY ed.), 40:17b–19b.
13. Sung Lien, 43:5a.
14. Others involved with the Chin-hua reforms included Northern Chinese and Uighurs whose positions were inherited; they were used by Yü Ch'üeh because of their honesty and willingness to work. See Hu Chu, *Ch'un-pai chai lei-kao*[ck] (*Chin-hua ts'ung-shu* ed., 1973),[cl] 18:18a–21a 19:16b–20a.
15. Yü Ch'üeh, *Ch'ing-yang hsien-sheng wen-chi*[cm] (SPTK ed.), 9:8ab.
16. Wang Wei, *Wang Chung-wen kung chi*[cn] (*Chin-hua ts'ung-shu* ed.), 6:39a.
17. Yü Ch'üeh, 9:8b.
18. Wang Wei, 6:40b; Yü Ch'üeh, 9:9a.
19. Lü P'u, *Chu-ch'i chi*[co] (*Hsü Chin-hua ts'ung-shu* ed.,[cp] Yung-k'ang, 1924), 2:2a–3a.
20. Tai Liang, *Tai Chiu-ling chi*[cq] (*Ch'ien-k'un cheng-ch'i chi* ed., 1866),[cr] 2:1a–2a; Hu Chu, 18:18a–21a.
21. Su Po-heng, *Su P'ing-chung chi*[cs] (*Chin-hua ts'ung-shu* ed.), 13:1a–5b.
22. Yü Ch'üeh, 9:9a.
23. Hu Chu, 18:18a–21a.
24. Wang I, *Mu-na-chai wen-chi*[ct] (*K'uo-ts'ang ts'ung-shu*,[cu] 2d ser., Chekiang, 1948), appendix, 4a–5b; Sung Lien, 48:15b–17a.
25. The quotations are from Sung Lien's biography of Wang I in *Sung Wen-hsien ch'üan-chi*, 48:15b–17a.
26. Wang I, 1:7a–8a.

59. See James C. Scott, *Comparative Political Corruption* (Englewood Cliffs, New Jersey: Prentice Hall, 1972), p. 21.

60. See Samuel P. Hays, "The Politics of Reform in Municipal Government in the Progressive Era," in Barton J. Bernstein and Allen J. Matusow, eds., *Twentieth Century America: Recent Interpretations* (New York: Harcourt, Brace, and World, 1969), pp. 34–58.

61. Tai Liang, 8:9a.

62. SYHA, Vol. 3, p. 1759.

63. Tai Liang, 15:3b.

64. *Ibid.*

65. T'ao Tsung-i, 10:8a: Yang Wei-chen, 24:6a–7b; YS, 188:11b–13a.

66. *Yü-yao-hsien chih* (Chekiang, 1919), 3:1b–2a.

67. Wu Ssu-tao, 9:1a-3a; Tai Liang, 15:2a-5b.

68. *Ming T'ai-tsu shih-lu* [db] (Academia Sinica, Taipei, 1962), vol. 4, p. 1564.

69. Hu Chu, 19:16b-20a, 18:18a–21a.

70. Sung Lien, 35:9b; Huang Chin, 9:10b–12a; Wang Wei, 7:1a–2b, 8:15a–16a.

71. Sung Lien, 34:12a–13a: Wang Wei, 18:15b-16a; Chang Meng-chien, *Pai-shih shan-feng i-kao* [ac] (*Hsü Chin-hua ts'ung-shu* ed.), 8:5ab.

72. Wang I, 1:4b–5b, 15b–16b, 3:1a–2b, 2b–4b; Liu Chi, *Ch'eng-i po wen-chi* [dd] (SPTK ed.), 8:22a–24b.

73. Romeyn Taylor, "Chang I," in L. C. Goodrich and Chaoying Fang, eds., *Dictionary of Ming Biography (1368-1644)* (New York: Columbia University Press, 1976), Vol. 1, pp. 90-94; Sung Lien, 35:3ab, 4b–5b, 17b–18a, 44:15ab, 49:3b–5b; Wang Wei, 2:11b–12b, 7:6b–8a, 13a–14b; Tai Liang, 3:6ab. For Chang I's father, see Sung Lien, 50:5b–6a. Shih-mo I-sun and his family are mentioned by many contemporary writers.

74. Wang Wei, in Ch'eng Min-cheng, ed., *Huang Ming wen-heng* [de] (SPTK ed.), 62:9–14a; Wang I, 1:1b–3a.

75. Huang Chin, 10:8b-9a; Sung Lien, 14:17a–18a, 19:16a–17a.

76. Sung Lien, 15:1a–2a, 34:6b–7b; Liu Chi, 5:26a–27a, 35b–36a.

77. Wei Su, B3:7b–10a.

78. Wang I, 3:8b–9b.

79. *Ibid.*, 3:14b–15a.

80. Sung Lien, 34:6b–7b, 48:15b–17a, Sung Lien in *Huang Ming wen-heng*, 70.5b–6a; Wang Wei in *ibid.*, 62:11ab; Wang I, appendix, 5a.

81. Liu Chi, 5:22b. See also Hok-lam Chan, "Liu Chi", *Dictionary of Ming Biography*, Vol. 1, pp. 932–38.

82. Wang I, 3:7b.

83. Liu Chi, 2:4a. See Matsukawa Kenji, "Ryū Ki Ikurishi no kenkyū," [df] *Hokkaidō daigaku bungakubu kiyō* [dg] (March 1972), 20(1):131–234.

84. Liu Chi, 2:9b–10a.

85. *Ibid.*, 4:14b.

86. *Ibid.*, 4:23a–24a.

87. *Ibid.*

88. *Ibid.*, 6:35a–36a.

89. Sung Lien, 43:4a–7a.

90. Liu Chi, "Hsing-chuang" (Account of Conduct), 2ab.

91. *Ibid.*, 7:30b–31b.

92. Liu Chi, "Hsing-chuang," 2ab, 8:22a–24b; Sung Lien, 27:9a–12a; Wang Hsing-i, *Liu Po-wen nien-p'u*[dh] (Shanghai: Commercial Press, 1936), p. 37.

93. Wang Wei, 4:3b–4b.

94. *Ibid.*

95. Liu Chi, 16:19b–20a.

96. *Ibid.*, 13:36b.

97. *Ibid.*, 13:36b, 39a.

98. *Ibid.*, 5:36b–37a.

99. *Ibid.*, "Shen-tao-pei ming" (Spirit-way Stele), 4a. Cf. Ch'ien Mu, "Tu Ming-ch'u k'ai-kuo chu-ch'en shih-wen chi,"[di] *Hsin-ya hsüeh-pao*[dj] (August 1964), 6(2):270ff.

100. Sung Lien, 27:9a–12a; YS, 188:11b; *Ming T'ai-tsu shih-lu*, vol. 1, pp. 107–8.

101. Mancur Olson, *The Logic of Collective Action* (Cambridge, Mass.: Harvard University Press, 1971), p. 14.

102. *Ibid.*, pp. 48, 50–51.

GLOSSARY

a 治

b 安

c 浙東

d 紹興

e 泰不華

f 餘姚

g 劉輝

h 小學

i 金華

j 烏由

k 士

l 鄉飲酒禮

m 葉琛（伯顏）

n 青田

o 處州

p 明倫堂

q 極高明軒

r 都

s 富民

t 闊左

u 保正

v 主首

w 柳貫

x 保甲

y 龍泉

z 周敦頤，太極圖說

aa 躬行實踐

ab 九佳

ac 民

ad 土滿帖木兒

ae 義勇民丁

af 邁里古思，邁（吳）善卿

ag 果毅軍

ah 慈谿

ai 陳麟

aj 豪右

ak 寓公

al 士大夫

am 鄉正

an 陸象山（九淵）

ao 趙偕，王約，向壽，王桓，
楊芮，周堅，烏斯道，烏本
艮

ap 楊簡

aq 趙德淵

ar 體

as 反觀

at 變化

au 用

av 眞實踐履

aw 公議

ax 儒

ay 靜明

az 艮心

ba 土堅

bb 張士誠

bc 方國珍

bd 義民

be 石抹宜孫

bf 濯心

bg 浦江

bh 永康

bi 義兵

bj 鄉兵

bk 章溢，胡琛

bl 湯思退

bm 秦檜

bn 范仲淹

bo 湯京

bp 湯楷

bq 季仁壽

br 季汶

bs 天機

bt 賓忽丁

bu 潘惟賢，葉仲賢

bv 郁離子

bw 自治

bx 招安

by 民情

bz 紛更

ca 吳成（成七）

cb 私

cc 公

cd 貢師泰，貢禮部玩齋集

ce 危素，危太僕集

cf 朱德潤，存復齋集

cg 涵芬樓秘笈

ch 程端禮，畏齋集

ci 四明叢書

cj 宋濂，宋文憲全集

ck 胡助，純白齋類稿

cl 金華叢書

cm 余闕，青陽先生文集

cn 王褘，王忠文公集

co 呂浦，竹溪集

cp 續金華叢書

cq 戴良，戴九靈集

cr 乾坤正氣集

cs 蘇伯衡，蘇平仲集

ct 王毅，木枘齋文集

cu 括蒼叢書

cv 黃溍，金華黃先生文集

cw 楊維楨，東維子文集

cx 陶宗儀，南村輟耕錄

cy 烏斯道，春草齋集

cz 宋元學案，世界書局

da 宋史

db 明太祖實錄

dc 張孟兼，白石山房遺稿

dd 劉基，誠意伯文集

de 程敏政，皇明文衡

df 松川健二，劉基「郁離子」の研究

dg 北海道大學文學部紀要

dh 王馨一，劉伯溫年譜

di 錢穆，讀明初開國諸臣詩文集

dj 新亞學報

Jan Yün-hua

Chinese Buddhism in Ta-tu: The New Situation and New Problems

ALTHOUGH BUDDHISM in the Yüan period faced different problems at different times and places throughout the empire, the problems and the experiences of the Buddhists in Ta-tu[a] (modern Peking) were unique and especially significant.[1] They were unique because this was the first great center of Chinese culture that was conquered by the Mongols. They were significant also because it was the capital city of the Jurchen-Chin dynasty and it played a leading role in the religious life of North China. Under these circumstances, the problems and experiences, success or failure of the Buddhists in Ta-tu were not only decisive for their own religious life, but also, to a degree, reflected the manner in which Chinese civilization reacted and adapted itself to the new situation under the Mongol conquest.

When the Mongols took over the capital city, then known as Yen-ching,[b] in 1215, the situation in North China was confusing and uncertain. The Buddhists had to struggle for survival during this critical period of political turmoil. They had to deal with the new rulers and to secure their understanding and support, which was essential under those circumstances. They had to deal with Taoist organizations which were influential and supported by the Mongols. They had to confront or to cooperate with the Tibetan priests who had become increasingly dominant in the Mongol court. All these problems were implicated in the survival and prosperity of the Buddhists in Ta-tu. Moreover, as Buddhism had become an essential part of Chinese civilization after its introduction to China in the first century, these developments should be meaningful for

understanding the reaction and transformation of the Chinese tradition
during the period of Mongol rule.

Buddhism had had its ups and downs under Chin rule, but enjoyed
a degree of prosperity in the capital city on the eve of the Mongol conquest. Even though certain restrictions had been imposed on Buddhist
ordination, some of the rulers, such as Emperor Chang-tsung[c] (r. 1190-
1208) had also publicly paid respect to Buddhist leaders. Other religions
like the Ch'ang-ch'un[d] sect of Taoist religion and other schools of
Buddhism such as the Disciplinary School (Lü-tsung[e]) were outshone
in the capital city by Ch'an[f] Buddhism, which received imperial patronage.[2]

In contrast with the Chin court, the Mongol attitude towards religions in the newly conquered territories was rather passive and indifferent. Though some Mongol rulers later bestowed honors on certain religious leaders, constructed temples and ordained new priests, none of this
took place in the capital city during the early decades of the Mongol
occupation. In fact, the threat to the survival of Buddhists as well as to
the rest of the people was real and serious. After the Chin emperor Hsüan-
tsung[g] (r. 1213–1224) abandoned the capital city and fled to the south
in 1215, under the Mongol invasion the former capital of the Chin dynasty fell into disarry. A contemporary writer has this description of the
situation: "Bravos rose up amidst the unrest, people everywhere had no
one to depend on."[3] The situation for the Buddhists was even worse, as
they lost most of their monastic properties and their novices, and many
of their establishments were seized by the Taoists. Furthermore, the new
rulers seemed very cool and unconcerned about the plight of the Buddhists at that time.[4]

Most historians of Chinese Buddhism have paid much attention to
Yin-chien[h] (1207–1257) as the Buddhist leader of this period, and have
attributed to him all the Buddhist achievements during the predynastic
phase of Mongol rule.[5] However, that impression is quite misleading. It
is true that Yin-chien was very influential in the Mongol court, but his
influence was felt only from approximately 1230 onwards, twenty years
or so after the Mongol occupation of Yen-ching. When the Mongol cavalry subdued the Chin defenders in the capital city, Yin-chien was only
a lad of thirteen years and just about to start his career. It was other
Buddhists like Hsing-hsiu[i] (1166–1246) and his associates who provided
leadership during the difficult period of transition.

HSING-HSIU AND HIS GROUP

Hsing-hsiu, also known by his title "The Old Man of Ten Thousand Pines" (Wan-sung lao-jen),[j] was the preeminent leader of the Chinese Buddhists when the Mongol forces subdued Yen-ch'ing. A native of Honan and the spiritual heir of the Ts'ao-tung[k] Ch'an master Hsüeh-yen [1] (i.e., Master Man,[m] d. 1206), he was highly acclaimed by his followers under the Chin dynasty. His reputation ascended to great heights when he was invited to the imperial palace and delivered a sermon to Emperor Chang-tsung in 1193.[6] According to the record, when Hsing-hsiu arrived at the palace, the emperor received him in person, offered him a seat, and listened to the monk preach religious truth such as he had never heard before. In appreciation of Hsing-hsiu's discourse, the emperor bestowed a silk robe on the monk, who was also paid homage by the palace ladies and officials. Precious donations were given, and an assembly for mass conversion was called. The Buddhist historians even hailed the event by claiming that "auspicious clouds appeared over the sky continuously for a few days. Thereafter the harvest came and people sang for happiness while traveling on the road."[7] This cordial relationship between the Chin emperor and the monk continued for the next few years; and under an edict of 1197, the latter was appointed the abbot of Ch'i-yin[n] Ch'an Monastery, situated at Yang[o] Hill. Thereupon, a hall of lotuses was constructed for the monk, and the emperor visited the monastery and honored the occasion with a royal poem.[8] Also, Hsing-hsiu's eminence as a scholar and religious leader attracted brilliant disciples. Some of them, like Yeh-lü Ch'u-ts'ai[p] (1189–1243), Li Ch'un-fu[q] (Li P'ing-shan)[r] (1185–1231) among the laymen, and Fu-yü[s] (1203–1275), Chih-wen[t] (1217–1267), Ts'ung-lun[u] (active thirteenth century) and a few others from the clergy, are good examples.

After the Mongols took over the capital city, relations between the new authority and Chinese Buddhist monks were cool and indifferent. The Mongol rulers were no doubt preoccupied with military affairs and not yet ready to take new initiatives in government. On the Buddhist side, the leadership had lost the protection of the Chin court and had not yet established a new relationship with the conqueror. Under these circumstances, the Buddists were probably forced to adopt a wait-and-see attitude. Hsing-hsiu described his situation in a letter dated 1223 to Yeh-lü Ch'u-ts'ai, then an influential scribe-secretary and astronomer-astrologer:

Since the military changeover . . . I have lived in retirement at Pao-en Monastery at Yen-ching [i.e., Ta-tu], and constructed a lodge there for myself, calling it "The Lodge of Leisureliness" (*ts'ung-jung an*ᵛ).[9]

From this we know that the monk kept a low profile during the early years of the Mongol occupation. It is impossible to know whether the low profile was self-imposed or arose from Mongol indifference. But it is clear that he neither enjoyed the prestige he had had in the past, nor attempted to ingratiate himself with the new ruler. As he was a man of integrity, it seems unlikely that he would have resorted to improper means to advance himself. This attitude was quite consonant with the Confucian custom, as the name of his lodge, *ts'ung-jung* ("at ease" or "at leisure"), suggests.[10]

Indeed Confucianism remained strong during Hsing-hsiu's time and the monk himself was well known for his knowledge of Confucian teachings. Nevertheless he was an earnest Ch'an Buddhist of the Ts'ao-tung school, and though it is said that he "embraced both Confucianism and Buddhism," more importantly he is described as "adept and thorough in the teachings of that school."[11] This assessment by a colleague of his has been verified by the words of the monk himself as well as by his disciple. When his disciple Yeh-lü Ch'u-ts'ai declared that it is proper "to govern the state by means of Confucianism, cultivate the nature by means of Taoism, and control the mind by means of Buddhism," the Master immediately criticized the remark as "tantamount to destroying the two in order to compliment the third," i.e., "subordinating Buddhism and Taoism in order to accommodate Confucian feelings."[12] This clearly indicates that the monk, though broad-minded, never wavered in his religious commitment. Another instance of this is found in the work of Li Ch'un-fu or Li P'ing-shan, the other outstanding disciple of Hsing-hsiu. Li wrote the *Ming-tao chi-shuo* ʷ (Collected Plaints Concerning the Way), which is the most significant Buddhist countercriticism of the Neo-Confucian attack on Buddhism. The work was written under the influence of, and encouraged by, the Master Hsing-hsiu himself.[13]

Though the monk maintained a low profile during the early decades of the Mongol occupation, it should not be thought that he was entirely inactive. As a Buddhist less attached to wordly affairs than the Confucians, he simply accepted the change of dynasties and concentrated on his writing and the training of his disciples. It was only later, when the situation of the former capital city became more stable, that he bagan to play a limited role in helping his colleagues and disciples to deal with the Mongol rulers.

The most important work written by Hsing-hsiu during this period was the *Ts'ung-jung (an) lu*[x] (Record of [the Lodge of] Leisureliness).[14] It is a collection of one hundred historical instances in which Ch'an masters attained enlightenment. The work was originally compiled by Cheng-chüeh[y] (1091–1157) of Mt. T'ien-t'ung,[z] and Hsing-hsiu enlarged it with critical notes and poems as well as instructions. When the work was completed, Yeh-lü Ch'u-ts'ai wrote a preface to the collection, which indicates that the work was done at the request of the monk's disciples and for the sake of their school. The preface is dated 1224, and this indicates that the work was compiled during 1218–1224, a period of uncertainty and difficulty.[15] There is no doubt that this record of Hsing-hsiu was not merely hagiographical exegesis, but an original interpretation of the Ts'ao-tung tradition. His intellectual contribution through this book gave new vitality to Ch'an Buddhism.

The warm reception of the *Ts'ung-jung (an) lu* encouraged Hsing-hsiu and his associate. So the monk followed up the effort and compiled another book on the same subject in 1230. This book, *Ch'ing-i lu*[aa] (Requested Instructions), was originally compiled by Cheng-chüeh, but Hsing-hsiu expanded it. It contained another ninety-nine instances of enlightenment in the Ch'an school, and is regarded as a supplement to the former record. These two collections by Hsing-hsiu are the first systematic expositions of Ts'ao-tung Ch'an Buddhism. Before that, the records of the Ts'ao-tung masters were written on a more individual basis. Against this background, these two compilations may be seen as works that established the school tradition on firmer ground. Before this, the rising popularity of the *kung-an* in Ch'an Buddhism had been represented mainly by such works as the *Pi-yen lu*[ab] of the Lin-chi[ac] school. It is true that the doctrine, style, and teaching techniques of Lin-chi Ch'an had proven attractive to many Chinese, yet the compilation of *kung-an* and their use in a textbook for Ch'an Buddhism also helped the spread of the school. Thus its historical significance was noted by Yeh-lü Ch'u-ts'ai, who spoke of these two works as completing "the tripod among the three schools of Ch'an Buddhism" (*san-tsung ting-shih*). [ad] The other two were the schools of Lin-chi and Yün-men. [ae][16]

The training of disciples was another important accomplishment of Hsing-hsiu during the early years of the Mongol occupation of Ta-tu. Eminent disciples destined to play important roles in the future were all trained by him during this difficult period. Yeh-lü Ch'u-ts'ai, Fu-yü, Chih-wen, and Ts'ung-lun are good examples.

According to Yeh-lü, Hsing-hsiu was the only Master who attained the "Concentration of Self-existence" (*ta-tzu-tsai san-mei*)[af] and was able to make judgments in matters of subtle doctrine and thus preserve the genius of the Ts'ao-tung school. [17] Yeh-lü also considered that the Master possessed all the good qualities and virtues of the other schools of Ch'an, yet was completely untainted by the defects of these schools. The quality of Hsing-hsiu's teaching was also testified to by his disciples. Yeh-lü writes that while away in Central Asia in the company of Chinggis during the Western campaigns, he dreamed of the Master and was touched by the remembrance of his untiring spirit and affections. [18]

For two decades after the Mongols took over Ta-tu, and when uncertainty no longer cast a shadow over the future of the Buddhists, Hsing-hsiu, it seems, still remained publicly inactive. This was probably not only because there was no demand for such activity on his part, but also because he preferred to concentrate on writing and training disciples. Except for a few instances, there are no reports of his public activity available to us. He yielded his leadership to masters such as Hai-yün, [ag] and came forward himself only when the clergy were in danger. He persuaded Hai-yün, for example, to plead with the Mongol authorities to stop the reintroduction of the qualifying examinations for Buddhist clergy. It is also reported that he was active in the appointment of Fu-yü to be the abbot of the Shao-lin Monastery. [19]

Among the disciples of Hsing-hsiu, Yeh-lü Ch'u-ts'ai occupies a special place since, as Chief of the Secretariat, he was the senior and the most influential non-Mongol official in the Mongol court, and he also had close connections with Buddhism during the early period of the Mongol establishment at Ta-tu. His personal faith and his advice to the Mongol rulers during the heyday of his career had an important influence on the course of events. Therefore, many of his activities drew the close attention of Buddhist monks.

Though the life and thought of Yeh-lü Ch'u-ts'ai have been discussed by Igor de Rachewiltz in an early symposium,[20] the main concern
of de Rachewiltz's paper was Yeh-lü's political career and ideology, not
his activities and thought as a Buddhist. In the main, Yeh-lü was responsible for four significant developments in relation to Buddhism.

The first was his role in the appointment of abbots to some key
monasteries in North China, including especially his effort in relation to
Master Hai-yün. According to the inscription of the Master, it was "in
the year of *wu-tzu* [i.e., 1228] [that] the Chief of the Central Secretariat,
the honorable Yeh-lü, Chan-jan chü-shih,[ah] recommended that the
Master [Hai-yün] be invited to take charge of the Ch'ing-shou[ai] Monastery. The request was granted."[21] Most later biographers of Hai-yün have
neglected to mention Yeh-lü's initiative and support of the monk. The
biographies of the Master compiled by Nien-ch'ang[aj] (1282–1344?), Ming-
ho[ak] (1588–1640) and Ching-chu[al] (1601–1654) respectively,[22] all fail
to mention this connection. Apart from this, Yeh-lü was also responsible
for some other appointments to Buddhist monasteries in the provinces
under Mongol control.[23] Because of his influential position at court, his
efforts in their behalf brought a favorable outcome for the Buddhists at
Ta-tu. His support for them gave them a sense of security in times of
uncertainty.

Literary compilations are another contribution of Yeh-lü Ch'u-ts'ai.
Most of the important Buddhist writings produced in his time were related to him in one way or another. He wrote prefaces or colophons to
many of the outstanding works compiled or written by his friends. The
most well-known pieces are the prefaces to the *Ts'ung-jung lu*, *Ch'ing-i
lu* and other works by Hsing-hsiu, as well as the *Ming-tao chi shuo* by Li
P'ing-shan.[24] His other Buddhist writings include epigraphical texts, records (*chi*) and also poems,[25] many of which are preserved in his collected
writings.

The next contribution of Yeh-lü Ch'u-ts'ai to Buddhism was his
advice to Chinggis Khan concerning the conscription of monks. According to a Buddhist biography of Yeh-lü, before Chinggis launched his
campaign against the Khwārezmian empire in Central Asia in 1219, a
proposal had been made to the commanders of the expedition that the
monks of Mt. Wu-t'ai and other Buddhist centers who were able-bodied
and well-versed in military tactics be conscripted into the expeditionary
forces. Yeh-lü contested the proposal strongly. He argued that those who

were faithful to their religion would observe the Buddhist precepts of non-killing, compassion, and forbearance. Should this be the case, they would protect the lives of other beings at the risk of their own, as had been taught by the King of Dharma (i.e., Buddha). What purpose would it serve to recruit them into the armed forces? If they did not follow their own doctrine and precepts, then they lacked commitment and failed to exemplify true practice. If they could act contrary to the teachings of the Buddha, how could they be counted on for loyal service to the ruler? Therefore, they should not be asked to join the expedition. The great Khan accepted his advice.[26] Although it is not clear how many monks were spared from the proposed military service by virtue of Yeh-lü's intercession, this decision was undoubtedly an important one for the Buddhist clergy. There is no doubt that an overwhelming majority of Chinese Buddhist monks would have been reluctant to enter the Mongol military service, whether for conscientious or for selfish reasons.

Another initiative taken by Yeh-lü relevant to Buddhist affairs was his proposal for examining the clergy. The proposal alarmed Yeh-lü's teacher Hsing-hsiu and the Buddhist leader, Hai-yün, and in the end nothing came of it. Nevertheless, it shows that Yeh-lü's personal faith did not impair his judgement as a statesman. He thought that an examination of the clergy would not only reduce their numbers and be beneficial to the economy of the empire, but would also raise the level of the clergy and reform the religious life of Buddhists.[27]

Though Yeh-lü had no long acquaintance with Buddhism, through his study of Ch'an under Master Hsing-hsiu, his understanding of the tradition became very thorough and critical. He was able to perceive the historical task of Ch'an Buddhists at this time, and to persuade his Master to strengthen the Ts'ao-tung Ch'an tradition by compiling the *Ts'ung-jung (an) lu* and *Ch'ing-i lu*. This intention was clearly indicated in the colophon he wrote for Hsing-hsiu's *Ch'ing-i lu*. There Yeh-lü pointed out that among the three prevailing schools of Ch'an Buddhism at this time, the Lin-chi tradition was represented by the records of *Chi-chieh lu* and *Pi-yen lu*; and the Yün-men Ch'an tradition was preserved in the *Chüeh-hai hsüan-lu*, yet the Ts'ao-tung Ch'an tradition had no *kung-an* collection to represent it. With this in mind he successfully persuaded the Master to compile these works, which came to be included in the *Tripitaka* and had a lasting influence on the later development of Chinese Buddhism.

Yeh-lü not only had an historical vision of the Ts'ao-tung tradition, but also had an analytical and critical knowledge of Ch'an Buddhism at large. In one of the prefaces he had written, Yeh-lü stated that while he was attending Wan-sung in Ta-tu, he had the opportunity to examine "the principles of various schools."[28] He found that "each of the schools had its own unique merit, but disadvantage followed advantage when the latter emerged."[29] In his view, the intertwining of advantage and disadvantage was a natural condition of all *dharma* (things or laws). What is this intertwining? Yeh-lü analyzed each Ch'an school as follows:

In the school of Yün-men, the enlightened ones attain it out of [a paradoxical combination of] reticence and incisiveness (lit. "wisecracks," *chin-ch'iao*);[am] and the deluded ones lose it out of discrimination and impulsiveness (*shih-ching*).[an] In the school of Lin-chi, the illuminated ones attain it out of headlong daring (lit. "steepness," *chun-pa*);[ao] and the obfuscated ones lose it out of recklessness (*mang-lu*).[ap] In the Ts'ao-tung school, the wise ones attain it out of fine insight (*mien-mi*);[aq] and the stupid ones lose it out of [involvement in] minute details (*lien-hsien*).[ar][30]

This is an astute analysis of Ch'an Buddhism in North China, as it explicitly points out the respective strengths and weakness of the three influential schools. In Yeh-lü's view each of these schools has its unique approach and is capable of solving the religious problems of its followers. This capability may, however, turn into a weakness if it is overdone; that is, if it is pursued without regard to the attendant circumstances and conditions. The inclusion of Yeh-lü's own school and the pointing up of its characteristic weakness indicates the degree of objectivity and critical spirit achieved by Yeh-lü in his understanding of religion.

As a disciple, Yeh-lü held the highest esteem for his master, Hsing-hsiu, but this does not mean that their views were identical. We have seen Hsing-hsiu's criticism of the disciple, which reveals precisely the point of difference between the two. For Yeh-lü, the original teachings of the Three Sages were identical, though the style of the different schools (*tsung-feng*)[as] varied according to times and circumstances. He considered that Taoism and Confucianism illuminated the Chinese classics from within and without, while Buddhism distinguished between appearance and emptiness through the teachings of the expedient and the real. In a poem he said that someone without adequate understanding might stress the differences among the three, while a wise man with a broader outlook would see the harmony among them.[31]

On another occasion Yeh-lü expressed his syncretic approach even more explicitly. He states:

The Way of our Confucius is for governing the world, the Way of Lao Tzu is for nourishing the nature, and the Way of Buddhas is for cultivating the mind. This is a universal opinion, in the past as well as in the present. Apart from these [doctrines], the rest is all heresy.[32]

This explicit statement provoked the Ch'an Master's criticism of his disciple. Yeh-lü, however, responded with an interesting explanation. In a later letter to his master, he said that his statement had been an "act of adaptation" (*hsing-ch'uan*)[at] and should not be construed as subordinating the Buddhist Way. He further stated that the Confucian Way, though supposedly capable of governing the world, was inadequate for controlling the mind, which actually means that it is merely the dregs of the Way. In order to support his explanation, Yeh-lü quoted from the *Great Learning*. He stated: "according to Tai's classic text those who wished to bring order to their state . . . would first rectify their mind. There is never a case wherein one's mind is rectified and yet the state remains in disorder. From this we know that the governing of the world is a byproduct of the controlling of the mind."[33] This statement is significant because, firstly, it deals with the relationship between the mind and governance, and secondly, it connects the doctrines of Confucianism and Buddhism. His identifying of Buddhism with the control of the mind, and his giving precedence to the control of the mind over the governing of the world is a direct challenge to Confucianism. No wonder Neo-Confucian thinkers of the subsequent period had to give such priority to the problem of the mind. Unless Confucianism developed a satisfactory philosophy of mind, the Buddhist claim to the superiority of their own philosophy of the mind would carry great force.

HAI-YÜN, THE NEW LEADER OF THE BUDDHISTS

About two decades after Ta-tu came under the control of the Mongols, and at a time when Hsing-hsiu and other leading figures were lying low in their activities, the most active monk was Yin-chien, the well-known Hai-yün ta-shih.[au] Like Hsing-hsiu, the new leader was a Ch'an Buddhist, yet his personality, political connections, and contributions in many

ways differed from those of Hsing-hsiu. In the first place, Hsing-hsiu
appears to have had a broad interest in Chinese religion generally, and
displayed a remarkable literary and scholarly bent, while Hai-yün seems
to have been a man of action. In contrast to Hsing-hsiu's compilation of
books and attention to the education of youth, Hai-yün devoted himself
more to the revival of Buddhist monasteries and to dealing with Mongol
rulers and officials. As far as can be seen from the material in his biography, he wrote very little and produced no disciples of any great eminence. Liu Ping-chung[av] (1216–1274) is the only exception, and his
contributions were political in nature rather than religious.[34]

The source of Hai-yün's influence was his early connection with
Mongol officials. As the biography of Hai-yün in the *Fo-tsu li-tai t'ung-
tsai*[aw] is the most comprehensive account, modern scholars have constantly turned to it for its wealth of detail, yet it contains a number of
mistakes, and the treatment of Hai-yün's connection with the Mongol
rulers is one example. According to this biography, the Master was 13 at
the time Emperor Chinggis Khan was engaged in the campaign for the
conquest of the world. The master then resided at Ning-yüan,[ax] and he
saw His Majesty from amidst the crowd upon the fall of the city.[35] As
Kunishita Hirosato[ay] pointed out, this claim is contradicted by the official history.[36] Now an inscription concerning Hai-yün has been discovered which states that "when the Ning-yüan city first fell [into Mongol
hands], the Master and his teacher Chung-kuan[az] were both captured
. . . .[37] and Emperor Chinggis, then in Samarkand, sent a messenger to
the Grand Preceptor [*T'ai-shih*, i.e. Mukhali (1170–1223)]. . . . ." From
this passage it is clear that Hai-yün's first contact with the Mongols was
not directly with Chinggis Khan. Nevertheless his early association with
the Mongol rulers launched a successful career that provided a useful
link between the Buddhists and the rulers of Ta-tu.

Although at first Hai-yün's connection with the Mongol court was
quite limited, he gradually enlarged his contacts and achieved a high
standing. His first significant involvement was with Chancellor Hsia-li.[ba]
It is recorded that in the fall of 1233, Hsia-li was ordered by Ögödei (r.
1229–1241) to go to Yen-ching on an official mission. As Hsia-li had
heard of Hai-yün's reputation, he paid him a visit and received "pure
commandments" (*ching-chieh*)[bb] or discipline for verbal and bodily conduct from the master. Hsia-li was known for his stern attitude towards his
subordinates, and therefore the officials of Yen-ching were fearful of him.

It was in such a context that Hai-yün advised Hsia-li that "in the city of Yen very few people have survived the siege. . . . They resemble the grass and plants that remain after a bleak frost. They cannot revive unless the warm sun of spring appears."[38] He further said that "people are the foundation of a country; how can a country be a country when there are no people?" He continued, "a humane and altruistic mind (*jen-shu chih-hsin*)[bc] is the root of good government; the compassion taught by the Buddhas will be damaged should the sentient beings be left to suffer." The inscription states that "although the emissary could not accept this advice, he had high esteem for the admonition."[39] This indicates the limits of Hai-yün's influence, on the one hand, and the difficult situation with which the Buddhists were confronted, on the other.

The next significant move of Hai-yün was his protection of K'ung Yüan-ts'o[bd] (1179?–1252?), a fifty-first-generation descendant of Confucius. In 1190 K'ung inherited the title Duke of Yen-sheng[be] from his father, who had been honored by the Chin ruler as a gesture of patronage toward Confucianism. When the Mongol army captured the Chin Southern capital, Pien,[bf] (modern Kaifeng) in 1233, K'ung lost his position and became a refugee. During this time, however, Yüan Hao-wen[bg] (1190–1257), the Chin literary celebrity, submitted a letter to Yeh-lü Ch'u-ts'ai pleading with him to seek out talented scholars and grandees among the refugees for employment in the new government. He produced a list of fifty-four such individuals and K'ung Yüan-ts'o was one of them.[40] Accordingly, Yeh-lü Ch'u-ts'ai accepted Yüan's plea and rescued a few score of former leading Chin scholars and grandees, including the fifty-first lineal descendant of Confucius. It was "upon Yeh-lü Ch'u-ts'ai's recommendation that K'ung was restored by an imperial edict to the title of Duke Yen-sheng and to his traditional privileges."[41] According to the biography of Hai-yün, however, the credit for this is due to Hai-yün's persuasiveness. It is recorded that K'ung first went to Yen-ching and visited the monk with a letter of introduction from the honorable Yen (i.e., Yen Shih,[bh] 1182–1240), then a myriarch commander at Tung-p'ing under the Mongol aegis. The monk then spoke of the matter to the authorities, enumerating the traditional privileges that had been accorded to Confucius' family. He explained the political significance of supporting the K'ungs and requested the authorities to restore the traditional honors and privileges to Confucius' descendants. As a consequence, the rank was restored and sacrifice to the sage was allowed to continue. In addition, Hai-yün secured the continuation of family sacrifices to Confucius' disciples such as Yen Hui and Mencius, and persuaded the Mongol authorities to extend tax exemption to students who studied Confucian classics.[42] It is worth noting that Hai-yün invoked essentially the Confucian argument in recommending the restoration of Kung's hereditary title and privileges.

Hai-yün's efforts to restore the privileges of Confucius' family are ignored by the *Yüan shih* [bi] as well as by modern scholars,[43] yet evidence from Buddhist sources on the matter is quite substantial. After the Mongols' conquest of Pien, most of the leading Confucian scholars fled east and took shelter at Tung-p'ing.[bj] In desperation, they tried their best to present their case to the Mongol authorities through different channels. Yeh-lü aided their cause at the central court, while Hai-yün supported it at Ta-tu.

The most important contribution of Hai-yün to the Buddhist community at Ta-tu was his success in remonstrating against the reintroduction of the examination of the Buddhist clergy. The growth of the clergy population and its impact on the national revenue was a constant problem to various dynasties in imperial China, and it was no different under Mongol rule. As early as 1229, soon after Ögödei was elected to the Mongol throne, he issued an edict ordering that Buddhist and Taoist monks below the age of fifty should pass an examination on the scriptures of their religions. Unless they could do this, they would not be qualified to remain in the clergy and would thus be subject to taxation.[44] According to one source, as stated in the biography of Kuo Pao-yü [bk] he advised Chinggis Khan that "Buddhist and Taoist [monks] were of no benefit to the country and harmful to the people; they should all be banned."[45] The question of examining the clergy became more serious in 1235–36 and it made the Buddhist clergy in Ta-tu increasingly worried.[46] The matter was so urgent and worrisome that it forced even inactive leaders, such as Hsing-hsiu, to take up the cause. Buddhist leaders in the city visited Hai-yün and argued that any examination of clergy would be disastrous because religious teaching had long been suspended and most of the monks were illiterate. They jointly requested Hai-yün to intervene. It seems that Hai-yün was not at all certain whether he would be able to handle the affair successfully. His initial reaction to the request was cautious and diplomatic. On the one hand, he told the monks that they should urge their colleagues to attend the proposed examinations as the imperial decision must reflect deep consideration of the matter. He also complained that monks at that time were "giving little attention to observing the commandments and disciplines, had largely neglected to learn the ritual, and lived in a manner far removed from the Tao."[47] Obviously this response was political in tone, more like the pronouncement of a government official who supported clergy examination than of a monk who opposed it. On the other hand, when he met the Mongol officials, his antiexamination stand was clear and unambiguous. The conversation between Hai-yün and Hsia-li was sharp and incisive:

> The Chancellor said: "I have received a holy edict to send officials to take charge of the examinations on the scriptures. Those who are able to read will be allowed to continue as clergy; and those who are illiterate will be ordered to return to the laity."
>
> The Master responded: "I am a rustic monk myself, I never look at scriptures and do not know a single word."
>
> The Chancellor asked: "If you cannot read, how could you become a senior monk?"
>
> The Master rejoined with: "Is the honorable Great Official able to read [the scriptures]?"

(As this was uttered in the presence of many officials from different places and ranks, they were all shocked by the Master's retort.)

> The Chancellor again said: "What should be done?"
>
> The Master said: "How can the clergy be examined like young school boys? The state ought to encourage moral cultivation and worship the Three Jewels [of Buddhism], thus to revere heaven and extend the rule of the dynasty. . . ."[48]

His arguments successfully convinced Hsia-li and the latter reported this to Sigi-Khutakhu, the imperial messenger. As a result a compromise was arrived at, that "the examination would take place, but no candidates would fail."[49] An edict was also issued, declaring the restoration of Chinggis Khan's policy towards the Buddhists, i.e., the clergy were exempted from taxation.

According to Nien-ch'ang, in 1236, the Mongol officials intended to brand people on their arms. Hai-yün forcefully argued to Sigi-Khutakhu that people are not cattle. If they have submitted to becoming subjects of the empire they will have no other place to go. It is therefore improper to brand them like animals. His intervention stopped the move.[50] Kunishita points out that bodily branding was a tribal custom of the Mongols, and should not be misunderstood as a deliberate insult to the

Chinese, as Hai-yün himself acknowledged to Sigi-Khutakhu.[51] Yet whatever the justification of the Mongol's move might be, as far as the Chinese inhabitants of the capital city were concerned, Hai-yün's expression of anxiety over the matter, and the position he took, certainly reflected the Chinese sentiment. It can therefore be imagined that the monk's successful intervention won him respect among the local people.

The Master himself received a few more honors in subsequent years: in 1237 the two empresses of the late Chinggis gave him the title of Kuang-t'ien chen-kuo ta-shih[bl] (The Master who Illuminates Heaven and Pacifies the Empire); and he was again ordained as Abbot of Ta-ch'ing-shou[bm] Monastery in Yen-ching. Then in 1242 he was summoned by Khubilai Khaghan (r. 1260–1294) to his headquarters to give instructions in Buddhism.[52] Thus, as time went on Hai-yün's official position improved. He became Registrar of Buddhist Clergy in 1247 with very generous emoluments, and was called by Khubilai to Karakorum. His position as Registrar was once more confirmed when Möngke (r. 1251–1259) was elected to the throne in 1251. From the Buddhist viewpoint the new position held by the monk marked the highest point of the relationship between the Chinese Buddhists and the Mongols, as no other Chinese monk had ever held such a high position. As far as his achievements are concerned, however, it is only recorded that he secured for the Buddhists exemption of taxation and labor service in accordance with previous practice.[53]

One of the most important results of Hai-yün's association with Khubilai, however, was the recommendation of his disciple, Liu Ping-chung, to the service of the latter. In years to come Liu was destined to play an important political role in the establishment and consolidation of the Yüan dynasty.[54] Many aspects of the relationship between Hai-yün and Liu resemble that between Hsing-hsiu and Yeh-lü Ch'u-ts'ai. Isofar as its benefits to the Buddhists are concerned, however, Liu's contribution is dubious. While his influential position in the Mongol court must have made Buddhists feel secure, Liu's concrete support of Buddhism was much less apparent than Yeh-lü's had been. This was probably because, with his unique background and his shrewdness as a politician, Liu preferred to act behind the scenes rather than befriend the Buddhists openly. He was moreover, a syncretist who dabbled in Taoism and Confucianism. His only known contribution to Buddhism, it seems, was his support of monk Chih-wen when he participated in the Buddhist-Taoist debate on *Hua-hu ching* [bn] in 1258. Yet even in this debate his role was rather passive. He never acted as a spokesman for the Buddhist side, but behaved more like an uncommitted neutral observer.[55] Judging from his later interest in Taoism, one wonders whether his support for Buddhism was ever of a sectarian kind. Nevertheless while Liu gave little concrete assistance to the Buddhists, he did live up to the spirit of Buddhism. In the spirit-way epitaph composed by Wang P'an[bo] (1202–1293) in Liu's memory, it is stated that:

His Majesty [i.e., Khubilai] was divine in military matters with superb judgment, ever victorious over his enemies on the battlefield. Yet, deep in his mind there was humanity and love. The Venerable [i.e., Liu] often praised [His Majesty] by saying: "With Heaven and Earth to love life is a virtue; Buddhists regard compassionate assistance to sentient beings as the Mind." There were innumerable lives saved through Liu's skillful help and protection.[56]

It is also stated that before Khubilai's election to the throne, when he spent most of his time in his headquarters at Karakoram, many scholars traveled from afar to see the Prince. Many of them came with plans and recommendations designed to secure for themselves coveted positions. Liu alone never begged for anything. Whenever he was asked by Khubilai for advice, he always recommended qualified Chinese scholars for appointment. Consequently, many outstanding persons were recruited into Khubilai's service on his recommendation, and some of them contributed importantly to the establishment of the Yüan dynasty.[57]

DEFENCE WITHOUT AND CONSOLIDATION WITHIN

With the death of Hai-yün, the Chinese Buddhists of Ta-tu lost their most experienced leader. Thereafter, no other Chinese Buddhist monk ever attained the high stature and had the strong influence on Mongol authorities which the late master had had. This situation largely arose from the change in attitude of the Mongol court, as the Confucian elite began to play a greater role in the civil service and Tibetan priests had control over religious affairs. In comparison with the Confucians and Tibetans, Chinese Buddhists no longer enjoyed a preeminent position at the capital. Even under these circumstances, however, the younger generation of Chinese Buddhist leadership was still able to defend its religion from without and to consolidate its community within.

Of those who made an effort in this direction, Fu-yü, Chih-wen, and Ts'ung-lun were the most outstanding. Fu-yü was the senior of the three, and his contributions should be dealt with first. After he learned Ch'an Buddhism from other masters, Fu-yü joined Hsing-hsiu for "higher attainment" and worked under the Master's personal supervision for more than a decade. Soon after the demise of the Chin state in 1232, he was made abbot of the Shao-lin monastery and was called in for personal consultation by Khubilai while the latter was still a prince. In 1248, he was summoned to Karakorum by Ögödei Khan to preside over the Hsing-kuo Monastery and he had an audience with the emperor. Impressed by his calibre, Ögödei appointed him Superintendent of Buddhist Teaching (*Shih-chiao tsung-t'ung*).[bp] It was under his administration that two hundred and thirty-six defunct monasteries were restored and assigned to monks and nuns.[58] Fu-yü was the Buddhist spokesman in the 1258 debate with the Taoist representative. According to Hsiang-mai[bq] (fl. 1291), as early as 1255, Fu-yü had instigated the debate by reporting to Prince Arig Böge, at Karakorum, that Taoists had "insulted" Buddhism by fabricating the story of Lao Tzu's conversion of the barbarians. A Buddhist source claims that Li Chih-ch'ang[br] (1193–1256), the head of the Ch'ang-ch'un sect of Taoism, had participated in and lost the 1255 debate; a Taoist source confirms that Li was at Karakorum during that year, but makes no mention of the debate with the Buddhists at all.[59]

The Buddhists claimed that they won the 1255 debate and that the Mongol court at Karakorum took action to restore the Buddhist properties occupied by the Taoists. Yet the disputes between the two, which were mainly over rights to monastic properties, dragged on through 1255 and 1256.[60] This led to the 1258 debate which Khubilai personally presided over at Karakorum. Fu-yü was the spokesman for the Buddhists, and Chang Chih-ching,[bs] (1220–1270) was the Taoist representative.

The 1258 debate was an unfortunate event for the Taoists, as they were confronted by four opponents, i.e., Khubilai (who was more inclined to favor Buddhism), the Tibetan priests, the Chinese Buddhists, and the Confucian scholars at court. Phags-pa (1239?–1280), the Tibetan Imperial Preceptor (*Ti-shih*),[bt] played a crucial role in the debate. With his stature and influence in the Mongol court, his knowledge of Buddhism (especially its Indian and Tibetan background), and his sharp questioning, he helped the Buddhists win the debate. Phags-pa's contribution to the debate with the Taoists has been vividly described in an inscription concerning him:

When the Taoists took the *Shih chi* (Records of the Historian) and other works as a reference in the hope that they might win the debate by showing the impressive number of books [on their side], Pandita Phags-pa, the Imperial Preceptor, asked:

"What is this book?"

"This is the book of the rulers of privious dynasties," the Taoist replied.

"You are now discussing religious doctrine," his Majesty said, "what is the use of referring to the rulers of previous dynasties?"

"In our India (T'ien-chu) we do have such books [discussing religion]. Do you know them?" asked the Preceptor [Phags-pa].

"I have never heard of them", said the Taoist.

"Let me recite from the Indian king Bimbisara's hymn in praise of the Buddha for you. It reads as follows:

> 'None is comparable to Buddha in the heavens or the world,
>
> Nor in the ten worldly directions.
>
> I have seen all beings in the world,
>
> And none of them compares to Lord Buddha.'

"When this hymn was uttered, where was Lao Tzu at that moment?" [The Imperial Preceptor asked.]

The Taoist failed to answer the question . . .

The Imperial Preceptor further questioned:

"Has the *Shih chi* recorded the story of Lao Tzu's converting the barbarians?"

"No, sir."

"What is the scripture preached by Lao Tzu?"

"It is the *Tao-te ching*."

"Is there any other scripture apart from this"?

"No, sir."

The Imperial Preceptor then concluded:

"As this event is not recorded in the *Shih chi* nor is it mentioned in the *Tao-te ching*, the claim is obviously false.

The Taoists were at a loss to carry on the argument. Yao Shu,[bu] the Secretary, declared:

"The Taoists are defeated!"[61]

Although Yao Shu (1203–1280), the Confucian scholar, had only a limited and neutral role in the debate, the facts he presented to the court indirectly contributed to the Buddhist victory. For example, when he testified that the doctrines of humanity and righteousness (*jen i*)[bv] "are the teachings of Confucius," his statement, in fact, refuted the Taoists' claim that much of the Confucian moral teachings originated with Lao Tzu. Consequently, the Taoists again lost the debate. This led to the burning of forty-five Taoist texts, while seventeen Taoists were forcibly converted to the Buddhist clergy, and two hundred and thirty-seven temples under Taoist occupation were returned to the Buddhists.[62]

Among the Buddhist participants, Ts'ung-lun and Fu-yü deserve special attention. Ts'ung-lun probably had the longest record of participation in the controversies with the Taoists, including the final debate in 1281. Fu-yü was the one who initiated the debate with the Taoists. He was also a good teacher and organizer. When Buddhist monks gathered at Ta-tu in accordance with an edict of 1271, one-third of the assembly were Fu-yü's disciples. His biographers paid high tribute to his ability and devotion to the teaching of young monks, saying: "In his guidance and support of young scholars there is never any letup."[63] In many respects, his teaching has a poetic quality that is typical of Ch'an Buddhism. After he retired to Mt. Sung in his old age, he no longer attended social affairs, but engaged himself in the work of religious transmission. One episode may be quoted to show the spirit of Ch'an as well as the skill and quality of his teaching:

A monk asked:
"What was the intention of the Patriarch [i.e.., Bodhidharma] in coming from the West?"
The teacher answered:
"I will tell you when the Stalactite Mountain is nodding."
"What is the Way upward to honor and veneration?"
The Master answered:
"Egrets in the sand-pit are distrubed by fishermen's songs. Flying out from the reeds, they leave no trace to follow."[64]

The other Buddhist who participated in the debate with the Taoist representatives was Chih-wen, better known as monk P'u-an,[bw] another of Wan-sung's disciples and a personal friend of Liu Ping-chung. He was recommended to Khubilai by Liu, but declined the offer of a government position. He told Khubilai that he was interested in spreading Buddhism in the country, and not in gaining official position. However, after Khubilai's campaign to Yün-nan against the Ta-li[bx] kingdom in 1253, Liu Ping-chung again recommended his friend. Consequently, Chih-wen received the title of Fo-kuo P'u-an ta Ch'an-shih[by] and was appointed general supervisor of Buddhist affairs over several provinces, in which role he promoted and protected Buddhist interests with great zeal. Whenever Buddhist properites were encroached upon by members of other religions or local landlords, he made an effort to have the properties returned to the Buddhists. Chih-wen had a role in the Buddhist-Taoist debate but it seems that it was not a major one; after this he withdrew from the scene and retired shortly before his death in 1267.[65]

The two aforementioned leaders of Buddhism, besides participating in the Buddhist debate with the Taoists, had personal connections with Khubilai and had some influence in Mongol officialdom. Yet all these happened before Khubilai's enthronement. After Phags-pa became the State Preceptor (*Kuo-shih*)[bz] in 1260, the position of Chinese Buddhists in Ta-tu gradually declined. No Chinese monk ever attained high rank nor had the personal confidence of the Mongol emperor. Moreover, after the 1258 debate with the Taoists, the Tibetan priests, especially Phags-pa and his associates, often acted as judges before Khubilai. Under these circumstances, Chinese Buddhist monks seem to have become more cautious in their dealings with the Mongol court, searching for a way to deal with the Tibetans. This was necessary because, although the Tibetan priests and Chinese monks had some common traditions, in many respects Tibetan Buddhism differed from Chinese. The earlier confrontation between Ch'an monks and Indian Buddhists at Lhasa during the eighth century had already brought out this difference.[66]

With this in mind, we should note an occasion on which the Chinese monks were summoned by Khubilai to explain Ch'an Buddhism to the emperor and the Imperial Preceptor. The monk who gave the explanation was Ts'ung-lun, another disciple of Hsing-hsiu. This was a significant event philosophically and historically, though it has been left almost untouched by modern scholarship. In the biography of Ts'ung-lun,[67] it is recorded that in 1272 an edict summoned him to the imperial palace to lecture on Ch'an Buddhism. His lecture was based on the *Ch'an-yüan ch'üan*[ca] (Explanations on the Source of Ch'an) by the Master Kuei-feng (i.e., Tsung-mi,[cb] 780-841).[68] He quoted from the book and stated that:

> Ch'an is an Indian term, its complete form is *dhyāna*. The Chinese translated it as "thinking-subtle-cultivation" (*ssu-wei-hsiu*).[cc] It is also known as "quiet thinking." All these are a general designation of concentration-wisdom (*samādhi-prajñā*). It means the source that is the true nature of the original enlightenment of all the sentient beings. It is called the Buddha-nature, and also known by the term Mind. . . .[69]

The text goes on to say that though the Mind itself is universal without any differentiation, yet different gradations do exist in the practice of *dhyāna* meditation. The gradations are: (1) those who practice it in order to be reborn into a higher caste, (2) the concentration practiced by ordinary people to achieve happiness, (3) the Hinayanist concentration for No-self, (4) the Mahāyāna concentration for twofold emptiness, i.e., No-self and No-*dharma*, and (5) those who achieve sudden realization of one's own Mind as originally pure and free from defilement. In the latter, one has pure wisdom and the whole of the true nature within oneself; and if one practices the concentration with this realization, it is the supreme concentration. It is also known as the cool and pure concentration of Tathāgata, and what has been transmitted from [Bodhi] Dharma to later generations, one after the other, is this cool and pure concentration of Tathāgata.[70] The conversation went on as follows:

The Emperor asked, "Formerly, when a question was asked, no answer was given in spoken word or writing. Why have you spoken thus in your present lecture?"

The Master answered: "The principle (*li*) itself is inexpressible in words, I am trying to explain it by citing concrete examples (*shih*)."[71]

The Emperor asked: "Why is the principle inexpressible in words?"

"Because the principle is united with the spirit (*shen*).[cd] It is like a man eating honey, who could say that the honey is purple or white if asked to describe its color, but if asked to describe its taste, would find it difficult to put this into words," the Master replied.

The Emperor turned to the Imperial Preceptor [i.e., Phags-pa] and asked: "Is the reply right or wrong?"

The latter said, "This is certainly no different from the most profound teaching of the Perfection of Wisdom."

Then the emperor asked about the *kung-an*[ce] of the Ch'an partriarchs. The Master quoted the "banner and wind" *kung-an*[72] of the sixth patriarch (i.e., Hui-neng,[cf] 638–713):

"One evening when the wind was stirring up the temple banner, he heard two monks arguing. One said it was the flag that was moving, the other that it was the wind." The Sixth Patriarch said, "It is neither the banner nor the wind that is moving; it is only your own mind that moves."[73]

The Imperial Preceptor [commenting on the *kung-an*] said, "It is really the wind and banner that move. Why is it said that the mind moves?"

The master replied: "Because all things are nothing but the Mind only, and the ten thousand *dharmas* are nothing but Consciousness only. Is it not the Mind that moves?"

The biography records that "the sharp debate continued until evening."[74]

From a doctrinal viewpoint, the reference to Tsung-mi's *Ch'an-yüan ch'üan* is interesting because some Ch'an monks had reservations about the work during the T'ang period.[75] Even in the Northern Sung, there was at least one influential monk of the Ch'an school who regarded Tsung-mi as "a partisan of knowledge and understanding," and the work as "fraught with the language of contradiction. . . . It is no different from what one gets through vulgar gossip."[76] One has to remember that these remarks were spoken by Tzu-ning,[cg] the abbot of the famous Ching-te[ch] Monastery at Mt. T'ien-tung. Now, it was about two centuries later that Ts'ung-lun lectured to the Mongol emperor and the Imperial Preceptor on this same book. This reflects the changed situation of Buddhism in Yüan politics. Tsung-mi's philosophy as presented in this book is, on one level, a dialectical understanding of conflict and harmony between doctrinal and practical Buddhism and also among doctrinal sects themselves. On another level it attempts the same for sectarian practitioners. This dialectical understanding is known as *ho-hui*,[ci] or "harmonization and consummation," which is achievable through comparative study. On the one hand it is through exclusive analysis that the differences between the schools are manifest; on the other, it is through inclusive syncretism that an understanding of their universality is established. When understanding is achieved through both these processes, one would have a universal view which negates sectarianism; and one would also have a particular preference as to the most suitable religious means, which would facilitate the work of salvation. This philosophy assigns each of the Buddhist schools a proper place, pointing out both the usefulness and limitations of each at the same time.[77]

There is no doubt that such a philosophy served the Buddhist cause well during the Yüan period. This is because it connects doctrine and practice without difficulty, and because its tolerant attitude towards all sects would be helpful in reconciling and consolidating the Buddhists from within. It seems that Ts'ung-lun performed well before the emperor, and as a result of this encounter, Tsung-mi's book appeared in a new edition, the four-*chüan* edition with prefaces contributed by Wei-ta,[cj] Teng Wen-yüan,[ck] and Chia Ju-chou,[cl] respectively, printed in 1303.[78] According to Teng, in the twelfth year of Chin-yüan (1275), Khubilai called Phags-pa and other eminent monks to the Kuang-han palace and asked questions about the essence of Ch'an Buddhism. The monks presented the *Ch'an-yüan ch'üan* as their reply. The emperor was very pleased, so he ordered that printing blocks for the book be prepared in order to transmit the book to future generations.[79] Chia Ju-chou confirmed the date of the gathering and gave more details. He claimed that in the first lunar month of 1275 Khubilai invited the Imperial Preceptor to the Ch'iung-hua[cm] Island; Liu Ping-chung, the Grand Guardian, was also present. His Majesty thereupon summoned eminent monks in the capital, and asked them about the conflicting interpretations between Ch'an and doctrinal Buddhism. The late Master Hsi-an Yün[cn] and others, eight in all, gave answers to the questions raised in terms of the text of the *Ch'an-yüan ch'üan* by Kuei-feng Tsung-mi, and these, it is said, greatly pleased the emperor.[80] This story seems authentic but the date is definitely wrong. Liu Ping-chung passed away on September 20, 1274,[81] so there is no possibility that he could have been present at a meeting in 1275. The event referred to is probably the 1272 encounter in which Ts'ung-lun was the spokesman, and the other monks played their part in the preparation of the printing blocks. In any case, Tsung-mi's philosophy had great influence on the Ch'an Buddhists at Ta-tu, and the acceptance of this philosophy also reflects the changing needs of the times.

Two features of Ts'ung-lun's part in this debate are worth nothing. In the first place, the debate with Khubilai Khaghan and Phags-pa had earned him a reputation as a skillful speaker. In one of the prefaces to his book, Ts'ung-lun writes that he has "expressed in language the truth of the inexpressible. This will enable those who have never heard [the truth] to hear it." Someone has commented that "It is not that the Honorable Lun was so given to speech, but only that the Tao needed to be discussed. He therefore had no choice but to speak."[82] Secondly, when the controversy was concluded, an edict was issued on December 2, 1281, ordering the burning of false Taoist texts such as the *Hua-hu ching*, at the Ta-min-chung Monastery in Ta-tu. Ts'ung-lun was given the honor of starting the fire and he did it with a hymn before he set fire to the Taoist texts.[83] After it was done, he composed a poem on the spot, expressing the Buddhist's gratitude for the imperial decision.[84]

Ts'ung-lun is also known for his two compilations: one is called *K'ung-ku ch'uan-sheng*[co] (Echoes in the Empty Valley); and the other is *Hsü-t'ang hsi-t'ing*[cp] (Stories Heard in the Vacuous Hall). These two works were originally composed by I-ch'ing[cq] (1032-1083) and Te-ch'un[cr] (1064-1117), respectively, of the Sung dynasty. Ts'ung-lun enlarged upon the texts with his own appraisal in hymn form.[85] The style and purpose of his writing closely followed those of his teacher Wan-sung. In this respect, Ts'ung-lun is the only monk who was a true successor to the literary tradition of Wan-sung.

THE DOMINANCE OF TIBETAN PRIESTS

The formal establishemnt of the Yüan dynasty marks the beginning of the decline of Chinese Buddhist influence on the Mongol rulers. Though there was a new generation of leaders among Chinese Buddhists, none of them had a personality to match Hai-yün's nor connections with the Mongols comparable to his. In contrast with this, a new and powerful Tibetan Buddhist leader had emerged in the court, namely Phags-pa. Along with the difference in leadership, there was a change in the political atmosphere. As the Mongols faced the need to maintain their dominant position over the Chinese, it was natural for them to look to Tibetan priests for religious leadership rather than rely on the Chinese.

One may ask what attracted the Mongols to the Tibetans. Part of the answer is that the Tibetan form of Buddhism had many elements lacking in Chinese Buddhism, especially in Ch'an Buddhism. The Tibetan priests had impressed the Mongols by "the power, authority, and prestige of the religious hierarchy."[86] The colorful ceremonies and superior magic in Tibetan religion appealed to the Mongol mind more than the subtle philosophy and unconventional conduct of the Ch'an Buddhists. Morever, form a racial viewpoint, the Mongols felt a closer affinity to the Tibetans.

The one who built up Tibetan influence at the Mongol court was Phags-pa.[87] He had joined Khubilai in 1253 when the latter was age 15. His position at the Mongol court had been helpful to the Buddhists in their debate with the Taoists in 1258. After the establishment of the Yüan dynasty in 1260 he was appointed the State/Imperial Preceptor and in 1270 he created the Mongol script called the Phags-pa Script.[88] In the biographical account of Phags-pa, written by the Han-lin academician Wang P'an, there is one paragraph which describes the honors enjoyed by the Tibetan monk as well as one of the reasons for his success in the Yüan court:

In the eleventh year of Chih-yüan [1274], His Majesty [Khubilai] sent a special message to summon the Preceptor, and he returned to the capital at the end of the year. Upon his arrival, princes and lords, ministers and officials, scholars and common people all went out of the capital to welcome him. People constructed a great platform for burning incense and presented pure offerings. An elegant umbrella of flowers covered the platform and great religious music was performed. All people knelt down at the reception. The streets which he passed through were all decorated with colored silks and ornaments. Thousands upon thousands watched and worshipped him as if a Buddha had appeared in the world. At that time the imperial armies had just successfully crossed the River [i.e., the Yangtze] with flying speed, and the empire was unified in a short time. Though it was achieved by the effort of the sagely king and virtuous minister; yet it was also due to the invisible assistance given by the Preceptor. . . .[89]

The "invisible assistance" mentioned above refers to the alleged magic power of the Tibetan priest. There was a similar story about an earlier instance when Khubilai deputed general Bayan (1236–1294) to attack South China, and the mission failed. The emperor then asked the Tibetan priest Tampa why the protecting gods did not help. Tampa replied that "without an invitation to serve, a man will not go; except in response to a prayer, a Buddha will not speak." The emperor therefore prayed, and the Sung dynasty soon submitted.[90] Miraculous powers claimed for the Tibetan religion were no doubt one of its great attractions for the Mongol ruler.

The Chinese reaction to the dominance of the Tibetans might be characterized as a mixture of limited cooperation, passive acceptance, silent rejection, and a certain degree of resentful accommodation. Cooperation was limited to those matters in which some benefit may have accrued to the Chinese Buddhists. The best example is the cooperation between the Chinese and Phags-pa in the Buddhist-Taoist debate in 1258 discussed earlier. Further evidence of cooperation between the Chinese Buddhists and Tibetan priests came in the form of praise for those priests who had made some contribution to the welfare of Buddhism. The case of Sarpa (d. 1314) is one example. It is recorded that during Khubilai's reign, "although offices [for the regulation of Buddhism] increased in number, discipline actually deteriorated." According to government regulations, local officials were not supposed to interfere with clerical affairs, but abuses increased, especially in South China. It was in these circumstances that Sarpa was deputed to South China on the recommendation of Phags-pa, to become the provincial director of clergy. "After he arrived there, he abolished the measures that he considered to be superfluous and harsh, and his policies were tolerant, so the people enjoyed peace."[91]

The Chinese Buddhists' attitude toward the office of religious affairs was generally passive. This was, of course, nothing new, although the confrontation with a new alien authority gave it a different dimension. An illustration of this is the attitude of the monk Wen-ts'ai[cs] (1241–1302), an outstanding scholar in Hua-yen,[ct] who had become well known when he was the abbot of the Pai-ma[cu] Monastery at Lo-yang.[92] When Emperor Temür (Ch'eng-tsung, r. 1294–1307) built the Wan-shou Monastery on Mt. Wu-t'ai,[cv] Wen-ts'ai was offered the first abbotship of the monastery upon the recommendation of a Tibetan. The monk declined the offer, saying that he considered his abbotship at the Pai-ma Monastery already beyond his ability, so how could he be the abbot of the newly built imperial monastery? He concluded with the remark that "To overreach one's limitations in order to gain a high position will bring misfortune. To act without awareness is not enlightened. Confronted with these two temptations, I must respectfully decline the offer."[93]

Sometimes, the silent and passive reaction to the Yüan rulers' decision could be construed as a rejection. The best illustration of this is the reaction to a translation of a Sarvastivadin book of discipline, *Ken-pen shuo-i-ch'ieh-yu-pu ch'u-chia shou-chin yüan chieh-mo i-fan*.[cw][94] When the work was trnaslated into Chinese by Phags-pa in 1270, the Imperial Preceptor declared that the purpose of the translation was "to impart and promulgate the disciplinary rules over China."[95] Yet in the spirit-way epitaph of Lien Hsi-hsien[cx] (1231–1280), a Confucian scholar-official of Uighur origin, it is said that Lien was pressed by the Emperor to receive the new disciplinary precepts from the Imperial Preceptor. The inscription states that "When he was told by His Majesty to receive the precepts from the Imperial Preceptor, to read the Buddhist scriptures, to open his mind and have his spirit and wisdom benefitted thereby, Lien replied that 'I am honored by your instruction, but we already have received Confucius' precepts long ago.' His Majesty asked, 'What precepts of Confucius?' He replied, 'They are the loyalty of ministers and the filial piety of sons.' "[96] Inspite of pressure from the Mongol court, the effort to impose this discipline imparted by the Imperial Preceptor on the Chinese Buddhist community probably had little effect. When this is contrasted with the impact of monastic rules compiled by Chinese monks, such as the *Pai-chang ch'ing-kuei*,[cy][97] the passive rejection by Chinese Buddhists of the rules imposed by the Tibetans becomes quite clear.

The Mongol rulers' tendency to favor Tibetan priests incurred some resentment among Chinese monks. The crimes and abuses committed by Yang-lien-chen-chia,[cz] such as looting the tomb of the Sung emperors and raping the Chinese women, etc., in South China are notorious in Chinese history.[98] In the north too resentment certainly existed but to a lesser degree. In the biography of Liao-hsing[da] (d. 1321) it is stated that:

At that time because Shih-tsu [Khubilai] favored and gave honor to the monks from the West, the number of their followers flourished. Some of them wore high caps ornamented with red feathers on top, and were accompanied by guards and horses with a lofty and arrogant manner when they were on the road. Their manners were comparable to those of lords and princes. No monk in the country, even the most famous, dared to be disrespectful to them. Some made obeisance by pulling at the clothes and touching the feet [of these Tibetan monks].

Seeing the situation, Liao-hsing commented before his followers:

I have heard that a gentleman's love for the people is measured in keeping with proper decorum. How can one lower oneself by this kind of self-abasement? If one lowers himself, he must intend either flattery or deceit. I am striving for the Tao by myself. Why should I beg anything from them?[99]

The compilation of the Chih-yüan catalogue of Buddhist scriptures (*Chih-yüan fa-pao k'an-t'ung tsung-lu*)[db] affords a contrasting example of the Chinese Buddhists' acceptance of Tibetan dominance. It is a work of collaboration between the foreign and the Chinese monks with the Tibetan priests in command. The catalogue was compiled between 1285 and 1287, under the direction of Khubilai. Only two Chinese monk-scholars (*Han-t'u i-hsüeh*)[dc] were named in his directive to be members of the editorial board.[100] Apart from the standard bibliographic features, the catalogue had its special characteristics: first, every scripture mentioned in the catalogue had been collated with the Tibetan collection of Buddhist scriptures. Annotations on each Chinese title were made to indicate whether it was identical to or different from the Tibetan version. This was done on the recommendation of the Imperial Preceptor and it may be regarded as symbolic of Tibetan dominance in scholarly matters. Second, many Chinese transliterations of Sanskrit titles were added to the translated titles in Chinese. For example, the catalogue has added the Sanskrit name *Ma-ho po-lo-t'i-ya po-lo-mi-t'an su-t'an-lo*[dd] (Mahāprajñā-pāramitā-sūtra) under the Chinese title *Pan-jo pu.*[de] It further explains that it was necessary to provide a Sanskrit title because the name was lost

when the Master of the Tripitaka (i.e., Hsüan-tsang, 602–664) translated
the book into Chinese. A few Sanskrit terms till remained in transliteration because they were untranslatable. Comparison was therefore made
with the Tibetan version, and notations made as to whether the title was
available in Tibetan. If it was available in Tibetan, the Sanskrit transliteration was given; if not, the Chinese title remained as it was.[101] In other
words, the Chinese Buddhist scriptures were verified by reference to the
Tibetan collections.

From a scholarly viewpoint, this was a laudable practice introduced
into Chinese Buddhist scholarship; politically, it was evidence of Tibetan
dominance. This political significance becomes more explicit when the
handling of Phags-pa's own translations in the catalogue is considered. In
these cases, neither the Sanskrit transliteration nor the Tibetan sources
are referred to.[102] This difference in treatment indicates that the authority
and knowledge of Phags-pa were viewed as unquestionable. It is only the
Chinese translations that were subject to verification.

All these new translations of the Buddhist scriptures in the Yüan
period up to that date were included in the collection of the *Ta-tsang
ching*[df] (Tripitaka). The Chinese Buddhists' acceptance of the catalogue
and the new translations was probably customary since they took any
effort to edit and collect Buddhist scriptures as indicating support of the
religion. Morever, there are quotations in the catalogue where adjectives
favorable to previous Chinese dynasties remain intact. Thus, designations
such as "The Great T'ang" (Ta T'ang),[dg] and especially "The Great Sung"
(Ta Sung),[dh] are still retained in it.[103]

CONCLUSION

The Chinese Buddhists in Ta-tu had been confronted with a new and
serious situation at the beginning of the thirteenth century. Their religious life was threatened, monastic properities were occupied by the
Taoists, and there was uncertainty with regard to the new Mongol rulers.
The Buddhist leaders reacted to the circumstances with patience and diligence, not only surviving but even, to some extent, prospering during
this transitional period. They were able to maintain their religious life,
continue the transmission of teaching, recruit new novices and regain
properties occupied by the Taoists. Moreover the Buddhists were not only

able to serve their own purposes, but even to help the Confucian scholars, officials, and common men of Ta-tu at crucial moments.

The Buddhists' assistance to others might raise a question as to whether the Ta-tu Buddhists saw themselves as Buddhists first or as Chinese first. There is no clear answer to this, partly due to the fact that Buddhist tradition had always regarded helping people in general as a principal aim, and partly because the capital city had been under foreign rule since long before the Mongol conquest. Moreover, whatever the reasons might have been for their assistance to other groups, by their nonsectarian attitude they must have increased their prestige and influence among the masses of the region.

What are the reasons for the Buddhist success during this period? The first reason would seem to be the quality of Buddhist leadership. Taking Hsing-hsiu as an example, his courage and integrity were highly respected by all. When the Chin emperor Chang-tsung visited Hsing-hsiu's temple, the latter refrained from the corrupt custom of giving presents to the throne; and when he accepted royal gifts, he refused to kneel down as the imperial messenger instructed him to do.[104] One may also recall his "wait and see" attitude when the city was occupied by Mongols. In the case of Yin-chien, his appearance was described as "dignified"; he "feared nothing and his conversational gifts were extraordinary."[105] Among the lay Buddhist leaders, Yeh-lü Ch'u-ts'ai created a favorable impression with his frankness in replying to Chinggis Khan as well as with his physical appearance, magnificent beard, and sonorous voice.[106] Liu Ping-chung also struck Khubilai by his knowledge and insight.[107] Their personal qualities may have differed from one another, yet their personalities impressed the Mongols deeply. As a result, the Buddhists of Ta-tu were able to establish communication with Mongol rulers and officials and gain their respect in the predynastic phase of Mongol conquest.

A second reason for their success was the scholarship of the Buddhist leaders. Most of the high-ranking monks were well known for their knowledge of the school to which they belonged, and some of them, especially Wan-sung, Hai-yün, and Ts'ung-lun, were good scholars of the Chinese tradition in general. This broad knowledge enabled them to offer appropriate responses whenever the occasion demanded, and to make a wide appeal to other religions, hence gaining respect from the public.

A third reason for their success, though a passing one, was the Mongol attitude towards Buddhism. When the Mongols first conquered the city, there seems to have been no definite official policy on religions. As time went on, liberal support for all major religions was practiced on an *ad hoc* basis. Later, when more Chinese territory came under Mongol control, and stronger Buddhist leadership appeared, the Mongols had to appoint officials to deal with the situation. The appointment of Yin-chien to head the Buddhists and of Li Chih-ch'ang to head the Taoists, are examples of this.[108] Apart from the desire to control things, the Mongols also expected to derive spiritual benefits from the conduct of religious services. The biography of Yin-chien (Hai-yün) records that during his first meeting with Khubilai the Prince explicitly asked the monk: "Is there any law in Buddhism that would bring peace to the world?" The answer of the monk was affirmative. He said that the peace of the world depended on the happiness of the people, and the happiness of the people depended on man's policies and Heaven. Both man and Heaven are not separate from the mind, though man does not know the distinction between the two. Buddhism teaches the distinction and thereby enables man to apply correct policies. This answer is far from the orthodox line of Buddhism, but it does show how shrewd the monk was in presenting Buddhism as useful to the eager Mongol prince. In answering another question, the monk advised Khubilai that he should perform all the meritorious acts of a king as prescribed in the Buddhist scriptures; that he should search for virtuous men (*ta-hsien*)[di] and great Confucian scholars (*shuo-ju*)[dj] to assist the king; and that Buddhism should be recognized as the highest religion among the three Chinese traditions.[109] When this is read in the context of the Mongols' sponsorship of religious festivals and ceremonies with the aim of securing benefits for the empire, the political significance of the Mongols' support of Buddhism becomes more clear.[110]

The success of Buddhists during the period was, however rather limited. They succeeded in adapting themselves to the new situation but solved only some of the problems that arose. Having no plan of their own, they accepted what befell them, made some adjustments, but were unable to improve the situation appreciably. They made themselves available to serve the Mongols in religious ceremonies and administration, and got some benefits in return, but were not in a position to influence Mongol policy. This is especially clear with the establishment of the Yüan dynasty, from the reign of Khubilai Khaghan onwards, when the Chinese Buddhists helplessly watched the rise and domination of Tibetan priests in the government.

One may well ask: beyond their mere physical survival what spiritual progress did the Chinese Buddhists in Ta-tu make during this period? And, what mark did they leave on the history of Chinese Buddhism overall? The most important achievement of the Buddhists was the maintenance of Buddhist schools in Ta-tu which provided instruction in the religion. Apart from this, monks like Hsing-hsiu and some of his disciples also made original contributions to Ch'an Buddhism. Hsing-hsiu is well-known for his doctrine of "reality and illusion are not two, things (*shih*)[dk] and principle (*li*)[dl] mutually illuminate each other" (*chen-wang pu-erh, shih-li shuang-chao*).[dm][111] Ts'ung-lun's deep understanding of the different approaches and common end of Ch'an schools, and his appreciation of Tsung-mi's philosophy, helped the Buddhists develop a more harmonious relationship among themselves. His reference to different Ch'an masters, including some of the schools other than his own, shows his open-mindedness in religious thought.[112] The books on Ts'ao-tung Ch'an Buddhism compiled by Hsing-hsiu and Ts'ung-lun had a lasting influence and were of historical significance. The works completed the literary development of the so-called "five houses" of Ch'an Buddhism in China. Without these Yüan collections, the picture and the place of Ts'ao-tung tradition in Ch'an Buddhism would be seen quite differently.

The compilation of Ch'an Buddhist writings marks one of the transformations of the tradition. Though Ch'an Buddhism insisted that the written word cannot be entrusted with the transmission of religious truth, as time went on Ch'an established a literary tradition of its own. This tendency, beginning in the T'ang dynasty, continued throughout the Sung period, and then the Yüan compilations made their own contribution to this development. His own understanding of the transformation is expressed by Ts'ung-lun in these terms: "Principle is manifested through language, and without language the ultimate truth would become unattainable. Language does not go beyond principle, and without principle language cannot fulfill its proper end."[113] Thus Ts'ung-lun distances himself from the distrust of literature found in early Ch'an monks, and gives qualified approval to literary scholarship. In his book he confesses his astonishment over the breadth of experience and depth of insight expressed in the poems of Tu Fu[dn] (712–770). He comments that "If secular literature can attain so much, how much more should our true, supreme and wonderful Tao do for the liberation of the world?"[114] In other words, not only are language and literature necessary to express religious truth, but religious writings should be able to achieve greater breadth and depth than secular ones.

This relatively open attitude of Ch'an monks not only was extended to other sects of the Buddhist religion, but was found also in their constant reference to other Chinese philosophical works, especially Taoist and Confucian texts. This is true of the books compiled by Hsing-hsiu, and especially of those by Ts'ung-lun. This reference to other teachings should not, however, be understood to mean that Buddhists had embraced other faiths at the expense of their own religion; it only indicates that they recognized the usefulness of other writings as expressive of the understanding of religious truth. This relative open-mindedness was also found in Hsing-hsiu's lay disciples, Li P'ing-shan and Yeh-lü Ch'u-ts'ai.

In his criticism of the Neo-Confucian philosopher Chang Shih [do] (1133–1180), Li claims that the Neo-Confucian concept of "the total Mandate of Heaven" is what the Buddhists called "the Mind." [115] He further pointed out that Neo-Confucian terminology can all be traced to Buddhist and Taoist sources. Similarly, Yeh-lü also considered that "the doctrines of the Three Sages had a common origin, and that the different traditions of their schools developed only to meet the exigencies of the times." [116] Believing that the ends of Confucianism and Buddhism are the same, he sees the differences between them as being merely in the practical order. He urged the followers of the two schools not to ridicule each other because the Confucian teachings of rites and music and Buddhist doctrines of cause and effect represent merely terminological differences (*chia-ming*). [dp][117] Though there was constant reference to other religions and occasional equating of certain concepts among the three Chinese traditions, what emerged was still far short of a systematic philosophical synthesis. Nevertheless this interaction between Buddhism and other traditions served to foster a degree of mutual appreciation, and to lessen hostility at least on the philosophical level, if not on the institutional.

In Yüan Buddhist thought the focus is on the doctrine of Mind. Though always central to Buddhist thought, the concept of Mind developed a Ch'an coloration during this period. This is reflected in the frequent reference to the thought of Tsung-mi by Yüan and Ming thinkers. According to Tsung-mi, "all the sentient beings possess the emptiness of True Mind (*chen-hsin*), [dq] and the Nature is originally pure from the beginningless past." [118] He further states that "the Mind is clear and bright without any obscurity, self-knowing clearly and distinctly. It will remain imperishable throughout future time." This Mind, though absolute, is still subject to defilement when thought arises, but whether one becomes deluded or enlightened, the Mind itself never changes.[119] This was expressed by Hsing-hsiu in terms of the nonduality of "reality and illusion."[120] And this seems to be the reason why Yeh-lü Ch'u-ts'ai could believe that "the Way of Buddha is for cultivating the Mind" while at the same time Confucianism, "though inadequate for controlling the Mind, is for the governing of the world."[121]

With this emphasis on the absolute Mind, the balance of understanding and practice in religious life, and the appreciation of other religions, Yüan Buddhism passed on a living tradition to Ming thinkers and contributed to the syncretic tendency in later Chinese thought.[122]

NOTES

Abbreviations used in notes:

FTTT   *Fo-tsu li-tai t'ung-tsai,* by Nien-ch'ang, *Taishō,* vol. 49.

HTC   *Hsü Tsang-ching,*[dr] (Taipei: Chung-hua fo-chiao hui, rep. 1971).

Lun-chi   *Ch'en Yüan hsien-sheng chin nien-nien shih-hsüeh lun-chi,*[ds] ed. Chou K'ang-hsieh[dt] (Hong Kong; Ch'ung-wen shu-tien, 1971).

MKSC   *Ming Kao-seng chuan,*[du] by Ju-hsing,[dv] *Taishō,* vol. 50.

PHKSC   *Pu-hsü Kao-seng chuan,*[dw] by Ming-ho, HTC ed., vol. 134.

SPTK   *Ssu-pu ts'ung k'an* (Shanghai: Commerical Press, 1936).

T   *Taishō shinshū daizōkyō*[dx] (Tokyo: Taishō issaikyo kankōkwai, 1924–1932).

Wen-chi   *Ch'an-jan chü-shih wen-chi,*[dy] by Yeh-lü Ch'u-ts'ai, SPTK. ed.

WTHL   *Wu-teng hui-yüan hsü lüeh,*[dz] by Ching-chu, HTC, vol. 138.

YS   *Yüan shih,* by Sung Lien[ea] et al. (Peking: Chung-hua shu-chü, 1976).

1. Ta-tu, the Yüan capital in modern Peking, was known as Yen-ching under the Liao and the Chin. It was the Southern Capital (Nan-ching[eb]) of the former, and the Central Capital (Chung-tu[ec]) of the latter. Following Khubilai's enthronement, it was designated in 1264 as the national capital of the new dynasty. During the next decade, extensive construction work was undertaken to build a new city in the northeast of the former Chin capital. The Buddho-Taoist, Liu Ping-chung, one of the most influential advisers to Khubilai in these early years, has been credited with recommending the site of the new capital and helping draft the blueprint for the construction of the new city. It was renamed Ta-tu or "Great Capital" in 1272, but the construction of the new city was not completed until 1292, two years before Khubilai's death. Throughout this paper, I use the name Ta-tu in order to maintain consistency, although many of the events narrated here occurred before 1272 when the capital was known as Yen-ching or Chung-tu. For a modern account of Ta-tu, see, among others, Chu Ch'i,[ed] *Yüan Ta-tu kung-tien t'u k'ao*[ee] (Shanghai: Commerical Press, 1936); Komai Kazuchika,[ef] "Gen no Jotō narabi ni Daitō no heimen ni tsuite,"[eg] *Toa ronsō*[eh] (1940), 3:129–40; G. N. Kates, "A New Date for the Origin of the Forbidden City," *Harvard Journal of Asiatic Studies* (1942–43), 7:180–202; Hok-lam Chan, "Liu Ping-chung (1216–74): A Buddhist-Taoist Statesman at the Court of Khubilai Khan," *T'oung Pao* (1967), 53:133–34, and note 73, as well as the report on the recent excavations of the remains of Ta-tu published in *Kao-ku*[ei] (1972), 1:19–20, and *Wen-wu*[ej] (1977), 5:65–72.

2. For Buddhism under the Chin dynasty, see Kenneth K. S. Ch'en, *Buddhism in China: A Historical Survey* (Princeton: Princeton University Press, 1964), pp. 411–14; Makita Tairyō[ek] et al., *Ajia Bukkyō shi Chūqoku hen,*[el] vol. 2, ed. Nakamura Hajime[em] (Tokyo: Kosei shuppansha, 1976), pp. 68–69. For

Taoism under the Chin dynasty, see Ch'en Yüan, *Nan-Sung ch'u Ho-pei hsin tao-chiao k'ao*[en] (Peking: Chung-hua shu-chü, 1962).

3. See Yüan Hao-wen, "Tung-p'ing hsing-t'ai Yen-kung shen-tao pei," in *I-shan hsien-sheng wen-chi*[eo] (SPTK ed.), 26:1b.

4. It is stated in Yeh-lü Ch'u-ts'ai, "Yen-ching Ta-chüeh ch'an-ssu ch'uang-chien tsang-ching chi," *Wen-chi*, 8:28b: "At the beginning of the Chen-yu reign [1213–1217], the imperial armies in the southern campaign had subdued the capital city. After the war, there were no young novices, officials never sympathized with the situation [of the Buddhists], and monastic buildings were all occupied by resident people."

5. For a general account of Buddhism under the Yüan period, see, among others, Nogami Shunjō,[ep] *Genshi Shakuroden no kenkyū*[eq] (Kyoto: Hoyū shōten, 1978); Kenneth K. S. Ch'en, *Buddhism in China*, pp. 414ff; Paul Demiéville, "La situation religieuse en Chine au temps de Marco Polo," in *Oriente Poliano* (Rome: Instituto Italiano per il medio ed Estremo Oriente, 1957), pp. 193–236; Makita Tairyō, *Ajia Bukkyō shi Chūgoku hen*, vol. 2, pp. 77–87, and Sechin Jagchi, "The Mongol Khans and Chinese Buddhism and Taoism," *The Journal of the International Association of Buddhism* (1979), 2(1):1–27.

6. This is mentioned in FTTT, 20:693c; WTHL, 1:429–30a.

7. FTTT, 20:693c; WTHL, 1:429c.

8. *Ibid.*

9. *Ts'ung-yung lu* (HTC, vol. 117), 1:322a.

10. *Chung-yung*, 19. The translation is from Wing-tsit Chan, *A Source Book of Chinese Philosophy* (Princeton: Princeton University Press, 1963), p. 107.

11. See *Wen-chi*, 8:21b.

12. *Ibid.*, 13:22a.

13. See my biography of Li Ch'un-fu in *Sung Biographies*, ed. H. Franke (Wiesbaden: Franz Steiner Verlage GMBH, 1976), vol. 2, pp 557–82. For details, see my article, "Li P'ing-shan and his Refutation of Neo-Confucian Criticism of Buddhism," in *Development in Buddhist Thought; Canadian Contribution to Buddhist Studies*, e.d R. C. Amore (Waterloo, Ontario: Wilfrid Laurier University Press, 1979), pp. 162–93.

14. The book is found in HTC, vol. 117, pp. 321–91.

15. See Yeh-lü's preface to this work in *Wen-chi*, 8:21a.

16. *Ibid.*, 8:23b. For the *Pi-yen lu* by K'o-ch'in (1063–1135), see R. D. M. Shaw's translation, *The Blue Cliff Records* (London: M. Joseph, 1961). For the background of these two sects of Ch'an Buddhism, see H. Dumoulin, *A History of Zen Buddhism* (New York: McGraw-Hill, 1965), pp. 132–36.

17. *Wen-chi*, 13:23b.

18. *Ibid.*, 6:12a.

19. See WTHL, 1:430b.

20. See Igor de Rachewiltz, "Yeh-lü Ch'u-ts'ai (1189–1243): Buddhist Idealist and Confucian Statesman," in *Confucian Personalities*, ed. A. F. Wright

and D. C. Twitchett (Stanford: Stanford University Press, 1962), p. 193.

21. See the text of the inscription published by Ch'en Yüan in *Lun-chi*, p. 24. I am grateful to Professor Hok-lam Chan who kindly supplied reprints of this text as well as his paper on Liu Ping-chung.

22. See FTTT, 21:703c; PHKSC, 12:109; WTHL, 4:461c.

23. Other references for Yeh-lü's contributions to Buddhist appointment can be found in *Wen-chi*, 7:17b–18a, 8:6b–11b.

24. *Wen-chi*, 8:23a–24a; 14; 13b–14b. For prefaces to other Buddhist works written by him, see *ibid.*, 8:17b–19a; 13:1a–11b. For Li P'ing-shan, see note 13 above.

25. *Wen-chi*, 8:24a–30a.

26. WTHL, 7:431b–c.

27. *Wen-chi*, 8:17a–b.

28. *Ibid.*, 13:23b.

29. *Ibid.*

30. *Ibid.*

31. *Ibid.*, 2:15a.

32. *Ibid.*, 8:19b.

33. See *Wen-chi*, 13:22b. For the original version, see *Li chi*[er] (SPTK ed.), 19:7b–8a; the translation of the quotation from *Great Learning* follows Chan, *Source Book*, p. 86.

34. For the career of Liu, see Chan, "Liu Ping-chung," pp. 89–146.

35. See FTTT, 21:702c.

36. Kunishita Hirosato, "Genshō no okeru teishitsu to zensō to no kankei ni tsuite,"[es] *Tōyō gakuhō*[et] (1921), 11:556–62.

37. See the text of the inscription, in *Lun-chi*, p. 23.

38. *Ibid.*, pp. 24–25.

39. *Ibid.*

40. Yüan Hao-wen's letter, dated May 1233, is included in *I-shan hsien-sheng wen-chi*, 39:1a. For details, see Yao Ts'ung-wu,[eu] "Yüan Hao-wen kuei-ssu shang Yeh-lü Ch'u-ts'ai shu ti li-shih i-i yü shu chung wu-shih-ssu jen hsing-shih k'ao"[ev] (*Kuo-li T'ai-wan ta-hsüeh*) *Wen-shih-che hsüeh-pao*[ew] (June 1970), 19:225–75, and *id.*, "Chin-Yüan chih-chi K'ung Yüan-ts'o yü 'Yen-sheng-kung chih wei'tsai Meng-ku hsin-ch'ao te chi-hsü,"[ex] *Bulletin of the Institute of History and Philology, Academia Sinica* (1969), 39:189–96.

41. See de Rachewiltz, "Yeh-lü Ch'u-ts'ai", p. 205, and Yao Tsung-wu, note 40.

42. *Lun-chi*, p. 25, and FITT, 21:704a.

43. See YS, 148: 3505–3507, and Yao Ts'ung-wu, "K'ung Yüan-ts'o," note 41.

44. de Rachewiltz, "Yeh-lü Ch'u-ts'ai," p. 202.

45. YS, 149:3521.

46. There are various dates for this event: YS *ch.* 149 dated it in 1234 (p. 2532), FTTT in 1255 (21:703c). Since the inscription is the earliest source, it should be more reliable. See *Lun-chi*, p. 25. However, since much time was taken

in processing, the decision may have been made long before it reached the Buddhist community.

47. FTTT, 21:703c.
48. *Ibid.*, 703c–4a.
49. *Ibid.*, 704a.
50. *Ibid.*
51. Kunishita, 'Gensho . . . teishitsu to zensō", pp. 573ff.
52. FTTT, 21:704b.
53. *Ibid.*, 704c.
54. Chan, "Liu Ping-chung", pp. 89–146.
55. *Ibid.*, pp. 129–30. For the historical background of the Buddhist-Taoist dispute, see E. Zurcher, *The Buddhist Conquest of China* (Leiden: E. J. Brill, 1959), pp. 288ff. For an account of the event in the Mongol court, see Nogami Shunjō, *Genshi Shakuroden no kenkyū*, pp. 143ff; Kenneth K. S. Ch'en, "Buddhist-Taoist Mixtures in the Pa-shih-i-hua t'u," *Harvard Journal of Asiatic Studies* (1945–47), 9:1–12, and Joseph Thiel, "Der streit der Buddhisten und Taoisten zur Mongolenzeit," *Monumenta Serica* (1961), 20:1–80. For further reference, see Igor de Rachewiltz, "The Hsi-yü lu by Yehlü Ch'u-ts'ai," *ibid.* (1962), 21:11, note 9.
56. See Liu Ping-chung, *Ts'ang-ch'un chi*[ey] (SKCSCP, 4th ser., Taipei: Commercial Press, 1975), 6:10b. It is also quoted in FTTT, 21:706a.
57. Chan, "Liu Ping-chung," pp. 124–25, 132–33, 137–38.
58. WTHL, 1:430a–b.
59. See Hsiang-mai, (*Chih-yüan*) *Pien-wei lu*[ez] (T, vol. 52), 3:768ff. For an account from a Taoist viewpoint, see Ch'en Yüan, *Nan-Sung ch'u Ho-pei hsin tao-chiao k'ao*, pp. 55–60; see also Li's biography in *Ch'ang-ch'un tao-chiao yüan-liu* contained in *Tao-chiao yen-chiu tzu-liao*,[fa] ed. Yen I-p'ing,[fb] (Taipei: I-wen yin-shu kuan, 1974), vol. 2, pp. 173–181, esp. p. 174. For other studies on the Buddhist Taoist controversies, see note 55 above.
60. See (*Chih-yuan*) *Pien-wei lu*, 3:769b–770c.
61. FTTT, 22:722b. For Phags-pa, see note 89 below. For Yao Shu's role in this debate see Hok-lam Chan's biography in *Papers on Far Eastern History* (September 1980), 22:28–29.
62. See (*Chin-yüan*) *Pien-wei lu*, 3:771b–c. For the number of temples involved, see FTTT, 21:708c.
63. WTHL, 1:430b.
64. *Ibid.*, 430c.
65. Biography in Yü Chi,[fc] *Tao-yüan hsüeh-ku lu*[fd] (SPTK ed.), 48:1a; FTTT, 22:728a–9a. Also see PHKSC, 19:149; WTHL, 1:431a.
66. For the debate between the Indian Monks and the Ch'an Buddhists, see Paul Demiéville, *Le Concile de Lhasa, une controverse sur le quietisme entre bouddhistes de l'Inde et de la Chine au VIII siecle de l'ere chretienne* (Paris: Imprint nationale de France, 1952); G. Tucci, *The Minor Buddhist Texts*, pt. 2 (Rome: Instituto Italiano per il medio ed estremo Oriente, 1958). For

the historical significance of the debate at the Yüan court see my article, "Yüan-tai Ch'an-seng yü Hsi-tsang La-ma pien-lun k'ao,"[fe] *Fo-kuang hsüeh-pao*[ff] (1979), 4:163–71.

67. Biography in PHKSC, 18:149; see also WTHL, 1:430c–31a.
68. For Tsung-mi, see Jan Yün-hua, "Tsung-mi: His Analysis of Ch'an Buddhism," *T'oung Pao* (1972), 58:1–54. The most comprehensive study has been published by Kamata Shigeo,[fg] *Shūmitsu kyōgaku no shisōshi teki kenkyū*[fh] (Tokyo: Tokyo University, 1975).
69. From Kamata's edition in *Zen no goroku*, vol. 9: *Zengen shosen shutojo*[fi] (Tokyo: Chikuma shobō, 1971), pp. 13, 23.
70. *Ibid.*
71. The terms *shih* and *li* are basic concepts in Hua-yen Buddhist philosophy; they are usually referred to as phenomena and absolute. See Fung Yu-lan, *A History of Chinese Philosophy*, tr. D. Bodde (Princeton: Princeton University Press, 1953), vol. 2, pp. 341ff; Chan, *Source Book*, pp. 407ff; and F. H. Cooke, *Hua-yen Buddhism the Jewel Net of Indra* (University Park: Pennsylvania State University Press, 1977), pp. 55ff.
72. From P. B. Yampolsky, *The Platform Sutra of the Sixth Patriarch* (New York: Columbia University Press, 1967), p. 80.
73. *Ibid.* for a different version of the story, see *Tsu-t'ang chi*[fj] by Ching[fk] and Yün[fl] (Taipei: Kuang-wen shu-chü, 1972 ed.), p. 46a.
74. WTHL, 1:430c–d. It is interesting to note that a similar questioning of the Ch'an doctrine by Yüan officials also occurred in south China, where the work of Tsung-mi was also highly esteemed. See FTTT, 31:720a–21b.
75. See Jan, "Tsung-mi," pp. 25ff.
76. *Ssu-ming tsun-che chiao-hsing lu*[fm] (T, vol. 46), 895b.
77. See Jan Yün-hua, "K'an-hui or 'Comparative Investigation': The Key Concept of Tsung-mi's Thought," in *Korean and Asian Religious Tradition*, ed. C. S. Yu (Toronto: University of Toronto Press, 1977), pp. 12–24; and *id.*, "Conflict and Harmony in Ch'an and Buddhism," *Journal of Chinese Philosophy* (1977), 4:287–302.
78. This is the version included in T, vol. 48, no. 2015.
79. *Ibid.*, 397c.
80. *Ibid.*, 398a.
81. Chan, "Liu Ping-chung", p. 141.
82. PHKSC, 18:149a–b.
83. WTHL, 1:431a.
84. FTTT, 22:719b.
85. They are included in HTC, vols. 117 and 124.
86. From Ch'en, *Buddhism in China*, p. 148. About the reaction of the Chinese Buddhists to Tibetan dominance, see Nogami Shunjō, "Gen no Bukkyō ni kansuru ichi mondai"[fn] in *Tsukamoto hakase shōshu kinen Bukkyō Shigaku ronshu*[fo] (Kyoto: Tsukamoto hakase shōsu kinenkai, 1961), pp. 573–82.
87. For Phags-pa's biography, see YS, 202:4517–4518. It was based on the "Account of Conduct" composed by Wang P'an included in FTTT, 21:707b–c.

The latter has been studied by Nakano Miyoko[fp] in *Hsin-ya hsüeh-pao* (1969), 9(1): 93–119. For details of Phags-pa's career and other biographical accounts, see Nakano, *A Philological Study in the 'Phags-pa Script and the Meng-ku tzu-yün* (Canberra: Australian National University Press, 1971). On the political background of the rise of the Tibetan priest at the Mongol court, see Tsepon W. D. Shakabpa, *Tibet: A Political History* (New Haven: Yale University Press, 1967), pp. 61–70.

88. For the role of State Preceptorship in Chinese Buddhism, especially the Yüan period, see P. Pelliot, "Le Kuou-che," *T'oung Pao* (1911), pp. 671–76. There is an enormous literature on the Phags-pa script; see the bibliography listed in Nakano Miyoko, *Phags-pa Script*, pp. 152–65.

89. See FTTT, 21:707c.

90. *Ibid.*, 22:722b.

91. *Ibid.*, 729c.

92. The Pai-ma Monastery is claimed to be the first Buddhist monastery in China. See Zürcher, *Buddhist Conquest*, pp. 31–32.

93. See MKSC, 2:906b.

94. This translation is included in T, vol. 45, no. 1904.

95. FTTT, 21:705b.

96. From the inscription composed by Yüan Ming-shan[fq] (1269–1322), in Su T'ien-chüeh,[fr] *Kuo-ch'ao wen-lei*[fs] (SPTK ed.), 65:1a–16b. This statement appears on p. 14a. About the origin and career of this Central Asian, see Ch'en Yüan, *Western and Central Asians in China under the Mongols*, tr. Ch'ien Hsing-hai and L. C. Goodrich (Los Angeles: Monumenta Serica at U.C.L.A., 1966), pp. 245–47, esp. 222–23.

97. This work is in T, vol. 48, no. 2025; and HTC, vol. 111.

98. For the criminal activities of this notorious Tibetan priest in southern China, see Nogami, *Genshi Shokuroden kenkyū*, 240ff, esp. 251–58.

99. MKSC, 2:907b.

100. See the Chin-yüan catalogue, in *Chung-hua Ta-tsang ching*[ft] (Taipei: Hsiu-ting Chung-hua Ta-tsang-ching hui; 1965), vol. 1/73, p. 31809a.

101. *Ibid.*, p. 21810a–b.

102. *Ibid.*, p. 31851b.

103. *Ibid.*, pp. 31828a, 31829b, 31389a–b, etc.

104. See Yeh-lü's preface to *Shih-shih hsin-k'ai* in *Wen-chi*, 13:8b–9a.

105. See FTTT, 21:702c.

106. Igor de Rachewiltz, "Yeh-lü Ch'u-ts'ai," pp. 191–92.

107. Chan, "Liu Ping-chung," p. 117.

108. YS, 3:45.

109. The full text of the conversation is recorded in FTTT, 21:704b.

110. For the religious ceremonies sponsored by Mongols, see FTTT, 21:704c; YS, 5:88, 6:110, 7:142, etc.

111. For Hsing-hsiu's contribution to Ch'an Buddhism, see Nukariya Kaiten,[fu] *Zengaku shisō shi*[fv] (Tokyo: Genkosha, 1923–25), vol. 2, pp. 422–23.

112. For example, there are a number of instances of Ch'an Masters from the

Yün-men, Lin-chi, and other schools apart from these examples from the Ts'ao-tung school. See *K'ung-ku chi*, in HTC vol. 117, p. 266.
113. *Ibid.*, p. 290c.
114. *Ibid.*, p. 320a–b.
115. FTTT, 20: 698c.
116. From de Rachewiltz, "Yeh-lü Ch'u-ts'ai," p. 209.
117. *Wen-chi*, 3:6b.
118. From Kamata's edition (note 70), p. 131.
119. *Ibid.*, pp. 217–18. This doctrine was originally started by the writing of *The Awakening of Faith*. See Y. S. Hakeda's translation (New York: Columbia University Press, 1967), pp. 43ff.
120. Cf. note 112.
121. Cf. note 33. See also *Wen-chi*, 13:22b.
122. For the lineage of the Ts'ao-tung Ch'an school after Hsing-hsiu, see Nu-kariya, vol. 2, pp. 582ff. On the interactions and certain parallels of concepts between Ming Neo-Confucianism and Buddhism, see pp. 613ff. See also Araki Kengo,[fw] *Mindai shisō kenkyū*[fx] (Tokyo: Sōbunsha, 1972), and Tokiwa Daijō,[fy] *Shina ni okeru Bukkyō to Jukyō Dōkyō*[fz] (Tokyo: Tōyō Bunko, 1966), pp. 409ff; Kubota Ryōon,[ga] *Shina Ju Do Butsu sangyō shi-ron*[gb] (Tokyo: Tōhō shoin, 1931), pp. 609ff.

GLOSSARY

a 大都
b 燕京
c 章宗
d 長春
e 律宗
f 禪
g 宣宗
h 印簡
i 行秀
j 萬松老人
k 曹洞
l 雪巖
m 滿
n 棲隱
o 仰
p 耶律楚材
q 李純甫
r 李屏山
s 福裕
t 至溫
u 從倫
v 從容菴
w 鳴道集說
x 從容錄
y 正覺
z 天童
aa 請益錄
ab 碧巖錄
ac 臨濟
ad 三宗鼎峙
ae 雲門
af 大自在三昧
ag 海雲
ah 少林
ai 慶壽
aj 念常

ak 明河
al 淨住
am 緊俏
an 識情
ao 峻拔
ap 莽鹵
aq 綿密
ar 廉纖
as 宗風
at 行權
au 海雲大師
av 劉秉忠
aw 佛祖歷代通載
ax 寧遠
ay 圈下大慧
az 中觀
ba 厦里
bb 淨戒
bc 仁恕之心
bd 孔元措
be 衍聖
bf 汴
bg 元好問
bh 嚴實
bi 元史
bj 東平
bk 郭寶玉
bl 光天鎮國大士
bm 大慶壽
bn 化胡經
bo 王磐
bp 釋教總統
bq 祥邁
br 李志常
bs 張志敬
bt 帝師

bu	姚樞	de	般若部
bv	仁義	df	大藏經
bw	普安	dg	大唐
bx	大理	dh	大宋
by	佛國普安大禪師	di	大賢
bz	國師	dj	碩儒
ca	禪源詮	dk	事
cb	圭峯（宗密）	dl	理
cc	思惟修	dm	眞妄不二，事理雙照
cd	神	dn	杜甫
ce	公案	do	張杙
cf	慧能	dp	假名
cg	子凝	dq	眞心
ch	景德	dr	續藏經
ci	和會	ds	陳垣先生近廿年史學論集
cj	惟大	dt	周康燮
ck	鄧文原	du	明高僧傳
cl	賈汝舟	dv	如惺
cm	瓊華	dw	補續高僧傳
cn	西菴贇	dx	大正新修大藏經
co	空谷傳聲	dy	湛然居士文集
cp	虛堂習聽	dz	五燈會元續略
cq	義青	ea	宋濂
cr	德淳	eb	南京
cs	文才	ec	中都
ct	華嚴	ed	朱偰
cu	白馬	ee	元大都宮殿圖考
cv	五台	ef	駒井和愛
cw	根本說一切有部出家受近圓羯磨儀範	eg	元の上都並びして大都の平面に就いて
cx	廉希憲	eh	東亞論叢
cy	百丈清規	ei	考古
cz	楊璉眞加	ej	文物
da	了性	ek	牧田諦亮
db	至元法寶勘同總錄	el	アジア仏教史中国編
dc	漢土義學	em	中村元
dd	麻訶鉢囉提亞波囉密怛蘇怛囉	en	南宋初河北新道教考
		eo	遺山先生文集

Chün-fang Yü

Chung-feng Ming-pen and Ch'an Buddhism in the Yüan

INTRODUCTION

LIKE THE LIAO and Chin, the Yüan dynasty also supported Buddhism. The Mongols who conquered China and established the Yüan dynasty were originally followers of shamanism, a pantheistic animism widely practiced by the nomadic peoples of north Asia. But when the Mongols came into contact with Tibetan Lamaism (the Sa-skya-pa sect) they were much attracted by the magical powers and impressive rituals of the new religion. When Khubilai became the Khaghan in 1260, he named Phags-pa (1239?–1280) the Imperial Preceptor (*Ti-shih*);[a] and declared Lamaism the state religion.[1]

In the eyes of later historians, the Yüan dynasty stood out as a period when Buddhism received particular patronage. The *Yüan shih* devoted *chüan* 202 to an account of Buddhism and Taoism ("Shih-Lao chuan").[b] Aside from the *Wei shu*, (History of the [Northern] Wei) this is the only other instance in which a monograph on Buddhism and Taoism was accorded a place in an official dynastic history. The preface says:

The religions of Buddhism and Taoism have been practiced in China for more than a thousand years. Their ascendance and decline have often been connected with the likes and dislikes of rulers. Therefore, it is noticeable that during the Chin, Sung, Liang, and Ch'en, Buddhism was most conspicuous, whereas the same was true of Taoism during the Han, Wei, T'ang, and Sung. With the rise of the Yüan, Buddhism was richly patronized. Furthermore, the power of the Imperial Preceptors was unparalleled. Taoist magicians, making use of their prayers and sacrifices, took advantage of the times and flourished. But [compared to the Buddhists] the Taoists had only one tenth of [their influence].[2]

After describing the career of Phags-pa, creator of the Mongol script under Khubilai, the activities and imperial patronage of some twelve other

Lamaist Imperial Preceptors under subsequent rulers are given. The Ming compilers marveled at the special treatment bestowed on these powerful lamas. They remarked,

In one hundred years, there was no limit to the extent the court respected and trusted them. From the emperor and empress down to the imperial concubines and princes, all accepted the Buddhist precepts and paid obeisance to the Preceptor. During formal meetings, when all ministers and officials stood in rows, the Imperial Preceptor alone was permitted to sit on a special seat at the side [of the Khaghan].[3]

Several scholars have studied the unique institution of the Imperial Preceptor during the Yüan.[4] In short, an Imperial Preceptor was the head of Lamaism, the state religion of the Mongols, as well as the chief leader of the Chinese Buddhist sangha. He was regarded as the ecclesiastical head of the Yüan empire, just as the Khaghan was its political head. He had the overall administrative authority over Tibet. He could order a general amnesty by petitioning to the Khaghan.[5] Finally, unlike earlier dynasties, when only the emperor had the right to bestow titles on outstanding monks, the Imperial Preceptor during the Yüan had this same prerogative and thereby further signaled his independence.

When the lamas received such trust and patronage, abuses of power occurred. The 'Shih-Lao chuan" recorded with meticulous detail the infamous deeds of a Yang-lien-chen-chia,[c] who was the highest Lama official in South China, with the title of "Superintendent of Buddhist Teaching South of the (Yangtze) River" (*Chiang-nan tsung-she chang Shih-chiao*)[d] during the reign of Khubilai.[6]

In Ch'ien-t'ang and Shao-hsing, he dug up some 101 graves of the Sung royal family as well as those of Sung ministers. He killed four civilians. He accepted numberless pretty women and jewels from people. Moreover, he robbed and stole a lot of treasure which included: 1,700 ounces of gold, 6,800 ounces of silver, 9 jade belts, 111 pieces of large and small jade objects, 152 miscellaneous precious objects, 50 ounces of large pearls, 116,200 *ting* of cash, 23,000 *mou* of rice field. He shielded 23,000 households of ordinary people from paying taxes.[7]

On the economic side of Lamaism, we are supplied with statistics of extravagant spending:

[During the reign of Ayurbarwada] in Yen-yu 4th year (1317), the Commissioner in Charge of Religious Affairs (*hsüan-hui shih*)[e] reported the ingredients in units of catties required for Buddhist rituals conducted in the palace chapel in each year amounted to 439,500 catties of flour, 7,900 catties of oil, 21,870 catties of

ghee, and 27,300 catties of honey. During the thirty-year Chih-yüan reign [of
Khubilai Khaghan, i.e., 1264–1294], each year some hundred and two rituals
for worshipping and sacrificing to Buddhas were observed, but in the Ta-te 7th
year (1303) under Temür, the number was increased to more than five hundred.[8]

The Ch'ing historian Chao I[f] (1727–1814) wrote about the "excesses" of Yüan emperors in their patronage of Buddhism. Citing the
number of monasteries built and statues cast, he stated that the cost of
religious construction projects exceeded that of building imperial villas
and detached palaces. Cataloging the yearly expenditure, he calculated
that the expense of conducting Lamaist rituals went beyond officials'
salaries and soldiers' pay. Pointing out the frequent amnesties for the sake
of achieving religious merit, he felt that the lamas exercised their power
more arbitrarily than a powerful general or an insubordinate minister.
Chao I then sternly concluded, "Since lamas controlled the policies of
the Court and wasted the wealth of the empire, it was no wonder that
critics have said that half of the Yüan empire was lost in the hands of
monks. This should serve as a lesson."[9]

Perhaps reflecting the interests of these traditional historians, most
studies of Yüan Buddhism have centered upon the institutional, legal,
and social aspects of Buddhism.[10] The relationship between the court
and Buddhist monks, Lamaist as well as Chinese, has also attracted some
scholarly attention.[11] As Nogami Shunjo rightly pointed out, there has
been a tendency among scholars to confine their attention to Lamaism
when they deal with Buddhism in the Yüan, and the relationship between Lamaism and what he calls "Han Buddhism" has remained a
scholarly blind spot.[12] However, "Han Buddhism," or the indigenous
Chinese Buddhist tradition itself, has remained little explored.[13]

The imperial patronage of Buddhism was in fact extended to the
Chinese sangha in South China.[14] Chinese Buddhists in the Yüan were
classified as in the Sung, into three schools: Meditation (Ch'an),[g] Doctrine (Chiao),[h] and Discipline (Lü).[1][15] Ch'an was represented by only
Lin-chi and Ts'ao-tung, the other three Ch'an schools having declined
by this time. The Doctrinal schools included T'ien-t'ai, Hua-yen, and
Fa-hsiang. Among them Hua-yen was the strongest, having received much
stimulus during the Chin from the support given by the eminent Ch'an
master Wan-sung Hsing-hsiu[j] (1166–1246).[16] During the Yüan, three
monastic codes corresponding to the three types of Buddhist monasteries
were compiled: Hsing-wu[k] wrote the Lü-yüan shih-kuei[l] (Rules for Lü

Monasteries) in 1325, Te-hui[m] (1142–1204), compiled the *Pai-chang ch'ing-kuei ch'ung-pien*[n] (Revised Edition of the *Pure Rules of Pai-chang*)[17] in 1335, and Tzu-ch'ing[o] published his *Tseng-hsiu Chiao-yüan ch'ing-kuei*[p] (Extended Edition of the *Pure Rules for Monasteries of the Doctrine School*) in 1347. Buddhist historiography also made some progress in the Yüan. Nien-ch'ang[q] (1282–1344?) wrote the *Fo-tsu li-tai t'ung-tsai*[r] (Comprehensive Records of Buddhist Patriarchs in Successive Generations) in 1341, Chüeh-an[s] (1286–1355), wrote *Shih-shih chi-ku-lüeh*[t] (Brief Compilation of Buddhist History) in 1354, and P'u-tu[u] (1259–1340), in order to differentiate the Pure Land from other heterodox popular movements such as the White Lotus and White Cloud, had earlier compiled the *(Lu-shan) Lien-tsung pao-chien*[v] (Precious Mirror of the Lotus Sect [from Mt. Lu]) in 1308.

The Ch'an school, however, was the most important. Some of the Ch'an masters of the Yüan showed concerns similar to those of their predecessors in the Sung: they emphasized what was unique in Ch'an, but they also advocated harmony between Ch'an and other Buddhist schools, both the philosophical schools and the Pure Land. They believed in the truth of Buddha, but they were open to Confucianism. They placed the highest premium on awakening, but they were also strong upholders of the monastic discipline, believing that only through a disciplined life could one finally reach a breakthrough to awakening. Chung-feng Ming-pen[w] (1263–1323), whose life covered the major part of the Yüan, exemplified these tendencies.

LIFE OF CHUNG-FENG MING-PEN[18]

Chung-feng Ming-pen was the inheritor of a distinguished Ch'an lineage: he was the eighteenth-generation heir of Lin-chi. His master was Kao-feng Yüan-miao[x] (1238–1295), who achieved great repute as a serious Ch'an master after he had sat in solitary retreat for seventeen years in a place called "Gate of Death" (*ssu-kuan*)[y] on Mt. T'ien-mu in modern Kiangsu. Kao-feng in turn inherited the dharma from Hsüeh-yen Tsu-ch'in[z] (1214–1287), the disciple of Wu-chün Shih-fan[aa] (1178–1249).[19] These monks all belonged to the Yang-ch'i branch of the Lin-chi school, which split into two branches early in the Northern Sung dynasty under two influential monks: Yang-ch'i Fang-hui[ab] (992–1049) and Huang-lung

Hui-nan[ac] (1002–1069). Early on the Huang-lung branch was very strong, counting among its followers prominent literary figures and statesmen such as Su Shih (1036-1101), Huang T'ing-chien (1045–1105), Wang An-shih (1021–1096), and Chang Shang-yin (1043–1121). However, it was eclipsed by the Yang-ch'i branch in the Southern Sung dynasty, around the time of Yüan-wu K'o-ch'in[ad] (1063–1135), author of the celebrated *Pi-yen lu* (The Blue Cliff Records) and a leading patriarch of the Yang-ch'i lineage.[20] Yüan-wu had five disciples, among whom Ta-hui Tsung-kao[ae] (1089–1163)[21] was most famous. Chung-feng Ming-pen and his predecessors were the lineal heirs of Hu-ch'iu Shao-lung[af] (1077–1136)), another disciple of Yüan-wu and a fellow monk of Ta-hui.

Monks belonging to this lineage of Ch'an Buddhism were noted for their intense concern with the proper pursuit of cultivation and advocated the use of *kung-an*[ag] as the most effective way to reach awakening. Under this teaching the so-called *kung-an Ch'an* or *k'an-hua Ch'an*,[ah] which emphasized dwelling upon the *hua-t'ou*[ai] (the critical phrase in a *kung-an*) as the focal point of a Ch'an practitioner's training, came to full development. For these monks, *kung-an* came to represent the true essence of the Ch'an vocation. Yet interestingly, together with the heightened sense of self-consciousness of what uniquely was Ch'an, there was also a tendency toward the notion of the "universalization" of Ch'an. In other words, for these monks, there was really no contradiction between Ch'an and other Buddhist schools. On the contrary, Ch'an, in replicating the experience of the religious awakening of Buddha, actually were viewed to contain the other Buddhist schools, which were systems of explaining the Truth revealed in the same religious experience. The "universalization" of Ch'an was also manifested in its confident stance vis-à-vis non-Buddhist teachings. Yang-ch'i Ch'an had its home base in Kaifeng (Honan), former Northern Sung capital, and from the beginning had close ties with the political and intellectual elites of the day. Since these Ch'an monks attracted followers from among the Confucian literati, it was natural for them to compare Buddhism with Confucianism. Consequently, they were frequently engaged in a kind of ecumenical dialogue. When one reads these discussions, one is often struck by the note of authority which pervaded them. They were not apologists for Buddhism. They did not feel it necessary to justify Buddhism. Even though not all Ch'an monks would be so blunt, many of them probably would have shared the sentiment of Hai-yün Hsing-hsiu[aj] (1202–1257). When asked by Khubilai to rank the Three Teachings, he reportedly answered: "Our Buddha is the most excellent among all sages, the Buddha Dharma is the most real among all teachings, and only Buddhist monks harbor no deceit among men. Therefore, it has been the case from ancient times that Buddhism was the highest among the Three Teachings."[22]

In many ways Cung-feng Ming-pen was a true heir of the Yang-ch'i tradition. He was the youngest of seven children born to the Sun[ak] family. During his grandfather's time, the family moved from Hangchow to Ch'ien-t'ang. On the eve of his birth, his mother dreamed of the Buddhist monk Wu-men K'ai[al] arriving at the house with a lantern.[23] He was a very serious child, delighting in sitting in the lotus position and singing Buddhist chants from the time he was a mere toddler. When he played, he was always pretending to officiate at Buddhist services, which greatly astonished the neighbors. He started school at age 7, reading the *Analects* and *Mencius*, but before he could finish the latter, at the age of 9, his mother passed away and he stopped attending school. From 15 on he began to set his heart on leaving the householder's life. He observed the five precepts for a Buddhist layman, and recited daily the *Lotus Sutra*, *Sutra of Perfect Enlightenment (Yüan-chüeh ching)*[am] and the *Diamond Sutra*. He also practiced austerities: making burn marks on his arm in his fervent worship of the Buddha and walking around during the night to keep himself awake. When he felt drowsy he would knock his head against a pillar. He would often go up to the top of Mt. Ling-tung (Mountain of Spiritual Grotto) and sit in meditation. When he was about 20 he was reading the *Transmission of the Lamp*, and became deeply puzzled by a passage which recorded a conversation between Amradarika, guardian of the amra tree and wife of Bimbisara, and Mañjuśrī. She asked Mañjuśrī, "Since we clearly know that birth is in truth no-birth, why then are we still caught in the cycle of transmigration?" Ming-pen was advised by a monk named Ming-shan to go to Kao-feng Yüan-miao of Mt. T'ien-mu[an] to seek his instruction. Kao-feng was noted for being cold and unapproachable,[24] and usually did not accept disciples easily. But when he saw Ming-pen, he was impressed and wanted to give him the tonsure right away. However, because Ming-pen's father did not give him permission, he studied under Kao-feng as a lay disciple for three years.

In 1286, when he was 24 years old, Ming-pen was reading the *Diamond Sutra* and suddenly understood its deep meaning. When he turned to other sutras or Confucian texts he could also grasp their significance.

But Kao-feng told him that this was only intellectual understanding, not true awakening. The next year, with the help of a pious woman named Yang,[25] he finally received the tonsure from Master Kao-feng at the Shih-tzu yüan[ao] Monastery on Mt. T'ien-mu and accepted the full commandments for a monk the following year. During these years he worked hard at his meditation. When he was 27 he had a pseudoenlightenment: while meditating on a waterfall he thought he had an awakening, but when he asked Kao-feng for verification, he merely received a beating and was driven out of the room. After this he sat during the day and waited on the Master at night. He was so single-minded that very often the day would dawn without his realizing it. As so often happened with Ch'an enlightenment, Ming-pen's own breakthrough also occurred in a seemingly fortuitous fashion. At that time there was a rumor circulating among the people that the government intended to recruit young men and maidens. Ming-pen asked Kao-feng, "What would you do if officials came here to ask you for young men and maidens?" Kao-feng said, "I will simply give them a taste of the bamboo stick."[26] Hearing this, Ming-pen was said to have suddenly become awakened. To certify Ming-pen's enlightenment, Kao-feng gave him a self-portrait with the following caption,

> My face is inconceivable,
> even Buddhas and patriarchs cannot have a glimpse,
> I allow this no-good son alone
> to have a peep at half of my nose.[27]

After he attained awakening, Ming-pen remained at the Shih-tzu yüan Monastery for the next seven years until 1295, when his master Kao-feng passed away. During this period, he served as attendant for the sick (t'ang-chu),[ap] treasurer (k'u-t'ou),[aq] and precentor (wei-na),[ar] and worked as a liaison between patrons and the monastery. While busily engaged in monastic duties, he already had the wish to relinquish all the ties and live as a true mendicant. In 1292, Kao-feng's lay disciple Ch'ü T'ing-fa,[as] the Commissioner of Salt of the Kiangche province, donated 270 ch'ing of land on the Lotus-flower Peak of Mt. T'ien-mu and built a monastery named Ta-chüeh ssu[at] (Monastery of Great Enlightenment) for Kao-feng. When Kao-feng was about to die, he asked Ming-pen to head the monastery. But, wanting to be free of administrative entanglements, he declined and recommended another monk. After the funeral of Kao-feng, Ming-pen left T'ien-mu and started a life of wandering. He was in Wu-men (present modern Wu county, Kiangsu) in 1296, and the next year he visited Mt. T'ien-chu in Anhwei. In the winter of the same year he returned to Nanking and lived in a grass hut in retirement for ten months.

In 1298, he built the first of a series of retreats which all bore the name "Illusory Abode"[28] (*Huan-chu an*)[au] in Pien-shan of Lu-chou (present K'ai-p'ing county, Liao-ning). Sutdents started to flock to him, although Ming-pen was far from eager to establish a monastic center. He constantly moved about from one place to another and never tried to put down permanent roots anywhere. Twice he refused to head the Ling-yin[av] and Ching-shan[aw] monasteries of Hangchow, two of the five most famous Ch'an monasteries, the so-called "Five Mountains" (*wu-shan*).[ax][29] In 1299, he moved back to Wu-men and built the second retreat of Illusory Abode on Mt. Yen-tang[ay] in Chekiang. Students followed him there and during the next two years a sizeable following grew up around him. But his life took a new turn when in 1302 the abbotship of Ta-chüeh ssu became vacant and Commissioner Ch'ü insisted that Ming-pen take up the post. The biographer says that Ming-pen ran away in consternation. From Mt. T'ien-mu, however, he could not completely cut himself off. He spent one year (1304) living near the tomb of his master Kao-feng, and the following year took care of the affairs at Shih-tzu yüan monastery. In 1308 the future emperor, Ayurbarwada, asked him to come to the Eastern Palace. When he declined, the heir apparent bestowed on him the title Fa-hui Ch'an-shih[az] (Ch'an Master of Dharma Wisdom) and a robe woven in gold. This was the first of several imperial honors which were to come to Ming-pen. In 1309, trying to sequester himself, Ming-pen went to live on a boat in I-chen (Kiangsu). He wrote ten poems describing his amphibian life. One of them reads,

> I am tired of talking about the "former three's" and the "latter three's."[30]
> Boat-dwelling is indeed superior to living in a retreat house.
> Since there is no fixed location, this is the real "ten-foot square" room.[31]
> And a living monastery is characterized by not abiding anywhere.
> I conduct my morning service in the watery kingdom by a village shrouded in mist.
> I do my evening meditation on the moonlit bank and flowering creek.
> Sometimes a guest knocks on the prow of my boat and asks about Tao.
> But there is no need for the ascetic to talk any nonsense.[32]

The next year he was asked to go back to T'ien-mu, but after one year he again went to live on a boat on Wu-chiang (the Wu-sung River, the largest tributary of Lake T'ai). A lay disciple, Ch'in Tzu-tsung, had a temple built for him, but Ming-pen ran away to the north and tried to live incognito in P'ien-liang (modern Kaifeng, Honan). Hwever, he was discovered by monks and lay people in the area and they vied in paying him respect, saluting him as "The Ancient Buddha from South of the Yangtze" (*Chiang-nan ku-fo*).[ba] This apparently so discomfited him that in the spring of 1312 he went up to Mt. Liu-an (30 *li* west of present Hou county, Anhwei) and built a hut for himself.

Judging from the ten poems he wrote while dwelling in the mountain, Ming-pen felt very much at peace with his surroundings. One poem reads,

> What love and what hatred is there in my breast!
> I only feel ashamed that I am capable of nothing.
> Picking up broken clouds I mend my torn cassock.
> Climbing to a high cliff I sit on withered ivy.
> Surrounded by a thousand peaks—a room of half the normal size.
> Made leisurely by the experience of myriad realms—one monk alone.
> Aside from this ready-made *koan*
> There is no Dharma to be passed from lamp to lamp[33]

His idyllic retreat, like others before it, was only temporary. In the fall, when Darkhan Toghon[bb] (1292–1328),[34] Right Director of Kiangche Branch Secretariat, who later became Chief Councilor of the Central Secretariat, came to pay him respect, Ming-pen immediately decided to flee to a boat in Tung-hai chou (present Tung-hai county, Kiangsu). The following year, 1313, the abbotship of the Ta-chüeh monastery became vacant again. Mr. Ch'ü, the original patron of the monastery, had died in the same year and his son obtained the consent of the Hsüan-cheng yüan[bc] (Bureau of Buddhist and Tibetan Affairs)[35] to appoint Ming-pen as abbot. Ming-pen promptly declined and recommended another monk. Two years later he was offered the abbotship of Ling-yin ssu on the recommendation of the same Darkhan Toghon. Fearing that he would refuse again, Toghon had the Chief of the Central Secretariat add his own plea, saying, "Since the Master is noted for your virtue we feel you have an obligation to go along with popular sentiment and establish yourself as the head of a big monastery in order to help the cause of Buddhism."[36] Ming-pen's answer was naturally negative. He argued his case with great persuasiveness:

To be an abbot a person must be blessed with three things, namely, virtue, popularity, and wisdom. Virtue is the essence while the other two are function.

If a person is sound in his essence but deficient in function, he is still acceptable, even though he would not be skillful in his dealings with the community nor would he be perfect in administrative finesse. However, if he is lacking in virtue, even if he were a wonder-worker, his popularity and wisdom would not help him in any way. Now if a person is deficient in both essence and function, it would be a great shame to have him bear the empty title of abbotship. I know that in reality I am such a person, that is why I do not dare to assume the name.[37]

After this the officials allowed him to beg off on the excuse of illness and he returned to Mt. T'ien-mu. In 1316 Emperor Ayurbarwada ordered the Hsüan-cheng yüan to recommend famous monks for commemoration and an audience with the emperor. Just before the messenger arrived at Mt. T'ien-mu, Ming-pen stole away to Chen-chiang. A lay disciple, Chiang Chün,[bd] built him yet another retreat named Illusory Abode in 1317. In this year Ming-pen composed a set of monastic codes called *The Pure Rules of Huan-chu* (*Huan-chu ch'ing-kuei*).[be][38] In the preface he stated:

When people's hearts are preserved in the Way they are naturally correct and proper even though there are no rites or laws to guide them. What need is there for monastic codes? But alas the people's hearts have for a long time not been anchored in the Way and the monasteries have been in a state of disorder for over five hundred years. Master Pai-chang [Huai-hai,[bf] 749-814] tried to correct the situation by establishing the system of the "public monastery." However, from that time until now abuses cannot but have crept in. As we now live together in a retreat house, we must try not to break any regulations in our daily life. I dare not hope to imitate earlier models of monastic codes, but I have compiled a rule book consisting of ten sections to be used as a standard reference by both the host and the guests of the retreat. I intend this as a rule book for my own group but do not presume to share it with other people.[39]

Ming-pen had built his first retreat in 1298, nineteen years earlier. At the first retreat as well as at subsequent ones, Ming-pen undoubtedly had had disciples with him and some sort of community rules governing their daily life must already have been in use. So even though the *Pure Rules of Huan-chu* was composed in 1317, it probably was a final codification of the earlier unwritten regulations. We will examine this work in some detail later.

In 1318 the emperor, unsuccessful in summoning Ming-pen to court, bestowed more honors on him. Ming-pen was given the title of Fo-t'zu Yüan-chao Kuang-hui Ch'an-shih.[bg] The Shih-tzu yüan of Mt. T'ien-mu, the monastery with which Ming-pen was most intimately associated, was renamed "Shih-tzu Cheng-tsung Ch'an-ssu" (Shih-tzu, the Ch'an Monastery of Orthodox Lineage) and a stele recording this event was erected with a text composed by Chao Meng-fu (1254–1322),[bh] the famous painter and Hanlin scholar, by imperial command. In 1322, when Ming-pen was 60 years old, he was appointed by the Branch Bureau of Buddhist and Tibetan Affairs (*Hsing Hsüan-cheng yüan*) to head the famous Ching-shan Monastery. He delined and went thirty *li* away to Mt. Chung-chia which was isolated and difficult to reach. Still, it is said that his faithful followers would ford streams, scale cliffs, and brave the danger of tigers to visit him everyday. Feeling sorry for them, Ming-pen soon returned to Huan-chu an. He passed away the next year (1323), at the age of 61. In the autobiography he wrote the year before, Ming-pen reviewed his life and said:

Since I became a monk, thirty-seven years have now passed. When I first entered the sangha, my original purpose was to practice austerities and give up all material comforts. It is my life-long regret that I have failed to live up to this deal. Furthermore, I am unlettered in my scholarship and unenlightened in my meditation. However, due to karmic circumstances I became talked about by people who have nothing better to do. The reason that I have always admired the eremitic way of life is not because I am eccentric and try to set myself above ordinary men. Rather it is because I feel that I would let the faithful down because of my failings.[40]

Ming-pen was posthumously honored by Emperor Khoshila, who granted him the title "Ch'an Master Chih-chüeh" (Chih-chüeh ch'an-shih)[bi] in 1329, and by Emperor Toghan Temür who granted him the title State Teacher P'u-ying (P'u-ying kuo-shih)[bj] in 1334. In the same year the emperor granted the petition of one of Ming-pen's disciples, who asked that Ming-pen's collected writings, *Chung-feng ho-shan kuang-lu*[bk] (Extended Records of Monk Chung-feng) in thirty fascicles, be included in the Buddhist Tripitaka. The collected works consists of Ming-pen's sermons, individual instructions to disciples, letters, poems, commentaries on the *Diamond* and *Śūrangama* sutras, and essays on various topics. Aside from the *Kuang-lu*, there is also the *Tsa-lu*[bl] (Miscellaneous Records) in three fascicles, which contains Ming-pen's sermons and essays not collected in the *Kuang-lu*. These two works are the primary sources for an understanding of Ming-pen's thought.

Ming-pen was a central figure in the history of Ch'an Buddhism. Many of his ideas reflected the concerns of the Ch'an monks in the Yüan

period. His ideas in turn also exerted deep influence on Ch'an monks in
the Ming and later. Despite his eremitism, Ming-pen had attracted an
international following. Among the disciples who either came to him in
person or wrote to him for instructions were Japanese, Koreans, Tibetans,
Mongols, Western Asians and Annamese. Because of Ming-pen, the
kingdom of Nan-chao (in Yunnan) was converted to Ch'an Buddhism.
His portrait was carried back to the capital and he was venerated as the
first patriarch of Ch'an Buddhism there. Ming-pen was the teacher to
Japanese Zen monks who later established a lineage in his name (the
Genjū lineage named after the Huan-chu an) in Kamakura Japan.[41] His
writings have also remained popular among Japanese Zen monks ever
since that time. Indeed, Ming-pen has perhaps been even better known
abroad than in his own country.

This paper focuses on Ming-pen's contribution to Ch'an Buddhism
and his role as un upholder of monastic discipline. First I shall discuss
his thought about Ch'an Buddhism: what was wrong with the Ch'an
practices of his day, what is truly Ch'an, what is the relationship of Ch'an
with the philosophical schools, with Pure Land, with Confucianism, with
Discipline; and finally in what sense can one say that Ch'an is the essence of Buddhism or that Ch'an is synonymous with the Way? I will
then discuss Ming-pen's views on monastic discipline by an examination
of the *Pure Rules of Huan-chu.*

MING-PEN, THE CH'AN MASTER

First let me present two quotations:

When I first entered the sangha, which was around the Kai-ch'ing [1259] and
Ching-ting [1260–1265] eras [of the Sung], monasteries such as Ching-tz'u[bm]
usually had four to five hundred monks. The abbot was, needless to say, above
reproach. Among the ordinary monks, if there were one person who drank even
though he should do so rather infrequently, he would have been ridiculed by his
colleagues. One seldom heard of other offenses aside from drinking. But now
from top to bottom everyone is loose and has no sense of shame. Discipline is
the root of order (*li-fa*)[bn] for the monastery. If the root is cut off then there is no
way that branches and leaves can survive. Alas, when the body of the Way (*tao-
t'i*)[bo] weakens, the power of discipline (*chieh-li*)[bp] diminishes. When the power
of discipline diminishes, order within the sangha is lost.[42]

Very often I hear complaints from people who have failed to accomplish any-thing. Instead of blaming themselves for lack of effort, they say that Buddhism has declined and the monasteries have come upon hard times. They complain that there is no good teacher to guide them nor strict friends to help them. They talk about the inconveniences of bathing or the inadequacies of food. They blame the laxity of monastic rules and the noisiness of the surroundings. They say that because of all these their effort in meditation cannot help but suffer. But to use these as excuses for not working hard is like the farmer who gives up farming on account of the untimeliness of rainfall. How can he hope to have a harvest in the fall? [43]

In the first place, Ming-pen deplores the general decline of monastic discipline, and in the second, the lack of dedication and purpose of in-dividual monks. For Ming-pen, the condition of Buddhism in his day was far from satisfactory. Yet we do not find in his writings too much talk of "mo-fa," [bq] (Degenerate Age of the Law), a theme much favored by Chinese Buddhists since Sui and T'ang times. The idea of the Three Ages should ideally arouse, in the faithful, both eschatological expecta-tions and a sense of intense existential urgency. But it is also possible for a person less committed to Buddhism to use it as an excuse. Since Ming-pen lived in the age of *mo-fa*, it was no wonder to him Buddhism is in such a sorry state. Yet, if *mo-fa* is an historical necessity, can any human effort make the slightest difference? Instead of resorting to apology Ming-pen turned to very specific causes. Neglect of discipline and the failure to exert oneself stood out before all else. He used the example of human physiology to illustrate the state of Buddhism. We all know that the way to nourish our bodies is to preserve our original breath (*yüan-ch'i*). [br] The health of the body rests with the pulse-rate of the blood (*mai*) [bs] and the security of the pulse rests with our original breath. Similarly, the three Buddhist schools of Doctrine, Ch'an, and Discipline constitute the body of Buddhism, whereas training in the disciplinary rules (vinaya), medi-tation and wisdom, constitutes the heart blood of Buddhism. The perse-cutions suffered under the "three Emperors Wu" [44] damaged only our body, but as long as the pulse remains, the body (i.e., the Buddhist schools) can always recover. Conversely, even if the body appears healthy, as represented by the gorgeous structures of monasteries and the wealth of temple lands, when the inner life weakens due to the neglect of the disciplinary precepts, meditation and wisdom, then Buddhism will surely die no matter what patronage and protection it may enjoy. [45]

Turning to Ch'an Buddhism, Ming-pen's criticism was equally specific and penetrating. He was most critical of two tendencies among his
fellow Ch'an Buddhists: sectarianism and the attempt to reach awakening
intellectually. In his writings he constantly praised Lin-chi and quoted
him often, along with Bodhidharma, as an authority in matters of Ch'an
practice. However, he did not feel that the Lin-chi school was superior
to the other schools. On the contrary, for Ming-pen, the so-called five
schools of Ch'an were no more than five different paths for reaching the
same goal or, to use his imagery, "five different containers of the same
Way."

The five schools are different in regard to the men who founded them, but are
not different in regard to the Way. Have you not heard that the transmission of
the teaching by the Buddha and patriarchs is compared to the transmission of the
lamp? If you really understand the meaning of "transmission of the lamp," you
will never think that the Way can be divided into five. I would like to cite the
example of the lamps we use. There are paper lanterns, oil-cup lanterns, glass
lanterns, lamps lit by candles, and then torches. All these are called lamps. But
because the utensils used differ, the lamps look different. Yet despite the difference, they all can extinguish the gloomy darkness shrouding the long night of
samsara.[46]

The differences among the five schools were mainly due to the different
personalities of their founders. Consequently, the language and techniques each school employed in teaching students also differed. Ming-
pen characterized the style of Kuei-yang as "cautious and strict" (chin-
yen),[bt] Ts'ao-tung as "delicate and refined" (hsi-mi),[bu] Lin-chi as "penetrating and sharp" (t'ung-k'uai),[bv] Yün-men as "lofty and classic" (kao-
ku)[bw] and Fa-yen as "simple and clear" (chien-ming).[bx] Yet he was sure
that none of the founders had any conscious intention of establishing a
separate school. A school naturally came into being when like-minded
individuals were attracted by the style of one meditation center, stayed
together and formed a distinctive tradition. Therefore, Ming-pen regarded the sectarian bickering of the different Ch'an schools as utterly
ridiculous and felt that "if the patriarchs of the five schools should know
of this in their great silent samadhi, they would surely cover their noses
in laughter."[47]

Perhaps even more damaging than sectarian rivalry was the tendency
in Ch'an circles to intellectualize and verbalize, which really threatened
the very life of Ch'an. In an ironic passage which reminds one of the

Chinese proverb, "adding feet to a drawing of a snake," or in a more profound way, of the destroying of Chaos by his well-intentioned yet totally misguided friends in *Chuang Tzu*,[48] Ming-pen described his fellow Ch'an monks this way:

One man came along and put a stroke on the head of Ch'an. Another put a stroke at the feet of Ch'an; a third put a stroke in the heart of Ch'an. Finally, yet another man came over and put three more dots on top of the three strokes. When we look at it, the Ch'an thus decorated bears no resemblance to its original face. Later on more people came along and added more dots and strokes to those already there. Occasionally, they would put some of the dots and strokes in the wrong places, and they would start to criticize each other and give names to these, calling them Tathāgata Ch'an (*Ju-lai Ch'an*),[by] patriarch Ch'an (*tsu-shih Ch'an*),[bz] literary Ch'an (*wen-tzu Ch'an*),[ca] heretical Ch'an (*wai-tao Ch'an*),[cb] sravaka Ch'an (*sheng-wen Ch'an*),[cc] worldling Ch'an (*fan-fu Ch'an*),[cd] . . . Ch'an of shouts and sticks (*pang-ho Ch'an*).[ce][49]

The result of creating names and attaching labels was to stir up "the wind of opinions" (*chih-chien feng*),[cf] to churn "the sea of inchoate passions" (*tsa-tu hai*)[cg] and further agitate one's consciousness and discrimination.[50] The intellectual approach to spiritual cultivation was by no means limited to young monks who did not know any better. Ming-pen claimed that even teachers in many monasteries committed the same mistake. In their eagerness to produce heirs, these teachers would explain to their students the meaning of those *kung-an* or *hua-t'ou* contained in the various Ch'an texts as if these were primers used in elementary schools. This was, of course, counterproductive, for the very purpose of these *kung-an* was to force one not to use one's intellect to understand them. One must devote one's whole being to a *kung-an* and become totally absorbed in it. Only then could one penetrate through it. Before one reached this state, there was nothing another person could do to help. "Even if Śākyamuni or Bodhidharma should show you what this is all about by splitting open his liver and gall, it would simply obstruct your mind's eye even more!"[51]

The Way of Ch'an

The famous painter Chao Meng-fu and his wife were Buddhists and admirers of Ming pen.[52] After Chao passed away, Ming-pen recalled their relationship in an informal sermon delivered in Chao's memory. Ming-pen remembered that he first met Chao and his wife in 1304 when he had been invited to stay at Chao's residence in Wu-lin. After that time, Chao had often asked Ming-pen about Ch'an cultivation. He was particularly puzzled by the fact that if, according to Buddhism, we were originally endowed with enlightenment, then why was it that we were in fact not enlightened. Chao sometimes became so anguished over this paradox that he would burst out in tears. In recalling the past, Ming-pen used the opportunity to talk about the real meaning of "innately sufficient endowment" (pen-lai chü ts'u),ᶜʰ and he emphasized the critical importance of effort (kung-fu)ᶜⁱ in Ch'an cultivation. He first remarked that ever since Buddhism was introduced to China, the literati had been much attracted to it. This was the case during the Yüan. But most of them approached Buddhism intellectually, and only a minority would be willing to work seriously at meditation. Even in the latter case, they usually could not succeed because they misunderstood the meaning of "innate endowment" and "not relying on anything outside oneself" (pu-chia wai-ch'iu).ᶜʲ Relying on their cleverness and talent, they assumed that awakening was an easy matter and did not bother to strive harder. Ming-pen then delivered the central message of the sermon:

To speak of "innate endowment" is like saying that flour is contained in wheat or cooked rice is contained in grain. . . . Confucians also say that benevolence and righteousness do not come from outside one's mind. Therefore Mencius says that they are innate in me, but are not obtained from outside. But, if one does not really practice the virtues and never for one moment forgets this even in times of difficulties and suffering, he will merely have the innate mind of benevolence and righteousness. This is why the Buddha and patriarchs have compared the innately endowed enlightenment to the luster of an old mirror, which, due to lack of attention and care, becomes covered with the dust of love and hatred. During many lives and innumerable kalpas, the mirror has not been polished, and now, even if it originally had the nature to shine, it in fact could not do so. The best tool for polishing the mirror is none other than the hua-t'ou.⁵³

When Ming-pen compared the mind of original enlightenment to a mirror, it was exactly the way Shen-hsiu, the leader of Northern Ch'an, had put it.⁵⁴ It is ironic that Ming-pen, an orthodox Lin-chi master who traced his spiritual ancestry to Shen-hsin's opponent Hui-neng, would choose the same imagery and emphasize the necessity of polishing the mirror. But, for his time, this was definitely called for. There was already too much verbiage and empty talk. What was needed was serious effort.

For Ming-pen, the Way of Ch'an is a spiritual journey consisting of three stages. It starts when one becomes keenly aware of one's mortality and experiences samsaric dread (*sheng-ssu*).[ck] But this consciousness of the precariousness and fragility of one's physical existence should not create morbid obsession. Instead, it should be followed by a strong sense of faith (*hsin*).[cl] "Faith" in Ch'an Buddhism is quite different from faith in other religions. Essentially, it is a firm belief that there is a way out of one's anxiety and suffering. It is also an unshakeable conviction that "I" can accomplish the task of my own salvation. The final stage is, of course, awakening (*wu*),[cm] when one suddenly and fundamentally realizes that samsara, which originally causes so much fear and pain, now has no hold on one. As Ming-pen describes it,

We should know that samsara originally has neither essence or nature. It is only because we are ignorant of our own mind (*tzu-hsin*)[cn] that we deludedly drift with transmigration and feel as if there were really samsara. This is like water congealing into ice when cold air accumulates, but again turning into water when cold air suddenly disappears. When the mind is beclouded by ignorance, samsara is delusively wrought into being. But when one awakes from ignorance, one realizes the stillness of one's mind. In this case, if one should want to search for samsara, one would be like a man who has woken up and tried to recapture the events of his dream. How can this ever be done? Thus we know that samsara is originally void but we can realize this only through awakening; that nirvana is originally real but we do not know it because of our ignorance.[55]

The Way of Ch'an is a journey from ignorance to enlightenment. The entire endeavor is sustained by an effort which is generated and fueled by the *kung-an* or *hua-t'ou* one is forced to struggle with. Since this is the case, the *hua-t'ou* plays a crucial role in the Ch'an of Ming-pen.

Confrontation with Mortality

In the literature of Ch'an Buddhism, one often comes across the phrase, "Birth and death are great matters" (*sheng-ssu shih ta*).[co] Many Ch'an monks were said to have started their search for enlightenment when they were overwhelmed and completely taken over by the power of this phrase. What does it really mean? Therefore, to state to anyone that this is so should logically produce hardly any effect. Unless a person is himself visited with a fatal illness or confronted with the death of a loved one, the knowledge of his mortality will always remain an intellectual concept. He will live from day to day supported by a blind faith in his own existence. It is this congenital blindness to the truth of samsara that binds one forever to the cycle of birth-death-rebirth. Therefore, the first and most difficult step in one's liberation is to have the courage to face one's mortality. Ming-pen, in a letter to a monk in Korea, discussed the relationship between man's samsaric condition and the sense of "doubt" (*i*)^{cp} or what we may more freely interpret as "existential questioning."

What I call "the sense of doubt" is simply this: When you realize that you really do not know anything about this "Great Matter of Birth and Death," you stop every other thought and concentrate your mind entirely on this question. Why have I come down to the present from the remote past of uncountable kalpas? What was I like in the past? Why do I flow from the present to the unforeseeable future? Is there ever going to be an end? When you look at this question squarely in the face, this is "doubt." From the beginning, all Buddhas and patriarchs started their existential questioning at this point. When one dwells on this question without any rest, in the end one will naturally block the wondering of the mind, extinguish the agitations of passions and delusions, cut off one's intellectual discriminations, and forget the distinction between the subject and object. At that moment one will suddenly be in accordance with Reality and all one's doubts will burst open and disintegrate. Formerly, worthies did not "look at" any *hua-t'ou* or ponder on any *kung-an*. They also did not sit on a meditation cushion and pretend to be doing something special. The only important thing to them was to find out the meaning of samsara. For this they would walk three thousand *li* or five thousand *li*. And when they met a teacher, without bothering to take off their straw sandals they would blurt out, "I have come to find out why life and death are great matters, why life is impermanent and death comes in a flash." One thousand people acted this way and ten thousand people also acted this way. They left the householder's life because of this question. They wandered from place to place to seek instruction also because of this question. For them to seek the Way was for no other purpose than to solve this question.[56]

When one becomes totally absorbed in this existential question, one reaches the state which Ming-pen calls "Great Doubt" (*ta-i*).^{cq} It is experienced as a physical sensation:

When your breast is filled with the matter of life and death, you cannot push it aside no matter how hard you try. It is just like a man near starvation. Even if he should try to stop himself from grasping for food, he could not do so. . . . Under the pressure of the Great Doubt, a person naturally forgets to eat and gives up sleep. His body and mind become unified. Moreover, he is not aware of this sense of Great Doubt himself. He naturally is absorbed in the doubt and cannot have any rest. This is like the story about a former worthy who was standing in the courtyard deeply engaged in contemplating the word "wu." A sudden downpour came and he got soaked, yet he was not aware of his being wet. It was only when another monk called him that he woke up and discovered that he was wet with rain. This shows that his effort had become so pure and proficient that he could forget the external environment completely. This then is the Great Doubt. When you are in the midst of Great Doubt, as soon as the thought arises in your breast, "this is the Great Doubt," you are already in error. This is no longer the Great Doubt.[57]

In another case, Ming-pen stated that the ideal reaction to one's samsaric condition should be instinctive and automatic.

One becomes angry when one hears another person's malicious scolding. As soon as the sound enters one's ears, his heart of anger suddenly flares up and his body, mind, the external world, seeing, hearing, and feeling all become angry. He becomes so angry that he will not be able to eat or sleep. Even if he manages to sleep, he will dream of anger. He may even form a lifelong grudge and hatred against the person and cannot forget about the anger for one second. . . . In learning the Way, we want to end this matter. When we hear someone mention the two words "birth and death," we should react to it as if we were being scolded. We should not wait to check scriptures or quote treatises, nor should we deliberate and ponder over it. Rather, as soon as we confront the fact of our mortality, we should lodge this fact securely in our breast. We should not be able to push it aside or pretend it was not there. We should vow to ourselves that unless we reach sudden awakening we will never give up even if we die. With such determination, what great tasks are we not able to accomplish?[58]

For Ming-pen, courageous and honest confrontation with our samsaric condition constituted such a crucial step that he called it the essence of Ch'an. "The realization of samsara is the marrow of Ch'an. Ch'an is the eye of samsara."[59]

Faith

The realization of one's mortality, of course, does not always impel one toward spiritual enlightenment. On the contrary, an ordinary person's natural reaction to the knowledge of his own death will probably be either depression or hedonism. This is why Ming-pen put a great deal of stress on "faith." He said that when a person grounded his faith in his own mind (i.e., mind of original enlightenment), then awakening would not be a difficult matter. For when faith is so grounded, it will work like the force which drives a hungry man to seek for food. It will not give him a moment's leisure but drive him toward enlightenment.[60] This faith can be further analyzed in the following way:

In learning the Way, one should be equipped fully with five kinds of correct faith (*cheng-hsin*).[cr] The first is to believe that, within one's own heart, there is a master who experiences happiness, anger, sorrow, and joy, and that there is not even a hair of difference between him and the Buddhas of the past, present, and future. The second is to believe that during innumerable kalpas we have been bound up with samsara through sounds and forms, loves and hatreds, taints and habits. Within the four elements of our body, we transmigrate each instant and there is no time when we are standing still. The third is to believe that because of their kindness, ancient masters have handed down some words and phrases which can cut us free from the bonds of samsara. The fourth is to believe that as long as we devote ourselves to the daily effort of meditation, as long as our mind is concentrated and our thought unified, there surely will be a day when we reach awakening. The fifth is to believe that birth and death, which are impermanent, are no trivial matters. If we do not make up our minds to seek deliverance from the three painful realms of rebirth [animals, preta, hell] there is no way that we can escape from suffering.[61]

When faith is thus defined, it essentially means faith in one's own Buddha-nature, in the law of karma and samsara, and in the certainty of deliverance through one's work with a hua-t'ou.

The Role of Hua-t'ou in Ch'an Awakening

As Ming-pen had made clear, people in former times embarked on their spiritual journey on the strength of "existential questioning" alone. They had neither the aid of hua-t'ou, nor even the need for constant sitting. This agrees with what little we know of the early history of Ch'an. The systematic use of kung-an as a teaching device was a very late phenomenon and it did not figure as a regular part of instruction in Ch'an meditation before the tenth century, when the compilation and creation of kung-an became popular. According to Ming-pen, a kung-an was a "senseless and tasteless phrase" (wu-i-wei hua-t'ou)[cs] which a master made up to stop the student's excessive intellectual approach to Ch'an. When this senseless and tasteless word or phrase was drilled into a person's consciousness, it would make him feel as if "he had swallowed a hairy chestnut or drunk poison."[62] The purpose of this was to artificially create the "Great Doubt" which should naturally arise in a man if he were less burdened with intellectual baggage.

Before a student of the Way opens up his mouth to speak [the master] throws to him a senseless and tasteless word. He tells you to forget about body and mind, and every worldly concern and thought. He orders you to even forget about Ch'an, Buddha Dharma, language, and words. You should only generate a sense of Great Doubt concerning this hua-t'ou, absorb yourself in it and penetrate it. While you are thus engaged, do not think that you are doing it for the sake of understanding the Buddha Dharma, nor for the sake of gaining awakening, nor yet for the sake of achieving omniscience. The sole reason for your endeavor is because you cannot bear to live with the question of life and death. When the riddle of the *hua-t'ou* is broken, the mystery of life and death will also be dissolved. . . . Therefore, aside from life and death there is no other *hua-t'ou*, and aside from *hua-t'ou* there is no other life and death. Although the ancients became awakened to the Way through questioning life and death, and people in the present time become awakened to the Way through questioning *hua-t'ou*, the Way thus realized is the same despite the difference in the means which leads them to this realization.[63]

Since the *hua-t'ou* is no more than a device to create the essential sense of unrest and existential questioning, it follows that all *hua-t'ou* have the same effect if used properly. Ming-pen's own teacher, Kao-feng, was reported to have used only the *hua-t'ou*, "All dharmas return to the One, but where does the One return to?" During the thirty years he taught, he did not use any other *kung-an*.[64] Ming-pen himself did not seem to favor any particular *hua-t'ou*. For him, it was not which *hua-t'ou* to use, but *how* one should work at it. Ming-pen did not regard even the most famous *hua-t'ou* as sacrosanct. He made this humorously clear when he commented on the *kung-an* about Chao-chou's cypress tree. We recall that once Chao-chou was asked by a monk about the meaning of "Bodhidharma's coming from the West" (code words for the true meaning of Buddhism, and thus a question that is unanswerable). To this Chao-chou answered, "The cypress tree stands in the court-yard." Ming-pen said that there was no deeper significance behind the cypress tree. Chao-chou could have answered with "water flows leisurely in the creek," or "peach blossoms are red on the hill."[65]

The greatest obstacle one encounters in working with a *hua-t'ou* is the lack of single-mindedness. Ming-pen called this "second thought" (*ti-erh-nien*)[ct][66] or "stolen mind" (*t'ou-hsin*).[cu][67] As soon as one becomes aware of anything other than the *hua-t'ou*, one has already fallen into error. This other thought could be noble and virtuous. It could be one's awareness of how well or how poorly one is engaged in meditation. Yet this mere awareness destroys the identity between one and one's *hua-t'ou*. It can only be hopeless and deadly.

MING-PEN: THE RECONCILER OF TRADITIONS

We noted earlier that Ming-pen was averse to sectarianism within Ch'an Buddhism. He was equally opposed to divisiveness between Ch'an and

other Buddhist schools. Similarly, he argued for the compatibility between Buddhism and Confucianism, even though for Ming-pen this
compatibility did not imply that the two teachings were the same.

The first important Buddhist advocating the harmonization of
Buddhist schools was Yung-ming Yen-shou[cv] (904–975). Using mind as
the basis, he brought about a synthesis between philosophical schools,
i.e. the T'ien-t'ai, Hua-yen, and Wei-shih, which were known as *chiao-
men*,[cw] and the Ch'an, which was known as *tsung-men*.[cx] His advocacy
of the dual practice of Ch'an and Pure Land exerted considerable influence on later Buddhists, including Ming-pen. The Sung monk Ch'i-
sung[cy] (1007–1072), who was famous for his defense of Buddhism against
its Confucian critics, argued most forcefully for the compatibility of the
three teachings. He used the metaphor of crossing the ford to illustrate
the difference between the three teachings: some go through the ford with
their clothes on because the water is deep, others hold the clothes up
because the water is shallow. The Confucians produce sages to rule the
secular world, but the Buddhists produce sages to administer the monastic world. The two teachings occupy "separate realms"—they complement each other, but do not come into conflict.[68] Both Yen-shou and
Ch'i-sung were Ch'an monks. While the former defended Ch'an against
criticisms by other Buddhist scholars (whom Ming-pen referred to as
"Tripitaka scholars"), the latter defended Buddhism against the criticisms
of Confucians. Ming-pen respectfully called these two masters the "walls
and embankments of the buddhas and patriarchs" and paid them high
praise.[69]

Ming-pen found that Ch'an was fully compatible with Disciplinary
and Pure Land Buddhism, since all three schools taught ways to end
samsaric entrapment. Ming-pen thought Discipline the same as the Way
(another name for Ch'an). They were one in essence, even though they
differed in name. He said,

Discipline is the Discipline of the Way, and the Way is the Way of the Discipline. There are two names but there is only one principle. Why do we observe
discipline? It is because we want to end samsara. Why do we study the Way? It
is also because we want to end samsara. If our determination to end samsara is
strong, then even though we do not receive any precepts, we naturally observe
discipline. Even though we do not follow the Way, we naturally make progress
in the Way.[70]

In a letter written to a disciple in Yün-nan, Ming-pen started out by
saying that the three groups of pure precepts (*san-chü ching-chieh*)[cz] were

chief among all the precepts in the Vinaya. They were: (1) whatever worked for goodness (she-shan fa),[da] which Ming-pen interpreted to mean that one must cultivate everything which was good; (2) whatever pertained to dignified deportment (she-lü-i),[db] which he interpreted to mean that one must stop everything which is evil; and (3) whatever benefitted sentient beings (jao-i yu-ch'ing),[dc] which, according to Ming-pen, meant that one should save all sentient beings from samsara. Ming-pen compared these three groups of pure precepts to the ferry on which all buddhas and patriarchs of the past, present, and future went across to the other shore, or to the embryo in which they matured into buddhas and patriarchs. These precepts were indispensable for our release from samsara and entry into nirvana. Having established the central importance of the Vinaya precepts, Ming-pen proceeded to show that these very precepts could be contained in the Ch'an meditation on kung-an or hua-t'ou. He says,

When your mind and heart are filled completely with the hua-t'ou you are meditating on, you think of neither good nor evil. Since you have forgotten both good and evil, what need is there to talk about cultivation [of the good] and stopping [of the evil]? Moreover, when you are intensely concentrating on the hua-t'ou, you do not see any sentient being who is to be saved. This is benefitting sentient beings even though there is no actual being to be benefitted. Thus, although the hua-t'ou of Ch'an is not called the three groups of pure precepts, it in fact contains these pure precepts. There is no separation between the two.[71]

Ming-pen spoke of the identity between Ch'an and Pure Land:

Pure Land is the Mind and Ch'an is also the Mind. In essence they are one, but in name they are two. . . . Moreover, the reason we engage in Ch'an meditation is in order to end samsara (liao sheng-ssu).[dd] The reason we practice Buddha-invocation (nien-fo)[de] and follow the Pure Land teaching is also to end samsara. Among the teachings established by the Sage, there are a thousand paths and ten thousand tracks. But all the teachings have one thing in common, namely, their ultimate goal is to end samsara.[72]

Ming-pen wrote 108 poems (corresponding to the number of beads in a rosary used in nien-fo) entitled "Longing for the Pure Land" (Huai Ching-tu shih).[df] Some of them express the identity between the Pure Land and the Ch'an paths:

There is no need to talk about Pure Land aside from Ch'an.
One should know that there is no Ch'an outside of the Pure Land.
When one has solved these double kung-an,
A five-petaled lotus opens on the Bear Ear Mountain.

Amitābha Buddha lives in the West, while the First Patriarch comes from
the West.
To call on the Buddha and to do Ch'an meditation is of the same purport.
Once the ball of doubt accumulated for aeons is broken wide open,
The flower of the heart blooms in the same fashion.[73]

Ming-pen also wrote some songs extolling people to call on Buddha's
name. One of them goes like this:

This very mind is already the Buddha.
With this very mind one can become the Buddha.
Buddhas of the three ages have all realized that their mind is the Buddha.
Sentient beings in the six realms of rebirth are originally Buddhas.
But because of ignorance and delusion they are unwilling to believe in the
Buddha.
Do not forget to call the name of the Buddha whether you are happy or
unhappy, lucky or unlucky.
He who puts on clothes and he who eats food are no other than the Bud-
dha.
There is Buddha everywhere,
There is Buddha in movement, there is Buddha in quiescence.
There is Buddha in the midst of busy affairs, there is Buddha during the
time of leisure.
There is Buddha when you lie down, there is Buddha when you stand up.
There is Buddha in the good, there is Buddha in the bad.
There is Buddha in life, there is Buddha in death.
Remember the Buddha in every idea (*nien-nien*).[dg]
Remember the Buddha in each thought (*hsin-hsin*).[dh]
I urge you to call on the Buddha who is yourself (*tzu-chi fo*).[di]
Turn around quickly and do not seek after other Buddhas.
When your every thought is clear, who is not a Buddha?
I hope all people will take refuge in themselves who are already Buddhas.[74]

As this song makes clear, Ming-pen's understanding of *nien-fo* does
not postulate a distinction between the Amitābha Buddha, who is the
object of religious devotion, and the faithful devotee, who calls on the
name for salvation. On the contrary, he urges us to realize the identity
of our mind and the Buddha. So in calling on the name, we are not
calling on an Other, but rather we are returning to our true nature which
is already the Buddha. Like the *hua-t'ou* used in Ch'an meditation, the
name should serve as the focal point of our mental concentration under
all circumstances: when we are busy or leisurely, happy or sad, engaged
in daily affairs or during a time of sickness and suffering. When *nien-fo*

is practiced in this fashion, it is clearly no longer an expression of one's piety and faith, but a means to end all discursive thought and to arouse the "feeling of doubt" (i-ch'ing),[dj] the critical mental tension that drives one to reach awakening.

However, although Ming-pen says that the two paths lead to the same goal, he does not think it is good for a person to engage in both. On the contrary, a Ch'an practitioner should only engage in Ch'an meditation and a Pure Land practitioner only in nien-fo. According to Ming-pen, it is only through "one door" that we can enter into anything deeply.[75] If a person should attempt to practice Ch'an and Pure Land simultaneously (chien-hsiu)[dk] he will end up achieving nothing. For in the words of T'ien-ju Wei-tse[dl] (d.1354), who was a disciple of Ming-pen and an important Ch'an monk in his own right, this unfortunate person would be like the foolish man astride two boats. Not only would he fail to get into either boat, but he would surely fall into the water when the boats started to move.[76] Anyone who is serious about religious cultivation must specialize in a specific discipline.

Sectarian divisiveness and rivalry among Buddhist schools was a conspicuous feature of T'ang and Sung Buddhism. By Ming times, much of this had become history, and the slogans of "Ch'an Chiao ho-i"[dm] (harmonization of Ch'an and philosophical schools) or "Ch'an Ching shuang-hsiu"[dn] (dual cultivation of Ch'an and Pure Land) were no longer a novelty. Therefore, observers like Sung Lien (1310–1381) could write:

Ch'an and Chiao originally do not represent two separate doors. If we practice according to the philosophical schools, we must practice the six perfections of which meditation (ch'an-ting)[do] is one. Because sentient beings have different capacities, the Buddha therefore accommodated them by giving different instructions. It was truly unfortunate that people in later generations set up their own schools and attacked each other. Thus the scholars of the philosophical schools ridiculed the Ch'an practitioners as stagnating in emptiness and stillness (tai-yü k'ung-chi).[dp] The Ch'an practitioners, on the other hand, also ridiculed the scholars of the philosophical schools as being mired in terminology (ni-yü ming-hsiang).[dq] Controversies continued without end and what purpose in fact did they serve?[77]

The fact that such sentiment did become widespread in the Ming was perhaps because Ming-pen and others like him, following the example of Yen-shou, vigorously emphasized the need for transcending sectarian rivalries.

For Ming-pen, the differences between Ch'an and the philosophical schools were mainly differences in means or tactics, not in fundamental intention or goal. He neatly characterized them this way: "Ch'an is the philosophical school which dispenses with words, while the philosophical schools are Ch'an which uses words."[78] He tried to clarify the difference in another way. Whereas the other Buddhist schools all stress learning (*hsüeh*)[dr] and thereby provide a door through which a person can enter, Ch'an alone does not encourage intellectual effort or scholarly accomplishment. For this reason, Ch'an has been called a separate transmission.[79] In an essay entitled, "Night Conversations at a Mountain Hut" (*Shan-fang yeh-hua*),[ds] Ming-pen strikingly compared the different Buddhist schools to the four seasons of the year. Each was of course different from the others, yet each was also indispensible to the others. He went on to say:

The Esoteric school is the spring, T'ien-t'ai, Hsien-shou [Hua-yen], and Tz'u-en [Fa-hsiang] are the summer, the Lü School of Master Tao-hsüan is the fall, and the school which has singly transmitted the teaching of Bodhidharma [Ch'an] is the winter. If we discuss the matter from the standpoint of principle, people only know that Ch'an is a separate transmission aside from the other schools, but they do not know that the other schools also constitute a separate transmission aside from Ch'an. When we bring them together and return them to the source, the Esoteric school makes clear the Buddha-mind of great compassion which saves and relieves our suffering, the philosophical schools explain the Buddha-mind of great wisdom which reveals and imparts Truth, the Lü school upholds the Buddha-mind of great action which is dignified and solemn, and the Ch'an school transmits the Buddha-mind of great enlightenment which is perfect and complete. They are like the four seasons. Just like the four seasons, they should not be mixed (*hun*).[dt] [80]

MING-PEN'S VIEWS ON CONFUCIANISM

Long before the time of Ming-pen, other Buddhist thinkers had been engaged in the movement known as "Three Teachings in One." Ch'i-sung's views on the compatibility between Confucianism and Buddhism have been mentioned earlier in this paper. I will now discuss briefly the view of Tsung-mi[du] (780–841) and Ta-hui, for we can find interesting resonances of them in the writings of Ming-pen. In his famous essay, "On the Original Nature of Man" (*Yüan-jen lun*)[dv] Tsung-mi speaks of the different approaches the three sages (Confucius, Lao Tzu, and the Buddha) use and the way they complement each other. Confucianism and Taoism are provisional (ch'üan)[dw] doctrines, whereas Buddhism consists of both real (shih)[dx] and provisional doctrines. But, he concludes, "In going to the roots of things, Buddhism—since it examines all phenomena and, using every means, investigates their principles in an attempt to reveal their nature—decisively leads the other schools."[81] Whereas the other teachings establish proper conduct for oneself, says Ch'i-sung, only Buddhism can get to the origin of man. Ta-hui, on the other hand, uses the concepts of t'i (essence) and yung (function). The three teachings are the same in essence, for they are all based on the same luminous Mind and all sages, Confucius, Lao Tzu, and the Buddha, want men to achieve recognition and realization of the "correct mind" (cheng-hsin).[dy] As he puts it, "The mind of bodhi (p'u-t'i-hsin)[dz] is just another name for the mind of loyalty and righteousness (chung-i-hsin)."[ea][82] The insight a person achieves after enlightenment will equalize and eliminate all mundane distinctions. Ta-hui describes this state to a Confucian scholar:

If one achieves a genuine breakthrough, then one realizes that a Confucian is no different from a Buddhist, and a Buddhist is no different from a Confucian; a monk is no different from a layman, and a layman is no different from a monk; an ordinary man is no different from a sage, and a sage is no different from an ordinary man. In fact I am you and you are I; Heaven is earth and earth is Heaven; waves are the same as water, and water is no different from waves. Kumis and rich butter are but one taste; bracelets and hairpins are both melted from gold.[83]

However, even though the three teachings are the same in essence, there is a difference in their actual function, namely, each teaching has its specific realm of reference and its particular relevance. Both Tsung-mi and Ta-hui, despite their conciliatory attitude to non-Buddhist teachings, like to reserve the highest place among the three teachings for Buddhism. We may regard this as the application of the original intrafaith p'an-chiao[eb] (classification of Buddhist teachings), as developed by the T'ien-t'ai and Hua-yen schools, to an interfaith setting.

Ming-pen acknowledged the differences between Buddhism and Confucianism. Both Buddhism and Confucianism are methods to develop the Mind, but the Buddhist Way is sudden, and that of Confucianism is gradual:

The Confucian Way is to govern the mind (chih-hsin)[ec] and cultivate the mind (hsiu-hsin),[ed] whereas the Buddhist Way is to brighten the mind (ming-hsin)[ee] and to awaken the mind (*wu-hsin*).[ef] Governing and cultivating imply gradual-ness, whereas brightening and awakening imply suddenness. The mind is, of course, the same. But the sudden approach is surely different from the gradual approach. This is because the worldly and the otherworldly are different. If our Buddha should decide to talk about the worldly Way, he would surely not forget to mention the theory of "rectifying the mind" and "making the will sincere." Suppose Confucius should decide to talk about the otherworldly Way, how can one be sure that he would not mention "emptiness of Mind" or "perfection of enlightenment"? When a person does not understand the great skill-in-means a sage employs in establishing his teaching, he will argue senselessly and merely add confusion.[84]

In a manner reminiscent of Ta-hui, he says that all virtues issue from the Mind, and he then proceeds to pair the Confucian virtues with different aspects of the Mind:

There are eight items which are central to the governing of the world, i.e. Way, virtue, benevolence, righteousness, propriety, music, punishment, and govern-ment. But none of the eight is apart from the miraculous function of our One Mind. When the Mind is unobstructed, it is the Way. When it is correct, it is virtue. When it is compassionate, this is benevolence. When it is level and fair, it is righteousness. When the Mind is centered, this is propriety. When it is harmonious, this is music. When the Mind is straight, there is punishment and when it is bright there is government. Not only these eight, but in fact all good deeds which benefit the world and bring blessings to people, are possible only because of the manifestation of the miraculous function of this One Mind of ours. When ordinary men lose their miraculous function they are confused and become perverse. Therefore, sages have to establish teachings to correct them.[85]

Ming-pen wrote two interesting short essays in which he attempted to contrast and compare Buddhism with Confucianism. One essay was entitled "On Preventing passion and recovering nature" (*Fang-ch'ing fu-hsing*)[eg] which he wrote at the request of the painter Chao Meng-fu. The other essay was entitled, "Admonition on filial piety" (*Ching-hsiao*),[eh] which he wrote to a monk who felt guilty because he had not visited his parents for twelve years. In the first essay, Ming-pen tells us that Confu-cianism, being a worldly teaching, teaches us how to prevent the arising of passion, but Buddhism, being the otherworldly teaching, teaches us how to recover nature. There is obviously an implied value judgment which is immediately reinforced by Ming-pen's applying the Taoist expressions of "*yu-wei*" and "*wu-wei*" to Confucianism and Buddhism respectively. Like Tsung-mi, Ming-pen believes that the Buddhist teach-ing is more thorough. Therefore, although he appreciates the effort of Su

Ch'e^{ei} (1039–1112) to match the idea of centrality from the *Doctrine of the Mean* with the state of neither good nor evil spoken of by Hui-neng, and the attempt of Ta-hui to compare the Buddhist Trikaya to the opening sentences in the *Mean*, i.e., nature, the Way, and education, he nevertheless feels that the two teachings are not identical. Matching of concepts could be a helpful device, but it should not obscure the underlying differences.

In the second essay, "Admonition on Filial Piety," Ming-pen at first plays on the pun *"hsiao"* which can mean either filial piety or imitation depending on the homophone one uses. Filial piety is essentially imitation. Since our parents nurture and love us, we in turn should nurture and love them. But, he goes on to say, there are two ways of nurturing and two ways of love. "To serve parents with grain and meat, to clothe them with fur and linen is to nourish their physical body." "To inquire after one's parents morning and evening and not dare to leave them for any length of time is love with form." To nurture the parents' physical body and to practice "love with form" is the filial piety appropriate for a householder. Yet for a monk, he shows his filial piety through the nurturing of the parents' dharma nature and the practice of "formless love." What are they? "To discipline oneself with purity and restraint, and to cultivate blessedness and goodness for them [the parents] is to nourish their dharma nature." "To engage in meditation effort whether walking or sitting, to vow to realize the Way within the span of this life and, with this, to repay the kindness of parents, is what I call formless love." Moreover, Ming-pen says that the former, mundane, type of filial piety has a time limit, for we can love and serve our parents this way only when they are alive. But the latter, Buddhist, type of filial piety has no time limit, for our dedication to meditation and discipline is not altered by the existence or death of our parents. Ming-pen asserts that even sages and worthies cannot fulfill both types of filial piety simultaneously. Therefore, his advice to the conscience-stricken monk is to imitate the example of Śākyamuni. By leading a pure and disciplined life, by serious and sustained effort at meditation and, finally, by achieving enlightenment, a monk can hope to fulfill the requirements of filial piety. This is possible because of the Buddhist doctrine of "transference of merit" which enables a son to use the merit accrued from a sanctified life to benefit his parents spiritually.

It is clear from the above discussion that Ming-pen was keenly aware of the differences between Buddhism and Confucianism. However, he was not disheartened by the differences. He believed firmly in the primacy of Ch'an enlightenment, but he also believed that a person could achieve genuine spiritual realization through other teachings. As in his reservation concerning the joint practice of Pure Land and Ch'an, however, he again emphasized the importance of entering into the Way through "a single door." In one place Ming-pen described the enlightened state transcending sectarian distinctions most movingly: "The most precious thing is to penetrate deeply into Truth from one single door and attain self-realization. When enlightenment occurs, all fences break down. Only then will one suddenly see that the sages of the three teachings have always been holding hands outside words and symbols. There is no separation between the mundane and the supramundane."[86]

MING-PEN, CREATOR OF A MONASTIC CODE

In 1317, when Ming-pen was 55 years old, he wrote the code for his monastery, Huan-chu an, the *Pure Rules of Huan-chu*. As Ming-pen made clear in the preface, the code was primarily intended as a set of house rules for his own monastery. It predated the other three codes of the Yüan—the *Lü-yüan shih-kuei* by eight years, the *Pai-chang ch'ing-kuei ch'ung-pien* by eighteen years, and the *Tseng-hsiu Chiao-yüan ch'ing-kuei* by thirty years. The creation of codes was perhaps not unrelated to the reported general laxity of monastic discipline at that time. As indicated earlier, Ming-pen lamented the decline of strict discipline in some famous monasteries of which he had personal knowledge. We get a similar picture from contemporary legal codes concerning the regulations for monks. For instance, under the year 1317, the *Yüan tien-chang*[ej] (Institutes of the Yüan) reads:

Monks and nuns are people who have left the household life. Accordingly they ought to stay in the monastery and carry out their religious cultivation. But in recent years the pure rules have become either relaxed or not observed. Consequently, the incense and lights [of the faithful] have become extinguished. From now on, monks must perform the morning and evening worship and recite the sutra two times each day. On the four fast days, *ssu-chai-jih*[ek] [the 1st, 8th, 15th, and 23rd of the month], the abbot should lead the assembly offering incense, pray for the emperor's long life, and recite scripture. Monks must not be lazy or desultory. The abbot must be vigilant in his supervision. He should not allow monks to leave the gate of the monastery to go to tea houses and wine shops in the marketplace. The abbot of a monastery must be appointed from senior monks. Monks should not be allowed to build their own private houses or to own their own storehouses. They should not drink wine and eat meat. Nor should they keep wives and concubines and behave in the same way as worldly men. [If they do so] they corrupt the Buddhist tradition.[87]

Ming-pen's reclusiveness and repeated refusal to be the abbot of large and famous monasteries undoubtedly arose from his disapproval of the worldliness and materialism found in these places. Therefore he preferred to dissociate from them and live in his own Huan-chu an, a name implying retreat and retirement. But to live in retreat (chu-an)[e1] could also lead to abuses. Far from the gaze of public scrutiny, the solitary monk was bereft of supervision and guidance and he could very easily go astray. Ming-pen wrote a letter of admonition to a monk who was thinking of going into retreat:

In recent years, morals have declined and people's hearts have become unstable. There is the fad of "living in retreat" (chu-an) which can be an excuse for leading a comfortable and lazy life. There are no rules and proprieties to restrain one and there are no fellow monks to hold one in check. So if you want to sleep you just sleep, and if you want to leave, you just get up and leave. After living this way for a long time, a person will become self-indulgent and depart from the orthodox way.[88]

Ming-pen wrote the *Pure Rules of Huan-chu* because he felt the need to regulate the monks' lives and to instill in them a sense of discipline. The creation of monastic codes therefore fulfilled a practical function. But I think it also served a more fundamental purpose. The creation of monastic codes, like the compilation of *kung-an* records or the collection of the lives and deeds of exemplary monks, which can be conveniently called "role model" literature,[89] was connected with what I would call the crisis of authority inherent in Buddhism, particularly Ch'an Buddhism. These were attempts of Ch'an monks to create alternative sources of authority when the actual, personal, charismatic authority of the enlightened masters was not available. It is interesting to note that the collection of *kung-an*, the compilation of "role model" literature and the writing of monastic codes all started in the tenth and eleventh centuries. This was a time of what one may call the "post-charismatic" age of Ch'an, when the great T'ang masters had all passed away and observers of the monastic order began to be alarmed by signs of its decline. It is also interesting to note that most Ch'an masters, both Chinese and Japanese, emphasized the importance of the monastic codes. Pai-chang, who was credited with the creation of the first such code, the *Pure Rules of Pai-chang*, as well as Ta-hui, Ming-pen, Dōgen, and Hakuin, are but a few examples. Like the *kung-an* records and "role model" literature, the monastic codes were stressed in the hope that they could provide a basis for disciplined living in which meditation could be properly conducted and out of which enlightenment—the life of Ch'an, could arise.

Buddhism, in theory, only recognizes the authority of an enlightened teacher who in his religious life has succeeded in replicating the original and exemplary breakthrough to Reality as Buddha did. What happens, then, in the absence of an enlightened teacher? I suggest that the monastic codes, the *kung-an* collections, and the sayings and deeds of enlightened masters contained in the role-model literature were different ways developed to meet the crisis of authority. When the charismatic authority [90] of enlightened masters was unavailable, these served as substitutes.

The Pure Rules of Huan-chu is divided into two parts. The first part takes up almost six-sevenths of its entire length and is called "Jih-yung hsü-chih"[em] (Daily Tasks Everyone Must Know). It contains ten topics which cover every aspect of the monastic life. They range from the daily schedule of the monastery to the care of the sick and the conduct of funerals for the deceased members of the community.

The first section is entitled "daily schedule" (*jih-tzu*).[en] Here at the beginning of the code Ming-pen makes clear that meditation is to be the primary task for the community. Meditation is then the "daily task" (*jih-yung*). There are altogether four periods of meditation sitting (*tso-ch'an*)[eo] interspersed throughout a day and night which are divided into six blocks of time: the early day (*ch'u-jih*),[ep] the midday (*chung-jih*),[eq] and the late day (*hou-jih*),[er] then the early night (*ch'u-yeh*),[es] the midnight (*chung-yeh*),[et] and the late night (*hou-yeh*).[eu][91] During the time for meditation, one should be quiet and still. No conversation, reading, washing, or mending of clothes is allowed. One can leave his seat only to go to the rest room. When he does so, he must walk carefully as if he were treading on thin ice or facing a precipice—so that he will not disturb his neighbors.

The second section is called "monthly calendar" (*yüeh-chin*).[ev] It lists month by month all the holidays and festivals celebrated throughout the year. As might be expected, we find here some of the most important and significant dates for Buddhists to remember.;[92] More striking is the emphasis placed on religious services on behalf of the emperor. For instance, on the first and the fifteenth or each month, monks are to conduct a special service in which they first offer congee, then recite the *Ta-pei chou,*[ew] and pray for the welfare of the ruler. Moreover, a whole month (from the third of the second month to the third of the third month) is also devoted to the prayers for the emperor's longevity. This is called "T'ien-shou sheng-chieh"[ex] (Imperial Festival for the Long Life of Heaven) or the "Chin-kang tao-ch'ang"[ey] (Bodhimanda of the Diamond of Unlimited Life.) During this month, every morning after the congee offering and the recitation of the *Ta-pei chou,* the monks are to take turns reading a set of sutras[93] in front of the Buddha image in the main hall until the time for evening meditation. A bell is struck twice, once when the service begins and once when it ends. Each time the bell is struck, the abbot goes to the main hall to offer incense. The treasurer provides tea and fruit for the people who work in the main hall. The celebration of imperial birthdays and commemorative services on the anniversaries of deceased emperors were started in the T'ang dynasty.[94] The participation of Ch'an monks and monasteries in the imperial cult in the Sung and the Yüan had also been noted with interest by Japanese visitors.[95] Ming-pen is here therefore following this long tradition of reciprocal relationship between the imperial court and the sangha: monks pray for the emperor's welfare in the hope of receiving his continued protection and patronage. But in Ming-pen's case there is an indication that this is done not merely out of a sense of expediency. Ming-pen speaks to his fellow monks about the vastness of imperial grace (*huang-en*)[ez] which enables them to carry out a life of religious cultivation. Monks are feeble and weak and thus incapable of being independent. But for the protection and support of the state, they would be utterly lost and become vulnerable to the attacks and persecutions of the unfriendly. Therefore, monks should repay the imperial favor by leading vigilant, disciplined, and dedicated lives.[96]

The third section of the *Pure Rules of Huan-chu* is called "yearly regulations" (*nien-kuei*)[fa] which gives directions on three things. The first is the performance of "sheng-chieh" (imperial festival) which I have just described. The second is the observance of the "four holidays" (*ssu-chieh*)[fb] which are: the beginning of the summer retreat on the fifteenth of the fourth month (*chieh-chih*), [fc] the end of the summer retreat on the fifteenth of the seventh month (*chieh-chih*), [fd] winter solstice (*tung-chih*), [fe] and the New Year (*sui-ch'ao*). [ff] Ming-pen says that the last two festivals are now secular holidays, but the first two days have special significance for Buddhists and should be celebrated. To do so, ninety days are to be set aside (from the thirteenth of the fourth month to the thirteenth of the seventh month) for the conduct of "Śūraṅgama assembly" (*Leng-yen hui*). [fg] Under the leadership of the abbot, the monks are to thank the deities and spirits for their protection of the monastery. The third entry in this section is entitled, "yearly plan" (*sui-chi*). [fh] Ming-pen, citing the famous dictum of Pai-chang, "If you do not work for one day, you should not eat for one day," reminds the monks of the importance of manual labor. Ming-pen urges the monks to exercise the utmost seriousness whether working in the fields, in the maintenance of the temple and the temple grounds, or in other tasks, such as the preparing of soy sauce, vinegar, and preserved vegetables.

The fourth section is called "models in dealing with society" (*shih-fan*)[fi] which provides sample supplications (*shu*)[fj] which Ming-pen wrote to be read on the various festival days, prayer meetings for rain (*ch'i-yü*)[fk] and for sunshine (*ch'i-ch'ing*), [fl] liturgies commemorating deceased emperors and lay patrons, as well as a dedicatory essay on the birthday of the Earth God (*T'u-ti*). [fm]

The fifth section is called "planning and management" (*ying-pan*)[fn] which discusses the two main concerns in the life of the community: food and shelter. Food and shelter are necessary, but monks should not be choosy about the taste of the food or the spaciousness of their living quarters. The monks in charge of such things, however, must be diligent in planning ahead and managing well. For instance, they should see if the grain stored is sufficient, if the rooms need repair, and if the utensils and equipment are adequate. The persons so charged should be frugal, knowing when and what to save, and also enterprising, knowing when and how to seek donations from patrons.

The sixth section is called "household customs" (*chia-feng*)[fo] and covers a wide range of topics such as regulations about receiving travelling monks and lay visitors, appointments to and retirement from monastic duties, reward and punishment, begging and manual labor.

The seventh section is called "titles and duties" (*ming-fen*). [fp] There are five positions in Huan-chuan. What would be the position of the abbot in other monasteries is assumed by two people, *an-chu*[fq] (master of the temple) and *shou-tso*[fr] (the person who takes the first seat). They are equal in rank and share duties, the former taking care of ceremonial and ritual matters while the latter directs meditation. They are assisted by the *fu-an*[fs] (deputy abbot). The fourth is the steward (*chih-k'u*)[ft] and the last is the chef (*fan-t'ou*).[fu] Ming-pen criticizes the proliferation of monastic administrators in his time[97] and stresses flexibility and streamlining of duties. For instance, there is no need to appoint a guest prefect because the deputy abbot can take care of the guests along with his other duties. Exchange of functions (*hu-yung*)[fv] is allowed among the various officers when necessary.

The eighth section is "practice and cultivation" (*chien-lu*)[fw] where Ming-pen lays down the guidelines for the monks' dealing with outside society (*wai-yüan*)[fx] and their own internal relations (*nei-yüan*).[fy] Since a monk's main duty is to carry out his own cultivation, he should have a minimum of other engagements. So Ming-pen is not in favor of the monks' going to lay people's homes. When their parents and teachers are ill or die, brief visits are allowed. Ming-pen also disapproves of the monks exchanging letters and poems with lay people. Also included in this section is an essay for the instruction of novices.

In the last two sections, "care of the old and sick" (*she-yang*)[fz] and "funerals" (*chin-sung*),[ga] Ming-pen recommends the Pure Land Practice of *nien-fo*. Sermons on the Pure Land are given to the sick. If the patient is critically ill and cannot call on the Buddha's name himself, the other monks should do this for him. After a monk dies, his personal belongings should be disposed of through an auction held in the monastery.

The second main part of the Pure Rules is called "*K'ai kan-lu men*"[gb] (Opening the Door of Sweet Dew). *Kan-lu men* (amatadvava) is a Tantric term denoting the way to immortality or the release from samsara. This section contains a long liturgical text written by Ming-pen for use in the ritual of feeding hungry ghosts. The text bears the title, "P'u-shih fa-shih wen"[gc] (Essay on the Universal Bestowing of Dharma Food). Even though it is interspersed with mantras and invocations of Tantric deities, the text is essentially a long sermon on Buddhist morality and philosophy, truth being the "food" bestowed on the hungry ghosts in this ritual. It begins with a gatha from the *Avatamsaka Sutra*: "If one wants to understand all the Buddhas of the three generations, one should observe the nature of

the dharma realm and realize that everything is created by the Mind."
This gatha is conventionally called "the gatha which shatters hell" (p'o
t'i-yü chi),[gd] for when one recites this gatha to the infernal judge (ming-
kuan),[ge] it is said that the illusory phenomena of hell will disappear.
Ming-pen, however, says that this explanation does not go far enough,
for in fact is one truly understands the meaning of this gatha one will not
only shatter hell, but also shatter the ten dharma realms (shih fa-chieh).[gf]
For, "There is no buddha in the three generations, and the dharma realms
have no intrinsic nature. Yet they are nevertheless established, depending
on this One Mind"[98] (san-shih wu-fo, fa-chieh wu-hsing, i tz'u i-hsin,
erh chieh chien-li).[gg] Thus, to obtain a correct view of everything through
the cultivation of the mind is the most important thing. The text then
outlines the steps one should take in this direction: confession and repentance (ch'an-hui),[gh] taking the three refuges, receiving the five precepts, and finally the development of the bodhi mind (fa p'u-t'i-hsin).[gi]
Ming-pen also mentions the 10 precepts, the 48 bodhisattva precepts, the
250 great precepts, and the 3 groups of pure precepts. He says that the
precepts are like the ocean. The farther we go into the ocean, the deeper
we enter into it. As long as our faith does not relapse, all the various
precepts will naturally find a place in our life. Since the text is written
for the benefit of laymen (to be read aloud during the ritual of feeding
the hungry ghosts), Ming-pen explains the significance of taking the three
refuges and the meaning of the five precepts in great detail, but he only
lists the other precepts without explanation. The text stipulates the recitation of the Heart sutra and ends with the request that the merit accrued
be transferred to all the spirits in the ten directions so that they can all
achieve Buddhahood.

Attached to this liturgical text is another text to be used specifically
on the Ullambana festival (yü-lan-p'an).[gj] Ullambana means "utensils
hanging upside down" (tao-hsüan-chi),[gk] a metaphor describing the extreme suffering of beings in hell. Ming-pen says that originally the true
dharma realm is undifferentiated (p'ing-teng)[gl] and there are neither buddhas nor sentient beings. So why is there suffering? The answer is that
suffering comes from ignorance. Ignorance gives rise to the mind of delusion (wang-hsin)[gm] and distorted views (wang-chien).[gn] As a result, people form an external world of ten realms differentiated by either purity or
defilement. They also create an internal world of the eight kinds of con-

sciousness distinguished by either enlightenment or delusion. The way to untie beings from the suffering of "being hung upside down" is again for them to follow the steps outlined in the previous text: beginning with repentance and ending with the arising of the bodhi mind. Ming-pen refers to these steps as wonderful skill-in-means (*shan-ch'iao fang-pien*).[80]

The *Pure Rules of Huan-chu* ends with the liturgical text used in the Ullambana festival. Despite the divergent topics covered in Ming-pen's code, there is nevertheless an underlying theme running through them all. That theme is the central importance of mind cultivation. The code opens with a call for the strict observance of the meditation schedule and ends with an appeal to the suffering hungry ghosts to repent and develop the bodhi mind. Ming-pen uses every opportunity to reiterate this central theme. We find matter-of-fact instructions on etiquette, ritual directions, and daily hygiene side by side with the most profound discussion of the nature of Mind. Ritual is not to be detached from meditation and meditation is not to be separated from the conscientious performance of daily tasks. What Ming-pen says here is of course not entirely new, other Ch'an masters had said similar things. What is striking though is his manner of expressing it—through the medium of a code. All through the *Pure Rules* we sense Ming-pen's presence—encouraging, pleading, chiding, and cautioning. In creating the code, might not Ming-pen be trying to leave this body of rules as a last testament of the enlightened master, and as the heritage of the Ch'an tradition to which he had so devoted his efforts?

Ming-pen chose to lead the life of a recluse, yet in the end he achieved great fame, both in Yüan China and in countries abroad. Still, even though he could count many foreigners as his disciples, he remained curiously insular and intensely "Han" Chinese. He does not seem to have shown much interest in Tibetan Buddhism. Historical events touched him lightly and left few traces in his work. His only real passion was his love of the Ch'an tradition. He felt keenly the fact that he inherited an illustrious Ch'an heritage. He wanted nothing less than to preserve it and pass it on. His emphasis on *hua-t'ou*, his views on the harmonization of the Buddhist schools, and finally his creation of a monastic code can all be seen as efforts directed to this goal. In the final analysis, we can say that he achieved the goal, for he became an important torch-bearer of that tradition. Ming-pen was a central figure not only in Yüan

Buddhism but also for later periods. Monks in the Ming such as Chu-hung would look upon him both as a preserver of the Ch'an tradition and as a key figure in the increasingly popular movement for the harmonization between Ch'an and other Buddhist schools.[99]

APPENDIXES

I. Preventing Passion and Recovering Nature

When nature arises there are passions. When passions are born there is karma
(*yeh*).[gp] In response to karma there are things. Myriad things come into being as
a result of passion and karma. They are born at the appropriate places and they
die accordingly. Success and failure, disaster and blessing are all a dream. The
teaching of our Buddha shows people that although all beings are based in nature, there is a difference between the worldly and the otherworldly. The worldly
teaching tells us how to prevent passion (*fang-ch'ing*),[gq] but the otherworldly
teaching tells us how to recover our nature (*fu-hsing*).[gr] Preventing passion is to
do something (*yu-wei*)[gs] but to restore our nature is to do nothing (*wu-wei*).[gt] The
two should not be confused. Mr. Su Ch'e, in his preface to the commentary on
Lao Tzu[100] said that what the Sixth Patriarch meant by "neither thinking about
good nor thinking about evil" could be matched with "when joy, anger, sorrow,
and happiness do not arise, it is centrality" as found in [the *Doctrine of*] *the
Mean*. He also said that centrality was the same as what the Buddhists called
Buddha nature, and harmony was what Buddhists called the six perfections (*liu-
tu*)[gu] and myriad deeds (*wan-hsing*).[gv] Mr. Su concluded by saying, "When centrality and harmony are established, heaven and earth will be stabilized and the
myriad things will be nourished. Can these be accomplished without Buddhism?"
This is similar to Master Miao-hsi's [Ta-hui's] answer to a question posed by the
nephew of Chang Tzu-shao in which he compared the Buddhist concept of the
Three Bodies (trikaya, *san-shen*)[gw] to that of "what heaven mandates is called
nature, when we follow nature, it is called the Way; to cultivate the Way is called
teaching" as found in [the *Doctrine of*] *the Mean*. [What Ta-hui was doing here]
was to use a temporary expedient in order to shake him [Chang Tzu-shao] loose
from emotional attachment. For the truth of the Three Bodies is surely not limited to this explanation.

I have heard that the teaching of the Confucians called [the *Doctrine of*] *the
Mean* is to enable the feelings of men to achieve absolute centrality. Only then
will the way of regularity (*ching-ch'ang chih tao*)[gx] be able to be transmitted
without end. This is true not only for the mind of man. In fact, all things in the
world are born and transformed because they are endowed with centrality. If there
is no centrality, then even the most insignificant thing will not be able to nourish
itself. Internally, we use it to regulate the self, and externally, to rule the state.
Thus we cannot forget centrality even for an instant. Suppose it did not exist,
then the myriad things in the world would all expire as a consequence. How can
man alone exist? This is because centrality is the central axis in establishing life
and transformation (*sheng-hua*).[gy] This is why sages and worthies singled it out
to illumine it and treated centrality as the foundation of their teaching. When
we apply this principle to the parent, it is filial piety. When we extend it to the
ruler, it is loyalty. When we use it in the conduct of affairs, it is benevolence;
when we spread it among men, it is education, and when we transmit it in the

world, it is the Way. Therefore, the Way refers to the essence of centrality. Centrality is contained in the junction before the arising of joy, anger, sorrow, and happiness. When the emotions arise and their expressions hit the mark (*chung-chieh*)[gz] it is called harmony. When we talk about centrality we refer to this "hitting of the mark." If one goes too far or not far enough, in either case one does not hit the mark. But when one hits the mark of centrality one thus knows that the myriad things are nourisned even though they do not expect to be so nourished, and heaven and earth are established in their positions (*wei*)[ha] even though they do not expect to be so established. Since passions and karma are endless, how will life-and-death [samsara] come to an end? The worldly teaching reaches the highest level with this idea.

Buddhism, as the teaching dealing with the supramundane world, differs from this. How can I say this? The Sixth Patriarch said, "When you are thinking of neither good nor evil, what is your original face?" This is the essence of recovering nature. But Tzu-ssu said, "Centrality is before the arising of joy, anger, sorrow, and happiness, harmony is the hitting the mark after their arousal." This is then the best teaching about preventing passion. But "reaching centrality and harmony," "establishing heaven and earth," and "nourishing myriad things," are all responses to passion and karma. These things do not really exist in nature and principles (*hsing-li*).[hb] Tzu-yu [Su Ch'e] certainly knew the difference. Then why did he misquote this passage? [I think] by "what Heaven endows in us is called nature," Tzu-ssu was talking about the essence of centrality; by "to follow the nature is called the Tao," he was talking about the function of centrality; by "to cultivate the Way is called education" he was finally talking about the necessity of our following both essence and function [of centrality] and achieving an accord with it. "The Way cannot be departed from even for one instant. If it can be departed from it is not the Way." We must make each stirring of thought and each movement of the mind (*Chü-nien tung-hsin*)[hc] stay in the realm of centrality without departing from it even for one second. The theory of preventing passions reaches its height with this.

The pure Dharmakāya with which both the sage and the common man are endowed is our original nature. The perfect Sambhogakāya is the supernatural powers and brightness of the Dharmakāya. The myriad Nirmānakāyas are the impartial manifestations of Dharmakāya everywhere. Dharmakāya is like the sun. Sambhogakāya is like the rays of the sun, Nirmānakāya is like the universal illumination by the rays of the sun. Nature has no knowledge (*wu-chih*)[hd] and does nothing (*wu-wei*). The theory of recovering nature reaches its height with this. It is rather hard to equate this idea with "following nature and cultivating the Way." Yet Miao-hsi made the learning of recovering nature conform to the teaching of preventing passion, and Su Ch'e made the teaching of preventing passion conform to the learning of recovering nature. A Buddhist and a Confucian, each employed skill-in-means in their exegesis and tried to reconcile the ideas of the two schools. But if I do not point out the underlying differences, the ultimate truth will differ [from our understanding of it].

Tsa-lu, (ZZ, 2.27.4), 3:392d–393e

II. Admonition on Filial Piety

All parents of this world nurture and love their children. Therefore sages and worthies teach us to be filial to our parents. Filiality (hsiao)[he] means imitation (hsiao).[hf][101] Children imitate parental nurturing and repay their parents with nurturing. Children imitate parental love and repay their parents with love. Therefore, filiality cannot be exceeded by nurturing, but it reaches its utmost with love. However, there are two ways of nurturing and two ways of love. To serve parents with grain and meat, to clothe them with fur and linen is to nourish their physical body. To discipline oneself with purity and restraint, and to cultivate blessedness and goodness for them is to nourish their dharma nature. The nourishment of their physical body follows human relationship, but the nourishment of their dharma nature conforms to heavenly principle. Even sages and worthies cannot perform both. That is because there is a difference between being a householder and being a monk. If one is a householder but fails to nourish the physical body of his parents, he is unfilial. If one is a monk but fails to nourish the dharma nature of his parents, he is also unfilial. This is what I mean by the two ways of filiality. To inquire after one's parents morning and evening and dare not leave them for any length of time is what I call love with form (yu-hsing chih ai).[hg] To engage in meditation effort whether walking or sitting, to vow to realize the Way within the span of this life and, with this, to repay the kindness of parents is what I call formless love (wu-hsing chih ai).[hh] Love with form is near and intimate, but love without form is far and inaccessible. But if a person feels no love, he cannot even reach the near, not to mention the far and inaccessible. One cannot fulfill both the easy and the difficult types of love. This is because there is a difference between remaining in the world and leaving the world. To remain in the world but not carry out the love with form is unfilial. To leave the world but not to carry out the formless love is also unfilial. This is why I say that there are two ways of love. Furthermore, the mundane type of nurturing and love has a time limit, but the otherworldly type of nurturing and love has no time limit. Why does the former have a time limit? Because we can only love our parents when they are alive. When they die, this love vanishes. Why does the latter have no time limit? Because my mind of studying the Way is not altered by the existence or death of my parents. Parents are the great foundation (ta-pen)[hi] of my physical form. Yet is my physical form something I only have in this life? From innumerable kalpas until now, I have transmigrated in the three realms [of desire, form, and formlessness] and have received forms as numberless as the grains of sand. The so-called foundation of physical form fills the universe and pervades the cosmos. All that I see and hear could be the basis of my previous existences. There is no way to take account of my parents' labors and sufferings. That I should fail to repay their kindness may cause my parents to fall into other realms of rebirth and suffer the pain of transmigration. Thus the Way is no other than filial piety, and filial piety is no other than the Way. When a person does not know how to be filial but says that he wants to study the Way, that is like seeking water while turning his back on it.

If someone is unable to practice this but is only able to nourish the parents' physical body and to love them with form, can we call this filial piety? I would say that this is the filial piety of a householder. The reason we monks cannot engage in worldly filial piety is because we have entered the gate of emptiness and silence and have put on the monastic robe. We may try to emulate the otherworldly filial piety of the Great Sage of the Snowy Mountain [Sākyamuni]. Suppose we should make a mistake in one single thought (*i-nien yu-chien*)[hj] we would then lose both benefits [of the worldly and otherworldly filial love]. This is the height of unfilialness.

Tsa-lu (ZZ, 2.27.4), 1:366b–d

NOTES

1. For a general introduction to the religious situation in the Yüan, see Kenneth Ch'en, *Buddhism in China, A Historical Survey* (Princeton: Princeton University Press, 1964), pp. 418–21, Makita Tairyō, *Mishu no Bukkyō. Sō kara Gendai made,* in Nakamura Hajime et al., *Ajia Bukkyōshi. Chōgoku han,*[hk] vol. 2 (Tokyo, Kosei shuppansha, 1976); "Yüan-shih Men-ku-ko-han-men ho-i hsin-yang lo Tu-fan te fo-chiao" in Chang Man-t'ao,[hl] ed. *Chung-kuo fo-chiao shih lun-chi* (Taipei, Ta-cheng ch'u-pan-she, 1977), vol. 5, pp. 369–81.

   For a general discussion of Mongolian-Tibetan relationships see Herbert Franke, "Tibetans in Yüan China" in John D. Langlois, Jr., ed., *China Under Mongol Rule* (Princeton: Princeton University Press, 1981, pp. 296–328; Ch'en Yüan, *Western and Central Asians in China under the Mongols,* tr. Ch'ien Hsing-hai and L. C. Goodrich (Los Angeles: Monumenta Serica Institute, 1966); Josef Kalmas, *Tibet and Imperial China,* Occasional Paper 7, Australian National University (Canberra, 1967).

   Among studies dealing with Lamaism, one should consult Paul Demiéville, "La situation religiouse en Chine au temps de Marco Polo," *Oriente Poliano* (Rome: Instituto Italiano per il medio ed Estremo Oriente, 1957), pp. 193–236; Heather Karmay, *Early Sino-Tibetan Art* (London: Aris and Philips, 1975); Giuseppe Tucci, *Tibetan Painted Scrolls,* 2 vols. (Rome: La Liberia Oello Stato, 1949).

2. YS (Peking: Chung-hua shu-chü, 1976), 15:4517.

3. *Ibid.,* 4520–21.

4. Inaba Masanari deals with the time of each successive Imperial Preceptor in "Gen no teishi ni kansuru kenkyū—keitō to nanji wo chūshin toshite,"[hm] *Ōtani daigaku kenkyū nenpō* (June 1965), 17:79–156. Nishio Kenryū has examined the careers of the Imperial Preceptors at the close of the Yüan dynasty in "Genmatsu teishi no jiseki,"[hn] *Ōtani gakuhō* (January 1969), 48(3):65–84. See also Paul Ratchnevsky, "Die mongolischen GroBkhane und die buddhistische kirche," in Johannes Schubert and Ulrich Ungar, eds., *Asiatica, Festschrift Iriedrich Weller zum 65. Gegurtstag gewidmet* (Leipzig, 1954), pp. 489–504.

5. Nogami Shunjō, in "Gendai Butsuto no menshū undō,"[ho] *Ōtani gakuhō* (1959), 38(4):1–12, discusses the frequent amnesties requested by imperial preceptors. He combed through the YS and tabulated 27 amnesties from Temür to Toghon Temür covering the years 1295 to 1354. They were declared on request from Imperial Preceptors, from commissioners of good works, for the sake of securing the emperor's and empress dowager's recovery from sickness or to create merits. In the amnesty, prisoners sentenced to death or flogging were often freed. For instance, according to *Hsin Yüan shih* (Tientsin, 1930 ed.), 103:14b, "Hsing-fa chih" (Penal Institutes), in Yüan-chen first year (1295) on the request of the Imperial Preceptor, three

men sentenced to death and forty-seven sentenced to flogging were freed. See Nogami, p. 2. Chao I quoted from the same passage but exaggerated the figure, giving 30 and 100 respectively. He goes on to say that because of this custom, people grew bold: "Slaves and maidservants who killed their masters and wives or concubines who killed their husbands were often let off their crime fortuitously." See *Kai-yü ts'ung-k'ao*[hp] ch. 18, in *O-pei chü'an-chi* (Shanghai: Commercial Press, 1957), vol. 2, p. 142.

6. Nogami Shunjō, "Soka to Yorenshinka—Gendai shukyōshi no ichimen,"[hq] *Ōtani daigaku kenkyū nenpo* (1958), 11:1–26. For the biography of Sang-ke and Yang-lien-chen-chia, see YS, 205:4570; 202:4521. The two Tibetan monks have been regarded as arch villains by Chinese historians and held up as notorious examples of Lamas abusing their privileges. But Yang-lien-chen-chia was also active in spreading his religion by contributing to artistic projects in the South. He "was responsible for the carving of a group of esoteric Buddhist stone sculptures at the caves of Feilai Feng [Fei-lai feng] situated on the outside walls of the Qinglingdong [Ch'ing-lin-tung] at Feilai Feng. Tokiwa and Sekino say that the inscription giving his name as Chief Doner, dated the 29th year of Zhizheng [Jen-ch'en], 1292. (*Shina Bukkyō shiseki*, 5:102." Karmay, *Early Sino-Tibetan Art*, p. 24.

7. YS, 15:4521.

8. *Ibid.*, p. 4523.

9. Chao I, *Kai-yü ts'ung-k'ao*, p. 354. Another historian, Chang P'u (1602–1641)[hr] echoed the same sentiment but attributed the fall of the Yüan to the moral depravity of Toghan Temür, who practiced Tantric sexual rites under the direction of Lamas. "After Toghon Temür occupied the throne for a long time, Khama, Tughlugh Temür, and others recommended monks of Tibetan esoteric religion and as a result, men and women shared the same palace, ruler and ministers jested with each other. Thus the country was lost in the Chih-cheng period [1341–1368]. Are not the disadvantages of Buddhism extreme? . . . Lamas such as Chia-lin-chen persuaded the ruler saying that human life was short and one should be initiated into 'esoteric samadhi of great joy' (*pi-mi ta-hsi-lo ch'an-ting*).[hs] Toghon Temür listened and consequently forgot about the world. When small men delude rulers, they always make them indulge in desires. . . . When Confucius wrote the *Spring and Autumn Annals* he said that when China followed the way of the barbarian she would retrogress, but when barbarians followed the way of the Chinese, they would progress. The worshipping of the Buddha in the Yüan was a custom of the barbarians. . . . They kept the teaching of the barbarians and hoped to control the population of China. This was why the Yüan could not last long." See Chang P'u's postscript to Ch'en Pang-chan and Tseng Mou-hsün's *Yüan-shih chi-shih pen-mo* (Shanghai: Commercial Press, 1935), p. 115. See also Franke, "Tibetans in Yüan China" p. 327.

10. On the institution of the sangha administration, see Nogami Shunjō, "Gen no senseiin ni tsuite,"[ht] in *Asiatic Studies in Honor of Dr. Haneda* (Kyoto: Kyoto University, 1950), pp. 779–95, and "Gen no kudosushi shi ni tsuite,"[hu]

Shina Bukkyō shigaku (1942), 6(2):1–11; Ohyabu Masaya, "Gendai no osho no tomoku ni tsuite,"[hv] *Tōhō shūkyō* (October 1973), 42:52–68. On the Yüan legal statutes concerning Buddhism, see Ohyabu Masaya, "Gendai no hōsei to Bukkyō—zeiryo sosho, minken shinko kankei no kitei,"[hw] *Shigaku kenkyū* (March 1972), 86:1–35. On the tax exemption privileges enjoyed by Buddhist monasteries and Taoist temples, see Otagi Matsuo, "Genchō ni okeru butsuji dokan no zeiryō yumen ni tsuite,"[hx] in *Essays on the History of Buddhism Presented to Professor Zenryū Tsukamoto* (Kyoto: Tsukamoto hakase shōsu kinenkai, 1961), pp. 242–55. On the economic activities of monasteries, see T'ao Hsi-sheng, "Yüan-tai ti fo-ssu t'ien-yüan chi shang-tien,"[hy] *Shih-huo* (1935), 1(3):108–14; Chü Ch'ing-yüan, "Yüan-tai ti ssu-ch'an,"[hz] *Shih-huo* (1935), 1(6):228–31. On the social aspects of Buddhism, see Nogami Shunjō, "Gendai Ramakyō to minshu,"[ia] *Rikishi kyōiku* (1966), 14(8):8–13.

11. Relationship between the early Khaghans and Chinese Ch'an monks is treated in Kunishite Hirosato's "Gensho ni okeru teishitsu to zensō no kankei ni tsuite,"[ib] *Tōyō gakuhō* (1921), 11:547–77; (1922), 12:89–124, 245–49. The Buddhist beliefs of the Yüan imperial family are treated by Fujishima Tateki in, "Genchō koki no Bukkyō shinko,"[ic] *Indogaku Bukkyōgaku kenkyū* (March 1968), 16(2):309–13.

12. Nogami Shunjō, "Gen no Bukkyō ni kansuru ichi mondai—Ramakyō to Kanjin Bukkyō,"[id] in *Essays on the History of Buddhism Presented to Professor Zenryū Tsukamoto*, p. 573.

13. For this reason, Professor Jan's article in this volume is especially valuable. There are a number of Buddhist sources which are useful in helping us to get a sense of what Chinese Buddhism was like in the Yüan. Among others, one can cite *Fo-tsu t'ung-chi* (Record of the Lineage of the Buddhist Patriarchs) by Chih-p'an, *ch.* 48; *Fo-tsu li-tai t'ung-tsai* (Comprehensive Records of Buddhist Patriarchs in Successive Generations) by Nien-ch'ang, *ch.* 36; and *Shih-shih chi-ku lüeh hsü-chi* (Continuation of the Brief Compilation of Buddhist History) by Huan-lun, *ch.* 2–3. The above are all in vol. 49 of *Taishō shinshuū daizōkyō* (hereafter abbreviated as T) (Tokyo, 1924–1934). *Wu-teng yen-t'ung* (Strict Lineage of the Five Lamps) by Fei-yin[ie] in *Dainihon zokuzōkyō* (hereafter abbreviated as ZZ) (Kyoto, 1905–1912), 2B, 12:1–5 and *Chih-yüeh lu* (Pointing to the Moon) by Ch'ü Ju-chi,[if] *ch.* 7, contain information on Ch'an Buddhism. On Pure Land Buddhism in the Yüan, see *Ching-t'u sheng-hsien lu* (Record of Sages and Worthies of the Pure Land) by P'eng Shao-sheng,[ig] ZZ, 2B, 8:2.

14. Nogami, "Gen no Bukkyō ni kansuru ichi mondai—Ramakyō to Kanjin Bukkyō." Nogami pointed out that the patronage of Han Buddhism was especially noteworthy during the reigns of Temür and Khaishan around 1294 to 1310. His study centers around the career of the Hua-yen monk Liaohsing[ih] (d. 1321) of Mt. Wu-tai. See also Nishio Kenryū, "Genchō no Konan toji ni okeru Bukkyō,"[ii] *Bukkyō shigaku* (October 1971), 15(2):84–104.

15. A monk's affiliation was indicated by the way he was addressed. For instance, a Ch'an monk, whether he belonged to the Lin-chi or the Ts'ao-tung lineage, was addressed as "elder" (*chang-lao*)[1j] A monk belonging to the *Chiao* school, whether T'ien-t'ai, Hua-yen, or Fa-hsiang school, was addressed as "master lecturer" (*chiang-chu*).[1k] See Ohyabu Masaya, "Gendai no osho no tomoku ni tsuite," p. 62.

16. He was active under the Chin emperor Chang-tsung (r. 1190–1209) who invited him to lecture in the palace. Wan-sung wrote the *Ts'ung-jung lu*[1l] (T 2004), a major Ts'ao-tung text. He was known to have advocated the harmony between Ch'an practice and Hua-yen philosophy, and the compatibility between the Three Teachings. He had many disciples, among whom there were Li Ch'un-fu (P'ing-shan)[1m] (1185–1231), ‑Yeh-lü Ch'u-ts'ai[1n] (1189–1243 and Fu-yü[1o] (1203–1275) who played a major role in the controversy with Taoists under Möngke and Khubilai Khaghan. See the article by Professor Jan included in this volume.

17. Even though this code is called "revised" (*ch'ung-pien*), which implies that there is an original "Pure Rule of Pai-chang" upon which the present work is based, recent Japanese scholarship has questioned if there ever was such a code written by Pai-chang. It seems that the Yüan code is a synthesis of various monastic codes compiled in the Sung, the earliest being the *Ch'an-men kuei-shih*[1p] (1103). After searching through the extant Buddhist literature of the late T'ang and Five Dynasties, Japanese scholars have failed to find any mention of a Pai-chang code. In the writings of Pai-chang's contemporaries and disciples, neither the term of *Pai-chang ch'ing-kuei* nor the fact that Pai-chang had compiled any code was mentioned. See Kondō Ryōichi, "Hajō shingi no seiritsu to sono genkei,"[1q] *Hokkaidō Komazawa daigaku kenkyū kiyō* (November 1968), 3:19–48, especially 21–30, and his "Hajō shingi to Zen'on shingi,"[1r] *Indogaku Bukkyōgaku kenkyū* (1969), 17(2):328–30.

18. The primary sources for a biography of Ming-pen follow. A short autobiography written by Ming-pen himself found in *T'ien-mu Chung-feng ho-shang kuang-lu*[1s] (reduced ed. Kyoto, 1884) (hereinafter abbreviated as KL) contained in the Japanese Manji (卍) edition of Tripitaka 31·10·6 & 7·18, p. 653b–d. Tsu-shun, "Yüan ku T'ien-mu-shan Fo-tz'u Yüan-chao Kuang-hui Ch'an-shih Chung-feng ho-shan hsing-lü,"[1t] in *ibid.*, 30, pp. 686c–688d. Yü Chi, "Yu Yüan ch'ih-tz'u Chih-hsüeh Ch'an-shih Fa-yün t'a-ming,"[1u] *ibid.*, 30, pp. 688d–689c. Sung Pen, "Yu Yüan P'u-ying kuo-shih tao-hsing pei,"[1v] *ibid.*, 30, pp. 689d–690d. Tzu-jung, "Chung-feng P'u-ying kuo-shih,"[1w] in *Nan-Sung Yüan Ming Ch'an-lin seng-pao chuan*[1x] (ZZ 2B.10.4), 9:350d–352a.

19. For the life and activities of Wu-chun Shih-fan, see Fukushima Shummō, *Dai Sō Keigan Butsuken Mujun Zenshi,*[1y] published on the 700th Memorial Anniversary of the Master's Death by Tōfukuji Temple (Kyoto, 1950), pp. 1–122. Both Wu-chun and Hsieh-yen had connections with Kamakura Zen circles, for several of their disciples came to Japan and established Zen sects

there. See also Abe Choichi, "Nansō kōki zenshuū no dōkō—Kokin haka no shakai taki tachiba o chūshin toshite,"[iz] *Bukkyoō shigaku* (September 1972), 16(1):1–20.

20. For a discussion of Ch'an in Sung and the Huang-lung and Yang-ch'i branches of Lin-chi school see Yanagida Seizan, "Chūgoku Zenshu shi,"[ja] in Nishitani Keiji et al., eds., *Kōzazen* (Tokyo, 1974), vol. 3, pp. 88–106. See also Abe Choichi, "Sōdai Ōryūha no haten,"[jb] *Komazawa shigaku* (November 1962), 10:32–37.

21. Kajiya Sōnin, "Daiei"[jc] in *Kōzazen*, vol. 3, pp. 259–74; Abe Choichi, *Chūgoku Zenshushi kenkyū*[jd] (1963), pp. 467–85. See also the author's "Ta-hui Tsung-kao and 'Kung-an Ch'an,' " in *Journal of Chinese Philosophy* (1979), 6:221–35. Ta-hui is the subject of a Ph.D. dissertation by Miriam Levering, "Ch'an Enlightenment for Laymen: Ta-hui and the New Religious Culture of the Sung" (Harvard University, 1978).

22. *Fo-tsu li-tai t'ung-tsai* (T 49), 21:704b. Even though this work offers the most comprehensive account of the life of Hai-yün, it also contains certain inaccuracies, as pointed out by Professor Jan in his article. Hai-yün was also mentioned by the Taoist Ch'ang-ch'un chen-jen in his travel accounts. Hai-yün was reported to have had a meeting with Shih T'ien-hsing, a Chinese general under the Mongol general Mukhali, and they discussed the relationship between China and Buddhist philosophical schools. Hai-yün said that they were like the two wings of a bird, or like the relationship between warriors and scholars, for they were equally important. Hai-yün was regarded as "Speaker of Heaven" (bö'e, kao-t'ien-jen),[je] the most respected title given to a shaman, by Chinggis Khan. See Arthur Waley, tr., *The Travels of an Alchemist, the Journey of the Taoist Ch'ang-ch'un from China to the Hindukush at the Summons of Chingiz Khan* (London: George Rutledge, 1931), pp. 6–8, 29–30.

23. This could be the monk Wu-men Hui-k'ai[jf] (1183–1260), the author of *Wu-men-kuan*,[jg] an anthology of forty-eight *kung-an* with his own commentaries. The text says, "Wu-men k'ai-tao-che."[jh] Yet it is curious that the mother should recognize the identity of the monk who died three years before Ming-pen's birth. Wu-men's arriving at the house with a lantern is, of course, highly symbolic. The transmission of the mind in Ch'an Buddhism is referred to as the transmission of the lamp (i.e., lamp of wisdom). Arriving at the house with a lantern would imply that Wu-men was thereby entrusting the Ch'an transmission to Ming-pen.

24. Kao-feng's strictness can be seen from this account of his interview with a wealthy lay patron. Ch'ü T'ing-fa, who was the Commissioner of Salt in Chekiang and Kiangsu, admired Kao-feng and came to pay him a visit on the second month of 1291. At that time Kao-feng was secluded in his cave called "Gate of Death" on top of Mt. T'ien-mu. The only way to get to the cave was by riding in a basket pulled by pulleys. When Ch'ü arrived after much physical exertion, Kao-feng's first words to him were, "Do you come here for sightseeing or for the Buddha Dharma?" To which Ch'ü answered

that he had come for the sake of Buddha Dharma. Kao-feng threw down the bamboo stick he was holding and demanded if Ch'ü knew what the Buddha Dharma was. When Ch'ü answered no, the master reprimanded him, saying, "Unless you go into the tiger's lair, you will not be able to get hold of the tiger's cub." See "Ch'u Yun-shih T'ing-fa tsu ku Yao-shih tao-ch'ang tui-ling hsiao-tsan," *KL* 570a. See also Sheng Ju-tzu, *Shu-chai lao-hsüeh tsiung-t'an*[ji] in *Li-tai hsiao-shuo pi-chi hsuan: Chin, Yüan* (Shanghai: Chung-hua shu-chü, 1958) pp. 79–80. As we have seen earlier, Ch'ü Ting-fa had become a very important supporter of Kao-feng. He donated 270 *ch'ing* of land and built the Ta-chieh cheng-teng ch'an ssu on the Lotus Peak of Mt. T'ien-mu in 1292. When Kao-feng died in 1295, Chung-feng recommended a disciple called Tsu-yung to take care of the temple. See Fujishima Tateki, "Genchō Bukkyō no ichi yōsō—Chūhō Mimpon o meguru koji tachi,"[jj] *Ōtani gakuhō* (November 1977), 57(3):16.

25. Her name was Yang Miao-hsi.[jk] This lady used to be a palace maid (*kung-jen*) during the last years of the Sung. She believed in Taoism and was in fact a Taoist priestess. Recognizing that Ming-pen was not an ordinary youth, she persuaded his father to let him join the sangha. Later, when Ming-pen was ready to go forth into the homeless life, Yang donated the monk's robes and other implements to enable him to receive tonsure. She asked Ming-pen to give her a little bit of the hair shaved off at the tonsure for safekeeping. She kept the hair in a clean room and worshipped it with incense. After several years she discovered that sariras had grown from the hair shavings. They gradually increased in number and amounted to more than fifty pieces. The sariras were five-colored and brilliant in luster. All who saw them them were astonished. Yang was converted to Buddhism as a result of this miracle and offered the sariras to the Yün-chü Ch'an-an[jl] on the Mountain of Seven Treasures in Hangchow. In the winter of 1334 a stupa was built to house the hair and the sariras. Ming-pen's famous disciple, T'ien-ju Wei-tse, wrote an account to record the story: "P'u-ying Kuo-shih she-li-t'a chi" in *T'ien-ju Wei-tse Ch'an-shih yü-lu* (ZZ.2.27.5), 6:458 a–b.

26. Bamboo stick (*chu-pi*)[jm] was a stick about one foot and five inches. It was wrapped in rattan, and then lacquered. A Ch'an master used it as a teaching device striking students who were negligent in meditation. It was also a symbol of the master's authority. See Nakamura Hajime, *Bukkyōgo daijiten* (Tokyo, 1975), 955c.

27. *KL*, 30:686d.

28. The Huan-chu an at Wu-men fell into disuse during the disorders at the end of Yüan. Monk Yüan-yen restored it in the first year of Hung-wu (1368) of the Ming and asked Sung Lien to write an essay recording the history of the temple. In this essay, Sung Lien related Ming-pen's explanation of the term "Huan-chu": "What is revealed by the clear water is the essence of illusion (*huan-t'i*),[jn] what is reflected by the bright mirror is the traces of illusion (*huan-chi*).[jo] When illusion is extinguished and awakening reaches emptiness, this is the supreme height of transcendental awareness. We should

abide in this samadhi which resembles illusion (ju-huan san-mei).[jp] Therefore, I will name the temple 'Illusory Abode' (or 'Abiding in Illusion')." Sung Lien, "Wu-men ch'ung-chien Huan-chu ch'an-an chi," in *Sung Wen-hsien kung ch'uan-chi*[jq] (SPPY ed.), 29:5a.

29. Lin-chi Ch'an reached an uncontested position of supremacy among Buddhist schools in the Southern Sung. It was widely accepted by the court, officials, and literati and underwent what Imaeda Aishin[jr] calls "aristocratization." As a result, some secular bureaucratic features were adopted by the Ch'an monasteries. The system of "five mountains" (wu-shan) was a new creation reflecting this change. According to this system, official monasteries (kuan ssu)[js] in the country were classified into three ranks. The highest were the "five mountains" which were Ching-shan, Ling-yin, T'ien-t'ung, Ching-tz'u, and A-yü-wang.[jt] The second in rank were the "ten caityas" (shih-ch'a)[ju] and the lowest were the "various monasteries" (chu-shan)[jv] which were thirty-five in number. Citing Sung Lien as his source Imaeda said that this system of temple classification was proposed by Shih Mi-yüan in the time of Emperor Ning-tsung (r. 1195–1225). The various temples being thus classified resembled bureaucratic posts in civil service. A monk first had to serve as an abbot in the temple of the lowest rank and if he distinguished himself by his talents, he would then be promoted to head a temple in the next higher rank. When a monk became an abbot of one of the five mountains, he would be regarded with great admiration just as if a common man should become a great general or famous minister. Sung Lien lamented this stress on hierarchy as a secularization of Ch'an, for in former days all temples were equal in status. Perhaps because of abuses, the Ming emperor T'ai-tsu elevated the Lung-hsiang chi-ch'ing ch'an-ssu of Ch'ien-tang (present Nanking) to a rank above even that of the "Five Mountains" and renamed it T'ien-chieh shan-shih ch'an-ssu. Since the Ming, the "Five Mountains" system has not been much in use in China. The story was considerably different in Japan, however, where the *gozan* system was established by Japanese Zen monks during the Kamakura period, using the Chinese model, and took deep root. Imaeda Aishin, *Chūsei Zenshūshi no kenkyū*[jw] (Tokyo: Tokyo daigaku shuppankai, 1970), pp. 141–46. The Japanese *gozan* system is treated by Martin Collcutt, *The Zen Monastic Institution in Medieval Japan* (Ph.D. diss., Harvard University, 1975).

30. The phrases "ch'ien san-mei" and "hou san-mei"[jx] occur in the 35th chapter of *Pi-yen lu*. According to Nakamura's explanation, it describes the state of basic wisdom (keng-pen chih),[jy] transcending the intellect. See *Bukkyōgo daijiten*,[jz] p. 844d.

31. Ming-pen is here contrasting the real abbot's room, which is not located in any fixed place, with the conventional one, which is represented by the "ten-feet square room" and forms part of a monastery.

32. *KL*, 29:682b.

33. *Ibid.*

34. He was an important supporter of Ming-pen. He was a son of Kharghasun,

a distinguished minister during the reigns of Khubilai and Temür. His biography was attached to that of his father (YS, 136:3295). He became censor-in-chief in 1313, regional administer of Kiangche in 1320, and left chancellor of the province in 1325. While he was friendly with Ming-pen during the years 1320 to 1323 (the year Ming-pen died), he was the left chancellor of the province and concurrently in charge of the Bureau of Buddhist and Tibetan Affairs. See Fujishima Tateki, "Genchō Būkkyō no ichi yōsō," p. 22.

35. The Bureau of Buddhist and Tibetan Affairs was founded in 1264. It was unique, having no precedent in Chinese bureaucratic traditions. See Franke, "Tibetans in Yüan China," pp. 311–14.

36. *KL*, 30:686d.

37. *KL*, 30:687a.

38. This is included in ZZ 2.16.5, pp. 486b–506b.

39. ZZ 2.16.5, p. 486b.

40. *KL*, 18:653d.

41. According to Collcutt," . . . the Genjū lineage comprising the followers of Japanese monks like Kōsen Ingen (1295–1374) and Muin Genkai (d. 1358), who had journeyed to Yüan dynasty China to study Zen under the monk Chung-feng Ming-pen at his hermitage, the Huan-chu an (Genjū'an). The pioneers of this lineage in Japan prized Chung-feng's reclusiveness, advocated his blend of Pure Land and Zen and quit the official *gozan* monasteries for provincial retreats where they acquired reputations for severe Zen meditative practice. By the late fifteenth century monks of this lineage had attracted a wide following and enjoyed the patronage of *sengoku daimyo*. Since monks of this lineage were permitted to hold dual *inka*, that is, to inherit other Zen transmissions, with the growing popularity of this branch of Rinzai Zen, many monks affiliated with the Genjū lineage were invited to head the very *gozan* monasteries which early members of the lineage had left in disgust because of their formalized and literary character." See Collcutt, *Zen Monastic Institutions*, p. 182.

42. *KL*, 11:611d.

43. *Ibid.*, 11:607c.

44. The persecutions of Buddhism under the "three Emperors Wu" refer to the three attempts of rulers whose names all contain the character "Wu" to proscribe Buddhism. Emperor Wu of the Northern Wei tried to suppress Buddhism in 446, Emperor Wu of the Northern Chou did likewise in 574–577, and finally Emperor Wu-tsung of the T'ang carried out the most extensive persecution in 845, which was known as the Hui-ch'ang persecution. See Kenneth Ch'en, *Buddhism in China*, pp. 147–51, 181–94 and 226–32. Ch'en says on p. 232: "The persecution of Buddhism in 845 was undoubtedly the most widespread of its kind in China. The earlier instances in 446 and 574–577 were largely limited to North China, in those regions under the control of the Northern Wei and Northern Chou, and were not responsible for any lasting bad effects on the religion. The Buddhist communities

in south China were not touched at all. The T'ang proscription, on the other hand, was effective throughout the empire, and because it damaged the Buddha sangha permanently, it is one of the significant events in the history of Buddhism in China."

45. KL, 18:649c.

46. KL, 11:605d–606a.

47. *Ibid.*

48. Chuang Tzu tells this poignant tale succinctly in *ch.* 7 of the work bearing his name: "The emperor of the South Sea was called Shu [Brief], the emperor of the North Sea was called Hu [Sudden], and the emperor of the central region was called Hun-tun [Chaos]. Shu and Hu from time to time came together for a meeting in the territory of Hun-tun, and Hun-tun treated them very generously. Shu and Hu discussed how they could repay his kindness. 'All men,' they said, 'have seven openings so that they can see, hear, eat, and breathe. But Hun-tun alone doesn't have any. Let's try boring him some! Every day they bored another hole, and on the seventh day Hun-tun died." *The Complete Works of Chuang Tzu,* tr. Burton Watson (New York: Columbia University Press, 1968), p. 97.

49. KL, 4:579d.

50. *Ibid.*

51. KL, 11:607a.

52. Chao Meng-fu painted portraits of Ming-pen in addition to writing letters to him. For instance, there is one portrait kept in the Jishoin Temple of Kyoto. Ten letters written in Chao's famous calligraphy are kept in the National Palace Museum in Taiwan and one letter is kept in the Art Museum of Princeton University. In these letters Chao addresses Ming-pen as his teacher and refers to himself as Ming-pen's disciple. He questions Ming-pen concerning various aspects of Buddhism. Curiously, though, except for an eulogy accompanying a portrait of Ming-pen, there is no reference to the monk in Chao's collected work, *Chao Wen-min kung Sung-hsüeh-chai ch'üan-chi,*[ka] 10 *ch.* (1882 ed.).

53. KL, 2:570b–c.

54. See Philip B. Yampolsky, tr., *The Platform Sutra of the Sixth Patriarch* (New York: Columbia University Press, 1967), p. 130.

55. KL, 18:647b.

56. *Chung-feng ho-shang tsa-lu* (hereafter abbreviated as TL), (ZZ 2.27.4), 2:380d.

57. *Ibid.*, p. 385d.

58. KL, 20:659c.

59. KL, 20:659d.

60. KL, 18:647a.

61. KL, 20:659c.

62. KL, 4:575b.

63. TL, 2:380d–381a.

64. KL, 1:558a–b.

65. TL, 3:392c–d.

66. KL, 4:583b; TL, 3:390d–391a.
67. TL, 1:365d–366a.
68. Miriam Levering, "Ch'an Enlightenment," p. 121.
69. KL, 11:604c.
70. TL, 3:388a.
71. KL, 4:582b.
72. KL, 11:605d.
73. TL, 3:393b and 396a.
74. TL, 1:367c–d.
75. KL, 11:605d.
76. *T'ien-ju Wei-tse Ch'an-shih yu-lu,*[kb] (ZZ 2.27.5.), 2:416a. For a general discussion of the joint practice of Ch'an and Pure Land, see the author's *The Renewal of Buddhism in China: Chu-hung and the Late Ming Synthesis* (New York: Columbia University Press, 1981), pp. 47–57.
77. Sung Lien, "Shih-shih hu-chiao-pien hou-chi," in *Sung Wen-hsien kung ch'üan-chi*, 35:14b.
78. KL, 19:654a–b.
79. KL, 11:603b–c.
80. *Ibid.*
81. See Tsung-mi's "On the Original Nature of Man," in Wm. Theodore de Bary, ed., *The Buddhist Tradition* (New York: Modern Library, 1969), p. 181. See also Levering's dissertation, chap. 3, "Ta-hui and Confucian Teachings: Three Teachings Return to One."
82. *Ta-hui P'u-chüeh Ch'an-shih yu-lu*[kc] (T 47), 22:912a.
83. *Daie sho*, tr. by Araki Kengo[kd] (Tokyo, 1969), p. 145. See the author's article, "Ta-hui Tsung-kao and *Kung-an* Ch'an," *Journal of Chinese Philosophy* (1979), 6:229, and also Levering's dissertation, chaps. 3 and 4.
84. KL, 5:58b–590a.
85. *Ibid.*
86. KL, 11:610d.
87. *Yüan tien-chang*, ch. 33, cited in Ohyabu Masaya, "Gendai no hōsei to Bukkyō," p. 18.
88. KL, 4:583c.
89. This includes not only biographies of eminent monks but particularly anthologies of pertinent sayings and exemplary deeds of earlier Ch'an masters. These works were studied as a substitute for the actual words and actions of a living master. I have in mind in particular the *Ch'an-lin pao-hsün*[ke] (Treasured Teachings of the Ch'an Monastic Tradition) compiled by Ta-hui. I discussed these and related ideas in greater detail in my paper, "The Concept of Authority in the Buddhist Traditions," delivered at the Annual Meeting of the Association for Asian Studies, Los Angeles, 1979.
90. For the discussion of "charisma," see Max Weber, *The Theory of Social and Economic Organization*, tr. and ed. with an introduction by Talcott Parsons (New York: Free Press of Glencoe, 1964), pp. 358–59.
91. *Ch'u-jih* begins at 6 A.M., *chung-jih* at 10 A.M., *hou-jih* at 2 P.M., *ch'u-yeh*

at 6 P.M., *chung-yeh* at 10 P.M., and *hou-yeh* at 2 A.M. Each lasts four hours. Meditation is carried out in four periods: 8–9 P.M., 3–4 A.M., 9–10 A.M. and 3–4 P.M. The four-period meditation was first mentioned in the *Ch'an-lin pei-yung ch'ing-kuei*[kf] (1311) but must have been in use long before this. Both Eisai (1141–1215) and Dōgen (1200–1253) mentioned it.

92. The holidays celebrated include the following: the Buddha's birthday on the 8th of the 4th month, Kuan-yin's birthday on the 19th of the 2nd month, the Buddha's Enlightenment on the 8th of the 12th month, the Buddha's nirvana on the 15th of the 2nd month, Bodhidharma's death on the 5th of the 10th month, Master Kao-feng's death on the 1st of the 12th month, the Ullambana festival on the 15th of the 7th month, and the Tuan-yang festival on the 5th of the 5th month, which is actually not a Buddhist holiday.

93. A list of the sutras used is provided in the *Pure Rules.* They are: *Avatamsaka, Lotus, Yüan-chüeh ching, Diamond, Ch'ing-lien-hua ju-i pao-lun-wang shen-chou*[kg] (The Divine Dharani of the Blue Lotus Precious Cakravartin Who Grants Desires) and *Hsiao-tsai miao-chi-hsiang shen-chou*[kh] (The Divine Dharani of Manjusri Who Does Away with Disaster). See ZZ 2.16.5, p. 489a.

94. Kenneth Ch'en, *Buddhism in China*, pp. 276–77.

95. For instance, Dōgen observed that, in the Ch'an monasteries he visited, prayers were offered during the daily chanting of the sutras for the welfare of the ruler, the peace of the nation, and the prosperity and security of patrons. "In addition, on the first and the fifteenth day of each month and around the anniversary of the emperor's birthday, a special ceremony of invocation for the imperial well-being was held." He also said, "In the Yüan dynasty, when the Ch'an sect found it expedient to be particularly obsequious towards the imperial court, some monasteries displayed tablets reading 'Long Live the Emperor,' 'Gracious Years to the Empress,' and 'A Thousand Autumns to the Crown Prince.' " See Collcutt, pp. 281–84. There was no indication that these tablets were kept at Huan-chu an.

96. KL, I:560d–561a.

97. "The *Ch'an-yüan* code (1103) made provision for only four stewards, one of them the prior (*kan'in*)[ki] being responsible for financial matters. By the time Dōgen visited China a century later, six stewards were the norm: 'In monasteries there have always been six stewards.' The two additional stewards were both divided between a *tsusu,*[kj] *kansu,*[kk] and *fusu.*[kl] This development suggests that during the Southern Sung dynasty, not only had formalization of Ch'an monastic bureaucratic structure taken place—six stewards to balance six prefects—but, more important, a single financial officer had been insufficient to cope with an expansion in the volume and complexity of economic affairs as Ch'an monasteries were drawn more intimately into a monetized local economy." See Collcutt, p. 360. Ming-pen's reduction of monastic personnel at Huan-chu an was a reaction against this proliferation of bureaucratic structure. Just as his repeated refusal to head some of the monasteries which belonged to the "five mountain" category, this action can

be seen as a criticism against the Ch'an monastic tradition which had evolved from the Sung.

98. ZZ 2.16.5, p. 503b.

99. See the author's *The Renewal of Buddhism in China*, p. 53.

100. When Su Ch'e was 42, he was exiled to Yün-chou[km] (modern Kiangsi), where there were many monasteries. He became friendly with a monk called Tao-ch'üan,[kn] who was living on Mt. Huang-po and was a third-generation disciple of Master Tao-hsüan. Tao-ch'üan at first felt that there could absolutely be no mutual understanding between Buddhists and Confucians. Su told him that it was not so. Su's discussion consisted of this passage quoted by Ming-pen. At the end of the talk, Tao-ch'üan was convinced. During his subsequent five-year-stay in the area, Su would show Tao-ch'üan each chapter of his commentary on *Lao Tzu* when he was finished with it. Su Ch'e's commentary, *Tao-te-ching chü,*[ko] which I consulted, is in Yen Ling-feng,[kp] *Wu-ch'iu-pei-chai Lao Tzu chi-ch'en ch'u-pien* (Taipei: Yi-wen yin-shu-kuan, 1965), pt. 10. This story is found in "T'i *Lao Tzu Tao-te-ching* hou," in vol. 5 of the book just cited, pp. 2a–b.

101. The same idea is found in Ch'i-sung's essays on filiality. He wrote twelve essays on this subject. In the third one, "On the Origin of Filiality" (*Yüan-hsiao*),[kq] he talks about filiality being the same as "imitation." See *Hsin-chin wen-chi*[kr] (SPTK ed.), 2:36.

GLOSSARY

a 帝師

b 釋老傳

c 楊璉眞加

d 江南總攝掌釋教

e 宣徽使

f 趙翼

g 禪

h 教

i 律

j 萬松行秀

k 省悟

l 律苑事規

m 德輝

n 百丈清規重編

o 自慶

p 增修教苑清規

q 念常

r 佛祖歷代通載

s 覺岸

t 釋氏稽古略

u 普度

v 蓮宗寶鑑

w 中峰明本

x 高峰原妙

y 死關

z 雪巖祖欽

aa 無準師範

ab 楊歧方會

ac 黃龍慧南

ad 圓悟克勤

ae 大慧宗杲

af 虎丘紹隆

ag 公案

ah 看話禪

ai 話頭

aj 海雲行秀

ak 孫

al 無門開

am 圓覺經

an 天目山

ao 獅子院寺

ap 堂主

aq 庫頭

ar 維那

as 瞿霆發

at 大覺寺

au 幻住庵

av 靈隱

aw 徑山

ax 五山

ay 雁蕩

az 法慧禪師

ba 江南古佛

bb 脫歡

bc 宣政院

bd 蔣均

be 幻住清規

bf 百丈懷海

bg 佛慈圓照廣慧禪師

bh 趙孟頫

bi 智覺禪師

bj 普應國師

bk 中峰和尚廣錄

bl 雜錄

bm 淨慈

bn 禮法

bo 道體

bp 戒力

bq 末法

br 元氣

bs 脉

bt 謹嚴

es	初夜	ge	冥官
et	中夜	gf	十法界
eu	後夜	gg	三世無佛，法界無性，依此一心，二皆建立
ev	月進		
ew	大悲呪	gh	懺悔
ex	天壽聖節	gi	發菩提心
ey	金鋼道場	gj	盂蘭盆
ez	皇恩	gk	倒懸器
fa	年規	gl	平等
fb	四節	gm	妄心
fc	結制	gn	妄見
fd	解制	go	善巧方便
fe	冬至	gp	業
ff	歲朝	gq	防情
fg	楞嚴會	gr	復性
fh	歲計	gs	有爲
fi	世範	gt	無爲
fj	疏	gu	六度
fk	祈雨	gv	萬行
fl	祈晴	gw	三身
fm	土地	gx	經常之道
fn	營辦	gy	生化
fo	家風	gz	中節
fp	名分	ha	位
fq	庵主	hb	性理
fr	首座	hc	舉念動心
fs	副庵	hd	無知
ft	知庫	he	孝
fu	飯頭	hf	效
fv	互用	hg	有形之愛
fw	踐履	hh	無形之愛
fx	外緣	hi	大本
fy	內緣	hj	一念有間
fz	攝養	hk	牧田諦亮，民衆の仏教く宋から現代までフアジア仏教史，中国編
ga	津送		
gb	開甘露門		
gc	普施法食文	hl	張曼濤，中國佛敎史論集
gd	破地獄偈	hm	稲葉正就，元の帝師に関す

jr 今枝愛眞

js 官寺

jt 徑山，靈隱，天童，淨慈，
    阿育王

ju 十剎

jv 諸山

jw 中世禪宗史の研究

jx 前三昧，後三昧

jy 根本智

jz 佛教語大辭典

ka 趙文敏公松雪齋全集

kb 元如惟則禪師語錄

kc 大慧普覺禪師語錄

kd 荒木見悟，大慧書

ke 禪林寶訓

kf 禪林備用清規

kg 青蓮華如意寶輪王神咒

kh 消災妙吉祥神咒

ki 監院

kj 都寺

kk 監寺

kl 副寺

km 筠州

kn 道全

ko 道德經註

kp 嚴靈峰，無求備齋老子集成
    初編

kq 原孝

kr 譚津文集

Liu Ts'un-yan and Judith Berling

The "Three Teachings" in the Mongol-Yüan Period

WU CH'ENG[a] (1249–1333), a leading Neo-Confucian thinker, was so affected by the prevailing syncretism among Yüan dynasty intellectuals that he wrote:

Since Chin and T'ang times, Buddhism, Confucianism, and Taoism have been called the Three Teachings. However, to venerate them on equal terms without any discrimination is the virtue of the Great Yüan.[1]

The interflow of the ideas of the Three Teachings: Confucianism, Taoism, and Buddhism in the Yüan was stimulated by a variety of forces generated long before the Mongol conquest, but the Yüan syncretic tendencies were also the product of the unique cultural, political, social, and ethnic tensions which accompanied Mongol rule. Each of the three religions had to make its peace with the alien rulers, and the process of peacemaking and compromise produced pragmatic forces encouraging syncretism both within each of the three religions and among them.

THREE TEACHINGS PRIOR TO THE MONGOL CONQUEST

The Three Teachings had been actively competing for patronage and support since Wei-Chin times (220–420). In that period interest in the study of the *Lao Tzu* and the *Chuang Tzu* and the abstruse discussions of the scholarly Neo-Taoist thinkers offered an opportunity for erudite Buddhist monks to introduce their doctrine to Chinese intellectuals and to gain increasing numbers of followers from that community. However, Confucianism, with its intricate relationship to Chinese culture, state, and society, was still the dominant philosophy. Taoism and Buddhism were competing to penetrate into the lower strate of the society by means of religious trappings such as rituals and stories of heaven and hell; they also sought to gain ascendancy by means of forged scriptures and coop-tion of each other's deities.

Open debates between representatives of the Three Teachings com-peting for political recognition were held during some of the Six Dynas-ties (222–589) and the T'ang (618–907).[2] Some of these were light-hearted occasions generating a spirit of conviviality, but some led to serious ar-gument.[3] Though these debates did not greatly diminish ideological con-flict among the Three Teachings, they provided a context in which dif-fering views were presented and discussed. Few intellectuals could be wholly ignorant of the claims of other schools.

Nomadic or seminomadic tribes who succeeded in ruling parts of North China also patronized the Three Teachings, but being non-Han peoples and not tied to native traditions, they tended to favor Buddhism and/or Taoism over Confucianism. The Khitans, who succeeded in oc-cupying a small part of north China and founded the Liao dynasty (947–1125), saw the advantage of ruling the Chinese through Han bureaucratic institutions. However, although Confucian and Taoist temples and prac-tices were well established in the Liao territory Buddhism was the most popular of the Three Teachings during the Liao.[4] Of the many favors granted to the Buddhist monks, two are noteworthy: the appointmet of a number of Buddhist monks to official posts, and the "Double Tax Payers" (*erh-shui hu*)[b] system, which favored Buddhist orders.[5]

In many ways the administration of the Jurchen Chin (1115–1234) in North China resembled the Liao bureaucratic system although it was far more sinicized. Though the number of Buddhist monks and Taoist priests to be ordained each year was officially restricted, this policy was counterbalanced by the fact that even in the early days of Emperor Shih-tsung[c] (r. 1161–1189), ordination certificates, reverential titles, and pur-ple cassocks were available for purchase from the government.[6] The le-nient attitude of the Jurchen court towards the Three Teachings was re-flected in the attitude of the Confucian scholars and officials towards their Buddhist and Taoist rivals.[7]

The South, which continued under Han Chinese rule, remained more staunchly Confucian, although the influence of Buddhism and Taoism was by no means insignificant. There, supporters of the orthodox school of Confucian teaching continued to reject any admixture of Buddhist customs and habits in their rituals and other social functions.

These feelings were also extended to some native beliefs, such as shamanism and sorcery, and particularly to religious Taoism. For years the term *erh-shih*[d] (two teachings) had been a derogatory one in scholarly works. The main objections were not ideological, but rather institutional and economic.[8] Yet, despite this antagonism, one of the most important developments during this period was a growing tolerance among Confucians towards the other two teachings. This was in part pragmatic, for the general conditions at the time were favorable to syncretism, and would have made suppression difficult.

During the sixty years of disturbances and upheavals preceding the establishment of the Northern Sung (960–1126), many Confucian scholars fleeing to the mountainous areas of north and northwest China took refuge in temples. There they had opportunity to read and have close personal contacts with their members. Because of this exchange of ideas, new approaches to and questions about classical Confucian texts were generated, giving rise to new directions in Confucian thought.[9] During the Southern Sung (1127–1279), despite the general weakening of the national strength, Taoist religious institutions prospered. Confucian scholar-officials' tolerance towards Taoism reflected official participation by Confucians in Taoist worship at government level,[10] and also their common interest in the *Book of Changes*. In addition, the popularity of Ch'an Buddhism reached unprecedented heights, strengthening the general pressures for syncretism. Sung scholar-officials, despite their predominant Neo-Confucian background, had moved closer to Buddhism not only as a religion, but also as a philosophy. During the time of Lu Hsiang-shan[e] (1139–1193) the influence of Ch'an among his followers was so intense that the distinction between their practice and that of the Ch'an Buddhists became negligible. It would be impossible to distinguish the *Yü-lu*[f] (*Tao-tsang*[g] no. 1016) of the Taoist patriarch Pai Yü-ch'an[h] (1134–1220), the venerated Fifth Master of the Southern School, from the *yü-lu* of a Ch'an monk, if one did now know it was written by a Taoist. From the Buddhist side, Ta-hui Tsung-kao[i] (1089–1163), a Ch'an leader, advocated discussing Ch'an in a Confucian context, further blurring the distinctions of the Three Teachings at this time.[11]

On the even of the Mongol invasion, then, in the North the Three Teachings were competing for the patronage of alien rulers as well as the Chinese populace, whereas in the South there had been great strides toward a syncretism of the Three Teachings in large part because of the influence of Ch'an Buddhism on the Neo-Confucianism and Taoism of the day.

THE MONGOL GOVERNMENT AS A STIMULUS TO SYNCRETISM OF THE THREE TEACHINGS

Prominence of Tibetan Buddhism

The Mongol dynasty was the first foreign dynasty to succeed in conquering the entire Chinese empire. As in the case of the earlier Liao, and to some extent the Jurchen Chin, they felt more at home with Buddhism than with Confucianism. Because the Mongols, with their nomadic heritage, had practiced a shamanistic form of religion, replete with rituals and magic, they were most at home with the ritualistic and magical Buddhism of the Tibetans. In the time of Möngke (Hsien-tsung, r. 1251–1259), when the capital was still in Karakorum, there was a Tibetan "State Preceptor" (*Kuo-shih*),[j] Na-mo,[k] at his court.[12] Khubilai (r. 1260–1294), in his capital Yen-ching (Ta-tu,[l] modern Peking), created some religious offices for Taoists, but on the whole the most venerated and highest status among the religious leaders was that of the Tibetan "Imperial Preceptor" (*Ti-shih*)[m] and "State Preceptor," and numerous privileges were enjoyed by him and his followers.

Tibetan lamaism must have impressed the Mongols by the richness of its symbolism and ritual as compared to their shamanism. One instance from the *Yüan shih* will serve to illustrate this point:

In the seventh year of Chih-yüan[n] [1270], Emperor Shih-tsu [Khubilai] followed the advice of Phags-pa [1239?–1280], the Imperial Preceptor, and installed a white parasol behind the imperial seat in the Great Hall of Brilliance (*Ta-ming tien*).[o] The parasol was made of white satin, with Sanskrit [Tibetan?] words written on it. It was said to pacify and subdue the wicked and the devil, as well as protect the state and the monasteries. Since then, on the fifteenth day of the second month of each year, there was a White Parasol Service held in the Great Hall. Processions from different departments and societies were to gather there to lead the Parasol on its rounds inside and outside the Imperial City as a means of exorcising evil spirits and receiving blessings.[13]

And then follows the detailed description of the lavish ritual, equipment, and personnel involved in this ceremony:

The Eight Garrisons [under the Chief Military Commission] assigned 120 parasol-drummers, 500 cavalrymen in armor as horsesoldiers at the rear [of the processions]; and another 500 men, either served as pullers of the carriage on which a sedan chair of Kuan Yü[p] [of Han, the God of War] who acted as [patron saint] of the Holy Altar was placed, or performed miscellaneous errands on the road. The Bureau of Buddhist and Tibetan Affairs (Hsüan-cheng yüan)[q] had 360 Buddhist monasteries under its jurisdiction. Its duties were to provide Buddhist statues and altars, pennants, pendant streamers, portable precious shades, carriages, drums and standard bearers [for this occasion]. There were 360 altars to be provided, each with 26 carriers and holders [of various objects], as well as 12 monks playing the cymbals. The Ta-tu District was to organize 120 teams of men called the Great Societies of the Golden Gate (Chin-men ta-she)[r] representing a variety of professions. The Department of Music (Chiao-fang ssu)[s] and the Office of Harmonious Clouds (Yün-ho chü)[t] took care of the 400 musicians who made music with clappers, cane drums, Tartar horns (pi-li),[u] dragon flutes (p'i-p'a),[v] zithers, and lutes. The Office of Harmonious Prosperity (Hsing-ho chü)[w] took charge of 150 courtesans, who were to perform in group plays. The Office of Harmonious Blessings (Hsiang-ho chü)[x] took charge of acrobats, men and women, altogether 150 members. The Department of Phoenixlike Deportment (I-feng ssu)[y] took charge of three groups of light music performers, the Han-Chinese, the Muslims, and the people from Ho-hsi,[z] each group consisting of three teams, for a grand total of 324 persons. All the participants in this festival were dressed in new and attractive robes; the armor, the insignias, and the equipment were all fine and bright, and provided officially. The processions extended for more than thirty li, with their members wearing shining dresses embroidered with gold, jade, and pearl patterns. Crowds of men and women poured into the streets of the capital to watch.[14]

The partiality of the Mongol court toward Tibetan Buddhists was resented by the Chinese, who felt the native Chinese population was made to suffer unjustly. One Chinese official expressed his outrage over the disruptions caused by these foreign monks, as recorded in the Yüan shih:

In the second year of T'ai-ting[aa] [1325], Li Ch'ang,[ab] a censor from the Shensi branch [of the Censorate] memorialized: "Recently I took a trip passing through the prefectures of P'ing-liang, Ching-ning, Hui-chou, and Ting-hsi.[ac] I saw traveling Tibetan monks wearing round-shaped signs in gold representing a tally [pass], and riding in a continuous stream. They numbered several hundred. As the post-lodges could not accommodate so many visitors, they stayed in the houses of common folk. This resulted in the eviction of husbands and rape of women. In the Feng-yüan[ad] [Shensi] District alone, from the first to the seventh month of the year, 185 trips were made by the Tibetan monks riding to and fro. Over 840 horses were used by them; this figure exceeded by 60 to 70 percent the normal use [of horses] by imperial princes and provincial officials. Post-lodge attendants had no one to turn to to air their complaints, and censors did not dare to utter a word. Moreover, the round passes were normally issued only to messengers reporting emergencies on the frontier; how could these monks be permitted to wear them: I begged [the court] to rectify the rules governing the movement of the Tibetan monks en route and during their stay at the post-lodges, and permit the censors to impeach the monks for their crimes." There was no response.[15]

The government, indeed, went out of its way to protect these monks from the Chinese populace. An edict was issued about 1288 warning that "should anyone strike a Tibetan monk he would have his hands cut off; should anyone revile a Tibetan monk, he would have his tongue plucked out." Although this law was abolished in 1309,[16] favoritism towards Tibetans pressured the ministers at court and native Buddhists to maintain a certain degree of cordiality with them.[17]

The Difficulties in Establishing Confucianism at the Yüan Court
If the Mongols were slow to embrace Chinese religious and philosophical ideas, preferring instead the ritual grandeur of Tibetan Buddhism, the Confucians were slow to accept or serve an alien dynasty. In the *Sung-Yüan hsüeh-an* are included about one hundred Confucian scholars who were active between 1279 and 1367; quite a few lived in the early Yüan but refused to serve the new dynasty. Some took up teaching so that Chinese students could be educated in traditional values.

However, some Confucians, concerned for the survival of Confucian ways, served the Mongols in order to protect scholars from persecution and to introduce Confucian ideas, practices, and policies gradually in the Mongol Court. In the early years, there was considerable cause for concern about the survival of Confucians. The Mongols were well known for their harsh treatment of captives and for the massacre of survivors of cities which would not surrender.[18] Usually only technicians and craftsmen were spared, since they were useful to the conquerors. Confucian scholars, with a few exceptions,[19] did not fare well at the hands of invading Mongols.

Nevertheless, in the reigns of Chinggis, Ögödei, and Möngke, there were some Han-Chinese, Khitan, Hsi-hsia, and Chin officials serving the Mongol conquerors who sought to save Confucians and Confucian temples. The *Yüan shih* records, for instance, that in the spring of 1215 a Confucian temple in the city was destroyed in the battle over the Middle Capital of the Chin (modern Peking). Wang Chi[ae] (d. 1240), the Pacification Commissioner, rebuilt the temple and in its corridors displayed several ancient stone drums originally from Ch'i-yang[af] (in Shensi).[20] This gesture of appeasement held great significance for Han-Chinese and other sinicized people. Another Chinese named Chang Jou[ag] (1190–1268), one of Ögödei's favorite commanders of the Han Army in the Mongol forces, also saved some Confucian scholars from slaughter after the fall of the last Chin capital Ts'ai-chou[ah] in early 1234.[21]

Yang Wei-chung[ai] (1205/6–1260) was able to convince the Neo-Confucian Chao Fu[aj] (c.1206–c.1299) to go and teach Neo-Confucian doctrines at the Mongol court, as depicted in the following account of his *Yüan shih* biography:

In the year *i-wei*[ak] [1235], Emperor T'ai-tsung [Ögödei, r. 1229–1241] ordered Prince Köchü to lead an army to attack the Sung. Because the city of Te-an[al] [in modern Hupei] had resisted till its fall, several tens of thousands [of men and women] were taken captive and killed. Yang Wei-chung was then in charge of the affairs of the Central Secretariat in the military quarters. [At the same time,] Yao Shu[am] [1203–1280] received an imperial command to seek out [among the captives] by the army [those distinguished] Confucians, Buddhists and Taoists, physicians and fortune-tellers [for the court]. Whenever they saw Confucian scholars in custody, they released them. Chao Fu was one of those. Yao Shu spoke to him and realized that he was an extraordinary man. [Chao did not wish to] go to the north, as all the members of his family and clansmen had been massacred. He bade farewell to Shu. However, Shu urged Fu to stay with him in his tent, fearing that he might commit suicide. When Shu woke up [during the night,] the moon was bright, Chao Fu was gone, and only his pajamas remained. [Yao Shu] immediately went out on horseback shouting his name and searching for him among the corpses piled up on the plain, but could not find him. When he reached the waterside, he found Chao Fu there, barefooted, with disheveled hair, wailing, sighing to Heaven, and about to drown himself. Yao Shu then exhorted him that dying would not help matters. He said: "If you live, you may have descendants perpetuate [your teaching] for a hundred generations. Follow me to the north, nothing will happen to you!" Chao Fu reluctantly went along. There had been no proper communications between north and south for a long time, and Confucian works published in the south were unknown to the northern scholars. Chao Fu then wrote down from memory all the commentaries written by the Ch'eng brothers [Ch'eng Hao, 1032–1085, and Ch'eng I,[an] 1033–1107] and Chu Hsi[ao] [1130–1200] [for Yao Shu]. On Chao Fu's arrival in Yen-ching, more than a hundred scholars went to study under him and he also had an audience with Khubilai, then an imperial prince at court. . . .[22]

Not only did Chao Fu bring Neo-Confucian teachings to the Mongol court, but Yang Wei-chung became so interested that he began the process of establishing formal Neo-Confucian studies in north China. According to the same account:

Yang Wei-chung, while listening to Chao Fu's discourses, became interested in Confucian doctrines. [Then in 1238] he and Yao Shu set up the Great Ultimate Academy (*T'ai-chi shu-yüan*)[ap] and a temple in honor of Chou Tun-i[aq] [1017–1073] [in Yen-ching], with tablets of the two Ch'eng brothers, Chang Tsai[ar] [1020–1077], Yang Shih[as] [1053–1135], Yu Tso[at] [1053–1123], and Chu Hsi as members of the temple, to share in the sacrifices. They selected more than 8,000 *chüan* of Confucian works [written by these scholars] and invited Chao Fu to lecture on them.[23]

Among the most renowned Confucian advisers to the Mongols was Yeh-lü Ch'u-ts'ai[au] (1189–1243), a descendant of the imperial Liao family. Although "erudite in many [Chinese] classics," he was particularly interested in Ch'an Buddhism, and he was a colleague of the Chin syncretist Li Ch'un-fu (or Li Ping-shan,[av] 1185–1231).[24] Among Yeh-lü Ch'u-ts'ai's contributions to the early Mongol administration were the recognition of K'ung Yüan-ts'o[aw] (1179?–1252?) as the fifty-first-generation descendant of Confucius in 1233, along with a hereditary title and post,[25] and the introduction of examinations in 1237 for scholars competing for the posts of executives or taxation officers in occupied towns and cities.[26] The last measure was more important than the first, as it could have paved the way for the formal reinstitution of state examinations to select scholar-officials. However, as late as the reign of Khubilai Khaghan, despite the many capable Chinese advisers at the court, state examinations had not been reintroduced. This was a serious issue, for "due to the suspension of the examinations, scholars found no means to enter the state service. Some went to study law and articles to become government clerks. Others took up a variety of professions, such as personal servants to officials, small peddlers, craftsmen, traders, and merchants."[27] It was only in 1313–1315, under Emperor Ayurbarwada (Jentsung, r. 1311–1320), that the civil service examinations for the *chin-shih* degree were finally introduced in the Yüan empire. Two examination halls were provided in Yen-ching: one for the Mongols and the Se-mu (i.e., miscellaneous aliens), and the other for the Han-Chinese. Commentaries on the Classics written by Chu Hsi, the Ch'eng brothers, Ts'ai Ch'en[ax] (1167–1230), and Hu An-kuo[ay] (1074–1138) dominated the prescribed curriculum. The old commentaries, with the exception of the *Book of Rites* (*Li chi*),[az] had either fallen into oblivion or were kept on the list only for consultation.[28] The reintroduction of the state examinations was seen by Neo-Confucian scholars as a triumph in the struggle between the Chinese ministers and the conflicting elements at the court. However, although the Confucians had finally won the examination issue, their position at court was fundamentally different during the Yüan. Among the Neo-Confucians, apart from the Han-Chinese scholar-officials, there were young men from the Tangut Hsi-hsia, the Uighurs, the Mongols, the Ärkä'un, and the Muslims, not to mention the sinicized Khitans and Jurchens. Their mutual contacts and acquaintances contributed to the coexistence of the Three Teachings.

Given the persistently foreign flavor of the Yüan court, and its continuing interest in Tibetan Buddhism, Chinese religious leaders seeking the patronage and approval of the court learned early that any divisions within the ranks of Buddhism, Taoism, or Confucianism only annoyed the Mongols, who were not inclined to listen to bickering Chinese. During the Sung Confucian scholars had been outspoken in their opposition to the other two teachings, but no more than two or three isolated cases of this are recorded in the *Yüan shih*.[29] Under the Yüan, in fact, an attitude of coexistence and compromise served the best interests of all Three Teachings. As a result, despite the influence of the Tibetan monks, the joint efforts of the Confucian scholar-officials and the Taoist priests prevented Mongol China from enforcing one single creed. And the same attitude of compromise applied to different sects within each teaching. There were practical pressures for accommodation, not only to Mongol tastes, but to other doctrines as well. In its relative aloofness from Chinese ways, the Mongol government provided a strong incentive for syncretism. The lavish patronage of Tibetan rituals showed that the Mongols were willing to support religious activities, and Chinese intellectuals sought that support for native traditions.

BUDDHISM AND SYNCRETISM IN THE YÜAN

As we have seen, while Buddhism played an important role in the Mongol court from the very beginning, it was Tibetan Buddhism, and not Chinese Buddhism, which was dominant. Tibetan monks were highly placed political and religious advisors, and members of the Chinese Buddhist sects found it difficult to circumvent their influence. Many

Buddhist monks allied with the Tibetan lamas mainly for their own protection, relying on their shared Buddhist convictions. Ch'an masters were more active than the others in courting the Tibetans, though the voice of the followers of the Hua-yen[ba] School was not unheard. Many Confucian scholars at the court and in the provinces had personal relationships with the Ch'an monks, and early Han-Chinese advisers to the Mongols were also Ch'an Buddhists. By cultivating the support of Tibetans, Ch'an Buddhists not only overcame antipathy to Ch'an ideas at court, but also established themselves as the dominant Chinese Buddhist school.

In the Yüan, there were three main Buddhist schools in China: Ch'an, Hua-yen, and Vinaya. The Vinaya School was not particularly prosperous, so that the basic competitors were Hua-yen and Ch'an. Around 1288 Hua-yen priests requested Khubilai to evict the Ch'an priests from famous Buddhist monasteries in the South and replace them with members of the Hua-yen Sect. Ch'an leaders in the South sought help from their colleagues in the North as well as those Tibetan friends who were known to sympathize with them. For instance, the Tibetan Yang-lien-chen-chia,[bb] known as Superintendent of Buddhist Teaching (*Shih-chiao tsung-t'ung*),[bc] was an important participant in the debate. Yang-lien-chen-chia was hated by the Chinese because of his exhumation of the Sung royal tombs in Shao-hsing[bd] (1285), but this animosity did not prevent Ch'an monks from seeking his support.

In the 1288 debate, the Ch'an school was represented by Miao-kao[be] (1219–1293), and the Hua-yen school by Hsien-lin,[bf] known to have been well versed in the Buddhist treatise *Po-fa lun*[bg] (On the Hundred Divisions in the Phenomenal Realm). The discourse, held in the presence of Khubilai, was from time to time interrupted by the explanations of Yang-lien-chen-chia (supporting the Ch'an position), while Monk Ching-fu,[bh] Ch'an Abbott of the Ling-yin[bi] Monastery, Hangchow, pulled at Miao-kao's robe whenever he thought the words he used might cause a misunderstanding.[30] In the biography of Miao-kao we read his version of the debate:

There were people slandering the Ch'an doctrine at the capital. The master Miao-kao said: "A very grave thing is happening to the teaching of the *dharma*. I have to protest against it and fight the charges until I die." So he went to Yen-ching. There was an edict ordering members of several schools to gather at the court and debate before the Emperor. Emperor Shih-tsu [Khubilai] asked: "What is the main principle of Ch'an?" The Master respectfully replied "It is pure, intelligent, wonderful, and all-embracing. Its body is empty and quiet, and is not to be approached via perception, feeling, thinking or any other means of discrimination." The Emperor questioned him on further points and the Master related the deeds of the earlier patriarchs of the West as well as those of the East, and the episodes dealing with Te-shan's[bj] [780–865] rod and Lin-chi's[bk] [d. 866] shout, and his whole statement consisted of 2,000 words. Then he was summoned to appear before the imperial couch and debate face to face with his opponent. The debate went on and on for quite a long time, and finally the opponent lost his ground and was silenced. Emperor Shih-tsu was pleased.[31]

Even if the Ch'an victory was not as clear-cut as Miao-kao claims, Ch'an had definitely established itself at court.

The influence of the Ch'an Buddhists and their association with the Tibetan religious leaders is reflected in the records dealing with the burning of the apocryphal Taoist scriptures in 1258–1259 and 1280–1281. As in many "doctrinal" debates, the issue of the scriptures masked the real issue: monastic property.

After the fall of the Chin many deserted Buddhist monasteries had been repaired, adapted, and occupied as Taoist monasteries by the Ch'üan-chen[bl] priests under the patronage extended to them by the Mongol rulers after their Patriarch Ch'iu Ch'u-chi (i.e., Ch'ang-ch'un,[bm] 1148–1227) had been given an audience by Chinggis Khan in Samarkand in 1222. The Buddhist monks hoped to regain control of some 230 monasteries lost to the Taoists in this way.

To regain court patronage, they claimed that Taoist scriptures were forged. In the first instance, in the great debate between the Buddhist monks and Taoist priests mainly of the Ch'üan-chen Sect, the native monks were represented by Fu-yü[bn] (1203–1275), Abbot of the Shao-lin[bo] Monastery at Karakorum, Chih-wen[bp] (1217–1267) and Monk Tzu-tsung,[bq] who was none other than Liu Ping-chung[br] (1216–1274), Khubilai's principal adviser. Both were of the Ch'an school. The Tibetan monks were represented by Phags-pa and Na-mo. According to the (Chih-yüan) Pien-wei lu (Rectification of False Charges Against Buddhism During the Chih-yüan Period) by Hsiang-mai[bs] (fl. 1291), both Tibetan leaders and the Confucian advisor Yao Shu spoke in the debate supporting the Ch'an monks. On the Taoist side, led by Chang Chih-ching[bt] (1220–1270), leader of the Ch'üan-chen Sect and successor of Li Chih-ch'ang[bu] (1193–1256), more than two hundred priests from several Taoist monasteries in north and northeast China failed to stand up to the Buddhists. The Buddhist victory was witnessed by several eminent Confucians.[32]

In the second instance, in 1281, among those present on the Buddhist side were Ho-t'ai-sa-li,[bv] the Superintendent of Buddhist Teaching, and on the Taoist side, Ch'i Chih-ch'eng[bw] (1219–1293), head of the Ch'üan-chen Sect, Chang Tsung-yen[bx] (d. 1291), the Thirty-sixth Celestial Master from Kiangsi, and Li Te-ho[by] (d. 1284) and Tu Fu-ch'un,[bz] both leaders of the Ta-tao[ca] Sect. The Ch'an Buddhists were represented by monks Ts'ung-lun[cb] and Chi-hsiang,[cc] who actually set the aprocryphal scriptures on fire, with Ts'ung-lun uttering a short verse confessing the penitence of those who had committed the sin of forgery, a ritual in accordance with the Buddhist tradition.[33]

Satisfied with the decision of the court, and the burning of some, if not all, forged texts, Ch'an monks turned their attention to the financial rather than the ideological issue. Even in the heat of controversy Monk Fu-yü still praised Lao Tzu as "the worthy man of the East," and in his memorial to the court he did not raise any objection to the coexistence and parallel development of the Three Teachings.[34]

Not all Buddhists were engaged in competing with Taoists or Confucians; many were sufficiently well versed in the doctrines of the other schools to comment on all Three Teachings and their philosophical or doctrinal interrelationships. One example is the monk Hsing-hsiu (alias Wan-sung,[cd] 1166–1246) who had been recommended by Yeh-lü Ch'u-ts'ai as "versed both in Confucianism and Buddhism." He wrote in his *Ts'ung-jung (an) lu*[ce] (Record of [the Lodge of] Leisureliness):

Confucianism and Taoism take *ch'i*[cf] as principle. The followers of Buddhism take mind as the root. Master Kuei-feng[cg] [Tsung-mi, 780–841] once said: "The primordial *ch'i* generated from the mind is controlled by the perceived division of Alayavijñāna." I, Wan-sung, say that the above is the orthodox teaching of our Ts'ao-tung[ch] School and the life and veins of the Buddha.[35]

Monk P'u-tu[ci] (1259–1340), a follower of the Pure Land School with some T'ien-t'ai[cj] background, asks in his *Lu-shan Lien-tsung pao-chien*[ck] (Precious Mirror of the Lotus Sect from Mt. Lu) (Preface 1312): ". . . [In instructing people] could one not say that the teaching of Buddha is complementary to the teaching of Confucius, as the surface and lining of a garment are to each other?" In another instance, he argued that the teaching of the Pure Land was "very useful to the dissemination of the doctrines of the Duke of Chou and Confucius. Its help to imperial sovereignty is indeed far-reaching."[36]

Chih-ch'e[cl] (fl. 1333), a Ch'an monk from Szechwan, in his *Ch'an-tsung chüeh-i lu*[cm] (Resolving Doubts in Ch'an Buddhism) quoted very freely from the *Book of Documents*, the *Analects*, and the *K'ung-tzu chia-yü*,[cn] not to mention some anecdotal accounts from historical works. In a double-column note he matched the five Buddhist commandments with the five Confucian human relationships, i.e. "not killing" with "humanity," "not stealing" with "righteousness," and the like.[37]

Miao-ming's *Che-i lun*[co] (A Treatise to Dispel Doubts), written in 1351, may be taken as representative of Buddhist works of syncretical nature towards the end of the Yüan. The author was originally a Confucian scholar from Shensi and in this work cited liberally from all Three Teachings, including popular religious Taoism.[38] He wrote:

Therefore, although the sages might have lived in different countries, when they were aroused by the same stimulus, they would speak as if through the same mouth. However, the illnesses of the people were different in degree, and therefore the medicines for their treatment were also different in dosage. But the compassion and will to cure the sufferings and bring them [the people] security and peace was shared by all of them [the sages].[39]

He tried to reconcile Taoist nonaction with the attainment of Buddha-nature: "The meaning of the character *tao* is 'to lead,' 'leading people to the state of nonaction (*wu-wei*)[cp] '. . . the Dharmakāya of the threefold body of a Buddha is nonaction."[40]

Nien-ch'ang[cq] (1282–1344?), a Buddhist historian, played an important role both in the relations of Chinese monks to Tibetans and in the development of the Three Teachings. In 1323 he was in Yen-ching as one of the calligraphers ordered to copy with gold ink the Buddhist scriptures for the court. Because of his duties, he had come to know the Imperial Preceptor Kun dga'blo gros rgyal mts'an dpal bzan po, and studied Tantrism under him. He was also a compiler of one of the chronological accounts of Buddhism in China, the *Fo-tsu li-tai t'ung-tsai*[cr] (Comprehensive Records of Buddhist Patriarchs in Successive Generations), an important contribution to the syncretic process of the Three Teachings.[41] For instance, in this work Nien-ch'ang quoted, nearly in full, Li Ch'un-fu's *Ming-tao chi-shuo*[cs] (Collected Plaints Concerning the Way), a key work on the syncretism of the Three Teachings written at the end of the Jurchen Chin. Its original separate edition is now a rare book.[42]

TAOISM AND SYNCRETISM IN THE YÜAN

Taoism functioned in the Yüan, as it had for over a millennium, at many levels, basically divisible into philosophical and religious Taoism. The philosophical legacy of Lao Tzu and Chuang Tzu continued to influence relatively open-minded Confucians and Buddhists as well as Taoists. Institutionally, however, Taoism was represented by the schools of religious Taoism, whose intellectual record was not impressive, at least in the eyes of Confucians and Buddhists.

From Kan Chi^ct (fl. 200) and Chang Ling^cu (fl. 156) of the Later Han to Lu Hsiu-ching^cv (406–477), T'ao Hung-ching^cw (452–536) and K'ou Ch'ien-chih^cx (d. 448), the Taoist leaders relied mostly on religious trappings to attract the lower strata of society. Plagiarized Buddhist scriptures deified Lao Tzu over a broad religious audience. In the Six Dynasties, religious Taoism produced no masters comparable to the Confucian Wang Pi^cy (226–249) or the Buddhist Seng-chao^cz (384–414). During the T'ang Taoists were repeatedly bested by their Buddhist opponents in debates at court.

However, in the Sung and Chin periods, in the development of Ch'üan-chen Taoism under Wang Che^da (1113–1170), religious Taoism began openly to incorporate elements from Confucian and Buddhist thought; their inferior status was a stimulus to syncretism. Other sects of Taoism were also active in this period, but it was the legacy of Ch'üan-chen which was dominant in the Yüan.[43]

Wang Che's teaching was more ethical than religious, stressing purity and reticence in the tradition of Lao Tzu, and in addition loyalty and filiality, reflecting Chinese "national" consciousness. Wang drew parallels with the two established religions and identified his own Taoism with traditional religious Taoism in order to gain support and avert government suspicion of new religions. His disciple Ma Yü^db (Ma Tan-yang, 1123–1183) describes his teacher's respectful behavior toward other religious leaders as stemming from his belief in the unity of the Three Teachings:

The Master [Wang Che] was on his journey to Tung-mou.^dc Whenever he saw a monk [or a Taoist priest] on the road, even if he was not acquainted with him, he would bow to him. A follower asked: "You do not know each other, why should you bow to the man?" The Master said: "The principle of the *Tao* is to be meek and humble, and deferential to others. The Three Teachings have a common entrance [leading to the Way], though they often use their own separate doors. Confucius once said: "[If the search for riches is sure to be successful,] though I should become a groom with a whip in hand [i.e., to take a humble position] to get them, I will do so." What is wrong then if I merely bow to someone?[44]

A poem in his *Ch'ung-yang ch'üan-chen chi*[dd] (Sayings about Preserving the Nature by Master Double Yang, Preface 1183), reads:

The gate to Confucianism and the door to Buddhism share the same approach,
The Three Teachings have always been governed by the same principle.
Perfect enlightenment will bring you entry and exit.
True understanding will let one be broad-minded and unbiased.
For cultivation of the spirit, the *ch'i* and the vitality of us Taoists are the best,
The Sun, the Moon, and the Stars are alike.
Having achieved discernment, mastered texts, and obtained purity,
One watches the vast void above the clear sky.[45]

The Three Teachings are also frequently discussed in the works of his close disciples, such as Ma Yü, Wang Ch'u-i[de] (fl. 1197), T'an Ch'u-tuan[df] (1123–1185), and Hao Ta-t'ung[dg] (fl. 1178). Of the seven distinguished disciples of Wang Che, Ch'iu Ch'u-chi was the most famous and the first to establish relations with the Mongols. In 1188 he was summoned by Emperor Shih-tsung of the Chin to explain the chapter on "The Spirit of the Valley" in the *Lao Tzu*. However, Ch'iu asked the Emperor to fast for seven or at least five days before he listened to it. The Emperor was unwilling to submit to such an ordeal, even though Ch'iu lowered his request to three days.[46] Three decades later (1222), he met Chinggis Khan and tried to use that connection to further the interests of the Ch'üan-chen Sect.

Although Ch'iu did not write about the Three Teachings, Yin Chih-p'ing[dh] (1169–1251), his disciple and successor as the Patriarch of the Ch'ang-ch'un Monastery, wrote of how each of the Three Teachings taught subduing one's *ch'i* in order to let the original illuminated brightness of the mind function:

The Master [Yin] said: "To be commonplace is equivalent to [the attainment of] the Real Constant. The mind is capable of responding to myriad changes, without being moved by [external] objects. Constant response and constant quietude will gradually lead one to the Way and the commonplace is the Way. The reason that many people cannot appreciate being commonplace is because they are not the masters of their minds. Their emotions are influenced by [external] objects and their *ch'i* scatters about in the myriad apertures of the world. Mencius put this rightly: 'The will is the leader of the *ch'i.*' If one is able to control one's *ch'i,* not letting it be scattered about, then it will be transformed into brightness, and the accumulation of such brightnesses will form the Great Brightness. The Master Ch'iu Ch'u-chi once said: 'The Great Brightness is enshrouding the purple-gold lotuses.' The lotuses here allude to the mind, where the intelligence and discernment reside. One will be able to reach the stage [of Great Brightness] only when one is able to be commonplace first. The 'dual medium' taught by Confucius is also meant to be commonplace. There is also the saying: 'The original nature of the Buddha does not imply enlightenment, nor have the masses been led astray. Wherever one's mind is stirred, there is a commonplace thought, it is the *bodhi* and nothing else.' [In the *Lao Tzu* we have:] 'Woe to him who wilfully innovates while ignoring what is constant,' and 'Knowledge of the constant is known as discernment!' " Then his disciples asked: "Do you mean that our teaching is no different from that of the Buddhists?" The Master said: "In principle there is no difference." The teaching of the Buddha, the teaching of our doctrine, and the conventional teaching [i.e., Confucianism] all contain wonderful principles. If one is able to grasp this with one's mind and nature, the Way will be perceived automatically. When that time comes, even the mind and nature may be forgotten.[47]

Some Taoists, however, took a disdainful attitude toward other religions in the Yüan. Ting I-tung[di] (fl. 1300) collated a collection of Sung and Yüan commentaries on the *Lao Tzu* in which he opposed Confucian and Buddhist interpretations of the work. He wrote:

There have been so many scholars interpreting the *Lao Tzu.* The Confucian scholars interpret it in accordance with what they believe to be the *tao.* [The works of] Ch'eng T'ai-chih[dj] [Ching Ta-ch'ang, 1123–1195] and Lin Chu-ch'i[dk] [Lin Hsi-i, fl. 1261] belong to this category. The Buddhists interpret it in accordance with what they believe to be the *hsing*[dl] (nature). [The works of] Su Ying-pin[dm] [Ch'e, 1039–1112] and Pen-jan Tzu[dn] [Shao Jo-yü, fl. 1159] belong to this category. None of them has grasped its real meaning. For the *tao* of the Confucianists is the way of arranging for our daily life and affairs, and the *tao* of Lao Tzu is the principle of voidness and spontaneity. How is it possible for us to force upon it a Confucian interpretation? The *hsing* of the Buddhists is the nature of complete nakedness, while the *tao* of Lao Tzu is the wonderful abstruseness of both the spirit and the body. How is it possible for us to force upon it a Buddhist interpretation?[48]

If some Taoists were disdainful of Confucianism and Buddhism, however, many members of the Ch'üan-chen and the Cheng-i[do] Sects, the mainstays of Taoism, advocated a friendly and reconciliatory attitude, particularly after their defeat in the debates over forged texts. The Ch'üan-chen priest Lin Tao-huang[dp] (alias Ch'ang-huang, fl. 1294) published a

"Diagram of the One and the Same Origin of the Three Teachings" (San-chiao t'ung-yüan p'i-shuo)[dq] in the form of a circle, the center of which is marked yüan-i[dr] ("the original one") with three lines of equal length radiating from it and indicating the syncretism of the Three Schools.[49] Lin's diagram symbolizes the syncretic openness of his school.

There were Yüan Taoists known for their use of Confucian and Neo-Confucian ideas in interpreting Taoism. Teng Ch'i[ds] (fl. 1298), in his commentaries on the Lao Tzu, cited Shao Yung's (1011–1077) Huang-chi ching-shih shu[dt] (Supreme Principles Governing the World) alongside "canonical" teachers of the Southern School and Ch'üan-chen Taoism.[50] Tu Tao-chien[du] (fl. 1306) was indebted to Shao Yung in his Hsüan-ching yüan-chih fa-hui[dv] (Further Studies in the Philosophy of Lao Tzu), and his interpretation of the Lao Tzu incorporated material from the Book of Changes, Book of Documents, and Mencius.[51]

The syncretic flavor of Yüan Taoism, however, is perhaps clearest in the writings of Li Tao-ch'un,[dw] a Ch'üan-chen priest whose works incorporate elements of all Three Teachings, especially his collection entitled Chung-ho chi[ds] (Collected Essays on the Doctrine of the Mean). In his essay "The Essential Teaching of Abstruseness" (Hsüan-men tsung-chich),[dy] he illustrated the "Essential Teaching" by drawing a circle with the following explanation:

The Buddhists call it yüan-chüeh[dz] ("complete enlightenment"), the Taoists "the Golden Pill," and the Confucians "the Great Ultimate." What is meant by the nonultimate and also the Great Ultimate is what is beyond reach and is still within reach. The Buddhist work describes it as "motionless" like "thusness," and "clear" like "the constant knowledge"; the Book of Changes says that it is "still and unmoving, but when acted upon, it penetrates forthwith"; and the Taoist text says that "when both the body and the mind are motionless, the true sign of the nonultimate will appear as the wonderful root of the Great Ultimate." From this we know that what is thought to be desired by the Three Teachings is tranquility and quietude. It is what Master Chou [Tun-i] described as "the mastery of quietude." For the state of the human mind is tranquil and quiet. Before the mind feels anything, everything in it is the principle of Heaven, which is calm and profound. It is the abstruseness of the Great Ultimate. When it feels, it is the movement of the Great Ultimate and is bound to be one-sided. While the mind is in the state of tranquility and quietude and care is given to what it nourishes, the principle of Heaven will remain constantly bright within one, and one's mind will be calm, intelligent, and clear. When it moves, it is the master of itself and is capable of making a suitable response to all things. When one is thoroughly familiar with the cultivation of the mind, one's responses will be spontaneous.

Then the thusness of the nonultimate will be recovered and the wonderful response of the Great Ultimate understood. All the principles of Heaven and Earth and of the myriad things will be epitomized in one.[52]

Li also wrote an essay entitled "A Eulogy of the Diagram of the Great Ultimate" (*T'ai-chi-t'u sung*)[ea] with an explanation of the Diagram of the Great Ultimate.[53]

CONFUCIANISM AND SYNCRETISM IN THE YÜAN

The Confucians and the Mongols started out from a base of mutual suspicion and distrust. On the Confucian side, the Mongol rulers were foreigners who did not embrace Confucian moral values and educational policies in their style of ruling; hence Confucians believed it was not ethical to serve the regime. Other Confucians felt called upon to educate the Mongols in Confucian values, and this was all the more important because the Neo-Confucian philosophy which had emerged in the South during the Southern Sung was virtually unknown in the North where the Mongols had their base. The transforming influence of these teachings was not going to affect government unless some Confucians took up an active role.

From the Mongol side Confucianism seemed to them, at least at first, to be simply another Chinese religion. In 1235 Yao Shu had been ordered "to seek out . . . [distinguished] Confucians, Buddhists, Taoists, and physicians and fortune-tellers for the court." It is obvious from Ögödei's order to Yao Shu that in the eyes of the Mongols a Confucian enjoyed the same status as a follower of the other two teachings, i.e., that of a religious preacher. Shamanism had been the dominant religion in their tribal life, and the subtle distinction between a religious preacher and a cultural and ethical mentor, who was simultaneously a political administrator, was not quite clear in their mind. Thus:

When Hsien-tsung [Möngke, r. 1251–1259] came to the throne, Kao Chih-yao[eb] [d. after 1268] had an audience with him and told how the Confucian scholars had learned the teachings of Yao, Shun, Yü, T'ang, King Wen, and King Wu.[ec] Since antiquity, those responsible for the empire who followed the teachings of these wise rulers were able to maintain order; those who did not, failed. Confucian scholars should be exempted from the corvée so that they could study. The Emperor asked: "How do the Confucians compare with the shamans and practitioners of medicine?"[54]

Also in the second year of Möngke's rule (1252), the official Chang Te-hui[ed] (1195–1274) and the ex-Chin scholar-poet Yüan Hao-wen[ee] (1190–1257) asked Prince Khubilai to accept the title of "Grand Patriarch of the Confucian Teaching" (*Ju-chiao ta tsung-shih*).[ef] The title "Grand Patriarch" has distinctively religious connotations, and they apparently tried to manipulate the Mongols' belief in Confucianism as a religion to advance their cause.[55]

It took time for the Mongols to understand the social position of Confucianism and for Neo-Confucian ideas to be accepted in North China. Hsü Heng[eg] (1209–1281) had a role in both. He had benefitted by the commentaries on the Classics written by the Ch'eng brothers and Chu Hsi, brought to the north by Chao Fu and Yao Shu. When Khubilai was still a prince in charge of the administration of the Shensi and Honan areas, Hsü Heng was made an educational intendant in the prefectures of Huai-chou[eh] and Meng-chou.[ei 56] After Khubilai ascended the throne, Hsü became Chancellor of the Imperial College at Yen-ching, the new capital. Among Hsü's students there were a number of very bright young Mongol scholars as well as Central and Western Asians, some of whom had come to serve the court as hostages. One of his former students, An-t'ung[ej] (1245–1293), was the Chancellor of the Right in the Central Secretariat in 1265.[57]

As an orthodox Neo-Confucian at the court of alien rulers, Hsü Heng tried to reconcile his service of the oppressive Mongols with his sense of Confucian duty, citing Confucius as his authority against loyalist claims that the Mongols did not have Heaven's mandate to rule. He said:

The mind of the sage is the mind of Heaven and Earth. But in one's everyday conduct, it should be guided by rituals and righteousness. Whether or not they [the conquerors] had received the mandate is not the main concern. If we took the view that whoever was opposed by Confucius could not have been favored by Heaven, I am afraid that this view would be too idealistic and not supported by the facts of history. For instance, [Confucius] had refused to meet Chao Chien-tzu[ek] at a time when the family of Chao was on the ascendant. He had memorialized the ruler to send troops to punish Ch'en Heng[el] [because of his regicidal action] at a time when the clan of Ch'en was prospering. We could condemn [these two men] as unrighteous, but if we say that they were not favored by Heaven, then this would be untrue. . . . This is what I can see at present.[58]

Perhaps because he worked so hard to establish Confucian teachings, he was critical of Buddhist Teachings. He abhorred religious Taoism, disliked philosophical Taoism (i.e., the *Lao Tzu*), and tried very hard to avoid Buddhism. He said: "I am sure that Taoism cannot lead one to enjoy long life or become an immortal. For everything in the world there is a model; for this [immortality or longevity] there is none."[59] Condemning the activities of the Taoist priests of the early Yüan, he said:

Lao Tzu spoke of purity and nonaction as a means through which the people would be spontaneously rectified and transformed. Judging by the present situation, [the Taoists] are unable to take care of even their own mouths, let alone the governing of the world. The fact is that they too have set up offices empowered with the authority to control their members, and levy heavy taxes accompanied by other kinds of adroit means of extortion. Their regulations are numerous. Purity and want of desire, oh my Lord![60]

Theoretically he denounced the *Lao Tzu* as less substantial than the teaching of the *Doctrine of the Mean*.[61] We read in his *Yü-lu:*

The definitions for *tao, te,*[em] humanity, righteousness, rites, and intelligence found in the *Lao Tzu* are entirely different from the definitions given by us Confucians. [The *Lao Tzu*] advocates withdrawal and retirement instead of putting everything on the board. Our principles are open and just, and the rules and regulations are known to everyone.[62]

Despite his allegations that the philosophy of Lao Tzu had some drawbacks, Hsü Heng in his personal conduct was known to have benefited by the practice of it. He admitted that the *Lao Tzu* might be useful in time of disturbances:

Lao Tzu is a book written for a time of decay. Following this course leads to harsh laws and cruelty. One who reads it should know its good points as well as its weaknesses. [Since its appearance] subsequent generations have been even more degenerate and insensitive, unable to compare with the Golden Age of the Three Dynasties, which was honest and pure. [The *Lao Tzu*] might be useful if one put it into practice as Chang Liang[en] [d. 189 B.C.] and Emperor Wen Ti[eo] [r. 179–157 B.C.] did in the Former Han.[63]

In his famous "Five Points on Current Affairs" (*Shih-wu wu-shih*),[ep] a long memorial presented to Khubilai Khaghan, Hsü Heng used the teachings of Lao Tzu to suggest more flexible and gentler approaches to governance:

Your servant had heard that boldness is important in fighting for the world, and withdrawal and retreat are important for keeping it. Without boldness, the world will not submit to you; without practicing withdrawal and retreat, you will be unable to keep what you have got. There are different tactics to handle different situations. This is what the ruler of men should examine.[64]

In his private communications and contacts with friends, his own philosophy of history and destiny sometimes sounds more Taoist than Confucian. For instance, he says in his "Letter to Tou Mo" (1196–1280) (*Yü Tou hsien-sheng shu*),[eq]

Fate is conditioned by time, and time by general tendency. The general tendency cannot be resisted, and the [opportune] time cannot be flouted. If one bends to and obeys them, no matter whether one advances or retreats, is staying at home or serving the state, is lucky or unlucky, is gaining or losing, one can be right all the time. . . . Contrariwise, if one wishes to impose one's own will [on destiny], starting before it is known, acting before the time is ripe, it will be tantamount to a man pulling out a seedling in the mistaken hope of helping it to grow, or to one who wants to do the chopping for the Master Carpenter. Pulling out the shoots hurts the grain, and chopping wood for the Master Carpenter hurts one's own hand.[65]

This is similar to what is said in his *Yü-lu*:

All the affairs in the world from ancient times to the present can be interpreted as the warring of two sides against one another. They can also be likened to the vying for superiority between the *yin* and the *yang*, the hard and the soft, or to the wrestling between two sides. If one wins, the other will lose, and vice versa. However, it is often the case that the winner will not stop on reaching the limit and will fight on until he goes too far. The loser will not regain his strength until he has suffered to the extreme. Because each side is not content with its lot, fighting and retaliation continue and never cease.[66]

In South China, where Neo-Confucianism was more firmly established, syncretic tendencies were even more marked. While Hsü Heng was from the North, Wu Ch'eng (1249–1333) came from the South. His native place was Ch'ung-jen, Fu-chou[er] (Kiangsi). At the end of the Southern Sung he was about 30 years old. In the course of his early pursuit of Neo-Confucianism he had studied under three teachers: Tai Liang-ch'i[es] (*chin-shih* of 1238), Ch'eng Jo-yung[et] (*chin-shih* of 1268), and Ch'eng Shao-k'ai[eu] (1212–1280).[67] Both Tai and Ch'eng Jo-yung were scholars who followed Chu Hsi's commentaries of the Classics, but Ch'eng Shao-k'ai had originally been a follower of Lu Hsiang-shan's school. Later he argued that Chu Hsi and Lu Hsiang-shan shared much common ground.[68] Some time between 1314 and 1320 he built a Tao-i[ev] Academy in Hsin-chou,[ew] Kiangsi, to commemorate the contributions of these two great scholars and his own syncretical views. To some extent, Wu Ch'eng's syncretism must have been derived from Ch'eng Shao-k'ai.

While studying under Ch'eng Jo-yung at the Lin-juᵉˣ Academy, Fu-chou, Wu had a classmate, Ch'eng Chü-fuᵉʸ (1249–1318). Ch'eng Chü-fu later went over to the Yüan as a hostage after his uncle had surrendered the city of Chien-ch'angᵉᶻ (Kiangsi) to the Mongols. In 1286 Ch'eng Chü-fu, partly in response to continued guerrilla resistance in the area, was sent to the South by Khubilai to recruit Chinese scholars to serve him. The edict in this case was written in Chinese and not in Mongol in order to show Khubilai's sincerity and admiration for Chinese culture.[69] Wu went to Yen-ching the next year, but returned home after a stay of less than one year without committing himself to a post in the capital. On his return he accepted some minor jobs at home and in 1302 revisited Yen-ching. In 1309 he was appointed a Proctor at the Imperial College in the capital, and in 1311, he became the Director of Studies. Thus he reconciled himself over time to serving the Mongol administration.[70]

Wu was educated in the thought of the orthodox Ch'eng-Chu School. However, his praise of Lu Hsiang-shan shows his profound admiration. In his "Preface to Lu Hsiang-shan's *Yü-lu*" he says:

The teaching [of Master Lu] is as bright as broad daylight, and his words as loud as a thunder-clap. Even when one reads them more than a hundred years after his time, one still feels as if one is being taught by him personally . . . There are many scholars here and there at present who have shown admiration for the Master. But I wish to know, is there anyone who really understands his sayings? Is there anyone who really wants to put his words into practice?[71]

However, he saw Lu Hsiang-shan's teaching, not as unique, but as a focus on the naturally endowed sagely mind taught by many Neo-Confucians, whether followers of Chu or Lu. "The cultivation of one's mind . . . was a common heritage [from the ancient sages] to Shao, Chou, Chang, and the Ch'eng brothers. Those who believe that Mister Lu worked alone in this field do not really understand the teaching of the Sages."[72] He sought to reconcile Chu's investigation of the principles of things, and Lu's honoring the moral nature by not losing the original mind:

In man's daily communications and social contacts there are myriad changes and thousands of variations, each of them a new discovery of the mind. If every response one makes is in the direction of Principle, then one understands what "not losing one's original mind" means. The cultivation of the mind is not merely sitting in quietude and abandoning all the other things.[73]

In an essay entitled "Bidding Farewell to Mr. Ch'en Hung-fan"[fa] he wrote:

The process of learning advocated by Chu Hsi was reading and discussing. The teaching of Lu Hsiang-shan was grasping of true knowledge and putting it into practice. As a matter of fact, reading and discussing are the means for searching for true knowledge and preparing for practice, and the grasping of true knowledge and practicing it cannot be entirely severed from reading and discussion. The teachings of these two masters are but one.[74]

Wu Ch'eng's syncretic attitude did not function only with regard to Confucianism; he was open to philosophical Taoism as well. In an essay entitled "The Studio of Deep Quietude" (Yüan-mo chai chi)[fb] he states:

If there is something contrary in the Chuang Tzu to our teachings with regard to human relationships and common sense, we should, of course, not follow it. However, if in its depth of philosophical approach there is something agreeable to our teachings, we may still follow it. In doing so, we won't be following Chuang Tzu but our sages.[75]

He also compared the sayings in the Chuang Tzu with those of the Sung Neo-Confucians:

Master Ch'eng said that "if one's nature was quiet, one was capable of learning." The venerable Chu-ko [Liang][fc] [181–234] said that "without quiescence one's scholarship could not be accomplished." The quiescence required there was easy for everyone to strive to achieve. Master Chou [Tun-i] said that "the sage regulated [the myriad affairs] by the principle of the Mean, rectitude, humanity and righteousness, considering tranquility [quietude] to be the ruling factor": and in the Chuang Tzu it is said that the state of quiescence is reached when none of the myriad affairs is capable of disturbing one's mind. The quietude required here is more difficult to achieve, and one may not be able to do it unless one has grasped the teaching of the sage. The Great Learning says: "That calmness [quietude] will be succeeded by a tranquil repose." It is just the same as what has been pointed out by Master Chou and the Chang Tzu.[76]

The fact that Wu Ch'eng was very fond of the Chuang Tzu and the Lao Tzu may be supported by essays about them included in his collected works.[77] His Commentaries on the Lao Tzu and his Edited Texts of the First Seven Chapters of the Chuang Tzu are included in the Taoist Canon (Tao-tsang, nos. 392–393 and 497 respectively).

He was less interested in religious Taoism, but followed in the footsteps of Chu Hsi, who before him had written a commentary on the Ts'an-t'ung-ch'i[fd] (1197) using a Taoist pseudonym.[78] He deliberately sought out Taoist masters with a reputation for lofty virtue and an ascetic spiritual life. All in all, Wu Ch'eng was a Yüan Neo-Confucian who had less regard for doctrinal labels than for the quality of religious life and philosophical reflection. He represents the apogee of Confucian syncretism in the Yüan.

CONCLUSION

During the Yüan period there were tensions and hostilities between the three teachings of China in their various schools, but the need to court Mongol patronage and avert repression of native traditions stimulated openness and tolerance. The situation demanded the reconciliation of divergent philosophies and hostile religious factions. When in 1291 a Ch'an monk, Hsiang-mai, compiled his (*Chih-yüan*) *Pien-wei lu* to record the events of the debate on the doubtful authenticity of the Taoist scriptures, he summarized his views as follows:

Confucianism, Taoism, and Buddhism are the Three Teachings known to the world. [As to the ultimate goal of] punishing the evil and encouraging the good, it is common to the three of them [and it does not matter which course one takes]. As to their essential ideas, I cannot say that there is not much difference between them. There has been a consensus on this since Han-T'ang times, and there is no need for others to make free statements without careful thought. The merit of Lao Tzu's philosophy is humility in order to avoid harm. The teaching of Confucianism places primacy on loyalty and filial piety and serving people. When loyalty and filial piety prevail in the country, families can be protected and individual lives prolonged. When humility prevails, controversy can be resolved and danger averted. When compassion prevails, many lives can be saved and the aim of life and nature fulfilled. They are complementary like the surface and lining of a garment, reflecting one another like the rays of the sun, the moon, and the stars, and supporting one another like the three legs of a tripod. But there is a difference in some degree. The Taoists believe in texts which are forged. Their aim is to establish a superstructure embracing past and present and superseding both Confucianism and Buddhism.[79]

All three teachings have a place, he believes, so long as one does not try to dominate. Popular literature was also influenced by syncretic trends and the "Sages of the Three Teachings" cropped up in Yüan drama as well as in other writings.[80] Thus the Yüan dynasty in Chinese history was a great period of syncretism and assimilation.

The extraordinary ability and adaptability of the Three Teachings, despite the altercations, brings to mind a poem written by a talented wife of Chao Meng-fu[fe] (1254–1322), a famous calligrapher and painter of the early Yüan who declined an invitation to serve the Mongol government.[81] This poem, though personal, seems to illustrate the interrelationship between the Three Teachings so aptly that I would like to quote it in conclusion:

> Twixt you and me
> There's too much emotion,
> That's the reason why
> There's such a commotion!
> Take a lump of clay
> Wet it, pat it,
> and make an image of me,
> and an image of you.
> Then smash them, crash them,
> and add a little water.
> Break them and remake them
> into an image of you,
> and an image of me.
> Then in my clay, there's a little of you.
> And in your clay, there's a little of me.[82]

NOTES

Abbreviations used in notes:

T   *Taishō shinshū daizōkyō*[ff] (Tokyo: Taishō issaikyo kankōkwai, 1924–1932).
TT *Tao-tsang* (Shanghai: Commercial Press photolithographic ed., 1924–1926).

1. *Wu Wen-cheng chi*[fg] (SKCSCP 2d ser., Taipei, Commercial Press, 1971), 49:3a.
2. The existing records are found in the *Chi ku-chin fo-tao lun-heng*[fh] (Record of Debates between Buddhists and Taoists Past and Present), a work compiled by Monk Tao-hsüan[fi] (596–667), included in T no. 2104.
3. One resulted in an altercation between the famous Monk Hsüan-tsang[fj] (602–664) and some thirty-odd Taoist priests in 647 at the court of Emperor T'ang T'ai-tsung (r. 627–649) during consultations on some of the problems encountered in the process of translating the *Lao Tzu* into Sanskrit. See *Chi ku-chin fo-tao lun-heng, chüan ting,* 386.
4. See Karl A. Wittfogel and Feng Chia-sheng, *History of Chinese Society: Liao* (Philadelphia: American Philosophical Society, 1949), pp. 291–309; also *Liao shih*[fk] (Peking: Chung-hua shu-chü, 1974), 37:441; 14:156; 22:267; 115:1527.
5. *Ibid.,* 8:94; 20:24; 22:266, 270; 25:295; 60:931. For "er-shui hu" and taxation in Liao times in general, see Wittfogel and Feng, pp. 335–345. See also Nogami Shunjō, *Ryōkin no Bukkyō*[fl] (Kyoto: Heirakuji shōten, 1953), pp. 244–60.
6. *Chin shih*[fm] (Peking: Chung-hua shu-chü, 1975), 50:1124; 10:241; 46:1030. Cf. also *ibid.,* 14:319. Such practices became necessary later because of excessive military expenditures.
7. The leading Chin scholar-official, Hanlin Academician Chao Ping-wen[fn] (1159–1232), was severely criticized for the admixture of the two teachings in his essay "On the Origin of the Doctrine" (*Yüan-chiao*)[fo] in Huang Tsung-hsi's SYHA (SPPY ed.), 100:4a. This essay is included in his *Hsien-hsien lao-jen Hu-shui wen-chi*[fp] (SPTK ed.), 1:1a–2b. For his biography, see *Chin shih,* 110:2426. Li Ch'un-fu (P'ing-shan), a distinguished Chin advocate of syncretism, grouped together Lao Tzu, Confucius, Mencius, Chuang Tzu, and the Tathāgata as the Five Sages of the world in his *Ming-tao chi-shuo.* He was also well known for his outspokenness in regard to Neo-Confucianism and Buddhism. See his biography in *Chin shih,* 126:2734 and SYHA, 100:2b–3b. For studies on Li Ch'un-fu, see the paper by Jan Yün-hua included in this volume, note 13.
8. Thus, Fan Tsu-yu[fq] (1041–1098), in his "Essay on the 'Doctrine of the Mean' " (*Chung-yung lun*),[fr] commented: "The words in the *Lao Tzu* and the *Chuang Tzu* show too much concern for oneself and too little concern for others" (SYHA, 21:6a). And Ch'en Ch'un[fs] (1153–1217) also said: "Rituals and regulations are the main part of the institution where the principle and righteousness are embodied. Each item and every detail reveal a careful

consideration of the ancients. Were we to put them aside, would we not be in danger of falling into the state of emptiness and nonbeing of Buddhism and Taoism?" (SYHA, 68:7a). Wei Liao-weng[ft] (1178–1237), a scholar and statesman of the Southern Sung, summarizing the situation at the end of the dynasty, lamented: "Emptiness and void—these are the elements harmful to *tao*. But the present situation is again different from what it was when the Buddhist and Taoist teachings begin to thrive. It is the huge expenses for the penitential masses and the costly extravagance in building their monasteries . . . that are the worries of the gentlemen of the time" (SYHA, 80:7b).

9. Ou-yang Hsiu[fu] (1007–1072), the famous historian and man of letters, was the first to cast a skeptical eye on the authenticity of the "Ten Appendices" (*Shih-i*)[fv] to the *Book of Changes*. Ssu-ma Kuang[fw] (1019–1086), another great historian and Confucian scholar, in his article "I Meng"[fx] (Doubts about Mencius), criticized severely the arguments contained in the *Mencius*. See SYHA, 4:8b–11b and 7:5a–12b. Cf. Ch'ü Wan-li, "Sung-jen i ching ti feng-ch'i,"[fy] *Ta-lu tsa-chih*[fz] (August 1964), 29(3):23–25.

10. Posts with high responsibilities (i.e., appointments as imperial envoys or supervisors at the Taoist monasteries) were usually offered to retired officials at various levels as a mark of good will on the part of Sung emperors. See Akizuki Kan'ei, "Shōyōsan Gyokuryō Banjukyū to Sōdai jinshi,"[ga] in *Yoshioka Yoshitoyo hakushi kanreki kinen Dōkyō kenkyū ronshū*[gb] (Tokyo: Gakushō kankōkai, 1977), pp. 533–44.

11. SYHA, 40:10a.

12. For the title of the State Preceptor, see Paul Pelliot, "Le kuou-che," *T'oung Pao* (1911), 12:671–76. For the reading of the name of Na-mo, see Iwai Hirosato, *Nisshi Bukkyō shi*[gc] (Tokyo: Tōyō Bunko, 1950), p. 510.

13. YS (Peking: Chung-hua shu-chü, 1976), 77:1926.

14. *Ibid.*

15. YS, 202:4522; see also *ibid.*, 12:242; 130:3166; 144:3438. Cf. Giuseppe Tucci, *Tibetan Painted Scrolls* (Rome: Libreria dello stato, 1949), vol. 1, pp. 31–32.

16. YS, 23:512, 202:4522.

17. There were some brave souls who refused to accept second place to the Tibetans, as seen in the following story: "[It was about 1329], the Imperial Preceptor [Rin c'en grags pa] arrived in the capital. There was an edict that courtiers and officials of the first grade and below were to ride on white horses and greet him outside the city. The ministers were ordered to bow to him most reverently and offer a drink. Po-chu-lu Ch'ung[gd] [1279–1338, a Jurchen] advanced holding a cup of wine in his hand and said: 'The Imperial Preceptor is a follower of Śākyamuni and the master of all Buddhist monks under Heaven. I am a follower of Confucius who is the teacher of all Confucian scholars under Heaven. Perhaps we do not need to bow to each other.' The Imperial Preceptor laughed, took the cup which Ch'ung had offered him and drank it all. All other people trembled with fear" (YS, 183:4222).

18. The biography of Li Te-hui[ge] (1218–1280) in YS, 163:3818, for example,

states that the purpose of such massacres was plunder. One, however, must also take into consideration the psychological effect of such a genocide calculated by the Mongols when planning their war strategy.

19. For instance, when during the siege of the Chin capital Pien (Kaifeng, Honan) in spring 1232 the Mongols requested its surrender, one of their demands was to send "members of twenty-seven families, including those of the Hanlin Academician Chao Ping-wen, K'ung Yüan-ts'o (a descendant of Confucius), and the wife and children of [the Chin generals] who had already submitted to the Mongols, and several tens of women skilled in embroidery, as well as bow makers and falconers." See *Chin shih*, 17:386.

20. YS, 153:3612. See also Sun K'o-k'uan, *Yüan-tai Han wen-hua chih huo-tung*[gf] (Taipei: Chung-hua shu-chü, 1968), pp. 331–37.

21. YS, 147:3474; Sun K'o-k'uan, pp. 279–83.

22. YS, 189:4313ff. See also the paper by Wing-tsit Chan included in this volume, esp. notes 2 and 3.

23. YS, 189:4314.

24. *Ibid.*, 146:3455. Cf. Igor de Rachewiltz, "Yeh-lü Ch'u-ts'ai (1189–1243): Buddhist Idealist and Confucian Statesman," in *Confucian Personalities*, ed. A. F. Wright and D. C. Twitchett (Stanford: Stanford University Press, 1962), pp. 189–216.

25. YS, 146:3459. In Chin times, besides an imperial edict in 1127 proclaiming the absolute necessity of holding the *chin-shih* examinations both in the North and the South (former Sung territory), another significant imperial favor shown to Confucianism was the bestowal in 1140 of the hereditary title Yen-sheng kung[gg] (The Duke Perpetuating the Line of Sagehood) upon K'ung Fan[gh] (d. 1142), the alleged forty-ninth-generation descendant of Confucius. See *Chin shih*, 3:57; 4:76. On the latter, see Yao Ts'ung-wu[gi] in *Bulletin of the Institute of History and Philology, Academia Sinica* (October 1969), 34:189–96. See also the paper by Jan Yün-hua included in this volume, note 40.

26. YS, 146:3461.

27. *Ibid.*, 81:2017.

28. *Ibid.*, 81:2019. See also Abe Takeo, "Gendai chishikijin to kakyo,"[gj] *Shirin*[gk] (November 1959), 42(6):113–52.

29. For example, YS, 195:4412, 197:4452.

30. *Fo-tsu li-tai t'ung-tsai* (T no. 2036), 22:720. Chih-p'an, *Fo-tsu t'ung-chi*[gl] (T no. 2035), 48:435, recorded that the Emperor was somehow displeased with the words of the Ch'an masters, but it could have been a partisan view. The *Shih-shih chi-ku lüeh hsü-chi* by Huan-lun[gm] (T no. 2038), 1:907, tallies with the *Fo-tsu li-tai t'ung-tsai*. For the notorious activities of Yan-lien-chen-chia, see Nogami Shunjō, *Genshi Shakuroden no kenkyū*[gn] (Kyoto: Hoyū shōten, 1978), pp. 240ff, esp. 251–58.

31. *Hsü Chih-yüeh lu*[go] (Sequel to the Records of Pointing at the Moon) (Taipei: Chen-shan-mei photolithographic ed. of 1886, 1968), 4:17a. Cf. Nishio Kenryū "Genchō no kōnan tōji ni okeru Bukkyō,"[gp] *Bukkyō shigaku*[gq] (October 1971), 15(2):84–104.

32. For instance, Yao Shu, other ministers, such as Tou Mo, Chang Wen-ch'ien[gr] (1217–1284), and the famous Uighur Confucian scholar Lien Hsi-hsien[gs] (1231–1280). See *Pien-wei lu* (T no. 2116), 4:771. Professor Ch'en Yüan erred in suggesting that Monk Fu-yü was from the Shao-lin Monastery of Mt. Sung (Honan); see his *Nan-Sung ch'u Ho-pei hsin tao-chiao k'ao*[gt] (Peking: Chung-hua shu-chü, 1962), p. 57. For Liu Ping-chung's role in this debate, see Hok-lam Chan, "Liu Ping-chung (1216–74): A Buddhist-Taoist Statesman at the Court of Khubilai Khan," *T'oung Pao* (1967), 53(1–3):128–30.

33. *Pien-wei lu*, 5:776ff. See also Paul Demiéville, "La situation religieuse en Chine au temps de Marco Polo," *Oriente Poliano* (Rome: Instituto Italiano per il medio ed Estolmo Oriente, 1957), pp. 193–236; Erik Zürcher, *The Buddhist Conquest of China* (Leiden: E. J. Brill, 1959), pp. 288ff; Kenneth K. S. Ch'en, "Buddhist-Taoist Mixtures in the Pa-shih-i-hua t'u," *Harvard Journal of Asiatic Studies* (1945–47), 9:1–12; Joseph Thiel, "Der streit der Buddhisten und Taoisten zur Mongolen-zeit," *Monumenta Serica* (1961), 20:1–80, and Nogami Shunjō, *Genshi Shakuroden*, pp. 143ff.

34. *Pien-wei lu*, 3:769.

35. *Ts'ung-jung (an) lu* (T no. 2004) 1:228. For Tsung-mi, see Jan Yün-hua, "Tsung-mi, His Analysis of Ch'an Buddhism," *T'oung Pao* (1972), 58:1–54.

36. *Lu-shan Lien-tsung pao-chien* (T no. 1973), p. 343.

37. *Ch'an-tsung chüeh-i lu* (T no. 2021), p. 1013. This comparison had been initiated in the fifth century by Emperor Wen Ti (r. 424–453) of Liu-Sung, and it appeared also in the essay "On the Origin of the Tao" (*Yüan-tao lun*)[gu] written by Emperor Hsiao-tsung[gv] (r. 1163–1189) of the Southern Sung, as well as in the writings of Ch'i-sung (1007–1072), a Ch'an monk of the Northern Sung. See *Fo-tsu li-tai t'ung-tsai*, 20:692; Ch'i-sung, *Hsün-chin wen-chi*[gw] (T no. 2115), 16:737.

38. For example, the *Tao-shih fa-lun ching*,[gx] the *Ling-pao hsiao-hun ching*,[gy] and the *Chin-ch'üeh ch'ao-yüan ching*.[gz] These works are not found in the *Tao-tsang*.

39. *Che-i lun* should probably read *Hsi-i lun*.[ha] Cf. T no. 2118, 5:815.

40. T no. 2118, 1:800.

41. Ch'en Yüan criticizes the work as less reliable than other Buddhist histories. See *Chung-kuo fo-chiao shih-chi kai-lun*[hb] (Peking: K'o-hsüeh ch'u-pan she, 1957), pp. 137–38.

42. *Fo-tsu li-tai t'ung-tsai*, 20:695–699. Cf. note 7.

43. In the early Chin (1140), the teaching of the T'ai-i[hc] Sect had been prevalent in Honan. The Ta-tao Sect became popular in Hopei around 1150. The Cheng-i, the Mao-shan, the Hun-yüan,[hd] and other sects were active in the South. See Ch'en Yüan, *Nan-Sung ch'u Ho-pei, passim*, and Sun K'o-k'uan, *Yüan-tai tao-chiao chih fa-chan*[he] (Taichung: Tunghai University, 1968), *passim*. Because of the greater influence of the Ch'üan-chen in Yüan times, we shall concentrate solely on it.

44. *Tan-yang chen-jen yü-lu*[hf] (TT no. 728), 1:1b. The quotation of Confucius'

saying comes from the *Analects*, 7. See James Legge, *The Chinese Classics* (Hong Kong: Hong Kong University Press rpt., 1960), vol. 1, p. 198.

45. *Ch'ung-yang ch'üan-chen chi* (TT no. 793), 1:8a–b.

46. Yin Chih-p'ing, *Ch'ing-ho chen-jen pei-yu yü-lu*[hg] (TT no. 1017), 3:6b–7a.

47. *Ibid.*, 1:3b–4a. For the quotation from Mencius, see James Legge, vol. 2, p. 188.

48. Liu Wei-yung, *Tao-te chen-ching chi-i ta chih*[hh] (TT no. 432), 1:1b–2a. Cf. TT no. 433, 4:21a.

49. *Hsüan-tsung chih-chih wan-fa t'ung-kuei*[hi] (TT no. 734), 1:7a.

50. *Tao-te cheng-ching san-chieh*[hj] (Three Commentaries on the *Tao-te ching*) (TT no. 371), 3:21a–b, 3:27a. For an anthology of Shao Yung's writings, see SYHA, ch. 9–10, and W. T. de Bary et al., eds., *Sources of the Chinese Tradition* (New York: Columbia University Press, 1964), vol. 1, pp. 460–65.

51. *Hsüan-ching yüan-chih fa-hui*[hk] (TT no. 391); Tu Tao-chien, *Tao-te hsüan-ching yüan-chih*[hl] (TT no. 390), preface, 4b.

52. The essay has a preface by Tu Tao-chien dated 1305. See *Chung-ho chi* (TT no. 118), 1:1b–2a.

53. *Ibid.*, 1:3b–13b.

54. YS, 125:3072ff. Cf. Ch'ien Hsing-hai and L. C. Goodrich, tr., *Ch'en Yüan, Western and Central Asians in China under the Mongols* (Los Angeles: Monumenta Serica at U.C.L.A., 1966), p. 19. Kao Chih-yao came from a Tangut family who had adopted a Chinese name. Many of the Hsi-hsia people had studied classical Chinese and Chih-yao had a *chin-shih* degree from that kingdom.

55. YS, 163:3824. Cf. Yao Ts'ung-wu in *Ta-lu tsa-chih* (February 1963), 26(3):6–9, and Hok-lam Chan, "Liu Ping-chung," p. 120, note 42.

56. On An-t'ung, see YS, 126:3082. See also Igor de Rachewiltz, "Muqali, Bōl, Tas and An-t'ung," *Papers on Far Eastern History* (March 1977), 15:56–58.

57. On Hsü Heng, see YS, 158:3716; SYHA, 90:1b. Cf. the references cited in Wing-tsit Chan's paper included in this volume, note 12.

58. *Lu-chai i-shu*[hm] (SKCSCP 4th ser.) (Taipei: Commercial Press, 1973), 8:1a–b.

59. *Ibid.*, 2:24b–25a.

60. *Ibid.*, 2:28a.

61. *Ibid.*, 5:2b.

62. *Ibid.*, 1:17b.

63. *Ibid.*

64. *Ibid.*, 7:17b.

65. *Ibid.*, 9:3a–b. The classical allusions in the last part of this passage come from *Mencius* and *Lao Tzu*. See James Legge, vol. 2, p. 191, and D. C. Lau, tr., Lao Tzu, *Tao-te ching* (London: Penquin Books, 1963), p. 136. For Tou Mo's biography, see YS, 158:3730.

66. *Lu-chai i-shu*, 1:26b–27a.

67. On Wu Ch'eng, see YS, 171:4011; SYHA 92:1a. Cf. the references cited in

David Gedalecia's paper included in this volume, esp. note 1. For Tai Liang-ch'i, Ch'eng Jo-jung, and Ch'eng Shao-k'ai, see SYHA, 66:7a; 83:4a; 84:6a.

68. *Ibid.*, 84:6b.
69. On Ch'eng Chü-fu, see YS, 172:4015; SYHA, 83:10a. For his mission to south China to recruit scholars for the Mongol court, see Sun K'o-k'uan, *Yüan-tai Han wen-hua*, pp. 345–63.
70. See note 67.
71. *Wu Wen-cheng chi*, 17:14a–b.
72. *Ibid.*, 48:13b.
73. *Ibid.*
74. *Ibid.*, 27:18b.
75. *Ibid.*, 5:4a.
76. *Ibid.*, 63:1a–b. For Chu-ko Liang's quotation, see *Chu-ko Wu-hou wen chi*[hn] (*Cheng-i t'ang ch'üan-shu*[ho] ed., 1868), 1:22a. For Chou Tun-i's, see *Chou Lien-ch'i hsien-sheng ch'üan-chi*[hp] (*Cheng-i t'ang ch'üan-shu* ed.) 1:2a. For that of *Chuang Tzu*, see James Legge, *The Sacred Books: The Texts of Taoism* (New York: Dover Publications, 1962 rep. of 1891 ed.), p. 330. For that of the *Great Learning*, see James Legge, *The Chinese Classics*, vol. 1, p. 357.
77. *Wu Wen-cheng chi*, 1:36b–38a, 17:13a.
78. *Ibid.*, 15:5b; 58:2b. Chu Hsi's commentary is found in TT no. 623, *hsia*, 8a.
79. *Pien-wei lu* (T no. 2116), 2:763.
80. Fan Tzu-an, "Ch'en Chi-ch'ing wu-shang chu-yeh chou,"[hq] Act I, 3a, in *Yüan-ch'ü hsüan*[hr] (SPPY ed.), vol. 3. An immediate example of amalgamation which can be seen in North America is the thirteenth- and fourteenth-century frescoes (from Shansi) donated by Sir Joseph Flavelle to the Royal Ontario Museum, Toronto, in which images of bodhisattvas and Taoist polar-gods are found on the same walls.
81. See F. W. Mote, "Confucian Eremitism in the Yüan Period," in *The Confucian Persuasion*, ed. A. F. Wright (Stanford: Stanford University Press, 1960), pp. 236–38.
82. It was written by Madame Chao (Kuan Tao-sheng,[hs] 1262–1319) when her husband in his middle age thought of taking a concubine. Moved by the poem, he changed his mind. This poem is found in Shen Hsiung, *Ku-chin tz'u-hua*,[ht] *chüan hsia*, included in T'ang Kuei-chang, ed., *Tz'u-hua ts'ung-p'ien*[hu] (Taipei: Kuang-wen shu-chü rep., 1967), vol. 3, p. 780. Translation follows Lin Yutang, *The Importance of Living* (New York: Reynal Press, 1937), p. 183.

GLOSSARY

a 吳澄
b 二稅戶
c 世宗
d 二氏
e 陸象山
f 語錄
g 道藏
h 白玉蟾
i 大慧宗杲
j 國師
k 那摩
l 燕京（大都）
m 帝師
n 至元
o 大明殿
p 關羽
q 宣政院
r 金門大社
s 郊坊司
t 雲和署
u 箏簇
v 琵琶
w 興和署
x 祥和署
y 儀鳳司
z 河西
aa 泰定
ab 李昌
ac 平涼、靜寧、會州、定西
ad 奉元
ae 王檝
af 岐陽
ag 張柔
ah 蔡州
ai 楊惟中
aj 趙復
ak 乙未
al 德安

am 姚樞
an 程顥、程頤
ao 朱熹
ap 太極書院
aq 周敦頤
ar 張載
as 楊時
at 游酢
au 耶律楚材
av 李純甫（屛山）
aw 孔元措
ax 蔡沈
ay 胡安國
az 禮記
ba 華嚴
bb 楊璉眞加
bc 釋教總統
bd 紹興
be 妙高
bf 仙林
bg 百法論
bh 靜伏
bi 靈隱
bj 德山
bk 臨濟
bl 全眞
bm 丘處機（長春）
bn 福裕
bo 少林
bp 至溫
bq 子聰
br 劉秉忠
bs 祥邁，［至元］辯僞錄
bt 張志敬
bu 李志常
bv 合台薩哩
bw 祁志誠
bx 張宗演

by 李德和   dm 蘇穎濱（轍）
bz 杜福春   dn 本然子（邵若愚）
ca 大道   do 正一
cb 從倫   dp 林道晃（常晃）
cc 吉祥   dq 三教同源譬說
cd 行秀（萬松）   dr 元一
ce 從容（庵）錄   ds 鄧錡
cf 氣   dt 邵雍，皇極經世書
cg 圭峯（宗密）   du 杜道堅
ch 曹洞   dv 玄經原旨發揮
ci 普度   dw 李道純
cj 天台   dx 中和集
ck 廬山蓮宗寶鑑   dy 玄門宗旨
cl 智徹   dz 圓覺
cm 禪宗決疑錄   ea 太極圖頌
cn 孔子家語   eb 高智耀
co 妙明，折疑論   ec 堯舜禹湯文武
cp 無爲   ed 張德輝
cq 念常   ee 元好問
cr 佛祖歷代通載   ef 儒教大宗師
cs 鳴道集說   eg 許衡
ct 干吉   eh 懷州
cu 張陵   ei 孟州
cv 陸修靜   ej 安童
cw 陶弘景   ek 趙簡子
cx 寇謙之   el 陳恒
cy 王弼   em 德
cz 僧肇   en 張艮
da 王嘉   eo 文帝
db 馬鈺（馬丹陽） ep 時務五事
dc 東牟   eq 與寶先生書
dd 重陽全眞集   er 崇仁，撫州
de 王處一   es 戴艮齊
df 譚處端   et 程若庸
dg 郝大通   eu 程紹開
dh 尹志平   ev 道一書院
di 丁易東   ew 信州
dj 程泰之（大昌） ex 臨汝書院
dk 林竹溪（希逸） ey 程鉅夫
dl 性   ez 建昌

fa 陳洪範

fb 淵默齋記

fc 諸葛亮

fd 參同契

fe 趙孟頫

ff 大正新修大藏經

fg 吳文正集

fh 集古今佛道論衡

fi 道宣

fj 玄奘

fk 遼史

fl 野上俊静，遼金の佛教

fm 金史

fn 趙秉文

fo 原教

fp 閑閑老人滏水文集

fq 范祖禹

fr 中庸論

fs 陳淳

ft 魏了翁

fu 歐陽修

fv 十翼

fw 司馬光

fx 疑孟

fy 屈萬里，宋人疑經的風氣

fz 大陸雜誌

ga 秋月観暎，逍遥山玉隆万寿宮と宋代人士

gb 吉岡博士還暦紀念道教研究論集

gc 岩井大慧，日支佛教史

gd 孛朮魯翀

ge 李德輝

gf 孫克寬，元代漢文化之活動

gg 衍聖公

gh 孔璠

gi 姚從吾

gj 安部健夫，元代知識人と科擧

gk 史林

gl 志磐，佛祖統紀

gm 幻輪，釋氏稽古略續集

gn 續指月錄

go 元史釈老伝の研究

gp 西尾賢隆，元朝の江南統治しこおける仏教

gq 佛教史學

gr 張文謙

gs 廉希賢

gt 陳垣，南宋初河北新道教考

gu 原道論

gv 孝宗

gw 契嵩，鐔津文集

gx 道士法輪經

gy 靈寶消魂安志經

gz 金闕朝元經

ha 析疑論

hb 中國佛教史概論

hc 太一

hd 茅山、混元

he 元代道教之發展

hf 丹陽眞人語錄

hg 清河眞人北遊語錄

hh 劉惟永，道德眞經集義大旨

hi 玄宗直指萬法統歸

hj 道德眞經三解

hk 玄經原旨發揮

hl 道德玄經原旨

hm 魯齋遺書

hn 諸葛武侯文集

ho 正誼堂全書

hp 周濂溪先生全集

hq 范子安，陳季卿誤上竹葉舟

hr 元曲選

hs 管道生

ht 沈雄，古今詞話

hu 唐圭璋，詞話叢編

Index

Neo-Confucian Studies

Modern Asian Literature Series

Translations from the Oriental Classics

Studies in Oriental Culture

Companions to Asian Studies

Introduction to Oriental Civilizations